Social Differences and Divisions

edited by Peter Braham and Linda Janes

The Open University

Blackwell
Publishing

First published 2002 by Blackwell; written and produced by The Open University

Blackwell Publishers

108 Cowley Road
Oxford OX4 1JF
UK

238 Main Street
Cambridge, Massachusetts 02142
USA

Index compiled by Isobel McLean

Edited, designed and typeset by The Open University

Printed and bound in the United Kingdom by the Alden Group, Oxford

British Library Cataloguing in Publication Data

A catalogue record for this book is available from The British Library.

Library of Congress Cataloguing in Publication Data

A catalogue record for this book has been requested.

ISBN   0 631 23309 1 (hbk)
        0 631 23310 5 (pbk)

1.1

Contents

Preface   vii

Social differences and divisions: introduction
Peter Braham and Linda Janes   ix

Chapter 1   'Place, lifestyle and social divisions'
Linda Janes and Gerry Mooney   1

Chapter 2   'Social exclusion and class analysis'
Mike Savage   59

Chapter 3   'Understanding gender divisions: feminist perspectives'
Linda Janes   101

Chapter 4   'Race, power and knowledge'
Karim Murji   159

Chapter 5   'Citizenship'
Bryan S. Turner   205

Chapter 6   'Social justice'
Peter Braham   249

Chapter 7   'Education, housing and social justice'
Peter Braham and Norma Sherratt   291

Readings in social differences and divisions   345

Acknowledgements   384

Index   388

The Open University Course Team

Hedley Bashforth, Tutor Panel Member and Author
Melanie Bayley, Editor
Tony Bennett, Joint Course Chair, Author and Book Editor
Peter Braham, Author and Book Editor
Lene Connolly, Print Buying Controller
Margaret Dickens, Print Buying Co-ordinator
Richard Doak, Tutor Panel Member and Author
Molly Freeman, Course Secretary
Richard Golden, Production and Presentation Administrator
Peter Hamilton, Author and Book Editor
Celia Hart, Picture Researcher
Sue Hemmings, Author
David Hesmondhalgh, Media Author
Karen Ho, Course Secretary
Rich Hoyle, Graphic Designer
Jonathan Hunt, Co-publishing Advisor
Denise Janes, Course Secretary
Linda Janes, Author and Book Editor
Yvonne Jewkes, Tutor Panel Member and Author
Tim Jordan, Author and Book Editor
Hugh Mackay, Author
Liz McFall, Author
Margaret McManus, Copyrights Co-ordinator
Gerry Mooney, Author
Karim Murji, Author
Janet Parr, Tutor Panel Member and Author
Steve Pile, Author and Book Editor
Winifred Power, Editor
Peter Redman, Author
Roger Rees, Course Manager
Halimeh Sharifat, Course Manager Assistant
Norma Sherratt, Author
Elizabeth B. Silva, Author
Kenneth Thompson, Joint Course Chair, Author and Book Editor
Diane Watson, Author and Book Editor
Emma Wheeler, Production and Presentation Administrator
Kathryn Woodward, Author

Consultant Authors

Mitchell Dean, Macquarie University
Celia Lury, Goldsmiths College
Jim McGuigan, Loughborough University
Mike Savage, University of Manchester
Merl Storr, University of East London
Bryan S. Turner, University of Cambridge

External Assessor

Rosemary Pringle, University of Southampton

Preface to the series

Sociology and Society is a series of four books designed as an introduction to the sociological study of modern society. The books form the core study materials for The Open University course *Sociology and Society* (DD201), which aims to provide an attractive and up-to-date introduction to the key concerns and debates of contemporary sociology. They also take account of the ways in which sociology has been shaped by dialogue with adjacent disciplines and intellectual movements, such as cultural studies and women's studies.

The first book in the series is *Understanding Everyday Life*, whose aim is to 'defamiliarize' our relations to everyday life by showing how the perspectives of sociology, cultural studies and feminism can throw new light on, and prompt a reflexive attention to, varied aspects of day-to-day social life that are usually taken for granted. The book is designed as a means of illustrating and debating different aspects of everyday life in a number of key sites – the home, the street, the pub, the neighbourhood and community – and in various social activities, such as work and consumption, and teenage romance.

The second book, *Social Differences and Divisions*, in addition to looking at class, which sociologists have treated as one of the central forms of social stratification, also explores social differences and divisions based on gender, 'race' and ethnicity. The book then examines the concepts of citizenship and social justice – concepts that both reflect and influence the perception of social divisions. Finally, the book contains case studies of two key sectors – education and housing – which highlight significant divisions and inequalities; it also looks at the social policies that have been designed to address them.

Social Change, the third book, shows how, from sociology's early concerns with the transition to industrial and democratic social forms to recent debates over the rise of information, networked or global societies, sociology has been centrally concerned with the nature and meaning of social change. However, the book seeks to frame these debates through an explicit examination of the spaces and times of social change. Social transformations are exemplified and questioned by looking at the ways in which societies organize space–time relations. The topics and examples include: urbanism and the rhythms of city life, colonialism and post-colonialism, the alleged transition from industrial to information society, new media and time–space reconfiguration, intimacy and the public sphere, and the regulation of the self. Finally, it examines new perspectives on how sociology itself is implicated in social change.

The last book in the series, *The Uses of Sociology*, discusses the various ways in which sociology is practised and the consequences of sociological activity for public affairs. It explores the main debates in sociology concerning its social purposes. Comparing and contrasting different sociological traditions in sociological thought, it examines a variety of their engagements with 'the social'.

The relevance of sociological knowledge is considered in relation to government, the public sphere (including the media), economic life, social movements, 'race' and ethnicity. The book also considers related questions, such as whether sociology is a science or a cultural endeavour, and whether sociological research and analysis can be detached and unbiased. Finally, it considers different views of what Max Weber called the 'vocation' of sociology, and asks whether sociologists have taken the role of prophets – criticizing present social arrangements and envisaging possible future developments.

Although edited volumes, each of the chapters has been specially commissioned for the series in order to provide a coherent and up-to-the- minute introduction to sociology. Each chapter is accompanied by a set of extracts from key, previously published, readings that are relevant to the chapter topic. At the end of each book there is also a set of 'generic' readings selected for their broader relevance to the overall themes of the book. Together these supply a wider view of the subject, with samples of historically important writing as well as of current approaches. Throughout the chapters, key terms and names are highlighted. These can be further studied by consulting a sociological dictionary, such as *The Blackwell Dictionary of Sociology* or *The Penguin Dictionary of Sociology*. The overall approach taken is interactive, and we hope general readers will use the activities and the questions based on the readings in order to engage actively with the texts.

Tony Bennett
Kenneth Thompson
on behalf of The Open University Course Team

Social differences and divisions: introduction

Peter Braham and Linda Janes

In March 2001 the BBC recorded a large number of 'hits' on its website following reports about changes in the way data about social class were to be collected and interpreted in the 2001 Census. The occupational classification system that had been used previously to measure class position had been modified to take account of changes in employment structures and the relationship between occupation and social class since the 1991 Census. The BBC website enabled individuals to check their own position with a couple of clicks and there were complaints as people took exception to their allocated positioning. Skilled tradespeople, for example, remained low on the list and some of them objected that this misrepresented their class position in terms of consumption. Interest in the BBC 'social class' website suggests that many people are concerned with class differences in 2001, and specifically with their own location in the hierarchical scale of class status and division.

Social class is a prime example of social differences and divisions that are the topic of this book, which focuses mainly on the UK although some wider, comparative examples are included. We hope that, like the visitors to the BBC website, readers and students will respond with interest to the discussions of contemporary, intersecting social differences and divisions in this volume and find the different theoretical perspectives brought to bear on them illuminating.

The idea that society is divided into distinctive social groups, each uniting people through their particular and shared experiences and interests that mark them as different from, and possibly in conflict with, other groups, has been a long-standing and taken-for-granted sociological understanding. We would be surprised therefore to come across empirical or theoretical work that did not pay attention to the influence of social divisions, particularly to those of class, gender and 'race'/ethnicity, which are usually seen as the core triumvirate of divisions of sociological concern. However, from the mid-1980s onwards recognition of the relevance of a wider range of key social differences came to the fore, and divisions including those based on sexuality, health, disability, age, nationality and religion began to receive more attention.

Recognition of social divisions has therefore become a ubiquitous aspect of sociological inquiry, yet the term 'social division' does not appear in two of the most popular current dictionaries of sociology. Instead, definitions are provided for several related terms such as 'stratification', 'inequality' and 'life-chances' that have historical precedence in the theorizing of social difference and division within the field of sociology. Stratification has typically referred to studies of structured, systematic social inequalities between groups of people. For example, Weber explained status hierarchies in traditional and feudal societies through stratification and also applied it to the analysis of modern, industrialized class-based societies in which the 'life-chances' of an individual to share in economic and cultural resources are shown to be unequally distributed. Although relating originally to economic inequalities, stratification studies have also incorporated other divisions such as 'race' and gender (Huber and Spitze, 1983; Crompton and Mann, 1986). Since the end of the 1980s, with the recognition of the complex interconnections between and within different aspects of social identity, difference, stratification and inequality, the umbrella term of 'social divisions' has become a commonplace referent for this broad area of sociological inquiry. Geoff Payne (2000), for example, describes 'social divisions' as a 'middle-range' perspective in terms of its underpinning assumptions about how the social world operates, locating it between contrasting perspectives of structural-functionalism, Marxism and post-modernism. To explain this further, post-modernism sees society as characterized by rapid and uneven change across social, political, economic and cultural dimensions which works to undercut the operation of macro structural processes and relationships such as those of class, gender and 'race': thus social structures are seen as increasingly fragmented, complex and contradictory. In stressing continuing socially constructed divisions linked to systematic inequalities in terms of power and resources, a social divisions perspective eschews the individualist and relativist conceptualizations associated with post-modernism. At a simple level, a structural-functionalist perspective holds to a view of society as essentially cohesive and integrated, in which people interact and negotiate with each other within institutional frameworks towards the common good. Within this model any differences are seen to be socially productive rather than divisive. Marxism, in contrast, represents society as essentially conflictual, divided principally by social class. The working class stands in a position of structural exploitation by the ruling class and the notion of social division is combined with economic division in relation to ownership of the means of production. Within this two-class model, opposition is explicit and inevitable, leading eventually to revolutionary change.

These traditions are represented by 'The manifesto of the Communist Party', by Karl Marx and Friedrich Engels (Reading A)[*] and by 'Class, status, party', by Max Weber (1946/1922) (Reading B). The Communist Manifesto famously describes the history of pre-bourgeois societies as the 'history of class struggle' between oppressor and oppressed, but argues that in bourgeois society the class antagonism had increasingly become a struggle between two great classes, the bourgeoisie and the proletariat. The view of a two-class model of society based on ownership or non-ownership of the means of production, as portrayed in the Communist Manifesto, was replaced in Marx's later work by a more sophisticated and complex scenario within which a number of class fractions

[*] The Readings referred to in this Introduction represent different schools of approach to the study of social differences and divisions. As such, they raise issues which span the concerns of the different chapters rather than being limited to any single chapter. For this reason, these readings are located at the end of the book, arranged in the order indicated here. This Introduction provides a context and setting within which they should be read.

were in conflict. Nevertheless, the application of the two-class model to contemporary capitalism has been criticized for being incapable of fitting the middle class into its schema and because of changes in the ownership of the means of production. In 'Class, status, party' Weber provides an alternative to Marx's concept in that class is defined, not in terms of the means of production, but in terms of a common market position that is linked to shared life-chances. On this basis it is possible to speak of different housing classes consisting, for example, of owner-occupiers or tenants in the private sector (addressed in Chapter 7 of this volume), as well as classes in terms of possession of key marketable skills. In addition to this, Weber posits the idea of status groups defined in terms of honour attributed to them or in terms of common lifestyle.

A social divisions perspective sits somewhere between these conflictual and cohesive models. On the one hand, it does not see society as functionally integrated around an accepted status quo but seeks to question and explain the normative assumptions and beliefs which apparently hold society together at a structural level and which thereby veil social divisions and the operation of power. On the other hand, it does not see class as necessarily the primary social division, and division as therefore primarily economic, but emphasizes the operation of intersecting and multiple social divisions which persist over time but are not always fixed and immutable.

In exploring social divisions, we need to consider some fundamental questions. Firstly, what are the key characteristics of social divisions? How do they come about, and what sustains them? Secondly, how are social divisions distinct from related categories, such as social differences and social inequalities? Thirdly, if society is fragmented by a multiplicity of social divisions into groups with oppositional interests within and between them, how is it that social cohesion is maintained at all? And, equally important, we should keep in mind the dual, but interdependent, focus of our analysis: on social divisions as structural, lived, social relations and social divisions as constructed categories of analysis within sociology.

What are social divisions?

The fact that societies are made up of individuals who share characteristics with some and are different from others is a commonsense observation which even young children notice. In this sense a world divided into groups – distinguishable on the basis of characteristics such as gender, age, ethnicity, nationality, religion and affluence – is a seemingly ready-made framework through which we understand the world. Everyone is included in the membership of these different groups and we make sense of our identities through our inclusion in some groups and exclusion from others. The first vital point for sociological analysis, however, is that these group categories are neither natural nor biological, but *socially*, as well as historically, constructed. For example, whilst being a man or a woman has a biological dimension, what it means to be a man or a woman – how it is possible to live and make sense of that biology – is socially constructed according to dominant beliefs in a society at a particular juncture or era. As Simone de Beauvoir wrote in 1949, 'One is not born, but rather becomes, a woman.' Our membership of social groups is bound by rules, conventions, histories and institutional sanctions, both implicit and explicit, that are socially determined. Typically these patterned constructions are persistent and constraining, although because they are social in character they are open to challenge and resistance, and can change over time. The changing discourses of femininity and masculinity since the 1950s are salient illustrations of this kind of change. Gender roles have changed, demonstrating that domesticity does not reside in women's genes, nor bread-winning in those of men; thus in the UK women now outnumber men in the labour force for the first time in peacetime. This, then, is the social aspect of social division.

Division in this sense requires at least two sides – for example, to be black or white, male or female, in good health or ill, heterosexual or homosexual – and this often implies a hierarchical relationship in which one category is advantaged precisely because it is more highly valued, in relation to its opposite, at a structural, social level. Since the two sides are constructed in relation to each other, to belong to one side is defined in terms of not belonging to the other. In this sense the two sides of social divisions can be seen as mutually constitutive: one side exists only in relation to its opposite and is defined by its difference from this opposite. A social divisions perspective is therefore often associated with a commitment to exposing and analysing social disadvantage, and the notion of clear-cut, embedded divisions can be strategically useful in such a project. In particular it facilitates a focus on the normative, privileged side of a bipolar division, for example on the invisible privilege of whiteness in a particular society. However, there are often more than two sides in social divisions to confuse a simple analysis in terms of the 'underdog'. A social division in terms of black or white, for example, ignores the many shades in-between and the differences between 'non-white' ethnicities. This example is particularly instructive for an examination of the way in which social divisions have been analysed because, for a prolonged period in the UK, the vital division here was thought to be between an undifferentiated white population and an undifferentiated black population. Differences in the circumstances of the 'black' population between those of African-Caribbean origin and those whose origins were from the Indian sub-continent, and indeed differences within the Indian sub-continent population, were neglected.

Social divisions are also matters of identity – or to put it in another way, identity and social division are closely interconnected issues (see Bradley, 1996). We are all a complex amalgam of multiple aspects of identity and members of several different socially divided groups and although disadvantage tends to multiply across group categories, this is not necessarily the case. Social divisions often connect and overlap in ways that reinforce disadvantage, but can also operate in contradictory ways. It is therefore unhelpful to think in terms of discrete differences and divisions added together in the constitution of identity and of each of us made up of, for example, separate elements of gender + 'race' + class + sexuality and so on. Identity is more accurately represented as combining these elements in dynamic mutual constitution. Thus, for a black British woman, gender, 'race' and nationality are intersecting dimensions of identity, constructed in relation to and dependent on each other, rather than being hermetic elements sitting side by side. Recognition of the complexity of differences within and between divisions, and the constantly shifting and contradictory nature of individual identifications and positions, points towards the critical insights of post-modernism and the celebration of difference, and away from a purchase on collective, structural disadvantage and inequality. But a sophisticated social divisions perspective must take these complexities of identity on board whilst holding on to an analysis of specific social processes that lead to social outcomes in terms of material and cultural inequality (Anthias, 1998).

Difference, division, inequality?

Social divisions therefore refer to substantial, entrenched and patterned differences between people that run through a society and which influence their present and future prospects – their life-chances. In this respect they are distinct from the more neutral descriptor of social difference which does not necessarily imply a hierarchical, value-laden division. Thus we may be members of differently located social groups, for example of a political party, Friends of the Earth or the Countryside Alliance and, although it is actually through our activities in these 'everyday' social environments that we experience the impact of the more substantial social divisions of society, these memberships are unlikely to have the impact on our life-chances that major social divisions such as class, gender, 'race'/ethnicity, age, religious affiliation have.

Social divisions also relate closely to social inequalities although the two terms should not be conflated as one. Social divisions often result in inequalities of material and cultural resource, in which case inequalities are an outcome of social division. A key element within social divisions is the operation of social power, both in terms of the direct influence of legal and social policy frameworks that construct and maintain social divisions, and in terms of the more indirect constraining impact of dominant cultural assumptions and beliefs.

Payne depicts social divisions as being society-wide distinctions between two or more groups of people that, among other things:

- are perceived as being substantially different materially or culturally

- are long-lasting and sustained by dominant cultural beliefs, the organization of social institutions and individual interaction

- confer unequal access to resources – and thus different life chances and life styles

- engender shared identities in terms of perceived difference from those in an alternative category of the same social division

(Payne, 2000, pp.242–3)

This summary raises a host of issues, but let us highlight just two contrasting points. It should be understood that, though social divisions can be pervasive and forceful in the aggregate, they need not and do not apply to every individual case. Thus the divisions between social classes in terms of morbidity, mortality, housing tenure, educational attainment and so on, do not apply to every member of these social classes. Therefore, many children from working-class families reach university, and many children from middle-class families fail to reach university, even though the educational divide has favoured the latter over the former and continues to do so despite attempts to produce equality of opportunity. Social divisions are therefore to be comprehended at the aggregate level, rather than at the individual level, even though it is also the fact that specific individuals are affected by them. By contrast, some divisions operate equally at both aggregate and individual levels and then the individual *and* the group might stand on the wrong side of a social divide. For example, a black landlord in the southern USA during the 1940s would not have been received by a white tenant at the front door even though he had called to collect rent. The reason was simple: the status as landlord counted for little or nothing compared to racial status. In this case the racial divide created a rigid line sufficient to overcome social divisions that would otherwise hold sway. The rigidity of the colour (or caste) line is explored by Gunnar Myrdal (1962; Reading C). Myrdal describes a society in which a 'Negro' was unable to pass across the caste line by legitimate means. The crucial point was that Negroes were subject to certain disabilities not because they were poor or uneducated, but because they were 'Negroes', defined at that time in the United States as a person with any trace of 'Negro' ancestry. In this instance 'race' had become the central axis of social relations. Thus a belief that discrete 'races' existed and that they stood in a fixed relation to one another, was taken to justify racial discrimination, exclusion, disadvantage, exploitation and segregation. Myrdal distinguishes between 'class struggle' – which he viewed as too simplistic and which he felt exaggerated the bonds of solidarity supposedly shared by members of the same class – and the 'caste struggle' – which he viewed as a tangible gulf that divided the (US) population into antagonistic camps.

Even as biological conceptions of separate 'racial stocks' have retreated, 'race' remains a powerful force for social division insofar as particular cultural, ethnic or national groups can be depicted as possessing 'essential' characteristics and treated accordingly. Moreover, attempts to correct such divisions are often constructed in terms of the very distinctions that are the object of contestation. The idea of a meritocratic society which is colour-blind and blind to other demarcations that are held to be irrelevant to the ability to perform a particular task is difficult to realize in the face of pre-existing social divisions. And so we encounter racial quotas and ethnic monitoring being employed to ameliorate racial inequality and injustice and the use of racial categories in the Census to help measure racial inequality; and in other contexts we find schemes to remedy gender imbalance and of rewarding universities for accepting students from certain postcodes as a way of ameliorating social class inequalities.

Social divisions: falling apart or holding together?

If contemporary society is characterized by increasing fragmentation and social division, what is it that keeps it from disintegration? Sociologists differ on this point, but the underlying explanation is generally agreed to lie in the relationship between multiple identities and cross-cutting and contradictory divisions discussed above. Thus if social divisions rarely reinforce each other, this limits the potential for significant challenge to the social order, maintained through dominant institutional discourses and frameworks. This has been demonstrated in relation to gender divisions, where divisions between women with respect to class, sexuality and most strongly to 'race', mitigated against a united women's political movement (see Janes in Chapter 3 of this volume). Equally, racial divisions have often made it extremely difficult to persuade white workers that they have basic interests in common with black or immigrant workers. For individuals, membership of constituencies across different groups and categories often means that a consistent position of opposition and challenge in terms of a specific social division is problematic. But even if, as Anthias (1998) suggests, social divisions often operate in mutually reinforcing ways, multiply disadvantaged groups have little social power to generate change, and privileged groups are constructed in relation to these disadvantaged groups, and hold more power with respect to maintaining the status quo (Lorde, 1984).

Outline of this book

This book is concerned with different conceptions of power, status, class, 'race'/ ethnicity and gender, and how they interrelate; the individual chapters focus on an analysis of social divisions and related inequalities of social outcome in specific contexts and on their explanation at a conceptual and theoretical level. There are substantive chapters on class, gender and 'race' and in this respect the book conforms to a sociological approach that is well established. In other respects the book is less conventional. In beginning with a chapter about the impact of place in relation to life-chances and lifestyle, it draws on the increasing synergy between sociology and geography in explanations of social life and highlights an underlying form of social division and related inequality which is beginning to receive more attention, not least through the concern with social exclusion. According to Lister (1990, p.47), by providing a 'common floor' the welfare state is the institutional embodiment of social citizenship rights. These rights raise questions about the limitations on the social citizenship rights of those excluded by poverty. Indeed, Lister quotes a description of poverty as being 'a condition of partial citizenship', insofar as the poor lack resources to meet expectations of others in the workplace or the family and because their ability to make choices is curtailed.

Later chapters focus on broader topics of citizenship and social justice now at the forefront of sociological and political debate, partly as a consequence of various aspects of European integration. These topics provide a fertile framework for analysing the historical development of key social divisions. The final chapter goes on to explore ways in which ideas about social justice influence contemporary approaches to education and housing, and how this relates to continuing social divisions.

The framework for the book is established in Chapter 1, **'Place, lifestyle and social divisions'** by Linda Janes and Gerry Mooney, which illustrates the extent to which 'place' is central to the construction, maintenance and representation of social differences and divisions. The chapter first seeks to demonstrate how 'life-chances' are influenced by where we live, especially in terms of access to education, employment and healthcare and the operation of what is now known as the 'postcode lottery'. Mooney and Janes then look at two contrasting examples of contemporary 'places' by examining the phenomenon of 'gated communities', communities built within and outside some of the world's big cities. Such communities are expressly designed to include some and exclude others through elaborate physical barriers and surveillance systems. Finally, the chapter looks at two different communities: first, the new urban development of Celebration in Florida, a community that is designed to reinstate traditional community values of inclusiveness – a town without walls – although the authors argue that certain social exclusions operate here at a more symbolic level; then the development of another community based on barriers of inclusion and exclusion – Manchester's Gay Village – in the context of theoretical explanations of social difference and division in terms of a 'lifestyle' community.

If this book had been written twenty years ago, social class – as one of sociology's foundational concerns – would undoubtedly have filled more pages in its own right, being viewed from within the sociological tradition as the key determining social division on which others ultimately depended. We still see class as critically important, but now we prefer to interrelate social class with other social divisions which change the ways in which class itself is constituted and experienced. This is the point of departure for Mike Savage in Chapter 2, **'Social exclusion and class analysis'**. Savage's chief concern is to explore the continuing contemporary relevance of social class as a primary social division at a time when some prefer to speak of 'social exclusion'. He argues that this approach implies that all but a few are included in an inclusive society, implicitly undivided by class, and that any 'problem' actually lies outside society rather than being integral to it (see Morris, 1995; Levitas, 1998). Savage goes on to argue that this discourse serves to obscure the extent to which material class divisions remain deep-rooted in our society and that, whilst class awareness is reducing, inequalities are actually increasing. For Savage this is the contemporary conundrum of class. To complete his analysis, Savage examines three classic theoretical perspectives on class – those of Marx, Weber and Bourdieu – and evaluates the relevance of each to the contemporary nature of social class divisions. Whilst acknowledging insights of continuing relevance in the analyses of Marx and Weber, Savage argues that Bourdieu's more cultural theory – particularly his deployment of concepts of cultural and economic capital, habitus and field – provides a more adequate analysis of contemporary class relations.

As we said earlier, from a sociological perspective, the core triumvirate of social divisions are class, gender and 'race'/ethnicity. Chapter 3 explores gender divisions and Chapter 4 explores divisions associated with 'race', though later chapters also address all three of these interconnected divisions.

In Chapter 3, **'Understanding gender divisions: feminist perspectives'**, Linda Janes looks at the different ways in which feminist theorists have analysed and explained gender divisions and inequalities. She begins by questioning popular evocations of gender equality associated with the notion of 'post-feminism' before evaluating the different accounts of the relationship between gender and power offered by liberal, socialist and radical feminism. Janes then analyses the impact of the black feminist critique of the mainstream political and theoretical movements. This analysis should be seen in the context of our earlier point about social divisions and social cohesion, for it illustrates how the recognition of differences amongst women, and of identity as multiple and intersecting across social divisions, threatened a united feminist political challenge to the established order. Janes goes on to examine the critical merging of insights between feminism and post-structuralism and post-modernism as feminism, like sociology, turned to more cultural explanations of power in the 1990s. However, as she explains, many feminists remained sceptical about what they saw as the abandonment of concern with women's material inequalities in favour of cultural, yet apolitical explorations of difference and identity and some sought to counter this trend. Beverley Skeggs' (1997) ethnographic work – which draws on Bourdieu's cultural theoretical framework in material and cultural terms, and which Janes examines at some length – can be seen as an example of reinstating class in feminist analysis.

In 'Only contradictions on offer: feminism at the millennium' (1999; Reading D), Lynne Segal, a key socialist feminist commentator on the intellectual and political project of feminism over the last thirty years, offers an analysis of the state of the movement at the turn of the twenty-first century. In a wide-ranging review Segal evaluates feminist gains – citing women's growing economic independence and expectations in relation to autonomy and choice in their lives across public and private spheres together with feminist global connections supporting women's struggles worldwide – against remaining, or indeed re-emerging challenges. Here she highlights the erosion of welfare benefits in the USA and in the UK impacting on lone mothers and older women in particular, the threat to women's reproductive rights worldwide, and the retrenchment of patriarchal, family values from both the political left and right. Like Skeggs, Segal eschews the extreme theoreticism of some feminist post-modernism and its irrelevance to the everyday political struggles of many women, whilst holding to the value of the productive insights brought to feminism in its broad remit by the cultural dimension of understanding. Finally, Segal rejects the arguments of the 'new feminist' commentators of women's empowerment as over-optimistic, individualistic and politically naïve. She concludes that, in spite of its contradictions, feminism remains a legitimate political enterprise because 'its most radical goal, both personal and collective, has yet to be realized: a world which is a better place not just for some women, but for all women…[and]… that would be a far better world for boys and men, as well' (p.375 below).

The contention that 'race' is a central organizing element of society, rather than one that is contingent upon other social divisions, is the starting-point for Chapter 4, **'Race, power and knowledge'**, by Karim Murji. Murji argues that racial categories are unstable and questionable, rather than being obvious and immutable – as they may seem at first – especially through their equation with skin colour. According to Murji, 'race' is a construct that we *learn* to 'see', code and name, and though the idea of 'race' may crumble when subject to scientific scrutiny, it remains powerful as a social construct. Thus it has real effects: certain groups are assumed to have an 'essence' in common and this influences allocation of resources and patterns of inequalities. Using the concept of 'racialization' to describe the way in which 'race' categories and 'race' thinking are applied to different groups, Murji shows how the US Census has manifested a concern with defining those deemed 'non-white' – and has had a particular fascination with degrees of blackness. Thus while non-white racial categories have fluctuated over time, the Census has treated the category 'white' as undifferentiated and unchanging.

As Bryan S. Turner argues in Chapter 5, **'Citizenship'**, citizenship rights are significant in terms of social divisions and differences because, ultimately, they determine who is 'inside' and who is 'outside' a society and how tightly national borders are defended. According to Mitchell and Russell (1994), there is a difference between the UK and other EU countries in granting full citizenship rights to migrants and their descendants, though they note that the UK has become much less liberal about entry rights and access to citizenship, while other EU countries have become more liberal. As they explain, since the 1980s the problem of immigration into the EU has come to be seen increasingly in terms of asylum-seekers and the need to identify and exclude 'bogus' refugees, who are in reality 'economic migrants'. This perception has led to the characterization of 'Fortress Europe' and a range of new measures to tighten pre- and post-entry checks and to discourage refugees from attempting entry (Mitchell and Russell, 1994, pp.139, 143–8).

Yet social citizenship is wider than who is admitted to a country. It also concerns who it is that gains access to specific benefits and privileges of citizenship. In this sense citizenship encompasses criteria of membership, identity, inclusion and participation, and the allocation of resources that is contingent on these criteria. As Mitchell and Russell note, though the UK is in advance of other EU countries in combating racial discrimination, there is substantial evidence of differential access in the UK to what is termed the *de facto* rights of citizenship – for example, disadvantaged access to public housing for members of minority ethnic groups (see Chapter 7 of this volume).

In his analysis of citizenship, Turner explores the work of the English sociologist, T.H. Marshall, who divided citizenship into three aspects – civil, political and social. As Turner points out, there are several weaknesses in Marshall's approach to citizenship, if we apply it to contemporary British society. One weakness is that Marshall assumed a relatively homogeneous population in which regional, cultural and ethnic divisions counted for little alongside social class divisions. By contrast, Mitchell and Russell (1994) highlight cultural differences within citizenship, in the light of which substantial sections of the UK population seem unwilling to accept as citizens minorities who are 'culturally distinct and visibly different from themselves', and they refer to the apparent desire on the part of some minorities to 'live apart' and the implications that this might have for common citizenship (pp.153–4).

Another weakness in Marshall's approach, according to Turner, is that he assumes that the rights of citizenship accrue passively through universal rights. In Turner's opinion, citizenship has accrued traditionally through the key processes of war, reproduction and work. Thus the route to social citizenship came through paid work in the formal labour market, war-time service or the production of children within the family – which, in turn, led to welfare entitlements and the provision of education. Turner argues that these elements of entitlement to citizenship have been attenuated by various developments: thus, for instance, the labour market has changed substantially, in part because labour market flexibility has led to the casualization of the labour force and because there has arisen an 'underclass' of the permanently unemployable. In addition, Turner argues that the relationship between reproduction and entitlement has altered in significant ways. For example, the birth rate has declined markedly and this has threatened the state's objective in securing the connection between reproduction and citizenship (hence increasing reliance is placed on immigration to sustain the population). What makes Turner more optimistic is the prospect that new forms of social citizenship – not specifically situated within the nation-state – are emerging. Here he refers to attempts to counter global pollution (leading to environmental citizenship on a global scale), the increasing attention paid to the rights of aboriginal peoples and to cultural rights (which he describes as 'post-national' citizenship rights) and the challenge to family-based rights through new forms of households based on changing forms of 'sexual citizenship'.

The way in which the distribution of and access to unequal rewards and resources is justified, especially in respect of the least advantaged in society, and the principles used to support improving their condition, are explored by Peter Braham in Chapter 6, **'Social justice'**. Though the focus here is on distributive justice, this encompasses a multitude of overlapping concepts that can be related to social justice in general – including need, merit, fairness, equity, equality, equality of opportunity and equality of outcome. Yet, even if the goal of social justice is interpreted in terms of equal opportunity, this simply raises fresh complexities of policy and practice: for example, why is it that achieving the goal of providing equal opportunity in education – which is far from being a weak objective – has resisted so many educational reforms? This issue is raised here and discussed further in Chapter 7. Braham focuses on several facets of social justice with reference to 'race' and immigration – inequality, perceptions of inequality and the interventions needed to achieve social justice. To this end he considers the extent of racial discrimination, the argument that under-achievement harms not just the individual but also the wider society, and the propensity to treat all minority ethnic groups as similarly disadvantaged. Finally, he considers how approaches to social justice might vary according to whether poverty and deprivation are ascribed to structural societal forces or whether they are seen as the result of individual choice and behaviour.

This issue is also the focus of 'Social class and underclass in Britain and the USA' by Gordon Marshall (1997; Reading E). According to Marshall, there are many critics who suggest that class analysis is flawed because it neglects substantial sections of the population, notably the economically inactive. In particular, the question arises as to whether the large numbers of impoverished welfare dependants, who 'have fallen through or dropped out of the class structure entirely' constitute a distinct group – an underclass – that needs to be addressed separately in class analysis. As Marshall explains, the attention paid to the underclass has its origins principally in US debates. These debates focused on two supposedly interrelated phenomena, namely, the high rate of youth unemployment and the growing incidence of one-parent households, each of which was believed to be especially prevalent in the US black population. In both the USA and the UK there has been strong and often acrimonious disagreement about whether the alleged characteristics of underclass life are cause or consequence of weak labour market position. In other words, the dispute centres on the process of causality between, on the one hand, structure and deprivation and, on the other hand, behaviour and attitudes.

However, the present position of ethnic minorities in the UK cannot be properly understood in isolation from the genesis of post-Second World War immigration to the UK and the so-called rigidification of the social-job structure that ensued. The class position of immigrant workers in western Europe is the central focus of the reading by Stephen Castles and Godula Kosack (Reading F). Castles and Kosack reject the view that immigrants – whether or not distinguishable by the colour of their skin – constituted a 'new proletariat', separate from the indigenous working class. In their view, only if 'classes' were replaced by 'status groups' could immigrants be treated as a separate group, in which case their disadvantaged circumstances would consign them to being one of the lowest status groups. Instead, Castles and Kosack depict immigrant workers as belonging to the same working class as indigenous workers, though they recognize that for various reasons it is a divided working class. These divisions reflect the material differences between immigrant and indigenous workers in terms of incomes, housing and so on, as well as the subjective responses of hostility and prejudice that these objective differences engender.

In the final chapter, Chapter 7, **'Education, housing and social justice'**, Norma Sherratt and Peter Braham examine inequalities in education and housing, taking into account issues of social justice, difference and division raised in earlier chapters. Their point of reference is the Beveridge Report of 1942, which set out a blueprint for the welfare state and called for the abolition of the 'five giants' of want, ignorance, disease, squalor and idleness and which gave particular attention to how the position of the least advantaged in society could be ameliorated. The idea was that education would banish ignorance and deliver equal opportunity and the provision of adequate, affordable housing would help to end squalor and want. The principles underlying the welfare state are explored by T.H. Marshall (1981; Reading G). He explains that the creation of a democratic welfare state demanded intervention in spheres such as education and health in which different life-chances prevail and which operate to create and sustain class distinctions. However, Marshall argues that the fundamental principle of the welfare state is that the market value of an individual cannot measure their right to welfare. In his words, the central function of welfare is to 'supersede the market'. The difficulty that ensues is that whereas welfare depends on altruism, the market (and much of politics) depends on an appeal to self-interest and it is this, in Marshall's view, that complicates the task of solving the 'problem of economic inequality'.

With regard to education we may ask a series of questions. For example, what are the differences in levels of educational attainment between groups and how do we account for them? Which groups have been regarded as educationally disadvantaged and why? How far does education reflect existing social divisions and how have concepts of social justice and equal opportunity helped to erode or eradicate such divisions? Can we compensate for inequalities outside the education system and on what basis and to what degree? There are various matters that need to be confronted, some of them quite familiar, others less so. The issue of why it is that the expansion of education has not translated readily into equalizing opportunity, so that, for example, the proportion of children of working-class origin entering university has remained much the same even though the total number going to university has increased dramatically, is familiar enough. Perhaps not so familiar is the issue of how far an emerging 'market approach' serves to preserve middle-class educational advantages and so – contrary to the aims of the Education Act 1944 – tends to redistribute educational opportunities from the *less* to the *more* privileged.

As far as housing is concerned, the chief social divisions relate to the gulf that exists between owners and non-owners – a gulf that reflects different approaches to the provision of housing, namely, housing to satisfy need and housing to produce gain. Improvements in the quantity and quality of housing have not ended inequality between housing 'haves' and 'have-nots'. While the provision of housing by non-market sources has increasingly been treated as a safety-net for the less advantaged, owner-occupation, though it is often described as a communal benefit (best captured by the phrase 'a property-owning democracy'), it is above all a benefit for individual families insofar as it constitutes a substantial and growing capital asset. Housing tenure has attracted sociological attention in terms of its effect on widening existing inequalities – especially via wealth generation – and insofar as it may represent an increasingly significant division in society, in which certain groups are concentrated on problem estates and in problem areas. Council – or social – housing has passed through successive stages, and these stand as an example of fluctuating inequalities and changing attitudes to social justice: first, as a notable benefit of citizenship (from which certain groups were generally excluded); then, with the large-scale sale of council housing, as an opportunity to acquire a valuable asset; and, finally, as the location of the less skilled, the unemployed and those in receipt of welfare. The volume therefore ends as it began – by looking at social divisions in terms of 'place'.

In summary, then, the underlying argument of this volume is that social differences, which often but not always result in social divisions, which again may or may not give rise to social inequalities, are a fundamental aspect of contemporary societies. Because such differences and divisions are social and structural in character, they persist and reproduce over time, but are not immutable. The structural relationship between divisions can change, as has happened in gender relations in the latter half of the twentieth century, and individuals can also move across some divides, although such social mobility is irregular and slow. Cross-cutting affiliations to different socially divided groups can operate to reduce the likelihood of general social unrest, and those on the 'wrong' side of several social divisions have little social power to challenge dominant regulations and practices. Whilst the individual chapters each take a specific social division or an issue underlying approaches to social divisions as their main topic, a key overarching focus is the interconnected, mutual constitution of social differences and divisions over time.

References

Anthias, F. (1998) 'Re-thinking social divisions', *Sociological Review*, vol.46, no.3, pp.505–35.

Beauvoir, S. de (1953) *The Second Sex*, London, Jonathan Cape. First published in France in 1949.

Beveridge Report (1945) *Social Insurance and Allied Services*, Cmnd 6404, London, HMSO.

Bradley, H. (1996) *Fractured Identities: Changing Patterns of Inequality*, Cambridge, Polity Press.

Castles, S. and Kosack, G. (1973) *Immigrant Workers and Class Structure in Western Europe*, London, published for the Institute of Race Relations by Oxford University Press.

Crompton, R. and Mann, M. (1986) *Gender and Stratification*, Cambridge, Polity Press.

Huber, J. and Spitze, G.D. (1983) *Sex Stratification: Children, Housework and Jobs*, New York, Academic Press.

Levitas, R. (1998) *The Inclusive Society?*, Basingstoke, Macmillan.

Lister, R. (1990) *The Exclusive Society: Citizenship and the Poor*, London, Child Poverty Action Group.

Lorde, A. (1984) *Sister Outsider*, Trumansburg, NY, Crossing Press.

Marshall, G. (1997) *Repositioning Class: Social Inequality in Industrial Societies*, London, Sage.

Marshall, T.H. (1981) *The Right to Welfare and Other Essays*, London, Heinemann.

Marx, K. and Engels, F. (1960/1848) 'The manifesto of the Communist Party' in *Marx, Engels, Lenin – The Essential Left: Four Classic Texts on the Principles of Socialism*, London, Unwin Books.

Mitchell, M. and Russell, D. (1994) 'Race, citizenship and "Fortress Europe"' in Brown, P. and Crompton, R. (eds) *A New Europe? Economic Restructuring and Social Exclusion*, London, UCL Press.

Morris, L. (1995) *Social Divisions*, London, UCL Press.

Myrdal, G. (1962) *An American Dilemma*, Vol.2: *The Negro Social Structure*, New York, Harper and Row.

Payne, G. (ed.) (2000) *Social Divisions*, Basingstoke, Palgrave.

Segal, L. (1999) *Why Feminism? Gender, Psychology and Politics*, Cambridge, Polity Press.

Skeggs, B. (1997) *Formations of Class and Gender*, London, Sage.

Weber, M. (1946) 'Class, status, party' in Gerth, H. and Mills, C. Wright (eds and trans.) *From Max Weber: Essays in Sociology*, London, Oxford University Press (originally published as *Wirtschaft und Gesellschaft*, 1922).

Place, lifestyle and social divisions

Linda Janes and Gerry Mooney

Contents

1	**Introduction**	**2**
	Aims	4
2	**Place, the postcode 'lottery' and unequal life-chances**	**5**
3	**Sociology and place**	**20**
	3.1 Representing place	22
4	**Utopia/Privatopia: making places for the new millennium**	**24**
	4.1 Gated communities	24
	4.2 Celebration: new urban paradise in 1990s' USA	27
	4.3 Trouble in paradise	29
5	**Place and lifestyle**	**33**
	5.1 Manchester's Gay Village	33
	5.2 Lifestyle: place, identity and consumption	35
6	**Conclusion**	**38**
	References	**39**
	Readings	
	1.1: Seán Damer, 'Problem places and problem people' (1989)	42
	1.2: Andrew Ross, 'Sure tried' (1999)	46
	1.3: Douglas Frantz and Catherine Collins, 'Truman didn't sleep here' (1999)	49
	1.4: Ian Taylor, Karen Evans and Penny Fraser, 'Out on the town: Manchester's Gay Village' (1996)	53

1 Introduction

Consider, for a moment, the question, 'Why do I live where I do?'

What factors have influenced this dimension of your life? If you have moved often, how would you account for these moves?

To what extent are you happy with your location? Would you live elsewhere if you were free of any constraints?

Answers to these questions will be myriad and, we think, strongly influenced by our changing relationships to factors of social difference and division that are the subject of this book. For example, if we live in a city, the promise of cultural diversity, social exchange and the mix of public and private amenities that the density and intensity of a modern city can provide may have positively drawn us to urban living. We may have moved to a particular city for a job, or because of a partner's job. We may value proximity between home and work. We may have a sense of belonging to a particular cultural or ethnic community that is based in our city or we may value the sense of anonymity in a crowd. However, we need quite a high level of economic resource to take full advantage of cultural benefits as city residents. We may instead live in a part of a city that has been devastated by de-industrialization and the displacement of communities over the last twenty years or so; we may live with a fear of crime and violence that is the 'other' side of representations of city life.

life-cycle,
class,
gender,
ethnic group,
sexualities

Our sense of what constitutes a safe environment is likely to be different depending on our age (or stage in the **life-cycle**), **class**, **gender**, **ethnicity**, **sexuality**, mobility and whether we live alone or are responsible for children, to name just some of the key variables. Whilst the appeal of urban life is possibly strongest amongst young people, it is also the case that members of this group can be drawn to the city for less positive reasons. The breakdown of caring relationships in both domestic and institutional contexts, the effects of unemployment and racism, drug culture and social exclusion are among the factors that push young people, in particular, to cities where they may become part of the population defined as 'homeless'. The same material space of the city can therefore represent very different environments to groups of people who experience it in different ways.

If we live in the countryside, to take the obviously contrasting case, we may have been attracted by ideas of increased private and public space and by the belief that rural areas have greater 'community spirit' and involvement, less pollution and reduced traffic. Here again our experiences of rural life will depend to some extent on our position in relation to interconnecting social differences and divisions. Many rural dwellers – particularly older and disabled people – have become disillusioned and isolated as public transport has declined and shops and other services have closed down in response to retail park competition and reductions in public social provision. In addition, cultural and ethnic diversity is still not very apparent in rural Britain and village life is often characterized as insular and regulatory, with neighbours providing support and surveillance in possibly equal measure.

The better-off amongst us may be able to afford a version of the benefits of both worlds by living, like our nineteenth-century counterparts, outside the city and working within it. Nowadays this usually depends on maintaining expensive (for individuals and the environment) private transport. Even for this group, however, the problem of isolation for children, especially teenagers, is often a particular problem. Feminist research has demonstrated how, for many middle-class mothers now in part-time or full-time employment, the remainder of their time can be totally accounted for by their continuing responsibility for domestic work, and the more recent requirement to provide transport for children – to and from school, health-linked and extensive social activities (McDowell and Pringle, 1992).

Single mothers and households dependent on state benefits are amongst those who have least choice about where they live. In media representations, as well as often in actuality, they occupy the derelict and neglected tower-blocks without working lifts or landing lighting or they live in other forms of inferior private or residual public housing.

These suggestions of some reasons why we live where we do are very simplified caricatures of the usually complex processes that contribute to decisions, impositions and compromises about where we live. They also assume a UK context. Lifted to a global scale, factors of influence would be much more varied. However, we could make two general points:

- that where we live is influenced by interacting and changing factors of social difference and division which affect, to a greater or lesser extent, the levels of choice we have in the matter;

- where we live is seen to 'count' as a contributory marker of identity and difference.

This introductory discussion has served to foreground place as a relevant topic in the exploration of social differences and divisions. However, you may well be wondering why 'place' is the first topic we examine in a book with an apparently clear-cut sociological focus on social divisions, which are conventionally thought to highlight class, gender, ethnicity, sexuality, age, disability – to name the most commonly analysed social categories. Place is surely a geographical rather than a sociological category? We would argue that this distinction does not hold and that the notion of place involves both the social and the spatial. Tim **Jordan (2002)**[1] has argued that places can be socially constructed and completely detached from physical spaces, using rave and internet communities as examples. Here we emphasize the symbolic dimension of constructed places, albeit still linked to physical spaces. Places are made and remade by interacting social groups operating in the context of changing structural opportunities and constraints, and places mean different things to different people. Place, therefore, seems to be a very appropriate starting-point in a discussion of social differences and divisions because places – cities, towns, villages, suburbs, community enclaves – are the locations in which the whole range of social differences are actively lived. In fact, differences are constructed in, and themselves construct, place (Bridge and Watson, 2000). Middle-class children growing up in gentrified areas of inner-city renovation, for example, are likely to secure levels of education and cultural and economic advantage with which to foster further gentrification. And, once such an area is convincingly represented as successful, it is likely that its success will grow.

[1] A reference in bold type indicates a chapter in a book, or a book, in the *Sociology and Society* series.

The Introduction to this book discussed the differently inflected meanings of the terms social difference, social division and social inequality. These different and distinctive formulations of power relations are demonstrated in the examples of place we examine in this chapter. Differences can be constituted in places in ways that lead to polarization, inequality and exclusion or, alternatively, in ways which constitute sites of resistance and the celebration of identity. In addition, differences are not simply registered at the social, cultural or economic level; they are also constituted symbolically with groups inscribing places with particular meanings and discursive practices (Bridge and Watson, 2000, p.253). This chapter is therefore centrally concerned with place both as a site and as a signifier of social differences, divisions and **inequalities**. Taking the example of place, in relation to marketing, inequalities in health, the divided city, consumption and lifestyle among other issues, our concern is to explore not only the ways in which place features as a signifier of wider social divisions but how place, in relation to the social divisions of class, gender, ethnicity and sexuality, is an integral part of social differentiation. The central argument that unfolds in the next section is that where one lives can have a major impact on one's life-chances. Section 3 focuses on the impact of place stigmatization. Section 4 will focus on two contemporary, differently differentiated constructed places – the phenomenon of gated communities and the new town of Celebration in Florida, planned and developed by the Disney Corporation during the 1990s. In section 5 we will focus on Manchester's Gay Village. Throughout the chapter we emphasize not only that places are actively made but that social divisions and differences are also constructed through place as well as reflecting such divisions.

equality

AIMS

The aims of this chapter are:

1   To analyse the ways in which 'place' is constituted in relation to social differences, divisions and inequalities through the study of a range of different examples.

2   To evaluate the influence of where we live on our 'life-chances' and to examine ways in which data about where we live are collected, interpreted and used.

3   To analyse how places are both sites and signifiers of social differences and divisions.

4   To examine the concept of 'lifestyle' with respect to the constitution of place.

5   To apply the concept of cultural capital in explaining relations between lifestyle and place.

2 Place, the postcode 'lottery' and unequal life-chances

How many of you reading this arose this morning to discover that more unsolicited mail – 'junk' mail – had been delivered? While there may be a widely-held belief that this kind of mail is randomly distributed, in fact unsolicited post is rarely random but is highly targeted, not only on you or your family but also on your place of residence. A vast array of information about places is gathered and used by a range of organizations in contemporary societies. The importance attached to place of residence is exemplified by the operations of insurance companies. The type of place in which you reside, as classified by its postcode, plays a major role in the premium one is expected to pay – if, indeed, insurance will be provided at all. In this respect alone your postcode can say much about you.

Today, relatively sophisticated marketing techniques are employed to identify particular market segments, or niches: groups of people who can be distinguished not only in terms of their income, employment or consumption patterns, but in terms of their general social attitudes and outlook. Place of residence is often central to such systems of classification.

ACTIVITY 2

Take a few minutes to compare the profiles of the two different areas provided below as produced by the management consultancy firm, CACI. When you have done so, answer the following questions:

1 What do they tell us about the place in question?

2 In what ways are the places differentiated?

3 How representative are such profiles likely to be?

TYPE 8 HOME OWNING AREAS, WELL-OFF OLDER RESIDENTS

These are areas of classic seaside retirement bungalows. Although they are found all over Britain, the largest concentrations are in the Isle of Wight, Dorset, Sussex (East and West) and Devon. 44 per cent of the population of Christchurch is ACORN Type 8.

Demographics

These neighbourhoods have very high proportions of elderly people and very few children. Almost 40 per cent of the population is aged 65 and over and over 50 per cent of households are either pensioner couples or single pensioners. With almost 18 per cent of the population suffering a long-term illness (a level 50 per cent above average), health care is a major issue.

Socio-economic profile

40 per cent of the population are retired. Of the working population, the majority are professional and white-collar occupations. Other key features of the socio-economic profile are above average levels of self-employed, home-based and part-time workers.

Housing

Almost 60 per cent of homes are owned outright in ACORN Type 8. This is a level almost 2.5 times the national average. There are very few rented homes, and few flats or terraced homes – over half the houses are detached with a further quarter being semi-detached.

Food and drink

The proportion of people who do grocery shopping daily is 52 per cent higher than average. Most grocery shopping trips are made by car. Freezer ownership is slightly above average and consumption of frozen ready meals is well above average. Consumption of frozen foods such as beefburgers and fish fingers, however, is low. Consumption of most packaged and fresh foods is low, except tinned and packet soup and fresh fish. Beer consumption is well below average but consumption of sherry, port and vermouth is high.

Durables

Car ownership rates are modest – the majority of households have only one car. The proportion of people who have owned their car for five years or more is almost double the average, while there are many fewer new cars than average. Cars tend to be medium sized and priced. 61 per cent more people than average are buying video cameras. Other durables purchased more frequently than average in these areas are washer/dryers, dishwashers, built-in ovens and hobs. Twice as many homes as average are having secondary glazing fitted.

Financial

The income profile peaks in the £5–10,000 and £25–30,000 bands. The proportion of people earning over £40,000 is less than half the average. Ownership of National Savings Certificates is over twice the national average, while share ownership is 40 per cent higher than average. Credit cards are more popular than debit cards. Mortgage and hire purchase ownership are below average.

Media

Daily paper readership is largely concentrated on three titles – *The Telegraph*, *The Express* and *The Mail*. All are read much more by people in this ACORN Type than on average. *The Sunday Express* is the most popular Sunday paper with 62 per cent above average readership. Other Sunday titles with above average readership are *The Sunday Telegraph* and *The Mail on Sunday*. ITV viewing is medium and commercial radio listening is light.

Leisure

Winter holidays are much more popular than average, as are European destinations. The proportion of people staying in their own holiday home or timeshare is 78 per cent above average. Gardening is a popular activity and 82 per cent more people than average have a greenhouse. Propensity to visit pubs, clubs and wine bars is low, while the proportion of people eating out regularly is slightly above average. Steakhouses, in particular Berni Inns, are very popular. Participation rates in all sports except bowls are below average but people are more than twice as likely as average to go to theatres and art galleries regularly.

Attitudes

People in this ACORN Type are much more likely than average to believe that a woman's place is in the home. They are generally content with their standard of living and are not terribly concerned with searching for low prices when shopping. They like to holiday off the beaten track. They are more likely than average to respond to direct mail, but are not particularly keen on other forms of advertising.

TYPE 45 LOW RISE COUNCIL HOUSING, LESS WELL-OFF FAMILIES

These low income council neighbourhoods are concentrated mainly in Merseyside. 34 per cent of the population of Liverpool is in this ACORN Type. They are also found to a lesser extent in the major conurbations, central Scotland and parts of Wales.

Demographics

The age structure of these neighbourhoods is very close to the national average, though there are above average proportions of children. The incidence of large households and of single parent households are both above average. 17 per cent of the population suffer from a long-term illness – this level is 40 per cent above average.

Socio-economic profile

The unemployment rate is just over double the national average, but the male unemployment rate is even higher. Nearly 47 per cent of households have no working residents. The proportions of people working in services and in manufacturing are fairly close to the national average. The socio-economic profile, however, is biased towards the lower status occupations with around double the national proportion of unskilled workers. A third of workers use public transport to get to work – 2.1 times higher than average.

Housing

50 per cent of homes are council rented. 29 per cent are being bought, and 11 per cent are owned outright. Compared with the national profile, this is a strong bias towards council renting. By far the most common type of home is the terraced house, which accounts for 67 per cent of all dwellings. The remainder are split roughly equally between semi-detached houses and purpose-built flats.

Food and drink

The proportions of people both doing grocery shopping on foot and daily grocery shopping are higher than average. 42 per cent more people than average are regular freezer centre users while over twice as many people as average are heavy users of frozen beefburgers. Other products which are consumed more heavily than average are brown sauce and ketchup, tinned steak, tinned/packet soup, crisps and snacks, bacon and sausages. Consumption of fresh food, especially fruit, is extremely low. In addition to having a relatively poor diet, people here are three times more likely than average to be heavy smokers – the highest levels of smoking of all the ACORN Types. Consumption of all alcoholic drinks except draught lager and vodka is below average.

Durables

Car ownership is very low, with almost 60 per cent of households having no car. The proportion of new cars is very low, as is the proportion of cars costing more than £10,000. Despite the low incomes, purchase levels for a range of durables are high – computer games and games systems, bicycles, gas cooker, microwaves, washing machines, tumble dryers and fridge freezers. The proportion of homes having new central heating installed is 32 per cent higher than average.

Financial

A quarter of people have an income of under £5,000 per annum. Under 2 per cent earn over £30,000 per annum. As might be expected from the number of durables being purchased, 27 per cent more people than average have a hire purchase agreement. Ownership of other financial products is low, especially interest-bearing current accounts, investment products, debit cards and personal pensions.

Media

2.3 times more homes than average have cable television but the ownership of satellite television is 30 per cent lower than average. *The Mirror* and *The Sun* are the most widely read daily papers. *The Star* and *The Daily Record* also have higher than average readership levels in these neighbourhoods. *The News of the World* has the largest Sunday readership while *The Sunday Mirror*, *The Sunday People* and the Scottish Sunday titles all have above average readership. Both ITV viewing and commercial radio listening are heavy.

Leisure

49 per cent of people in these areas do not have a holiday at all. Holiday camps are 36 per cent more popular than average among those who do take holidays, while caravanning has slightly above average popularity. People in this ACORN Type are as likely as average to go to pubs and clubs regularly, but less likely to eat out. They do not participate in sporting and other activities very much – the only activities showing above average popularity are bingo, betting and darts.

Attitudes

People in these neighbourhoods are much less likely than average to be interested in exercise and a healthy diet. Despite being careful to budget when shopping, they are more likely than average to buy a new brand when they see it. They are more likely than average to enjoy television and radio commercials.

Source: CACI, 2000

As we can see, places and people in these profiles are being grouped and differentiated according to certain social, economic and demographic criteria. Utilizing the ACORN classifications, to which we return a little later, there is considerable emphasis on housing tenure and also on income and, as we would expect, on lifestyles and patterns of consumption. Additionally these profiles provide generalizations about the attitudes that are held to be representative of the locales concerned. Note the claim, for instance, that residents in Area Type 8 (that is *'Home Owning Areas, Well-Off Older Residents'* (for a full listing of this classification refer to Table 1.1 below)) 'are much more likely than average to believe that a woman's place is in the home'! In the ACORN classification places are being distinguished on the basis of a wide range of discriminators with some indications of social composition of the areas concerned on the basis of household composition, income (often utilized as a proxy for class), ethnic 'mix' and age profile. In this process of classifying places, then, a particular 'sense of place' is produced (on this see Massey and Jess, 1995).

The kinds of information about places provided by organizations such as CACI are invaluable to companies who are concerned to identify potential customers. However, the differentiation of people and social groups by place of residence is not something that is unique to commercial market research. It is not uncommon for a person's behavioural characteristics, voting preferences or a range of other attributes, to be 'read off' from where they live. 'Postcode discrimination' by employers, whereby residents in a particular area are actively discriminated against in recruitment processes, is one notable example of this, but in everyday commonsense narratives where you live is often presented as a defining characteristic of the type of person that you are. In this respect geography forms part of the toolbox of daily discriminators that we employ to make sense of the world around us.

ACTIVITY 3

To begin to explore some of these issues more fully, read carefully the short article from *The Guardian* on postcode inequalities reproduced as Figure 1.1. When you have done so, answer the following questions:

■   On what bases are places being differentiated here?

■   What does this tell us about geographical inequalities in Britain in the late 1990s?

One of the key features of British society during the past two to three decades is the extent to which Britain is increasingly divided geographically (see Byrne, 1999; Pacione, 1997; Philo, 1995). This widening geographical (or *spatial*) divide is widely interpreted as being indicative of growing social and economic inequalities in general – of *social polarization* – between rich and poor, black and white, male and female. In the *Guardian* article, places are being demarcated in relation to household income. The contrasting fortunes of different areas are clearly highlighted but note also the claim that the evidence provided lends weight to the argument that a *'north–south divide'* is a prevalent feature of contemporary British society (see Mohan, 2000). While by no means a novel idea, the notion of a north–south divide is one of the most commonly used geographical metaphors today, highlighting inequalities between groups of people in different parts of the UK. It is a description dating back to the mid-1980s, referring to the developing political and economic situation and the differential impact of de-industrialization across the country. Deepening unemployment and recession in the north was contrasted with the development of new high-tech and service-based industries in the south, albeit in uneven and fragmented pockets. The political map also reflected this material economic division with Conservative constituencies dominating in the south (and in rural areas) and Labour in the north (and in the cities). This political pattern has now changed, particularly with the 1997 and 2001 elections, but we would argue that the material and symbolic geographical divide is still very much alive.

Postcodes chart growing income divide

Paul Baldwin

Liverpool is the poorest place to live in the country, according to a new survey showing wide variations in household incomes across the nation down to individual postcodes. Nine of the 20 poorest postcodes are areas of Liverpool.

High incomes are concentrated in the central London postcode areas of Barbican, Blackfriars, Belgravia, east and west Temple, and Embankment, where four in 10 homes gross in excess of £50,000. Of the top 20 postcodes, only one – Slough in Berkshire – is outside London.

In contrast, well over 80% of households in Liverpool's Edge Hill, Birkenhead, Bootle, Middlesbrough, Leicester and central Belfast get by on less than £13,000.

The detailed picture of the prosperity of the nation shows that the wealth disparity between London and many towns beyond Watford Gap has become unbridgeable.

At the extremes, householders in Sunderland, at £16,100, have just over half the amount of their counterparts in West London. At county level, the people of Surrey enjoy an income of £29,700, 71% higher than those living in Tyne and Wear (£17,400) while the Prime Minister resides in a Whitehall area where the £45,900 income is higher than the average in his North-east constituency of Sedgefield.

The findings are part of the largest and most detailed survey of gross house-

hold incomes ever undertaken in the UK. It was carried out by market research group CACI.

A spokesman said the result reflected the view that people are reasonably optimistic about the state of the economy but he added: 'The argument has been made that the rich are getting richer and the poor are getting poorer.

'Average household incomes in greater London are 40% higher than those in the north of England. It would appear that the last three years has not seen a decline in the north-south divide.'

'There are political parties and pressure groups that are not satisfied with the official government case. They suggest that the economic boom is an illusion. Many also contend that the encouraging broad brush statistics cover a worrying trend towards an increasing polarisation.'

He claimed that CACI figures, based on household income, gave a truer picture of the real prosperity of a nation than traditional markers such as the unemployment register or the movements in the housing market.

Today's survey comes three years after the original and shows overall that the national average household income has risen by 9.7% – well above inflation.

The survey also throws up some moderate surprises. While Surrey, Berkshire and Buckinghamshire hold the top three slots for highest average income by county – rising more than 11% on

the same survey in 1998 – the Borders and Durham also saw income growth of more than 11% over the same period.

Sheffield and south Yorkshire fare badly along with Dyfed and Mid-Glamorgan but perhaps the grimmest data come from the Western Isles where real incomes fell over the three years.

The poorest towns and cities in the country are Sunderland, Truro, Sheffield, Plymouth and Swansea, with an average household income of £18,000 or less.

Huddersfield is one northern town which has risen in prosperity, with a 13.1% income growth over the past three years, rising 10 places in the towns' league table. With an average household income of £20,800, it is now nearly as prosperous as Bath.

Economist David Starkey, fellow of Fitzwilliam College, Cambridge, said the study seemed broadly in line with expectations but added: 'Although there are extremes of income you have to consider other factors such as the relative prices of property to get a genuinely realistic picture.

'Generally we all got much better off but there is about 10% of the population that is seriously left out.

'The whole Blair experiment is sort of working. We are on a knife edge but as long as things like car manufacturing do not go down and we don't start seeing really sharp cut-backs, we may be just about all right.'

Figure 1.1 Source: The Guardian, 25 October 1999

life-chances   Differences in **'life-chances'** (to borrow a term coined by the early twentieth-century German sociologist, Max Weber) in relation to housing, education, employment and health, are only too visible a reminder that modern societies are characterized by division and inequality. One of the most evident aspects of such differentiation is in relation to geography. The ways in which we talk in everyday language is 'routinely spatially marked' (Keith and Pile, 1993, p.16). Place can be viewed as a geographical manifestation of social divisions and inequalities. We hear continually of places *of* high unemployment and *of* poverty among other descriptions. Consider also how frequently we make or hear assumptions being made about particular places. We commonly talk of places having a 'strong sense of community' or having 'none' at all; of 'good places' and of places best avoided. And, as Marxist geographer David Harvey reminds us, such representations have real effects:

> Evaluative schemata of places, for example, become grist for all sorts of policy-makers' mills. Places in the city get red-lined for mortgage finance, the people who live in them get written-off as worthless ... The material activities of place construction may then fulfil the prophecies of degradation and dereliction. Similarly, places in the city are dubbed as 'dubious' or 'dangerous' again leading to patterns of behaviour both public and private, that turn fantasy into reality.
>
> (Harvey, 1996, pp.321–2)

This reference to place, that is the use of a geographical or spatial referent, not only serves to render key aspects of social divisions and social inequality as more visible, but can also compound and reinforce such inequalities. However, we wish to go further than this to argue that place does not simply reflect these social divisions and the inequalities they give rise to, but is itself part and parcel of those very social divisions. Thus different groups of people can find themselves advantaged or disadvantaged depending on the place in which they live. Inequalities of class, ethnicity or gender, for instance, are often compounded by patterns of geographical differentiation – or segregation. Place matters, then, but only in relation to other social relations to which it is central.

Thus far we have side-stepped the issue of how place is to be defined. As with the notion of 'community' (see **Jordan, 2002**), with which it is often, though confusingly, interchanged, defining what place is can be very difficult. At one level it can refer to a geographical location, but beyond this it is important to acknowledge that places can have multiple meanings, meanings that may not be attributable to simple location. These meanings can vary between different groups and the ways in which places are identified and represented is something that is consistently fought over: for instance, the external labelling of a place often conflicts with the 'sense of place' of those who live there, particularly if the label is negative and stigmatizing. We return to this later in the chapter but at this stage it is important to take with you, as you progress, this idea of place as contested and fought over.

community

Let us return to the issue of place classification. During the last two decades of the twentieth century, marketing and promotional techniques have developed apace and along with them there have been significant developments in the use of *geodemographic* systems, that is systems for targeting potential customers in particular areas who exhibit similar behavioural patterns in relation to, for example, shopping. You have already met one of the most widely used geodemographic systems in Activity 2 above – ACORN, **A C**lassification **o**f **R**esidential **N**eighbourhoods. This is:

> ... based on the idea that 'birds of a feather flock together', it gives recognition to the fact that people with broadly similar economic, social and lifestyle characteristics tend to congregate in particular neighbourhoods and exhibit similar patterns of purchasing behaviour and outlook ... .
>
> (Wilson, Gilligan and Pearson, 1992, p.202)

Table 1.1 The *acorn® targeting classification 2000

ACORN categories	Percentage of population	ACORN groups	Percentage of population
A THRIVING	19.0	1 Wealthy Achievers, Suburban Areas	14.0
		2 Affluent Greys, Rural Community	2.2
		3 Prosperous Pensioners, Retirement Areas	2.8
B EXPANDING	10.4	4 Affluent Executive, Family Areas	3.4
		5 Well-Off Workers, Family Areas	7.0
C RISING	9.0	6 Affluent Urbanites, Town & City Areas	2.5
		7 Prosperous Professionals, Metropolitan Areas	2.5
		8 Better-Off Executives, Inner City Areas	4.0
D SETTLING	24.5	9 Comfortable Middle Agers, Mature Home Owning Areas	13.7
		10 Skilled Workers, Home Owning Areas	10.8
E ASPIRING	13.9	11 New Home Owners, Mature Communities	9.9
		12 White Collar Workers, Better-Off Multi-Ethnic Areas	4.0
F STRIVING	23.1%	13 Older People, Less Prosperous Areas	4.4
		14 Council Estate Residents, Better-Off Homes	10.9
		15 Council Estate Residents, High Unemployment	3.6
		16 Council Estate Residents, Greatest Hardship	2.4
		17 People in Multi-Ethnic, Low-Income Areas	1.8

Source: CACI, 2000

ACORN types		Percentage of population
1.1	Wealthy Suburbs, Large Detached Houses	2.2
1.2	Villages with Wealthy Commuters	2.8
1.3	Mature Affluent Home Owning Areas	2.7
1.4	Affluent Suburbs, Older Families	3.4
1.5	Mature, Well-Off Suburbs	2.9
2.6	Agricultural Villages, Home Based Workers	1.5
2.7	Holiday Retreats, Older People, Home Based Workers	0.7
3.8	Home Owning Areas, Well-Off Older Residents	1.5
3.9	Private Flats, Elderly People	1.3
4.10	Affluent Working Families with Mortgages	1.8
4.11	Affluent Working Couples with Mortgages, New Homes	1.3
4.12	Transient Workforce, Living at their Place of Work	0.3
5.13	Home Owning Family Areas	2.5
5.14	Home Owning Family Areas, Older Children	2.6
5.15	Families and Mortgages, Younger Children	1.9
6.16	Well-Off Town & City Areas	1.1
6.17	Flats & Mortgages, Singles & Young Working Couples	0.9
6.18	Furnished Flats & Bedsits, Younger Single People	0.5
7.19	Apartments, Young Professional Singles & Couples	1.4
7.20	Gentrified Multi-Ethnic Areas	1.1
8.21	Prosperous Enclaves, Highly Qualified Executives	0.9
8.22	Academic Centres, Students & Young Professionals	0.6
8.23	Affluent City Centre Areas, Tenements & Flats	0.7
8.24	Partially Gentrified Multi-Ethnic Areas	0.8
8.25	Converted Flats & Bedsits, Single People	1.0
9.26	Mature Established Home Owning Areas	3.4
9.27	Rural Areas, Mixed Occupants	3.4
9.28	Established Home Owning Areas	3.9
9.29	Home Owning Areas, Council Tenants, Retired People	3.0
10.30	Established Home Owning Areas, Skilled Workers	4.3
10.31	Home Owners in Older Properties. Younger Workers	3.2
10.32	Home Owning Areas with Skilled Workers	3.3
11.33	Council Areas, Some New Home Owners	3.7
11.34	Mature Home Owning Areas, Skilled Workers	3.3
11.35	Low Rise Estates, Older Workers, New Home Owners	2.9
12.36	Home Owning Multi-Ethnic Areas, Young Families	1.0
12.37	Multi-Occupied Town Centres, Mixed Occupants	2.0
12.38	Multi-Ethnic Areas, White Collar Workers	1.0
13.39	Home Owners, Small Council Flats, Single Pensioners	2.3
13.40	Council Areas, Older People, Health Problems	2.1
14.41	Better-Off Council Areas, New Home Owners	2.0
14.42	Council Areas, Young Families, Some New Home Owners	2.7
14.43	Council Areas, Young Families, Many Lone Parents	1.6
14.44	Multi-Occupied Terraces, Multi-Ethnic Areas	0.7
14.45	Low Rise Council Housing, Less Well-Off Families	1.8
14.46	Council Areas, Residents with Health Problems	2.1
15.47	Estates with High Unemployment	1.3
15.48	Council Flats, Elderly People, Health Problems	1.1
15.49	Council Flats, Very High Unemployment, Singles	1.2
16.50	Council Areas, High Unemployment, Lone Parents	1.5
16.51	Council Flats, Greatest Hardship, Many Lone Parents	0.9
17.52	Multi-Ethnic, Large Families, Overcrowding	0.5
17.53	Multi-Ethnic, Severe Unemployment, Lone Parents	1.0
17.54	Multi-Ethnic, High Unemployment, Overcrowding	0.3

(Note: ACORN and CACI are registered trademarks of CACI Limited.)

Note in Table 1.1 the use in the ACORN system of a range of sociologically inspired categories including groups defined as 'thriving', 'rising', 'aspiring', 'better-off executives' or 'council estate residents, greatest hardship'.

Classification systems such as ACORN provide descriptions of neighbourhoods that summarize their households' demographic and socio-economic profile thereby allowing, in theory at least, for better identification and targeting of niche groups by marketing agencies. Note the demarcation of areas with a 'multi-racial' population and the significance attached to family type and age in the measures of classification adopted. There is a strong emphasis on occupations, housing tenure and on income, which are used to generate a picture of the social class make-up of the area in question. Importantly, however, any idea of class as such is notable by its absence from ACORN and other similar systems of classification. In its report, *Blurring Demographics,* The Henley Centre, one of Britain's leading management consultancies, claims that class is losing its salience. Instead of class-based measures of social differentiation, it argues that:

> A more effective approach to classification is to identify the drivers of a particular market's demand, and then to segment consumers along these lines. By being sensitive to the intricacies of consumer identity, companies can engender higher levels of trust and loyalty, as well as generating valuable insights for marketing communications and branding.
>
> (The Henley Centre, 2000)

Such arguments tend to reflect the idea of a consumer-oriented society that is characterized by the declining significance of class. This is taken up by Mike Savage in Chapter 2.

In addition to these commercially driven systems, a large and diverse range of public and statutory organizations also hold data organized in relation to place/ geographical segmentation. Other bodies that use geodemographic approaches or discriminators include the Higher Education Funding Council for England (HEFCE), which categorizes places in terms of the take-up of post-school educational provision. Here, again using postcode analysis, places are grouped into several 'lifestyle neighbourhoods' where, for example, there may be low levels of educational attainment, high unemployment and relatively little progression to post-school education or, by contrast, where there is high take-up.

Classifications of place and/or of specific groups of people in relation to particular places can be used for different purposes, and there is often a tension between them. Arguably they increase the surveillance of particular social groups by those who are more powerful. On the other hand, while the kinds of systems explored here can be *potentially* useful in diverting resources to disadvantaged sections of the population (though they can also be used to discriminate), and to addressing problems such as concentrations of ill health, the means by which areas are demarcated are far from neutral. Such systems, and the measures upon which they are founded, are often cloaked in discourses of objectivity: the claim that the methodologies employed and the systems of place identification and classification represent in some senses simple value-free, technical exercises. But there is no one index or system of classification, and the choice of which one to employ is far from academic. In relation to the systems employed by public agencies, the decision to utilize one schema as against another can have implications for the choice of policies that may be subsequently pursued. Not only are these classifications based on particular assumptions, often influenced by impressionistic and anecdotal pictures of particular places (and the people who live there), but the results are frequently open to sharply contrasting interpretations.

Local authorities expend considerable efforts in identifying and designating 'deprived places', often utilizing the ten-yearly Census and other data collected along postcode lines. There is a long history of 'area-based' urban policy premised on the understanding that places can be distinguished and demarcated in relation to a range of social indicators, such as income, housing tenure and family composition, benefit take-up and levels of crime (see Atkinson and Moon, 1994). All too often such policies have been based on the view that particular groups of people in disdvantaged or 'deprived' places are to 'blame' for the 'social problems' that are prevalent. Thus 'problems' in an area frequently come to be represented as 'problems' *of* an area. Arguably, however, this focus on deprived places or neighbourhoods took on a new significance with the election of the Labour government in 1997. The Social Exclusion Unit, established by Labour within a few months of its election victory, outlined the government's proposals for 'neighbourhood renewal' (see Cochrane, 2000; Social Exclusion Unit, 1998, 2000). The publication of the SEU Report, *Bringing Britain Together,* in 1998 represents one of the clearest signs of Labour's approach to the 'problems' of 'socially excluded' places. Crime is highlighted as a particular issue in such areas, with juvenile crime, general 'lawlessness' and 'anti-social' behaviour singled out for special mention. Additionally, 'family breakdown' and low educational attainment are also pinpointed as key issues to be addressed. Furthermore 'place' has come to play a more significant role in Labour's social policies in general. In its 1999–2000 Annual Report the government made great play of its success in improving social and economic conditions, 'widening opportunities', across the length and breadth of the country (Prime Ministers' Office, 2000). Residents in England and Wales could, through the internet, check on progress in their particular locales in relation to health provision, school budgets, employment and, once again, in relation to the 'fight against crime' (http://www.annualreport.gov.uk/inyourarea/): see Figure 1.2.

Place, and the fortunes of different places, continues to be a major political issue, as we noted previously with the re-emergence of the long-standing debate over a north–south divide in 1999–2000. It is perhaps not too difficult to understand the Labour government's keenness for area measurement and place-based policies given the considerable amount of evidence that points to widening and deepening social and geographical inequalities in UK society – inequalities that became sharper and more profound in the 1980s and 1990s (Mackintosh and Mooney, 2000).

One of the most thoroughly investigated dimensions of this relates to the relationship between place and patterns of ill health and death rates. Health sociologists among others have produced a wide array of evidence to support the claim that place of residence and patterns of morbidity and mortality are closely related.

Postcode guide to services at grassroots

The annual report is on the internet for anyone to see how their city, town or village is doing. Website visitors can put in their postcode and discover progress reports on their schools, hospitals and police forces. Here we pick the postcodes for Tony Blair and William Hague's constituency bases. The Liberal Democrat leader, Charles Kennedy, lives in Scotland, not covered by the website, so we look at how the party's home affairs spokesman, Simon Hughes, fares.

Tony Blair
Constituency: Sedgefield
Postcode: TS29 6DU

The prime minister's constituency is one area where his mantra of education, education, education should be chanted. The north-east has the highest levels of unemployment and the lowest levels of GCSE results; it was perhaps as a result of these unwelcome statistics that the area benefited from the New Deal for Schools.

The local education authority budget allocation for 2000–01 is £212.26m, up £9.24m on last year. The number of infants in classes larger than 30 is down from 6,123 in 1997 to 1,330 – 81% of pupils – this year. The area has four Beacon-status schools but also four with serious weaknesses.

The local health authority budget allocation is up by 6.52% on last year at £453m.

In-patient waiting lists have dropped to 11,656, but only by 845 since 1997, a decrease of 6.75%. However, out-patients waiting for an operation have nearly tripled from 1,997 to 5,922.

In Durham the average time from arrest to sentence for persistent young offenders has been cut by 33 days, a fall of 27.5%. Notifiable offences between October 1998 and September 1999 dropped to 49,180, compared with 52,474 a year earlier.

Police numbers in the area have stayed almost constant: 1,555 in 1999, compared with 1,559 in 1998.

The report says that, thanks in part to the New Deal, long-term youth unemployment has fallen by 56% in Sedgefield since 1997, while unemployment in the north-east fell from 9.9% in February–April 1999 to 8.5% in the same period this year.

William Hague
Constituency: Richmond
Postcode: DL7 8EG

The leader of the opposition's constituency appears to have done rather well. Richmond has more than 760 foreign-owned companies employing 100,000 people, although areas of high unemployment remain, including in South Yorkshire which has qualified for EU funding worth £760m in the next few years.

The LEA budget allocation for 2000–01 is up from £219.37m to £232.15m, and while there are still 1,500 infants in classes with more than 30 pupils, this is down from 4,808 in 1997. Six schools have achieved Beacon status; however, there are eight schools in special measures or with serious weaknesses.

The health authority budget allocation is up 6.52% on the previous year, bringing the total for 2000–01 to £453m. People waiting for in-patient operations are down from 15,315 in 1997 to 14,611. However, there has been a rise in those awaiting out-patient treatment from 3,644 in March 1998 to 5,005 in 2000.

The average time from arrest to sentence for persistent young offenders in North Yorkshire has been cut by 33 days, or 26.4%. Crime is down by only 0.1% on notifiable offences. There were 66 fewer police officers in 1999 than in 1998, a drop of nearly 5%, in the North Yorkshire force.

Unemployment in Yorkshire and the Humber fell from 6.9% in February–April 1999 to 6.3% in the same period this year, and long-term youth unemployment has fallen by 56% in Richmond since 1997.

Simon Hughes
Constituency: North Southwark and Bermondsey
Postcode: SE1 3UJ

An inner-city Lib Dem constituency in London highlights the stark differences in how effectively the government is tackling the varying problems faced by rural as against urban constituencies.

In Southwark attempts to reduce class sizes appear to be working, with 410 infants, 4.63%, in classes larger than 30, down from 800 in 1997. The LEA budget allocation for 2000–01 is £130.40m, up £6.59m on last year, and four local schools have achieved Beacon status.

However, there is a high level of failing schools, with 17 in special measures and with serious weaknesses.

In-patient waiting lists have dropped markedly from 19,261 in 1997 to 17,371, but this is accompanied by a big increase in out-patients waiting to be treated: 6,432, compared with 2,612 in March 1998.

The crime rate, at 13.11 of offences per 100 of population, is above the national average of 9.98 offences and has increased by 8.7% from 920,095 notifiable offences in London between October 1997 and September 1998 to 1,000,380 for the following year.

The average time from arrest to sentence for persistent young offenders has been cut by 57 days, a fall of 35.6%, but the number of officers in the Metropolitan police has dropped from 26,106 to 25,885.

Long-term youth unemployment has fallen by 63% in North Southwark and Bermondsey since 1997, while unemployment in the London region fell from 7.8% in February–April 1999 to 7.4% in the same period this year.

Figure 1.2 Source: The Guardian, 14 July 2000, p.8

Table 1.2 Constituencies where people are most and least at risk of premature death (mortality rates under 65) in Britain (1991–95)

Rank	Name	Obs<65	SMR<65	Pop<65	Avoidable (per cent)
	Ratio of 'worst health' to 'best health'	**2.3**	**2.6**	**1.0**	
1	Glasgow Shettleston	1405	234	50,740	71
2	Glasgow Springburn	1438	217	57,007	69
3	Glasgow Maryhill	1432	196	67,246	65
4	Glasgow Pollok	1313	187	62,257	64
5	Glasgow Anniesland	1176	181	56,757	63
6	Glasgow Baillieston	1267	180	66,076	62
7	Manchester Central	1597	173	94,191	61
8	Glasgow Govan	1028	172	57,286	61
9	Liverpool Riverside	1458	172	78,573	60
10	Manchester Blackley	1421	169	78,573	60
11	Greenock and Inverclyde	1051	164	54,050	59
12	Salford	1285	163	72,681	59
13	Tyne Bridge	1297	158	76,678	57
14	Glasgow Kelvin	828	158	50,304	57
15	Southwark North and Bermondsey	1214	156	76,811	56
	'Worst health' million	*19,210*	*178*	*1,003,923*	*62*

Rank	Name	Obs<65	SMR<65	Pop<65	
1	Wokingham	588	65	80,936	
2	Woodspring	620	65	74,251	
3	Romsey	593	65	73,300	
4	Sheffield Hallam	481	66	61,865	
5	South Cambridgeshire	636	66	79,401	
6	Chesham and Amersham	673	67	76,914	
7	South Norfolk	710	69	79,820	
8	West Chelmsford	674	69	79,820	
9	South Suffolk	601	69	79,820	
10	Witney	675	69	82,975	
11	Esher and Walton	705	69	83,333	
12	Northavon	742	70	88,333	
13	Buckingham	593	71	70,344	
	'Best health' million	*8291*	*68*	*1,004,147*	
	Britain	556,957	100	47,587,310	

Notes: The population of each constituency is estimated for 1993 from 1991 mid-year ward statistics updated by the 1996 ONS age/sex mid-year estimates of population for local authority districts. The mortality figures are assigned to constituencies through the postcodes of the deceased.

Obs<65: Number of deaths under the age of 65

SMR<65: Standardized Mortality Ration for deaths under 65

Pop<65: Number of people in constituency under the age of 65

Avoidable: % of deaths which would not have occurred if the 'worst health' areas had the death rate of the 'best health' areas.

Source: Shaw *et al.*, 1999, Table 2.1, p.14

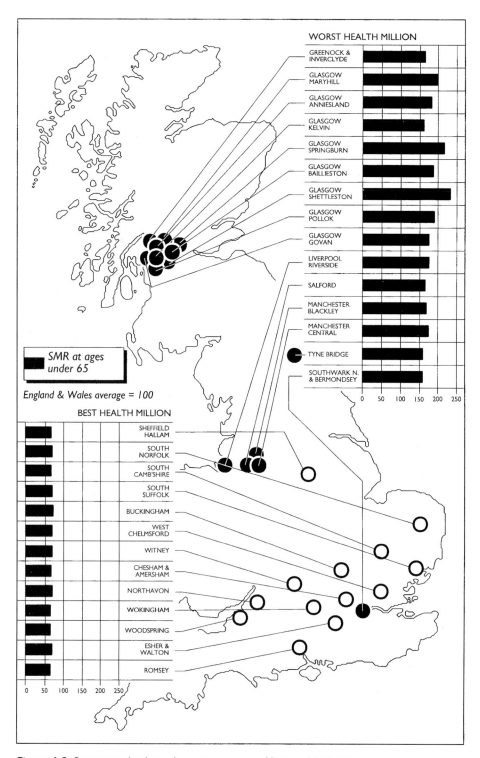

Figure 1.3 *Premature deaths in the extreme areas of Britain, 1991–95*
Source: Shaw et al., 1999, Figure 2.1, p.15

Social scientists from the University of Bristol investigated this by focusing on the 1997 Parliamentary Constituencies (Shaw *et al.*, 1999; Mitchell *et al.*, 2000): see Table 1.2 and Figure 1.3. Supporting the findings of previous research, they concluded that the death rates for the one million 'worst health' people were 2.6 times greater than those living in constituencies with the 'best health' million. In accounting for this they argued that there was a particularly close relationship between the social class composition of an area and death rates:

> Differences in the social class structure of constituencies explained about the same amount (8%) of variation in mortality in the whole of Britain in the early 1990s as they did in the early 1980s. These results suggest that, contrary to popular beliefs, there has been little or no decline in the importance of social class in determining the patterns of mortality in Britain (Britain is certainly not becoming a classless society).
>
> (Mitchell *et al.*, 2000, p.19)

Indeed, not only do Mitchell and colleagues claim, against the views of organizations such as The Henley Centre, that class still matters, they argue that geographical inequalities in Britain's health reached their highest recorded levels in the late 1990s. It is the relationship between geography and other social divisions that matter here: the widening health gap has accompanied the growing income and wealth divide between the richest and poorest sections of the population. The evidence provided by the Bristol researchers adds to widespread concerns that a *postcode lottery* in health care (and also in educational provision) exists in contemporary Britain. Where one lives plays a part not only in one's overall standard of health and life expectancy but in general quality of life. Using the ACORN system in 1996 the Department of Health examined what it termed area *'variations'* (as opposed to inequalities) in health across England. It concluded that there was a marked difference in patterns of morbidity, that is ill health, between the ACORN categories and a 'general tendency for health to deteriorate from Category A to Category F ...' (Department of Health, 1996). In addition, where you live can matter immensely in the provision and quality of health care. Access to such care can vary significantly between different places. In 1999 the Westminster government and the Scottish Parliament both announced proposals to end the postcode health 'lottery', particularly through the launch of the National Institute for Clinical Excellence that would set down national guidelines for health care and treatment.

There is a complex interplay of factors at work in creating the patterns of ill health and life expectancy between different places. This involves the social divisions of class, gender and ethnicity, as well as age, and processes of discrimination and oppression, such as racism and sexism. We should not forget in addition the ongoing controversies over how such inequalities are to be defined, measured and theorized, issues that are explored in subsequent chapters in this volume.

SUMMARY OF SECTION 2

This section has shown that:

1   There are a number of different classifications of place in operation that can be used for different purposes, from market research through to the identification of 'deprived' areas.

2   The mapping of place through systems such as ACORN tends to be premised upon particular sets of assumptions, values and political judgements about certain places.

3   Schemes for the classification of place often produce overly homogenized views of places that work to obscure their internal social composition, divisions and differences.

4   There are marked dfifferences between areas in relation to patterns of health, educational provision and attainment.

5   Place is something that is actively made – and contested.

---

3 Sociology and place

While the classifying and mapping of places may have reached new levels of sophistication in the 1990s, there is a long history of classifying places in sociology, particularly though not exclusively in the sub-discipline of urban sociology (Savage and Warde, 1993). Place has occupied a central position in sociology and in other forms of social investigation in Britain since the mid to late nineteenth century. Victorian social research was successful in establishing ways of measuring, mapping and identifying areas within cities that were commonly regarded by the ruling classes of the period as those of the 'dangerous classes' or 'residuum' (Mooney, 1998, pp.54–60). Nineteenth-century social reformers such as Charles Booth developed techniques of mapping places on the basis of statistical difference between places: see Figure 1.4.

These techniques can be related to a more significant concern with the surveillance of the 'lower' social classes. In this respect **Tony Bennett and Diane Watson (2002a)** have referred to Mary Poovey's notion of the 'ocular penetration' of the lives of the poor, rendering them as – potentially at least – more visible and potentially controllable. Arguably the kinds of methods developed during this time – tied as they often were to concerns with the surveillance and regulation of poor people – have been a dominant feature of social investigation since then, with sociology often playing a significant role. Exploring the working classes in their place of residence was all too often an essential component of these sociological studies. In other ways nineteenth-century explorations of the lives of the poor lived through the 'community studies' of the 1950s and 1960s (see **Jordan, 2002**). More recently we can see the continuing concerns with the lives of the poor in the more journalistic and popular 'travelogues' that have become a more distinctive and visible genre in the late twentieth century. Widely-read books such *Danziger's Britain*, subtitled 'a journey to the edge', or Nick Davies' *Dark Heart* which proclaims to provide 'the shocking truth about hidden Britain', or Wilson and Wylie's *The Dispossessed*,

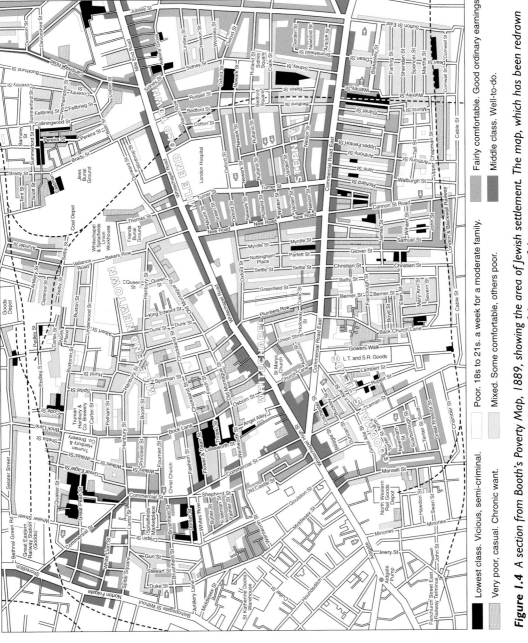

Figure 1.4 *A section from Booth's Poverty Map, 1889, showing the area of Jewish settlement. The map, which has been redrawn and simplified, shows the predominant social class composition of the streets of the area.*

Legend:
- Lowest class. Vicious, semi-criminal.
- Very poor, casual. Chronic want.
- Poor. 18s to 21s. a week for a moderate family.
- Mixed. Some comfortable, others poor.
- Fairly comfortable. Good ordinary earnings.
- Middle class. Well-to-do.

represent a blurring of the distinction, often fuzzy in any case, between academic-informed discourse with the more voyeuristic approach of some forms of journalism (Danziger, 1996; Davies, 1997; Wilson and Wylie, 1992). These examples – and there are plenty of others both in written form and as well as in television documentaries – could perhaps tentatively be termed 'popular (or populist!) sociology'. Whatever the media, however, they tend to share – and through this we can observe the continuing legacies of past methods of social and sociological investigations – an interest in those aspects of working-class life deemed to be 'pathological'.

The interest in patterns of social segregation in the city has a long history in sociology. While in Britain a strongly empirically based tradition of social investigation was established and developed from the late nineteenth century, in the United States during the 1920s and 1930s the Chicago School of sociology was pioneering new methods of social research. As American urban sociologist Ed Soja points out, the Chicago School was also concerned to provide empirically based measures through which different places in cities could be demarcated (Soja, 2000, p.86). These places – or, to use the term coined by the Chicago sociologists, *natural areas* – could be marked by the distribution of particular populations, such as ethnic groups, or by the incidence of social problems, such as crime rates.

The Chicago School of sociology was influential in securing a place for *urban* sociology within the wider discipline. But through its methods and its concern to conduct detailed ethnographic studies of groups within inter-war Chicago, the School was influential beyond the confines of the urban sociology of the time. The influence of its mapping techniques laid the basis for the geodemographic systems developed later in the century. Additionally it helped to identify place as a legitimate and useful concern of sociological research.

3.1 Representing place

One of the key themes which runs through the discussion thus far is that a sense of place, along with geographically based inequalities, is an important element in how we see the world around us: its differences and forms of divisions. How particular places are constructed and represented reflects unevenness in power relations in society. This is all too evident if we consider the ways in which certain places acquire negative labels.

READING 1.1

Now read the extract from Séan Damer's study of 'Wine Alley' in Glasgow which you will find reprinted at the end of the chapter as Reading 1.1. When you have done so, answer the following questions:

1   What factors contributed to the labelling of some housing estates as 'problem places'?

2   What might be the consequences of such labelling for the people who live there?

In his studies of place stigmatization in Glasgow, Séan Damer focuses on two housing estates in different parts of the city that had acquired negative reputations during the post-Second World War period (Damer, 1989, 1992). The Moorepark housing estate was more popularly know by the derogatory name 'Wine Alley', while the since-demolished Blackhill estate had a city-wide reputation as a place of poverty and violence. Class-based and ethnicity-based forms of discrimination combined here, with Blackhill's population comprising a significant number of people from a Catholic Irish background. Damer's work points to the diverse sources of these negative reputations. These include, in addition to local folk-wisdoms, the state, at all levels, the police and law enforcement agencies, the media and, importantly, academic social science (in Damer's terms, the *social-democratic* representation).

The labelling of places as problem or deviant locales carries widespread consequences for the people living therein. We have referred already to postcode discrimination by employers. This is how one resident of the Kelvin Flats estate in Sheffield expressed their own experience in this regard:

> As soon as I have written a letter [of application] and I have written where I live, I have not heard from them. And also when I have been for interviews, these people say 'well!'. I never put Kelvin Flats on my letters of application [now], because I know I won't hear anything. So I have gone to an interview to give them the opportunity to see me first, rather than judging what sort of person I am from where I live. Their faces dropped. I look for it and I have seen it, their face drops when you say 'I live at Kelvin.'
>
> (quoted in Lawless and Smith, 1998, p.212)

In addition to such discrimination in finding employment, 'financial exclusion' also results in far-reaching problems for residents. Andrew Leyshon and Nigel Thrift argue that during the 1990s there has been a process of financial withdrawal by financial institutions away from poorer social groups and poorer places as they sought to recoup losses incurred through the deregulation of credit in the 1980s (Leyshon and Thrift, 1997, p.226). The practice of 'red-lining' areas on the map, whereby financial institutions actively discriminate against certain places and thus make it difficult for residents to obtain credit or loans, has long been noted. The Office of Fair Trading has prohibited the 'scoring' of areas (often on the basis of court judgements relating to debt) while the Commission for Racial Equality has claimed that such practices tend to discriminate against areas with high proportions of people from minority ethnic backgrounds (Ludgate Public Affairs, 1999). Yet red-lining and other related place-based exclusions still occur, albeit implicitly. Leyshon and Thrift argue that the 'character' of an area or place frequently played an important role in this process. They concluded that 'spaces of financial exclusion' are emerging in modern societies such as the United Kingdom which are clearly linked to place, class, gender and ethnic backgrounds and affecting job prospects and income levels.

The studies by Damer in Glasgow and by other sociologists in Manchester and Sheffield (Taylor *et al.*, 1996) highlight that there is no one sense of place but multiple stories. Place is something that is fought over, and *for* – a theme to which we return in later sections. Damer discusses the ways in which people, often in the most difficult of circumstances, struggle to forge some sense of collective identity and support and – while acknowledging both the limitations of the term, as well as its more negative aspects and connotations – 'community spirit'. Against employer discrimination, financial exclusion and processes of labelling and stigmatization, people in places constructed as problem locales actively fight for a different sense of place from that employed by state agencies, the media and, indeed, often by academics.

To conclude this section it is important to understand that the geography of place both reflects and contributes to the structures of social difference, divisions and inequalities that are considered throughout this book. Whether we are talking about the housing estates in the studies referred to above, or places of power – for example, the City of London – we cannot understand place without beginning to develop an understanding of the ways in which society is divided. But, in turn, in focusing on place, we are also unpicking the social relations that underpin it. Places are part and parcel of the social structure of a society – they are socially produced and reproduced in ways that are often highly iniquitous.

SUMMARY OF SECTION 3

This section has:

1 considered the construction and meaning of place in relation to social differences and divisions in the UK context, in particular how the ascription of a postcode to an individual can serve as a shorthand signifier that condenses a range of assumptions about social characteristics, lifestyle and status. Postcodes operate as powerful signifiers that have real effects, not least as facilitators of social surveillance for wide-ranging purposes.

2 examined the ways in which 'life-chances', specifically those linked to education and health, are influenced by where we live and looked at some examples of how places become linked to particular representations.

In the remainder of the chapter we are going to consider some examples of contemporary places in terms of their very differently planned construction and development with regard to social differences and divisions.

4 Utopia/Privatopia: making places for the new millennium

In section 4 we move away from the issue of social division through place in the United Kingdom to a more global context, to consider some examples of places that have been actively constructed in relation to social differences and divisions. A key focus here will be the relationship between inclusion and exclusion in these community developments: does inclusiveness in relation to certain social groups inevitably mean exclusion of others?

4.1 Gated communities

Half an hour later, as I turned onto Gateway Terrace, I thought that *community* was a strange word for a collection of houses that isolated people so thoroughly. Each house – if that's what you call something with twenty rooms and four chimneys – was set so far back behind trees and fences that you could only see fragments of facades or gables. There weren't any sidewalks, since no one could possibly walk to town – or rather, mall – from this distance. […] I stopped the battered Skylark at the gate and looked for a way in. A large sign told me the premises were protected by Total Security Systems and that the fence was electrified so not to try to climb over it. I wondered if one of those spikes at the top had caused the damage to Nicola Aguinaldo's abdomen …

(Paretsky, 1999, p.71)

In this extract, V.I. Warshawski, Sara Paretsky's fictional feminist detective, is, as usual, pursuing the interests of the poor and exploited against the evil and corrupt activities of corporate Chicago. A young Latino housemaid has been killed and V.I. suspects the woman's previous employer, a big-shot corporate boss whose out-of-town residence she is therefore trying to access. Strategic literary stereotyping aside, the quote neatly evokes a type of 'gated' community that has developed since the 1980s within, or just outside, some cities in the world,

Figure 1.5 *The entrance to a gated community in China: this is a global phenomenon, and a symptom of societies with wide social differences*

in response to particular constellations of conditions. Gated communities are characteristically self-segregated, prestige residential areas enclosed within high walls and electrified fences and protected by electronic surveillance, with remote-controlled gates that are often supervised (guarded), through which only residents have automatic access. They have developed largely in response to escalating fears about violent crime and threatened safety in large cities where the effects of material inequalities and social divisions are most intensely represented. Gated communities vary in emphasis and the extent to which the symbolic exclusivity they represent is reinforced by physical barriers. Some emphasize an exclusive, luxury lifestyle in residential communities that foreground leisure facilities and property values. Some gated enclaves within cities are less prestigious and promote the idea of secure, semi-private neighbourhoods and territory for middle-class people. (See Figure 1.5.)

Although a growing phenomenon in Europe, Canada, South America and the USA (Blakely and Snyder's 1997 analysis of the development of gated communities is titled *Fortress America*), early and high-profile examples were developed in Los Angeles, Johannesburg and Cape Town. These have been linked to the idea of 'white flight' from areas of perceived urban, racial conflict (Robinson, 1999).

Protecting cities by erecting walls to keep outsiders out is clearly anything but a new idea. It seems ironic to think now that in Roman cities of the UK such as Chester and York, the walls currently promoted to embrace as many heritage visitors as possible were originally designed to exclude people. Similarly, attempts at re-ordering space within cities to counter congestion and conflict – and with the aim of socially engineering proximity and detachment between people according to categories of class, culture, religion and ethnicity – have a long history in nineteenth-century urban redevelopments such as Paris and Chicago, as well as in colonial cities. A famous instance in the British context were the Cutteslowe Walls in Summertown, a suburban district of Oxford, built

Figure 1.6 One of
the two Cutteslowe
Walls that blocked
roads through
adjoining estates in
Summertown,
Oxford, 1935

in the 1930s to separate a middle-class, private housing estate from its
immediately adjacent working-class, council estate neighbour: see Figure 1.6.
The Cutteslowe Walls became the subject of intense local political demonstration
and dispute which eventually led to their demolition in 1959 (Collison, 1963).

However, contemporary social theorists such as Blakely and Snyder (1997),
Davis (1994) and Caldeira (1996) argue that gated communities are a distinctive
development of post-modernity, which are developing in response to the anti-
urban idea, often fuelled by the media, that big cities are now out of control because
of the potential conflicts between and within their vast, socially divided populations.

ACTIVITY 4

Pause for a moment to consider the following questions and to jot down your
ideas.

1   What do you think those in favour of gated communities might argue are their
    benefits?

2   What do you think their critics might argue in response?

COMMENT

Arguments in support of gated communities are likely to note that:

■   they provide safe residential environments for people with security for their
    property, thus delivering what might be seen as a fundamental right of citizenship.
    Those enjoying these benefits are more likely to fulfil their role as responsible
    citizens and positive contributors to society.

■   gated communities are likely to be homogeneous, so their members are more
    likely to share values and therefore foster new community links and networks
    of common purpose.

- where class, ethnicity and other factors are sources of conflict and incompatible differences, gated communities may provide a pragmatic solution, at least for some people.

Conversely, critics are likely to focus on the effects of gated communities on those excluded. For example:

- establishing ring-fenced areas of protected security can have a destabilizing effect on neighbouring areas because the perceived crime and violence that those inside gated communities are seeking to avoid are displaced onto areas outside their boundaries. This happens at both the social and symbolic level, because the negative representation of 'no-go areas' as dangerous can easily become a self-fulfilling prophecy.

- rigid spatial divisions between communities make social divisions and inequalities concrete and absolute, as crossing the boundaries between them is increasingly perceived as dangerous. This is likely to have a pernicious effect on commitment to any shared rights and responsibilities of citizenship as social and cultural diversity are perceived in terms of hierarchical difference and negative 'otherness'.

- in addition, gated communities provide open season for property developers and security firms to exploit the concerns of people who are fearful of their security and feel they can buy a solution by excluding those who seem to pose a threat.

To summarize, then, gated communities represent a contemporary example of the construction of place on the basis of unequal and hierarchical social division rather than of difference in the sense of diversity. They *in*clude residents on the basis of significant wealth and social status and actively *ex*clude others (except as low-paid service-workers), thereby constructing and reinforcing social inequalities. Powers of exclusion operate through the direct and material boundaries of walls and security systems but exclusivity is also maintained at the representational level – by the social meanings signified by gated communities. The excluded are kept out as much by the representation – the messages generated – as by the walls themselves.

4.2 Celebration: new urban paradise in 1990s' USA

The development, by the Disney Corporation, of the new town of Celebration in Osceola County, Florida – 15 miles south of Orlando and close to their three theme parks – is ostensibly based on very different principles from those underpinning the development of gated communities. As opposed to insular enclosure, Celebration seeks to offer openness in terms of both the built and social environment. Walls and gates are certainly not apparent in Celebration because the town is constructed to promote close community involvement and interaction between neighbours. Houses are densely arranged, without the large separating lawns that we typically associate with middle-class residential developments in the USA (ubiquitous in movies, even if we haven't seen them for real), so that residents can hardly avoid meeting each other on the adjacent front porches that are a distinctive feature of most dwellings. Also the town was designed to attract visitors – at one level it is self-consciously another Disney attraction – who are required in order to support the retail economy in the new town.

The story of Celebration is fascinating, not least because it was exactly that – a story covered endlessly in the national US media, an ambitious social experiment that has been subjected to continuing public scrutiny. It is also of significant interest to academics and social theorists, and thereby for the methodological practice of sociology. Our account here is informed by two ethnographic accounts of the development of Celebration: *The Celebration Chronicles: Life, Liberty and the Pursuit of Property Value in Disney's New Town* by Andrew Ross (1999) and *Celebration, USA* by Douglas Frantz and Catherine Collins (1999).

Planned 'new town' developments have been increasingly commonplace since the Second World War, based on the idea that 'communities' will thrive if the built environment is designed to support the complex mix of community needs in terms of housing, education, health, transport, employment, cultural amenities and so on. Celebration is not novel as a new town development per se but because of its connection with Disney and the way in which it was promoted in this respect. Disney already owned the land on which Celebration was built and – according to Ross's and Frantz and Collins' accounts – the idea for a new town was the brainchild of a Disney executive who eventually managed to pitch it successfully to his boss. It related back to a pet project of Walt Disney himself – a fantasy **Utopian** community called ur-EPCOT which encompassed communitarian ideals and family values. The appeal to Disney was the combination of a potentially hugely lucrative development project in an area where they already had vast interests, and the opportunity to promote their reputation as a corporation committed to the public good, most particularly to family life – suppliers of paradise in both the real and the fantasy worlds.

Utopia

Once committed to the project, Disney established a separate development company for Celebration that set about planning the new town as a distinctive example of New Urbanism. New Urbanism is a contemporary philosophy and practice relating to urban development based on a neo-traditional approach using traditional building styles and materials, and on 'a fundamental belief that the design of the physical environment has a fundamental effect on social behaviour' (Ross, 1999, p.78). Rejecting high-rise modernism and suburbia, New Urbanism sees the solution for modern living as lying in a return to the scale of small-town life, updated to take account of contemporary social and environmental concerns and advantage of new technologies. The focus is on high-density, socially mixed population in the belief that proximity to others fosters civic responsibility and involvement (in contrast to the philosophy underpinning gated communities), and on a car-limited environment. Walking downtown is easy from all residential areas, apartments are built above shops in the downtown area to ensure that it does not become an empty space at night: access for car parking is built only from the backs of houses.

Celebration was planned for 20,000 residents, to be gradually recruited to the town as it developed through several phases, and to cost US$2.5 billion over ten years, $100 million of which would be the start-up funding from Disney. The five cornerstone commitments were to Place, Community, Health, Education and Technology. The extensive market research that Disney undertook to find out what types of houses 'Celebrationites' might prefer confirmed New Urbanist convictions. Traditional styles were much the most popular and a *Celebration Pattern Book* of vernacular house styles – including the Classical, the Colonial

Revival and the Cottage – was developed. There were four basic models in a price range from US$120,000 to $1 million with some variations within each. In addition there were apartments for rent but, significantly, no accommodation was developed for public ownership and distribution. The Health Centre emphasized a community role promoting wellness rather than curing illness. Celebration School, a key promotional selling-point for the town, initially offered a progressive educational philosophy based on mixed ability and mixed age group learning in interactive 'neighbourhoods' rather than traditional classrooms. The emphasis was on providing an education appropriate to the contemporary world where skills of debate, performance and portfolio development were foregrounded, as opposed to those of rote learning and written presentation in relation to tests. 'Learning neighbourhoods' had a mix of open and closed areas designed for different activities, comfortable seating, large tables, lots of computer terminals and electronic equipment, but no desks. In the original plan, all Celebration homes were to be electronically linked to the school.

The downtown area had priority investment from Disney – a glitzy downtown would be a key draw for potential residents and visitors alike – and an impressive range of gliterati architects (Philip Johnson, Charles Moore, Cesar Pelli, Robert Venturi and Denise Scott Brown amongst them) were commissioned to design Celebration's civic buildings. They were given clear briefs for post-modern styles that would complement the town's commitment to neo-traditionalism.

Figure 1.7 New homes on Celebration Avenue: traditional verandahs and picket fences

Disney financed a high-profile marketing campaign for the town that drew massive interest. By the time Phase 1 development was complete in 1995, 351 houses were sold and 123 apartments rented in a lottery which five thousand people attended and which, according to Ross, now has a place in American cultural myth. Claiming you were present at the Celebration lottery, apparently, is like claiming you were at the Woodstock music festival in 1969!

Figure 1.8 *'Isn't this reason enough for Celebration?': billboard advertising the new development*

ACTIVITY 5

So, how close does Celebration seem to Utopia to you? Spend a few minutes noting down what you think might be the benefits and the drawbacks of this planned new urban community, designed to integrate socially mixed people.

4.3 Trouble in paradise

In addressing the question posed in Activity 5, Ross's answer is that Celebration is 'both the best and worst of towns' (1999, p.325). It is a crime- and violence-free town with almost full employment, for those who want it, provided largely by Disney in the surrounding area. It is a clean, potentially healthy, aesthetically distinctive environment and the residential planning does promote contact, involvement and investment in the community. Ross describes how actively some residents pursue community in this sense, taking up community-based positions on civic committees, and some referring specifically to the ideal of **Gemeinschaft** (or community) when interviewed (see **Hamilton, 2002**).

Gemeinschaft

However, significant flaws were also apparent. Residents typically paid 25 per cent more for property in Celebration than equivalent houses would have cost elsewhere, on plots that were much smaller, in order to provide New Urban high density (as well as more income for Disney). They paid this for the value-added benefits offered by the promised Utopian community, but disillusion soon set in due to poor construction work. Many Celebrationites had reservations about the restricted range of house designs, not to mention the regulation requiring white-lined curtains, and when the houses were shoddily built it added insult to injury. They were reluctant to make too much fuss in the glare of media scrutiny for fear that property values would immediately plummet. The downtown plan for chic retail outlets meant that there was no supermarket or video store in town, so residents had to shop out of town for everyday items.

Both Ross and Frantz and Collins focus strongly on the conflicts over Celebration School, which many early residents listed as their main reason for coming to Celebration. Opening on a note of high optimism related to offering a distinctive education relevant to the contemporary world, it quickly fell from grace in the town when students failed to achieve high grades in standard national tests. Bitter conflicts ensued between the school and parents, and between parents, who were completely divided in their views about what education should deliver. The struggles gave rich pickings for the media that fanned the flames and, within a year of opening, over half of the school's staff had left and many students had been withdrawn.

Celebrationites might be keenly aware of the material divisions represented by the difference between The Estate House and The Cottage, but with the cheapest house priced at US$120,000 many people are totally excluded from this social experiment. Although Celebration's focus is on the nuclear family, the town has a gay community and inclusively incorporates some same-sex couples and single parents, according to these commentators. However, in spite of the planners' attempts to market the town as culturally and ethnically inclusive by featuring an Hispanic child in preview video advertising and placing advertisements in the minority press, the town is almost entirely white.

ACTIVITY 6

Based on what you have read about Celebration so far, consider why you think the town failed to attract an ethnically mixed population. When you have done so, go on to read Ross's explanation.

READING 1.2

Now read the extract 'Sure tried' which is taken from Chapter 11 of *The Celebration Chronicles*.

Ross's account describes Disney's attempts to promote ethnic diversity as superficial, paying liberal lip service to a policy of inclusion but without any positive follow-through action to secure and maintain it. For example, the architecture and design were thought to be culturally alienating – reminiscent of plantation development and with an emphasis on peace and quiet. Crucially, the cost of property and accommodation, which had a generally discriminatory effect, impacted particularly in relation to ethnicity. Ross comments elsewhere that if Disney had adopted a more creative attitude towards financing Celebration property for both purchase and rent – by setting up Housing Associations, for example – then their declared commitment towards a mixed community could have been achievable. Ross also identifies the different attitudes towards ethnic inclusivity demonstrated by white Celebrationites, from entrenched racism and bigotry through tolerant indifference to positive regret at Celebration's monocultural character. The school was initially an important counter-influence because it was open to non-resident students and drew in a proportion of children from multi-ethnic backgrounds outside the town, as well as some teachers. But the general controversies and conflicts that developed around the school undermined its 'beacon' effect in respect to ethnic diversity that, in Celebration, represented a clear social division.

READING 1.3

Before leaving Celebration we would like you to turn to Reading 1.3, an extract from 'Truman didn't sleep here' which is the final chapter of Frantz and Collins' *Celebration, USA*. In it they evaluate the relative success and failure of the project. How would you summarize their judgements for and against?

Frantz a0nd Collins found that Celebration is an 'authentic', living and breathing town in spite of its association with Disney 'pixie dust'. The town design, buildings, layout, architecture and so on *could* work to deliver what the concept envisioned, but there are problems both in the material quality of construction and in the demand for uniformity and acceptance of control that buying in to the community concept involves. Buying-in came most easily to the early 'pioneers'. Even amongst (what turned out to be) a very undifferentiated community in the socio-economic terms, there were significant differences of expectation and conflicts of view, particularly over the school. But the public processes of debate and involvement that challenged the imposition of regulations and controls were beginning to have some effects and Frantz and Collins clearly feel that Celebration can provide a worthwhile model for further New Urbanist projects.

SUMMARY OF SECTION 4

1   Gated communities are constructed on the basis of social division rather than more neutral social difference. They are exclusive in terms of private wealth and status. Their exclusivity operates at both material and symbolic levels; walls and security systems function as both physical and representational boundaries.

2   Celebration provides a contrasting example of apparent openness and inclusivity – a community without walls. Here again the built environment, in this case without walls rather than depending on them, functions at both material and symbolic levels; the two are mutually constitutive.

3   In spite of its signature of social diversity and inclusiveness promoted by Disney, Celebration implicitly excludes certain social groups; it is predominantly a white, middle-class town.

4   The more modest achievement of the Celebration project is perhaps that the town provides a community that is socially differentiated, albeit within an overall context of middle-class sameness. Older people, single and gay people live alongside the predominant heterosexual families, linked through their shared commitment to the community revival philosophy of the project and to shared 'lifestyle' interests.

5   In spite of directed advertising, the town failed to draw an ethnically mixed population and remains a 'white' town. In this instance the superficial representational message signifying Celebration as ethnically inclusive did not connect with its intended audience.

5 Place and lifestyle

5.1 Manchester's Gay Village

In section 5 we are going to look at the example of a very different type of place: one that has been made anew right in the middle of an old, British city – Manchester's Gay Village. In contrast to the examples of gated communities and Celebration in the previous section, large-scale new building developments – separate or segregated – have not taken place, and the Gay Village is not necessarily the place where the gay people who use it actually live. It is instead an area of the city that has become a social centre for gay people, primarily for men, to meet and spend leisure time. It is therefore a place that relates specifically to the social division of sexuality, and also to lifestyle: in the village, the gay men's community meets in the context of consumer culture.

Figure 1.9 *Canal Street in Manchester's Gay Village*

READING 1.4

Now turn to Reading 1.4, 'Out on the town' by Ian Taylor, Karen Evans and Penny Fraser. This is an account of Manchester's Gay Village, based on interviews with eight gay men who identify as members of the community.

Consider the following questions as you read, and note down your answers:

1 What do the authors identify as the key characteristics of the Gay Village and who is it for?

2 What factors influenced its development?

3 Why, according to their respondents, did it develop in Manchester, rather than in London or another northern town?

The Gay Village is an inner-city area of Manchester that has been the target of recent urban redevelopment. It has been actively remade as a social and leisure-based enclave where gay men socialize and, most importantly, feel safe from homophobic harassment. It operates inclusively rather than exclusively – i.e. people gather there in an open-ended and voluntary way and there are no barriers to keep anyone out, but the establishing culture appeals specifically to young, gay, white men and less so to lesbians. The 'places' that constitute the community are places of leisure consumption – bars, clubs, restaurants and so on – so the village is linked to the 'pink pound', in this instance the spending power of gay men. It is 'a place for males with money who like to drink' (Taylor *et al.*, 1996, p.187).

The Gay Village developed as the result of a specific coincidence of economic and cultural circumstances. The development boom of the mid-1980s, when entrepreneurs were looking for new 'niche' markets to extend leisure-based consumption articulated with a wider cultural (and legal) context of liberalizing attitudes towards homosexuality. But the specific cultural context at the time was one of backlash because of the moral panic over AIDS and the Thatcher government's emphasis on 'family values'. Consolidating a collective community against the backlash was an important factor. The establishment of a separate, but open, development, underpinned by market and consumer confidence, and the transformation of an area that had historical links with the hidden gay community of previous years, was the result. A profitable alliance between political and commercial development agencies and the successful gay business sector was also an important dimension.

Respondents thought that the village had developed in Manchester, rather than elsewhere, because it has a history of incorporating different communities and a reputation for 'friendliness', although they recognized that this did not extend throughout all areas of the city. Certainly, the use of terms such as 'European' and 'cosmopolitan' suggest a more positive attitude towards ethnic and cultural difference than the kind of language often applied in, and about, such places, represented as zones of negative cultural difference conceptualized as, for example, ghettos.

5.2 Lifestyle: place, identity and consumption

In this section and in section 4 we have spent some time considering descriptions of three different examples of contemporary places and accounts of how they came about. We have also analysed how they relate to ideas about social difference, division and inequality. Now we will look finally at the light a more theoretical, sociological explanation might throw on these constructions and transformations of place.

In all three examples – gated communities, Celebration and Manchester's Gay Village – it is clear that traditional theories of social class (to be discussed in Chapter 2) are relevant. These communities are upper- or middle-class developments, in the sense that they depend on significantly or relatively high levels of income, or other economic advantage, to take part. Poorer people are definitely excluded, but neither inclusion nor exclusion rests only on economic status. For example, as we have learned, these places are also largely white. Regardless of the marketing of Celebration directed at middle-class ethnic diversity, black people have not gone to live there. Early research suggests that they do not identify with the culture and 'lifestyle' of the town. It is therefore exclusionary in terms of the informational 'messages' it gives about what living there means, and who you are if you live in Celebration. But sufficient economic resource is not an adequate reason for white people to live there. Celebration's appeal is directed at quite particular, neo-traditional, cultural values based on a 'lifestyle' of New Urbanism.

Similarly, although Manchester has an area-based community called the Gay Village, it is gay men rather than lesbians who use and identify with it. In seeking to explain this, the authors of Reading 1.4 quote Adler and Brenner's (1992) argument that women are typically poorer than men – fewer women could afford to participate in the consumption-based social activities in the village – but also that the wider dominant 'culture of masculinity' means women tend to develop 'a less transparent culture built around networks and trusting relationships' (p.187). Here again, interacting factors of both economic division and symbolic, cultural meaning are in play. The division of age is also a factor recognized by the gay men interviewed in this study. They feel that the consumer lifestyle of the Gay Village is likely to be less inclusive as they get older, regardless of income.

In these examples there is therefore an emphasis on buying into particular forms of lifestyle with respect to place, albeit in contexts that are also subject to economic and social inequalities and exclusions. The sociologist Mike Featherstone makes the following comment about current interest in the concept **lifestyle** and practices associated with '**lifestyle**':

> The term 'lifestyle' is currently in vogue. While the term has a more restricted sociological meaning in reference to the distinctive style of life of specific status groups (Weber, 1968; Sobel, 1982; Rojek, 1985), within contemporary consumer culture it connotes individuality, self-expression, and a stylistic self-consciousness. One's body, clothes, speech, leisure pastimes, eating and drinking preferences, home, car, choice of holidays, etc. are to be regarded as indicators of individuality of taste and sense of style of the owner/consumer. In contrast to the designation of the 1950s as an era of grey conformism, a time of *mass* consumption, changes in production techniques, market segmentation and consumer demand for a wider range of products, are often regarded as making possible a greater choice (the management of which itself becomes an art form) not only for youth of the post-1960s generation, but increasingly for the middle-aged and the elderly.
>
> …
>
> The concern with lifestyle, with the stylization of life, suggests that the practices of consumption, the planning, purchase and display of consumer goods and experiences in everyday life cannot be understood merely via conceptions of exchange value and instrumental rational calculation. The instrumental and expressive dimensions should not be regarded as exclusive either/or polarities, rather they can be conceived as a balance which consumer culture brings together. … Rather than unreflexively adopting a lifestyle, through tradition or habit, the new heroes of consumer culture make lifestyle a life project and display their individuality and sense of style in the particularity of the assemblage of goods, clothes, practices, experiences, appearance and bodily dispositions they design together into a lifestyle.

(Featherstone, 1991, pp.83, 86)

ACTIVITY 7

What do you make of Featherstone's explanation of 'lifestyle'? Can you relate it to the examples of place we have studied?

In our view, Featherstone adopts a rather 'triumphalist' tone, which seems significantly to undersell – in this extract, at least – the restrictive operation of unequal material and social relations and to suggest that lifestyle choices are more open than they often are. But he does precisely identify the symbolic values of consumer goods and practices that operate independently of, but articulate with, their instrumental and use values. In terms of our examples of place, we can see how buying in to Celebration, or spending time in the clubs and bars in Manchester's Gay Village, are expressions of 'lifestyle' in Featherstone's sense. They are consumption activities that operate as complex and condensed signifiers that communicate – to others as well as back to the generating consumers themselves – who they are.

In pushing this analysis further, Pierre Bourdieu's influential concept of **cultural capital** (Bourdieu, 1986; see also **Bennett, 2002**), linked to the notion of lifestyle, is also useful. Bourdieu suggests a model of social class that is based on related aspects of different metaphorical 'capitals'. These are neither solely based on, nor reducible to, differentials in economic relations of power.

cultural capital

Beverley Skeggs provides the following clear summary that identifies Bourdieu's four forms of capital:

(i) *economic capital:* this includes income, wealth, inheritance and financial assets

(ii) *social capital:* capital generated through relationships with others, links with influential groups

(iii) *cultural capital:* this can exist in three forms – in an embodied state, that is in the form of long-lasting dispositions of the mind and body; in the objectified state, in the form of cultural goods; and in the institutionalized state, resulting in such things as educational qualifications […]

(iv) *symbolic capital:* this is the form the different types of capital take once they are perceived as recognized and legitimate. Legitimation is the key mechanism in the conversion to power. Cultural capital has to be legitimated before it can have symbolic power. Capital has to be regarded as legitimate before it can be capitalized upon.

(Skeggs, 1997, p.7)

The argument is that in any individual's (or group's) social context, their levels of symbolically legitimated economic, social and cultural capital articulate to provide changing levels of power and 'distinction' depending on the overall amount of symbolic capital in the mix at the time. Thus a high level of economic capital does not automatically guarantee overall 'distinction' or power in a social field, because cultural or social capital may not be correspondingly high. For example, there was significant economic capital in Celebration, but this did not, on its own, control what happened there. In that context specifically, cultural capital with respect to the promotion of new urbanism and progressive education – constituted as a lifestyle – also had a high level of symbolic legitimacy. Bourdieu's model provides a dynamic way of understanding how the complexities of power relations work – which counters the notion of a static and determining ascription of social class per se, and which emphasizes the role of changing symbolic meaning and value over time.

The idea of cultural capital is perhaps particularly relevant in the example of the Gay Village. Here, place was transformed for a subordinate social group through the promotion of consumer lifestyle. Featherstone argues that:

> It makes sense to talk about the genesis of taste for lifestyles and cultural goods in terms of the possession of volume of cultural capital as well as economic capital. To attempt to map taste purely in terms of income is to miss the dual principles in operation, for cultural capital has its own structure of value, which amounts to convertibility into social power, independent of income or money. The cultural realm thus has its own logic and currency as well as rate of conversion into economic capital.
>
> (Featherstone, 1991, p.89)

Economic capital was important in the constitution of the Gay Village, as demonstrated by the emphasis on the role of gay entrepreneurs. However, cultural capital, which translated into development of the area in a specific way that represented a safe but exciting place of consumer 'lifestyle' for gay men, was equally and independently important. In this instance, cultural capital – symbolically legitimated in a particular lifestyle context – has been converted into social power.

SUMMARY OF SECTION 5

1   Manchester's Gay Village is an example of place transformed through the coincidence of economic and cultural factors. It does not exist as a fixed and delimited material space of residence (as gated communities and Celebration do) but as a changing area of leisure-based consumption constituting a safe environment for gay men.

2   It exemplifies the spatial constitution of social difference in positive terms that affirm gay male identity. The ways in which the Gay Village is represented in terms of its cultural meanings have operated, in concert with economic investment, to foster its particular development. It provides a further example of place as both a material site and symbolic signifier.

3   We have seen how sociological theories of lifestyle and cultural capital can throw explanatory light on why and how the Gay Village developed as and when it did, and on the power relations that underpin it.

6 Conclusion

In this first chapter of *Social Differences and Divisions* we have argued that place is central to the construction, maintenance and representation of social differences and divisions. In section 2 we analysed ways in which our life-chances are influenced by where we live and looked at how private and public agencies collect, construct meanings in relation to, and use information about, people based on their place of residence. In particular, we examined how access to education, employment and health care can be influenced by where we live in ways that construct social divisions in unequal terms. In section 3 we considered some of the ways in which a concern with place has been central to sociology.

In section 4 we examined two contemporary 'places' – the global phenomenon of gated communities and the new urban development of Celebration in Florida – as places differently constituted in relation to social division and difference. Finally, in section 5 we examined the development of Manchester's Gay Village in the context of theoretical explanations of social difference in terms of a lifestyle community.

A key theme of the chapter has been the constitution of places as both sites and signifiers of social differences and divisions. Places are the material spaces in which social differences and divisions are made and remade, but they also exist as cultural representations of meaning, and the meanings of places, as well as their material spaces, can be contested, struggled over and changed. The examples of places we have considered demonstrate how power operates in different ways in the construction of place with regard to social differences and divisions. Gated communities and the postcode health lottery, for example, manifest the operation of power in terms of direct exclusion and regulation, thereby demonstrating the constitution of place in terms of social division and inequality. Manchester's Gay Village, and to some extent Celebration, demonstrate the making and re-making of places in terms of social difference and diversity, drawing on lifestyle connections in which power operates in a more diffuse way and cultural capital is as relevant as economic capital.

Our discussion of place, as the location where categories of social difference and division are shaped, experienced and changed, sets the scene for the substantive explorations of these intersecting categories in the following chapters of this book.

References

Adler, S. and Brenner, J. (1992) 'Gender and space: lesbians and gay men in the city', *International Journal of Urban and Regional Research*, vol.16, pp.24–34.

Atkinson, R. and Moon, G. (1994) *Urban Policy in Britain*, Basingstoke, Macmillan.

Bennett, T. (2002) 'Home and everyday life' in Bennett, T. and Watson, D. (eds) *op. cit.*.

Bennett, T. and Watson, D. (2002a) 'Understanding everyday life: introduction' in Bennett, T. and Watson, D. (eds) *op. cit.*.

Bennett, T. and Watson, D. (eds) (2002b) *Understanding Everyday Life*, Oxford, Blackwell/The Open University. (Book 1 in this series.)

Blakely, E.J. and Snyder, M. (1997) *Fortress America,* Washington, DC, The Brookings Institution.

Bourdieu, P. (1986) *Distinction: A Social Critique of the Judgement of Taste*, London, Routledge.

Bridge, G. and Watson, S. (eds) (2000) *A Companion to the City,* Oxford, Blackwell.

Byrne, D. (1999) *Social Exclusion*, Buckingham, Open University Press.

CACI (2000) *The ACORN User Guide Index*, London, CACI Limited.

Caldeira, T. (1996) 'Fortified enclaves: the new urban segregation', *Public Culture,* vol.8, no.2, pp.329–54.

Cochrane, A. (2000) 'New Labour, new urban policy?' in Dean, H., Sykes, R. and Woods, R. (eds) *Social Policy Review 12*, Newcastle upon Tyne, University of Northumbria/ Social Policy Association.

Collison, P. (1963) *The Cutteslowe Walls: A Study in Social Class*, London, Faber & Faber.

Damer, S. (1989) *From Moorpark to 'Wine Alley': The Rise and Fall of a Glasgow Housing Scheme*, Edinburgh, Edinburgh University Press.

Damer, S. (1992) *'Last Exit to Blackhill': The Stigmatization of a Glasgow Housing Scheme*, University of Glasgow, Centre for Housing Research, Discussion Paper no.37.

Danziger, N. (1996) *Danziger's Britain: A Journey to the Edge*, London, HarperCollins.

Davies, N. (1997) *Dark Heart: The Shocking Truth about Hidden Britain*, London, Chatto & Windus.

Davis, M. (1994) 'Beyond Blade Runner: urban control – the ecology of fear', Westfield, NJ, Open Magazines Pamphlet Series.

Department of Health (1996) *Health Survey for England, 1996*, http:// www.officialdocuments.co.uk/document/doh/survey96

Featherstone, M. (1991) *Consumer Culture and Postmodernism*, London, Sage Publications.

Frantz, D. and Collins, C. (1999) *Celebration, USA: Living in Disney's Brave New Town*, New York, Henry Holt and Co.

Hamilton, P. (2002) 'The street and everyday life' in Bennett, T. and Watson, D. (eds) *op. cit..*

Harvey, D. (1996) *Justice, Nature and The Geography of Difference*, Oxford, Blackwell.

Henley Centre, The (2000) *Blurring Demographics*, http://www.henleycentre.com

Jordan, T. (2002) 'Community, space and the everyday' in Bennett, T. and Watson, D. (eds) *op. cit..*

Keith, M. and Pile, S. (1993) 'Introduction: the politics of place' in Keith, M. and Pile, S. (eds) *Place and the Politics of Identity*, London, Routledge.

Lawless, P. and Smith, Y. (1998) 'Poverty, inequality and exclusion in the contemporary city' in Lawless, P., Martin, R. and Hardy, S. (eds) *Unemployment and Social Exclusion*, London, Jessica Kingsley.

Leyshon, A. and Thrift, N. (1997) *Money/Space*, London, Routledge.

Ludgate Public Affairs (1999) *Tackling Social Exclusion in Financial Services, Volume 2: Credit Scoring*, London, Ludgate Communications.

McDowell, L. and Pringle, R. (1992) *Defining Women: Social Institutions and Gender Divisions*, Cambridge, Polity Press.

Mackintosh, M. and Mooney, G. (eds) (2000) 'Identity, inequality and social class' in Woodward, K. (ed.) *Questioning Identity: Gender, Class, Nation*, London, Routledge/ The Open University.

Massey, D. and Jess, P. (eds) (1995) *A Place in the World?*, Oxford, Oxford University Press/The Open University.

Mitchell, R., Dorling, D. and Shaw, M. (2000) *Inequalities in Life and Death*, Bristol, Policy Press/Joseph Rowntree Foundation.

Mohan, J. (2000) *A United Kingdom?*, London, Arnold.

Mooney, G. (1998) 'Remoralizing the poor'?: Gender, class and philanthropy in Victorian Britain' in Lewis, G. (ed.) *Forming Nation, Framing Welfare*, London, Routledge/The Open University.

Pacione, M. (ed.) (1997) *Britain's Cities*, London, Routledge.

Paretsky, S. (1999) *Hard Time*, New York, Random House.

Philo, C. (ed.) (1995) *Off the Map: The Social Geography of Poverty in the UK*, London, Child Poverty Action Group.

Prime Minister's Office (2000) *The Government's Annual Report, 1999–2000*, London, The Stationery Office.

Robinson, J. (1999) 'Divisive cities: power and segregation in cities' in Pile, S., Brook, C, and Mooney, G. (eds) *Unruly Cities?*, London, Routledge/The Open University.

Rojek, C. (1985) *Capitalism and Leisure Theory*, London, Tavistock.

Ross, A. (1999) *The Celebration Chronicles: Life, Liberty and the Pursuit of Property Value in Disney's New Town*, New York, Ballantine Books.

Savage, M. and Warde, A. (1993) *Urban Sociology, Capitalism and Modernity*, Basingstoke, Macmillan.

Shaw, M., Dorling, D., Gordon, D. and Smith, G.D. (1999) *The Widening Gap*, Bristol, Policy Press.

Skeggs, B. (1997) *Formations of Class and Gender*, London, Sage.

Sobel, E. (1982) *Lifestyle*, New York, Academic Press.

Social Exclusion Unit (1998) *Bringing Britain Together: A National Strategy for Neighbourhood Renewal*, Cm 4045, London, The Stationery Office.

Social Exclusion Unit (2000) *National Strategy for Neighbourhood Renewal, A Framework for Consultation*, London, The Stationery Office.

Soja, E.W. (2000) *Postmetropolis*, Oxford, Blackwell.

Taylor, I., Evans, K., and Fraser, P. (1996) *A Tale of Two Cities: Global Change, Local Feeling and Everyday Life in the North of England – A Study in Manchester and Sheffield*, London, Routledge.

Weber, M. (1968) *Economy and Society*, 3 vols, New York, Bedminster Press.

Wilson, R.M.S., Gilligan, C. and Pearson, D. (1992) *Strategic Marketing Management*, London, Heinemann-Butterworth.

Wilson, R. and Wylie, D. (1992) *The Dispossessed*, London, Picador.

Readings

 Seán Damer, 'Problem places and problem people' (1989)

(i) The 'images'

In the late 1980s in Britain, it is a commonplace to remark the existence of whole large areas in our cities containing 'problem' populations. These populations constitute a problem for the state because of their dependency, which is economic, social and political. The last couple of decades has seen a series of larger and larger government action programmes designed to wean these populations from their dependency. It would be fair to say that these programmes, whether aimed at 'deprived areas', 'inner cities' or 'peripheral estates', have simply not worked. Yet we are so familiar with the rhetoric of large-scale problems requiring large-scale solutions that we forget that this definition of 'the urban problem' is but the latest in a process at least a century old. In the 1950s, 1960s and early 1970s, the rhetoric focused on 'problem tenants/families/estates'. Individual, familial and community pathology was the name of the game. Local-authority officials and social scientists have made a living for decades peddling spurious definitions and analyses of these terms. Only last year, yet another book was published on 'The Problem Estate' (Reynolds, 1986). Whatever their intentions, many allegedly objective media stories and programmes convey a series of 'images' of these housing estates and their people. These images are familiar; they are of dereliction, poverty, degradation, 'corruption', vandalism, violence, educational and employment failure and inarticulacy. In a word, they are negative. But, they are negative in a special way; they uniformly *stigmatize* the locals as in some sense responsible for the mess they are in. ...

...

The iconography of problem people congregated in problem places is so strong in British society – perhaps particularly strong in Calvinist Scotland – that the most subliminal of media cues can trigger off a chain reaction in our minds. Consider the sheer range of such places: Blackhill, Barrowfield and Teucherhill in Glasgow; Craigmillar and Wester Hailes in Edinburgh; Ferguslie Park in Paisley; Mains o' Fintry in Dundee; the Raploch in Stirling; Meadowell in North Shields; Cantril Farm in Liverpool; Hulme and Moss Side in Manchester. The list is endless. Not all readers will have heard of all these places, but many readers will have heard of at least some of them. Will readers recognize one feature that all of these developments have in common? They are all council housing estates, containing working-class people. ...

(ii) The representations

Having introduced the widespread media imagery of so-called problem estates and problem people, I now turn to *representations* of them. By this, I mean explicit or implicit attempts purporting to make sense of the 'reality' underlying these images. Three categories are considered: firstly, the 'state'; secondly, the 'social-democratic'; and thirdly, the 'filtering-down', representations. These three categories roughly correspond respectively to centrist, Fabian and thoroughly reactionary positions on the parliamentary spectrum.

(a) The state representation

This representation refers to the official explanation of problem places and people in both central- and local-government circles.

The first official mention of problem families or problem tenants that I can find appears in a government report of 1930 (CHAC, 1930). This report appears in the context of both the Depression and the national campaign against slums, and so the language reflects the official concerns of the inter-war period:

> In our opinion the grading and placing of tenants of different standards are of the highest importance and if rightly handled have many possibilities ... Bad habits are not easily broken and when these habits govern the behaviour of a small community, such as sometimes exists in a slum street, they persist for want of better

alternatives. The bad tenant will learn more readily by eye than by ear; example is better than precept. We therefore favour the principle of separating unsatisfactory tenants from one another, so far as this is possible, and interspersing them amongst families of a good type; and we recommend the adoption of this policy.

(CHAC, 1930, para.27)

At the same time, the same report accepts that a major problem of many tenants moving into slum clearance estates was lack of money:

A number of tenants whom we questioned told us that they had no money for extra furnishings and were afraid to purchase by deferred payments for fear of falling into arrears. It is clear that many people do not possess enough furniture to make their new house into a home.

(CHAC, 1930, para.39)

The report continues:

Some tenants are thriftless and careless in their domestic habits, but are susceptible of permanent improvement under the combined influence of environment and instruction in hygiene and cleanliness. Such tenants require visiting more frequently, the close supervision being gradually relaxed as the standard improves.

The remainder, a small minority, represents what may be called the hard core of the problem of management. It consists of tenants who must be kept under constant supervision to prevent deterioration in standard and those of sub-normal types without the will or mental capacity to help themselves, the halt and the maim of society with a heritage of misfortune not always of their own making
...

(CHAC, 1930, paras 36–7)

and:

For the rest a careful watch must be kept on the small minority of tenants who are really troublesome. There is the tenant who considers the local authority fair game for exploitation and is always finding excuses for not paying rent; the tenant who allows his children to maltreat the house; the quarrelsome tenant who is never happy unless quarrelling with the neighbours, or with his wife. There is the tenant who drinks or gambles, so that both family and landlord are compelled to go short; the tenant whose mental capacity does not permit the reception of new ideas; and the tenant who must be taught the necessity of keeping home clean and tidy. Each offers an individual problem of housing psychology; no two can be handled quite alike. But all must be dealt with sympathetically and with understanding.

(CHAC, 1930, para.39)

So there it is: the designation of the 'difficult' or 'problem' tenant, the first official report in British history.

The next problem became what to do with these tenants as 'sympathy and understanding' seldom seemed to work. A government report of 1933 notes the Dutch practice of segregating 'problem tenants' in a special sort of training camp, but rejects the idea for Britain. In a section entitled 'The problem of undesirable tenants', it says:

We are not satisfied that the number of tenants is other than relatively very small in this country, and we are disposed to think that the policy of isolating them is open to objection.

(HMSO, 1933, para.19)

But this report goes on to say that there is a small number of 'undesirable tenants' who, if not provided for or if refused by the Local Authority, cause trouble wherever they go.

In the post-war years, the edges of the 'problem family/tenant' profile become much sharper, while those of the 'problem estate' also begin to harden rapidly. This was in part a function of the experiences of the war, and in part a function of the nation's housing problem at the end of the war. In the first instance, various 'units', like the Family Service Units, sometimes composed of conscientious objectors, and frequently middle-class, had gone to work in the inner areas of our major cities and had rediscovered the atrocious living conditions experienced by some sections of the working class, and the terrible effects of such experience. Besides, the general condition of the British working class had been dramatically revealed to the middle-class by the behaviour of children evacuated from the great cities. It was from these encounters that the notion of the 'problem family' crystallized.

Administrators – the government, local authorities, housing managers – and sociologists began to pay increasing attention to the problems surrounding the lives of the poorer sections of the urban working class. It was here that the second factor came into play. During the six years of the war, there had been no house building, little maintenance, and considerable bomb damage. Much of this damage and decay affected working-class neighbourhoods. The post-war administrators had much the same worries as their predecessors of the previous generation: how to ensure that 'difficult tenants' would respect the property in the massive new housing estates going up all round the country. For the housing managers, the perennial problem was how to get the rent in. …

…

'Problem families' are similarly selected out for definition in the post-war period. The notions of the 'problem family' and 'problem tenant' are not isomorphic. A careful reading of the contemporary literature would suggest that all problem families were likely to be problem tenants in so far as they were in local-authority property, whereas all problem tenants were not necessarily problem families. The following describes the characteristics of the 'problem family':

> Those families in whose case there is social defectiveness to such a degree that they require supervision and control for their own well-being and that of others …
>
> Families presenting an abnormal amount of sub-normal behaviour over prolonged periods with a marked tendency to back-sliding. Those who for their own well-being and that of others require a substantially greater degree of supervision and help over long periods than is usually provided by existing services.
>
> (Wofinden, 1950, p.5)

Another commentator said:

> The essential feature of the problem family is that the standard of living as judged by Western civilisation is shocking; and that the parents make no effort to improve these standards. They might be described as 'social recidivists'.
>
> (MacIntosh, 1952, p.194)

The 1950 report cited above went on to suggest that some sort of 'halfway house' between the slum and the slum clearance estate be established for these 'problem families', for if they did not learn household management techniques they were going to become 'problem tenants', who might – although these words were not used yet – produce 'problem estates':

> By adopting such a procedure, it might be possible to prevent housing estates becoming populated with too many problem families.
>
> (Wofinden, 1950, p.41)

So it would be fair to say that there was widespread official concern in the 1950s that the 'peripheral' housing estates being constructed on the outskirts of our towns and cities as part of the post-war reconstruction plan would not [sic] be smashed by the activities of a few intractable families, and that further, a sense of 'community' could be developed in these estates which would assist in the incorporation of these 'problem families'. This concern at this particular historical juncture was most probably a function of the sheer scale of slum clearance during this decade, razing the rotten physical structure of Britain's inner cities and exposing the compounded problems of workers trapped there. …

…

(b) The 'social-democratic' representation

The term 'social-democratic' is being used here as shorthand for all accounts offered by the social science disciplines and their applications, as to a greater or lesser extent, they all operate within the same paradigm. It is important to spend at least a little time on these accounts, for it is the great *raison d'être* of sociology that it transcends the 'commonsense' explanations of social phenomena offered by the legendary [sic] man-in-the-street. (This latter phrase is not without significance for, as we shall see, not only are the sociological accounts sexist, but the 'filtering down' accounts are grossly patriarchal.)

Social workers, sociologists and other social scientists seem really to have become concerned with 'problem families' and 'problem tenants' in a systematic manner only after the Second World War. What strikes me from a review of their writings on the topic is the closeness of academics' work to the categories used by officials. To put it another way, academics and officials alike appear to have shared the same paradigm. The tendency, especially in sociological writing, is to relativize the 'problem family/tenant' notions while simultaneously accepting uncritically the validity of the notions as such. Thus Philip and Timms (1953), in possibly the first sociological paper on the topic, suggest that the 'problem family' is both an administrative category and a challenge to social work, and note that there is little historical understanding of the genesis of the term. Kuper (1953, pp.79–80) suggests that stereotypes of the 'lower class' or 'scruffy' way of life are abroad in official circles, but makes a distinction between the 'roughs' and the 'respectables'. It appears from the text that the terms may be Kuper's rather than his informants, although he does say that he derived the criteria for 'respectability' from the 'respectables' amongst his informants (*ibid.*, p.80)! Baldamus and Timms produce a bland analysis of the 'problem family' and conclude that:

> Such families were characterised by sets of beliefs and values at variance with the established culture; it therefore seemed important to understand such families as constituting a group with a cultural life different from the rest of society, that is, a separate sub-culture.
>
> (Baldamus and Timms, 1955)

The influence of functionalist sub-cultural theory is evident here while the tenor of the article makes it plain that such families are 'not quite right', that this independent culture is in fact 'dysfunctional' in the wider society. Various other papers seem to follow whatever was sociologically fashionable in describing the characteristics of the 'problem family/tenant' so that eventually we reach an account which Dave Byrne delightfully characterizes as all about: 'families who (*sic*) are anomic, retreatist, failed innovators and who live in a culture of poverty' (Byrne, n.d., p.6).

But, as stated above, the academics share a basic orientation with the officials: whatever the causes of the 'problem' behaviour, these families need to be dealt with; they require treatment. …

…

(c) The filtering-down representation

The filtering-down representation of 'problem tenants' and 'problem estates' is reproduced more or less tenuously in the official literature, for example, in 'Council House Communities' (SHAC, 1970), without a doubt the most systematic of the studies of the 'problem' or 'depressed estate' phenomenon. The difference lies in the degree of camouflage of offensive language. In Glasgow, this version used to be the orthodoxy in Corporation circles, particularly in the Housing Management and Public Health Departments, and is still given an airing from time to time in the local press. It is seen as a genuine and non-problematic explanation of certain 'types' of people.

Noting that most 'problem' or 'depressed' housing estates are inter-war (or immediately post-war) slum-clearance estates, and that typically, most 'problem tenants' are to be found in such estates, the story goes like this: the first tenants of such estates came from terrible housing conditions, they were very poor, were from large families, were short on domestic skills, were unused to a 'proper' house, did not respect authority or property, were accustomed to a wildly extrovert and irresponsible way of life, were enmeshed in a drunken

and criminal subculture, and so on. The worst of these tenants constituted a core of 'problem families' or 'anti-social' tenants whose behaviour eventually drove the substantial numbers of 'respectable' families in these estates to emigrate. Thus these estates began to acquire a bad reputation among the potential tenants of local authorities, and consequently 'respectable' families would refuse to accept a tenancy in them. With this twist in the spiral of the bad reputation, the estates came to be used by local authorities as 'dumping grounds' for thoroughly 'unsatisfactory' tenants or 'problem' cases deemed unworthy of better accommodation. As the number of 'unsuitable' and 'unsatisfactory' families and individuals increased in any one scheme, so vandalism also increased, local authority services began to be provided with less than enthusiasm and the estate came to assume the characteristics of a 'ghetto'. This resulted in the flight of any 'respectables' left in the neighbourhood, the total impossibility of letting houses there and the final, unequivocal status of the estate as a 'problem', which again in turn finally ensured its more-or-less abandonment by the local authority and its rapid decline to a state of total dereliction. …

…

In reviewing the literature, then, it has become plain that there is a powerful theme concerning British working-class life: some sort of dichotomy between those who live in estates or developments which the state stigmatizes, and those who are fortunate enough to live elsewhere. The former areas tend to be referred to as 'problem estates' or 'depressed' areas, or latterly, 'areas of multiple deprivation', while their inhabitants are called 'rough', or 'problem families', or 'deprived', multiply or otherwise. The latter are 'normal' or 'respectable'; not being stigmatized, they do not seem to be categorized so powerfully. In the heyday of the late 1960s and early 1970s, there was a shift from a correctional perspective towards such places and people to a more liberal one. But with the advent of Thatcherism, a nakedly punitive attitude has re-emerged, shot through with blatant racism. What can be noted at this juncture is that the representation of this split has a long history in this country: it goes back to somewhere in the first half of the nineteenth century. Hobsbawm, speaking of the mid-nineteenth century, has expressed it thus:

> A fissure therefore ran through what was increasingly becoming 'the working class'. It separated 'the workers' from 'the poor', or alternatively 'the respectable' from 'the unrespectable'.
>
> (Hobsbawm, 1975, p.224)

The task now is to try to construct a scientific explanation of this phenomenon.

References

Baldamus, W. and Timms, N. (1955) 'The problem family: a sociological approach', *British Journal of Sociology,* vol.6.

Byrne, D. (n.d.) *'Problem Families': A Housing Lumpenproletariat,* Working Papers in Sociology no.5, University of Durham, Department of Sociology and Social Administration.

CHAC (Central Housing Advisory Committee) (1930) *The Management of Municipal Housing Estates,* London, HMSO.

HMSO (1933) *Report of the Departmental Committee on Housing* (*The Moyne Report*), Cmd. 4397, London, HMSO.

Hobsbawm, E. (1975) *The Age of Capital, 1848–1875,* London, Weidenfeld & Nicolson.

Kuper, L. (ed.) (1953) *Living in Towns,* London, The Cresset Press.

MacIntosh, J.M. (1952) *Housing and Family Life,* London, Cassell.

Philip, A.F. and Timms, N. (1953) *The Problem of the 'Problem Family',* FSU.

Reynolds, F. (1986) *The Problem Estate: An Account of Omega and its People,* Aldershot, Gower.

SHAC (Scottish Housing Advisory Committee) (1970) *Council House Communities: A Policy for Progress,* Report of the Sub-Committee on Amenity and Social Character of Local Authority Houing Schemes, Edinburgh, HMSO.

Wofinden, R.C. (1950) *Problem Families in Bristol,* Occasional Papers on Eugenics no.6, London, Cassell.

Source: Damer, 1989, pp.1, 2–6, 13–14, 18–20

 # Andrew Ross, 'Sure tried' (1999)

The draw for the Phase One lots in 1995 had attracted a crowd far exceeding the company's expectations, but there was one big letdown. As Peter Rummell recalled: 'I remember when we had the lottery for the first homes, people were camped out. One of our guys came back, reporting on the crowds, and he was shaking his head. There were five or six hundred people camping out and I think there was one black family in there. We were all disappointed. Sure tried.' Following the advice of James Rouse, who had worked hard to integrate Columbia [several Celebrationites had moved from Columbia in Maryland] in the 1960s (and who once served as a consultant for Walt's ur-EPCOT), TCC had advertised in minority publications, and had produced promotional literature that portrayed families and students of color going about their business in town and at the school. The video shown in the Preview Center for prospective home buyers focused disproportionately on non-white residents. There was nothing the company would have liked more than to see a diverse population in Celebration. But it flourished as a largely white-bread town during the pioneer years, and was likely to remain so for the near future. This had not been a foregone conclusion. Central Florida has its share of middle-class minority families living in upscale suburban communities. But they were not choosing to come to Celebration. After two years, the town had attracted only one African American homeowning family, while three single women were living in rented apartments (two of whom moved away shortly after I left town). Dawn Thomas, Town Hall's assistant community manager, and her son Eddie were full participants in the community, and were among the town's most popular residents. So, too, was Dorothy Johnson, an ex-teacher and librarian, who was a drama and opera fan and a regular attendee of the Celebrators retiree group meetings.

The third renter, Wanda Wade, a young teacher laid off in April, had virtually no involvement in the community: 'This town's too interesting for me,' she joked. She rarely went out at night, at least after she had been stopped and questioned by police on more than one occasion. 'I don't pass GO, I don't collect two hundred dollars, I go straight home to my little house, and hole up.' Wade says she hates labels – 'I tear labels off beer bottles after I buy them from the store' – but was quite clear about why the town's aspirations might not be appealing to African Americans: 'For a majority of us, this concept of perfection is not reality, it's not a realistic outlook on life. We haven't grown up like this, we haven't had exposure to it, and we're not comfortable with what's not real. African American parents wouldn't want to sugarcoat their kids' perception of reality in this way.' Referring to the common sight, around town, of bicycles unfettered by lock or chain, she conceded that she had 'never been in a neighborhood where people felt they could leave their bikes out in the front yard.'

The only black homeowners, Bob and Mountrey Oliver, had built a solid brick Colonial Revival mansion at the top of Longmeadow. They had moved from Torrey Pines, an exclusive development in the Dr. Phillips area of Orlando, where there were several black families. From the look of the promotional literature, they had expected at least 30 per cent minority population in Celebration, especially since the range of advertised housing prices was so broad. The Olivers, who moved partly because they did not want their children to grow up 'too bourgeois', faulted the media for portraying Celebration as all white, but reported what several of their black friends had said: 'Why spend $300,000 for such a small lot?' Forgoing a larger lot, it was implied, was an extravagance that white folks could more readily 'afford' to do. Materialism for the black middle class is harder to come by and thus more difficult to compromise. …

They had almost been joined in the ranks of homeowners by Beulah Farquarson, a feisty, self-described 'Harlem child', who withdrew her children from the school and herself from the town after signing builders' contracts. Farquarson, who sells time shares, had run twice for the school board (and once for county commissioner), and was collecting signatures for another bid, unsuccessful as it turned out. Described to me by another resident as a 'negative black person', Farquarson had little good to say about the reality of Celebration, although she praised some of the planning behind the town. When her children turned sour on the school (they 'signed themselves out'), there was no reason to stay, especially in a town that lacked black residents. She blamed the inflated price points. 'Black people aren't stupid. Folks here are starving their behinds off just to pay their utility bills. We are not a cash-flow people. Once we've made it, we stay put in our mansions and don't think about starting new communities. Besides, we aren't interested in a "community". Black folks grow up in a "culture", and it's a noisy one. Celebration's downtown is noiseless. It's a joke for us.' …

Celebration also had a sprinkling of South Asian physicians and a range of Hispanic residents – Cubans, Dominicans, Mexicans, Puerto Ricans, and South Americans – but none of them (with the exception of MENSA kingpin Joseph Palacios) figured among the town's most active citizenry or had forged a prominent role in the community. Minority students from Osceola County had a much more visible presence in and around town, and so it was the school, again, that provided the active ingredient of diversity in Celebration.

In my interviews with the mostly white residents, I always asked why they thought the town had not attracted more minority residents and whether their relative absence was a source of concern. These interviews were informal conversations, lasting for ninety minutes or longer, and mostly took place in residents' homes. I tried to ask the questions about race in a way that did not put anyone on the defensive, but they often did.

A few retirees were clear examples of 'white flight' from urban areas that they considered to have 'declined'. For one couple from Miami, the 'last straw' had been a [Drug Enforcement Agency] agent at their door asking to park a car in their driveway because he anticipated a shoot-out across the street – 'This was not the ghetto,' they explained to me. 'It was not Overtown, or Liberty City, it was a nice middle-class suburb, where Jackie Gleason lived.' 'We are so happy to have been delivered,' they declared, adding, 'We're not racist, but some people are used to living at a lower level of life, and what can you do? You try to be a model and hope they will follow.' Other stories from elderly residents about Miami typically distinguished between the good *exilio* Cubans and the bad new immigrants, starting with the 'social deadbeats and psychos' who came with the Mariel boatlift, as one prominent resident put it. 'Florida's public schools,' he continued, 'teach to the bottom third of each class, and these are mostly the Hispanics. The rest are bored to tears as a result, and they are the ones with the talent.'

Some residents' perceptions of Osceola County were not exempt from that notorious white rule that divides the good minority from the bad one. One Celebration businessman spoke of the recent 'Latin influx' in the county. 'These are not Latins from Long Island, mind you, they are from south of the border and Puerto Rico.' Slighting 'the Oriental families who own all the small hotels on 192,' he praised 'the original Osceola County folks, the white folks; they are good people, who put down roots.' …

Younger nester parents, born after the civil rights era, were less likely to make bigoted comments, and many felt they had moved from communities riddled with prejudice to a town that was much more tolerant. Several regretted the lack of diversity here – 'We need to be diluted' – and confessed to being embarrassed that there was 'very little coloring in town.' For a small number, usually those who had a spouse with a Latin background or who were Jewish, diversity was an aspect of community life that did register on their scale of priorities. For the majority of white residents, it did not. Most felt 'it was not natural' to identify others by skin color, and so it was not something to which they gave much thought. 'We don't really notice it.' Those who acknowledged that they did notice race, believed, however, that it was 'not natural' to try to integrate communities. In general, it was assumed that integration had been 'artificial' because it had been done 'for show' and had not happened 'naturally.' Diversity, as one put it, was 'good for the right reasons, and bad for the wrong reasons.' A typical pattern of response was to acknowledge outright that race was 'not an issue', to be followed by some qualification that veered way off track into the subconscious hinterlands of white, propertied America.

> 'I'm not prejudiced, though my parents were. I look at people as people. But I don't like to hear people complaining about slavery and all that, or using their color as a crutch. Though I know what it's like for them to feel left out. If I go out with my husband and his friends and they talk about football, I feel left out.'

> 'We don't really notice the color issue, but let me tell you, we resent people hanging clothes over the balcony, and that can happen in fancy homes too, but luckily it doesn't happen in Celebration.'

> 'I don't look at people as colored one way or another, and I don't think it's natural to do social engineering. You can't mandate an idea. Bussing screwed up in most cases. But you shouldn't have to be stepping over homeless people in order to feel like you live in the real world.'

> '90 per cent of us wouldn't mind. I don't know what Arabs or Hispanics or Blacks want, but they're welcome to live next to me. Here Christian, Jewish, and Muslim kids play together. Besides, the black people have progressed so quickly. I may have set them apart at one time, but since 1970 or so, they are like us.'

> 'I don't care myself, although this is a white ghetto. I would welcome more diversity as long as it doesn't drive the prices down.'

> 'We don't like the fact that this town is so unbelievably white, but we don't lie awake at night thinking about it. People are not willing to move out of their own culture just to experience other cultures.'

> 'It's just not an issue for us. We don't see it in terms of minority this or that. We're from Miami.'

For the most part, white Celebrationites were politely stumped when asked why the town had not attracted more minorities, but there were several theories offered. The architecture of the town, some of it directly evoking plantation houses, was perceived to convey the feel of an all-white community of yore and might be off-putting to non-whites. Disney, some said, was also considered the essence of white-bread family values and not very inclusive in its approach to the marketplace or to its own corporate culture. The theory of black middle-class materialism was echoed by at least one other resident: 'Blacks are smarter with their money, they work hard for it, they want a big lot, and a good-sized shelter, and don't want to plop down $300,000 for something that's so … small.' Other views aimed at being more sociologically acute:

> 'Members of ethnic groups don't often move freely from state to state because of their close-knit families and communities.'

> 'Minorities lose more of themselves than they gain when they move to places like this. They give up a lot of their own culture.'

> 'African Americans don't go out of their way to invite risks. This is a test community, and they already have enough tests in their lives. Their culture is less receptive to change or risk.'

Black tourists sometimes commented, when I asked them, that the town seemed a little 'scary', but this was a common observation on the part of many first-time visitors, of whatever racial background. Whatever distillation of 'white fear' resided among townsfolk was strangely reflected by a 'fear of Celebration' evinced by outsiders. But fear, I concluded, is not the signature mark of whiteness in Celebration. Indeed, liberal guilt about the community's demographics is widespread enough among residents to generate a veneer of regret. Instead, I found that the key to whiteness lay in the many comments I heard about the invisibility of race: it's 'not natural' to view people in terms of their skin color. In truth, nothing has ever been *natural* when it comes to race in America. What seems natural at any time and in any place usually corresponds to what white folks feel comfortable with seeing. At the end of the century, whites seem increasingly comforted by the notion that race is becoming invisible, once again. It had been so, for different reasons, before the ferment of the civil rights era, when minorities had simply been eclipsed from the public eye. Recently, the force of conservative opinion that a 'level playing field' has been achieved for all races has prepared the way for a new kind of color blindness. Today, white people are often at their most white when they believe that consciousness of race is not natural. In many ways, it is a belief that most defines us as white. Seventy years ago, what united whites was the perception that their racial designation was an outcome of biological nature, in the same degree as, but superior to, other ancestral groups. It is much less acceptable now to believe that biology is responsible for the differences between people. But white-skin privilege abides and goes unexamined when it's no longer 'natural' to think about someone's racial background and is perceived to be racist to do so. As Malcolm X pointed out, 'racism is like a Cadillac. There's a new model every year.'

It has been well over three decades since racial discrimination was publicly outlawed in housing, education, and public transportation. While no longer chronic, the patterns of segregation by race and income persist. Residential census maps still betray the grisly story of racial isolation. Every day, in the thousands of housing developments under construction, suburban white communities inch farther out from the increasingly diverse populations of the inner suburban rings. The ending of redlining and racially restrictive covenants, it turns out, did not make a truly radical difference to demographic patterns. The free housing market has produced an outcome today that is not so terribly different from the era of high segregation. But it's not natural to see it that way.

In late May, on a torrid Saturday afternoon, I turned out for a co-ed softball tournament organized as a fund-raiser for the PTSA. My own valiant home run had been disqualified because I forgot to drop the bat (why throw away a lucky bat?). Time was almost up, and my team had been hammered by the Osceola County sheriffs' team. A male resident on the sidelines began to taunt one of the opposing team's male players up at bat. 'Quit playing like a woman,' he jeered. Larry Haber, the captain of our side, responded loudly from the other side of the field, 'That's enough of that kind of talk. Cut it out!' The remark sliced through more than the sauna heat of the day. It was a public break with the male sporty camaraderie that had settled over the games, in spite of the presence of female players. A clumsy silence followed, before the pitcher swung her arm.

Haber's had been a mild form of gender treason, but brave enough in such a public setting. On reflection, it struck me that the sports field was a much easier place to break ranks with masculinity than with whiteness. But where could the latter occur in Celebration? As it happened, one white couple told me that the same heckler had made some apparently racist comments at a dinner party in his house. They felt uncomfortable and held their tongues rather than object to his remarks. The same scenario was probably being repeated a thousand times around the country in every setting where white folks gathered.

Celebration residents did not deserve to be singled out for these sad confirmations of white solidarity. For sure, it is a more tolerant and diverse place than many of the gated security zones that are the 'natural' outcome of market behavior at the end of this century. But this town had set itself up as a model of community and housing for the future, and it was springing up in full view of a nation that had long perfected the art of segregation through its housing practices and policies. Like Levittown and Columbia, it would be very closely watched, while other communities went about their all-white business as usual. What a pity, I thought, there were not more opportunities to break bread, let alone break ranks.

Source: Ross, 1999, pp.264–71

 # Douglas Frantz and Catherine Collins, 'Truman didn't sleep here' (1999)

One especially hot afternoon near the middle of August, Cathy was riding her bike back from the post office when a dark blue car with Pennsylvania license plates pulled up alongside her. The attractive woman who was driving rolled down the window and asked for directions. Before Cathy could respond, one of the four children in the car leaned across and said, 'Can you tell me where Truman lives?'

'Pardon me?' asked Cathy, who suspected some kind of tourist joke.

'Truman? Didn't you see the movie?' asked the mother.

'Oh, that Truman,' said Cathy, who had in fact seen the media satire *The Truman Show*. 'He was just a character. It was all make-believe. And anyway, it wasn't filmed here. It was filmed over in Seaside, which is on the panhandle.'

The mother and child were obviously disappointed, though Cathy could not figure out whether it was because they had the wrong town or because they had just learned Truman wasn't a real person. They drove off without saying thank you.

It was not the first time we had run into the misconception that the movie had been filmed in Celebration. Early in the summer, when *The Truman Show* was released in theaters, a surprising number of people assumed that the movie had been filmed where we lived. Friends from far away called and said they had seen our town in the movie. Even a few people who lived in Celebration were convinced that at least the downtown scenes had been shot in their hometown. It seemed to be a point of pride.

Perhaps the mistake could be excused. There were, after all, similarities between Celebration and the movie town called Seahaven. The world inhabited by Truman Burbank, the character played by Jim Carrey, had pretty houses and an orderly downtown. The sunrises were beautiful, and the weather was flawless. Everybody smiled placidly and waved and said hello. The only hitch, of course, was that nothing in Seahaven was real. Truman was the star of the twenty-four-hour-a-day television drama that had been on the air since his birth, thirty years earlier. Our favorite line was delivered by Ed Harris, who played Christoff, the show's creator; defending his town, he said: 'It's not fake. It's just controlled.'

The same might be said of Celebration. By the end of our year in Celebration, we had concluded that it was not fake, except for silly architectural idiosyncrasies like the dormers on many houses. It was genuine, without script or cue cards. It was, however, controlled by rules and regulations and the omnipresent guiding hand of the Disney Company through its surrogate, the Celebration Company.

Over the course of the year, our attitudes toward the rules had split along lines that would have been predictable to people who know us well. While Doug felt that people had understood the rules when they bought their houses and should accept them, Cathy had two concerns. On the practical side, she was annoyed by the inequality in enforcement of the rules. For instance, a fair number of people, including two on our street, had been allowed to buy houses that they did not intend to live in for months, even years, a clear violation of the regulations everyone signed. The result was gaps in neighborhoods, houses that sat empty, people who were not part of the community. Along those same lines, some people had been permitted to buy two lots, which had the same general impact.

Cathy's second concern was more philosophical. Restrictions can become coercive and can be used to stifle debate or dissent within a community. In the same way, the concept of good citizenship can be reduced to sterile definitions, such as keeping your grass cut to three and a half inches and paying community assessments promptly. Both sap the vitality of a community and impose conformity where diversity is necessary.

…

The debate over community restrictions resonates beyond the borders of Celebration. Historically, people with similar beliefs and values have bonded together to create new towns in America. Those that survived evolved over time, reaching beyond the initial common interests to embrace a broader definition of community. Today's manifestation of that instinctive tribalism is the increasing number of communities banding together to form private governments and community associations to impose restrictions on anyone who wants to live in them. The majority of these enclaves are built for the middle and upper-middle classes, making them 'privatopias' of privilege and exclusiveness and widening the gulf between the haves and the have-nots. In the narrow sense, these places fit the definition of community; like-minded people with common values and fears are using barricades to seal themselves off from the problems of the surrounding world. But in reality these places are often anticommunity cocoons. They breed isolation and conformity and promote the balkanization of America. Rather than a place where real-world problems are confronted and dealt with by diverse people in a well-defined public realm, the privatopia represents the same escapism and white flight that led to the suburbanization of the country.

Elements of these tendencies can be found in Celebration. The attempt to stifle debate over the school in the first year of the town's existence was a dramatic demonstration of the impulse toward conformity. You either loved everything about Celebration or kept quiet about it. Disney's decision not to build affordable housing or develop creative financing to open Celebration to low-income families reflected a narrow definition of who makes up a real town and underscored the elite nature of the town. The company's fear that the project would not be as popular with the middle class if it had room for poor people was probably accurate from a market standpoint, but a community is not just a commodity. The failure to include poor people in Celebration, and in neotraditional communities in general, is an act of separation and seclusion that contradicts the underlying philosophy of the town and reinforces the circular prophecy that the less we know about other people the more we will have to fear.

On the other hand, there were honest efforts on the part of the company and the residents to avoid creating an isolated enclave. The Celebration Foundation was a novel attempt to reach out to each other in times of need, both to those within the community and to those in the greater community outside the town, and to remind Celebration's residents that there were less fortunate people just beyond the borders. The foundation sponsored volunteer efforts to improve the shelter for battered women in nearby Kissimmee, regularly collected donations for various countywide social service programs, and organized volunteers when the tornadoes struck in early 1998. And when there was contact between the town and people from the outlying county, it seemed to go smoothly. The children bused to Celebration School from outside the town, who were much more diverse in terms of race and socio-economic status, were treated the same as the townies. That is what we heard from our own children, those children from outside Celebration, other parents inside and outside Celebration, and the teachers and administrators.

Architecture and planning also played a role in making Celebration more egalitarian. Because the houses looked basically alike and expensive homes were mixed in with apartments and less-expensive houses, people's homes were a sort of neutral ground, which helped to reduce the economic and social hierarchy. Unlike other subdivisions, where houses are segregated strictly by price, Celebration was laid out in a relatively democratic fashion. We have no way to prove it, but our theory is that this egalitarian planning contributed to the inclusiveness in the friendships made by our children at an age when many groups of youngsters form nasty little cliques based partly on how much money their parents earn.

...

Disney could have taken the safe route and developed another golf-course community on its property. Instead, the company did something truly innovative, banking on the public's even greater desire for community than for a golf course, and in the process, it tried to address a critical social ill by offering an alternative to fifty years of suburban growth that had been draining America of the sense of community and intimacy. The company went beyond merely employing some of the easiest neotraditional icons, like sidewalks and porches, and risked its brand name and used its savvy marketing ability to offer an alternative.

...

... Disney created a town where real people could come and live and test the alternative on a very public stage. Dreamers like Frank Lloyd Wright and Le Corbusier had only imagined their utopias. They counted on the power of their ideas to make up for the lack of resources, but, with the exception of the awful slums that now ring Paris in a perversion of Le Corbusier's vision, their concepts were not implemented. Disney, on the other hand, had made a contribution to the effort to create a new urban order, whether or not you liked it.

And we liked much of it. From a design and planning standpoint, Celebration marks the next step in the neotraditional movement. It represents the largely successful evolution into what Charles Fraser dubbed post-neotraditionalism. You *can* be isolated in Celebration, but unlike in traditional suburbs, you have to work at it. The design of the community, from the physical structure to the intangible attitudes of its residents, pushes people to confront life around them. It suggests mutual dependence in a country where planning has too often stressed independence. Celebration is human-sized and walkable. The front porches, though not entirely successful, and the closeness of houses to the sidewalk and street encourage us to look out on the world and to be part of the procession passing by. The average suburban household puts thirty thousand miles a year on its vehicles. In Celebration, we reduced our household from two cars to one and drove that one less than a thousand miles a month.

...

The report card on Celebration is not all A's and B's. Disney's desire to get the best return possible on its land was the driving force in building the town, and the company deserves to be criticized for the hype it generated and for the rapaciousness with which it sought to capitalize on the demand that it whipped up. To satisfy that demand, builders were pushed beyond their capabilities. ...

...

More complicated is the task of assessing responsibility for the outsized expectations that so many people brought to Celebration. The rhapsodizing literature and the inherent twinning of Disney's theme parks and its new town drew people with unrealistic dreams. Michael Eisner's hyped references to Celebration as the embodiment of Walt Disney's original dream of a real community at Epcot fueled the myth that living in Celebration would be the closest thing to living at Disney World. In the beginning, Celebration was a town where believing replaced knowing.

Not all the blame for the great expectations can be placed on Disney. America is, after all, the land of the quick fix. Too often in our society we look for external solutions to internal problems, and Celebration attracted more than its share of people who thought they could trade their old problems for a trouble-free life in a new town. Disney didn't create those unrealistic expectations, but it was guilty of capitalizing on them.

The company also can be faulted for failing to deliver on everything that it did promise. Complaints about builders are not unique to Celebration. Suits against builders and developers are filed regularly across the country. But Disney promised that it had found the best builders in the country, and people expected a level of quality commensurate with the promise and with what they had seen at Disney's theme parks.

Disney also had billed Celebration as a town where the latest advances in technology would enrich life for everyone. There were concrete pledges that residents would be linked directly to the school, neighbors, doctors, and shops through cutting-edge technology. But many of those assurances remain unfulfilled, and some of the technology described in Disney's promotional literature just didn't exist. ...

The most unrealistic expectations, however, were associated with the school. We admire Disney for its ambitious vision of a progressive school, a public school at that. Even after the uneven experiences of our two children, we remain believers in Celebration School's basic respect for individual learning abilities and the usefulness of interdisciplinary approaches to problem solving and an alternative form of assessing a child's knowledge, at least in the early years. But the school presented two serious problems from the day it opened. ...

During the first year, the teachers were ill prepared from the outset to handle so taxing a program. They lacked proper training in many required areas, from multidisciplinary teaching to how to monitor the progress of so many children on different tracks to ways in which to integrate technology into the classroom. Indeed, in a survey conducted by the school's PTA, the teachers themselves complained that they did not receive sufficient training in using computers.

The lack of training and the absence of uniform standards and methods translated into unevenness among the classrooms. We felt our children attended different schools. Some classrooms functioned smoothly and productively, as evidenced by our daughter Becky's first year at the school. Others were chaotic, as our son Nick discovered. Robert Peterkin

had cautioned at an early planning session for the school that it would take years to function smoothly, but residents expected to find what they had been promised from Day One – a model, world-class school.

The second major problem also was related to the expectations of parents, though in a slightly different way. Celebration was marketed as a new town with old-fashioned values. The architecture reminded people of the towns where they'd grown up, or the towns in which they would have liked to grow up. As a result, many people moved to Celebration expecting to find a school like the one they attended, or the one they would like to have attended. Instead, they were confronted with a radical departure from both past and present: there were no grades, no textbooks, and no written curricula. They walked into classrooms where as many as ninety kids, sometimes as much as six years apart in age, were clustered in groups, slouched on couches, or playing games on computers. There was even a bed in the middle of the media center. Though the literature had indicated clearly that the school would be a departure from what we had known as children, few parents were prepared for what they found, and many were left discombobulated.

'The difficulties are understandable, I think,' said Ronald Clifton, the former foreign service officer who was Stetson University's liaison with Celebration. 'It is a very complex school. It is trying to put into practice in one school the state-of-the-art innovations that you would find individually in other schools, but never in this combination. You probably won't find another school that has all of these aspects in one place.'

None of the problems Celebration was experiencing as a new town, from difficulties with the school to leaky roofs on the town houses, was a fatal flaw. They were growing pains, and they could be remedied with patience and effort.

But sometimes it took a lot of patience…

…

At the school, compromises were in place and most parents were holding their breath and their fire as the new year began. The quiet revolution over the summer was a milestone in Celebration's effort to make its own history. Parents had overcome the fears of retaliation and coalesced into a formidable and reasonable force for change, which is a pretty good definition of the beginnings of self-governance and democracy. People had taken their hands out of their pockets, not to point fingers but to work together.

Source: Frantz and Collins, 1999, pp.307–11, 312–13, 314–17

1.4 Ian Taylor, Karen Evans and Penny Fraser, 'Out on the town: Manchester's Gay Village' (1996)

One of the more striking features of the rapid changes taking place in Manchester's city centre in the late 1980s and early 1990s was the transformation of an old warehouse area by the city-centre canal into a series of winebars and restaurants dedicated to the use of the gay and lesbian populations – the so-called 'Gay Village'. In early 1995, in what was still a rapidly developing and changing area, there were 15 gay or mixed pubs and clubs, three cafés, a hairdresser, a taxi service and a shop in the core of the Village, and a number of other venues on its fringe. The development of the Village and, more recently, the production of a 'gay supplement' in Manchester's *City Life* magazine have identified Manchester as a mecca for gay people from elsewhere in the North of England, and has also distinguished Manchester from other cities in the North, like Sheffield. Few of these have witnessed any successful claiming of urban facilities specifically for the use of gay people.[1]

…

The public identity of the area as a 'Gay Village' began to be asserted, for the first time, in the mid-1980s – ironically at a time when the then Prime Minister, Margaret Thatcher, was leading an ideological offensive to reinstate a particular, Victorian idea of 'family values'. This highly visible campaign was readily turned towards criticism of gay lifestyles, especially when the first reports began to emerge of the HIV virus and subsequent deaths from AIDS in America. Gay politics and lifestyles were quickly coming to terms with this new threat, but anti-gay feeling was generally whipped up by the popular press. Many gay men talk of this time as one of 'withdrawal into the [gay] community', and this general feeling may have contributed to the withdrawal of gay venues into their 'own' space, geographically separate from areas of the city where homophobic encounters or even assaults were feared. The late 1980s was the time of the so-called 'Lawson boom', with considerably increased competition for city space and higher rentals, as entrepreneurs in the city moved to cater for the new leisure interests of a young professional class with money to spend. In Manchester, the 130 pubs in the city centre began to feel some competition, for the first time, from the spread of the wine bar and also from a rapid expansion in the number and range of city-centre restaurants. The Village itself, however, close to Chorlton Street bus station and the established locale

for prostitution, was not immediately recognised as ripe for development and improvement by mainstream development agencies: arguably, full recognition of its potential was delayed until the establishment of the Central Manchester Development Corporation in 1988. Given the cheap rents and property prices in the area, a clear market opportunity existed for gay entrepreneurs to take part in the process of gentrification of the city centre, but within a distinct urban territory and space.

The topography of the area colonised by the Gay Village undoubtedly aided its identification with this minority club scene. The area is one which sits among old, disused warehouses left over from the industrial heyday of Manchester, but it is also close to Piccadilly rail station (the main station from London), Chinatown (the largest such area outside London) and the main building of UMIST (the University of Manchester Institute of Science and Technology). It is by no means simply a residual wasteland, and, as in many North American developments – for example, the Marigny neighbourhood of New Orleans discussed by Lawrence Knopp (1990) – its close relationship to significant other civic, educational and leisure sites has been influential in its recent renaissance. The old warehouses which have been the material resource for the 'gentrification' of the Village area were located alongside the city's canal system and have proven to be easy conversion projects. The historical links of some streets in the area, especially around the Chorlton Street bus station, with prostitution – another socially censured activity, but one which presumably was widely patronised by many local men – may also have given some cachet to the area as a site of forbidden pleasures. Rather than acceding to an urban tradition in which 'forbidden sexualities' are only to be pursued in seedy and sordid surroundings, however, gay businessmen proceeded to brighten up the area and publicly identify its existence. They also tried to bring a sense of humour and defiance to the images which they emblazoned in lights on clubs (witness the limp-wristed Statue of Liberty on the side of the New York, New York public house), and certainly they have repopulated its dark, narrow streets and waterways. The Village has become a place in which gay sexuality is affirmed and supported. The canals and buildings, which had long been recognized as important symbols of Manchester's industrial heritage but were suffering from neglect, have been 'rescued' and given over to another use (in the language of the Marxist political economy adopted by Castells and others, given a new 'use value'). Certainly, the rescue of the canals and warehouses in the Village area has met with the wholehearted approval of key figures and agencies in the local 'growth coalition'. The Central Manchester Development Corporation's area of geographic responsibility shares a boundary with the Village along Canal Street and has launched projects opening up, repaving and lighting the walkways alongside the waterways. The CMDC has also provided grants for the cleaning of buildings on Canal Street. As in the Marigny neighbourhood of New Orleans, there is in effect an alliance of the agencies in the local political and commercial institutions that have the responsibility for the project of urban development and 'renaissance' with the interests of leading entrepreneurs from the local gay population.

...

Urban space and sexual preference

The reconfigured urban space and upgraded buildings that comprise the Gay Village – an enclave in the central city area where gay people can feel relatively secure – is a product of the initiative and energy of individuals and groups within the lesbian and gay 'community' in Manchester, imaginatively reappropriating that city-centre area of warehouses and canals as a centre of clubs, bars and restaurants. But this public colonisation of a central city space in Manchester is itself, of course, a product of the more general 'coming out' of homosexual and lesbian people over the last 30 years. We want to retrace some of this history here very briefly. But our overall argument is that the public affirmation of 'gay sexuality' which is so often proclaimed ... as the result of this process of liberalisation is actually much more apparent and straightforward in some localities (or 'urban enclaves') and cities than others, and the public expression of this particular sexual preference in the industrial North of England generally is especially problematic.

Gay sexuality emerged from 'the dark days' prior to 1968 into a heady combination of Gay Liberation in the 1970s, the subsequent celebration of gay lifestyles in the early 1980s, and the emergence of the pink economy that followed. The move from identification with 'homosexuality', which always promoted a pathological definition of this sexuality, denoting disease and abnormality of character, to one in which 'gayness' could be declared, and a recognition that same-sex preferences and desires

existed and were discussable, marked a turning point. The subsequent emergence of the more public gay 'scene' – particularly in San Francisco and some sections of other North American cities – is seen by many commentators as an alternative home to that provided by the family household in mainstream society, and a spatial alternative to the mainstream neighbourhood. Initially, the rhetoric of gay magazines insisted that these areas would become a kind of haven for the many thousands of people in each city of 'different' or diverse sexuality. This is not a promise we have been able to explore in depth in this research, but the work we have done suggests that whilst the culture of Manchester's Gay Village is accepting of the many 'badges' which lesbians and gay men have chosen to adopt to express their personalities and tolerates a mix of styles and ages in its clubs, it nevertheless caters, primarily, for males with money who like to drink. As our focus group respondent Bill remarked:

> Economics actually empower people in lots of ways. It's actually brought us together through having clubs and pubs, and people are actually aware that having a gay night brings a lot of people in. There is meant to be the pink elusive pound, but it's worth a lot of money. It's thrown around a lot, it's like gay men don't have families, supposedly. I feel quite frustrated when I do go out sometimes. I think this is it really. You do have pubs where you drink, and you have to spend money, or take drugs. There are clubs where you have to drink, and you spend money.

In some respects, however, little has changed for those who do not have the economic power to participate in the pink economy. Bill is unemployed at present and felt this restriction more than most:

BILL: There's a lot on the scene if you can afford to go out there. That's one issue, money. If you've got enough money to buy drinks ...

KAREN EVANS: What if you can't afford to go out, what do you do then?

BILL Well you go cottaging ... if you're looking for sex.

As if to underline the fact of economic inequality of means with respect to gay people's use of the Village, a 'cottage' has recently developed in a disused warehouse just to the south of the Gay Village. The co-presence of this hidden sexual economy alongside the Village itself is an important gloss on the Village's own self-confident descriptions. There is no question, however, that the Village 'scene' is a liberating experience for many, particularly those who must routinely hide their sexuality at work, in their day-to-day relationships or in other public places. At the same time, it is clear that the 'scene' itself brings a pressure to bear on individuals, demanding conformity to its particular image of gay sexuality, and it is arguable that this neutralises some of the diversity which exists within this expression of sexuality. There is an unmistakable sense, in particular, in which the Gay Village is another overwhelmingly 'male space' within the city, albeit in a territory where gay men do not feel the pressure of 'compulsory heterosexism'. Commentators on the growth of gay neighbourhoods and leisure facilities in North America confirm that a similar process of hegemonisation of the alternative space by gay men of the entrepreneurial class is at work. Castells (1983) argues that this process is an expression of an 'innate male territorial approach', whilst Adler and Brenner (1992) have argued that attention must be paid to the differential material resources available to men as against women, as well as recognizing that lesbian women, confronting the larger dominant culture of masculinity and the danger of male violence against them, may opt for a less transparent culture built around networks and trusting relationships rather than wanting to colonise space and territory. The main identity of the Gay Village is in this sense as a leisure space for gay men, and whilst lesbians do sometimes make use of its facilities, it is not their space.

...

There was some hope in the group with whom we were in discussion, who ranged from early twenties to early forties in age, that the gay community in Manchester would adapt and change, in line with their own changing, developing biography and the ageing process:

HAROLD: By the time we're 50 there's going to be a huge group of people that'll all be 50 and all want somewhere to go.

Bill thought this was already beginning to happen:

> I think in the end people will get pissed off with it ... going to the clubs for years and years ... I even get that at my age ... There will be an organic change within the gay scene and that's happening anyway.

Others were not so sure, and saw the Village as catering primarily for young gay people, including those who had never experienced the constraints of a 'closeted life' before the opening of the Village, and

certainly before the impact of the legislation of 1967. There was some awareness that the priority placed on the idea of 'a scene' directed at younger, high-spending gay consumers was, in some senses, a form of discrimination, driven by commercial or political and interest-group considerations. Some of the gay men taking part in our discussion felt ironically that the heterosexual society was in fact more accepting of a wide age-range of people, at least in its pub culture. There was some sense of a *ressentiment* here, with the more middle-aged gay men feeling they had had to suppress their sexuality, perhaps getting married and never feeling able to 'come out' as gay people at all, and resenting the freedom of young gay men.

There was energetic disagreement as to the extent to which older people were accepted on the gay scene at the present time. Pete, an employee of the National Health Service, who also stressed that his experience as a 'working-class' gay man might be different from that of middle-class users of the Village, pointed out:

> You look around the pubs in the Gay Village and they are not all the same. Each pub has got its own character. The Union and the Rembrandt do attract quite a lot of older men ... they feel comfortable in there. Those kinds of pubs were there a long time before 1968.

Sebastian felt that it was more acceptable within the gay 'scene' to go out in a mixed age-group than in heterosexual society:

> It's the only community where you can go for a meal with somebody twenty years older than you and still be acceptable.

Others felt strongly that this did not change the fundamental orientation of the Village towards a youthful clientele. Matt, a man in his twenties, agreed:

> It's just for young people ... what happens when you're 50 and you can't be going out, or you've got a gammy leg and you can't be dancing all night?

It was also agreed that lesbian women did not play a large part in the life of the Village. To some of our discussants (all of whom were male) this was because lesbians were excluded by gay men; to others it was due to the preferred lifestyles of lesbians being incompatible with those of gay men. It was admitted that men dominate the Village and that the women's 'scene' is relegated to occasional women-only nights in otherwise mixed or predominantly gay clubs. In a similar way the 'scene' was recognised to be heavily dominated by white men. In many ways the Village does not cater for minority tastes within its boundaries: it has grown up around a specific (white, male and middle-class) culture and it is in the interest of the gay, white, male entrepreneurs who have opened up the Village that their facilities continue to be heavily patronised by gay men who feel comfortable within that culture and who have 'discretionary income' to spend.

The Gay Village in the larger Manchester

Our research in Manchester included a survey, carried out in different sites around the city, eliciting information on responses to different parts of the city and to the city in general. One of our interview sites was directly adjacent to the Gay Village, and the people we spoke to there – many of whom had not ventured directly into the Village area itself – still associated the area with dereliction and unattractive buildings and had an image (a memory) of it as a depressing area. But at the same time, nearly all the people we interviewed thought they knew their way around the area and where the boundaries lay: it scored highly in terms of its 'readability'. Also, quite strikingly, it scored highest of all the six places in Manchester where we chose to carry out interviews in terms of perceived sense of safety. Ironically enough, four people interviewed in Manchester during our survey had had some experience of crime or 'trouble' in that area, but even these did not see the area as a particularly fearful place. The upgrading and gentrification of the area by gay entrepreneurs ostensibly catering for a minority lifestyle has created in the process an area of the city which is generally seen as one which it is safe for all to frequent, despite the continuing association of the general vicinity with female and male prostitution. It is widely acknowledged that heterosexual use of the area is quite high, as women in particular take advantage of an area which they can walk through without being harassed and pubs which they can use to meet up with friends (cf. Evans and Fraser, 1995).

Where such gay enclaves have not developed within cities, as in Sheffield, the lesbian and gay lifestyle has remained much more hidden from public view. It is of some significance in this respect that, whilst none of the people we interviewed during our street survey in Sheffield spontaneously referred to their own sexuality or volunteered a definition of themselves as 'gay' or 'lesbian', a small minority of people we interviewed on the streets of Manchester were confident enough so to do.

The few gay venues in Sheffield are scattered throughout the city. A pub used by lesbians and gays is situated near the railway station (prior to 1967, Manchester's gay pubs were also found near what are now called transport interchanges) and the remaining two are in sparsely populated areas, one being in Attercliffe, which has been heavily depopulated since the demise of Sheffield's steel industry. The pubs, like the areas in which they are found, are run down and unmodernised. The overwhelming impression is of a subordinated sexual minority in hiding, shirking the gaze of the larger public, and reticent about its own difference and diversity. Joseph Bristow, a gay man from Sheffield, writing in a recent collection of essays on gay life in Britain, comments on how:

> If one things strikes me about the gay pubs in my own city, Sheffield, it is the *ordinariness* of many of the clientele – they could be drinking and smoking almost anywhere.
>
> (Bristow, 1989, p.59)

The Gay Village in Manchester is confident of its own difference from the dominant culture and is committed, at least rhetorically, to a diversity of sexual identities. The local equivalent of San Francisco's Gay Pride parade is an annual carnival, complete with street floats, which ventures out through the city streets on August Bank Holiday weekend, returning into the Village for a weekend-long celebration. At other times of the year, on Friday and Saturday evenings, there are periodic, informal, showy displays in the Village area by transvestites and others, promenading along the canal sides in front of the various pubs and clubs.

Sheffield City Council, dominated as it has been historically by trade union representatives from the steel trades, has not supported lesbian and gay rights to the same extent as the City Council of Manchester. But the fact of City Council support alone cannot explain the growth and confidence in gay lifestyles in Manchester. Evidence shows that there was a thriving 'gay scene' in the city for some time before the election of the 'left Labour' council in 1981. Gay activists had already organised themselves politically and had eventually won support for the opening of a Gay Centre from the new Council, very soon after its election. Furthermore, the Council employed two gay men as equal opportunities officers in 1985. Many of our respondents in the gay community insisted that the Council's support was really just a confirmation of the ground that had already been won in Manchester in earlier years.

It is important for our argument in this book on difference in local culture to note how many of the gay people who participated in our focus group discussions had been attracted into Manchester as a result of positive exploratory visits from other cities (with frequent references to the tolerant atmosphere, especially in the city centre). Samuel was originally from Cardiff but moved to Manchester to be with a friend. He was well aware of Manchester's gay scene before he moved, and had already made comparisons with his own city:

> The biggest thing that has come over to me is, you go to Cardiff and there's an extremely, almost non-existent, gay scene. It's, like, two pubs, if they can be bothered to call themselves gay, and one club. It's like again, if you haven't got a strong circle of friends, you've had it. You might as well go and live in Outer Mongolia, there's a better gay scene there!

This gay person's shameful critique of his town of origin was accompanied by the assertion that Manchester is inherently different, in some way, to other cities. The gay men in our discussion group found this 'sense of difference' hard to articulate. However, there was some feeling that what is usually referred to as the 'local culture' of Manchester, although definitely resonant with the culture of work and manufacturing, was not as 'macho' as in other cities. Words like 'cosmopolitan' and 'European' were used to sum up its atmosphere. It is generally seen as a tolerant city, open to different ideas and different ways of living. …

…

The existence of the Gay Village plays an important part in the shaping of a culture of toleration for them, as gay men. But a part of the 'elective affinity' displayed for Manchester involved references to the welcome, it was believed, the city extends to other minority groups, symbolised (in a characteristically 'consumerist' perspective) by the existence of areas like Chinatown in the city centre and the cluster of nearly 50 Indian restaurants and foods shops on one stretch of the Wilmslow Road in Rusholme: physical areas-cum-'social spaces' that were read as evidence of Manchester people's toleration and celebration of minority cultures. Harold grew up within the Jewish community in Prestwich. He pointed out that the gay community is one of the many different 'communities' within the Greater Manchester area:

> We're not the only minority. There's loads, and loads of ghettoes. It all helps I think, like a flavour of everything.

Note

1   Claims have ben made for Newcastle upon Tyne as a centre of gay life for the North-eastern region of England, but the 'scene' in this city is mainly organised around a series of existing pubs (cf. Lewis, 1994).

References

Adler, S. and Brenner, J. (1992) 'Gender and space: lesbians and gay men in the city', *International Journal of Urban and Regional Research*, issue 16, pp.24–34.

Bristow, J. (1989) 'Homophobia/misogyny: sexual fears, sexual definitions' in Shepherd, S. and Wallis, M. (eds) *Coming on Strong: Gay Politics and Culture*, London, Unwin Hyman.

Castells, M. (1983) *The City and the Grassroots*, Berkeley, CA, University of California Press.

Evans, K. and Fraser, P. (1995) 'Difference in the city: locating marginal use of public space' in Sampson, C. and South, N. (eds) *Conflict and Consensus in Social Policy*, Proceedings of the British Sociological Association 1993 Conference, Basingstoke, Macmillan.

Knopp, L. (1990) 'Some theoretical implications of gay involvement in an urban landscape', *Political Geography Quarterly*, vol.9, no.4, October, pp.337–52.

Lewis, M. (1994) 'A sociological pub-crawl around gay Newcastle' in Whittle, S. (ed.) *The Margins of the City: Gay Men's Urban Lives*, Newcastle upon Tyne, Athanaeum Press.

Source: Taylor, Evans and Fraser, 1996, pp.180, 184–5, 186–8, 189–92, 193

2

Social exclusion and class analysis

Mike Savage

Contents

| I | Introduction | 60 |
| | Aims | 61 |

| 2 | Class awareness and identification | 61 |

| 3 | Class inequality | 66 |

4	The classical class analysis of Marx and Weber	70
	4.1 Marx	71
	4.2 Weber	73

| 5 | Class distinctions and class cultures | 76 |

| 6 | Conclusion | 82 |

| **References** | | 83 |

Readings

| 2.1: Mike Savage, Gaynor Bagnall and Brian Longhurst, 'Ordinary, ambivalent and defensive: class identities in the North West of England' (2001) | 86 |

| 2.2: Rosemary Crompton, 'The classic inheritance and its development: Marx' (1996) | 91 |

| 2.3: Rosemary Crompton, 'The classic inheritance and its development: Weber' (1996) | 94 |

| 2.4: Pierre Bourdieu *et al.*, 'The weight of the world' (1999) | 97 |

1 Introduction

Since 1997, the Labour government in the UK has stated its public commitment to reducing 'social exclusion' as part of its concern to foster an inclusive society. The language of social inclusion and exclusion is telling: the idea of social inclusion is bland and inoffensive, a deliberate pitch for the 'middle ground'. After all, who but extremists of one sort or another could possibly be in favour of the 'social exclusion' of particular peoples (though it is striking that on many substantive issues, such as dealing with asylum-seekers, a politics of social exclusion – though not phrased in these terms – remains evident). It is noteworthy that the language of inclusion and exclusion marks a subtle reworking of older forms of class politics. For much of its history, the Labour party pursued a politics phrased in terms of justice, redistribution and equality. An important undercurrent to this was the issue of class. This was a politics that recognized the entrenched nature of class divisions, and the existence of different interest groups within society. It was a politics concerned with changing (with differing degrees of effectiveness) the relationship between the classes. The language of social inclusion, by contrast, does not draw attention to divisions amongst the 'socially included' and implies a society where most social groups have been incorporated into a common social body, with shared values and interests, and no major issues to fundamentally divide them amongst themselves. Given this assumption, policy need only focus on bringing in those – few – outsiders who remain outside the social body (see Chapter 6 for a fuller discussion of these themes).

Seen in this light, the language of social inclusion and exclusion is entirely consistent with the language of 'classlessness' which was developed by the Conservative government in the 1990s, especially under John Major's leadership. The Labour party's leader, Tony Blair, does not think that class divisions are of pressing political concern (though some elements of his party continue to hanker after more traditional modes of class politics). In this chapter, we consider whether in the light of this new political agenda, it is useful to think that class is a fundamental social division. Insofar as class is still an entrenched social divide, it poses problems and difficulties for a politics of social inclusion. In section 2, I will argue that there is a general weakness in people's awareness of class, but I will also show that class divisions remain deep rooted, and if anything are becoming more marked. Hence, we have what I define as the 'conundrum of class'. Although the material importance of class to people's life-chances seems ever more important, people's recognition of the salience of class seems weak, and may even have faded in recent times. Class inequalities are routinely brushed aside, ignored and effaced, even by those most disadvantaged by them. It can be argued that this is different from people's everyday – though commonsense – awareness of inequalities linked to gender, place, generation, ethnicity and 'race'. The conundrum will lead me to explore how entrenched class inequality can go hand in hand with the cultural invisibility of class.

In section 4 we look at how we might explain this conundrum sociologically. I examine the contributions of the classical class theorists, Marx and Weber, and show that, whilst both thinkers continue to offer insights of major contemporary significance, there are significant problems with their accounts of class that reduce their use in considering its contemporary nature. Section 5 then considers whether the contemporary theory of Pierre Bourdieu (1984) offers a way of understanding the conundrum of class. Drawing especially on Bourdieu's account of cultural divisions in France, I unpack his concept of 'cultural capital' and place it in the broader context of his analysis of 'habitus' and 'field' in order to show that he offers a good way of understanding how class inequalities are routinely reproduced in a way that leads to them being largely unrecognized. You will be introduced to an outline of Bourdieu's concepts of field and habitus in order to show how they can lead to a very different approach to class analysis.

AIMS

This chapter aims to:

1   Explore the contemporary significance of social class with respect to the extent that people are aware of the continuing structural impact of class divisions in society and identify themselves personally in relation to such divisions.

2   Evaluate the different class theories of Marx, Weber and Bourdieu in terms of their salience in explaining the contemporary relevance of class divisions.

3   Examine the implications of debates about class for an understanding of contemporary politics.

2   Class awareness and identification

ACTIVITY 1

Before reading any of this chapter, or any of the associated readings, please consider these two questions:

■   It is sometimes said that we live in a classless society. Do you agree?

■   Do you think of yourself as belonging to any particular social class? If so, which one?

What were your responses to Activity 1? If you are typical of the British population, it is likely that you do not think that we live in a classless society. Survey evidence suggests that people certainly have a strong sense that British society is riven by class conflict: around 75 per cent of people in 1991 thought that social **class** mattered either 'a great deal' or 'quite a lot' in affecting people's opportunities. During the 1980s, when the Conservative party led by Margaret Thatcher was in government, the proportion of people feeling that class conflict was strong increased somewhat (see Abercrombie and Warde, 1994). With respect to the second question of Activity 1, it is also very likely that you have been able to define yourself as a member of a social class. Young (1992) found that only around 2 per cent of respondents interviewed by the British Social Attitudes Survey during the 1980s 'didn't know' what class they are in, and there has been no tendency over time for people to be less likely to allocate themselves to a class (Reid, 1998). Most surveys show that over 90 per cent of people identified themselves as members of one class or another.

class

Figure 2.1 *'I look up to him ...'. The classic sketch from* The Frost Report *in the 1970s satirizing the British class structure of upper, middle and working classes*

middle class, working class

If you are one of the majority who defined yourself as a member of a class, then you probably have a roughly even chance of saying you are **middle** or **working class**. Marshall *et al.* (1988) found that (when pressed) 3 per cent of people identified themselves as upper or upper middle class, 24 per cent claimed that they were middle class, 12 per cent that they were lower middle class, 11 per cent that they were upper working class, 38 per cent that they were working class, and 4 per cent that they were lower working class. What is striking is that even though the majority of the British labour force are in white-collar, non-manual occupations, more people defined themselves as 'working class' (58 per cent of the responses of those placing themselves in a class) rather than middle class (42 per cent), and these proportions have not changed much since Marshall *et al.* carried out their survey in 1984. Britain is relatively unusual in that most other comparable nations, such as the USA or Japan, see a much higher proportion of their populations claiming to be middle class.

ACTIVITY 2

Did you find it easy to do Activity 1? Did you find it easier to answer the first or second part of the Activity? Did you instantly know which class you belonged to? Was this something you had thought about much before? Is your sense of class identity important to you? How does your sense of class identity compare to your identification with your gender, ethnicity and generation?

My own guess is that you were able to answer the first part of Activity 1 fairly easily but had to think before answering the second. I also think it likely that few of you feel strongly that you belong to a particular social class. Though I expect that you could place yourself in a class when asked, I doubt that this is something you have given much conscious thought to. In short, I think it is likely that your sense of belonging to a class is ambivalent and uncertain. These expectations are drawn from research I have carried out on this issue with Gaynor Bagnall and Brian Longhurst (Savage *et al.*, 2001), some findings from which are included as Reading 2.1. Our in-depth interviews with 178 people living in four sites in and around Manchester (Ramsbottom, Cheadle, Wilmslow and Chorlton) indicated that around two-thirds of people did define themselves as a member of a particular class. Even so, the proportion of people who in no way identified with any class, around one-third, is significantly higher than is suggested by surveys. This may be due to the way that in-depth interviewing allows greater dialogue between interviewer and respondent than is possible in structured surveys. What our interviews also revealed was that even those people who did define themselves as members of classes did so ambivalently, with people prefacing their remarks with phrases such as 'I suppose I'm ... ' or 'probably I'm. ... ' Reading 2.1 also shows that significant numbers of respondents indicated that they had never thought about class before, whilst others switched between a working-class and middle-class definition of themselves in the course of the interview. This suggests that they had not thought through or reflected on their class identity with any precision. By contrast, they were able to articulate a sense of class as a political issue, as a topic which was relevant to the social and political structure of British society. When asked about whether Britain was a classless society, most respondents were emphatic that it was not. People had little difficulty in talking about class divisions, but did not like to think of themselves as members of particular classes.

(a) Ramsbottom

(b) Cheadle

(c) Wilmslow

(d) Chorlton

Figure 2.2 *Areas of Manchester where the survey was carried out*

Now read Reading 2.1 which gives more detail of the results from the survey by Savage *et al.*

From your experience, do the research results ring true? How do you explain the findings regarding the ambivalent nature of class awareness?

Savage *et al.*'s findings may appear to contradict the survey evidence mentioned above. Consider, for instance, the survey carried out by Marshall *et al.* (1988), the most important recent survey of class divisions in the UK, which claims that 'social identities are widely and easily constructed in class terms' (*ibid.*, p.145). The survey noted that few people articulate alternative identities to that of class, and whilst people don't have a radical **class consciousness**, they were emphatic that it was deeply felt. However, we need to be careful in interpreting this evidence. Saunders (1989) claims that Marshall *et al.* (1988) bombarded respondents with a series of questions which assumed the existence of class before asking them about their own class identity, a procedure which was likely to lead respondents to identify in class terms. Thus, Saunders emphasizes that the fact that people can define themselves as members of a class does not mean that such identifications come readily to them. When people are asked to think of themselves in terms of a series of social categories, then they may be able to place themselves within them, but it does not follow that such categories mean much to them (see also Pawson, 1989).

To give an example: when people are asked to place themselves not in social classes, but in ranked groups (with 1 at the top and 10 at the bottom), only 1 per cent 'did not know' which group they were in (see SCPR, 1992, pp.6, 15). Yet sociologists have rarely used this evidence to argue that people actually think in ranked terms rather than in terms of class (though see Prandy, 1997). Furthermore, Evans (1992), using the same survey data as Marshall *et al.* (1988), has also shown that most people's **attitudes** are not closely linked to their class identification: attitudes towards inequality and towards the 'worse off' (for instance unemployed people or low-paid workers) are not related to class. 'The class structuring of class consciousness … does not imply class structuring of concern for those on welfare, or opposition to the free market' (Evans, 1992, p.249). He concludes by noting that 'for those beliefs and values that do not involve obvious class-related costs and benefits – even when they involve egalitarian concerns – class appears to be relatively unimportant' (*ibid.*, p.254). It seems that few other beliefs appear to follow from the class labels people can give themselves.

When we examine it carefully, we find that survey evidence is therefore less emphatic in demonstrating the existence of class awareness than is sometimes claimed (for example by Reid, 1998). Taking this point even further, we could argue that people's responses to questions asked in surveys about class identification can actually be indirect ways of 'refusing' class identities. Consider, for instance, the Americans and Japanese, who are likely to see themselves as middle class. The reason for this may not be that people feel strongly that they are in fact middle class, but rather they may see the term middle class as the least loaded of the class terms that are offered to them. Claiming a middle-class identity is an indirect way of refusing, or minimizing, a class identity: by saying you are middle class you may be describing yourself as a typical, ordinary person, neither particularly well off nor particularly poor. In

class
consciousness

attitude

Britain, it is interesting that people are more likely to say they are working class than is the case in the US or Japan. However, the same argument can apply. Most people still tend not to define themselves as members of the 'extreme' classes, notably the 'upper-middle' class at the top (around 2 per cent of respondents) and the 'poor' class at the bottom (3–4 per cent of respondents) (see Marshall *et al.*, 1988). A reason why significant numbers of British people think they are working class may be because they think of themselves as 'working', like most other people: hence it is a claim to being ordinary and typical, not a claim to a specific strongly held working-class identity. Certainly in our research (Savage *et al.*, 2001) we found no cases of working-class identifiers who had a strong attachment to working-class institutions such as trade unions, the Labour movement, and so on.

We find support for this argument in other qualitative research that endorses the view that people's awareness of class is more complex and hesitating than survey evidence may suggest. Devine's (1992) study of the social identities of affluent manual workers in Luton emphasized that the identities of nation, region and ethnicity were all strong, and did not override notions of class but sat alongside them. Devine emphasized that most of her respondents saw themselves as 'ordinary', sometimes linked to phrases such as being 'ordinary working people'. More recently, Bradley's (1999) interviews with 198 employees in the North of England report that a surprisingly high proportion of her sample do not think in terms of class and have only a weak sense of class identity. Although many think of themselves as working class, this does not entail a strong attachment to the manual working class. This supports the arguments of Savage *et al.* (2001) that class identities are generally weak, even though people can think of themselves as belonging to a particular class.

How, then, can we conclude our account of class identities? We have seen that the term class has considerable popular currency, and that people do use the term both to identify themselves in class terms and also to make sense of political conflict. However, class does not seem to be a deeply held personal identity, nor does class appear to invoke strong senses of group or collective allegiance – though there are exceptions to this. (If you think you are an exception, and that you have a strong sense of class identity, spend a few minutes thinking why this might be and whether you think you are typical compared to your friends.) In general, personal class identification is relatively muted. While there continues to be consistent evidence that people tend to feel society is unjust, that inequalities are more marked than can readily be justified, and that people do not, in a sense, get what they deserve, there is very little evidence that these popular feelings turn into a radical class-conscious critique of contemporary society in which people feel that revolutionary changes in class relationships would alleviate these problems. Indeed, Marshall *et al.* (1988, p.190) emphasize that there is no evidence from their study that can 'be said to reflect a mature sense of developed class consciousness comprising class identity, class opposition, class totality and the conception of an alternative society'.

SUMMARY OF SECTION 2

Although the term class has popular currency and people apparently feel that society is unequal and divided by class, personal class identification and class consciousness is relatively muted.

3 Class inequality

In recent years, whatever people's perceptions of their class might be, there is no doubting that class inequality has hardened. People's destinies are as strongly affected, and perhaps more strongly affected, by their class background (whether this is measured by their parents' class, or their own) than they were in the mid-twentieth century. During this period, state intervention in many industrial capitalist nations led to the slow but distinct erosion of income and wealth inequalities. The development of progressive taxation, whereby the wealthy were taxed proportionately more than the poor, together with the development of non-commodified welfare services principally in the fields of health, education and housing, led to an attenuation of wealth inequalities (although these nonetheless continued to be marked). From the 1970s, the emergence of right-wing neo-liberal governments in many – though not all – capitalist nations, led to financial deregulation, the privatization of some government industries and services, and tax-cutting in favour of more affluent groups. The result has been a marked polarization of wealth and income in the UK and USA. Although several European nations (in particular Germany and Sweden) have resisted these trends, by maintaining their commitment to a redistributive regime, the US model (in stocks and shares, property and so on) has had far-reaching implications.

distribution of income and wealth

Inequalities in the **distribution of wealth** have increased significantly in the UK since the late 1970s (Joseph Rowntree Foundation, 1995). Tax cuts (notably the cut in tax rates for the wealthy from 83 per cent to 40 per cent), and soaring stock-market and property values, have allowed those who were already wealthy to accumulate their wealth massively. Wealth can be stored and accumulated (through investments or property, for instance) and it is therefore likely that it is more unevenly distributed than income. In the late 1990s, the top 10 per cent of the population owned 50 per cent of the nation's wealth, and during the 1990s the wealth of the most affluent 200 individuals doubled.

Income inequalities

Income inequalities have also increased substantially since 1980. There are growing differences between incomes accruing to those in professional, managerial and administrative employment (the middle class, or 'service class' to use the term popularized by Goldthorpe, 1982), and those in other occupations (the working class). Whereas economists usually argue that income differentials take the form of a statistician's curve, with most people earning incomes in the middle ranges, recent research actually suggests that there is a growing gap between the affluent and the less affluent. Thus, in the UK, in 1998, men in three occupational groups had weekly incomes significantly *above* the national average of £427.10. These were managers, who earned £626, professionals who earned £568, and associate professionals, such as nurses, who earned £516. Every other group earned considerably *below* the national average, with craft manual workers earning the next highest average, £360. There were actually rather few occupational groups earning around the national average: groups either earned considerably more, or less, than the average. The situation for female workers was identical. There is therefore evidence of a marked income gap based on class differences between managers, professionals and administrators, and other manual and routine non-manual occupations.

Take a look at Table 2.1 below. What reasons can you think of for the inequalities in pay between managers and professionals, on the one hand, and the rest of the occupations on the other? Do you think they reflect the esteem in which different occupations are held? Do you think they are caused by the skill levels of employees in these occupations? Are these inequalities linked to class-based power differences between these groups? If so, what kind of power differences?

Table 2.1 Figures on income differentials by socio-economic group in 1998

Occupational group	Men, full-time	Women, full-time
Managers and administrators	625.6	435.3
Professionals	568.4	458.4
Associate professionals	515.9	375.8
Clerical and secretarial	291.9	257.6
Personal and protective services	339.5	220.1
Sales occupations	339.6	231.0
Craft workers	360.4	217.7
Plant and machine operatives	332.9	228.6
Others	280.4	193.3
Average	*427.1*	*309.6*

Note: Figures for full-time weekly pay, for those whose income is not affected by absence.

Source: Savage, 2000, Table 3.3, p. 52

There has been – and still is – extensive debate about the reasons for income inequality. These are too complex to summarize fully here (though see Savage, 2000, Ch. 3). One reason we can examine here is **status**, where the rewards of the better-paid occupations are linked to the prestige of these jobs, since people think it right that people in these jobs are better rewarded. However, survey evidence shows that most people do not think it right that those in better-paid job should be as well rewarded as they are, and there are instances of highly esteemed jobs that are not relatively well paid – nursing, for example (Savage, 2000).

    The other main reason put forward to explain pay differentials is **human capital**. Here the argument is that, in a competitive labour market, those with skills and expertise are able to command a premium that allows them to earn increasingly more then those without such skills. Income inequality can thus be seen as a fair reflection of the amount of investment people have made into their skills and training. In fact, evidence suggests that the picture is considerably more complex than this. One important measure of skill – qualifications – shows only a slight association with income (Dale and Egerton, 1997), especially for men. There is growing divergence in people's income even if they have identical qualifications. Gosling *et al.* (1994) show that there is increasing income differentiation for workers with the same level of educational qualification. In 1978, of those who left school poorly qualified at age 16, the best-paid 10 per

status

human capital

cent earned 2.25 times more than the worst-paid 10 per cent. By 1992 this ratio had risen to nearly three times. Other research indicates that skills only appear to lead to increases in income when workers are in the kind of employment (such as in professional or managerial roles) that values such skills (Theodossiou, 1996). Rather than human capital being a just reward for people's investment in their skills, it actually accentuates class inequalities. Those in 'middle-class' jobs are able to increase their incomes by raising their skills, whereas those in manual or working-class employment get no such advantage – whatever skills they may possess. These findings suggest that the class perspective, which emphasizes that pay is linked to the kinds of jobs that people have, rather than the attributes of the people themselves, is increasingly important in explaining income inequalities.

We find further indication of the hardening of class inequalities when we look at health. If levels of health and morbidity (i.e. death) are related to class position, there can be no stronger evidence for the reality of class inequality. Many of those who have emphasized class inequalities, from **Friedrich Engels** in his pioneering study of class in Victorian Manchester, to Joseph Rowntree in his study of poverty in early twentieth-century York, have focused on inequalities in health as a key indicator of class inequalities. In the UK the National Health Service is relatively unusual compared to many other nations, in that it provides free or heavily subsidized health care at the point of delivery to patients, in an attempt to prevent level of income affecting quality of health care. This was part of the drive towards social citizenship (discussed in Chapter 5). However, it has

Engels, Friedrich

become increasingly clear over the past twenty years since the publication of the Black Report on Health Inequalities (Townsend and Davidson, 1982) that in fact class differences are persistent and enduring and subsequent research has emphasized the entrenched association between income levels and health (Wilkinson, 1996).

Most studies have focused on differences in male mortality rates. These have shown that male unskilled manual workers are more likely to die earlier than male professionals and managers. It also seems apparent that there have been few relative changes in mortality rates in the last fifty years, despite the public investment in the National Health Service. Bartley *et al.* (1996) indicate that men in the highest Registrar General's social class in 1981 had only two-thirds the chance of dying between 1986 and 1989 as the male population as a whole. Male unskilled manual workers were nearly one-third more likely to die than the population as a whole, indicating that they were twice as likely to die as men in the upper professional classes. Bartley *et al.* (1996) indicate that it is not just income levels that

Figure 2.3 Friedrich Engels, 1820–95

appear to cause this mortality, since poorly paid agricultural workers actually have better than average mortality rates. It may be that those who are routinely in positions of powerlessness vis-à-vis managers are more likely to die. Thus routine white-collar workers as well as manual workers fare worse than the norm.

Somewhat different pictures of health inequalities are provided if the focus is on women, or on long-standing illness rather than morbidity (Cooper *et al.*, 1998). Some researchers emphasize that income rather than class is the more fundamental cause of health inequalities. Nonetheless, it is still clear that recent research has established the enduring nature of health inequalities, even though there continues to be debate as what the precise causes of this are (see, for example, Popay *et al.*, 1998).

Let us take stock. There is a conundrum here. This is that class – defined here in terms of economic position – matters very greatly for people's **life-chances**. Whether one takes income, health, social mobility prospects or whatever, class matters. This poses real problems for a politics of social inclusion that suggests that all but those completely 'outside' society are part of a common social body. In fact, there are entrenched, indeed growing, differences even amongst those who are fully employed, which suggests class inequality continues to be a fundamental feature of contemporary social life. Indeed, the more significant that anything is for the quality of one's life (for instance health and education), the more closely associated it is with class inequality. However, the other side of the conundrum is that people appear routinely unaware of the salience and significance of class insofar as it affects their own lives and identities. Although people are aware of the existence of class inequalities, they do not by and large see themselves as belonging to classes or having distinct class interests. In this respect, any political party trying to appeal to class interests or class identities may well find it does not elicit much support from the electorate – even from those who might actually benefit from policies designed to lead to a reduction in class inequalities.

life-chances

SUMMARY OF SECTION 3

1 Class – in terms of economic position – matters greatly for people's life-chances. Measured by any material category – health, wealth, income, social mobility, morbidity, education – class represents a continuing and fundamental social division.

2 Despite political rhetoric about the 'classless' society, material class inequalities are in fact increasing rather than decreasing.

3 However, although people recognize that society is divided along class lines, they appear to be relatively unaware of the significance of class insofar as it affects their own lives and identities, and class identification is typically weak. There is therefore a conundrum around the issue of social class in contemporary society.

4 The classical class analysis of Marx and Weber

Marx, Karl
Weber, Max

Sociological class analysis has its roots in the work of **Karl Marx** and **Max Weber**. Throughout the twentieth century, the debate on class has drawn on the dialogue between Marx and Weber, with sociologists (as well as other social scientists and historians) staking out their positions on class by drawing on the arguments of these founders of sociology. Both writers continue to be inspirational sources for contemporary sociological reflection, and nearly all textbooks on social theory continue to emphasize their contemporary relevance (such as Hughes *et al.*, 1995; Craib, 1996). However, neither of their frameworks offers us a straightforward base for understanding the conundrum of class.

READING 2.2

Please read Reading 2.2, which summarizes the main elements of the class theory of Marx. When you have finished reading, write down the points that you think are relevant to understanding the conundrum of class analysis discussed in sections 2 and 3 of this chapter. How valuable do you think Marx's arguments are for understanding class in contemporary times?

Figure 2.4 Karl Marx, 1818–83

4.1 Marx

Let us firstly review the significance of Marx's ideas. There is no doubt that Marxist ideas continue to be highly pertinent to sociological thought. For much of the twentieth century, Marxism was a powerful and vibrant intellectual force, associated with the rapid rise of **communist** and **socialist** politics in many parts of the globe during the first half of the century; and especially in the second half of the century Marxism became respectable as an academic discipline, and laid deep roots in nearly all of the humanities and social sciences. It is striking that despite the collapse of the communist political project with the fall of the East European bloc in the 1980s, the intellectual relevance of Marxism has continued, albeit increasingly as an academic discourse with few roots in popular politics and culture. There are a number of ways in which Marxist insights help us understand the contemporary nature of class.

communism, socialist societies

Firstly, Reading 2.2 shows that Marx emphasized the *material* nature of class inequality, and the way that class interests polarized as **capitalism** developed. While the main class divisions we discussed in section 3 are rather different to those that Marx himself discussed, in general terms Marx's arguments about the entrenched nature of economic class inequality are borne out by current trends. I emphasized the main economic class differences between managers, professionals and administrators (the service class) on the one hand, and manual and routine white-collar and technical workers (the working class) on the other. Marx himself concentrated on the class divisions between employers and propertyless employees, and said little about managers, professionals or white-collar workers. However, as Crompton indicates in Reading 2.2, this in itself is not an overriding objection to Marx's arguments. Even though professionals and managers are not the owners of enterprises, they can still be said to 'service' their employers, and as a result can be distinguished from the working class. Indeed, this is where Goldthorpe's (1982) influential concept of the 'service class' is compatible with this Marxist argument.

capitalism

Secondly, Marx predicted the development of class-consciousness as workers became aware of their class situation and sought to transform this through political action. I have argued that this has certainly not happened, and we have seen in section 3 that most people today have a very limited sense of class identity. This has fundamental repercussions for Marxism, as Crompton notes (in Reading 2.2) when she refers to the debate on the base and superstructure approach. Marx emphasized that the working class were the emancipatory force who had the potential to overthrow capitalism: this claim allowed Marxists to appeal to class in order to connect with practical political struggles in many different parts of the world. Even in those nations where it was peasants rather than manual workers who stood at the vanguard of political struggle, it was possible to adapt the language of class to allow it populist and nationalist connotations. Class was therefore a key rallying cry within Marxist discourse. However, as Reading 2.1 suggests, today most people who see themselves as working class do so not because they recognize their exploited place in society but as a means of claiming that they are ordinary or typical members of society. This is of course a very different sense of class awareness to that deriving from the Marxist tradition.

Most Marxists have recognized that class awareness does not take the form that Marx hoped. Their response to this is to point to the tension within Marxism between its stress on both the structural powers of capitalism as a mode of production and on the significance of class. This dominant tendency within Marxism links economic and **social change** to the dynamics of capitalist development, and places particular emphasis on the structural power of capitalism to determine social change. It is the processes of capitalist production and capital accumulation that cause contradictions and crises within the capitalist system, and as a result drive historical change. Class conflict, if it is evident, is at most the means by which such deep processes surface and lead to social change. Class itself has no independent role in bringing about change and is the epiphenomena of deeper-seated structural forces. In this respect, recent Marxists have made little real play on the idea of class (see Savage, 2000).

social change

Thirdly, Marx's account of class is problematized by the limitations of the labour theory of value. The labour theory of value united Marxist analyses of capitalism with class. This was because it provided an explanation of how capitalism depended on the systematic *exploitation* of labour, and hence the creation of class divisions. Capital accumulation took place through the extraction of surplus value from workers who produced commodities. In this way, *capitalism generated profits through the same processes by which classes were formed*, and so there was a systematic link between capitalism and class in Marxist analysis. People came to recognize their class interests and their class identities through their involvement in capitalist employment relations. It was therefore the main way by which class formation – the link between class *in itself* and class *for itself* – could be registered.

The labour theory of value depends on distinguishing *productive* labour from *unproductive* labour, so that the former can be seen to have surplus value extracted from them by the latter. In early industrial capitalism, it seemed straightforward to regard manual labourers – who produced the commodities that were then sold for profit by capitalist enterprises – as the core body of productive labourers. During the twentieth century, however, as fewer people were employed in manual production, so it became more ambiguous as to who was actually carrying out productive work. Are workers involved in the 'service sector' (which at the end of the twentieth century comprised around two-thirds of the workforce in advanced capitalist nations) productive? Are housewives who carry out domestic labour for their husbands and children productive? For much of the 1970s, bitter disputes were waged on these questions but ultimately it proved impossible to determine a non-arbitrary way of delineating productive from non-productive labour.

Most Marxists decided that it was more useful to focus on capitalism as a social structure, rather than worry about how capitalism and class were intertwined. The 'regulationist' school of Marxism, associated with Aglietta (1979), Lipietz (1987), Boyer (1990) and others, turned their attention to broader processes of economic and political restructuring. In the process, they lost interest in the kinds of process of class formation that Crompton discusses in Reading 2.2.

I have suggested that popular views about class reflect current Marxist uncertainties on this issue. Most people are aware of class inequalities, but do not link their experience of work and employment to class in a straightforward way. This is consistent with a Marxism that no longer uses the labour theory of value as its cornerstone, and which recognizes that capitalism produces structural inequalities but that they are not rooted exclusively in the extraction of surplus value in the workplace. Yet, whilst this suggests that Marxism continues to be useful in accounting for the generation of structural inequalities through the trends in capitalism, it does not provide a way of understanding the specific kinds of class identities and awareness that we have discussed here.

READING 2.3

Please turn to Reading 2.3, which summarizes the key ideas of Max Weber. Do you find the classes as distinguished by Weber a useful way of understanding contemporary social divisions? Do you find Weber's ideas more useful than Marx's in thinking about the conundrum of class?

4.2 Weber

There are rather different issues concerning the fate of Weberian class theory in comparison to Marxism. Weberians have argued that Weberian approaches can provide a more secure foundation for class analysis than can Marxism (Marshall *et al.*, 1988; Goldthorpe and Marshall, 1992; Scott, 1996). As Reading 2.3 shows, Weber makes no claims about the existence of class consciousness, a point which may be better suited to the contemporary ambivalence of class identity. Weber emphasizes the distinction between class, status and command (see also Scott, 1996) and between class position and class formation. The first distinction allows Weberians to argue that there is no necessary connection between economic inequality (class), honour and reputation (status) and power (command). The related distinction between economic and social class allows Weberians to emphasize that there is no necessary reason to suppose that class has any intrinsic social importance. Economic class need not lead to social classes, nor need class be any more central than status

Figure 2.5 *Max Weber, 1864–1920*

or command. Whether class is socially significant is a contingent question that can only be answered by examining empirically whether classes have been formed as relatively enduring social collectivities.

In many respects, this seems a very useful foundation for unpacking the conundrum of class that we came across in section 2. Weberians would not be surprised by the fact that marked economic inequalities do not lead necessarily to awareness of class, and would argue that the relative weakness of class identities is entirely what they might expect. Given their emphasis on how class inequalities are related to market processes, they would also have no problems in relating increased inequalities to the increased role of market processes in economic and social life. However, there are three significant problems in the Weberian framework.

Firstly, as Reading 2.3 shows, a Weberian approach to economic class argues that differences in market rewards lead to economic class. However, as you saw in section 3, the idea of human capital, which is consistent with this market-based approach, does not explain economic class inequality. Rather, it is fundamental divisions in employment relations – as the Marxist approach would argue – that govern economic inequalities. We could argue that the Weberian position places too much emphasis on the role of market processes in affecting rewards, rather than examining how markets are themselves socially structured.

Secondly, a Weberian account of status draws attention to the way that esteem is not linked to economic class but is an independent force which structures life-chances. The concept of status seems to be of limited value in unpicking people's sense of class identity and group membership. While this may be consistent with the fact that people do not identify themselves as members of specific social classes on the basis of their economic position, it is also striking that today people rarely make status claims of any kind. People are wary of appearing to demonstrate openly their cultural superiority, or at least using overt and self-conscious methods. Rather, a common refrain is to emphasize one's ordinariness, one's common membership of the social mainstream. This is a peculiar kind of status claim since its importance resides in distinguishing yourself in terms of your *lack* of distinctiveness. The dominance of political discourses of 'social inclusion' may in fact impede specific social groups from advancing claims as to why they should be treated as special cases.

Finally, Weberian attempts to find a way of linking economic class to processes of class formation have proved problematic. Those Weberians who have sought to go beyond the simple point that there is no automatic association between economic class and social class have often tried to delineate the specific mechanisms that may, in certain cases, produce an association. This involves identifying the kinds of processes by which class collectivities can form around class positions (see Giddens, 1973). Three main processes have been highlighted, including political class formation, when political organizations mobilize on the basis of class, and socio-cultural class formation which refers to the extent to which distinctive class cultures are forged. Perhaps most importantly, demographic class formation, has been given especial importance in the work of Goldthorpe. This concerns the extent to which classes are self-recruiting and thereby form homogeneous class characters.

These common efforts have led to a substantial class-analysis programme, especially in the UK and parts of Europe (Goldthorpe *et al.*, 1980; Halsey *et al.*, 1980; Goldthorpe and Marshall, 1992; Marshall *et al.*, 1988). The exponents of this programme emphasize that the working class continues to be economically deprived. Furthermore, since most working-class people come from working-class backgrounds, it is possible to detect a process of working-class formation as children follow in their parents' footsteps. Through this inter-generational transmission of class, the working class continues to exist as a coherent social body, with shared cultures, values and lifestyles. This argument draws upon numerous studies of working-class life, mainly carried out from the 1950s to the 1970s, which emphasize the continued vitality of working-class culture in industrial communities. The community studies of Hoggart (1956), Dennis *et al.* (1956), Willmott and Young (1957, 1960) and Bott (1957) were all testimony to the existence of a clear and distinct working-class culture based on shared values and a sense of isolation from 'middle-class' society.

However, when examined carefully, although they point to evidence concerning the association between class position and life-chances, there is not much evidence that there are strong processes of working-class formation in Britain, or indeed any contemporary nation-state. The evidence from Reading 2.1 shows that working-class identities are not especially strongly held, nor do they lead to a clear and cohesive set of views in the way that the idea of class formation would suppose. Part of the reason for this is the way that cleavages of gender, age, 'race' and ethnicity interrelate with those of class (as discussed in the Introduction to this volume). By only considering the class position of women when they are in a higher social class to their male partners, Goldthorpe himself is not able to establish that manual women and men are linked together into a demographically formed class. Similarly, because manual work is increasingly performed by relatively young men (Egerton and Savage, 2000), it seems that significant numbers of manual workers are not carrying out manual work during most or all of their lives.

Weberian theory does not provide a theory of *why* class matters. Weberian approaches only suggest a set of procedures about how one might try to connect economic class with social class. They do not, in themselves, demonstrate that it is a particularly useful or worthy project to try to make this connection. This suggestion that Weberian scholarship does not actually demonstrate that class is especially salient leads on to a further, methodological point. Weber argues that it is inevitable that social values colour the kinds of topics that social scientists research; objectivity is only possible insofar as procedures can be laid down to eliminate subjective bias once particular topics have been chosen for study. However, when posing the key question as to 'why study class' (rather than ethnicity, religion, gender, consumption or indeed anything else), Weber himself gives no direct answer, since it is not possible to provide objective reasons for one's choice of subject.

Contemporary Weberians resolve this question in one of two ways. Firstly, they might note that since class is a live topical issue, and much discussed in political and social discourse, this is reason enough to study it. In earlier periods also, when class was a pressing political issue (partly as a result of the influence of Marxist politics), this would have been a reasonable response. However, in a period when the main intellectual discourse on class, that of Marxism, is in retreat, and class politics is muted, this reason does not seem a very good one. Secondly, as Goldthorpe and Marshall (1992) argue, since class analysis has always been prominent within the sociological tradition, it makes sense to continue to tease out the best procedural means by which class can be studied. However, the danger here is a kind of academic self-referencing. The argument seems to be that because in the past academics have studied class, so it should go on being studied in ever more rigorous ways. But this does not establish the relevance of its study to those (an increasing number) not socialized into its concerns.

Indeed, it is possible to detect a shift in the reception of class analysis in recent years. In the 1960s, debates on the changing nature of class were central to the understanding of social change in Britain. The argument that the working class was becoming middle class was not just of interest to sociologists, but also to political commentators, and led to a series of high-profile studies, culminating in Goldthorpe *et al.*'s (1968, 1969) famous **affluent worker** studies. However, by the 1990s, debates on class had become detached from these kinds of social

affluent worker

underclass

and political questions. A good example of this is the way that political discourse took up the idea of 'social exclusion', and showed an interest in debates about the '**underclass**', yet these were not issues that were addressed within class analysis (see Savage, 2000). Despite its sophistication, the Weberian tradition is of relatively little value in accounting for the particular manifestations of class inequality and class awareness that are currently found in the UK. This is not to say that it is of no value at all: it forces us to consider the complexity of the relationship between class inequality and class awareness, and prevents us from providing simplistic accounts of class formation. However, once this point is recognized it is still important to reflect on how connections are sustained and here it would appear that the Weberian tradition says little of substantive value.

SUMMARY OF SECTION 4

1   The classical class analyses of both Marx and Weber have some continuing pertinence with respect to present-day manifestations of class division but both also have significant limitations in explaining the contemporary conundrum of class identified in this chapter.

2   Marxism emphasizes structural economic inequality as a result of capitalist development, and this is largely borne out by current trends. However, the class-consciousness, action and struggle that were predicted by Marx as an inevitable consequence of class exploitation within capitalism are typically absent in the current conundrum of class in which people do not link their own experiences of work with class division and capitalist exploitation.

3   The Weberian argument that there is a possible – but not necessary – link between economic class and social-class formation chimes with the ambivalence that characterizes the contemporary conundrum of class. However, Weberian work that tries to establish links between economic and social class has failed to establish that such connections are especially important.

5   Class distinctions and class cultures

Bourdieu, Pierre

stratification

How, then, do we understand the conundrum of class? In this last section I will explore how the arguments of **Pierre Bourdieu** can help us. Bourdieu's ideas have become increasingly prominent amongst sociologists interested in the cultural dimensions of **stratification** in recent years (for instance, Featherstone, 1987; Savage *et al.*, 1992; Butler and Savage, 1995; Calhoun *et al.*, 1993). However, his work is complex and multi-faceted. In this section I do not seek to provide a systematic account of his views, but only those relevant to exploring the conundrum of class.

cultural capital

Bourdieu is best known for his arguments about the significance of **cultural capital** (see, for example, Bourdieu, 1984). Here he argues that some people are socialized into having the kinds of values and dispositions that allow them to appreciate forms of 'high culture', such as classical music, art, 'great literature'

Figure 2.6 *Pierre Bourdieu, 1930–*

and so forth. Bourdieu argues that the appreciation of such art forms is not a private matter linked to people's individual taste. In part this is because high culture is publicly sanctioned by being preserved and venerated in high-status museums, art galleries and theatres. These are also the kind of cultural forms which are celebrated by being given pride of place in the curriculums at schools and universities. Furthermore, Bourdieu claims that an appreciation of high culture is dependent on the denigration of low and popular culture, so that celebrating the music of Beethoven or Bach, for instance, involves the implicit downgrading of rap or dance music. High culture depends on the abstraction of 'art' from the daily necessities of life, and involves looking at art forms in a detached way, which can only be dependent on forms of cultural privilege. Possession of cultural capital does not just mean that people are able to appreciate classical paintings and so forth. By being based around abstraction, cultural capital bestows on its possessors the skills and attributes to perform well in the educational process and hence convert their dispositions into educational credentials that will allow them to move into privileged jobs. Thus, cultural capital allows people to sustain social advantage. It is a separate axis of stratification to economic capital.

It should not be assumed that cultural capital is simply concerned with an appreciation of art forms. Bourdieu emphasizes that its manifestations colour nearly all areas of social life, though in ways that are often not recognized. One example of this can be found in Warde's (1997) study of food consumption in the UK. We normally think of our taste in food as a matter of personal preference, or perhaps as a lifestyle choice (if we choose certain foods to lose weight or keep fit, for instance). But Warde shows that food taste systematically differs by social class, and that this is not just due to the different income levels of classes but appears related to the cultural capital that different occupational groups possess.

Look at Table 2.2 (derived from Warde, 1997) and work out the answers to the questions below:

■ Which occupational group consumes most of the following forms of food: fresh fruit; tea; sausages; and eating out?

■ Why do you think occupational groups seem to prefer different types of food?

Table 2.2 Expenditure (£s) per week and percentage of food expenditure, by socio-economic group of heads of household, for selected food items, 1988

| | Socio-economic group* | | | | | | | | | |
| | 3 | | 5 | | 9 | | 15 | | 12 | |
	£	%	£	%	£	%	£	%	£	%
Bread, rolls	2.11	3.7	1.58	2.6	1.59	4.0	1.89	4.0	2.05	4.5
Cereals	0.99	1.7	1.25	2.0	0.86	2.2	0.79	1.6	0.83	1.8
Beef and veal	3.62	6.3	4.02	6.6	1.58	4.0	2.16	4.5	2.35	5.2
Bacon and ham	0.79	1.4	0.78	1.3	0.62	1.6	0.84	1.8	0.84	1.8
Sausages	0.39	0.7	0.35	0.6	0.28	0.7	0.37	0.8	0.45	1.0
Cooked and canned meat	1.10	1.9	1.01	1.6	0.88	2.2	1.18	2.5	1.35	3.0
Poultry and game	2.27	4.0	2.37	3.9	1.50	3.8	1.65	3.4	1.57	3.5
Fish	1.39	2.4	1.50	2.5	0.93	2.4	1.00	2.1	0.90	2.0
Fish and chips	0.65	1.1	0.38	0.6	0.42	1.1	0.58	1.2	0.53	1.2
Milk – fresh	3.10	5.4	2.74	4.5	2.02	5.1	2.68	5.6	2.62	5.8
Fresh vegetables	2.16	3.8	2.85	4.6	1.50	3.8	1.66	3.5	1.37	3.0
Canned vegetables	0.51	0.9	0.39	0.6	0.44	1.1	0.56	1.2	0.60	1.3
Potato products	0.90	1.6	0.53	0.9	0.70	1.8	0.86	1.8	0.94	2.1
Potatoes	0.76	1.3	0.51	0.8	0.52	1.3	0.67	1.4	0.71	1.6
Fruit – fresh	1.95	3.4	2.56	4.2	1.44	3.6	1.40	2.9	1.29	2.9
Tea	0.60	1.0	0.32	0.5	0.38	1.0	0.53	1.1	0.47	1.0
Coffee	0.68	1.2	0.87	1.4	0.49	1.5	0.61	1.3	0.61	1.4
Sugar	0.32	0.6	0.26	0.4	0.20	0.5	0.30	0.6	0.32	0.7
Eating out	12.70		17.87		8.95		11.04		9.03	
		22.1		29.1		22.6		23.1		20.0
All food expenditure (£)	57.47		61.42		39.58		47.80		45.17	
Total expenditure (£)	297.00		370.05		233.44		244.44		–	
Food as % all expenditure		19.4		16.6		17.7		19.5		–
N households		152		81		395		349		733

Notes: * Socio-economic groups: 3: small industrial and commercial employers; 5: professionals, self-employed; 9: routine white-collar workers; 15: *petite bourgeoisie*; 12: skilled manual workers.

Source: Warde, 1997

There are clear differences in the spending patterns of different occupational groups. A contrast can be drawn between the 'healthy' eating of the professionals, and the 'traditional' eating of the other groups. We can see this both in terms of the actual amount of money professionals spend each week, and also the percentage of their total spending on food. Professionals spend most on fresh fruit, as well as fish (but not fish and chips!), and fresh vegetables. By contrast, small industrial and commercial employers have tastes that are similar to skilled manual workers, even though they are significantly wealthier than them: their diet relies more on bread and potatoes and cheaper kinds of meat. There are in fact quite marked differences in taste: employers spend almost twice as much a week on tea (for instance) than professionals. Professionals spend twice as much on fresh vegetables than skilled manual workers.

Warde discusses how these differences seem explicable in terms of the cultural capital of the professional middle class. Their distance from everyday practical exigencies of 'getting by' allows them to weigh up their food choice more abstractly, and leads them to question the value of conventional, 'staple' food. They are more interested in food that they know is healthier. Their food tastes show greater distance from tradition and habit, and take a more calculating, abstract form.

This example shows that people are not necessarily aware of such striking class differences in food tastes. This indicates a key difference between cultural capital and Weber's concept of status that we discussed in section 4. Whereas status refers to the attitudes of honour (or dishonour) people may have towards certain people, lifestyles or activities, cultural capital is more than this. It also involves the inculcation of particular skills and abilities that may bring with them potential rewards, *even though people may be unaware of this, or may misrecognize their cultural capital, or their lack of cultural capital.* Thus, it is not clear that there is greater honour in eating particular types of food in contemporary Britain (interestingly, as Warde suggests, beef, which is probably the most esteemed British dish, is proportionately the most popular food for all occupational groups!). Nonetheless, certain implications do follow from professionals' attachment to a more healthy diet, notably in terms of their lower morbidity rates.

Whereas status needs to be recognized as status in order for it to be status, cultural capital can be routinely misrecognized and yet still effective. Indeed, Bourdieu's point is that it is this misrecognition of cultural capital that is a fundamental force in making it so effective. It is precisely because high culture is defined as universal culture, the embodiment of greatness that goes beyond the specific condition of any particular social groups, that it can so effectively help sustain the privileges of intellectual cultural elites. The example of food consumption illustrates the power of this point. Eating fresh fruit and vegetables is part of the culture of the professional middle class, but it is also presented as the naturally healthy diet. The class basis of this form of food consumption is thereby disregarded, but it is held out as a norm that all groups should aspire to, even those with very different cultural frames and economic and social resources.

This argument is highly relevant to the conundrum of class I sketched out in sections 2 and 3. People's lack of class identification and their ambivalence about belonging to classes can be explained by the power of cultural capital. One of the most important recent studies to demonstrate the power of cultural capital is that of Skeggs (1997). She shows how young working-class women in the North-West seek to establish their respectability and their femininity by eschewing any reference to the disreputable working class. They thereby 'dis-identify' with class. As they seek to establish their place and win respect within the class system, they are *necessarily* unable to stand back from the assumptions and values of class to detachedly talk about the process that classifies them.

READING 2.4

Now turn to Reading 2.4, which is the account of Danielle, produced as part of Bourdieu *et al.*'s recent study of 'suffering', translated as *The Weight of the World* (1999).

Do you think Danielle sees herself as disadvantaged, and as 'suffering'? Why? Do you think the interviewer thinks Danielle is suffering? Do you see her as disadvantaged? Why do you think Danielle does not seem more aware of the difficulties of her life?

Bourdieu's book is a collection of interviews with a variety of French people from diverse walks of life: farmers, industrial workers, migrants, those living on the margins of society, and so forth. Bourdieu shows how these people rarely openly acknowledge their suffering, but rather seek to 'put a brave face on it'. In Reading 2.4, Danielle comes over as a proud woman, who does not wish to make a meal of her situation: 'I try to do my job; like every other occupation it has its good and bad sides'. It seems pretty clear, in fact, that the work is tough: working long hours, at night, with supervisors all around her, having to stand to do her work, performing repetitive and routine operations, with few promotional prospects. And in fact, if you read the interview carefully, there are glimpses where Danielle indicates that she is aware of this. In her asides, the interviewer implies that Danielle's situation is indeed bleak.

Danielle's account is included to show certain similarities to the responses given in Reading 2.1. Like the respondents discussed in Reading 2.1, Danielle is ambivalent about her social positioning and does not readily put her life story in terms of class. Bourdieu's explanation of this is that people's outlooks are encompassed by their *habitus,* their internalized, often unconscious, dispositions. These kinds of dispositions make people feel comfortable or uncomfortable in various kinds of situations, and people therefore adjust themselves by situating themselves within those *fields* with which they are comfortable. Bourdieu uses the metaphors of sports-playing to explicate his concepts of habitus and field. Simply, the habitus is the 'feel for the game', whilst the field is the 'game itself'. Thus, a skilled tennis player may realize that she is a poor chess player and concentrate her energies on tennis, where she feels most accomplished and 'at home'. In this way she gets ever more skilled at tennis but less skilled in other pursuits. And so it is with respect to social class. People can feel uncomfortable when they meet members of other social classes, and therefore they routinely avoid putting themselves in such situations. In this way people adjust their lives around their habitus, and this allows them to go about their daily lives often without reflecting consciously on class as a lived experience.

This is a rather different perspective on class to that which is used by Marx and Weber who both see the foundation of class as lying in the structure of economic inequality. For this reason they see classes as formed to advance economically determined class interests (as you saw in Readings 2.2 and 2.3).

This fundamental feature of their class analysis means that class is only pertinent for people's ideas and values if it can be shown that they are aware of their class position and can see how their economic interests are relevant to their identities and actions. For these classical writers, Danielle's story, as well as the evidence from Reading 2.1, poses problems. Some Marxists would see these stories as an example of how a dominant ideology can brainwash people into not recognizing their class interests. This argument, however, does not fully recognize that people do in fact reflect and think about their situations, as Danielle's story indicates. It would seem preferable to ground people's complex views and ideas in their everyday lives, in the way Bourdieu discusses.

Some writers have criticized Bourdieu for implying that cultural tastes can be simply seen as the product of a person's class (Halle, 1993; Lamont, 1992). However, Bourdieu's account is more subtle than this. He does not claim that people act almost unthinkingly according to their class background. Rather, they act intentionally, drawing on their experience of bodily awareness of being at ease or ill at ease. Willis's account of *Learning to Labour* (1977) remains a classic demonstration of this point, as he shows how working-class 'lads' who felt uncomfortable in an academic, middle-class school environment play up their independent, 'manly' qualities by embracing the world of manual labour. This leads them to take up 'dead-end' jobs with few prospects, which therefore ultimately reinforces their own subordination within the class system. Thus, maximizing one's sense of social ease may easily go against one's material, economic interests. This point also explains why class can be important even when people themselves seem relatively ignorant or unaware of class, as we have found to be the case in section 3 of this chapter.

The basic distinction that Bourdieu (1999) draws is that between those fields organized around physical, largely pre-reflexive skills (such as many sports) and those fields organized around intellectual attributes (which he terms the 'scholastic outlook'), as in many areas of cultural appreciation such as listening to classical music or reading 'high-brow' novels. Cultural capital depends on distancing itself from the immediate, superficial worlds of physical sensation, and hence exists in tension with them. Only some kinds of habitus can operate as capital. Since these reflexive, intellectual fields are better able to organize socially powerful institutions, such as the church, the education system, and indeed most activities of the state and corporate organizations, so those excluded from this habitus are excluded from much of public life, even though they may not be fully aware of this. Capital exists where a stake in a particular field has the power to lead to additional rewards in other fields. These are rewards which the participant may not be aware of at the time, especially since they are in other fields to those which she or he is currently engaged in. Thus the child who is able to do well at school may not be aware, or perhaps may be only dimly aware, that this will lead to occupational advantages later in his or her life, but this lack of awareness in no way detracts from the fact that his or her habitus conveys the power of capital. In some fields, skilled performers gain the rewards directly associated with their skills within that field. Outstanding footballers can command high incomes by virtue of their footballing prowess. But when people can acquire skills in particular fields that allow them to move effectively into other fields, we can see a process of accumulation, since skills lead to other skills. In contemporary capitalist societies such as Britain, it is the interconnection between cultural capital, the educational system and the labour market that is of prime importance in generating class inequality.

SUMMARY OF SECTION 5

1   The focus on the significance of cultural dimensions of social stratification in the work of Bourdieu, particularly his concept of cultural capital, provides a useful explanatory mechanism in relation to the contemporary conundrum of class.

2   Cultural capital depends on a network of publicly sanctioned cultural values permeating society, not on individual distinctions of taste.

3   Cultural capital bestows privilege on those identified with high cultural values, linked across all social fields – for example, education, employment, consumption.

4   Bourdieu draws a distinction between 'fields' organized around physical skills and prowess and those dependent on intellectual attributes. Cultural capital depends on distancing itself from the former and embracing the latter.

5   Bourdieu's theory chimes with the ambivalence and lack of class identification within the contemporary conundrum of class. Cultural capital often involves taken-for-granted, internalized assumptions about cultural values as shared and universal rather than specific, which results in people identifying themselves as ordinary rather than class-conscious.

6 Conclusion

It is widely recognized that the past quarter-century has seen a profound, deep-seated remaking of social relationships across the globe. The dramatic restructuring of the world economy – caused by the development of flexible modes of capital accumulation, the collapse of viable alternatives to capitalism, financial and institutional deregulation, the emergence of new forms of public and corporate governance, and new forms of virtual and digital communication – has produced a turbulent social world. Rapid mobility, new forms of risk and insecurity, the erosion of fixed social and territorial boundaries and the final eclipse of tradition have all been seen as elements of contemporary social change (see for instance Castells, 1996–2000; Giddens, 1990; Lash and Urry, 1994).

And yet, despite this turbulence, some things remain remarkably unchanged. I have shown that people's life chances continue to be governed by their social class position. There is virtually no aspect of a person's life that is not shaped by class: people's income, their job prospects, their housing conditions, leisure interests and social life continue to be associated with their class. If anything, people's destinies are more affected by their social class than was the case twenty years ago. Even in an age of great uncertainty, some things don't change!

Although social-class inequalities continue to be deep rooted, we cannot simply rely on classical class theory to account for the contemporary significance of class. Whereas both Marx and Weber focused on class formation (the processes by which classes formed as social collectivities which were able to shape social change), we currently see few signs of class formation of any kind. People tend to be ambivalent about their class identities, and there is little evidence that class is a strong source of collective identity. We need instead to focus on the conundrum of class, the lack of connection between structural class inequality and class awareness. This allows us to recognize the deep-rooted significance of class in a rather different way. The power and significance of class depends on and is necessarily linked to its non-recognition by participants. Bourdieu takes this simple, but powerful, insight and applies it to class analysis. It suggests a fundamentally different way of looking at the concerns of class analysis since it disrupts the class-formation problematic of Marx and Weber in favour of a 'dis-identification of class' model (see Skeggs, 1997). Classes are most powerful and significant not when there are high levels of class-consciousness and class identity, but when such awareness is in fact absent. This allows class inequalities to be routinely reproduced by people who would not consciously see themselves as members of classes. It also leads us to a form of critical sociology that needs to carefully unpick the complex meanings and values that lie behind what may appear to be straightforward social processes.

References

Abercrombie, N. and Warde, A. (1994) *Contemporary British Society*, Oxford, Polity Press.

Aglietta, M. (1979) *A Theory of Capitalist Regulation: The US Experience*, London, New Left Books.

Bartley, M., Carpenter, L., Dunnel, K. and Fitzpatrick, R. (1996) 'Measuring inequalities in health', *Sociology of Health and Illness*, vol.18, no.4, pp.455–74.

Bott, E. (1957) *Family and Social Networks*, Oxford, Oxford University Press.

Bourdieu, P. (1984) *Distinction*, London, Routledge.

Bourdieu, P. (1999) *Pascalian Meditations*, Cambridge, Polity Press.

Bourdieu, P. and Ferguson, P.P. (1999) *The Weight of the World*, Cambridge, Polity Press.

Boyer, R. (1990) *The Regulation School: A Critical Introduction*, New York, Columbia University Press.

Bradley, H.. (1999) *Gender and Power in the Workplace*, Basingstoke, Macmillan.

Butler, T. and Savage, M. (1995) *Social Change and The Middle Classes*, London, UCL Press.

Calhoun, C., LiPuma, E. and Postone, E. (1993) *Bourdieu: Critical Perspectives*, Cambridge, Polity Press.

Castells, M. (1996–2000) *The Rise of the Network Society*, 3 vols, Oxford, Blackwell.

Cooper, H., Arber, S. and Smaje, C. (1998) 'Social class or deprivation', *Sociology of Health and Illness*, vol.20, no.3, pp.289–311.

Craib, I. (1996) *Classical Social Theory*, Oxford, Oxford University Press.

Crompton, R. (1998) *Class and Stratification*, 2nd edn, Oxford, Polity Press.

Dale, A. and Egerton, M. (1997) *Highly Educated Women: Evidence from the National Child Development Study*, London, Stationery Office, Research Paper 25.

Dennis, N., Henriques, F. and Slaughter, C. (1956) *Coal is our Life*, London, Eyre and Spottiswoode.

Devine, F. (1992a) *Affluent Workers Revisited*, Edinburgh, Edinburgh University Press.

Devine, F. (1992b) 'Social identities, class identity and political perspectives', *Sociological Review*, no.40, pp.229–52.

Egerton, M. and Savage, M. (2000) 'Age stratification and class formation: a longitudinal study of the social mobility of young men and women', *Work, Employment and Society*, vol.14, no.1, pp.23–49.

Evans, G. (1992) 'Is Britain a class-divided society? A re-analysis and extension of Marshall *et al.*'s study of class consciousness', *Sociology*, vol.26, no.2, pp.233–58.

Featherstone, M. (1987) 'Lifestyle and consumer capitalism', *Theory, Culture and Society*, vol.4, no.1, pp.55–70.

Giddens, A., (1973) *The Class Structure of the Advanced Societies*, Basingstoke, MacMillan.

Giddens, A. (1990) *The Consequences of Modernity*, Cambridge, Polity Press.

Giddens, A. and MacKenzie, G. (1982) *Social Class and the Division of Labour*, London, Macmillan.

Goldthorpe, J.H. (1982) 'On the service class: its formation and future' in Giddens, A. and MacKenzie, G. (eds), *op. cit.*, pp.162–85.

Goldthorpe, J. and Marshall, G. (1992) 'The promising future of class analysis', *Sociology*, vol.26, pp.381–400.

Goldthorpe, J. with Llewellyn, C. and Payne, C. (1980) *Social Mobility and the Class Structure in Modern Britain*, Oxford, Clarendon Press.

Goldthorpe, J., Lockwood, D., Bechhofer, F. and Platt, J. (1969) *The Affluent Worker in the Class Structure*, Cambridge, Cambridge University Press.

Goldthorpe, J., Lockwood, D., Bechhofer, F. and Platt, J. (1968) *The Affluent Worker: Political Attitudes and Behaviour*, Cambridge, Cambridge University Press.

Gosling, A., Machin, S. and Meghir, C. (1994) 'What has happened to men's wages since the mid-1960s?', *Fiscal Studies*, vol.15, no.4, pp.63–87.

Halle, D. (1993) *Inside Culture: Art and Class in the American Home*, Chicago, University of Chicago Press.

Halsey, A.H., Heath, A. and Ridge, J. (1980) *Origins and Destinations*, Oxford, Clarendon Press.

Hoggart, R. (1956) *The Uses of Literacy*, Harmondsworth, Penguin Books.

Hughes, J., Martin, P.J. and Sharrock., W. (1995) *Understanding Classical Sociology*, London, Sage.

Joseph Rowntree Foundation (1995) *Inquiry into Income and Wealth*, 2 vols, York, Joseph Rowntree Foundation.

Lamont, M. (1992) *Money, Morals and Manners: The Culture of the French and American Upper Class*, Chicago, IL, Chicago University Press.

Lash, S. and Urry, J. (1994) *Economies of Signs and Spaces*, London, Sage.

Lipietz, A. (1987) *Mirages and Miracles: The Crises of Global Fordism*, London, Verso.

Marshall, G., Newby, H., Rose, D. and Vogler, C. (1988) *Social Class in Modern Britain*, London, Hutchinson.

Pawson, R. (1989) *A Measure for Measures*, London, Routledge.

Popay, J., Williams, G., Thomas, C. and Gatrell, T. (1998) 'Theorising inequalities in health', *Sociology of Health and Illness*, vol.20, no.5, pp.619–44.

Prandy, K. (1997) 'Class and continuity in social reproduction: an empirical investigation', *British Journal of Sociology*, vol.46, no.2, pp.340–64.

Reid, I. (1998) *Class in Britain*, Oxford, Polity Press.

Saunders, P. (1989) 'Left write in sociology', *Network,* no.44, pp.3–4.

Savage, M. (2000) *Class Analysis and Social Transformations*, Buckingham, Open University Press.

Savage, M., Bagnall, G. and Longhurst, B. (2001) 'Ordinary, ambivalent and defensive: class identities in the North-West of England', *Sociology*, vol.35, no.4, pp.875–92.

Savage, M., Barlow, J., Dickens, P. and Fielding, A.J. (1992) *Property, Bureaucracy and Culture: Middle Class Formation in Contemporary Britain*, London, Routledge.

Scott, J. (1996) *Stratification and Power: Structures of Class, Status and Command*, Cambridge, Polity.

SCPR (Social Community Planning Research) (1992) *British Social Attitudes: The Ninth Report*, Aldershot, Dartmouth.

Skeggs, B. (1997) *Formations of Class and Gender*, London, Sage.

Theodossiou, I. (1996) 'Promotions, job seniority, and product demand effects on earnings', *Oxford Economic Papers*, vol.48, pp.456–72.

Townsend, P. and Davidson, N. (1982) *Inequalities in Health: The Black Report*, Harmondsworth, Penguin Books.

Warde, A. (1997) *Consumption, Food and Taste: Culinary Antinomies and Commodity Culture*, London, Sage.

Wilkinson, R. (1996) *Unhealthy Societies: The Afflictions of Inequality*, London, Routledge.

Wilmott, P. and Young, M. (1960) *Family and Class in a London Suburb*, London, Routledge.

Willis, P. (1977) *Learning to Labour: How Working Class Kids Get Working Class Jobs*, Farnborough, Saxon House.

Young, K. (1992) 'Class, race and opportunity' in SCPR, *op. cit.*.

Young, M. and Wilmott, P. (1957) *Family and Kinship in East London*, London, Routledge.

Readings

 Mike Savage, Gaynor Bagnall and Brian Longhurst, 'Ordinary, ambivalent and defensive: class identities in the North West of England' (2001)

If we inductively examine people's accounts of class, a number of organizing themes, relatively constant across our sample, are revealed. We group them into four main points here for ease of juxtaposition though they are interconnected in various ways.

Ambivalent class identities

Juxtaposition of narratives of objective and subjective class

… people's sense of their own class ambivalence often goes hand in hand with a strong awareness of the existence of class inequalities. In this respect people seem to have little difficulty in talking about class 'out there', but do not like to think about class closer to home, with respect to their own sense of identity. When people talk about Britain becoming (or not becoming) a classless society, they can draw on a wide repertoire of ideas and idioms, but these then collapse as soon as they are asked to reflexively locate themselves in terms of class. Here are three examples:

> I think there is still the Establishment and the have's and the have not's. I think it's getting wider myself. You only have to drive through Levenshulme, Mosside, to see what people haven't got and drive through Prestbury to see what people have got. So I think there is a big divide myself. I think the middle classes, my perception from years previous is that there are three distinct classes. I think the middle's got a bit fuzzy, I think you've got lower-class people who've moved up and possibly upper class people who've been dragged down a bit, so to speak, but I think the two extremes are quite strong, the public school boy type. I think the Establishment still runs the country and I don't think that'll be broken myself.

> *And which class do you see yourself as?*

> I suppose middle.

> (C17)

Here we see how a fairly elaborate account of class divisions, and their possibly changing character is followed by a characteristic defensive rhetorical device, 'I suppose …', and hesitation in locating himself in terms of class. Another example from Ramsbottom indicates a similar kind of narrative structure in dealing with class.

> *There is some discussion these days about whether Britain is becoming a classless society or not – do you think it is?*

> No – I wish it was. Well the gaps, if what you hear on the television is true, the gaps seem to be getting wider between the richer and the poorer, whether it is or whether it's a fallacy I don't know. I know there's all the homeless they can't get jobs – I don't altogether believe that. I go into town and into the supermarket; they all have job adverts – not specialized jobs, they don't have to have a lot of qualifications, well any qualifications – there's work there – I think there is if they really want it. I may be wrong – that's how I see it. These homeless on the streets like you see in Manchester – I've seen them – I think a lot of the young people are maybe from split homes where they are not wanted – that is sad – and there is more and more of that. That does upset me but a lot just sleep because they want independence and I haven't a lot of patience that way. Families too easily split up, I think. Young people I think they are brought up at school to be your own person, you must do this and that whereas I think if they stuck with their families a bit more … I do think there comes a time when they reach 18 and they go to college or university, that is a good break and I think it does them good, but the younger ones, the 15 and 16 year olds there is no excuse for that. Is that what you want?

Do you see yourself as belonging to any particular social class?

No, we're middle class, working class. I don't know. I'm the same as I've always been.

(R63)

This quote (from a former activist in the Ramsbottom Conservative Party) indicates how the question on classlessness triggers off a long, rather rambling account of social change in contemporary Britain. The idea of class clearly means relatively little, nonetheless it is a hook on which to hang a series of general observations about the state of Britain. In this respect class is salient as a cue to thinking about the changing character of British society. However, when asked to place herself in terms of class, a clear hesitation ensues. The respondent offers both of the main classes as ones that she potentially belongs to before deciding that neither applies. A final quote usefully indicates the same kind of response structure.

Do you think Britain is becoming classless?

That's a tough one. In many ways yes. In the sense that I think many of the old boundaries of class, distinctions or the … the mechanisms that held the class system in place are being eroded by education, by change in the way we live, by other factors but I think those things change very slowly. I think a lot of the change may be superficial and people might … my perception is that people who are middle class or above would seem to like to hold on to something. That's a bit of a generalization because there are plenty of people I know who would … but in conversation when you scratch beneath the surface sometimes you pick out people wanting to have this sense of 'well, we've moved on' or 'we're …', you know, and I like to pursue that quite often in conversation just to see what people mean.

How do they react when you do pursue it?

Sometimes by … when they realize that you're on the hunt for something, by denial – 'oh, no, that's not what I meant' kind of thing and sometimes just by being quite … by being defensive about it, you know, sort of 'yeah, sure', you know, 'why shouldn't one be proud of x, y and z', you know. So, yes, it's being eroded. I think the class structure has been and is being eroded but there is I think an undercurrent of class which is probably still there.

Do you think of yourself as belonging to a particular class?

No. I was going to say I didn't … I wouldn't put myself as … I'm working class by background and upbringing and I'm still working so in that sense I'm still working class. I find a difficult … a difficult area to make distinctions in. Again it's a scale or a criteria that I prefer not to use so I don't find it helpful or meaningful.

How striking it is that having diagnosed the issue of defensiveness in others this respondent himself exactly duplicates the rhetorical device he exposes. Like the others he finds it fairly easy to talk about class 'out there', but is challenged when asked to place himself in terms of class. Not for these respondents (or indeed, for the majority of those we interviewed) are the reflexive self-identities that Giddens (1991) and Beck (1992) emphasise as characteristic features of late modernity. Rather, classes are talked about in ways that are defensive, which hence support the arguments of Bourdieu (1984) and Skeggs (1997) concerning the difficulty of 'naming' class. But we also see evidence in support of Marshall and Devine's emphasis that class is a cue for political reflections, and is a term that people still use to make sense of social and political change. In this respect, class is definitely not a term that is central to a sense of self-identity, though people seem to recognise, sometimes grudgingly, that it exists 'out there'.

(b) The individual and social structure

Our suggestion is that for our respondents, to place *yourself* in a class is to commit a category mistake. Classes are 'out there', part of the social fabric, whereas people themselves are 'individuals' who by definition cannot be parts of classes. We see here a particular articulation of individuality as standing outside classes. Some examples of this common pattern:

If you had to describe yourself as any particular social class, what would you describe yourself as?

Middle class, working class, middle class.

Sort of a bit of both?

Yeah.

Do you think of yourself in these terms?

No. I just think I am me, and this is how I am, take me or leave me, you know.

(C27)

Just as we have seen above (R63), this respondent offers both middle and working class as potential identifiers, and does not see any crucial distinction between them. She clearly does not routinely, or even occasionally, think of herself in terms of class. The following example indicates the same point, though it is striking that it is a person very different in terms of social location.

> I don't feel very class conscious, obviously I am somewhere in the middle, lower-middle I suppose ... I don't slot myself into any particular group. I like to think that I am just me.
>
> (W33)

What we see here is a version of the 'individualistic ethic'. Class pollutes this idea of individuality, since it challenges people's autonomy by seeing them as a product of their social background. Class, insofar as it exists at all for these respondents, does so as a set of external reference points through which the individual navigates. It would be a category mistake for people to refer to themselves in terms of classes, and this explains why people's ambivalence about class exists. A common version of this response is to talk about class identity in terms of a life history. Here the individual moves between classes in the course of his or her life. Class provides a set of external anchors for the individual and hence it is quite compatible with telling a life history – even though respondents were not encouraged to reply in these terms.

> I knew this would come up. A jumped up working class who has now entered the middle class. I hate to say it, I can't escape it, but I think we have become more middle class from humble origins. We're the class that grew up with working-class parents keen on education who pushed us and we all went to grammar schools and college and university and came out and suddenly found that we didn't belong where we came from.
>
> *So you wouldn't see yourself in any particular social class?*
>
> No, I'm a post-master's granddaughter, a railwayman's daughter. I've got no money.
>
> *But you wouldn't see yourself in any class?*
>
> My grandfather used to reckon he was middle class and my father was obviously working class.

> *But it's not something that matters to you?*
>
> No, I was horrified to find out how snobbish I was.
>
> (D4)

It is striking here how although this respondent is familiar with the idea of class, and does not find it difficult to phrase her life history in terms of transitions between classes, nonetheless, the idea that she herself 'has' a class is something that she greatly resists. A number of respondents speak of the way that they have origins in the 'working class' and are then able to talk about themselves as moving away from that distinct class category. Here is another example of this point:

> *Do you regard yourself as belonging to any particular social class?*
>
> Not really, no. I mean I come from a normal working-class family, my dad's always worked, my mum took on a traditional role, she finished work when she had us, so in that respect I would say from working class but with the work, the firm that I'm in, I'm working with people who aren't from working-class backgrounds, I mean for instance a partner that I had lunch with she was privately educated and her father was a solicitor and she's looking to move house and she was saying that she'd never lived in a house like this she wouldn't be able to cope with living in a new house with five bedrooms or whatever and that's not to say she's a snob, but it's just what she's been used to, so the kind of profession you're in you do tend to find people who are more middle class.

The idea of class invites respondents to make sense of themselves in a broader social context. It is a connecting device, whereby people locate themselves, but it is not an identity that is internalised.

(c)   The defensiveness of class identities?

One possible explanation for the accounts of class that we have provided is to see it as a form of defensiveness, along the lines indicated by Skeggs (1997) and consistent with Bourdieu (1984). The argument here would run that because people are threatened by thinking of themselves in terms of class, they seek strategies to displace class, which they do by seeing it as something outside themselves. There is certainly plenty of evidence that defensiveness appears to exist. The quotations used so far, D4, R63, W33 all seem to exhibit defensive reflexes. However, the issue of defensiveness is a very complex one that calls for careful examination. …

In general terms, people felt happier differentiating themselves from other classes rather than identifying themselves as a members of a class. This is also a distancing device.

> I don't feel I belong to any particular class. I'm middle class, I suppose, but there's a great lump of people in the middle class and I'm only not working class because I happen to have sufficient money to be middle class and do things middle-class people do.
>
> (W69)

> I suppose I am middle class.
>
> *Why do you say that?*
>
> Well, I am not working class, and I am not upper class, so I don't think there is anything else, is there?
>
> (W59)

Presenting your class relationally as well as preferring to talk about class 'out there', can all be associated with a form of defensiveness. But a further aspect of defensiveness needs full discussion, which is the idea of reflexive class identities.

(d)   Reflexivity and class identities

Perhaps the biggest variation in the way people responded to questions on class identity was between those who had the cultural capital to reflexively play around with ideas of class, compared to those who felt threatened by the ideas of class and lacked the cultural confidence to reflect on these terms. Graduates tended to have the knowledge to think about applying class labels to themselves, and had the confidence to reject them, or invert them. Here are some examples:

> On the old ABC thing? I think I come from a C sort of working-class, self-employed background, struggling to get the income and social life of a B, a profession, but if you look, like at the professions like teachers, when I was growing up firemen and policemen and so on, they were all professional.
>
> (R37)

> Using other people's criteria I suppose I'm middle class because I've had a tertiary education, but it's probably not to do with

middle class, and how would you say, how would you name a class that you belong to, I'm not sure, so I can't answer that one, but from the old criteria I would say middle class.

> (D14)

These are two examples of limited reflexivity. R37 knows the market research categories and is prepared to use them in thinking about himself. D14 is also aware that class is organized around external criteria and therefore that he might be middle class even though he does not think in these terms. The two following quotes take this reflexivity a stage further:

> *Do you see yourself in class terms?*
>
> No, my background is my father was a university lecturer and my mother was a teacher. We lived in a three-bedroom detached house with a garden.
>
> *What about now?*
>
> I like to think that I am not marked by the way I speak, but then again I probably am. If you were to pin me down I would say, pretend to be, lower-middle class.
>
> (D20)

> *If you had to describe yourself as belonging to any particular social class, what would you describe yourself as?*
>
> I wouldn't really … just for the reason again, with what I was saying … I generally know a lot of people from different walks of life and with different … I suppose some people would class some of these as very privileged and some less privileged. To me it doesn't really mean anything. I don't know where I would sit myself, probably working class.
>
> *But it is not a label you would pin on yourself?*
>
> Well I don't put any label on myself really. I think labels are pinned on you by other people.
>
> (D23)

In these cases the respondents are aware that class is a label, a set of criteria, and they are prepared to take the step of trying on these labels for size, so to speak. There is here a sense of the politics of labels, especially in D23. D20, by contrast is more playful and is prepared to 'pretend' to be lower-middle class. It is interesting to note that these reflexive class identities are somewhat stronger in Chorlton, the gentrifying area of urban Manchester where one might expect to find these kind of responses.

To summarise, the broadest division in our sample is between a defensive majority and two minorities: a small group of self-confident members of classes, and a somewhat larger (though still minority) group of reflexive class identifiers. Both these minority groups have cultural capital: the former have cultural capital of a more traditional type which invokes a fixed class hierarchy, the latter of rather newer type that prizes reflexivity. The dominant discourse on class identity is a variant of the defensive refrain, which spread across the social spectrum. We now unpack this a little more by examining its relationship to the discourse of being 'ordinary'.

Snobbishness and ordinariness

Skeggs (1997) emphasizes how her sample of working-class women wanted to appear respectable. In our sample this theme was not particularly strong. What seemed to matter more for our respondents was being 'ordinary'. Regardless of people's social practices, it proved very unusual for people to claim to be snobs, or to prefer elite culture, or wish only to mix with a select few. ...

> ... I would describe myself as a very normal, lower middle class person.
>
> *(Daughter interjects: I would say upper-lower class – no working class – upper-working class)*
>
> I get on with most people. I have found that there are nice people but obviously have come from very nice backgrounds, and also I know people that are perhaps in the poverty trap, but I wouldn't treat them differently.
>
> (C51)

> I, well, I don't know whether you'd put me as working class really, or I should imagine, I don't think we're middle class, but we, I don't know, I don't really know where we come in that really.
>
> *How would you describe yourself?*
>
> I'd just say ordinary ...
>
> (C12)

> I suppose everybody has their background, and their, you know, their parents have had a certain standard of living ... You know I treat everybody the same.
>
> (C60)

Here we have what might be termed 'omnivoric refrain'. This is the idea that people should be treated the same regardless of social position. Interestingly, this omnivoric refrain can be mapped onto both working-class and middle-class reference points. We have already seen above how some respondents offer both middle-class and working-class identification. This apparent ambiguity makes sense, however, when it is understood that respondents are using both these terms as part of a quest to appear 'normal'. Thus, middle-class identification can be linked into a claim to be in the middle, and hence normal.

> I suppose middle, middle of the road really. I'm not a snob if that's what you mean.
>
> (C27)

> I don't give it a lot of thought really, but I suppose I am really just middle of the road.
>
> (W23)

> I wouldn't put myself in the upper class and I wouldn't put myself in the working class to use the old distinctions, so by than definition I would be middle class.
>
> (W34)

> I most definitely would be middle class, but then most people are middle class. I suppose I am firmly middle of the middle. It sounds extremely boring.

If claiming to be middle class offers one way of establishing one's ordinariness, working classness can also be used to the same end. Here the logic works by establishing that working-class people are ordinary because they work. It is not that a particular kind of work is singled out, rather that the need to work is used to establish a certain common position.

> I suppose that I cannot deny I am working class, but I think the fact that my dad is a doctor, a GP and my mother has always brought in additional finances to the family, I feel like I have had to work.
>
> (D34)

> I would say that I am working class, I am working class, I sell my labour ... It just happens that I get paid quite a nice salary, not as much as some but I am OK, and I don't worry about paying the bills but I am working class.
>
> (D66)

I'd say working class. What we've had, we've had to work for, everything. We had to work and save up for it, we've had nothing given to us.

Do you think in these terms?

No, pretty average person, that does what everybody else does round here and copes.

(R12)

When I was growing up they used to say lower middle class, but I don't believe that. I'm working class, all my family have to work, so they're working class.

Well I labour so I must be working class. Like anybody who earns a hundred thousand or so, as long as they do a job they've got to be working class.

We can see then how ambivalent references to working-class or middle-class identities should be understood as rhetorical attempts to establish normalness.

References

Beck, U. (1992) *Risk Society*, London, Sage.

Bourdieu, P. (1984) *Distinction*, London, Routledge & Kegan Paul.

Devine, F. (1992) *Affluent Workers Revisited*, Edinburgh, Edinburgh University Press.

Giddens, A. (1991) *Modernity and Self Identity*, Cambridge, Polity Press.

Marshall, G., Newby, H., Rose, D. and Vugler, C. (1988) *Social Class in Modern Britain*, London, Hutchinson.

Skeggs, B.L. (1997) *Formations of Class and Gender*, London, Sage.

Source: Savage, Bagnall and Longhurst, 2001, pp.1–13

 2.2

Rosemary Crompton, 'The classic inheritance and its development: Marx' (1996)

Marx's aim was to provide a comprehensive analysis of capitalist society with a view to effecting its transformation; he was a committed revolutionary as well as a social theorist. In the *Communist Manifesto*, Marx and Engels (1962, p.34) describe the course of human history in terms of the struggle between classes:

> Free man and slave, patrician and plebeian, lord and serf, guild-master and journeyman, in a word, oppressor and oppressed, stood in constant opposition to each other, carried on an uninterrupted, now hidden, now open fight, a fight that each time ended, either in a revolutionary reconstitution of society at large, or in the common ruin of the contending classes.

There can be little doubt, therefore, as to the centrality of class in Marx's work, but, although the theme is constant, he nowhere gives a precise definition of the class concept. Indeed, it is somewhat poignant that his last manuscript breaks off just at the moment at which he appeared to be on the point of giving such a definition, in a passage beginning: 'The first question to be answered is this: What constitutes a class? – and the reply to this follows naturally from the reply to another question, namely: What makes wage-labourers, capitalists and landlords constitute the three

great social classes?' (Marx, 1974, p.886).

For Marx, class relationships are embedded in production relationships; more specifically, in the patterns of ownership and control which characterize these relationships. Thus the 'two great classes' of capitalist society are bourgeoisie and proleteriat, the former being the owners and controllers of the material means of production, the latter owning their own labour power, which they are forced to sell to the bourgeoisie in order to survive. However, Marx did not have, as has sometimes been suggested, a 'two-class' model of society. It is true that he saw the bourgeoisie and proletariat as the major historic role-players in the capitalist epoch, but his analyses of contemporary events made it clear that he saw actual societies as composed of a multiplicity of classes. That is, Marx used the term 'class' both as an analytical concept in the development of his theory of society, and as a descriptive, historical concept. For example, in his account of the (1852) Bonapartist coup d'état in France, 'The Eighteenth Brumaire of Louis Bonaparte' (1962a), a variety of social groupings are identified including the landed aristocracy, financiers, the industrial bourgeoisie, the middle class, the petty bourgeoisie, the industrial proletariat, the lumpenproletariat and the peasantry.

Marx's account of antagonistic class relationships did not rest upon ownership and non-ownership alone. Rather, ownership of the material forces of production is the means to the exploitation of the proletariat by the bourgeoisie within the very process of production itself. The key to Marx's understanding of this process lies in the labour theory of value, a concept which Engels described as one of Marx's major theoretical achievements. In a capitalist society, argues Marx, labour has to become a commodity like any other, but it is unique in that human labour alone has the capacity to create *new* values. Raw materials (commodities) such as wood, iron or cotton cannot by themselves create value; rather, value is added when they are worked on by human labour to create new commodities which are then realized in the market. The labour which is purchased (and therefore owned) by the capitalist will spend only a part of the working day in the creation of values equivalent to its price (that is, wages); the rest of the working day is spent in the creation of surplus value, which is retained by the capitalist. (Surplus value does not simply describe profit, but is distributed to a number of sources including taxes, payments to 'unproductive' labourers and new capital investment, as well as profits or dividends.) Thus even though the labourer may be paid at a wage that is entirely 'fair', that is, it represents the value of this labour in the market, and the worker has not been cheated or swindled in any legal sense (cheating and swindling *may* occur, of course) – he or she has nevertheless been exploited.

It has been emphasized that Marx was not just concerned to provide a description of the nature of exploitation in class societies, but also to give an account of the role of social classes in the transformation of societies themselves. Thus, for Marx, classes are social forces, historical actors. For Marx, men (and it should be said, women) *make* their own history, although not necessarily in the *circumstances* of their own choosing. Some commentators have suggested that for Marx a class only existed when it was conscious of itself as such. However, in *The Poverty of Philosophy* he appears to make an unambiguous distinction between a 'class in itself' and a (conscious) 'class for itself' (1955, p.195). This ambiguity in Marx's work has been of considerable significance in the development of sociological analyses of class.

Marx's account of the generation of human consciousness is central to his theory of historical materialism, the social-scientific core of Marxist theory. This is summarized in the Preface to *A Contribution to the Critique of Political Economy*:

> In the social production of their life, men enter into definite relations that are indispensable and independent of their will, relations of production which correspond to a definite stage of development of their material productive forces. The sum total of these relations of production constitutes the economic structure of society, the real foundation, on which rises a legal and political superstructure and to which correspond definite forms of social consciousness. The mode of production of material life conditions the social, political and intellectual life process in general. It is not the consciousness of men that determines their being, but, on the contrary, their social being that determines their consciousness.

> (Marx, 1962b, pp.362–3)

Two related – and contentious – insights may be drawn from this account. First, that it is the economic 'base' that determines the political and ideological 'superstructure' of human societies; and second, that it is material being that determines human consciousness, rather than vice versa. …

Marx's distinction between base and superstructure has been the subject of extensive debate. He has been widely accused of economic reductionism – the assertion that the economic base *determines* social, political and intellectual development. Such a mechanistic model would, indeed, constitute a gross oversimplification of the complexities of human behaviour, and in a letter written after Marx's death his collaborator Engels emphasized that the theory of historical materialism should not be interpreted as claiming that the economic situation was the *sole* cause of human behaviour. Rather, he argued that although it might be 'ultimately' determinant, at any particular moment, other social relations – political, ideological – would also be affecting human actions. The base/superstructure debate, however, was not closed as a consequence of Engels's invervention.

Marxist theory has developed in a number of different directions. By the 1970s two broad strands within Marxism relating to the base/superstructure debate had emerged: 'humanist' and 'scientific'. As Urry (1981, p.8) has noted, these perspectives incorporated 'the reproduction of certain of the problems which have already been encountered within orthodox sociology'. This was the structure/action debate; the contrast between, on the one hand, sociological perspectives which emphasize above all the significance of human action in explanations of social institutions and behaviour, and, on the other, the functionalist or structurally deterministic accounts of society which such 'action' approaches criticized.

Thus, humanist Marxism – as in, for example, the work of Gramsci – tends to treat the base/superstructure distinction as a metaphor which can all too easily be interpreted in a deterministic fashion. Gramsci emphasizes the value of Marx's analysis as a means of developing a critique of the dehumanizing aspects of modern capitalism, a critique which will ultimately enable the actor to transcend his or her 'alienation'. As with the action approach within sociology, therefore, a central role is given to the human actor.

'Scientific' Marxism was the self-assigned label of French structural Marxists such as Althusser (1969) and Poulantzas (1975). Althusser argued that ideology and politics were not determined by the economy in a mechanistic fashion, as some simplistic interpretations of Marx had assumed. Rather, they should be seen as conditions of its existence and are therefore 'relatively autonomous' – although, echoing Engels, Althusser held that the economic was determinant in 'the last instance'. The work of Althusser and Poulantzas was also characterized by a distinctive (rationalist) epistemology, or view of how knowledge about the world is acquired. Knowledge about the social world, they argued, does not proceed by observation but through theoretical practice or 'science' – of which Marxism was an example. Thus we do not 'know' classes by observing them but rather through the theoretical identification and exploration of the class structure, and individuals are the 'bearers' or 'agents' of these structures of social relations. This approach, therefore, emphasizes above all the primacy of identification and description of class *structures*. The manner in which individuals are distributed within these structures is, from their perspective, of comparatively minor importance; the important task for the 'scientist' is to identify the structure itself, and thus the 'real interests' of the individuals located within it. It is not difficult to see parallels here with functionalism and structural over-determinism in sociology (Connell, 1982). Different classes are being identified according to their 'functional' relationship to the capitalist mode of production as a whole, which is described in Marx's account of the exploitation of workers within the labour process and the way in which different groups in society are related to this process.

...

Throughout the 1980s, the debate on class continued amongst Marxist theorists. Structural Marxism no longer has the influence it once had – at least in part, it may be suggested, because of the electoral failure of the left during this period (see Preface in Benton, 1984). The collapse of 'state socialism' has also been widely interpreted as an empirical refutation of Marxist theory. The revival of Marxist scholarship in the 1960s was accompanied by an optimism of the left which persisted throughout much of the 1970s; the 1980s, however, witnessed the electoral rise of the 'New Right' – Thatcherism in Britain, Reaganomics in the United States. Political theorists including Przeworski (1985), Laclau and Mouffe (1985) and Wood (1986) have examined the possibilities of the development of socialism in these changing circumstances. Much of this discussion has involved a fundamental revision of some basic Marxist political ideas. In particular, the central place which the proletariat or working class occupied in Marx's original writings has increasingly been called into question. Wood (1986, pp.3–4) has summarized these revisions (which she describes, somewhat scathingly, as the 'New True Socialism') as follows: first, the absence of revolutionary politics amongst the working class reflects the fact that there is no necessary correspondence between economics and politics (that is, the link between base and superstructure is regarded as tenuous, even non-existent). Second, there is no necessary or privileged relation between the working class and socialism, and so a socialist movement can be constituted independently of class (thus dissolving the link between 'class' and 'consciousness'). Third, socialism is in any case concerned with universal human goals which transcend the narrowness of material class interests and may therefore address a broader public, irrespective of class. Thus the struggle for socialism can be conceived as a plurality of democratic struggleS, bringing together a variety of resistances to many forms of inequality and oppression (for example, those associated with gender and race).

These arguments amongst Marxist theoreticians have not been directly concerned with class and stratification research in sociology, but they have nevertheless had a considerable impact. The American sociologist Erik Wright (1989) has systematically developed both his 'class map' and his strategy of analysis in response to inputs from these sources. More generally, however, it may be suggested that contemporary debates within theoretical Marxism have contributed to more general arguments to the effect that 'class' is no longer a relevant analytical concept as far as late twentieth-century societies are concerned.

Marx, therefore, saw classes as real social forces with the capacity to transform society. His class analysis did not simply describe the patterning of structured social inequality – although an explanation of this structuring can be found in the relationships to the means of production through which classes are to be identified. His theories have been enormously influential and are open to a number of different interpretations. Two major problems have been identified which are still the focus of considerable debate within sociology: first, the relative significance of the 'economy' (or class forces) as compared to other sources of social differentiation in the shaping of human activities; and second, whether or not consciousness is integral to the identification of a class. As we shall see, the position of Max Weber, the other major theorist whose ideas have been central to the development of sociological perspectives on class, was rather different on both of these issues.

References

Abercrombie, N. and Turner, B.S. (1978) 'The dominant ideology thesis', *British Journal of Sociology*, vol.29, no.2, pp.49–70.

Althusser, L. (1969) *For Marx*, Harmondsworth, Penguin.

Benton, T. (1984) *The Rise and Fall of Structural Marxism*, London, Macmillan.

Braverman, H. (1974) *Labour and Monopoly Capital*, New York, Monthly Review Press.

Collins, R. (1971) 'Functional and conflict theories of educational stratification', *American Sociological Review*, vol.36, pp.1002–19.

Connell, R. (1982) 'A critique of the Althusseian approach to class' in Giddens, A. and Held, D. (eds) *op.cit.*.

Gerth, H. and Mills, C. (1948) *From Max Weber*, London, Routledge.

Giddens, A. and Held, D. (1982) *Classes, Power and Conflict*, London, Macmillan.

Laclau, E. and Mouffe, C. (1985) *Hegemony and Socialist Strategy*, London, Verso.

Marshall, G. (1982) *In Search of the Spirit of Capitalism*, London, Hutchinson.

Marx, K. (1955) *The Power of Philosophy*, Moscow, Progress Publishers.

Marx, K. (1962a) 'The eighteenth brumaire of Louis Napoleon' in K. Marx and F. Engels (1962) *op. cit.*.

Marx, K. (1962b) Preface to a contributions to the critique of political economy in Marx, K. and Engels, F. (1962) *op. cit.*.

Marx, K. (1974) *Capital*, vol. 3, London, Lawrence and Wishart.

Marx, K and Engels, F. (1962) *Selected Works*, Moscow, Foreign Language Publishing.

Marx, K. and Engels, F. (1970) *The German Ideology*, London, Lawrence and Wishart.

Poulantzas, N. (1975) *Classes in Contemporary Capitalism*, London, New Left Books.

Przeworski, A. (1985) *Capitalism and Social Democracy*, Cambridge, Cambridge University Press.

Turner, B. (1988) *Status*, Milton Keynes, Open University Press.

Urry, J. (1981) *The Anatomy of Capitalist Societies*, London, Macmillan.

Weber, M. (1976) *The Protestant Ethic and the Spirit of Capitalism*, London, Allen and Unwin.

Wood, E. (1986) *The Retreat from Class*, London, Verso.

Wright, E. (1989) *The Debate on Classes*, London, Verso.

Source: Crompton, 1996, pp.26–35

2.3 Rosemary Crompton, 'The classic inheritance and its development: Weber' (1996)

The contrast between Marx's and Weber's analysis of class may at times have been overdrawn, but it cannot be doubted that their approaches to social science were very different. Marx was a committed revolutionary, Weber a promoter of 'value-free' social science; and although Weber could not be described as an idealist, he was widely critical of Marx's historical materialism. Marx claimed to have identified abstract social forces (classes) which shaped human history – although, as we have seen, the extent to which Marx considered such structures *can* be identified independently of human action is itself a topic of much debate. Weber, in contrast, was an explicit methodological individualist. That is, he argued that all social collectivities and human phenomena have to be reducible to their individual constituents, and explained in these terms. As far as class is concerned, for Weber:

> We may speak of a 'class' when (1) a number of people have in common a specific causal component of their life chances, in so far as (2) this component is represented exclusively by economic interests in the possession of goods and opportunities for income, and (3) is represented under the conditions of the commodity or labour markets.
>
> (Gerth and Mills, 1948, p.181)

Thus, 'class situation' reflects market-determined 'life chances'. The causal components contributing to such life chances include property, giving rise to both positively and negatively privileged property classes (that is, owners and non-owners), and skills and education, giving rise to positively and negatively privileged 'acquisition' or 'commercial' classes. Weber was aware of the (almost) infinite variability of 'market situations' and thus of the difficulty of identifying a 'class', and his discussion in *Economy and Society* incorporates the listing of over twenty positively and negatively privileged, property and acquisition , classes. This empirical plurality is resolved by Weber's description of a '*social* class', which 'makes up the totality of those class situations within which individual and generational mobility is easy and typical' (Giddens and Held, 1982, p.69). He identified as 'social classes' (a) the working class as a whole; (b) the petty bourgeoisie; (c) technicians, specialists and lower-level management, and (d) 'the classes privileged through property and education' – that is, those at the top of the hierarchy of occupation and ownership. In short, at the descriptive level, Weber's account of the 'class structure' of capitalist society is not too different from that of Marx, despite the fact that their identification of the *sources* of class structuring (production relationships on the one hand, market relationships on the other) *are* very different.

Marx and Weber, however, differed profoundly as far as the question of class action was concerned For Weber, ' "classes" are not communities; they merely represent possible and frequent, bases for communal action' (Gerth and Mills, 1948, p.181) 'Associations of class members – class organizations – may arise on the basis of all … classes. However, this does not necessarily happen … The mere differentiation of property classes is not "dynamic", that is, it need not result in class struggles and revolutions' (Giddens and Held, 1982, pp.69–70). Indeed, in a passage which clearly refers to the Marxist notion of 'false consciousness' Weber writes that:

> … every class may be the carrier of any one of the innumerable possible forms of class action, but this is not necessarily so … That men in the same class situation regularly react in mass actions to such tangible situations as economic ones in the direction of those interests that are most adequate to their average number is an important … fact for the understanding of historical events. However, this fact must not lead to that kind of pseudo-scientific operation which has found its most classic expression in the statement of a talented author, that the individual may be in error concerning his interests but that the class

is infallible about its interests.
(Gerth and Mills, 1948, pp.184–5)

Weber's historical sociology, therefore, was developed in conscious opposition to Marxist theories of historical development – at least in its more economistic versions – as in Weber's analysis of the genesis of modern capitalism in *The Protestant Ethic and the Spirit of Capitalism*. In this book, he explored the unintended consequences of Calvinist ideology, and its impact on historical development, through an examination of the 'elective affinity' between Protestantism and the 'spirit of capitalism', which affected the development of capitalism itself. Weber argued that rational, ascetic Protestantism, as developed within a number of Calvinist churches and Pietistic sects in Europe and America during the seventeenth century, provided, through its rules for daily living (diligence in work, asceticism, and systematic time use) a particularly fruitful seedbed for the development of capitalism. It would be misleading to argue that Weber had developed his argument in order to advance an alternative, 'idealist', interpretation of history; he did not seek 'to substitute for a one-sided materialistic an equally one-sided spiritualistic causal interpretation of culture and of history' (Weber, 1976, p.183). However, as Marshall (1982, p.150) has argued, the question as to whether Marx's materialist or Weber's pluralistic account of the rise and development of capitalism is to be preferred is not, ultimately, an empirical one but, rather, a question of the 'validity of competing frameworks for the interpretation of social reality'. Although Weber's account of the rise of capitalism cannot be described as 'idealist', therefore, it does lead, inevitably, to an account of the relationship between the 'ideological' and 'material' realms of human activity which would be in conflict with Marx's analysis.

Weber's analysis is also to be distinguished from Marx's in that he not only denies the inevitability of class action and conflict, but also the identification of class as a primary source of differentiation in complex societies. For Weber, ' "classes" and "status groups" are phenomena of the distribution of power within a community' (Gerth and Mills, 1948, p.181), and in certain circumstances status may be the predominant source which regulates entitlements to material rewards. Status is associated with honour and prestige and, indeed, may often come into conflict with the demands of the market, where, to use an old phrase suitably adapted: 'every man (and woman) has his (or her) price'. In contrast: 'in most instances', wrote Weber, 'the notion of honour peculiar to status absolutely abhors that which is essential to the market:

higgling' (Gerth and Mills, 1948, p.193). Thus in Weber's analysis the feudal lord or abbot, for example, would belong not to a dominant class but to a status group. 'Status', in Weber's writings, is a complex concept. First, there is the meaning which has already been described: that which reflects the etymological link with 'estate' or '*Stände*' and describes positions which represent particular life chances or fates for the status group in question. Second, status groups have been identified as 'consciousness communities', as when, for example, Collins (1971, p.1009) describes status groups as 'associational groups sharing common cultures… Participation in such groups gives individuals their fundamental sense of identity'. Third, as we have seen in the previous chapter, status has been used to describe consumption categories or 'lifestyle', as the totality of cultural practices such as dress, speech, outlook and bodily dispositions (Turner, 1988, p.66).

The crucial differences between Marx's and Weber's accounts of class may be summarized as follows: first, for Marx, class relationships are grounded in exploitation and domination within *production* relations, whereas, for Weber, class situations reflect differing 'life chances' in the *market*; second, Marx's historical materialism gives a primacy to 'class' in historical evolution which is at odds with Weber's perspective on historical explanation; and finally (and following from this point), whereas for Marx class action is seen as inevitable, for Weber classes 'merely represent possible, and frequent, bases for communal action' (Gerth and Mills, 1948, p.181).

References

Abercrombie, N. and Turner, B.S. (1978) 'The dominant ideology thesis', *British Journal of Sociology*, vol.29, no.2, pp.149–70.

Althusser, L. (1969) *For Marx*, Harmondsworth, Penguin Books.

Benton, T. (1984) *The Rise and Fall of Structural Marxism*, London, Macmillan.

Braverman, H. (1974) *Labour and Monopoly Capital*, New York, Monthly Review Press.

Collins, R. (1971) 'Functional and conflict theories of educational stratification', *American Sociological Review*, vol.36, pp.1002–19.

Connell, R. (1982) 'A critique of the Althusseian approach to class' in Giddens, A. and Held, D. (eds) *op. cit.*.

Gerth, H. and Mills, C. (1948) *From Max Weber*, London, Routledge.

Giddens, A. and Held, D. (1982) *Class, Power and Conflict*, London, Macmillan.

Laclau, E. and Mouffe, C. (1985) *Hegemony and Socialist Strategy*, London, Verso.

Marshall, G. (1982) *In Search of the Spirit of Capitalism*, London, Hutchinson.

Marx, K. (1955) *The Power of Philosophy*, Moscow, Progress Publishers.

Marx, K. (1962a) 'The eighteenth brumaire of Louis Napoleon' in Marx, K. and Engels, F. (1962) *op. cit.*.

Marx, K. (1962b) Preface to a contributions to the critique of political economy in Marx and Engels, *op. cit.*.

Marx, K. (1974) *Capital*, vol.3, London, Lawrence and Wishart.

Marx, K and Engels, F. (1962) *Selected Works*, Moscow, Foreign Language Publishing.

Marx, K. and Engels, F. (1970) *The German Ideology*, London, Lawrence and Wishart.

Poulantzas, N. (1975) *Classes in Contemporary Capitalism*, London, New Left Books.

Przeworski, A. (1985) *Capitalism and Social Democracy*, Cambridge, Cambridge University Press.

Turner, B. (1988) *Status*, Buckingham, Open University Press.

Urry, J. (1981) *The Anatomy of Capitalist Societies*, London, Macmillan.

Weber, M. (1976) *The Protestant Ethic and the Spirit of Capitalism*, London, Allen and Unwin.

Wood, E. (1986) *The Retreat from Class*, London, Verso.

Wright, E. (1989) *The Debate on Classes*, London, Verso.

Source: Crompton, 1996, pp.26–35

Pierre Bourdieu *et al.*, 'The weight of the world' (1999)

With an employee from the central sorting post office – interview by Rosine

I never see the sun

— Ordinarily you work at night?

Danielle Yes, at night.

— From when to when?

Danielle From nine at night to five in the morning, you have to get used to the schedule. I leave here around seven, call my parents …

— You call your parents every day?

Danielle Almost every day, not for long, but it's regular, they've gotten used to it. We finish around five or five-thirty, I get the first metro, and for a woman, it's not the easiest thing in the world …You've got to like it, it's different. In the beginning I was a mail carrier, I've been doing this since '82 … May '82.

[She then explains why she chose to change from mail carrier to the night shift]

Danielle There are pretty many benefits, pretty much time off and you can call on other employees to fill in for you: so with a fill-in, plus certain regular leaves, you get a longer leave period, which means you can work for two weeks flat out and then take two weeks off.

— What do you mean 'flat out'?

Danielle You fill in for a co-worker. You work two nights out of three, and the third night, instead of taking your regular day off, you fill in for a co-worker, so that person will fill in for you when you want. Or sometimes you get two days off because you work Sundays; Sunday evening, that counts as three hours of CL – that's compensatory leave – because you get extra compensation for working from nine to midnight, which means that you get an extra day for working three Sundays. So you take that day, which Administration owes you, and then you get a co-worker to fill in for you, plus the regular day off … And then too you have a lot of free time. Before I met Serge I was a bit homesick, and I thought I'd use the time to go back to Aveyron more often. You need more than a weekend to go to the Aveyron.

— And that's when you met Serge?

Danielle No it was after that. I met Serge when I was working overtime in '84. I was on a night schedule, it wasn't bad, so I thought, why not stay. Serge wasn't very happy with me working nights but I told myself, I've taken a lot of things for him, he's going to take some things too and then that was the way things went. The ambience … except for standing up all the time, and it's true that a human being is made to sleep at night and work during the day …so there's an imbalance for the body but … the ambience … and all that …it's nice, that's all …

Standing up the whole time in one spot

— How does it work?

Danielle When you get there, there are steel bins, bins, you know, with like little pigeonholes … then there's a table called the 'opening' table, that's where the trucks unload, there are handlers or 'handler agents' – they're handlers for sure – who unload the trucks, the big postal sacks, they bring them over on little tables, the rolling carts; they bring them over to the opening table, and there's one guy who opens the sack and the others around the table separate the regular size letters from the little size, and they put them in little boxes, the big ones they put in baskets, you know, those metal baskets and then it's sorted by little slots.

The first time that I entered into these rooms, I said, golly it's huge, it's a factory … no, it's impressive, enormous …and then the small letters go in little plastic sorters, and it's sorted into little slots; and then there are different departments … to acknowledge receipt of registered letters … insured letters, all that goes in a sack with a red label, and it's called 'Reds' or loads, and is sorted at a higher level: GSAX, General Service Agent, they do the sorting in an enclosed office and they're marked in a small notebook and when you go to the distribution section, you have to have the addressee sign.

We remain standing up the whole time in one spot. In front of the setup, for four hours you sort the 15th arrondissement, that's all you do, and you've got to know your stuff … you have to know the Rue Vaugirard, how long that street is and how it turns … it's impossible for one mailperson to deliver the whole street which goes from the 6th arrondissement as far as the Porte de Versailles; it's a street crossed by several districts within the arrondissement, so you put districts 5 and 12 together … 14, 20 and you have to know. You have to know that a given street goes into a given slot.

— *It's already sorted a bit when it gets to the opening table, all Paris isn't in there?*

Danielle It's sorted for the 15th but there are also mistakes, letters that belong in the 17th but end up in the 15th, these are 'wrong addresses'; or letters where the sender got it wrong, for example, putting Boulevard Raspail [runs through the 6th and 14th arrondissements, next to the 15th in the 15th.

— *How many slots do you have to fill?*

Danielle Sixty-six plus three 'zones' plus 'bills', 'single address zipcodes' and 'wrong address', actually I'd say 75 slots and the same for the other employees. But, on the other hand, there's another department, the 'in and out' department is what they call it, for us it's the 'in' department, the 'out' department is in an annex, Rue François-Bonvin and there it's automated, there are PIMS, HMs … a Toshiba, there are machines, computers, so you do the zipcode, you run them through the PIM, and the agent'll do the zipcode 75014, the agent'll get a reject and then it ends up in the HM … in the … it goes in the slots … I can't exactly describe it … and afterwards it's sealed in plastic. That's the 'out' department.

— *And you're standing up all this time?*

Danielle That's right. Now they pay some attention because there are some older people who've been working at night for years, with leg problems; they contact phlebologists and all that … They realized how useful a stool could be, a stool adapted to the slot racks, but it's not really possible because the slot racks are so old. They could put in new slot racks but there are too many slots, it would be too fanned out, but there is a proposal to adapt seats to the slot racks, so sometimes we put two stools together, you know two bar stools one on top of the other, and we sit down, we're tired.

— *Do you stop in the middle?*

Danielle There is a small break from a quarter to one to two o'clock to eat a bite or rest.

— *And how many co-workers do you have?*
Danielle About 30.

— *Do you know them all?*

Danielle Yes. There are changes but I've known them all for a long time …there is an ambience, you end up liking each other … I even have a co-worker who … who is a big philatelist, he loves comics, he's very intense about a number of things. He can become postmaster …then prime minister, who knows!

— *There are supervisors with you?*

Danielle Yes, because there are several grades, the lowest grade is auxiliary, it's not even a classified position, then there's the mail delivery woman, you know, mail-man … then the agent or AXDA … then there's CDTX, that's the supervisor, an inspector for the routes, an inspector for the mail delivery people, but that's a supervisor; then there is the CT, the inspector in the head section like Serge, but that's part of the 'office'; there is the divisional inspector CTDIV and beyond that … all this comes under the rank of inspector.

— *And they are all in there with you?*

Danielle Yes, yes. Some are there.

— *But they don't do the same work?*

Danielle No, no. They give the orders, they register … they all have their particular job, but on the other hand the CTDIV [divisional inspector] is below the inspector and above the CDTX [supervisor] and then there is the inspector and then that's all … because the head inspector works in the day; the postmaster … with him he's already made the grade … then he can become postmaster [*She searches for the right word*], then prime minister, who knows!

— *How do the supervisors act with you?*

Danielle It's OK, they are nice enough, I try to do my job; like every other occupation it has its good sides and bad sides.

When I get up, night is falling

— *Especially for a couple …*

Danielle Yes, because you see each other …you see each other …let's just say that if Serge worked nights, it would work, but with him working days and me nights we see each other less often, necessarily we see each other less often. When I met Serge I was already working nights; he's always known me working nights.

— *You spend one night out of three at home?*

Danielle Yes, but I'm always coming out from under; we don't really live like people who … There, you can see for yourself, I've not gotten back to a regular schedule [*she has been on sick leave for three weeks following an operation*], I still don't sleep nights.

— *And vacations?*

Danielle Just the same; my time to sleep is from seven in the morning to three in the afternoon. Sometimes in the middle of winter I don't ever see the sun, I get up … not in total darkness … that's not the case when I get up, night is falling and I go off to work, I come back …it's still night, there are periods like that.

— *You must not see your husband.*

Danielle Well yes, because he works close by, he has a good schedule, I get to see him. And then he works in shifts, a morning or an afternoon, he had this morning off, he's working this afternoon. He has regular shifts: six in the morning to half-past twelve and twelve to six-thirty. Where it's the most serious is when he doesn't work mornings and he works afternoons: I get back, I'm tired and he's getting up, I find it hard to talk, and when he has to leave at noon, I get up and fix him something to eat, but I don't have my wits about me and he leaves just when I'm coming out from under. I don't have to [*fix him something to eat*] but he's so nice, a man's a man, I tell myself that he's not going to know how … well, he'll know what to eat but … I'm always wanting to take attention.

[*She talks about the problem of having a child.*]

Even though there are married women with children, to keep from paying daycare one or the other works at night, that happens a lot in my job; to raise their kid, not to pay daycare, one of them does daycare at night, the other during the day and the one who works at night takes the day. I have adapted myself, I was always with my family. My parents were everything for me, I adored my parents and I loved the countryside, nature, I missed it a lot and in Paris I felt stifled whereas here [*in Ulis*] it's 30 kilometers outside Paris, it's not very far … it's not really the country, it's in between.

I stayed in the Aveyron until I was 20, then I went to Rodez to study; it's a small town, I did the secretarial course, a sort of BEP-CAP as office secretary, but it's still a small town; next to the big city, Rodez is a big village. I would have been happy on the farm, but at my parents' place it's too hard, it's impossible to bring it up to date, we'd have had to build a house … with modern facilties … we'd have had to … and it's not even that, but such a small farm! because the terrain is too hilly and then they used to live well because they sold vegetables and fruits but now with fruit coming in from Spain through the Common Market, that's taken everything … and then for a woman … I would have liked it … but what can you do? My parents told me, 'It's not that we don't want to have you here, but you have to be ambitious, take your exams'; and then at that time they used to get a newspaper and I saw an announcement: sign up with this organization, I wrote in, I sent in all the information, all that …

— *You didn't know it was for the postal service?*

Danielle Yes I did, it was clearly marked. The newspaper was *Centre-Presse* or *Midi-Libre*, I don't know which. I signed up and I went to Rodez and there I was accepted under I can't remember which number. They notified me that I was accepted and that I could have a medical exam and 'you will be assigned to mail delivery in Paris,' but they didn't tell me where. They had asked me what region I preferred, Rouen, the North, Paris, or the East; so I put down the Paris region: I got Paris and I found out where only three months before I started working: 'you are assigned to the 15th arrondissement and start work in two weeks,' that's how I left.

Entry into Paris

Danielle In the beginning I stayed a few weeks with my aunt in Saint-Denis [working-class suburb north of Paris] [*This is the wife of Danielle's mother's brother, the owner of a café-restaurant first in Saint-Denis, then in Roissy nearby. He has lived in the Paris region for more than 30 years and has kept a house near her parents' home where they go for a few weeks in the summer and around the end of October, and which he has fixed up very nicely with an eye to retiring there.*]. Monsieur Reyrolle [*a neighbour close to her family*] took me to the train station at Rodez, I was really sad, I was only 20, but everybody's got to earn a living, so a bit of sadness … but that was later. My brothers and sisters had their lives, there I was, all alone in a studio apartment faced with all of life's problems, just starting work, a whole bunch of things like that, I was a bit lost. But even so, I liked the others at work, I used to go out, weekends I was never alone, well, yes, a couple of times … But I didn't have any real friends, we were more like acquaintances who did things together.

— *Don't I remember that you were in a residence at one point?*

Danielle In the beginning I was in a postal service residence, on the Boulevard Pasteur; it's a residence where they let you stay at least three months, and then you fend for yourself … it's the entry into Paris. Afterwards I lived in a residence where you could stay a little longer, there were only four of us, then of course there were always new arrivals, so you had to make room for the newcomers. Everyone, once they've adapted to Paris, everyone has to look for their own place; I looked for anything I could find … a small apartment, I found a studio … it was gloomy inside, Rue Firmin-Didot in the 15th near the Porte de Versailles, I was down in the dumps … then I was on the Rue Blomet, then I moved to the Rue Saint-Lambert [all in the 15th near the post office where she works] …

— *Why did you keep moving around?*

Danielle Because in the first place, I was bored, it wasn't open enough, there wasn't enough air, it was on the fourth floor and there was an elevator but it was gloomy and I couldn't get used to it. Then I was in a maid's room so I had no facilities at all. Then I said to myself, it's all well and good to go clean up at Yvette's [*her sister, who runs a café*], but it's a pain, find something of your own … But before that … to get back my deposit on the first studio, I had to pay double rent for a certain amount of time, the maid's room and the other rent. I lived in the maid's room, I lived there a year, and then another employee told me 'Dani, I found a studio at a good rent if you want to go have a look,' I said OK. There, there were all the facilities, there was a kitchen, a living room wing that was also the bedroom, a storage place, and a bathroom. I stayed there for a certain time, then I met Serge, we were in an F2 [two-room apartment] Rue Desnouettes and then we came here.

A kind of tranquillizer

— *Do you remember your first impressions when you got here from the country?*

Danielle Not really, but you're young, you don't see the whole, if I were starting out now, it would be harder, but at the time … I was a bit carefree … you tell yourself that you're going to meet people, you're going to get married, meet a Prince Charming, all a bit silly. So when you get here … but I'd already lived in Rodez, so I knew something of a city. I saw Paris … Yes of course, Paris is very beautiful but for someone from the provinces who comes on a visit; if I'd come as a tourist then, I would have stayed with friends, I'd have spent two months seeing all the monuments and all the things Paris has to offer, to take advantage of them, I would've appreciated it, but this way I saw Paris … I'll tell you … because you get here, perhaps no longer now, but at the time you always hoped to get a transfer, you wait, it's a wait, they tell you 'You're a trainee.' It takes a year to be classified, so you say 'fine for a year, I'll sacrifice a year and then I'll go back home.' What makes this not a good solution is because you're only here in passing, you don't look at things, you don't appreciate, you just want the year to end so you can go back home … all that. They mislead you at the start, to soften you up, a kind of tranquillizer. It's a bit like blackmail. So you don't want to adapt because you tell yourself that you'll have to get used to the provinces again, perhaps you won't be assigned where you want to go, in your parents' town or that it's going to take time. All that makes you think and then you float, you float a lot. I didn't have the same perspective in '76 as I do now.

— *Your mother always talked about the bag you had there.*

Danielle Yes, it was a satchel with straps. Now they have supermarket-type carts for nearby deliveries, and they have storage sites, postal service buses that take you around; which means you put half the round in a bag, and someone, a driver agent, that's an agent who drives a vehicle, takes you to a number halfway through your round. For example, if I'm doing the Rue de Bergères, I'll start out and fill my bag up to a given point, halfway along the route, then at that point my bag will be empty, so then I'll pick up the mail in a bag that this person will have given me. I was the one who sorted my route but it's true that it was … and three times a day! You worked every morning, you had to be at work at six, and if you got there late, you had to explain why, you got 'tickets' they're called, and getting marks and all stirs up lots of things. We worked every morning and every other afternoon; the worst day was when you had morning and afternoon, you did three rounds, one 'money round' with money orders, registered letters, insured letters, things like that, important things.

— *It's almost harder than at night.*

Danielle That's right. Serge would have liked me to … but where it wasn't bad was when, you know, the delivery person presents the calendar to the people on their route and there you got a small thank you amount which didn't hurt at the end of the year, it wasn't a whole extra month of salary but still … You paid three or four francs for the calendar and you offered it to the customer, to the individual, and the individual accepted or not, and would give a small present, 50 or 100 francs depending on what they could afford, and that's for you. That makes a little bundle at the end of the year whereas here you're paid for the 'thirteenth month,' it was a kind of extra month's salary. It's important when you work days.

— *But did you get very much out of it?*

Danielle Oh no! and then you have to like doing it, it's begging, it's different, you can't be ashamed of sticking out your hand all over the place, it's not an obvious thing to do.

Source: Bourdieu and Ferguson, 1999, pp.300–8

3

Understanding gender divisions: feminist perspectives

Linda Janes

Contents

1	**Introduction**	**102**
	Aims	104
2	**Is the future female?**	**104**
	2.1 Paid work	105
	2.2 Income	110
	2.3 Unpaid domestic work	112
	2.4 Parenthood	114
3	**Equality feminism**	**117**
4	**From equality to difference**	**120**
	4.1 'The personal is political'	120
	4.2 'Sisterhood is powerful'	125
	4.3 'Ain't I a woman?'	127
5	**From materiality to meaning**	**130**
6	**Reinstating class: materiality *and* meaning**	**135**
7	**Conclusion**	**138**
	7.1 And finally ...	139
	References	**139**
	Readings	
	3.1: **Nicola Charles, 'Women and class – a problematic relationship?' (1990)**	**142**
	3.2: **Harriet Bradley, 'Gender: rethinking patriarchy' (1996)**	**146**
	3.3: **Beverley Skeggs, '(Dis)Identifications of class: on not being working class' (1997)**	**150**

1 Introduction

This chapter is about social divisions of gender. It explores questions relating to differences between men and women and the extent to which gender differences constitute social inequalities. For example, are women and men equal, but different, or does difference actually mean inequality? And, if the social division of gender positions women as inferior to men, is that a universal inequality? Are all women, then, unequal to all men or are some women more equal than others? And what about differences amongst women, and amongst men – do they also constitute social divisions that we need to take account of in an analysis of gender and power? In exploring these questions this chapter focuses particularly on ways in which feminist commentators have explained **gender relations**, and differences and inequalities between men and women, and amongst women. It therefore highlights some of the ways in which feminist thinking has articulated with, and challenged, mainstream sociological thought.

sociology of gender

One of feminism's greatest strengths is its diversity and heterogeneity – in fact from the 1980s it has been customary to refer to feminisms in the plural, rather than to feminism. It is both a political movement, cutting across other collectivities of class, 'race' and religion for example, and a diverse body of theoretical perspectives which cuts across many academic disciplinary boundaries. As we shall see, the relationship between politics and theory in feminism is its essential life-blood, but not always easily negotiated. This chapter, then, provides a 'taster' to some of these political and academic debates, but it is inevitably restricted in scope historically and culturally; the quantitative 'evidence' we shall consider is based mainly on the contemporary UK and analysis is drawn from western feminism. It is therefore important, I think, to bear the limitations and specificity of its framework in mind as you read the chapter. For example, in *The Origins of Modern Feminism* (1985) the feminist historian Jane Rendall provides a comparative account of the development of political and intellectual social movements between 1780 and 1860 in France, England and the United States, which prioritized and theorized women's emancipation in a consolidated way for the first time. She locates these developments within the western context of **modernity** and the **Enlightenment**, but acknowledges also the long historical legacy of women's earlier recorded self-conscious awareness of sexual politics in, for example, the fourteenth and fifteenth centuries. Rendall notes that the first recorded use of the term 'feminism' in English, derived from the French, was in 1894, according to the 1933 *Supplement* to the *Oxford English Dictionary*, although the 1894 text does not contain the accepted modern meaning of the term (Rendall, 1985, p.1).

modernity, Enlightenment

In her chapter on gender in a recent textbook entitled *Social Divisions* (Payne, 2000), Pamela Abbott sets the framework for her analysis as follows:

> In identifying gender as an important social division, sociologists are going beyond arguing that men and women have different roles in society, and are typically found performing different jobs. We are concerned with explaining them – to provide theoretical accounts based on the idea that these differences are structural, are predominantly social in origin, and that men, as a category, have more power than women as a category. While there are considerable differences in these various theoretical accounts, [...] men are seen as able to

use their power to control resources, maintain their position of dominance vis-à-vis women and so are able to exploit women. However, although men are thus in a position of advantage, they are also structurally constrained by ideas of masculinity and what is expected as the correct way for a 'man' to behave.

(Abbott, 2000, p.55)

Abbott highlights several important points here. Firstly, she identifies the social and structural focus of sociological analysis of gender divisions. We are not so much concerned with differences and divisions between individual men and women, but with how divisions operate at a social and structural level between men as a category and women as a category; with how existing, but changing, socially constructed gender positions influence our lived experiences. In defining gender divisions as structural, we highlight the ways in which differences between men and women are assumed by and enshrined within institutional frameworks such as the law, the family, education, employment and the welfare state. These institutions are based on dominant cultural understandings about gender differences which they then reproduce, and it is very difficult for individuals to choose to challenge them in substantial ways. Secondly, in highlighting the social dimension, Abbott emphasizes the distinction between gender and sex differences. Sex differences refer to biological differences between men and women, whereas gender refers to differences that are socially inscribed. So, while the terms male and female refer to the biological sexes, masculinity and femininity are terms used to describe the social roles and behaviours linked to each gender. Biological difference – the argument that women are smaller and weaker than men (which is not, by any means, always the case either within or across cultures) – has often been used to justify unequal treatment of women as inevitably fixed in nature, but justification based on the socially constructed difference of gender is harder to sustain. Abbott makes a further important observation, however, that although masculinity is generally associated with power and advantage vis-à-vis femininity, men are just as constrained by gender identity as women.

Abbott's discussion goes on to acknowledge another key factor in the gender debate, the question of how gender interrelates with other social divisions. In terms of our social identities we are never only women or men, although gender seems to be an important dimension of identity for most people. Each one of us is a complex and changing amalgam of interconnected social identities of class, culture, 'race', ethnicity, nationality, sexuality, age – to name just some key aspects – and it is really impossible to separate gender from all the other dimensions. In analysing gender divisions, therefore, we need always to take account of the effects of other aspects of social difference and division. As the black feminist writer Audre Lorde memorably remarked from her own point of view, 'as a forty-nine-year-old Black lesbian socialist mother of two, including one boy, and member of an inter-racial couple, I usually find myself a part of some group defined as other, deviant, inferior, or just plain wrong' (Lorde, 1984, p.14).

Figure 3.1 *Audre Lorde*

To summarize, then, this chapter will explore the social division of gender in terms of differences and inequalities between men and women as social categories, taking into account the ways in which gender interrelates with other dimensions of social division. It will utilize, and evaluate, some feminist theoretical explanations of gendered power relations as a means of understanding gender divisions. Section 2 presents recent quantitative evidence relating to men's and women's participation in social life which we can use to inform our analysis of gender divisions. Section 3 reviews the perspective of equality feminism and the argument that women should aspire to equal treatment with men, based on the erasure of gender difference. Section 4 examines feminist analyses which address the issue of difference, both between women and men and, increasingly, between women themselves in explaining inequality. Section 5 provides an account of the shift in feminist analyses of gendered power during the 1990s, in debate with the concurrent, wider sociological focus on cultural explanations rather than material inequalities. Finally, in section 6, we review the example of a recent feminist research project in which both cultural and material gender inequalities are addressed and explained.

AIMS

The aims of the chapter are:

1 To assess some contemporary empirical data relating to gender differences and divisions in Britain.

2 To provide an account of different ways in which feminists have sought to explain social divisions of gender, women's subordination and the operation of gendered power.

3 To engage readers in an evaluation of the different theories and strategies introduced.

4 To evaluate two examples of feminist sociological analysis from the 1990s which seek to reinstate class as an intrinsic explanatory element in social divisions of gender.

2 Is the future female?

The woman question is answered. It is now understood that women can do anything that men can do. Anyone who tries to stop them will be breaking the law. Even the President of the United States, the most powerful person in the world, can be called to account by a young female nobody. Power indeed! The future is female, we are told. Feminism has served its purpose and should now eff off. Feminism was long hair, dungarees and dangling earrings; post-feminism was business suits, big hair and lipstick; post-post-feminism was ostentatious sluttishness and disorderly behaviour. We all agree that women should have equal pay for equal work, be equal before the law, do no more housework than men do, spend no more time with children than men do – or do we?

(Greer, 1999, p.5)

In this introduction to her much publicized book, *The Whole Woman*, Germaine Greer – often referred to as a 'celebrity' feminist, since her fame depends largely on her public identification with feminism – invokes the idea of a contemporary society in which gender inequalities have been successfully eliminated through the challenges of successive generations of feminism, which is therefore now redundant. These generations are represented through the negative stereotypes associated with the popular media and her heavy irony is not difficult to discern. She highlights the identity of the post-feminist, the beneficiary of the various challenges of feminism, a social movement that can now be consigned to history. The post-feminist woman lives in a world of gender equality, in which the future is female.

Greer's irony aside, I wonder how this post-feminist scenario chimes with your views and experiences? Do you think the future is female? Certainly, women's lives – in the developed West anyway – have changed greatly since, say, the 1950s in terms of their participation in relation to education, marriage, paid work, leisure and consumption. But what about domestic work and childcare: do you think women's responsibilities have changed there also? And what about men – have their lives changed as much? Thinking back to the chapter introduction, we should certainly be wary of generalizing, I think. Some women's and men's lives have changed more than others. Let's consider some recent quantitative evidence in the form of statistical data, recording differential gender participation rates in some of these crucial areas – paid work, income, domestic work and childcare – in the UK. The rest of this section will be based around activities in order to explore data in each of these areas.

2.1 Paid work

ACTIVITY 1

Consider the data in Figures 3.2–3.4 and Tables 3.1–3.3 carefully, and use them to answer the following questions about gender divisions:

1 How has the pattern of male and female rates of economic activity changed over the last thirty years?

2 What sorts of jobs do men and women typically do, and how have these patterns changed over the last ten years?

3 How do men's and women's participation in full-time, part-time, and temporary work differ?

4 How do divisions of ethnicity and age intersect with gendered patterns of paid work?

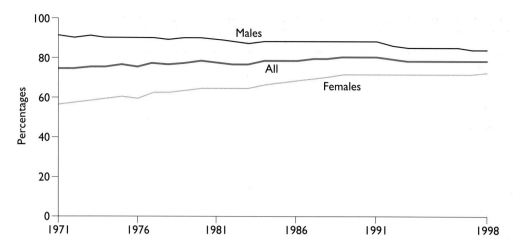

Figure 3.2 *Economic activity rates[1]: by gender, United Kingdom, 1971–1998*

Notes: [1]*Males aged 16 to 64, females aged 16 to 59. The percentage of the population that is in the labour force. Source of data: Labour Force Survey, Office for National Statistics*

Source: *Social Trends 30*, 2000, Chart 4.4, p.67

Table 3.1 Employees[1]: by gender and occupation, 1991 and 1999

	Males		**Females**	
	1991	**1999**	**1991**	**1999**
Managers and administrators	16	19	8	11
Professional	10	11	8	10
Associated professional and technical	8	9	10	11
Clerical and secretarial	8	8	29	26
Craft and related	21	17	4	2
Personal and protective services	7	8	14	17
Selling	6	6	12	12
Plant and machine operatives	15	15	5	4
Other occupations	8	8	10	8
All employees[2] = 100%) (millions)	11.8	12.4	10.1	10.8

Notes:

1   At Spring each year. Males aged 16 to 64, females aged 16 to 59.

2   Includes a few people who did not state their occupation. Percentages are based on totals which exclude this group.

Source of data: Labour Force Survey, Office for National Statistics.

Source: *Social Trends 30*, 2000, Chart 4.13, p.72

Table 3.2 Population of working age[1]: by employment status and gender[1], Spring 1999

	Males	Females	All
Economically active			
In employment			
Full-time employees	11.4	6.2	17.7
Part-time employees	0.9	4.6	5.6
Self-employed	2.2	0.7	3.0
Others in employment[2]	0.1	0.1	0.2
All in employment	14.7	11.7	26.4
Unemployed[3]	1.1	0.6	1.7
All economically active	15.8	12.3	28.2
Economically inactive	3.0	4.8	7.8
Population of working age	18.8	17.1	35.9

Notes:
1 Males aged 16 to 64, females aged 16 to 59.
2 Those on government employment and training schemes and unpaid family workers.
3 Based on the ILO definition.

Source of data: Labour Force Survey, Office of National Statistics.

Source: *Social Trends 30*, 2000, Chart 4.2, p.66

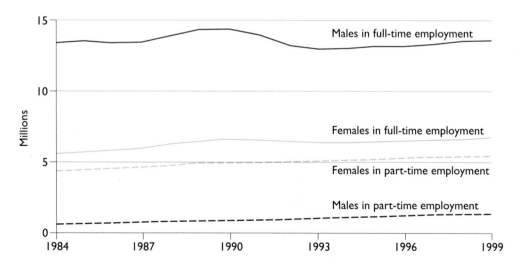

Figure 3.3 *Full and part-time employment[1]: by gender, United Kingdom, 1984–1999*

Notes: [1]*At Spring each year. Includes employees, self-employed, those on government employment and training schemes and, from 1992, unpaid family workers. Full/part-time is based on respondents' self-assessment. Source of data: Labour Force Survey, Office for National Statistics*

Source: *Social Trends 30*, 2000, Chart 4.10, p.70

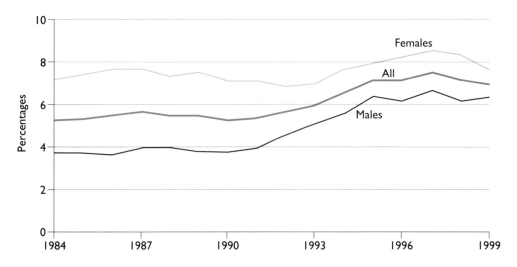

Figure 3.4 *Temporary employees[1]: by gender, United Kingdom, 1984–99*

Notes: [1]*As a percentage of all employees. Temporary employees are those who assess themselves to have either a seasonal or casual job, a job done under contract or for a fixed period, or were temporary for some other reason. At Spring each year. Source of data: Labour Force Survey, Office for National Statistics*

Source: *Social Trends 30*, 2000, Chart 4.16, p.73

Table 3.3 Economic activity rates[1]: by ethnic group, gender and age, 1998–99[2]

	Males				**Females**			
	16–24	25–44	45–64	All aged 16–64	16–24	25–44	45–59	All aged 16–59
White	79	94	78	85	71	77	71	74
Black Caribbean	74	88	72	81	53	78	68	72
Black African	53	84	81	77	34	67	55	59
Other Black groups	–	85	–	80	–	79		77
Indian	60	94	71	80	52	70	51	62
Pakistani	54	88	55	71	37	29	21	30
Bangladeshi	52	85	–	68	31	–	–	19
Chinese	31	83	70	62	–	65	66	62
None of the above[3]	54	82	82	75	55	59	69	60
All ethnic groups[4]	77	93	77	85	69	75	70	73

Notes:

1 The percentage of the population that is in the labour force.
2 Combined quarters: Spring 1998 to Winter 1998–99.
3 Includes those of mixed origin.
4 Includes those who did not state their ethnic group.

Source of data: Labour Force Survey, Office for National Statistics

Source: *Social Trends*, 2000, Chart 4.8, p.69

Figure 3.2 indicates the significant rise in women's participation in waged work since 1971 when 56 per cent of women between 16 and 59 were economically active compared to 72 per cent in 1999. Over the same period men's participation has declined from 91 per cent to 84 per cent. These patterns relate to the huge restructuring of the British economy in which manufacturing industries, the primary site of men's employment, have closed down, replaced by the service industry economy which employs large numbers of women. In 1999 there were more women than men active in the UK economy for the first time since the Second World War (Franks, 1999).

So women are primary workers in the new economy, but what sorts of jobs do they do? Table 3.1 demonstrates some clear divisions between men's and women's jobs, and some indications of gradual change. Men predominate in manual and craft-related occupations as well as in managerial and administrative work. Although women's participation in these more prestigious jobs is increasing, men's is not decreasing. Women predominate in selling and personal service work, as well as in secretarial and clerical occupations, although they do less of this work now than ten years ago. Table 3.1 does not delineate different levels within these occupational categories, but we know from other sources how few women there are in the most senior management and professional positions. The glass ceiling and the glass wall are popular metaphors that describe the difficulties women have in securing 'top' jobs in mixed professions or jobs at all in those associated solely with men (Franks, 1999; Segal, 2000).

Table 3.2 and Figures 3.3 and 3.4 present data relating to men's and women's differential participation across full-time, part-time and temporary work. Here we see that women are much less likely to work full-time, and much more likely to work part-time, than men. Whereas the proportion of men working part-time remains very small in relation to the number working full-time, there is a comparatively small difference between the number of women working part-time and full-time. However, although the absolute difference is very significant, since 1984 the number of men working part-time has more than doubled while the number of women in part-time work has increased by only one quarter. Women are also more likely to be in temporary jobs, although since 1997 there has been a convergence of likelihood. The most common explanation for the high numbers of women in part-time and temporary work is their primary responsibility for childcare and household management. Some

commentators argue that this demonstrates women's choice (Hakim, 1995), whilst others point to the lack of affordable childcare in the UK as the primary reason.

Finally, Table 3.3 indicates widely varied economic activity rates between ethnic groups, with the greatest variation amongst women. For example, 72 per cent of Black Caribbean women are recorded as economically active, compared to only 30 per cent of Pakistani and 19 per cent of Bangladeshi women. For men in these groups the difference follows the same pattern but is less marked.

2.2 Income

Have a look now at Figures 3.5, 3.6 and 3.7. What do they tell us about the differentials between men's and women's incomes?

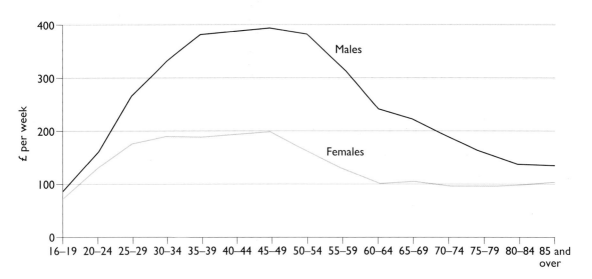

Figure 3.5 *Mean individual income: by gender and age, Great Britain, 1996–97*

Source of data: Family Resources Survey, Department of Social Security

Source: *Social Trends*, 2000, Chart 5.6, p.84

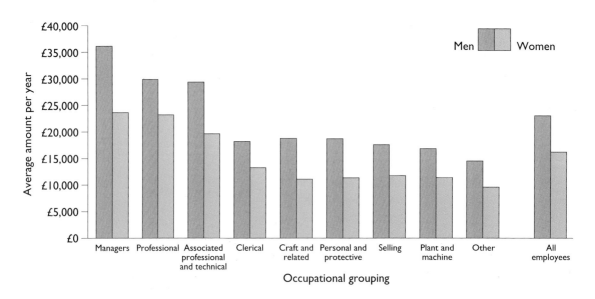

Figure 3.6 *Average gross annual earnings of full-time employees, Great Britain, 1997–98*

Source of data: Office for National Statistics, New Earnings Survey 1999, Tables A13 and A14

Source: EOC, 2000

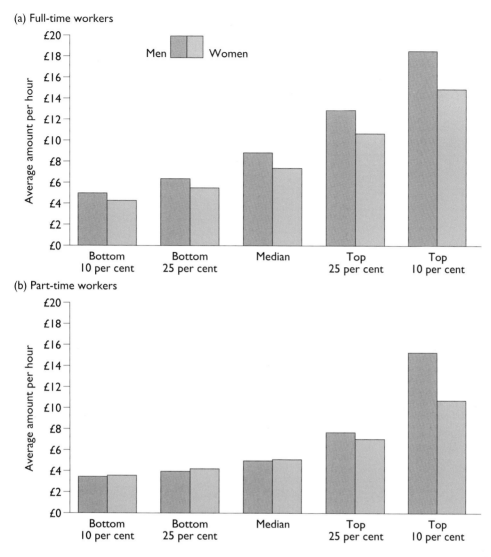

Figure 3.7 *Gross hourly earnings, Great Britain, 1999*

Source of data: Office for National Statistics, New Earnings Survey 1999

Source: EOC, 2000

Figure 3.5 indicates that, although young women and men start out earning similar incomes, men's earnings quickly outstrip women's and in mid-life, when both genders are earning their highest incomes, men's earnings are double those of women. The greater proportion of women in part-time work goes some way towards accounting for this differential but Figures 3.6 and 3.7 show that this does not offer a full explanation. In all occupational groupings, full-time women employees earn substantially less than men and the inequality is greatest in higher paid jobs. In part-time employment, men's and women's wages are closer to the top 10 per cent of earners, where men's hourly wage is one-third higher than women's.

2.3 Unpaid domestic work

Table 3.4, dating from 1994, shows the gender distribution of some typical household tasks. How would you characterize the divisions?

Table 3.4 Division of household tasks[1], Great Britain, 1994

	Usually the woman	About equal or both together	Usually the man	Always the woman	All couples[2]
Washing and ironing	47	32	18	1	1	100
Deciding what to have for dinner	27	32	35	3	1	100
Looking after sick family members	22	26	45			100
Shopping for groceries	20	21	52	4	1	100
Small repairs around the house	2	3	18	49	25	100

Notes:

1 By married couples or couples living as married
2 Includes those who did not answer and where the task was done by a third person.

Source of data: British Social Attitudes Survey, Social and Community Planning Research

Source: EOC, 1998

Would you agree that gender stereotypes appear to prevail, with women maintaining majority responsibility for washing and ironing and men for household repairs? Shopping, however, is an activity now shared equally in nearly half of households. In an earlier survey, in 1991, couples were asked about how they thought such household tasks should be allocated and revealed an interesting difference between attitudes and actions. For example, 62 per cent of couples thought that household cleaning *should* be shared equally, whereas it was only *actually* shared equally in 27 per cent of households. Feminists have argued that women's increased participation in paid work has not been balanced by men's increased responsibility for domestic work, and that this constitutes a significant inequality (Hochschild 1989, 1997; Franks, 1999; Jamieson,1998). However, some recent research based on international comparisons, suggests that there is a gradual convergence in the unequal levels of responsibility for domestic work undertaken by women and men (Gershuny, 2000; see also section 3 in **Hemmings, Silva and Thompson, 2002**). More equal sharing is more likely to occur between younger couples and in households with high levels of educational qualification.

Figure 3.8 *The washing-machine revolutionized laundry day in the 1950s, but most domestic work has remained the woman's job despite most women being employed outside the home.*

Figure 3.9 *Today's 'average housewife' does all the work previously done by a team of servants*

2.4 Parenthood

Finally, let's look at some statistics about parenthood. Study Tables 3.5 and 3.6 and Figure 3.10 and consider the following questions:

1 Who takes primary responsibility for childcare?

2 What is the impact of having children on mothers' rates of economic activity? What is its impact on the economic activity rates of fathers?

3 What is the impact of lone parenthood on women and on men in relation to employment?

Table 3.5 Providers[1] of childcare[2], Great Britain, 1996–97[3] (percentages)

	Pre-school age children	School age children in term time	School age children in holidays
Female respondent	82	78	77
Her partner	15	10	12
Mother/mother-in-law	11	7	12
Registered child-minder	6	2	2
Other relative	3	2	5
Private nursery/crèche	2	–	–
Person employed in respondent's home	1	2	3
Friend/neighbour unpaid	1	1	
Friend/neighbour paid	1	2	1
Day nursery/crèche run by employer	1	–	–
They look after themselves	–	5	5
Child's older siblings	–	2	2

Notes:

1 Percentage of dependent children cared for by each type of provider. More than one type of provider may be identified.

2 Respondents were mothers aged 16 to 69.

3 Main fieldwork took place between July 1996 and February 1997.

Source of data: Family and Working Lives Survey, Department for Education and Employment.

Source: EOC, 1998

Table 3.5 indicates that women continue to take primary responsibility for childcare, which is provided mainly by mothers themselves. However, grandmothers actually provide as much childcare as fathers do. Figure 3.7 demonstrates the significant impact that motherhood has on women's economic participation rates. In spite of the big rise in the employment of mothers with

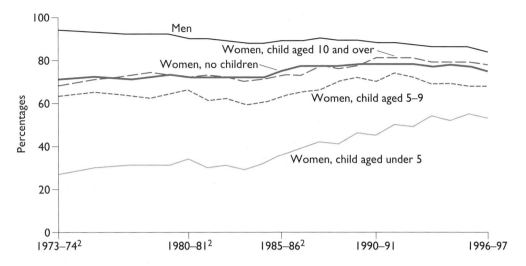

Figure 3.10 *Economic activity rates[1]: by age of youngest dependent child*

Source: EOC, 1998

Notes:

1   Women aged 16 to 59, men aged 16 to 64. The percentage of the population that is in the labour force.
2   Calendar years up to 1988.

Table 3.6 Employment and unemployment rates for parents[1], United Kingdom, 1997–98

	Employment rate[3]	Unemployment rate
Women		
Couple	68	4
Lone parent	43	16
Men		
Couple	89	5
Lone parent	59	14

Notes:

1   Women aged 16 to 59, men aged 16 to 64, with dependent children.
2   Combined quarters: Spring 1997 to Winter 1997–98.
3   All in employment as a proportion of the total population of working age.

Source of data: Labour Force Survey, Office for National Statistics

Source: EOC, 1998

young children since 1973 (much of which is part-time as we learned above), they are less likely to be in employment than are mothers of older children. Once children reach the age of ten, their mothers are as likely to be in employment as women with no children. Men's employment has declined over the same period, but their role as fathers is not a factor in this change. Table 3.6

shows that lone fathers are much less likely to be in employment than fathers with partners but significantly more likely to be in work than lone mothers. Ninety per cent of lone parents are mothers, and lone mothers are the only group of women less likely to be in work than thirty years ago. They constitute one of the poorest groups within the population.

■   ■   ■

I hope that this brief review of contemporary statistics provides some insight into Greer's skepticism about a post-feminist future in which gender equality has been achieved. In her book Greer draws on contemporary evidence in relation to women's position in paid work, the domestic sphere, sexuality, representation and reproduction, to argue against ideas that women have achieved equality with men, or that women's difference from men is adequately understood and supported in public policy or what is defined as the 'private' realm of the family.

SUMMARY OF SECTION 2

In assessing material inequalities between men and women in Britain, we can note the following summary evidence:

1   Women's paid employment has increased dramatically in the last thirty years, particularly employment of mothers, but much of their employment is part-time and/or temporary.

2   Ethnicity is a critical variable in relation to gendered rates of employment.

3   Men's employment remained constant until the late 1980s when economic restructuring cut many traditionally male jobs.

4   Women's income is less than men's across all full-time occupations. Part-time hourly rates are similar in lower and middle range jobs, but men earn more in higher-paid, part-time jobs.

5   Women retain primary responsibility for childcare, as well as for the majority of household domestic tasks, although here there is evidence of some gradual readjustment towards more equal sharing.

This introduction has suggested a picture – albeit only a partial version – of the kinds of gendered social divisions that sociologists, particularly feminists, have analysed, sought to explain and to challenge. Let's now move on to explore some of their explanations.

3 Equality feminism

> The Queen is most anxious to enlist everyone who can speak or write to join in checking this mad wicked folly of woman's rights, with all its attendant horrors on which her poor sex is bent.
>
> (Queen Victoria, 1870; quoted in Marlow, 2000)

Feminism is often described within contemporary social theory as a 'new **social movement**', referring to a social and/or political collective grouping focused on an identity which cuts across traditional groupings such as class or nationality. **Feminism** is certainly a movement focused on social transformation with women's emancipation at its core (Segal, 2000), although what emancipation might require has been the subject of much debate. However, it is definitely not new, and the origins of modern feminism go back to the mid eighteenth century as noted in the introduction above (Rendall, 1985).

social movement

feminism

In the UK context, a key 'foundational' text was Mary Wollstonecraft's *Vindication of the Rights of Woman,* published in 1792. Wollstonecraft addressed the issue of **inequality** between men and women and wrote in response to contemporary texts of liberal philosophers on the 'Rights of Man' and the establishment of citizenship. Within traditional liberalism 'man' is posited as a superior creature to animals because of his ability to reason, which is cast as the distinguishing feature of the modern, rational, individual human subject associated with the Enlightenment. Liberalism posits a subject of democratic citizenship who accepts a 'social contract' which provides rights and legal protection in the civic public sphere of politics and employment, in return for individual compliance and constraint in these fields. The social contract provides a mechanism for a baseline of equality against which individuals will secure differential advancement through competition (see Chapter 5 for a full discussion of citizenship). It is important to note, however, that liberalism tends to restrict its controlling interventions to the public sphere and sees the private realm (of home/family) as sacrosanct.

equality

Wollstonecraft argued that, although women were supposedly implicitly included under the 'human' umbrella of liberalism, they were in fact included only as second-class citizens. She saw women's exclusion from equal education and their consequent socialization for the domestic realm as resulting in 'impaired' reason, and therefore undermining their inclusion as equal, rational citizens of liberal democracy. Wollstonecraft was therefore one of the first feminists to identify the exclusionary effect of the apparently gender-neutral use of the term 'man', and to make the distinction between 'sex' and 'gender', both of which insights have informed feminist debates to the present day. She saw that women were denied access to equal education on the basis that their 'sex' – as biological females whose concerns were therefore 'naturally', essentially, linked only to domesticity and childcare – but pointed out that there was no necessary logic to that relationship. It was based on a social understanding or construction that made an automatic link between the biological level and the social level – between sex and gender as equivalent. Wollstonecraft argued that if women had access to the same education as men, they could learn 'reason' too, which was, in itself, an androgynous quality. Although the relationship between sex and gender has been conceptualized in many more sophisticated and reciprocal ways since, the recognition of a distinction between the two

Figure 3.11 *Direct action by suffragettes brought about a significant breakthrough in women's battle for equality*

opened up the pathway to potential social transformation for women. As Simone de Beauvoir expressed the point so succinctly in *The Second Sex* in 1949, 'One is not born, but rather becomes, a woman'. Sex is difficult to change, but since gender is socially constructed and operates at the level of ideas, change is easier to bring about (in theory, at least)!

Although Wollstonecraft was a critic of gender-blind liberalism, she was herself proposing change from within a liberal standpoint. In this respect, she advocated the eradication of prejudice and women's subordination through the extension of equal opportunities and rights to women as individual citizens, underwritten by legal reform.

These characteristic priorities have been associated with a continuing tradition of liberal feminism since Wollstonecraft's day and were central to the campaign for women's suffrage at the end of the nineteenth century. The 120 years linking Wollstonecraft to the suffragettes is often referred to as the 'first wave' of modern feminism. The history of women's struggle for the vote in Europe and the United States, and of the opposition they faced, still carries powerful resonance. Historians have documented the involvement of women of different social locations in the suffrage campaign. However, it is typically cast as a predominantly middle-class, white women's movement, conducted by the beneficiaries of liberal social and educational reform pioneered by Mary Wollstonecraft and later nineteenth-century thinkers such as John Stuart Mill and Harriet Taylor.

Figure 3.12 *Women's demands for equality have never been popular: suffragettes were viciously lampooned in the press*

ACTIVITY 5

We have seen that liberal feminism is concerned with mitigating inequalities between men and women in the public sphere through legal and institutional reform. Can you think of instances of such reforms?

Women's right to vote is obviously hugely important in this respect. After the Second World War the removal of marriage bars that enabled married women to continue working in banking and teaching, for example, is liberal reform addressing women's unequal treatment. In the 1970s the Sex Discrimination and Equal Pay legislation set a legal framework which ostensibly established access to equality in relation to waged work. However, as we saw in the introduction, thirty years on, some women are much more equal to men (which men?) than others, and even that assumes a narrow definition of equality linking it primarily to the public sphere.

ACTIVITY 6

Given that liberal reforms have had limited success for women, what do you think critics might suggest are the inherent problems in relation to liberal feminist strategies for equality?

A key weakness that critics identify is liberalism's assumption of a 'level playing-field', i.e. that if equal opportunities legislation is in place then everyone is free to benefit equally from it. However, if women are economically and socially dependent on men (or state benefits) they are not able to take advantage of formal equality in the public sphere of politics and work. It could be argued, then, that women might need more resources than men in order to participate as equals in the public sphere (Phillips, 1987). This point relates to liberalism's core reluctance to intervene in the private sphere of the family/household, which can be the primary site of women's inequality. If women cannot access or afford adequate childcare, for example, then equal opportunities at work or in training for work are of little use to them. Critics of liberal feminism have argued that for women, the public and private spheres are interdependent and that the separation between them is entirely false. Whilst most women would be unlikely to reject liberal feminism's gains, critics would argue that they don't go far enough, particularly since they function at an individual rather than a collective level. Gains have mainly benefited middle-class women operating in the public sphere and are based on the assumption that priorities in this area are universal priorities for all women. In addition, they assume that in order to be equal with men, women must accept male standards as normative and therefore operate like men. However, because liberals are generally less concerned with the private realm, no reciprocal role reversal is necessarily expected of men at home.

SUMMARY OF SECTION 3

1   Equality feminism, linked to the liberal tradition of thought, prioritizes social and legal reform – such as equal opportunity legislation – as a means of promoting equality at the individual level between women and men.

2   It seeks to minimize the differences between women and men, and those between women themselves. It accepts male standards as normative, and tends to focus on change in the public sphere.

3   Critics of liberal feminism argue that it fails to go far enough in addressing women's inequality by focusing less strongly on the domestic sphere, since, for women, the two are interdependent. Formal equality is not effective if women cannot reach the starting-line, for example if responsibility for childcare means that they cannot compete equally in the job market.

We will now move on to consider how socialist and radical perspectives within feminism have focused on gender relations in the private sphere, and on emphasizing rather than minimizing women's difference from men. However, as we shall see, it was the recognition of differences among women that shook the foundations of 'second wave' feminism during the 1980s.

4 From equality to difference

4.1 'The personal is political'

Modern feminism's second wave was a renewed social movement, part of the wide social upheavals generated at the end of the 1960s, linked to the civil rights movement and student protests across Europe and the United States. The period between the 'first-wave' struggles for suffrage (women achieved full suffrage in Britain only in 1928) and the 'second-wave' resurgence of feminism in the late 1960s is typically, although not universally, reviewed as a regressive period for women's politics. The two World Wars had enormous impact, drawing women into waged labour to an unprecedented degree, and then returning them to the home in peacetime on the back of a hugely influential ideology of domestic and familial responsibility in the service of post-war reconstruction. In 1963, however, Betty Friedan's *The Feminine Mystique* identified a 'problem with no name' for women. Although this was primarily a liberal feminist text, it highlighted the malign social and psychological effects – previously little acknowledged and therefore 'un-nameable' – of middle-class women's economic dependency on men in the home. In the second wave the domestic sphere became the focus of feminist critical debate, located – albeit differently by socialist and radical feminists – as a key site of women's oppression. The development of the Women's Liberation Movement (WLM) at this time depended significantly on thinking generated through the medium of consciousness-raising groups, where women's sharing of personal experiences across the public/private divide galvanized a new politicized collective consciousness. The slogan 'the personal is political' became the condensed representative signifier of the second wave.

Many women involved in the WLM were also active in left politics at the time and, defining themselves as Marxist or socialist feminists, were concerned with the failure of class-based politics and theory to address or explain gender

Figure 3.13 *Men minding the crèche at the first national meeting of the Women's Liberation Movement, 1970*

inequalities. Harriet Bradley highlights the theoretical difficulty, and the solution provided by socialist feminists:

> Marxist analysis tended to handle the issue of gender inequality either by seeing women as members of the exploited working class (which they are clearly all not) or as housewives contributing either directly or indirectly to capitalist profits (which again they are all not). Moreover, gender divisions were shown by comparative historical study to be characteristic of all societies, not just capitalist or even class-divided societies, and to be marked in the Soviet bloc where capitalism had been rejected. It became apparent that it was impossible to conceptualize gender adequately within the single framework of the capitalist mode of production.
>
> The solution taken by Marxist feminists was to combine an account of capitalism with an analysis of a parallel system of patriarchy. Sometimes this took the form of what was known as unified systems theory, discerning a single complex structure of capitalist patriarchy or patriarchal capitalism (Young, 1981). … However, there was a tendency in these accounts for gender issues to slide out of sight and class imperatives to come to the fore. For this reason most feminists preferred the 'dual systems' option, which conceives patriarchy and capitalism as two equivalent and analytically separable systems which, however, are always found in any concrete social context.
>
> (Bradley, 1996, pp.87–8)

Socialist feminists, then, accounted for women's inequality at the theoretical level through the systemic operation of **capitalism** and **patriarchy**, working in tandem. Given their location in relation to Marxism, socialist feminists tended to focus on women's economic inequalities, although there was a recognition that these were fundamentally linked across waged work and unpaid domestic

capitalism, patriarchy

division of labour, domestic labour

work through the unequal sexual **division of labour** which pertained in both arenas, regulated by a patriarchal state. The notion of unpaid **domestic labour** may seem a commonplace understanding now but, as Sheila Rowbotham, one of the most influential socialist feminists writing at the time, observed in reminiscence in 1989: 'I remember when it was not obvious that housework was work – hence the initial excitement created by this assertion.'

<hr>
ACTIVITY 7
<hr>

Given the conceptual underpinning of socialist feminism described above, and its focus on women's economic subordination, what areas of campaigning do you think socialist feminists would prioritize?

At the political level socialist feminist campaigns concentrated, in matters such as demands for nurseries, reproductive rights, education and skill training and against women's low pay and discrimination and harassment at work. The priority was to reduce women's inequality by restructuring society in ways that would allow them to participate in waged work on a more equal basis with men. Unlike liberals, socialist feminists advocated fundamental, revolutionary change. Academic socialist feminism produced a prodigious amount of literature supporting these arguments for change that revealed and analysed women's exploitation in particular contexts of paid and unpaid work. Ann Oakley's *Housewife* (1974) was a pioneering work which drew attention to the ways in which women's domestic unpaid work is devalued and invisible in relation to men's paid work and the influence this has on constructing women's subordination. Empirical feminist sociological research demonstrated the reproduction of women's inequality through the operation of vertical and horizontal gendered segregation at work. Arguments promoted by politicians and employers, as well as some social theorists, to justify women's concentration in part-time work in terms of 'fitting-in' with their domestic responsibilities and by their 'naturally' weaker identification with the waged workplace were called into question by the evidence that women usually had no alternative in the absence of affordable childcare. In addition, the ideological association between women and part-time work was demonstrated to reinforce its link with low pay.

The difficulty of adequately conceptualizing the relationship between gender and class inequalities, which was central to socialist feminism, was also rehearsed in the arena of mainstream sociology in relation to the large-scale national surveys conducted by John Goldthorpe and his colleagues, that were known as the Nuffield studies. These influential surveys aimed to describe the British class

aggregate data

structure in relational terms based on **employment aggregate** analyses collected over time. The controversy centred on how women's class status should be measured and included, and developed when it became clear that Goldthorpe's original scheme (1980), following previous convention, had been based solely on men with women included only as wives. Goldthorpe's approach was subject to extensive criticism (Stanworth, 1984; Crompton, 1993) on the grounds of sexist bias as it did not take account of women's increasing representation in the labour market, nor the position of single, independent women. Goldthorpe defended his position by arguing that the household was the accepted unit of class analysis and that it was therefore appropriate to 'count' class status from the position of the head of the household. He claimed that the fact that this was usually a man accurately reflected women's subordinate position with respect to the labour market and therefore took account of women's inequality rather than misrepresenting it. Eventually Goldthorpe shifted his position somewhat and later surveys were based on the position of the head of household regardless of gender, although the principle of women's inclusion as independent subjects was not acceded.

This debate took place mainly in the pages of the academic journal *Sociology*, but it did point to issues of wider interest for feminists concerning the different ways that men and women experience the lived relations of class. For example, Goldthorpe's relational scheme allocated a relatively high status to clerical work, on the basis that when men engage in this sort of work it is usually on their way 'up' to more administrative/managerial positions. One of his arguments against including women as individuals in his scheme was that the high numbers of women in clerical work would boost this status category disproportionately. This would falsely suggest increasing social mobility in the overall aggregate, because when women do clerical work it is more often as low-level, 'dead-end' jobs. Goldthorpe was proving the point that jobs have lower status when done by women and that the occupational class structure operates differently for women. He also argued, in defence of his original scheme, that women respondents usually identified themselves with their husband's occupational class position, rather than independently (Crompton, 1993). This debate illustrates the difficulties that sociologists have had in analysing women's class position and experience, not least because of uncertainties about where to start and what to count. It does, however, indicate that class identities are gendered in their construction.

In her article 'Women and class – a problematic relationship?' published in the journal *Sociological Review* in 1990, Nicola Charles provides a detailed argument about the relationship between women's class position and their subjective understandings of class, based on quantitative and qualitative analysis of interviews with 200 women. She is concerned with how classes are counted, but moves beyond this towards analysing what class means to women, how they locate themselves in relation to class identity. In this respect Charles is contributing to the feminist critique of Goldthorpe's traditional schemes of class analysis. The next reading is taken from this article but is only a small proportion of a long article. The first section presents an empirical analysis, supported by statistical evidence, linking women's subjective class classifications with variables of their own occupation, their partner's occupation, the age at which they left full-time education, and their status as 'only' housewives. The second section is Charles's article conclusion in which she relates this empirical information to more qualitative and subjective information gleaned from interviews (for which there is unfortunately not enough space here) about how women in the sample perceived themselves in relation to class.

Figure 3.14 *Women in the 1972 miners' strike showing support for the men, protesting at the Coal Board Offices in London (joined by Dennis Skinner, Labour MP for Bolsover)*

READING 3.1

Turn now to Reading 3.1, from 'Women and class – a problematic relationship?' by Nicola Charles. As you read, take particular care to ensure you understand the statistical information presented in the tables in the first half of the extract. Note down answers to the following questions when you have studied both sections of the extract:

1　How would you summarize the way in which occupational status relates to women's subjective perception of class, according to Charles' analysis?

2　What other factors (defined by Charles as 'variables') are important?

3　How does Charles characterize the relevance of her findings for the feminist critique of mainstream class analysis?

Charles's findings suggest that occupational status – both of women themselves and their partners – is only one of the factors that influences women's subjective perceptions of class. Parents' occupation is also important, so that women who feel there is a mismatch between their own background and that of their partner can find it difficult to assign their current family unit to a class. Women whose own occupations and/or those of their partners are in the higher status groupings are more likely to consider occupation to be a key marker of class. Women who have no current (paid) occupation are no less likely than those with occupations to perceive themselves in terms of class.

Other factors that were significant in women's perceptions of class were their level of education, position with respect to housing (owned or rented, and in what sort of area) and level of income with respect to consumption (what they could afford to buy). 'Needing to work' was also seen to be an important indicator of differential class.

Charles suggests that her findings have implications for the debate between mainstream class analysis and the feminist critique with respect to how women should be 'counted'. Her evidence suggests that it is not possible simply to read off women's class location from their partner's occupational position. On the other hand, it is equally problematic to classify all individuals on an independent occupational basis because this fails to take account of the effect of ties of kinship on women's perceptions of their class position.

We can see that Charles's main argument is that women's subjective experience of class should be central to comprehensive sociological class analysis, that materiality and meaning, therefore, are interconnected.

ACTIVITY 8

How would you evaluate Charles's analysis, on the basis of your reading of this chapter so far? Would you want to raise any criticisms?

It seems to me that she assumes women to be an undifferentiated category, beyond the issue of class differences. For example, we do not know if the women in the survey were all white or included women of different ethnicities; if they were all white, then their whiteness is taken-for granted, invisible. The key focus on the link – or lack of it – between women's occupations and those of their male partners, suggests that the women were all in heterosexual partnerships, so the question of single women's class identification, or the position of lesbians or widows say, remains unexamined. In a sense, it may be unfair to criticize Charles's work in this respect, since it seems likely that her research aim was restricted to making a contribution to the class/gender debate, for which the framework was already established. However, I would suggest that it is also a work of its time, and that a similar feminist research exercise conducted later in the 1990s would have specified its partiality more explicitly.

4.2 'Sisterhood is powerful'

Whilst patriarchy was seen to operate in concert with capitalism in socialist feminist understandings of women's subordination, for radical feminists of the second wave patriarchy was identified as the primary source of women's oppression. Radical feminists were interested in explaining women's oppression, solely as women rather than as workers. They therefore focused on issues of sexuality, marriage, motherhood and domestic violence against women, aspects of women's intimate experiences in the private domain. In distinction from the liberal project of constructing an androgynous society in which women would be like men and therefore equal to them, radicals affirmed women's commonality and emphasized their difference from men. The celebration of women's commonality – 'a bond which cuts across all boundaries' (Whelehan, 1995, p.87) – is invoked by the 'sisterhood is powerful' slogan, the title of an early radical feminist anthology by Robin Morgan (1970). Radical feminism prioritized politics above theorizing and sought to mobilize women at the grassroots level through consciousness-raising groups that eschewed hierarchical organization. It was a fundamentally revolutionary form of politics because of its focus on aspects of private experience which had never been seen as within the scope of politics before. In this respect it transformed understandings of what could be 'political' (Whelehan, 1995). It was therefore more controversial than liberal and socialist strands because more threatening to the status quo, particularly in its advocacy, in its most extreme forms, of women's personal and political separatism. It was this aspect of radicalism that was typically caricatured in the popular press. However, its emphasis on woman-centred culture led to the development of communes, businesses and women's festivals and its political strategies led to the establishment of rape crisis and women's aid centres and wider support networks. Radical feminism has therefore transformed the lives of many women in very real terms.

Figure 3.15 *One of the women from the Greenham Common women's peace camp, who had cut their way into the US military base, being apprehended (1984). The peace camp was a rallying point for politically active feminists and several large, women-only demonstrations took place there*

What do you think might be theoretical criticisms of radical feminism's focus on women's shared oppression under patriarchy and their fixed difference from men?

Radical feminism was criticized for assuming all women were oppressed in the same way, thereby ignoring differences between women of class, 'race', age and so on. Moreover it denied the possibility that women were ever in positions of power over other women. The idea of a fixed difference between men and women suggested an essentialized and an ahistorical notion of both femininity and masculinity which was in danger of returning both genders to a framework in which biology represented destiny, thus undermining critical feminist insights relating to the social construction of gender. However, in drawing previously hidden issues into the political domain, establishing a conceptual link between sexuality and the social control of women through violence and in foregrounding political debates about pornography and prostitution, radical feminism has been truly ground-breaking.

Figure 3.16 *Women's groups highlighted the need for, and went on to set up, refuges for women and children who were subjected to violence in the home, an issue ignored by police, government and local councils*

Turn now to Reading 3.2, which is an extract from 'Gender: rethinking patriarchy', Chapter 4 in Harriet Bradley's *Fractured Identities: Changing Patterns of Inequality*.

In this short extract Bradley reviews the relevance of three concepts – patriarchy, the sexual division of labour, and compulsory heterosexuality – which she identifies as being of the most influence in second-wave 'classic' feminist thinking and the development of a sociological account of gender.

■ As you read, make sure you understand why each concept is relevant to 'a sociological account of gender'.

■ Drawing on your understandings of the debates discussed above, as well as on Bradley's analysis, jot down your ideas on how liberal, socialist and radical feminism would differently evaluate the three concepts.

Liberal feminists would find these concepts less acceptable than either socialist or radical feminism because they imply a structural view of how society works, whereas liberals prefer an explanation based on individual liberty, protected and constrained by the rights and responsibilities of citizenship enshrined in the law. Therefore the idea of patriarchy, operating as a systematic form of oppression would not fit in their model. They would accept that a sexual division of labour might operate in the public domain because of negative stereotypical ideas about women's capacities and would seek to address this through policy reform. Sexuality – of any sort – would be located in the private realm, off-limits for liberals. For socialist feminists, patriarchy is a useful concept, explaining how women are systematically exploited under capitalism through the mutually reinforcing operation of the two systems. The sexual division of labour is central to their understanding of women's oppression, since it explains how capitalism and patriarchy work together across the interdependent public and private spheres. Sexuality is an important issue for socialist feminists who would recognize the social construction of heterosexuality as an oppressive structural force, but economic exploitation remains their key concern. Patriarchy and compulsory heterosexuality are foregrounded in the radical feminist explanation of women's oppression, concerned primarily with women's experiences in the private sphere. For them, the sexual division of labour is relevant – particularly women's unpaid work as daughters, wives and mothers – but less so than for socialists.

4.3 'Ain't I a woman?'

Radical feminism's assumption of an essentialized female identity pinpointed a key difficulty within second wave feminism generally which was its failure adequately to recognize differences among women and to incorporate theorization of difference into its political and intellectual frameworks. Alongside the three 'classic' strands of the second wave there was also a significant body of feminist work that drew on reworkings of Freudian psychoanalysis, looking to the operation of the unconscious to explain women's oppression. Juliet Mitchell (1975), for example, combined a Marxist account of economic aspects of gender inequality with a Freudian analysis of the psychic structures of oppression to explain why female subordination is so hard to eradicate in spite of feminist gains at the material level (Bradley, 1996). In addition, lesbian feminism, although often mistakenly elided with radicalism because of its focus on sexuality, has been a strong independent strand within the women's movement. Lesbians are interested in deconstructing heterosexuality, but conflating lesbian and radical feminism tends to suggest that this is their only interest, which is like assuming that socialist feminists are solely interested in women's relationship to production. So the voices of different women criticizing the mainstream movement for assuming too much sameness in women's positions and thereby excluding concerns of particular groups were already to the fore when the powerful critiques of black feminism provoked a crisis in academic and political feminism during the 1980s.

The story of Sojourner Truth, a black slave woman from Ohio, and the speech she delivered in 1852 still has powerful resonance today, in exposing the myth of sisterhood and women's undifferentiated experience of subordination:

> That man over there says that women need to be helped into carriages and lifted over ditches, and to have the best places ... and ain't I a woman? I have ploughed and planted, and gathered into barns, and no man could head me ... and ain't I a woman? I could work as much as any man (when I could get it) and bear the lash as well ... and ain't I a woman? I have born five children and seen them most sold off into slavery, and when I cried out with grief, none but Jesus heard ... and ain't I a woman?
>
> (quoted in Bhavnani and Coulson, 1986, p.83)

Figure 3.17 *Sojourner Truth*

Truth makes the point that she is no less a woman, even though her experiences of oppression have been quite different from those experienced by white women. During the 1980s black feminists went on to criticize the ethnocentric bias of mainstream feminism in which white, predominantly middle-class women's experience was the taken-for-granted normative base against which different women's experiences were judged as deviant (Lorde, 1984). The legacy of slavery and colonialism that provided the historical context of black women's feminism was unrecognized, or certainly inadequately theorized. For example, the focus in white feminism on analysing the family as a primary site of women's oppression ignored black women's experience of the family as a positive refuge against racism during slavery. Similarly 'Women's right to choose' campaigns for abortion ignored some black women's struggles against enforced sterilization. Socialist feminism's concern with the relationship between capitalism and patriarchy as the agents of exploitation failed to incorporate analysis of race. bell hooks (1987) criticized the feminist priority of gender equality in the following trenchant terms: 'If men are not equals in white supremacist, capitalist, patriarchal class structure, which men do women want to be equal to?'

Where black women's position was taken into account, there was a tendency to construct this in terms of a hierarchy of oppression which suggested that black and white women experienced sexist oppression equally, and that black women were further subjected to an additional layer of racist oppression. This understanding did not recognize that sexist oppression operated differently, depending on other aspects of identity. Harriet Bradley illustrates the point convincingly in the following scenario:

> Take, for example, the position of a twenty-year-old Afro-Caribbean woman, whose parents were manual workers, bringing up two children on her own in inner-city Birmingham, and having to choose between low-paid work as a hospital domestic and dependency on benefits. How do we start to explain her fate? Is it because of gender that she is faced with responsibilities for childcare with no help from a man and that she faces a limited range of labour market options? Or is it racism which means the only job she can find is the stereotypical 'servant' role which has historically been consigned to black women? Or is it class which has led her to leave school early with limited qualifications? Of course, it is all of these things, operating in mutual reinforcement.
>
> (Bradley, 1996, p.19)

White feminism thus tended to attribute absolute victim status to black women, weighed down by the triple oppressions of 'race', gender and class, which denied the diversity across and within different ethnicities. Whiteness itself was not recognized as an ethnicity. This was a label attached only to exploited minorities and the invisible but privileged identity of whiteness – which was the context of some women's direct exploitation of others – was taken for granted and unexamined.

Figure 3.18 *The Sari Squad picket protesting against the government's immigration policy during the Conservative party conference at Blackpool in 1983*

Pause for a moment to consider the implications that the recognition of differences and divisions between women might have for a women's political movement.

Clearly, the recognition of differences and division could threaten the notion of unity and common goals. If differences between women were so great, what could be the common agenda holding feminism as a collective movement together, politically or theoretically? Were equality and difference actually irreconcilable? Would fragmentation and polarization be inevitable? These were the challenges that feminism faced towards the end of the 1980s. The black feminist critique initiated these difficult questions; they were also reinforced by the changing context of social theory in general, and the influence of post-structuralism and post-modernism.

SUMMARY OF SECTION 4

1   Socialist feminists, in debate with traditional class analysis, explain women's inequality and exploitation through the joint power systems of capitalism and patriarchy, operating across the public and private spheres.

2   Radical feminists identify patriarchy as the primary mechanism of power in women's inequality.

3   In the 1980s black and developing world feminists posed a powerful critique of the universalism of the mainstream movement, underpinned by assumptions that all women were exploited in the same way, regardless of the significant social divisions between them.

4   The recognition of differences then became central to feminist analyses of gendered inequalities and power. This presented a theoretical challenge to the political unity of feminism.

5 From materiality to meaning

post-structuralism, post-modernism

Throughout the 1990s feminism turned towards the increasingly influential developments of **post-structuralism** and **post-modernism**. Both constitute wide-ranging areas of theoretical work, but here we are concerned only to highlight some of the ways in which feminism has engaged in dialogue with these schools of thought during the 1990s that have influenced new ways of understanding gender relations. Both schools of thought involve a 'turn to culture', thereby implying, perhaps, a turn away from material structures – hence the title of this section.

Post-structuralism offers the revolutionary idea that language has the power to *construct* our understanding of the world. Within post-structuralism, therefore, any concept – such as gender or patriarchy – is a social construct which is defined by the ways in which it can be described and iterated within language, and it cannot operate outside the limits imposed by linguistic definitions at a

point in time. Some commentators point to Foucault's concept of **discourse**   discourse
here, referring to 'a group of statements which provide a language for talking
about – i.e. a way of representing – a particular type of knowledge about a
topic' (Hall, 1992, p.291). Linked discourses construct discursive formations
which operate together to define and limit the ways in which it is possible to
understand a topic at any particular time and in any particular place. Discourses
are therefore always contingent and specific, although prevailing discourses
which achieve dominance construct a 'truth effect' whilst they remain dominant,
and are extremely powerful because they permeate all social institutions, and
the practices of groups within them. Foucault used the idea of dominant but
contingent discursive formations to challenge the absolute truth claims of modern
science, and to argue that such claims were in fact partial and specific.

Foucault was himself little interested in discourses of gender although we
can see how these ideas could provide fruitful ground for feminist analysis. For
example, conceptualizing gender as a specific and contingent discourse subject
to change over time facilitates an understanding of the reproduction of power
disparities and also the possibility of their renegotiation. A cluster of generally
accepted ideas about what constitutes appropriate femininity at a particular
moment, in effect a dominant discourse of femininity, maintains dominance
because we don't have the language to
articulate alternative possibilities outside the
established boundaries of our current
thinking. Over time, in response to the
impact of all sorts of influences, modification
in what it is possible to think and articulate
takes place, and prevailing discourses
change as a result. We could think here of
the way the typical representation of the
1950s' wife and mother – some of you may
be old enough to remember 'Katie' from the
Oxo adverts! – metamorphosed into the
many different women of today's cultural
representations. This is due to material and
economic changes but also to changes at the
cultural level of meaning, in what it is
possible to imagine, say and understand. In
fact, the cultural, discursive level is seen
within post-structuralism both to facilitate
and limit material change, rather than the
other way round. This reverses the Marxist
position in which culture is always ultimately
dependent on a material base. For example,
this kind of culturally shaped social change
is demonstrated by Table 3.7 which shows
the change between 1987 and 1994 in
attitudes towards women working.

As you will see, the shift in attitudes for
both men and women over this relatively
short time-span is significant. This suggests

Figure 3.19 *Oxo 'Katie' – the early incarnation: the bliss of
the full-time housewife cooking for her man*

Table 3.7 Attitudes towards women working, 1987 and 1994

	1987		1994	
	Women	**Men**	**Women**	**Men**
A husband's job is to earn the money; a wife's job is to look after the home and family				
Agree strongly	21	26	5	5
Agree	22	26	17	22
Neither agree nor disagree	19	19	17	16
Disagree	12	14	40	42
Disagree strongly	25	15	20	15
All	100	100	100	100
A job is all right, but what most women really want is a home and children				
Agree strongly	12	15	5	7
Agree	19	27	18	21
Neither agree nor disagree	20	23	23	25
Disagree	23	19	38	34
Disagree strongly	25	15	16	13
All	100	100	100	100

Source of data: British Social Attitudes Survey, Social and Community Planning Research
Source: EOC, 1998

that generally accepted ideas about what women should be and do – what we might call a dominant discourse of femininity – changed over this time at a cultural level. What constituted the meaning of appropriate femininity changed. Change in ways of thinking led to changes in practice – i.e. more women moved into the labour force. The key point about this model of social change is that culture has a shaping effect on material change rather than following it.

Foucault's model of discourse provides a more flexible and nuanced way of conceptualizing how power works in diffuse and multiple ways that can be productive rather than automatically repressive. Within this framework the concept of patriarchy, operating as a one-dimensional mechanism of oppressive male power, is rejected in favour of a model based on gendered power relations which are open to change, but which may also reproduce continuing inequalities. For feminists, these ideas usefully suggest how such gendered relations of power work in complex ways across institutional sites of family, work and the state, for example, and how they might change over time. The notion of dominant discourses – internalized as absolutely natural – can also explain how apparently oppressive and exploitative sets of relations can be experienced as pleasurable. However, they are less useful in explaining why, and in whose interests power works, since there is no originary source of power in Foucault's model. If power, as Foucault famously asserted, is everywhere, why do women continue to have so remarkably little of it? Isn't something more structural at work than dominant discourses resistant to change?

Patriarchy would not be valid as a concept in post-modernism because of the universalistic and ahistorical assumptions on which, arguably, it is commonly seen to be based. Like Foucault, post-modernism seeks to challenge the absolute claims of scientific knowledge that represented the key achievement of modernism. These are seen to depend on dualistic thinking in which objectivity is counterposed to subjectivity and linked to truth. Post-modernism also seeks to challenge notions of elitist expert knowledge and absolute truth, positing instead that knowledge claims are partial and dependent on the position and values of the knower. These challenges to universalist, objective knowledge and the privileging of particularity and positionality within post-modernism chime exactly with the challenge of difference within feminism promoted by the black feminist critique. Indeed, some feminists have noted that whilst post-modernists tend to claim that feminism has gained much from the insights of post-modernism, the reverse benefit is more accurately the case.

ACTIVITY 11

Can you suggest why a critique of 'dualistic thinking' (in terms of binary oppositions such as black/white, woman/man, objectivity/subjectivity) and the related argument that all knowledge is partial would appeal to feminists? Pause for a moment to write down your ideas.

Well, women have been conventionally defined in opposition to men, not just as their opposite but usually as their inferior. This is the problem of cultural binarism: one side of the relationship is typically seen as inferior to the other. Following on from that, we can consider how many pairs of binary qualities link what in western culture are taken to be less valued attributes with women and thus reinforce their inferior status. For example, women are associated with nature, men with culture; women with body, men with mind; women with emotion, men with intellect; men with objectivity, women with subjectivity and so on. Post-modernism's critique of dualism, arguing that we should think in terms of inclusive combinations rather than opposites (both/and, rather than either/or), offers more ground for changing women's relationship with negative, inferior meanings. Similarly, if all knowledge is partial, then male claims to absolute truth have no privileged status but merely reflect their own interests. However, women's truths are similarly partial – and thereby hangs the rub in the relationship between feminism and post-modernism which posits a pluralistic and relativistic model of society in which all truths are up for grabs. So whilst this facilitates the inclusion of diversity and difference that contemporary feminism seeks to integrate, its logical point of development is to suggest that no truth has more value than any other. Therefore conservative and repressive beliefs could hold equal currency with feminist challenges. A movement that is based on a principle of emancipation has necessarily to hold a position that some truths are better than others, for example that sexist oppression is wrong.

Moreover, post-modernism also challenges the notion of the unified and rational human subject, another key trope of modernist thought. Instead human subjectivity is characterized as de-centred, multiple and fluid, changing and unstable. Whilst these theories provided a framework for new feminist work on the construction of women's different contextual subjectivities, they also called into question the existence of the category 'woman' as a coherent entity and subject of feminism. So, to borrow Mike Savage's model from Chapter 2, post-structuralism and post-modernism offered a way out of the impasse in feminism at the end of the 1980s resulting from the black feminist critique, but simultaneously presented new conundrums. What could be the common aims of a social movement characterized by difference and diversity, in a social world where all truths are relative and the subject 'woman' no longer exists as a coherent entity?

During the 1990s, responding to these influences, feminist analyses tended to focus on the construction of gender relations and women's lived experiences across different sites. There was an expansion of interest across social sciences into cultural and literary studies as feminism became less the preserve of sociology in particular. This expanded remit under the umbrella of 'meaning' facilitated valuable critical work on new areas of gender analysis such as sexuality, subjectivity, representation and popular pleasures which sought to incorporate fully understandings of difference. The psychoanalytic strand established in the early second wave also expanded significantly in response to post-structuralism. What tended to fall out of focus here was the concern with material inequalities. Mary Maynard, for example, argued that 'simply to emphasize "difference" runs the risk of masking the conditions that give some forms of "difference" value and power over others' (1994, p.10). In addition, some feminists recognized that these newer theories, although possibly providing a more nuanced and sophisticated account of gender relations and power, were potentially exclusionary because of their intrinsic complexity. To quote Harriet Bradley again,

> While post-modernism has rightly pointed to differences in the experiences of working-class and minority ethnic women, there is an irony here. Current preoccupations with 'sexuality, subjectivity and textuality' may well serve to alienate these newly discovered constituencies further from middle-class feminism, as women further down the social hierarchy remain concerned with problems of poverty and over-work. Feminism would do well to recover some of its initial zeal in exposing material inequalities rather than retreating too completely into academic theoreticism.
>
> (Bradley, 1996, p.111)

SUMMARY OF SECTION 5

1   In the 1990s feminism, alongside mainstream sociology, turned towards cultural explanations of power.

2   Discourse emerged as an important theoretical concept, explaining the operation of power in terms of meaning, rather than material structures.

3   Feminism could gain from this explanation of power as socially constructed, historically specific and contingent because it meant power was always subject to resistance and change. Oppressive meanings linked to women's inequality could be open to challenge and change.

4   Some feminists were sceptical, arguing that material inequalities remained
     whilst others were diverted into academic discussions about difference
     and contested meanings.

In the final section of this chapter we are going to consider an example of
feminist work which I think aspires to Bradley's recommended aim, and which
integrates analysis of *both* materiality *and* meaning.

6 Reinstating class: materiality *and* meaning

This section is organized around another reading that is centrally concerned
with the relationship between women and social class, returning therefore to
issues of material inequalities which are sometimes eclipsed in post-modern
feminism. The reading is extracted from Beverley Skeggs' book *Formations of
Class and Gender* (1997). This is a study in the qualitative sociological tradition
based on an eleven-year ethnographic project (between 1982 and 1993) working
with a group of 83 working-class women living in a town in north-western
England. The women were initially students on caring courses in an FE college,
where Skeggs was herself a graduate student and junior lecturer, and the research
began in 1983 when they were sixteen. Skeggs – the importance of whose work
was highlighted in Chapter 2 – is fundamentally concerned with how women
experience class as a gendered identity, and with how identities are formed
through the mutual constitution of class and gender. Her research demonstrates
a thoroughgoing understanding and application of the nuanced insights of post-
modernism with respect to the construction of women's subjectivities, whilst
maintaining an absolutely clear focus on the material and cultural inequalities
of women's lives.

Skeggs deploys Bourdieu's theoretical framework of **cultural capital** (with   **cultural capital**
which you will now be familiar from your work on the previous two chapters)
to explain how the women in her study experience their interrelated identities
of class, gender and sexuality; how as subjects they are produced and produce
themselves in relation to these categories. She is not concerned, as Charles to
some extent is, with classifications between classes and simple subjective
recognition of class status, but with how the women actually experience working-
class identity on a daily basis; with what it means to them as an ever-present,
often unacknowledged, but none-the-less controlling element of surveillance
in their lives. (See **Bennett and Watson (2002)** for an extended sociological
analysis of everyday life in which the taken-for-grantedness of aspects of identity
are put under the microscope and deconstructed.)

Skeggs highlights the concept of respectability as a connecting theme for
her analysis, arguing that it constitutes a ubiquitous signifier of class, particularly
for women, who position themselves and others in relation to notions of 'being
respectable'. In terms of interpreting her research findings, Skeggs found that
respectability provided a useful analytical tool, a way of holding together
identifications of class, gender, 'race' and sexuality; that respectability was a

connecting factor which mediated all those categories. 'A respectable woman' represented the combination of these categories in particular and acceptable ways, which allowed the women to distance themselves from subject positions that they saw as socially negative.

Skeggs locates her work in terms of a commitment to reinstating class to feminist analyses, from which she claims it has 'almost disappeared, even from those claiming a materialist feminist position' (p.6). She cites claims of some feminists that the retreat from class has enabled other spheres such as the law and the state to come to the fore, but remains unconvinced:

> … it seems that the baby has been thrown out with the bath water. To abandon class as a theoretical tool does not mean it does not exist any more; only that some theorists do not value it. It does not mean that women would experience inequality any differently; rather, it would make it more difficult for them to identify and challenge the basis of the inequality which they experience.
>
> (Skeggs, 1997, p.6)

And, in explaining her personal motivation – as an academic feminist from a working-class background – for writing her book, she says:

> The writing of this book was fuelled by passion and anger. I watched 'class' analysis disappear from feminism and cultural studies as it became increasingly more of an issue for the friends I grew up with, the people I live(d) with and the women of this research. I felt caught in two worlds: one which theorized increased movement, access and playfulness and another which was regulated, circumscribed, denied and criminalized. As the differences between the two worlds widened (when fashions in postmodernism peaked) I used this book to try to make connections, to enable me to generate theory which can speak across the void, to make class matter.
>
> (Skeggs, 1997, p.15)

ACTIVITY 12

Before turning to the next reading, please look back to Chapter 1 (section 5.2) to refresh your memory with respect to Bourdieu's model of cultural capital as a framework for understanding class.

READING 3.3

Now, on the basis of this contextual introduction, turn to Reading 3.3 which is taken from Chapter 5 in Skeggs' book, '(Dis)Identifications of class: on not being working class'.

Consider the following questions as you read:

1   What does Skeggs mean when she describes class as a 'structuring absence' in the women's lived daily experience?

2   How does Skeggs use Bourdieu's theory of 'distinction' to explain the women's concerns with improvement and passing?

3   In what way does Skeggs link representations of the body with those of class?

4   How does Skeggs explain the women's social position in terms of cultural capital?

The 'structuring absence' of class refers to the women's attempts not to identify with being working class whilst simultaneously and constantly recognizing working class-ness as a controlling structure against which they try to position themselves as different. In this respect, awareness of working-class, feminine identity has a pervasive influence on their lives, whilst at they same time they attempt to resist identification with it and deny the relevance of class identity. Skeggs notes how the women sought improvement, initially through education, as a way of achieving difference and distinction in relation to others, and to appear to be other than working class. The attempts to achieve further aspects of distinction continued through their lives, with respect to their clothes, bodies and homes. The historical and popular representations of non-respectable working-class and pathologized femininity were the imaginary 'other' against which improvement and distinction could be achieved. By applying Bourdieu's model of cultural capital, Skeggs explains how the women tried to improve their tradeable assets through education, converting their caring skills into a more marketable resource.

The body is understood by the women to be extremely important because it functions to communicate their respectable feminine status to the world at large. Part of their cultural capital is vested in the skills and judgements they develop in relation to keeping fit and looking good. 'Letting go' is therefore recognized as failure in maintaining appropriate distinction which would be likely to result in loss of cultural capital, in Bourdieu's terms. Skeggs' overall argument, drawing on Bourdieu, is that these working-class women have very little economic or social capital that could be converted into symbolic capital worthy of exchange. Their key investments therefore have, of necessity, to be made at the cultural level, in particular in forms of 'respectable', heterosexual femininity which are more likely to provide positive symbolic exchange value in relation, for example, to marriage, motherhood and work. Her research delineates the complex ways in which the women negotiate the harsh material contexts of their lives at the level of identity and meaning.

In comparing Skeggs' research with the earlier work undertaken by Charles (see section 4.1) we can see that both contribute to the reinstatement of class in feminist analysis. Whilst Charles is still concerned with quantitative analysis to some extent, she also takes up the question of women's experience of class which is taken forward in Skeggs' detailed research. Both demonstrate a commitment to feminist work in which theoretical and political insight are equally important, in which materiality and meaning are given due weight, and in which therefore, as Skeggs says, the baby is not thrown out with the bath water.

SUMMARY OF SECTION 6

Skeggs' work provides an example of contemporary feminist research and analysis in which insights from earlier trends are synthesized and extended. Drawing on Bourdieu's model of power as cultural, symbolic capital, she reinstates class into feminist analysis of women's inequality, taking into account the complex ways in which the women of her research occupy culturally constructed identities.

7 Conclusion

We began this chapter with the contention that gender inequalities have been more or less erased in a 'post-feminist' developed world and that feminist politics are therefore now out-of-time, redundant. The singer and, latterly, film actor Bjork encapsulates this view neatly in her recent comment, 'My mother's generation were very much about screaming and shouting about being locked in a cage. Then the cage was eventually opened. My generation is more about ignoring it, stop moaning and get things done' (quoted in *Everywoman*, August 1995, p.10; cited in Greer, 1999, p.401). However, turning our attention to contemporary statistics (albeit restricted to Britain), we saw that although some convergence between women's and men's social positions is suggested, significant material inequalities between genders remain clear at the aggregate level, and the post-feminist world of independence and empowerment is not the context of all women's lives. The continuing entrenchment of inequalities led to the dry riposte to the notion of post-feminism from materialist feminists in the slogan emblazoned on T-shirts in the 1990s – 'I'll be a post-feminist in post-patriarchy.'

The chapter went on to explore different ways in which feminist theorists have sought to explain gender inequalities and the relationship between gender and power. The liberal feminist perspective focuses on democratic social and legal reform as a means of promoting formal gender equality. Equal opportunity legislation is now a key dimension of contemporary democratic politics, providing protection at an individual level for men and women (the Equal Opportunities Commission now receives as many claims from men as it does from women). But we saw that formal equality in the public sphere has limited impact on women in their roles as mothers and in the private sphere of the home. Women's subordination in these areas, as well as in relation to paid work, is the concern of the socialist and radical feminist perspectives in which the power systems of capitalism and patriarchy are differently analysed in accounting for gender inequality. Black and developing world feminists challenged the prioritizing of women's difference from men in the 1980s, criticizing the white, middle-class bias of mainstream feminism and its assumption of universality. They pointed to the significance of differences between women and the legacy of colonial power impacting very differently on black and white women. In the 1990s we saw a turn to cultural explanations of power in feminism, in dialogue with post-structuralism and post-modernism, and drawing particularly on the Foucauldian concept of discourse. Whilst this provided fertile ground and valuable insight for feminism, especially because power is always subject to resistance and negotiation in discourse and this opens up possibilities of change, some feminists came to think that an increasingly exclusive focus on cultural construction and difference eclipsed attention to continuing material inequalities. As Skeggs observes in explaining the motivation for her research which integrates close analysis of class inequalities with a cultural understanding of women's class identifications, 'it seemed that the baby had been thrown out with the bath water.'

7.1 And finally ...

What reflections might we have on the achievements of feminism at the beginning of the twenty-first century? Since claims for a post-feminist world of gender equality seem overstated and partial, maybe feminist theoretical explanations, as well as feminist politics, still have work to do. Certainly many women's lives have infinitely more potential for independence and autonomy than they had thirty years ago, due significantly to feminist challenges to thinking and to practice. Understandings of masculinity have also changed and some men have engaged enthusiastically in constructing more equal partnerships with women, with each other, and as pro-active, supportive fathers, as eager as some women to change constraining gender stereotypes.

However, women's autonomy remains everywhere under threat. For example, at the time of writing (January 2001) George W. Bush, in the first day of his Presidency, has directed his first legislative notification against women's abortion rights in the USA. The threat to reproductive rights remains perhaps the greatest threat to women worldwide. In addition, the contemporary focus on 'new genetics' in which a gene is pursued by scientists to account for every sort of condition and behaviour, from criminality to homosexuality, threatens to undermine feminist insights relating to social construction and return us to the idea that biology constitutes destiny. On the positive side, however, global alliances between feminists working internationally and stemming from the United Nations Fourth World Conference on Women in Beijing in 1995 have had significant beneficial effects and kept international issues relating to women at the forefront of political agendas.

In her book *Why Feminism?*, socialist feminist and academic Lynne Segal assesses the gains made by feminism over the last thirty years, and its continuing relevance today. She concludes:

Why Feminism? Because its most radical goal, both personal and collective, has yet to be realized: a world which is a better place not just for some women but for all women. In what I still call a socialist feminist vision, that would be a far better world for boys and men, as well.

(Segal, 2000, p.232)

References

Abbott, P. (2000) 'Gender' in Payne, G. (ed.) *Social Divisions*, London, Routledge.

Beauvoir, S. de (1953) *The Second Sex*, London, Jonathan Cape. First published in 1949.

Bennett, T. and Watson, D. (eds) (2002) *Understanding Everyday Life*, Oxford, Blackwell/The Open University. (Book 1 in this series.)

Bhavnani, K. and Coulson, M. (1986) 'Transforming socialist feminism: the challenge of racism', *Feminist Review*, no.23, pp.81–92.

Bradley, H. (1996) *Fractured Identities: Changing Patterns of Inequality*, Cambridge, Polity Press.

Charles, N. (1990) 'Women and class – a problematic relationship?', *Sociological Review*, vol.38, pp.43–89.

Crompton, R. (1993) *Class and Stratification: An Introduction to Current Debates,* Cambridge, Polity Press.

EOC (1998) *Social Focus on Women and Men,* Manchester, Equal Opportunities Commission.

EOC (2000) *Social Inequalities,* Manchester, Equal Opportunities Commission.

Franks, S. (1999) *Having None of It: Women, Men and the Future of Work,* London, Granta Books.

Friedan, B. (1963) *The Feminine Mystique,* London, Victor Gollancz.

Gershuny, J. (2000) *Changing Times,* Oxford, Oxford University Press.

Goldthorpe, J. (1980) *Social Mobility and Class Structure in Modern Britain,* Oxford, Clarendon Press.

Greer, G. (1999) *The Whole Woman,* London, Doubleday.

Hakim, C. (1995) 'Five feminist myths about women's employment', *British Journal of Sociology,* vol.46,no.3, pp.429–55.

Hall, S. (1992) 'The question of cultural identity' in Hall, S., Held, D. and McGrew, A. (eds) *Formations of Modernity,* Cambridge, Polity Press/The Open University.

Hemmings, S., Silva, E.B. and Thompson, K. (2002) 'Accounting for the everyday' in Bennett, T. and Watson, D. (eds) op. cit..

Hochschild, A. (1989) *The Second Shift,* New York, Viking.

Hochschild, A. (1997) *The Time Bind: When Home Becomes Work and Work Becomes Home,* New York, Metropolitan Books.

hooks, b. (1987) 'Feminism: a movement to end sexist oppression' in Phillips, A. (ed.) *Feminism and Equality,* Oxford, Blackwell.

Jamieson, L. (1998) *Intimacy,* Cambridge, Polity Press.

Lorde, A. (1984) *Sister Outsider,* Trumansburg, NY, The Crossing Press.

Marlow, J. (ed.) (2000) *Votes for Women: The Virago Book of Suffragettes,* London, Virago.

Maynard, M. (1994) '"Race", gender and the concept of "difference" in feminist thought' in Afshar, H. and Maynard, M. (eds) *The Dynamics of 'Race' and Gender: Some Feminist Interventions,* London, Taylor and Francis.

Mitchell, J. (1975) *Psychoanalysis and Feminism,* Harmondsworth, Penguin Books.

Morgan, R. (ed.) (1970) *Sisterhood is Powerful: An Anthology of Writings from the Women's Liberation Movement,* New York, Vintage Books.

Oakley, A. (1974) *Housewife,* London, Allen Lane.

ONS (2000) *Social Trends 30,* London, Office for National Statistics.

Phillips, A. (1987) *Divided Loyalties: Dilemmas of Sex and Class,* London, Virago.

Rendall, J. (1985) *The Origins of Modern Feminism: Women in Britain, France and the United States, 1780–1860,* London, Macmillan.

Rowbotham, S. (1989) *The Past is Before Us: Feminism in Action since the 1960s,* London, Pandora Press.

Segal, L. (2000) *Why Feminism?,* Cambridge, Polity Press.

Skeggs, B. (1997) *Formations of Class and Gender,* London, Sage.

Stanworth, M. (1984) 'Women and class analysis: a reply to Goldthorpe', *Sociology,* vol.18, no.2, pp.159–70.

Whelehan, I. (1995) *Modern Feminist Thought: From the Second Wave to Post-Feminism,* Edinburgh, Edinburgh University Press.

Wollstonecraft, M. (1975) *A Vindication of the Rights of Woman,* New York, Norton. First published in 1792.

Young, I. (1981) 'Beyond the happy marriage: a critique of the dual systems theory' in Sargent, L. (ed.) *Women and Revolution: The Unhappy Marriage of Marxism and Feminism,* London, Pluto Press.

Readings

3.1 Nicola Charles, 'Women and class – a problematic relationship?' (1990)

Women's subjective class

The ... area of concern ... on which I wish to focus here [is] the way in which women experience and understand class. Even though we asked only two questions specifically on class the women's responses were fascinating and throw light on the ways in which occupation and other factors are significant to women's conceptions of their own and their families' class identity.

The questions on class appeared in the context of a discussion of the women's and their partner's occupations. They were asked what social class they would say they were and why. ... [T]he women gave a wide range of responses and many reasons for assigning themselves to a specific class. In Table 1 we show the subjective class distribution of the sample.

Table 1 Subjective class of women

	Number	Percentage
Working class	80	40.0
Lower class	2	1.0
Upper working class	6	3.0
Total working class	88	44.0
In the middle	9	4.5
Lower middle class	13	6.5
Middle class	62	31.0
Total middle class	84	42.0
Other	15	7.5
Don't know	12	6.0
Missing information	1	0.5
Total:	200	100.0

As can be seen, the sample was divided almost exactly into two, one half considering themselves to be working class, the other middle class. Only 12 women were unable to place themselves in class terms at all. Although I wish to concentrate on women's perceptions of class it is perhaps useful to look at the relation between women's subjective class and the occupational class of themselves and their partners. This is shown in Tables 2 and 3.

If these tables are compared it can be seen that women's subjective class seems to be linked more closely to their partner's occupational class than to their own. This is to be expected, if Marshall *et al.*'s findings on the effect of partner's class on women's class identity, political allegiances and so on are accepted, and it indicates that men's status in occupational terms is significant for women's perceptions of their own class position (Marshall *et al.*, 1988). We are not here saying anything about whether or not a similar process occurs in the opposite direction; our data do not permit us to draw any conclusions on this.

...

In our sample there is a clear link between the age at which women left full-time education and their subjective class; this is shown in Table 4.

As can be seen, far fewer of those leaving full-time education over the age of 18 allocated themselves to the working class than did women who left school at the earliest opportunity, and the likelihood of a woman assigning herself to the middle class increases with level of education. As others have pointed out, women's level of education, their own occupation and even the occupation of their partners, are highly interrelated (Abbott and Sapsford, 1987, p.111). And, as they suggest, partner's occupational class may not operate as an independent variable but may itself be related to a woman's own level of education and occupation (Abbott and Sapsford, 1987, p.113). This indicates that women's subjective class may be as much influenced by their own background and

Table 2 Women's subjective class by own occupational class (number; and percentage in brackets)

Subjective class	Assigned class					
	I/II	IIIN	IIIM	IV/V	Student	Total
Working class	8 (19.0)	56 (53.8)	14 (48.3)	7 (41.2)	1 (50.0)	86 (44.3)
Middle class	25 (59.5)	39 (37.5)	9 (31.0)	7 (41.2)	1 (50.0)	81 (41.8)
Other	7 (16.7)	3 (2.9)	4 (13.8)	1 (5.9)	–	15 (7.7)
Don't know	2 (4.8)	6 (5.8)	2 (6.9)	2 (11.8)	–	12 (6.2)
Total	42 (100)	104 (100)	29 (100)	17 (100)	2 (100)	194 (100)

Table 3 Women's subjective class by occupational class of partner (number; and percentage in brackets)

Subjective class	Occupational class of partner						
	I/II	IIIN	IIIM	IV/V	No partner	Student	Total
Working class	14 (23.3)	10 (35.7)	47 (60.3)	14 (66.7)	2 (22.2)	–	87 (43.9)
Middle class	37 (61.7)	12 (42.9)	27 (34.6)	4 (19.0)	3 (33.3)	1 (50.0)	84 (42.4)
Other	4 (6.7)	2 (7.1)	4 (5.1)	1 (4.8)	3 (33.3)	1 (50.0)	15 (7.6)
Don't know	5 (8.3)	4 (14.3)	–	2 (9.5)	1 (11.1)	–	12 (6.1)
Total	60 (100)	28 (100)	78 (100)	21 (100)	9 (100)	2 (100)	198 (100)

Table 4 Age at which women left full-time education by subjective class (number; and percentage in brackets)

Subjective class	Age at which left full-time education						
	Minimum school leaving age		18		Over 18		All
Working class	75	(51)	9	(37.5)	4	(14.3)	88 (44.2)
Middle class	53	(36.1)	10	(41.7)	21	(75)	84 (42.2)
Other	10	(6.8)	2	(8.3)	3	(20)	15 (7.5)
Don't know	9	(6.1)	3	(12.5)	–		12 (6.0)
Total	147	(73.9)	24	(12.1)	28	(14.1)	199 (100.0)

occupation as by their partner's occupation, despite the observed link between the latter and women's subjective class.

The other two factors which seem to be important in this context are also linked to class. Owner occupation, for instance, increases as the class structure is ascended and renting decreases. This relation is true for women's and their partner's occupational class which suggests that, like education, it may not be an independent variable. As might be expected, those who live in rented accommodation are less likely to assign themselves to the middle class than are those who are owner occupiers (24.2 per

cent as compared with 46.5 per cent). There does not seem to be a significant difference between owner occupiers and those who rent in terms of assigning themselves to the working class; the figures are 42.8 per cent and 51.5 per cent respectively.

The [further] factor we have isolated is whether or not women are full-time housewives. This is important, first, because of the debate about the class status of housewives and, second, because in the women's accounts it becomes clear that a non-working wife is a sign of status which may have connotations in terms of class identity. There seemed to be little difference between women who were full-time housewives and those who were in paid employment as to their subjective class and this suggests that at least on the experiential level housewives should not be considered marginal to the class system. However, what is interesting is that women whose own occupational class was I/II were much less likely than the others to be occupied as full-time housewives. This is shown in Table 5.

There was no clear link between partner's occupational class and whether or not women were full-time housewives. This suggests that any observed relation between the status of women, in terms of whether or not they are full-time housewives, and their perceptions of class may in fact indicate a relation between women's occupational class, or, indeed, their level of education and the way class is perceived, rather than indicating a significant difference between women who are full-time housewives and those who are not. …

…

Conclusions

What emerges from this discussion is that women's occupational class is significant for the ways in which they perceive and understand class while the occupational class of their partners is significant for their allocation of themselves to a class. Secondly, it is clear that women who are full-time housewives do not feel that they are marginal to the class structure. They may be marginal to the occupational structure as it is conventionally understood, but class as is evident in the women's accounts, is not perceived solely in terms of occupation. Many factors enter into ways in which women understand and experience class and there is more than one way of perceiving class. It is from the qualitative material that these

perceptions emerged and they can be divided roughly into three groups; though it has to be stressed that none of these groups is mutually exclusive.

Thus, for one group of women occupational factors were of prime importance in understanding class, specifically the occupations of their partners, their parents and themselves. This reflects the findings of macro-studies but the qualitative material sheds light on the ways in which these factors are interrelated at the experiential level.

For women with a strong sense of their own class identity it seems to be their backgrounds and the occupations of their parents, particularly their father, which assume the most significance. Their partner's occupation can be significant, but if it is in conflict with their own background then the latter seems to be given more weight. Significantly, men's occupations seem to carry more weight than women's, both when women were talking about the class nature of their background and when they were discussing their subjective class. This emerges from our qualitative material and also confirms the quantitative findings of Marshall *et al.* (1988). The women who talk about their own class identity in this way often have difficulty in assigning their current family unit to a class because of the differences between themselves and their partners in terms of background, and/or conflict between their partner's occupation and their own background. There seems little in this sort of account to support the view that members of families necessarily share a class position, or that the current occupation of either or both partners can tell the whole story about their class identities. However, this group of women did relate class to occupation, albeit the occupations of their parents and even grandparents as well as their partners' and, less frequently, their own.

Table 5 Women's status as housewives by their occupational class (number; and percentage in brackets)

Women's status	Occupational class				
	I/II	IIIN	IIIM	IV/V	All
Housewife	15 (35.7)	66 (64.7)	19 (65.5)	14 (77.8)	114 (59.6)
Employed	18 (42.9)	28 (27.5)	9 (31.0)	4 (22.2)	59 (30.8)
Participating in informal economy	5 (11.9)	5 (4.9)	1 (3.4)	–	11 (5.7)
Other	4 (9.5)	3 (2.9)	–	–	9 (4.7)
Total	42 (21.9)	102 (53.4)	29 (15.1)	18 (9.4)	191 (100)

The second group of responses came from women who seemed to see society as divided into three groups, the rich and the poor at the extremes and everyone else in the middle. The ways in which they defined rich and poor were usually in terms of income and consumption, housing tenure being a very important factor, and there seemed to be some notion of a continuum whereby it is always possible to better yourself and move up the class structure. Class for this group was largely viewed as a function of income, the more you had, the more you were able to buy and the higher up the social scale you were. For these women class did not seem to be such a crucial part of their identity as it was for those in the first group.

A third group can also be identified who spoke about class in terms of the necessity of working. All who need to work for a living were working-class and the middle-class consisted of those who owned their own businesses. This is the view of class which links it to property relations although most of the women did not articulate it in this way. It is also a view which leads to the position that class no longer exists because everyone has to work for a living.

These different responses seemed to be related to women's occupational class. The first type of response was more likely to come from women in occupational classes I or II; the second was not class specific although a concern with housing, particularly the area in which it was located, was most likely to be voiced by women in occupational classes IV or V; the third type of response was most characteristic of women who were in occupational class IIIN, the 'intermediate' stratum. Thus these perceptions of class seem to bear a relation to women's occupational class. Additionally, partners' occupation does not seem to be significant in this context and women's level of education does. This quantitative material shows the importance of women's occupational and educational backgrounds to the ways in which they understand class and suggests that using partners' occupation only to define the class of married or cohabiting women is likely to cloud rather than clarify the processes which lead to class identity and class consciousness. On the other hand, income was more frequently included than any other factor in women's perceptions of class and did not vary with women's occupational class or any other variables looked at. Few women, even those who felt class to be irrelevant to them, were unable to place themselves in a class structure. This seems to indicate that women recognise that class structures society, although the way it impinges on an individual's life may be regarded as insignificant.

...

Women's perceptions of class therefore revolve around occupational classifications, classifications based on income and housing and classifications based on the 'need to work'. None of these systems of stratification fully describes the class relations of advanced capitalism although all bear a clear relation to it. Some of their perceptions do however bear a close relation to the way in which stratification theorists using occupational categories conceptualise class structure. Women, no less than men, perceive their society as being structured by class and themselves as occupying places within it, though these places do not necessarily coincide with those occupied by their partners. Housewives clearly do not feel themselves to be marginal to the class structure even though they may be temporarily marginal to the occupational structure of the public domain. This has implications both for 'conventional' stratification theory and for parts of the 'feminist critique'. For the former, it adds support to the argument that the class position of housewives cannot simply be read off from the occupation of their partners and suggests that women do not necessarily lose their own class identity either on marriage *or* on leaving the public world of paid employment. For the latter, it suggests that the problems of 'conventional' stratification theory cannot simply be solved by classifying all individuals on the basis of their own occupations. This, first, begs the question of the way in which housewives are to be assigned to a class and, secondly, assumes that ties of kinship have no effect on the class identity and class consciousness of the people involved. Finally, the way class is lived and understood by the women we spoke to involves many dimensions apart from their own and their partner's occupations; a consideration which may be relegated to the margins of any analysis which focuses too exclusively on the occupational dimension of class.

References

Abbott, P. and Sapsford, R. (1987) *Women and Social Class*, London, Tavistock.

Marshall G., Newby, H., Rose, D. and Vogler, C. (1988) *Social Class in Modern Britain*, London, Hutchinson Education.

Source: Charles, 1990, pp.54–6, 59–61, 83–5

3.2 Harriet Bradley, 'Gender: rethinking patriarchy' (1996)

I suggest that there is a danger of writing off the classic legacy and under-valuing its achievements. Whatever the theoretical limitations of 1970s feminism, its standpoints acted as stimuli for indispensable research into all aspects of gender relations. The liberal feminist standpoint promoted research into education and the state; socialist feminists explored the inequalities of gender in waged and domestic work; and radical thinking opened up the way to explore sexuality, and varying aspects of male violence. Without this rich basis of empirical evidence, contemporary feminism would not have been able to develop its understanding of the complexities of gendered power and its interrelation with other forms of oppression that are current preoccupations.

I want to highlight three of the key concepts of classic feminism: patriarchy, the sexual division of labour and compulsory heterosexuality. Insights gained from debates over these concepts have been vital to the development of a sociological account of gender.

Theorizing patriarchy

As has been implied, the analysis of patriarchy was in many ways the core contribution of 1970s feminism, although the concept has always been the target of critical attack. It was developed to indicate systemic arrangements which maintained male social dominance. The project of many feminist theorists, both Marxist and radical, was to develop a model of patriarchy analogous to the Marxian analysis of mode of production. Thus there were various attempts to distinguish the 'base' of patriarchy. For example, Hartmann (1981) argued that it lay in male control of female labour power, while Firestone (1971) considered that patriarchy arose from men's control of reproductive arrangements. Delphy (1977), taking domestic labour as central, suggested the alternative conception of two coexisting modes of production: the capitalist mode in which capital exploits the labour of the working class and the domestic mode of production in which men exploit the unpaid labour of women. The influence of Marxism is clear in all these versions. Sylvia Walby (1990) moved further away from the strict attempt to replicate the base/superstructure model of Marxism with her conceptualization of patriarchy which she defined as

'a system of social structures and practices in which men dominate, oppress and exploit women' (1990, p.20). She isolates six types of structure: paid work, domestic labour, sexuality, the state, violence and culture.

However, many feminists were unhappy with the concept, arguing that it tended to imply that *all* historical periods were characterized by male domination. Rowbotham's well-known critique (1981) is typical. She argued that the concept was too universalistic and ahistorical; it could not encompass variations in the balance of power between the sexes in different societies nor the different ways that power was exercised. The framework of patriarchy rules out the possibility of types of society where women and men are equal, or even where women are dominant.

One response was to explore historically exactly how and to what extent male power was exercised in various social contexts. Barrett suggested that the adjective 'patriarchal' should only be used to describe concrete historical instances in which 'male domination is expressed through the power of the father over women and over younger men' (Barrett, 1980, p.250). Walby, in a series of publications (1990, 1992, 1993), has developed an account of a move from 'private patriarchy' (that is, the control of women by individual men within the household) to 'public patriarchy', where women are subordinated in the public sphere (especially at work and within the state) by structures of segregation:

> In public patriarchy, women are not confined to the household and the mode of expropriation is more collective than individual, for instance, by most women being paid less than men. In private patriarchy the main patriarchal strategy is exclusionary, and women are not allowed into certain social arenas, such as Parliament, while in public patriarchy women are allowed in, but segregated and subordinated there.
>
> (Walby, 1993, pp.87–8)

While such accounts emphasize the variability of power relations, other problems with the concept are less easily solved, and have been highlighted by postmodernist critiques of classic feminism. Postmodernists see patriarchy as an inadequate way to conceptualize gendered power. It is a zero-sum concept: that is, it suggests that all the power rests with men, none with women. Contemporary feminists reject the portrayal of women as passive victims of male power. Recent conceptualizations emphasize the complexity of power relations between women and men, pointing out that some women are in positions of power over other women, and indeed, over men (for example, women of the aristocratic and bourgeois classes who employ servants of both sexes, or female employers and managers).

Despite these criticisms, feminists have been reluctant to abandon the term altogether. In part this is due to its important place in the history of second-wave feminist political campaigning: it has come to be a symbolic marker of a feminist position. It is a theoretical tool which feminist theorists have claimed and developed themselves, by contrast to, for example, the ideas of postmodern feminism, which has borrowed extensively from male writers such as Foucault and Derrida who have little specific interest in gender analysis. For these reasons many feminists continue to use the term. One strategy is to use it adjectivally ('patriarchal ideologies', 'patriarchal practices'), rather than as a noun with the implications of adherence to a system approach. The use of system theories has … been criticized … for the way it inevitably carries exclusions. But I see it as legitimate to speak of 'patriarchal relations' in reference to the gender differences which are the topic of this chapter.

The sexual division of labour

Those chary of the term patriarchy have preferred to use the alternative term 'sexual division of labour'. This term has proved acceptable to all feminist standpoints and is also the object of much current research within the social sciences under the influence of feminist analysis.

Initial explorations of the sexual division of labour in paid work drew on ideas from existing sociological theories. For example, Marxists took up the idea that women were part of the reserve army of labour drawn in and out of the labour force according to capitalist needs, although study of trends in unemployment suggested that, while possibly true in some historical periods, this did not fit women's labour market experience in the post-war decades: men have lost jobs rather than women in recent recession. Alternatively Humphries (1983) suggested that women, because they are used as cheap labour, constituted an 'ideal proletariat', a position that was criticized because of the history of collusions between employers and organized male workers to keep women out of 'men's jobs' (Hartmann, 1976; Bradley, 1989). Humphries's arguments about 'female proletarianization', however, merit reconsideration in the 1990s with the advance of women into the work-force. Beechey (1977) drew on the Marxian theory of value to suggest *why* female labour was cheaper, arguing that because women were habitually dependent on fathers and husbands the cost of the reproduction of their labour power was literally less; they could be paid a wage below what was considered necessary for male subsistence. An alternative to these and other Marxist formulations was to employ the Weberian framework of dual or segmented labour markets; this posits that the labour market is split into segments, between which it is difficult for workers to move, because of employers' requirements for different types of labour. Women can be seen to occupy secondary segments in the market, characterized by low pay, tight control, poor conditions and lack of opportunities. Workers in the secondary sector who can easily be hired and fired serve employers' need for flexibility, while they also rely on the stable commitment of a core of privileged primary workers, usually male and white.

While these approaches offer insights on employers' deployment of women, all slot women into pre-existing analyses of class, ignoring the gender dynamics which make such discriminatory practices possible. None of the theories is adequately able to explain why and how the sexes were segregated at work or account for the persistence of segregated structures (although dual labour market theory comes closest to doing so). The notion of gender segregation, both horizontal (the clustering of women and men in different sex-typed jobs and occupations) and vertical (the concentration of men in top grades in each occupation), became the central concern. Various factors were seen to contribute to the formation and maintenance of segregated structures: employers' motivations and attitudes; patriarchal and paternalist controls which treated women employees differently from men; the exclusionary policies and practices of trade unions and professional associations; ideologies or discourses of masculinity and femininity; work cultures which promoted preferences for same-sex workmates; sexual harassment which served to police the boundaries between men's and women's jobs (see, for example, Spencer and Podmore, 1987; Bradley, 1989; Witz, 1992). Cynthia Cockburn's studies (1983, 1985, 1991) have demonstrated the subtle processes through which jobs and workplaces become gendered. She highlights the role of technology and the way in which the association of men with technical competence serves to maintain gender hierarchies. Her research documents the resistance of men to the breakdown of segregation.

The domestic division of labour has also received much attention, starting with the pioneering studies of 'housework' by Oakley and others (Oakley, 1974; Hunt, 1980). Despite claims that marriages are becoming more symmetrical and domestic tasks being shared more equally, surveys persistently reveal that women still take the major share of housework and childcare even where both partners work (Martin and Roberts, 1984; Morris, 1990; Jowell *et al.*, 1992). Where the labour is displaced on to paid helpers, such cleaners, childminders and nannies are inevitably female. In this way the idea of women's responsibility for domestic labour persists and with it the view of women as 'naturally' orientated towards domestic life and motherhood (Crowley, 1992). More recent research indicates that, especially with the rise in male unemployment, many couples are beginning to renegotiate the domestic division of labour, with men taking more part (Wheelock, 1990; Morris, 1990; Brannen and Moss, 1991). But men remain selective in the tasks they undertake, and the ultimate responsibility remains with mothers. Child-rearing responsibilities are still a major reason for women's restricted labour market opportunities.

The many studies of the sexual division of labour reveal the extent and strength of gender segregation in contemporary societies. While feminist research has recently shifted towards the exploration of cultural aspects of gender, these studies remain the basis of our understanding of gender as a form of inequality.

Compulsory heterosexuality

While *all* classic feminist thinking encouraged a critical approach to long-standing notions of the public and the private spheres and sought to bridge the analytical gap between them, the radical standpoint in particular was the base for delving into personal relationships. The traditional view of the family, marriage and romance was that these were areas of freedom and individual fulfilment, set apart from the constraints of economic and public life (Zaretsky, 1976; Lasch, 1977). Feminists challenged this view, suggesting that marriage was an unequal contract in which women were trapped (Comer, 1974). Bernard (1976) suggested that men rather than women benefited from marriage, while wives suffered from the frustrations and isolation associated with the housewife role. The espousal of romantic ideals by

young unmarried women was shown to draw them into [the] same trap as their mothers (McRobbie, 1978; Westwood, 1984). In this way marriage and love were portrayed as social, not natural, institutions which served to further patriarchal dominance.

From this standpoint feminists were able to attack the view of emotions and sexual orientations as natural and given. In a famous essay 'Compulsory heterosexuality and lesbian existence' Adrienne Rich (1980) argued against the view that individuals were endowed with a fixed sexual identity. Rather, she claimed, heterosexual and homosexual desires and practices should be seen as points on a continuum of sexual behaviours.

Feminism divorces sexual behaviour from biological dimorphism, and suggests that individuals are potentially bisexual and androgynous; heterosexuality is so prevalent merely because it is socially constructed and learned as the norm of sexual behaviour. Those who reject the rules of 'compulsory sexuality' are liable to be stigmatized as abnormal, 'queer' and sick. However, those who accept the conventional version of sexuality also suffer, since their potential for exploring and expressing their individual sexuality in a variety of ways is suppressed. Rich laments the loss of the rich possibilities of warmer, more intimate bonds between women through such processes. Also, since the prevailing or 'hegemonic' version of male heterosexuality (Connell, 1987) encourages predatory, aggressive and sometimes violent sexual behaviour, the ideal of the male stud 'putting it about', compulsory hetero-sexuality contributes to the maintenance of male dominance.

Recent approaches to sexuality have emphasized the variety of straight, gay, lesbian and transsexual identities on offer, speaking in terms of 'heterosexualities' and 'homosexualities' rather than one prevailing sexual code. Moreover postmodern feminism is concerned to emphasize the pleasures and desires that can be enjoyed within sexuality even by women who accept the heterosexual norm unquestioningly. Nonetheless, the work of Rich and others speaking from the radical standpoint opened up the exploration of the way sexualities are socially constructed. The notion of 'compulsory hetero-sexuality' is still a very important insight into how we view sexual behaviour and the way some forms of sexual behaviour are accepted and others condemned. In such ways, classic feminist analysis laid the foundations for an understanding of gendered subjectivity.

References

Barrett, M. (1980) *Women's Oppression Today: Problems in Marxist Feminist Analysis*, London, Verso.

Beechey, V. (1977) 'Some notes on female wage labour in capitalist production', *Capital and Class*, no.3, pp.45–66.

Bernard, J. (1976) *The Future of Marriage*, Harmondsworth, Penguin Books.

Bradley, H. (1989) *Men's Work, Women's Work*, Cambridge, Polity Press.

Brannen, J. and Moss, P. (1991) *Managing Mothers*, London, Unwin Hyman.

Cockburn, C. (1983) *Brothers*, London, Pluto Press.

Cockburn, C. (1985) *Machinery of Dominance*, London, Pluto Press.

Cockburn, C. (1991) *In the Way of Women*, London, Macmillan.

Comer, L. (1974) *Wedlocked Women*, Leeds, Feminist Books.

Connell, R. (1987) *Gender and Power*, Cambridge, Polity Press.

Crowley, H. (1992) 'Women and the domestic sphere' in Bocock, R. and Thompson, K. (eds), *Social and Cultural Forms of Modernity*, Cambridge, Polity Press/The Open University.

Delphy, C. (1977) *The Main Enemy*, London, Women's Research and Resources Centre.

Firestone, S. (1971) *The Dialectic of Sex*, London, Jonathan Cape.

Hartmann, H. (1976) 'Patriarchy, capitalism and job segregation by sex', *Signs*, vol.1, no.3, pp.137–68.

Hartmann, H. (1981) 'The unhappy marriage of Marxism and feminism: towards a more progressive union' in Sargent, L. (ed.) *Women and Revolution: The Unhappy Marriage of Feminism and Marxism*, London, Pluto.

Humphries, J. (1983) 'The emancipation of women in the 1970s and 1980s', *Capital and Class*, no.20, pp.6–27.

Hunt, P. (1980) *Gender and Class Consciousness*, London, Macmillan.

Jowell, R., Brook, L., Prior, G., and Taylor, B. (eds) (1992) *British Social Attitudes: The Ninth Report*, Aldershot, Dartmouth Publishing.

Lasch, C. (1977) *Haven in a Heartless World*, New York, Basic Books.

McRobbie, A. (1978) 'Working class girls and the culture of femininity' in Women's Studies Group (eds) *Women Take Issue*, London, Hutchinson.

Martin, H. and Roberts, C. (1984) *Women and Employment: A Lifetime Perspective*, London, HMSO.

Morris, L. (1990) *The Workings of the Household*, Cambridge, Polity Press.

Oakley, A. (1974) *The Sociology of Housework*, Oxford, Martin Robertson.

Rich, A. (1980) 'Compulsory heterosexuality and lesbian existence', *Signs*, vol.5, no.4, pp.631–90.

Rowbotham, S. (1981) 'The trouble with "patriarchy"' in Feminist Anthology Collective (eds) *No Turning Back*, London, The Women's Press.

Spencer, A. and Podmore, D. (1987) *In a Man's World*, London, Tavistock.

Walby, S. (1990) *Theorising Patriarchy*, Oxford, Blackwell.

Walby, S. (1992) 'Post-modernism? Theorising social complexity' in Barrett, M. and Phillips, A. (eds) *Destabilising Theory*, Cambridge, Polity Press.

Walby, S. (1993) '*Backlash* in historical context' in Kennedy, M., Lubelska, C. and Walsh, V. (eds) *Making Connections*, London, Taylor and Francis.

Westwood, S. (1984) *All Day, Every Day*, London, Pluto Press.

Wheelock, J. (1990) *Husbands at Home*, London, Routledge.

Witz, A. (1992) *Professions and Patriarchy*, London, Routledge.

Zaretsky, E. (1976) *Capitalism, The Family and Personal Life*, London, Pluto Press.

Source: Bradley, 1996, pp.92–96

Beverley Skeggs, '(Dis)Identifications of class: on not being working class' (1997)

Class is a communist concept. It groups people as bundles and sets them against one another.

(Margaret Thatcher, *Guardian*,
22 April 1992)

Why do they take their class position so personally?

(Sennett and Cobb, 1977)

Class was central to the young women's subjectivities. It was not spoken of in the traditional sense of recognition – I am working class – but rather, was displayed in their multitudinous efforts *not to be* recognized as working class. They disidentified and they dissimulated. Theirs was a refusal of recognition rather than a claim for the right to be recognized. It was a denial of the representations of their positioning. This should not surprise us, for … the label working class when applied to women has been used to signify all that is dirty, dangerous and without value. In the women's claims for a caring/respectable/responsible personality, class was rarely directly figured but was constantly present. It was the structuring absence. Yet whilst they made enormous efforts to distance themselves from the label of working class, their class position (alongside the other social positions of gender, race and sexuality), was the omnipresent underpinning which informed and circumscribed their ability *to be*. This is a chapter about that relationship between positioning and identity. It is about the experience of class. Class operated in a dialogic manner: in every judgement of themselves a measurement was made against others. In this process the designated 'other' (based on representations and imaginings of the respectable and judgemental middle class) was constructed as the standard to/from which they measured themselves. The classifying of themselves depended upon the classifying systems of others.

Class is experienced by the women as exclusion. Whereas working-class men can use class as a positive source of identity, a way of including themselves in a positively valorized social category (Willis, 1977), this does not apply for working-class women. Warde (1994) asks if class in general ought to be defined by exclusion and deprivation, rather than by trying to locate attributes such as occupation and education which are shared by all class members. It is deprivations that persist over time even when actual occupations change or household composition alters. The exclusions occur because the women do not have *access* to economic resources and cultural ways to be anything other than working class. Their structural positioning does not enable access to productive resources. As this chapter will demonstrate they do not have any of the requisite capitals … to be middle class. The recent retreat from the study of class has been enacted by those who do have the requisite access and are claiming that their privilege is not an issue. However, access to knowledge is a central feature of class reproduction and it is very clear that those who want to dismiss class as a redundant concept want to abdicate responsibility from the relations of inequality in which they and the women of this study are very differently positioned. Class is absolutely central to how these women live their lives, exemplified in this chapter by their constant refusal to be fixed or measured by it.

The purpose of this chapter is to reinstate class back into feminist theory by showing how class informs the production of subjectivity. This is not just an analysis of subjective construction but an examination of how inequalities are consolidated, reproduced and lived as power relations. Class is primarily about inequality and exploitation. This chapter is divided into two sections. Drawing on the ethnography, the first section explores how the women articulate class, how it is informed by representation and how they are positioned by and position themselves in relation to class. The second section examines how the women lived class on a daily basis, analysing how they constructed their subjectivities through class-informed performances. It explores how attempts to escape class identifications through discourses of improvement and strategies of passing rarely succeed because of their lack of power to convert cultural capital into symbolic capital. Overall, it is a study of how social and cultural positioning generated denial, disidentification and dissimulation rather than adjustment. It is a study of doubt, insecurity and unease: the emotional politics of class.

Disidentifications

To me if you are working class it basically means that you are poor. That you have nothing. You know, nothing. [Sam, 1992]

The real working class are the ones you see hanging round the dole. They're dead scruffy and poor and they haven't a job but I guess they may be working if they are working class, they may be working. If they're working class they should be working so they work, I guess, in all the bad jobs. [Sheenah, 1992]

They're rough. You can always tell. Rough, you know, the women are common as muck you know, always have a fag in their mouths, the men are dead rough. You know. [Andrea, 1992]

Just poor, trying to get by on very little, it's not their fault there's no jobs anymore, they're the ones who are struggling. [Michelle, 1992]

The ones who batter their kids. [Pam, 1992]

It used to be you were working class if you worked in the railways say and it didn't mean you had no money, but now it's changed. Now it means that you don't work, like it's not those with the good jobs now it's those without jobs, they're the real working-class. [Lisa, 1992]

No doubt Thatcherism has informed this slippage from working to under-class and has influenced the construction of distinctions within the working class. The real working class for these women is something from which they are desperately trying to escape. It is why they are doing college courses. They want to be seen as different. …

…

Talking about class, however, is somewhat different from living it. Class connotations may be ubiquitous but they are rarely directly spoken by those who do not want to be reminded of their social positioning in relation to it. Class identifications were rare in the course of the research. As Berger (1980) notes, the identification 'I am' is more than a statement of immediate fact: it is already biographical. 'I am not' is similarly loaded. The following comments begin to chart the processes by which (dis)identification occurs:

Well I think I'm working class and I'll tell you why, it's because my mum has always had to work for a living. She really struggles to keep us well fed and clothed. Now I work in a garage at nights and the weekend to pay my way. She said she'd support me through college but I think she's supported us enough. She's worked herself to death. We must be working class. [June, 1983]

and later:

No, I don't think I'm working class at all now. Not after we bought the house and that … I expect I'm now middle class … but it's like when we go to Dave's business dos, but I don't really feel like some of them, you know the real bosses' wives with all their talk and that. I sometimes feel really frightened to speak in case I show him up. I expect they're really middle class so I'm not really like them, but I'm not like the rest of our family without two pennies to rub together. You know, I just don't think class is a very useful term. I think I'm probably classless. You know I'm not really one nor the other. I don't really fit. [June, 1989]

These two differently dated comments from June illustrate how she draws on her prior knowledge to make sense of class. The key to her first definition is work and struggle. She is primarily dependent upon her mother and so defines herself through her mother's labour. In the second comment there is a shift to ownership and labour is absent. As in the earlier comments poverty is *the* sign of working-classness and she is not poor. June is computing her class knowledge by the measurement of her difference from and similarity to others. She realizes that she is not like those who can speak in a different way. She is different from both and she has run out of defining features. Therefore for her the concept is redundant. Refusal and denial generate disidentification for Anita:

I think it's just daft trying to fit people into pigeonholes. They say because you live on a council estate that you must be working class. I remember all the stuff we did at college. But loads of people own their own houses and just because they're on council estates it doesn't make any difference. They own them. They're theirs. My mum and dad own their house now and even though my dad's unemployed now it still doesn't make him working class. He's going to set up his own business anyway he says. So they can't be working class. It's just a load of rubbish. [Anita, 1989]

Anita, who still lives with her parents, has a clear image of what it means to be working class. For her it is defined by house ownership and employment.[1] The knowledge she draws upon comes from academic representations, from lessons at college. Anita is adamant to resist the classifications she knows; she does not want to position herself where she can be measured in relation to others. Her comments show a clear awareness of the negative values associated with the working class. They also show that she knows that certain features of her family background would allocate her to the working class. She believes that ownership has superseded locality as the measure of class. (It should be remembered that this comment was made after 10 years of Thatcherism in Britain in which the government sold council houses with a long and strong ideological campaign to eradicate class as a social category but not as a social division.) Anita's vehement denial stands in opposition to the rare embrace of a class identity by Nicky:

> Yes. I'm working class and I'm proud of it. All the girls at work are. You'd have to be at our place the money we get paid. I can't bear those snobs who think they're better than you just 'cos they've got new windows and that. It looks stupid. They just don't want to own up to it. They're the same as us. They're bloody traitors, they're just snobs, that's what they are. [Nicky, 1989]

Nicky's local culture enables her to define herself with her workmates. She also uses economic criteria. She works as a care assistant at an EPH [Elderly People's Home]. As with the others she defines herself against an imaginary other – one signified here through windows (new windows were frequently put in place by those who had bought their council houses and wanted to signal that they were owners, hence different) – who make obvious attempts to construct their difference against people like Nicky.[2] Nicky's class politics are part of a larger historical internal working-class critique about those who appear to be buying out of their class (foreman rather than windows used to be the signifier). It is employment experience and economic criteria which have changed Angela's mind on her class position. Her first comment is made while she is still at college without responsibility:

> Well my dad, he's got his own window cleaning business with his brother and he's always got plenty of money, not just for himself but for us as well. My mum earns good money as well. If I see something I just go and tap him. He's as soft as shite. He'd give us owt. So, we've got plenty of money and that so we're middle class. [Angela, 1983]

Her second comment made six years later illustrates her changed position. She now has two children to support on her own. Her father's business collapsed and her mother lost her job at the local chemical plant:

> I never wanted to think I was working class, but there was this programme on recently and it made me think about it. Look I've got £77 coming in a week and £79 goes out. I can't pay off the poll tax, water and rent arrears. It can't go out if it doesn't come in. I had to see a solicitor for the debts that I run up when I had Jenna. The bailiffs were over last week. I have to buy things for the baby. I had nothing. So they took me to court and gave me seven days to pay. It was for about £500 but with the interest it flayed up to £1500. Well how could I pay so they sent them round. I haven't got nothing worth £1,000. Everything is second hand. So I said to him I've got no carpets in the kids' bedrooms and no wallpaper on the wall. The next door neighbour phoned the police. I don't have a phone no more. I know my rights. So, really what all this is about, why I'm telling you this, is it's stupid to think I'm not working class. I can't be anything else no matter how much hoity toity I put on. [Angela, 1989]

It is a television programme that instigates Angela's re-analysis of her economic situation. It speaks to her about her life. She evaluates herself in relation to the conditions in which she now finds herself. For her the cultural level of displaying class – being hoity toity – is minimal in relation to the economic conditions she endures on a daily basis. She cannot escape the fit between the representation and her life. June, Anita, Nicky and Angela all assessed themselves on the basis of their current position and all understood their background and economic circumstances through cultural discourses of classification. Charles (1990) found a similar diversity of factors for understanding and experiencing class by the women she researched. These understandings were not straightforward, they drew on fragmented understandings of popular representations of class.

Classificatory positions

…

It was a lot easier to identify the young women by what they were not. They were not middle class as defined culturally and economically (see Savage *et al.*, 1992). They were unlikely to pursue higher education;[3] their access to primary labour market jobs was severely limited;[4] their cultural knowledge and preferences were distinctly not high culture. Their leisure activities and consumption practices do not compare to Savage *et al.*'s (1992) descriptions of the middle classes. They were never in a position to disregard money, which Lamont (1992) and Bourdieu (1986) define as a major feature of the upper middle classes. They were never in a position to construct distance from necessity, which Bourdieu (1986) defines as a means of constructing distinctions. This difficulty of an accurate definition parallels with their difficulty in describing themselves as working class.

Class positions and class identity, however, are not the same. The young women had a clear knowledge about their 'place' but they were always trying to leave it. Bourdieu (1987) argues that the dispositions acquired as a result of social positioning in social space means that the occupant of a position makes adjustments to it: the sense of one's place must always be a sense of the place of others (Goffman, 1959). But what Bourdieu does not account for is the processes by which the adjustment is either made *or* resisted. Adjustment may not happen. There may not be a fit between positions and dispositions (McCall, 1992). When there is no legitimacy for a position – such as the White working-class sexualized women – therefore no symbolic capital – there may be no adjustment. They cannot adjust themselves to being in that category. This became apparent when exploring how the women constantly emphasized their movement from the category of working class through improvement.

Improving and passing

The first time I had heard such emphasis being put on improving was when I interviewed the mothers, many of whom were concerned that their daughters should improve upon their lives. Improvement is a means by which cultural capital comes to take on greater value outside of the local. It is when it can be traded in a wider context. Education was the means by which they could convert their caring capital into an economic resource in the labour market; the use of femininity was the means by which they could try and secure future resources through the marriage market. Improving narratives came to take on a greater significance through the course of the research. They related to many aspects of their lives and were always based on generating, accruing and/or displaying cultural capital. They wanted to and/or were involved in improving their appearance; their bodies; their minds; their flats/houses; their relationships; their future. Class was configured through the improvement discourse because in order to improve they had to differentiate themselves from those who did not or could not improve. They were continually making comparisons between themselves and others, creating distances and establishing distinctions and tastes in the process. As Bourdieu (1986) argues, distinctions constantly proliferate. The women had a strong sense of what they did not want to be, but were less sure of what they wanted to be. The knowledge available to them to enable them to resist being classified as working class was based on media and educational representations and limited contact with middle-class people. The middle-class people they met were usually in positions of authority (such as teachers, doctors and social workers). As Press (1991) notes from her research, the working-class women she interviewed learnt about middle-class lifestyles predominantly from television. Their desires not to be seen as working class are lived through their bodies, clothes and (if not living with parents) their homes.

The body and bodily dispositions carry the markers of social class. As Bourdieu (1986) notes the body is the most indisputable materialization of class tastes. Bodies are the physical sites where the relations of class, gender, race, sexuality and age come together and are em-bodied and practised. A respectable body is White, desexualized, hetero-feminine and usually middle class. Class is always coded through bodily dispositions: the body is the most ubiquitous signifier of class. The demands of femininity are such that ideal femininity requires a radical bodily transformation at which virtually every woman is bound to fail, adding shame to her deficiency (Bartky, 1990). When compounded with class, sexuality and race an enormous amount of regulation is faced. This is apparent in the women's comments about the fears presented to them through the bodies of the others that they don't want to be.

Relinquishing regulation and responsibility for bodies (they call it 'letting go') was a dominant theme in their distancing tactics:

> You know you see them walking round town, dead fat, greasy hair, smelly clothes, dirty kids, you know the type, crimplene

trousers and all, they just don't care no more, I'd never be like that. [Therese, 1983]

This is not dissimilar to dominant representations of working-class women documented by Rowe (1995) … Therese wants to display her distance from them, as does Marie:

> A woman down our way looks just like that, we call her Hilda[5] 'cos of the way she goes on, well her hubby left her and she was dead upset and surprised tell you surprised, I wasn't surprised, I wasn't surprised, I wouldn't be at all surprised if I looked like her and he walked out on me. [Marie, 1993]

The duty and obligation to take care of appearances for heterosexual relationships, as documented by Holland *et al.* (1991) takes on specific class and – by their absence – race manifestations:

> I like to keep fit. I think it's important to look after yourself. If you walk around looking all fat and scruffy people will think that you just don't care about anything, about yourself or about others. I mean how can you care about anything if you're prepared to let your body go to waste. [Wendy, 1989]

For Wendy the body is the carrier of class signals, of how she sees herself and wants to be seen. It is the external signal that tells others that she cares. … [T]hey function as descriptors of self. Wendy's body is a marked body, marked by class (and youth; these comments were made from the confidence of youthful bodies, when they were 16):

> We all go down to [X: the local sports centre] and do aerobics. It's a real laugh. We spend all night there. There's some women there though you wouldn't believe. They're huge. It takes them all their time to move from one position to the other. [Julie, 1983]

> Yea, they're always out of time, it's dead funny. They go bright red. Not just red; I mean bright red and by the end and they're all huffing and puffing. [Darren, 1983]

> It's dead sad really like if they'd have gone to aerobics in the first place it would be easy and they'd have never have ended up in that state. Your body's the only thing you've got that's really yours. They can even take the clothes off your back but your body it's there all the time. It's yours

and you have to take care of it. [Julie, 1983]

These comments suggest that these women do see and invest in their bodies as a form of cultural capital. It is the means by which they can tell others who they are. Julie pertinently points to the possessive relationship she has to her body; it is seen to be owned and invested in by the person who inhabits it. They regulate their bodies to make sure that they cannot be seen to be one who does not or cannot care. Fat signifies immovability; social mobility, they maintain, is less likely in a fat body … The working-class body which is signalled through fat is the one that has given up the hope of ever 'improving', of becoming middle class. It is the body which is recognized for what it is: a working-class body that is beyond the regulation and discipline required to be part of social and cultural exchanges. Historically, Bourke (1994) notes, the white working-class body did actually look significantly different from the middle-class body because it was shorter and less healthy. It still is less healthy and less likely to live as long; whilst the obvious differences have decreased, bodies still send off signals about class (see the Black Report 1982, Benzevale *et al.*, 1995; Joseph Rowntree Foundation, 1995). Bourdieu (1986) argues that bodily dimensions (volume, height, weight), bodily shapes (round or square, stiff or supple, straight or curved) and bodily forms (expressed through treating it, caring for it, feeding it, and maintaining it) reveal the deepest dispositions of class, gender and race. The texts of class, femininity, sexuality and race combine to produce a respectable body. It is one that is taken care of. It is the care of the self for the self and for others, a technology of individual domination of how an individual acts upon themselves in the technology of the self (Foucault, 1988). But also of how one deflects classification and deters the flow of cultural capital from the body.

The surface of their bodies is the site upon which distinctions can be drawn. Skills and labour such as dressing-up and making-up are used to display the desire to pass as not working class. Armstrong and Tennenhouse (1987) note how bourgeois women's desire was historically always coded (through dress, literature and visual arts) with respectability. Class is signified through elegance and sophistication which demonstrate a dissimulation from the working class but a simulation of the middle class. The fantasy of the 'other' (the middle-class, elegant sophisticate) becomes part of the construction of one's self. For instance, Mary makes clear distinctions between herself and other women and directly claims to be respectable. These are the ways in which class is spoken:

MARY: I do get dressed up, I get dressed up, I call it getting tarted up but I'm not tarty. Karen will ring up and say 'are you getting tarted up tonight?' I'm aware that I can't wear certain things that are too tarty say mini-skirts, they're tarty. I just can't wear them, they don't do anything for me, they don't suit me. They're not me, they're not my character, they're not me, they're … I wear classy clothes. I don't want to sound snobby but I like classical dresses, things that don't go out of fashion. I expect them to last five years. People comment on it all the time. John actually commented on it at my party. I had a long red skirt and a blouse and he said 'you look exquisitely elegant, you look totally different'. There was a girl here in a mini-skirt and a tight top and all the men were eyeing her and I said I should have worn my mini and boob tube to him and he says no, you're elegant … I like to look good, I like to have things no one else round here will ever have. I spend less money now that I've got the house, now I buy a dress for £70 or so every six months. It's better than £20 on a mini-skirt every month.

BEV: What's the image?

MARY: I don't know I've always wanted to be different. You see them round here with all the same clothes. My clothing says I'm different. I think my clothing says I'm respectable. I probably do it without thinking. I'm not aware of it, half the time if I throw on a pair of trousers and a blouse it works … Then I saw a girl I hadn't seen for ages and she said you look really elegant. (1991)

Mary clearly constructs herself as different, as respectable. This is validated through the responses given by others (and in this case not imaginary middle-class others) who help to validate Mary's difference. (I specifically don't use the term legitimate as her friends do not possess the symbolic power to legitimate her cultural capital; the validation is local.) Clothing is used by Mary as a vocabulary which conveys moral quality. …

…

Conclusion

By insisting on the centrality of class to the lives of the women I am trying to claim and legitimate one important aspect of their experience which they consciously try to disclaim. Even though they dissimulate from class, their dissimulations are reproduced through it. In so doing I want to suggest that class is not just a representation, nor a subject position which can be taken off a discursive shelf and worn at will or a social position which can be occupied voluntarily. Rather, I want to suggest that class is structural. It involves the institutionalization of capitals. It informs access to and how subject positions such as respectability and caring can be taken up. There is not a free fall or 'choice' over subject positions as Alcoff (1988) would suggest, but rather circumscribed access and movement between subject positions. At birth we are allocated into these spaces with their concomitant institutional organization such as the institutions of heterosexuality, the family and the racial and sexual division of labour. They pre-exist our agency but we contribute to their reproduction and reformulation; they frame our responses. Identities are not then reflections of objective social positions which is how class is often theorized (if at all). This, as Calhoun (1994) points out, would be to see identities always retrospectively. Nor are the social positions essential categories. Identities are continually in the process of being re-produced as responses to social positions, through access to representational systems and in the conversion of forms of capital.

This chapter has shown how social positions and cultural representations are entered into. These bring with them and enable access to differential amounts of capital. For White working-class women this capital is limited:[6] it is difficult to trade with it on a market in which symbolic delegitimation has occurred. Their experiences were dominated by exclusion from areas to trade their inherited capitals. They find it very difficult to trade on being working class and even more difficult to find anything positive associated with their working-class positioning. As the historical and contemporary analysis of class representations suggests, we should not be surprised that the women do not want to be recognized as such. However, the definitions of working-classness were by no means straightforward. When they did attempt to identify themselves they first had difficulties finding a discourse of class and, second, had problems with the methods of classification used to define it. This was paralleled in the academic accounts of class where no clear meaning is agreed upon and where classifications systems are strongly contested. The women tried to make sense of their class positioning through employment, background, housing and money. They had a strong sense that their social and cultural positioning was unjust. They did not adjust to their social positioning, as Bourdieu (1986) would suggest. Rather they made strenuous efforts to deny, disidentify and dissimulate. These were affective responses; class was lived as a structure of feeling. Class is still a hidden injury (Sennett and Cobb, 1977). They attempted to display their distinction from being classified as working-class through a variety of methods. To do so they made investments in their bodies, clothes, consumption practices, leisure pursuits and homes. These investments indicated a strong desire to pass as middle class. But it was only an imaginary middle class that they wanted to be. They did not want to take on the whole package of dispositions. Their responses to classification were informed by fear, desire, resentment and humiliation. They were individualistic responses produced through their own bodies and influencing their movement through social space. In this sense they become implicated in a similar mechanism to that which enabled the construction of the caring self. Their class subjectivity monitors itself dialogically through the real and imaginary experiences, perceptions and judgements of others.

It thus seems unlikely that the actions of these women are likely to lead to class politics, to class organization or even to class consciousness of a directly articulated form. These women are highly sensitive to issues of class and difference but they have no discourses available for them to articulate it as a positive identity.[7] Their class struggle is waged on a daily basis to overcome the denigration and delegitimizing associated with their class positioning. This is why representations are a key site in this class struggle; they are where symbolic violence occurs.[8]

Who would want to be seen as working class? (Possibly only academics are left.)[9] Within the field of cultural criticism working-class people have come to be seen as bearing the elemental simplicity of class consciousness and little more. They have always been the site for projected longings of the rebellious middle classes who put their investment in change in others rather than themselves. But these projections are here being refused. The women's consciousness of their classifications, their devaluing, their inability to get it right and their inability *to be* without shame, humiliation and judgement is part of the reason why they turn to respectability and responsibility as a means of establishing a valued and legitimate way of being and way of being seen.[10]

Notes

1 Thirty-nine per cent of the women are still single and 18 per cent still live at home. This is due to the lack of affordable housing, although two women own their own homes. Ownership is more likely if the women are married (31 per cent). Only a small number cohabit.

2 One of Britain's most popular soaps *Coronation Street* recently satirized the conversion of terraced houses by painting the outside of the house of the most working-class couple, the Duckworths, blue and yellow. The use of such a joke suggests the symbolic annihilation of those with aspirations within the working class to display their differences.

3 Initially none had any aspirations to pursue education after they finished at the further education college. As a result of lots of discussions and a trip to a university three did go on to higher education to do Sociology.

4 Through nursing and in-service courses one now works as a medical systems trainer. Two who pursued higher education work as qualified social workers.

5 Hilda comes from the character Hilda Ogden who was a caricature of pathological working class on the soap *Coronation Street*.

6 This formula of capitals can be applied to all social configurations. It cannot, however, tell us how these configurations will be experienced. That is the job of the researcher.

7 For Black working-class women access to an alternative positive identity (being Black) may be available.

8 Feminism has been (relatively) successful at challenging the negative valuing of women whereas Marxism, as the only coherent oppositional position on class, has been unable to generate such a popular struggle and is now itself under enormous discrediting attempts.

9 Lynne Pearce notes in personal communication that only once one has been given middle-class citizenship can one take pride in one's roots and not be ashamed because 'what I was is not what I now am'.

10 Alex Callinicos notes in personal communication in response to this chapter that resistance to the term working class should not be seen to detract from the increase in trade-union consciousness that is occurring in 1990s Britain. He points out that there are still 9 million trade unionists in Britain and he identifies a trend whereby workers who previously saw themselves as professional (such as teachers, bank-workers and nurses) are adopting trade-union methods of collective action.

References

Alcoff, L. (1988) 'Cultural feminism versus post-structuralism: The identity crisis in feminist theory', *Signs*, vol.13, no.31 pp.405–36.

Armstrong, N. and Tennenhouse, L. (1987) *The Ideology of Conduct: Essays in Literature and the History of Sexuality*, London, Methuen.

Bartky, S.L. (1990) *Femininity and Domination: Studies in the Phenomenology of Oppression*, London, Routledge.

Benzevale, M., Judge, J. and Whitehead, M. (1995) *Tackling Health Inequalities: An Agenda for Action*, Poole, Dorset, BEBC.

Berger, J. (1980) *About Looking*, London, Writers and Readers Publishing Cooperative.

Black Report (1982) *Inequalities in Health*, (ed.) Townsend, P. and Davidson, N., Harmondsworth, Penguin Books.

Bourdieu, P. (1986) *Distinction: A Social Critique of the Judgement of Taste*, London, Routledge.

Bourdieu, P. (1987) 'What makes a social class? On the theoretical and practical existence of groups', *Berkeley Journal of Sociology*, pp.1–17.

Bourke, J. (1994) *Working Class Cultures in Britain: 1890–1960*, London, Routledge.

Calhoun, C. (ed.) (1994) *Social Theory and the Politics of Identity*, Oxford, Blackwell.

Charles, N. (1990) 'Women and class – a problematic relationship', *Sociological Review,* vol.38, pp.43–89.

Foucault, M. (1988) 'The ethic of care for the self as a practice of freedom' in Bernauer, J. and Ramussen, D. (eds) *The Final Foucault*, Cambridge, MA, MIT Press.

Goffman, E. (1959) *The Presentation of Self in Everyday Life,* Harmondsworth, Pelican.

Holland, J., Ramazanoglu, C., Sharpe, S., and Thomson, R. (eds) (1991) *Pressured Pleasure: Young Women and the Negotiation of Sexual Boundaries,* WRAP Paper 7, London, The Tufnell Press.

Joseph Rowntree Foundation (1995) *Inquiry into Income and Wealth*, York, Joseph Rowntree Foundation.

Lamont, M. (1992) *Money, Morals and Manners: The Culture of the French and the American Upper Middle-Class*, Chicago, IL, University of Chicago Press.

McCall, L. (1992) 'Does gender *fit*? Bourdieu, feminism and conceptions of social order', *Theory and Society*, vol.21, pp.837–67.

Press, A. (1991) *Women Watching Television: Gender, Class and Generation in the American Television Experience*, Philadelphia, PA, University of Pennsylvania Press.

Rowe, K. (1995) *The Unruly Woman: Gender and the Genres of Laughter*, Austin, TX, University of Texas Press.

Savage, M., Barlow, J., Dickens, P. and Fielding, T. (1992) *Property, Bureaucracy and Culture: Middle-class Formation in Contemporary Britain*, London, Routledge.

Sennett, R. and Cobb, J. (1977) *The Hidden Injuries of Class*, Cambridge, Cambridge University Press.

Warde, A. (1994) 'Employment relations or assets: an alternative basis of class analysis', Paper presented to Lancaster Regionalism Group, 13 December, Lancaster University.

Willis, P. (1977) *Learning to Labour: How Working Class Kids get Working Class Jobs*, Farnborough, Saxon House.

Source: Skeggs, 1997, pp.74–6,77–9,81–5

4

Race, power and knowledge

Karim Murji

Contents

1	**Introduction**	**160**
	Aims	162
2	**The problem of identification**	**162**
	2.1 Vision and division	163
	2.2 Naming and categorization	166
3	**Racial governmentality**	**172**
	3.1 Racial categories in the census	172
	3.2 Racial knowledge and power	178
4	**Whiteness**	**181**
	4.1 Whiteness: dominant and fractured	181
	4.2 Eugenics: power and population	187
	4.3 The end of whiteness?	188
5	**Conclusion**	**190**
References		**191**
Readings		
4.1: Richard Jenkins, 'Categorization and power' (1997)		**193**
4.2: Sharon M. Lee, 'Racial classifications in the US census: 1890–1990' (1993)		**195**
4.3: U. Kalpagam, 'The colonial state and statistical knowledge' (2000)		**199**
4.4: Sheila Faith Weiss, 'Power through population: Schallmayer and population policy' (1987)		**201**
4.5: Jonathan W. Warren and France W. Twine, 'White Americans, the new minority?' (1997)		**202**

1 Introduction

At the beginning of his book, *Racial Conditions*, Howard Winant states that race is a fundamental feature of every aspect of life in the USA:

> Well over a century since the abolition of racial slavery ... concepts of race remain deeply embedded in every institution, every relationship, every psyche. This is true not only of such large-scale macrosocial relationships as the distribution of wealth or income, or segregation in housing and education, but also of small-scale microlevel relationships.
>
> (Winant, 1994, p.2)

Winant's view maintains that race is a key dividing line, and while this statement is about the US, it can be extended to argue that race is a fundamental and constitutive social division of many contemporary societies. This perspective is in **sociology of race** contrast to some other approaches in the **sociology of race**, which have placed race as a sub-set of other social relations and divisions, such as caste, class, stratification and status. Locating race as a central feature of social relations does not, however, mean that it is seen as standing apart from other social divisions. Indeed, we will see that class and gender relations cut across racial categories, and in terms of the broader theme of this book, it is in the intersection between these social divisions that measures for social justice should be located.

This chapter examines race as a social division by employing the distinctive concept of the 'labour of division' (Hetherington and Munro, 1997). This idea emphasizes the effort, or labour, entailed in the construction and maintenance of divisions. In other words, social divisions are constructions that require work to manufacture and maintain distinctive ways of 'seeing' the world. Vision, power and expertise are implicated in these constructions, as we will see in sections 2, 3 and 4.

The chapter is divided into three sections. In section 2, we will look at the apparent obviousness of racial identification. Race appears to be written on the body: it is a mark or a sign that is, seemingly, one of the clearest things about every individual. We question whether it is possible to maintain this view by probing the links between race and colour, and by querying and problematizing the words and descriptions applied to various racial minorities. Following from the question of terminology, section 3 examines the ways in which race has been delineated through official classifications such as the census. It links quantification to issues of authority and power in examining how racial categories are constructed and counted. Yet, the category 'white' is frequently overlooked and unquestioned in censuses and in section 4 we explore this further. How did **hegemony** whiteness achieve this **hegemonic** (or dominant) status where it manages to be 'unseen'? Through probing several facets of whiteness we will see that – like all racial categories – it is fractured and divided by other social divisions, and heterogeneous rather than homogenous. We will also see that it has been problematized as an object for intervention and regulation.

Understanding race as an object or phenomenon that is constructed socially through a labour of division employing vision, quantification and expertise focuses on the key role of power in making divisions. Within sociology there are a number **power** of distinctive perspectives on **power** (see Allen, 2000, for an overview). The

approach in this chapter draws upon the ideas of **Michel Foucault**, who stressed   Foucault,
the association between knowledge and power. Statistics, surveying, mapping   Michel
and the natural and the social sciences are significant as forms of knowledge that
have been instrumental in constructing race, as considered in sections 3 and 4.
The ideas of power-knowledge and the labour of division will be used to examine
the relationship between race and power in ways that may depart from the
conventional or everyday uses of the word race. The notion of race – which
seems to be something obvious and transparent – turns out to be rather unstable
and questionable, even while it has definite links to material differences between
groups of people. This is one of several paradoxes that comes up and you will
encounter others through an array of diverse settings including the US, the UK,
India and Germany. This wide range is intended to question what may be familiar
about race, and to 'unsettle' it as an idea.

As part of that unsettling, I would like to begin by thinking about the
relationship between race and ethnicity, two common or everyday words. An
ethnic group has a shared culture that includes language, customs and religion.   ethnic group
As a way of describing culturally distinctive groups, ethnicity is often preferred
to race because it is seen as something relatively fluid and chosen, while race
has often been an imposed social categorization, linked to supposedly fixed
features of the body. Because ethnicity is seen as a chosen form of group
identification it is often connected to the *positive* sense of distinctive cultural
identity and kinship. There are other reasons why ethnicity, rather than race,
can be preferred by sociologists and others. As Richard Jenkins (1997) points
out, while 'race relations' are frequently hierarchical and exploitative, ethnic
relations generally are not. He also adds that the idea of race, much more than
ethnicity, has been based upon explicit, though scientifically discredited, attempts
to define distinct racial 'types'.

While this seems straightforward, the notion of ethnicity as a chosen and
race as an involuntary identity is not so clear-cut. In section 2 we see that 'racial'
identities and even previously stigmatized terms and names can be reclaimed.
In other words, race is not necessarily imposed and ascribed – it can be voluntarily
chosen. For example, the novelist Mike Phillips (2001) points out that many
first- and second-generation West Indian migrants in the 1950s defined their
identity in terms of the island that they (or their parents) came from, as Jamaican
or Barbadian for instance. For Phillips, it was only in the 1960s and because of
the influence of radical 'Black Power' politics that being black became a more
prominent and dominant identity. In other words, a 'racial' identity (blackness)
stands over and above an ethnic one. Furthermore, it is a paradox that ethnicity
may not be chosen but imposed. For instance, in the UK the term 'ethnic minority'
is often a synonym for people of African, Asian and Caribbean descent. Yet,
what an 'Asian' ethnicity is – given the diversity of languages, cultures and
religions – is unclear (and the same point applies to the notion that there is an
'African' or a 'Caribbean' ethnicity).

A further paradox is that there are places where the idea of ethnicity is applied
in different ways. For instance, the separatist claims of the Basques in Spain, or
the Québecois in Canada are classed as assertions of ethnic identity or ethnic
nationalism. But, in the UK ethnicity is often regarded as an attribute of minorities
who are 'not white'; Scottish and Irish nationalism are not conventionally treated

as ethnic claims. Elsewhere, however, it is applied to white groups. In recent times the term 'ethnic cleansing' has been applied to violence between white people in the Balkan wars and between black people in Rwanda. These examples indicate that there is some ambiguity and overlap in the ways that race and ethnicity are used. In practice, both are sometimes related to, and conflated with, other terms including nationality, immigration and skin colour; both are or can be associated with culture and behaviour, as well as physical differences.

AIMS

This chapter aims:

1   To examine racial discourses, particularly in relation to how knowledge about race links to issues of power.

2   To consider the significance of what is seen and not seen as race, and its impact on thinking about social divisions.

3   Taking the example of the census, to highlight the role of quantification and accounting as particular ways of constructing and counting race.

4   To explore the frequently unquestioned category 'white', and in particular to show how, like all racial categories, it is unstable and intersected by the social divisions of class and gender.

---

2 The problem of identification

Michael Omi and Howard Winant (1994) state that an awareness of race forms part of everyday experience:

> One of the first things we notice about people when we meet them (along with their sex) is their race. We utilize race to provide clues about who a person is. This fact is made painfully obvious when we encounter someone whom we cannot conveniently racially categorize – someone who is, for example, racially 'mixed' or of an ethnic/racial group we are not familiar with. Such an encounter becomes a source of discomfort and momentarily a crisis of racial meaning.
>
> (Omi and Winant, 1994, p.59)

Omi and Winant suggest that race or racial identity is something obvious and immediately apparent – we can hardly fail to see it since it is manifestly visible. Their stress on the immediacy of identification by race, along with sex or gender, privileges these two categories as the most obvious signs of identity, presumably because they can be 'seen' in ways that other divisions can not. But is it apparent that we 'see' race (or gender) in this way? And who does the 'we' in this sentence refer to or include? These may seem bizarre questions to pose. However, it seems to me that Omi and Winant's statement raises two important issues, which they tend to gloss over and which ought to be examined further. These are:

1   What it means to regard race as visibly evident in the way they do, and

2   The names and terms used to categorize racial groups.

We explore these two issues now.

2.1 Vision and division

I would like you to write a list of the first five things you think of following the words 'I am … ', to describe yourself. Try to do this as spontaneously as possible and don't think about it too much!

This type of exercise is used to discern some of the main ways in which we think about what seem to be the most important features of our identities. There could be many possible answers to this question and the ones that you wrote may also reflect the context in which an exercise like this is carried out, indeed some of you may have regarded the identity of 'student' as significant. My point in asking you to complete this activity is to suggest that race may be an important aspect of some people's identity, but not of others. There are three aspects to this. First, when I did this, my race or ethnicity was not something that I listed, yet someone else of a broadly similar background did. Second, I wonder how many white people would think of listing this as an aspect of their sense of self? Yet, correspondingly, how many black or Asian people might have thought of themselves as 'raced' in these terms? Third, as we have seen, Omi and Winant seem to regard race and gender as forms of differentiation that are obvious, in ways that others are not. However, the boundaries of visibility and differentiation seem less clear to me. For instance, some individuals may have disabilities – such as being deaf – that are not visible. A person's social class may be inferred from a number of visual and verbal cues, including dress, posture, speech, and so on. But these can be learned and both played up and down, so the surmise made may not necessarily be correct. Age seems to offer less scope for confusion, though even here it may become harder to easily guess other people's ages. Even gender identity can be more questionable at times when androgynous and unisex styles are in fashion, or where gender is seen as a performed identity rather than an **essential** one.

essentialism

To turn to the question about who 'we' are, it is my contention that there are distinctive ways of seeing and understanding racial identities. The term race in the quote from Omi and Winant above seems to refer to visible racial minorities, or 'people of colour' – a term that has become increasingly common in the USA. But while visibility appears to be attached to skin colour, only some colours seem to count as race, namely, those attached to people who are 'not white' (I put it in quotes because it is an awkward term that groups a large number of people by what they are *not*). To approach this another way, consider the question raised by Donna Haraway (1992, p.53): 'what maintains the "normal" invisibility of the race of "whites", but not of people of "color"?

Spend a few minutes thinking about what responses occur to you in thinking about Haraway's question. Have a look back at the discussion of race and ethnicity in the Introduction.

Jenkins (1997) indicated that one of the features of race is that it has entailed explicit attempts to refine distinct 'types'. This knowledge production has usually 'othered' all those who are 'not white', making them objects of investigation and curiosity, as well as being used to justify exploitative social relations. The converse of this process of identifying 'them' is an idea of 'us' and, as this suggests, racial categories are relational. (We shall look at whiteness in more detail in section 4.)

Using 'people of colour' as an umbrella term for all people who are regarded as racial minorities does nevertheless throw up the problem of equating race with skin colours that are 'not white'. This is paradoxical because white is a colour, but whiteness is often absent in both conventional and sociological ways of thinking about the subject of race. Paradoxically, race and colour are often linked but the colour white seems to remain 'unseen' in racial terms. Its frequent invisibility is a sign of its dominant, hegemonic status and begins to alert us to the idea that vision is not a transparent act of seeing what is in front of us; observation is not a 'naked eye science' (Haraway, 1992, p.55).

There is however more to ideas of racial differentiation than merely what lies on the surface of bodies. Three examples illustrate the instability of linking race and colour, and seeing race as written on the body. First, Michael Banton provides an example of when race and colour do not connect. Though the following are admittedly unusual cases, there are times when a person's skin colour may change due to a medical condition:

> White people may become dark because of a kidney disorder, or the removal of their adrenal glands, or Nelson's disease following an attack of jaundice. The kidneys fail to break down the melanocyte-stimulating hormone from the pituitary glands. As a result, English people may find themselves regarded as Asians or blacks, and suffer discrimination. They have not changed their race. The discrimination is a reaction to skin colour. There are also changes in the opposite direction when Asian and black people contract forms of vitiligo and their skin lightens ... In Britain an Indian businessman whose skin lightened found that this helped him in his business life.
>
> (Banton, 1991, pp.119–20)

It is not entirely possible to ignore the way in which the 'English' in this quote stands in for white. Nevertheless, it should also be noted that Banton points out that skin colour may be independent of a raced identity, and that changes in colour may well be significant in terms of personal treatment as well as economic life-chances.

Second, considerations of racial difference have been linked to the distinction between the outer, observable differences between people – or phenotype – and the underlying genetic inheritance, or genotype. Race does correspond in some way to phenotypical differences among human populations though the relationship between them is not clear-cut. There may be any number of phenotypical differences between groups – for example, hair colour, facial features or body size. Because these are not necessarily coded as 'racial' differences, it is clear that phenotypical differences are not inevitably equated with race. Jenkins (1997, p.78) says they are a 'different orders of thing': 'phenotype is the material product of the interaction of genetic endowment (genotype) and environment, "race" is a cultural fiction'. In other words, race differences are not located in nature, and what is commonly seen as race (skin colour, for example) is not the same as observable visible differences between peoples since there are any number of clear differences and only some are counted as race. Banton (1991, p.117) makes the point in this way: 'People do not perceive racial differences. They perceive phenotypical differences of colour, hair form, underlying bone structures and so on. Phenotypical differences are a first order abstraction, race is a second order abstraction.' Race is a social construction that we have to learn to 'see', code and name as such.

For Robert Miles, the explanation of why some differences are coded as race lies in social structures and processes of domination and subordination. 'Race' (for Miles, always in quote marks to show that it is not a natural or scientific category) is a product of the meanings attributed to some aspects of physical appearance at some times, making it an historically and politically contingent construction, which has had changing meanings over time:

> The visibility of somatic characteristics is not inherent in the characteristics themselves, but arises from a process of signification by which meaning is attributed to certain of them. In other words, visibility is socially constructed in a wider set of structural constraints, within a set of relations of domination.
>
> (Miles, 1993, p.87)

Third, the idea that race is written on the body makes it a mark or a sign of skin, something that makes the body 'speak' its identity. Yet, as Paul Gilroy (2000) points out, bodies do not disclose their secrets in such transparent terms. In the violent conflict in Rwanda a number of Tutsis – who had had their identity cards changed to show themselves as Hutus – were said to have various physical features that gave away their real identity, such as being long limbed and having straight noses. But this led the militia into killing some Hutus who were said to be 'too tall' to be Hutu. When identification on physical characteristics became problematic, local villagers were required to attest the 'Tutsiship' of individuals (Gilroy, 2000). Paradoxically, to turn to another example, what is regarded as a sign of race and/or ethnicity may not be observable at all. Things that do not appear on the surface but refer to some real or imagined features inside the body have been treated as signs of a racial differentiation. Thus, despite outward physical similarities, there are said to be a number of subtle and perhaps ineffable means through which individuals are identified as either Protestants or Catholics in Northern Ireland, especially when it comes to deciding who should get a particular job (Jenkins, 1997). What the link between the observable and the unobservable may be is not straightforward, any more than the one between race and phenotype.

The obsession with – or fetish of – skin colour, physical appearance and the body is an instance of what Frantz Fanon (1986) in *Black Skin, White Masks* called 'epidermalization' meaning the inscription of race on the skin. This bodily or corporeal schema, Fanon stressed, is cultural and not genetic. Nonetheless, race is frequently used to refer to not just what is on the surface, but also to real or imagined underlying features of the body, as the visible external manifestation is linked with imputed and generally undisclosed features, such as blood and bones. In the name of science and social science these have taken the form of comparative investigations into brain size, physical features, hair and blood type, as well as intelligence tests and cultural differences. Nineteenth-century phrenology's use of skulls to establish mental capabilities and physiognomy's reliance on head and facial features to assess character indicate an obsessive preoccupation with differentiating the 'other' (Curtis, 1997). As we will see later, the process of 'othering' has been applied to white as well as black groups. All this points to the labour in making divisions and to the role of knowledge in producing systems of differentiation, categorization, and hierarchies that divide up peoples artificially and – equally artificially – group diverse peoples together in the name of race.

As Gilroy (2000, p.82) says, blood, bodies and cultural identity are all summoned in 'the fantastic idea of transmuting heterogeneity into homogeneity'. A name for that fantasy would be raciology, by which Gilroy refers to:

> ... the variety of essentializing and reductionist ways of thinking that are both biological and cultural in character ... [that underlie the] continuing power of 'race' to orchestrate our social, economic, cultural and historical experiences.
>
> (Gilroy, 2000, p.72)

The idea that possession of a certain skin colour could be a reason for classification into racial commonality seems even more peculiar if we ask what could be the basis for linking all white people as Caucasians, apart from a white skin? Instead of fixed and absolutist conceptions of identity as sameness, writers such as Gilroy argue for fluid and open forms of identification.

2.2 Naming and categorization

In this section, our concern is with the terminology of racial categorization. If, following Omi and Winant, we all classify people according to race, does this mean that we have innate perceptual and cognitive mechanisms to do so? For Omi and Winant (1994, p.60) these rules or schemes of classification are woven into the fabric of American society: they do not have to be explicitly stated, they just *are*: 'Everybody learns some combination, some version, of the rules of racial classification ... often without obvious teaching or conscious inculcation.' Building on this, Winant maintains that identity is colour-coded and problems in placing people according to that code are the source of feelings of unease and a form of cognitive dissonance for both the categorizer and categorized:

> Indeed, when one meets a person who is difficult to classify racially, the result is often a minicrisis of identity: not knowing to what race someone belongs is like not knowing to what sex the person belongs. For better or worse, without a clear racial identity a North American is in danger of having no identity.
>
> (Winant, 1994, p.3)

What are the names of these categories that are employed in classifying people? An immediate problem is that the categorization – indeed the terminology – of race has changed continually. Those usually called black people – generally, those of African and West Indian origins – have in the course of less than a century also variously been officially referred to or designated as 'negroes', 'coloureds', 'Afro-Caribbeans', 'ethnic minorities', and many colloquial names besides. These terms are not sequential and can in practice overlap. While some of these terms have come to be regarded as offensive (for instance the Macpherson report (1999) into the murder of Stephen Lawrence criticized the police for using the expression 'coloureds' to describe black people), they can also be reinscribed or reinterpreted.

Racial categorizations are not therefore simply imposed identities. Some groups or racial minorities who have traditionally been the object of racism may use race or racialized terms and identities as an expression of solidarity, to organize against exclusion and marginalization, and to develop counter-strategies. For example, the name of the 1980s' rap group NWA (Niggers With Attitude) re-claims a stigmatized label and uses it to critique the racially subordinated position of blacks in the US. Although the meanings of words can shift and be subverted, it may still be regarded as offensive to some and there are no simple guarantees about meaning. Thus, the use of the 'n-word' continues to be a matter of cultural controversy.

What matters here is that language and categories are not stable, have changed over time and remain matters of ongoing contestation. Meanings can be inverted to create a positive identity out of a stigmatized one and to form what Miles (1993, p.58) calls an 'imagined community of resistance'. Thus, the rise of Black Power in the US in the 1960s, the 'black is beautiful' slogan and the rise of Afro-centric political ideologies are all instances where blackness and Africa have been given different meanings and interpretations. These inversions of racial particularity replace shame with pride and, as Gilroy (2000) points out, these oppositional identities may not be given up lightly.

READING 4.1

To begin to locate the discussion in terms of power-knowledge, please read the extract 'Categorization and power' by Richard Jenkins (Reading 4.1 at the end of this chapter). Although Jenkins is discussing ethnicity in this extract, keep these questions in mind as you read:

1   How do power and authority interconnect with processes of external definition?

2   What is the significance of the distinction between groups and categories?

3   How does categorization contribute to group identity?

Jenkins underlines the idea that conceptions of 'us' and 'them' are part of an 'ongoing dialectic of identification'. In other words, there is a *transactional* or *interactive* association between self- and other identification. However, while groups may be able to define themselves, categories are defined by others, though categorization and group identity are inter-linked in four of the five scenarios outlined by Jenkins. Categorization may be imposed through force, but it may also be used to provide a sense of collective identity and a mode of organization and resistance. Categorizations may also be claimed through an imaginative association. For instance, a likeness can be drawn between the subordinated position of blacks and some white groups through the invocation of particular terms. In Roddy Doyle's novel and film, *The Commitments*, a humorous tone is used to make a serious point when Jimmy, the white manager of the eponymous rhythm-and-blues group, proclaims: 'The Irish are the niggers of Europe … Say it loud, I'm black an' I'm proud.'

Figure 4.1 Sacha Baron Cohen aka 'Ali G.'

To take the confusions of categorization and identity a step further consider the case of Ali G., the creation of Sacha Baron Cohen, a comedian of Jewish origins and a Cambridge University graduate, playing a proletarian Asian from Staines who seemingly wants to be, or pass as, a West Indian 'gangsta'. One of his catchphrases 'Is it 'cos I is black?' has been widely imitated by all kinds of people – black and white. How the identity of the 'Asian' (or 'British'? 'West Indian'?) Ali G. could be compartmentalized is imponderable. It could be that this is simply humorous and should not be taken seriously. Yet the popularity of Ali G. and his deliberately confused imbrication of race, culture and identity seem to signal something (but what?) about race in Britain at the turn of the millennium. And Ali G. is not alone in what is sometimes regarded as a post-modern world where the boundaries of identity seem more open than ever before, and more a matter of playfulness and pastiche than anchored in ritual and tradition.

If Ali G. plays with wanting to be black, how do we set his image alongside that of Michael Jackson, a pop singer of African-American origins who has gone through a prolonged process of skin-lightening? In his song 'Am I black or am I white?' he challenges those who believe the choice is between being one thing or the other. Terminological and linguistic confusions are multiplied if we try to think about how to locate people of 'mixed race': are new categories and terms needed to describe them? A common argument against the term 'mixed race' is that it suggests that there are 'pure' races in the first place, and this is also a case where there are not any easy answers about the 'correct' name. Could individuals who might be so described make up their own categories and names? Rather than be categorized as black or African-American, the golfer Tiger Woods refers to himself as 'Caublinasian', highlighting his mixed Caucasian/black/Asian origins. Yet, why is it that Woods has to account for and name his racial or ethnic identity, something that white people rarely do?

Figure 4.2 *'Am I black or am I white?'*

To ask another question: I wonder whether in naming people more emphasis should be placed on origins rather than identity? For example, I was born in (East) Africa but I am not sure if that makes me 'African'. By appearance I might be classified as 'Asian'. Yet Asian means different things in different parts of the world. In the UK it is largely used to include people whose roots lie in the Indian sub-continent, but in the USA it describes peoples from south-east Asia, including the Chinese, Japanese, Koreans, Vietnamese, etc. The term 'South Asian' is used to distinguish the former from the latter, but how useful is it to so designate all the Hindus, Sikhs and Muslims who have some connection to that part of the world? These are peoples who could easily be classified together for 'racial' purposes, yet, as these terms are intended to suggest, perhaps culture and religion are more significant aspects of identity than race. Furthermore, the examples used here indicate that there may be multiple forms of belonging and that 'routes' rather than 'roots' may be more significant to identity. One of these multiple forms of identity can be citizenship. My passport says that I am a citizen of the UK, but does that make me British? I suppose the answer depends on whether being British is a legal, national, or racial/ethnic status. In the late 1980s the then Conservative minister Norman Tebbit questioned whether black and Asian people in this country really were British, when he famously invoked his 'cricket test' and complained that many of the former peoples supported India, Pakistan and/or the West Indies rather than England. Years later, controversy about what 'Britishness' means rumbles on, for instance in the debate following the report of the Commission into the Future of Multi-ethnic Britain (Parekh *et al.*, 2000).

The sometimes unanswerable questions raised above are intended to signal that race, and racial categories and terminology, are inter-connected with a host of other terms such as ethnicity, nationality, citizenship, culture, religion, and skin colour. While we may all 'know' what race is and how it is used for classifying people, it seems to come close to collapsing the more we ask what it means in relation to identity, terminology and categorization. The paradox is that race is nonetheless a means of **stereotyping** that regards people in the same category as if they all have some 'essence' in common. It can and does result in forms of treatment and allocation that reproduce the facts of racial inequality. Social constructions can have real effects.

stereotypes

So far we have encountered a number of terms for describing various racial minorities. Have a look back at these. Are there others that you can think of? Make a list, then have a look at Table 4.1 below:

Table 4.1 Some classifications of human races

Buffon (1749)	American, Laplander, Tartar, South Asiatic, European, Ethiopian
Blumenbach (1781)	Caucasoid, Mongoloid, American Indian, Ethiopian, Malay
Cuvier (1790)	Caucasian, Mongolion, Ethiopian
Flourens (1839)	Caucasian, Mongolion, Negro, American, Malay, Hottentot, Boschisman, Papuan, Alfourou, Zealandic
Prichard (1848)	Caucasian, Mongolion, Negro, American, Esquimaux, Hottentot + Boschisman, Papuans, Alfourous + Australian
Boyd (1950)	Early European, European, African, Asiatic, American Indian, Australoid
Boyd (1963)	Early European, Laplanders, Northwest European, Eastern European, Mediterranean, African, Asian, Indo-Dravidian, American, Indonesian, Melanesian, Polynesian, Australoid
Coon (1965)	Caucasoid, Mongoloid, Australoid, Congoid, Capoid
Garn (1971)	Northwest European, Northeast European, Alpine, Mediterranean, Iranian, East African, Sudanese, Forest Negro, Bantu, Turkic, Tibetan, North Chinese, Extreme Mongoloid, Southeast Asiatic, Hindu, Dravidian, North American, Central American, South American, Fuegian, Lapp, Pacific Negrito, African Pygmy, Eskimo, Ainu, Murrayian, Carpenterian Australian, Bushman + Hottentot, North American Colored, South African Colored, Ladino, Neo-Hawaiian.

Source: E.H. Colbert and M. Morales, 1991. *Caucasoid, Mongoloid, Australian, Negroid* in *Evolution of the Vertebrates*, p.220.

Note: The eighteen- and nineteenth-century sources are from Smith (1859), Augstein (1996), and Molnar (1998).

Source: Blackburn, 2000, p.5

When I have asked students to do an exercise like this in the past, they often come up with terms such as 'Caucasian', 'Negroid', 'Asian', 'Chinese'. Words such as 'coloured' are rarer, perhaps reflecting changes in the use of language. Whatever names and terms are produced, race is something that evades closure through classification since there is no agreement about how many 'races' there might be. While the term 'Caucasian' is commonly used as a synonym for white, in its original meaning the idea of a 'Caucasian people' stretched all the way from southern India to Scandinavia. Hence, all kinds of people who might be regarded as 'Asian' could also be 'Caucasian'. Raciologies often use skin colour and physical features as the basis for classificatory schema. Here, the surface manifestations have been linked to underlying physical differences, as we saw earlier in section 2.1. Differences in brain size, cranial capacity, measurements of skull size and other features have been used as markers of racial differences. The purposes of differentiation are rarely neutral and lead on to hierarchical classifications of particular qualities said to be characteristic of each racial group. Investigations under the banner of science have produced a multitude of racial groupings – anything from three to ten to thirty classifications of human races (Blackburn, 2000). Many of these classificatory schemes date from the period of scientific racism and the extent of these investigations and schemes are another indicator of the labour of division.

There still are scientists attempting to categorize human populations racially (Kohn, 1996). Sports- and intelligence-testing have become the main areas where this carries on. These two fields reflect a persistent underlying theme: while black people have regularly been classified as inferior in terms of mental capacities they have correspondingly been accorded physical capacities in terms of strength, or other physical abilities. This distinction between mind and body (or intellect and physique) can be mapped on to the white-black dichotomy:

> In a broad range of popular and official discourses in the west, perhaps especially in the former white settler colonies like the US, *white* is a color code for bodies ascribed the attitude of *mind*, and thus symbolic power, not to mention other forms of power, in social practices like 'intelligence' tests. The *body* is coded darker.
>
> (Haraway, 1992, p.153)

The reason we are stressing the role of science is because the canons of scientific method – the observation and classification of regularities – are fundamental to the schemas and hierarchies of racial science. As techniques for placing and confining the physical body in a box or grid, racial knowledge acquires its apparent authority from science. The reason it can do this, David Goldberg (1997, p.28) argues, is because race-thinking and differentiation have historically been integral to the emergence of scientific authority: 'Race has been a basic categorical object, in some cases a founding focus of scientific analysis'.

The discussion of vision, observation and categorization can be linked through the notion of 'the gaze'. While Foucault (1977) does not make this argument in relation to race *per se*, he does advance the proposition that a key mechanism for the exercise of power is the medium of 'organized perception'. Through the study of various institutions – for example, prisons, hospitals and schools – Foucault uses the idea of 'the gaze' as the means through which individuals are made visible, classified and hierarchized. In particular, Foucault maintains that organized perception 'transformed the exercise of visibility into the exercise of power' (1977, p.187), and that the gaze operates through anonymous bureaucratic procedures that exercise a 'compulsory visibility' over those whom power is exercised – from individuals to the general population. Foucault's argument centres the role of vision in constructing and categorizing divisions. It emphasizes the link between power and knowledge and, in the next section, we look at the census as an example of a bureaucratic procedure that codes and counts what race is.

SUMMARY OF SECTION 2

In this section my aim has been to unsettle some taken-for-granted ways of thinking about race. The main arguments have been that:

1   Race is not simply about observing differences between peoples, since only some differences are coded as race.

2   Racial naming and categorization are unstable and changing.

3   Vision is involved in the production of divisions, through the links between categorization, science and power-knowledge.

3 Racial governmentality

3.1 Racial categories in the census

In this section, we examine in more detail officially encoded categories of racial/ethnic identification and their enumeration by looking at censuses. As Lee (1993, p.76) says, census categories are important because they 'represent political, legal and professional authority', and changes in classifications are reflective of 'demographic, political and ideological shifts in society'. Censuses quantify race and draw upon expert knowledge in defining and measuring it. At the end of this section, we will show how these can be regarded as instances of racial governmentality.

Our discussion will focus on the US census. There are a number of reasons for this. Firstly, unlike the UK, the US census has employed racial categories since its inception in 1790. This allows us, secondly, to look at the ways in which some of these categories expand, contract and change. Thirdly, it also enables us to look at what stays the same in the census, namely the category 'white', and to probe the significance of that as a supposedly undifferentiated group.

ACTIVITY 4

Please spend a few minutes studying Table 4.2 overleaf of racial categories used in the US census from 1790–1990.

As the table demonstrates, a key purpose of the race question in the census is to define all those who are 'not white'. Lee (1993) points out that of the eight groups listed in 1890 half alone apply to black or partially black populations. This fascination with degrees (or quarters and eighths, as in Quadroons and Octoroons) of blackness reflects a recurring fear about miscegenation and racial purity, particularly in the southern parts of the US. (Indeed, under Hitler German censuses were also fixated with seeking to differentiate degrees of Jewishness.) The effort – or labour – entailed in making and marking divisions is notable: the US Census Bureau instructed enumerators to be 'particularly careful to distinguish between blacks, mulattoes, quadroons and octoroons', specifying that black should be used only for those with 'three-fourths or more black blood' (cited in Lee, 1993, p.77). This rather complicated arithmetic was dropped in favour of what came to be known as the 'one drop' of blood rule, referring to the idea that anyone who had even a small amount of black ancestry was to be regarded as black. In 1910 and 1920 three-quarters of census categories were for 'non-whites'. The table indicates other variations in the content and number of categories. Melissa Nobles (2000, p.168) observes that: 'For 170 years, the Census Bureau's mission in regard to the race question was clear: define and then distinguish who was "white" from who was "non-white" and especially from who was "black"'. This is, however, only partially accurate. Actually, as the table shows, the prime concern and focus of the race question has been to categorize those deemed 'not white'. All these 'others' are defined through projected knowledge that produces the 'truths' of racial differentiation that the census creates and counts. The census does not just count *by* race, it also signals what counts *as* race.

READING 4.2

To follow this argument please turn to Reading 4.2 by Sharon Lee (1993). She identifies four issues in the interpretation of census classifications. Write brief notes on the questions below as you read:

1   What variations have there been in who has been regarded as white?

2   How have the census authorities dealt with non-standard responses?

3   What are some of the confusions of race and ethnicity created by the census?

In her article Lee reinforces the point about the considerable effort (or labour) the US census expends in providing many categories to classify and count all the 'non-white' varieties. Over time both the categories and purposes of the US census seem to have shifted. In the 1970 census respondents could self-identify on the race question, though enumerators were instructed to change answers such as 'Mexican', 'Moslem' or 'Brown' to 'White'! In the most recent censuses the number of categories has expanded and the question is no longer referred to as a race question, following expert advice that the word 'race' could be misleading, given the options provided (Lee, 1993).

A significant issue that Lee highlights is that who was regarded as white varied over time. For example, 'Asian Indians' were previously categorized as white but are now in the 'Asian or Pacific Islander' category. Meanwhile, people of a broadly similar ethnicity, Hispanics, can be placed into at least three categories – white, black or other. She also points out various confusions between race and ethnicity in the census. For instance, in 1930 the US census included the category 'Hindu', even though this refers to a religious rather than a racial grouping or identity. This is odd because religion is an aspect of identity that is usually suppressed in the US census. For Lee (1993) the absence of questions about religion reflects the distinction in the US constitution between church and state. Though this does not account for why 'Hindu' came up in 1930, it does have a significant consequence: it homogenizes (or, conversely, it fails to differentiate) the 'white' category by collapsing members of several religions (Christianity, Judaism, for example) into one racial grouping. It is also notable that the most recent UK census included a question on religion. It did so partly because of the force of two arguments. One was that 'Asian' and its sub-divisions failed to highlight distinctions in the socio-economic position of the main faiths that Asian people belong to. The second was that religion might be a more significant feature of self-identity than race, ethnicity or nationality.

Table 4.2 Racial categories used in the US census from 1790–1990

1790	1800	1810	1820	1830	1840	1850	1860	1870	1880	1890
Free White Males and Females	Free White Males and Females	Free White Males and Females	Free White Males and Females	Free White Persons	Free White Persons	White	White	White	White	White
All Other Free Persons, Except Indians Not Taxed	All Other Free Persons, Except Indians Not Taxed	All Other Free Persons, Except Indians Not Taxed	All Other Persons, Except Indians Not Taxed							
Slaves	Slaves	Slaves		Slaves	Slaves					
			Free Colored Persons	Free Colored Persons Gender Age	Free Colored Persons					
						Black (B)	Black	Black	Black	Black/Negro
						Mulatto (M)	Mulatto	Mulatto	Mulatto	Mulatto
										Quadroon
										Octoroon
								Chinese		Chinese
										Japanese

Source: Goldberg, 1997

1900	1910	1920	1930	1940	1950	1960	1970	1980	1990
White	White	White	White	White	White	White	White	White	White
Black (Negro or Negro Descent)	Black	Black	Negro	Negro	Negro	Negro	Negro or Black	Black (or Negro)	Black or Negro
	Mulatto	Mulatto							
			Mexican						
Chinese	Chinese	Chinese	Chinese	Chinese	Chinese	Chinese	Chinese	Chinese	Chinese
Japanese	Japanese	Japanese	Japanese	Japanese	Japanese	Japanese	Japanese	Japanese	Japanese
			Filipino	Filipino	Filipino	Filipino	Filipino	Filipino	Filipino
			Hindu	Hindu					
			Korean	Korean			Korean	Korean	Korean
								Vietnamese	Vietnamese
								Asian Indian	Asian Indian
								Guamanian	Guamanian
								Samoan	Samoan
						Hawaiian	Hawaiian	Hawaiian	Hawaiian
						Pan Hawaiian			
Indian	Indian	Indian	Indian	Indian	American Indian	American Indian	Indian (Amer.)	Indian (Amer.)	Indian (Amer.)
						Aleut		Aleut	Aleut
						Eskimo		Eskimo	Eskimo
	Other	Other	Other Races	Other Races	Other Race	Etc. (Inc. Asian Indians)	Other (Specify Race)	Other	Other Race
									Other API

The changing categories and the problems of re-classification by enumerators may be regarded as radically undermining the census and the administrative apparatus that constructs and uses it for planning and policy measures. Indeed, the US Census Bureau now warns against making comparisons between censuses. But what is the purpose of counting by race at all? The dangers of doing so are apparent in one of the two uses identified by Jenkins (1997). While censuses may not categorize named individuals, they do allocate individuals to categories and in certain cases, for example Nazi Germany and South Africa in the apartheid era, the consequences of such administrative processes are well known. On the other hand, Jenkins argues that census categorizations are vital for public administration and may serve to determine the targeting of resources to particular groups. Census numbers are both politicized and monetarized in shaping the distribution of government funds, as well as in claims made upon those funds (Rose, 1991). Both usages rely on knowledge and expertise to define, categorize and analyse the data, and the line between the benign and malign purposes of counting may sometimes be a thin one.

Despite his criticism of racialized categories and the administrative technologies of the census, David Goldberg (1997) argues that counting by race may be unavoidable because even as a rough and ready indicator it acts as a marker of past and present discrimination. Consequently, it also provides a reference point for measuring whether there have been improvements in the position of racialized groups over time. Both of these points are pertinent for issues of citizenship, social inclusion and social justice.

In the post-civil-rights era in the US, one purpose of counting by race is to enforce the legislation that is supposed to even-out some inequalities. What does this imply about using racial categorizations? Nobles (2000) identifies three positions:

1   In order to compare past and present would be an argument for keeping stable and unchanging categories.

2   Alternatively, if the purpose of the census is to capture and represent ethnic and racial diversity the old categories may be inadequate. This would be an argument for new and changing categories, as well as for increasing self-definition.

3   To produce broad, statistically useful and manageable categories that stand apart from both legislative need as well as the mobilizations of 'new' groups pressing to be represented in the census.

The last point seems an appealing and 'neutral' way to think about the census but, as Nobles recognizes, it would be hard to realize. There are two bigger problems with it: first, it would be at odds with the highly controversial nature of race-counting in the census; and, second, it suggests that statistical and categorical knowledge and expertise are purely technical and removed from the realm of politics.

3.2 Racial knowledge and power

Censuses provide a mode of racial categorization. The terms employed may or may not overlap with popular usage and with the terminology of racial science. In order to be useful, the categories need to be mutually exclusive, which is why the census avoids any way in which individuals can fit into more than one box or category. This has obvious shortcomings, as with the example of people of 'mixed race' who have been forced to be either one thing or another. (Though in 2000 the US census permitted people to tick more than one box or category.) The categories are not neutral descriptors: rather, as Goldberg (1997) argues, they impart assumptions, values and goals, they frame knowing, fashioning its content and they delimit the ways in which social relations are thought about. We can develop this point in four ways.

Racial naturalism

First, for all the changes and oddities of census classifications, the attempts to capture and confine something called race underline what Goldberg calls the principle of 'racial naturalism'. Haraway (1992, p.153) says that 'Race as a natural-technical object of knowledge is fundamentally a category marking political power through location in "nature"'. To follow the argument, consider Goldberg's response to the question of whether there should be a right to refuse to identify oneself in racial terms in the census:

> The denial of such a right implies (if it does not presuppose) that race is a primary, indeed, a primal category of human classification, one so natural … that it can be ignored only on pain of self-denial. Underlying the imperative of racial self-identification is the presumption of naturalism: one is expected to identify oneself as what one 'naturally' is. The democracy of self-naming is undermined by the authoritarianism of imposed identity and identification. Those resisting literally become the new 'Others'.
>
> (Goldberg, 1997, p.45)

Race is constituted as a pillar of identity and identification. Because of this, other ways of regarding individuals and groups – by religion for example – are relegated and hidden from view.

Discourse and power

Second, naming, recording and evaluating is an expression of power. As a result, in naming (or refusing to name) a group, or for an individual not to comply with the named categories, is a way in which existence is recognized or refused (Goldberg, 1997). Power here does not necessarily mean a repressive, censoring or controlling force. Indeed, Foucault was critical of classical sociology's notion that power is always a negative force. Instead, he argued that power is productive: it is a means of producing 'the truth'. The truth here refers to a system of ordered procedures for the production, regulation, distribution, and circulation of statements, or **discourses**. Power does not reside *outside of* social relations: it constitutes their organization. Thought works upon objects by means of inscription. It is through this process of recording that 'reality is made stable, mobile, comparable, combinable. It is rendered in a form in which it can be debated and diagnosed' (Rose and Miller, 1992, p.185).

discourse

Power–knowledge

Third, power cannot be conceived of as separate from knowledge. Foucault maintained that there is no power relation without a related field of knowledge, and no knowledge that does not presuppose power relations. The exercise of power perpetually creates knowledge and knowledge constantly induces effects of power. Thus, to come back to the census, the definition of what is to be counted, as well as the question of why count one thing rather than another, are not simply technical issues. Expert knowledge does not stand outside power-knowledge relations. Racial categories embody implicit assumptions about what phenotypical characteristics are signified as 'racial'. As Rose says:

> ... the technical processes which materialise the world – in graphs, figures and other traces – necessarily perform an act of simplification ... the[se] processes ... embody the expectations of the responsible technicians and officials; the discretion that they inevitably exercise is dissimulated by the claim that their expertise, whilst indispensable, is 'merely technical'. Expectations and beliefs are embodied in the framing of statistical enquiry, shaping what is counted in and in relation to what explicit or implicit theories. They are embedded in systems of classification adopted, for example ethnicity rather than race, nationality, ancestry, caste or religion.
>
> (Rose, 1991, p.680)

Enumerating objects of government

Fourth, censuses provide both a way of 'knowing' and a way of counting. Rose (1991) argues that numbers are essential to technologies of demographic government. The period since the seventeenth century has seen the growth of a new quantificatory era based on the key techniques of rationality, accounting and numericization. Rose (1991, p.676) asserts that in this 'domain of numbers' social quantification and statistics have been used to chart the 'moral topography of populations'. Particular objects of government, such as 'the insane', are delineated and enumerated through these techniques.

The last three points underline the relationship between power and knowedge; they are part of what Foucault meant by the term 'governmentality'. By this he means: 'the ensemble formed by the institutions, procedures, analyses and reflections, the calculations and tactics, that allow the exercise of this very specific albeit complex form of power, which has as its target populations' (cited in Abercrombie *et al.*, 2000, p.141). Those procedures, calculations and analyses include new technologies of governance such as censuses, statistics (what Foucault calls the 'science of the state') and the discourses of the social sciences. All are utilized in ways of 'knowing' and governing and managing populations. As Goldberg (1997) says, the racial categories and enumeration of the census can be seen as a formalized expression of racial governmentality because:

- Race is reflected and reproduced in administrative forms.
- Order and organization is provided by bureaucratic rationality.
- Data collection covers up ethical and political issues in the name of practicality.
- The knowledge it produces acquires status and authority, as uniformity and regularity are stressed and disorder is restricted.

Ethnic group question to be asked in England and Wales

What is your ethnic group?

◆ Choose one section from (a) to (e) then tick the appropriate box
   to indicate your cultural background.

(A) White

☐ British
☐ Irish
☐ Any other White background
   please write in below

[ ][ ][ ][ ][ ][ ][ ][ ][ ][ ][ ]
[ ][ ][ ][ ][ ][ ][ ][ ][ ][ ][ ]

(B) Mixed

☐ White and Black Caribbean
☐ White and Black African
☐ White and Asian
☐ Any other mixed background
   please write in below

[ ][ ][ ][ ][ ][ ][ ][ ][ ][ ][ ]
[ ][ ][ ][ ][ ][ ][ ][ ][ ][ ][ ]

(C) Asian or Asian British

☐ Indian
☐ Pakistani
☐ Bangladeshi
☐ Any other Asian background
   please write in below

[ ][ ][ ][ ][ ][ ][ ][ ][ ][ ][ ]
[ ][ ][ ][ ][ ][ ][ ][ ][ ][ ][ ]

(D) Black or Black British

☐ Caribbean
☐ African
☐ Any other Black background
   please write in below

[ ][ ][ ][ ][ ][ ][ ][ ][ ][ ][ ]
[ ][ ][ ][ ][ ][ ][ ][ ][ ][ ][ ]

(E) Chinese or Other ethnic group

☐ Chinese
☐ Any other
   please write in below

[ ][ ][ ][ ][ ][ ][ ][ ][ ][ ][ ]
[ ][ ][ ][ ][ ][ ][ ][ ][ ][ ][ ]

Figure 4.3 Ethnicity question from UK census, 2001

READING 4.3

U. Kalpagam provides an example of the governmentality approach in her depiction of colonial administration and statistical knowledge in nineteenth-century India. Please turn to her article now (Reading 4.3). Make brief notes on these questions as you read:

1   In what ways did the techniques of government of the colonial state differ from the pre-colonial?

2   What are the consequences of the concern with population?

This reading demonstrates the application of the conception of governmentality in a different context to the one we have been considering so far. In colonial India the key difference that Kalpagam identifies from the pre-colonial period is the 'vast documentation project' of charting and recording information to 'know' India scientifically. Using Foucault's definition of governmentality, she says this project required new institutions, procedures, calculations and tactics. Highlighting the link between power and knowledge, these instruments included censuses, surveys and mapping as the means by which the population was enumerated, classified and delineated. She argues that enumeration and classification transformed 'fuzzy communities' into firmly bounded ones, and qualitative attributes into 'hierarchically ordered facts'. For instance, instruments or techniques such as the census used and imposed a racial taxonomy, and in doing so re-ordered other forms of social groupings, such as kinship and lineage.

Kalpagam's account of colonial governmentality indicates that administrative and statistical techniques are not neutral instruments but rather that they serve to shape and constitute the social world. They define new objects of discourse and the kinds of interventions deemed to be required to regulate and manage populations. In this section we have used the US and UK censuses (see Figure 4.3) as instances through which race is constructed, delineated, and enumerated, and becomes the object of governmental interventions. As a technique of government the census is an example of power-knowledge in practice and while, as we have seen, it focuses upon racially 'othered' populations, the next section examines other modes of 'racial' regulation and interventions.

SUMMARY OF SECTION 3

The main arguments of this section have been that:

1   Census classifications reflect the persistent concern with defining racial 'others' and homogenize the category of whiteness.

2   Census categories and measures are not neutral and technical issues; they define, name and classify race authoritatively.

3   This process of governmentality is also evident in the colonial period, through quantification, classification and delineation.

4   Race is discursively produced through the effect of these institutional practices.

4 Whiteness

There is a potentially endless fascination with the multiple elaborations of the non-white categories in the census. Indeed, the concept of the labour of division is intended to draw attention to the energy expended in defining and maintaining conceptions of all the many varieties of 'the other'. As we have seen, conceptions of 'non-whiteness' have leapt about and proved to be far from consistent or stable in everyday language, in science and in official surveys. Newer categories multiply confusion and create new problems, rather than appearing as more precise and refined forms of measurement. This state of affairs tells its own tale and perhaps the key lesson is that the object that is being categorized evades definition because its boundaries are so unstable.

4.1 Whiteness: dominant and fractured

If we look back at the table of US census classifications, what *does not* change is of interest. Remarkably, over nearly two hundred years, one category stays almost totally unchanged, at least officially – the one labelled 'white' since 1850. To think about how curious that is, consider the fact that in the twentieth century the US was *one* of the centres of mass immigration. The first of two main waves of migration occurred from around the 1880s to the 1920s. This was dominated by people from southern, central and eastern parts of Europe. People from Asia and Latin America were most numerous in the second and subsequent wave (Lee, 1993). The multiple polyglot communities have all to some extent been 'Americanized' but it is still possible to discern distinct Swedish, Polish, British, Irish, Italian, Chinese, Korean, Jewish and Hispanic communities in the US. Significantly, some or many of these could be categorized as 'white', though some of the south-east Asian groups have – in the census at least – been differentiated from white since the nineteenth century. Given the conflation of race, ethnicity, skin colour and geographical origins in census classifications it might have been expected that white would not be treated as a singular term, particularly since there has been a seemingly unlimited concern with categorizing all the 'non-white' 'others'.

As this suggests, whiteness has remained largely unquestioned because it is the privileged viewing-point or the gaze that looks outwards at 'others' but is rarely itself the object of inspection. However, this does not mean that whiteness becomes totally unmarked and invisible. Rather, it operates relationally and relies on 'othering' for its meaning. As Haraway (1992, p.152) says, its 'race marking is *sotto voce*, but essential. White cannot be said quite out loud, or it loses its crucial position as a precondition of vision and becomes the object of scrutiny'. One way of testing this is to look back at Table 4.2. What is striking is that the census classifications have never been ordered alphabetically white remains at the top, always 'undivided, non-polarized, without distinction, and virtually without qualification' (Goldberg, 1997, p.53). If the listing followed a historical logic, 'American Indians' (or Native Americans) would be placed at the top; if demonstrating neutrality in hierarchy and classification was the intention, then an alphabetical system would be used.

We can get a sense of how whiteness acquired its contemporary meaning by following Bonnett's (2000) argument. He says that historical research shows the existence of colour-consciousness among the Chinese and among the people of the 'Middle East' (another odd term underlining the primacy of a Euro-centric vision, since where the middle east is depends literally on where one starts from): both saw themselves as, and were seen as, white. These white identities were not racialized in the modern sense. For the Chinese, skin colour was just one among a number of attributes of identity and being white was not conceived of in an exclusive manner. For them and Middle Eastern people a sense of being white was not destabilized by their encounters with Europeans. The latter were described as having 'ash'-like complexions and, in the Middle Ages, Europeans encountered by Middle Easterners were depicted as yellow, red and pale blue, as well as white.

Bonnett (2000) locates the emergence of racialized white identities at two main points. First, while whiteness did have earlier associations with purity and religion, it is notable that in the seventeenth century the idea of polygenesis (the idea that the groups or races of humankind have different lines of descent) associated blackness with the mark of Cain. The progeny of Ham (the son of Noah) were said to be marked with 'a black badge to symbolise loathsomeness' (Hannaford, cited in Bonnett, 2000, p.16). Second, the idea of race shifted from one marking a sign of nobility or breeding to a more inclusive notion of 'us', a process through which whiteness, Europe and Christianity became the pillars of white identity, to the exclusion of both non-whites and non-European whites. Hence, Bonnett points out that the Chinese came to think of themselves as 'yellow' rather than white.

Two brief examples give us a sense of this shift to a racialized and exclusionary whiteness. First, whiteness is accorded particular qualities that cut across the mind/body dualism – which associates white with the former and black with the latter – that we encountered earlier. For the eighteenth-century writer Charles White, there was no doubt about the intellectual superiority of white Europeans, but this was not the limit of their virtues as he observed that in: 'what other quarter of the globe shall we find the blush that over spreads the soft features of the beautiful women of Europe, that emblem of modesty, of delicate feelings, and sense?' (cited in Bonnett, 2000, p.18). This indicates at an internal fracture of whiteness in which women are coded as paler/lighter than men, a gendered differentiation examined in more detail below. Second, the idea of a common Caucasian race began to fragment. For example, in his *Peoples of all Nations* (1922), the anthropologist Sir Arthur Keith claimed that the European end of the Caucasian race was the 'cradle-land of the blond man; [while] at its Indian end we can find people showing distinct Australoid and Negroid traits' (cited in Bonnett, 2000, p.18). Both examples highlight the power of ideas in producing racialized whiteness, so it is important to note that other sociologists would emphasize the significance of material forces, including conquests, colonialism and exploitation. For example, Haraway (1992, p.153) maintains that: 'The concept of race ... was inextricably woven out of the history of the conjunction of knowledge and power in European and Euro-American expansion and economic and sexual exploitation of "marked" or "colored" peoples.'

Despite its dominance, whiteness, like all racial categorizations, is unstable and divided internally. As the Introduction to this book emphasized, with respect to *all* social divisions, cleavages of gender, nationality, class and religion intersect it. Particular fractions of whiteness either have to be protected as its 'essence', or excluded as 'other'. For Bonnett (2000, p.26) the reason for this is that whiteness because of 'its excessive and fetishistic nature ... is constantly endangered by groups (for example, women, the Irish, and the working class) who fail to live up to' its demands. We explore the ethnic, religious, national, class and gendered instabilities and fragmentations of whiteness in the remainder of section 4.

Let us return to the census for a moment: the apparently homogenized category 'white' seems doubly anomalous when there is historical evidence that, in the US, people of Slavic, Mediterranean and Italian origins have explicitly been seen as a race apart. For instance, Italian immigrants were called the 'Chinese of Europe' and in the South forced to attend all-black schools (Warren and Twine, 1997, p.205). Such depictions once again call into question the association of race with skin colours that are not white since some white people can also be treated as a racially differentiated sub-set of the population:

> Many physical characteristics (both real and imagined) have been and continue to be signified as a mark of nature and of 'race'. Moreover, cultural characteristics have also been, and continue to be, signified as to the same end. The reification of skin colour therefore mistakenly privileges one specific instance of signification and ignores the historical and contemporary evidence which shows that other populations (Jews, Irish people, etc.) have been signified as distinct and inferior 'races' without reference to skin colour.
>
> (Miles, 1993, p.87)

Miles (1993) maintains that the way to understand this signification is through the concept of 'racialization'. By this he refers to the process by which a particular group, or its characteristics or actions, is identified as a collectivity by its real or imagined phenotypical characteristics, or 'race'. The concept is also used to indicate the ways in which social structures and ideologies become imbued with racial meanings. As Miles shows, the idea of racialization connects race-thinking in ways that may be linked to cultural or physical characteristics. So instead of thinking about race as a product of colonial and imperial encounters, Miles argues that a racialization of the interior served to racialize particular sections of the white population.

ACTIVITY 5

Some instances of white groups being regarded as racialized have already been mentioned – have a look back at these. Can you think of any other cases of whites being racialized? For instance, look at the advertisement in Figure 4.4. Can you tell what nationalities are being stereotyped here?

We have encountered the idea of racialization earlier in the chapter, but the reason for raising it here is to allow you to to think of it particularly in relation to whiteness. To examine racialization, Miles uses the example of the response to Jewish migration in the nineteenth century. Anti-Jewish pogroms or massacres in Eastern Europe led to Jewish migration into other parts of Europe, including Britain. Campaigns against the re-settlement of Jews exaggerated the scale of immigration

Figure 4.4 *Dreamcast advert: 'Take on Johnny Foreigner online'*

and demanded laws to control and limit the numbers of Jewish refugees. These campaigns promulgated views that Jewishness was an hereditary and irremovable quality of blood; and that Jews were an 'alien race', associated with crime, disease, perversion and part of an international conspiracy to undermine civilized societies. In other words, as Miles says, 'the migrant population has been signified as a distinct category or type of human being by reference to real or alleged biological characteristics, a signification that has usually been accompanied by an explicit or implicit use of the discourse of "race"' (Miles 1993, p.135).

Religion is an internal division within whiteness, though it figures in different ways. On the one hand, the depiction of Jews as other defines them as not quite white. Physical features such as nose shape and size have been a recurring feature of attempts in imaginative works – and in racial science – to characterize and differentiate Jews from Gentiles. On another hand, religion features in the making of distinct national identities, for example in the argument that the modern identity of Britain depended on and was formed out of the self-conscious separation and distancing of Protestantism from the European Catholic majority, in ways that made the latter 'other'.

Irish people, for instance, have been a key 'other' for the British/English, and been subordinated within a racial hierarchy that has inferiorized them. We have already had a sense of how Catholicism was a fracture within English/ British whiteness. What is of significance here is the differential cultural and biological racialization of the Irish. For instance, the American Encyclopaedia of 1860 said that the US population 'contained elements of both northern and southern races of Europe, the first represented by the English, Scots and Germans and the second by the Celtic Irish'; elsewhere, the latter were described as 'savage, grovelling and bestial, lazy and wild, simian and sensual' (Knobel, cited in Warren and Twine, 1997, p.203). Thus, regarded as a separate and inferior 'Celtic race', physically distinguishable from the 'superior Anglo Saxons', conflicts between these two groups were described as race wars. Henry Louis Gates recounts a tale from 1973 when a member of the House of Lords spoke of 'distinct and clearly definable differences of race' between Irish Catholics and Protestants, claiming that 'any Englishman' could tell them apart (cited in Warren and Twine, 1997, p.203). It seems, however, that this capacity was not just limited to the English as, in the nineteenth century, the German writer Friedrich Engels observed that: 'Whenever a district is distinguished for special filth the explorer may safely count on meeting chiefly those Celtic faces, which one recognises at the first glance as different from the Saxon physiognomy of the native' (cited in Cohen, 1988, p.72).

Racializations of the Irish combine a sense of biological distinctiveness ('simian' and differing from 'Saxon physiognomy'), as well as cultural differentiation ('lazy', 'filth'). Like Jews, it was by no means clear that they were regarded as white. Indeed, the Irish have been depicted with ape-like features linking them to 'African savages' and to traditions of political dissent that tie them to the 'wandering Jew' (Cohen, 1988). As Cohen points out, this double stereotype

> … is actually encoded in the special name given to the Irish – Milesians, descendants of the legendary Spanish King Milesus. This 'race' was supposedly the product of interbreeding between the Moors and the Marrains, that is, between Africans who had Hispanic roots and Spanish Jews … This hybrid status did more than confirm the Irish as a 'monstrous race'. It set them apart, made them a special case.
>
> (Cohen, 1988, p.74)

In British race-thinking the Irish stood in as the 'missing evolutionary link between the "bestiality" of Black slaves and that of the English worker' (Cohen, 1988, p.74). They were 'white negroes', and in this sense could be seen as providing the model for slavery and colonialism. The simianization, or ape-like representation, of the Irish is notable because it demonstrates a continuity within racialized thought and Curtis (1997) has shown how these images were persistent throughout Victorian times. Thus, both the Irish and black people 'were constructed as objects of knowledge as "primitives", more closely connected to the apes than the white "race"' (Haraway, 1992, p.153): see Figure 4.5.

Figure 4.5

IRISH IBERIAN.　　　　ANGLO–TEUTONIC.　　　　NEGRO.

The Iberians are believed to have been originally an African race, who thousands of years ago spread themselves through Spain over Western Europe. Their remains are found in the barrows, or burying places, in sundry parts of these countries. The skulls are of low, prognathous type. They came to Ireland, and mixed with the natives of the South and West, who themselves are supposed to have been of low type and descendants of savages of the Stone Age, who, in consequence of isolation from the rest of the world, had never been out-competed in the healthy struggle of life, and thus made way, according to the laws of nature, for superior races.

Racializations that could be deemed 'closer to home' were focused on the lower or working classes in the Victorian era. Sometimes connected with views of the Irish, both were effectively racialized as 'other'. The racialized nature of class relations is apparent through the conception of the dangerous classes conceived as a racial sub-stratum or 'residuum' of the population. Fears about mob rule in Victorian Britain focused heavily on the concentration of the poor in urban areas, promiscuity, and population explosion. In these discourses, 'a new topography of urban degeneration emerges featuring sewers and cesspits, swamps and jungles, rookeries, and so on, all of them "fertile" breeding grounds of crime and vice of every kind' (Cohen, 1988, p.71). The themes of dirt, lack of hygiene and manners, and itinerancy formed the Victorian conception of racial hierarchy that combined social, moral and physical distinctions (Malik, 1996).

social Darwinism

As reflected in nineteenth-century **social Darwinism**, racial-thinking simultaneously invoked and transcended biology. Colour and social distinctions were linked by the governing classes of England who came to regard:

> The Irish and non-European native just as they had, quite openly, regarded their own labouring classes for many centuries: as thoroughly undisciplined, with a tendency to revert to bestial behaviour ... and by occasional but severe flashes of violence; vicious and sly, incapable of telling the truth, naturally lazy and unwilling to work unless under compulsion.
>
> (Bernard Semmel, cited in Malik, 1996, p.97)

A distinctive form of 'class racism' underlay the class-based codes of appropriate breeding and civility. To the extent that these codes also informed ideas about the civilizing mission of colonialism, there are clear links between racism 'at home' and abroad. The lower classes were deemed 'white trash', a designation signalling the consistent inter-linking of race and class (Wray and Newitz, 1997).

Finally, gender also fractures and intersects whiteness. The quote from Charles White indicated how white women are located in a particular space of the white (male) imagination. The gendered articulation of whiteness is most marked in fears about 'race mixing' and miscegenation, especially about sexual relations between white women and black men, as we also saw in Reading 4.2.

For instance, Henry Champley's *White Women, Coloured Men* (1936) fetishizes whiteness by essentializing it as something universally desirable in the bodies of white women. Describing and worrying about what he calls the 'coloured people's' discovery of the white women as 'a marvel … a wonder … as an idol worthy of being desired above all else', Champley issues this stark warning: 'Beware, White Race! The Coloured Races have discovered your supreme treasure, the White woman!' (cited in Bonnett, 2000, p.25). As Bonnett shows, this was tied in with fears of 'race suicide', and a feeling that the era of the authority of white men was coming to an end. Titles such as *Passing of the Great Race* (1916) and *The Rising Tide of Color Against White World Supremacy* (1920) exemplify this attitude. These discourses placed women in the position of what Ware (1992) calls 'conduits of the essence of the race', symbolizing biological and moral continuity and transmission. It is part of a code of breeding where race and racial continuity are invoked through ideas of inheritance and heritage (Cohen, 1988). The worries about 'race suicide' and 'degeneracy' are particularly apparent in the eugenics movement, which provides another illustration of the intersection of class, gender and race and power-knowledge.

4.2 Eugenics: power and population

Eugenics refers to a political strategy that seeks to 'improve' the reproduction of supposedly superior hereditary traits among particular sections of the population, while discouraging or preventing reproduction among those considered inferior – sometimes forcibly through sterilization. Many notable people in Europe and North America subscribed to these ideas at one time. Reflecting the concept of power-knowledge, it is important to note that eugenics is not a tale of manipulation by evil men, rather it is one of individuals committed to progress through research and reform (reaffirming our earlier point about science and race). I want to look now at one of the founders of German eugenics, Wilhelm Schallmayer (1857–1919). In his case, the intersection of class, gender and race is most apparent in arguments for an elevated conception of motherhood, including the suggestion that girls should be taught from an early age the importance of reproduction according to biological fitness for the survival and prosperity of the German race and nation (Weiss, 1987). In the following reading, however, it is the theme of rational management of population in Schallmayer's eugenics that is significant:

> He was the first person to clearly articulate the technocratic/managerial logic behind German eugenic thought, indeed eugenic thought in general: the idea that power or 'national efficiency' is essentially a problem in the rational management of the population.
>
> (Weiss, 1987, p.4)

In 1891 Schallmayer spelt out a strategy for saving Germany and the West from dangers of 'degeneration'. He advocated placing limits on the reproduction of 'hereditary degenerates', those 'asocial' individuals who were deemed the least productive, including criminals, alcoholics, and the insane. The corollary of this was to boost the reproduction of the 'fittest' who because of later marriage, birth control and excessive individualism were delaying childbearing. Schallmayer's concern – and that of eugenicists in general – was that this trend could signal a national decline, or degeneration, into mediocrity as the fittest reproduced less, while the unfit carried on. To prevent this he proposed a policy for the management of population growth to increase national efficiency.

Please turn to Reading 4.4, 'Power through population' by Sheila Faith Weiss. Consider these questions as you read:

1   Why were population management and quality important to Schallmayer?

2   What measures did Schallmayer and other eugenicists propose to deal with the problem of population quantity and quality at the time of the First World War?

Weiss stresses that, unlike some other German eugenicists, Schallmayer did not base his view on presumed racial superiority, or believe that eugenics was about the improvement of one race at the expense of another. In this he was at odds with the idea of 'race hygiene', and particularly of Aryan supremacy, a lineage that fed into the later Nazi period. However, a clear line of continuity between Schallmayer and these other strands is in the language of rational management of population and national efficiency. For Weiss (1987, p.157), the relationship between population and power in eugenics invokes a 'technocratic conception of population as a natural resource' that should be subjected to rational control.

Although Weiss does not do so herself, this argument can be re-stated in the language of governmentality. The stress on power through population and the control of reproduction is an instance of the Foucauldian idea of 'bio-power'. Foucault uses the concept of bio-power to refer to the various regulations and interventions of the body that focus on it as 'imbued with the mechanisms of life and serving as the basis of biological processes: propagation, births and mortality, the level of health, life expectancy and longevity, with all the conditions that can cause them to vary' (Foucault, 1979, p.139). Through seeking to manipulate and manage the quality and quantity of the population, statistical, demographic and scientific expertise and power-knowledge constitute the groups and objects of governmental regulation and intervention. Eugenics – with its reliance on science and rationality – provides an instance of this process. The logic of eugenics suggests that 'hereditary degenerates' would die out through processes of natural selection, being less suited for survival; or, in other words, that nature would take its course. Yet, eugenics has always been more prescription than mere description: it requires *active* intervention and control in population management. The supposedly objective, scientific and natural bases of eugenics validated the authority and power of established and emerging professions and human sciences – including biology, anthropology, psychology, sociology, criminology and social work.

4.3   The end of whiteness?

In September 2000 a front-page story in *The Observer* claimed that by the end of the twenty-first century whites would be a minority in Britain (see Figure 4.6 below). Based on work by an unnamed demographer using a projection of birth rates and immigration, the analysis is statistically questionable. What is more significant is that it suggests that all white people have something 'racially' more in common with each other than they do with people across the divide of skin colour. *The Observer* story reproduces concerns in the US where the process of whites becoming a minority has been feared for some time. However, the US provides another way of looking at whiteness and the process of 'minorization' which suggests that the boundaries of whiteness can be both exclusionary and fluid.

UK Whites will be a minority by 2100

Last days of the white world

by Anthony Browne

Whites will be an ethnic minority in Britain by the end of the century. Analysis of official figures indicate that, at current fertility rates and levels of immigration, there will be more non-whites than whites by 2100.

It would be the first time in history that a major indigenous population has voluntarily become a minority, rather than through war, famine or disease. Whites will be a minority in London by 2010.

In the early 1950s there were only a few tens of thousands of non-whites in the UK. By 1991 that had risen to 3 million – 6 per cent of the population. The population of ethnic minorities has been growing at between 2 and 4 per cent a year. Net immigration has been running at record levels, with 185,000 newcomers last year.

Government forecasts suggest that immigration on its own will be responsible for half the growth of the British population over the next couple of decades.

New immigrants, who are on average younger than the population at large, also tend to have higher fertility rates. In contrast the population of white British citizens is static. Their feritility rate is very low – at under 2 children per woman – and there is overall emigration of British citizens.

The analysis of the figures showed that if the population of ethnic minorities grows at 4 per cent a year, whites will become a minority before 2100. The demographer who made the calculation wished to remain anonymous for fear of accusations of racism.

Figure 4.6 *Front page,* The Observer, *3 September 2000*

READING 4.5

Please turn to Reading 4.5, an extract from an article by Warren and Twine. Consider these questions as you read:

1 How did whiteness come to incorporate Catholics and Celts in the nineteenth century?

2 How do they suggest the Irish and Chinese 'became white'?

3 In what other ways do they suggest that whiteness is a fluid category?

Warren and Twine indicate that groups such as the Irish and Chinese who were once racialized as 'other' in the US have become 'whitened' over time. They say this has occurred because 'blackness' has been positioned as the main racial referent; as blacks became 'blacker', so various groups seem to have become more 'white', sometimes by adopting more 'white' attitudes and social patterns. Whiteness is therefore not an essence but a flexible designation. Like all raced categories it is not a fixed state of being, but a matter of becoming. Whiteness is an historically and socially constructed category – other divisions intersect it; it is unstable and fluid. But, at the same time, it is also dominant.

SUMMARY OF SECTION 4

This section has investigated whiteness as a racial category. The main arguments have been that:

1   Whiteness became dominant through processes of excluding others, including non-European whites, Jews and the Irish among others.

2   Class and gender divisions intersect whiteness, and vice versa.

3   Eugenics reflects a concern about the decline of whiteness. Its programme for the rational management of population signals the application of governmental regulation and intervention to whiteness.

4   The boundaries of whiteness are both exclusionary and flexible.

5 Conclusion

We began this chapter by locating race as a key social division but also one that contains many paradoxes. The idea of race – what features count or are signified as race, which groups are and are not 'raced' – varies over time. Racial names and labels also vary, and their meaning is not necessarily fixed at their point of origin. Furthermore, official categories of race classification – and the reasons for collecting data in this way – are also open to fluctuation (though as we saw in sections 3 and 4, categories such as white shift less than others do, at least in official classifications). Nevertheless, despite all this fluidity and flux (and as you will see in Chapters 6 and 7), race clearly figures in terms of material divisions, where there is extensive, but also uneven, evidence of racial inequalities. Whether race or racism solely accounts for these disparities is problematic. I have argued that race is always fractured and complicated by class and gender relations and it is in the articulation between these divisions that understandings of social divisions and differences need to be situated.

One of the main concerns of this chapter has been to contest any implicit expectation or assumption that issues of race concern only 'non-whites'. In sections 2 and 3 we have stressed that using race in a limited way that equates with it colours that are not white serves to bring particular groups into vision, making them the objects of scrutiny, classification and regulation. Hence, section 4 considered that some white groups have also been regarded in racialized ways, as in the case of the Irish, Italians and Slavs among others. The core issue linking these sections is the way in which racial thinking operates as a form of essentialism – defining people as members of groups on the basis of some real or imagined commonality. Discourse and power – including classification, expertise and authority – are crucial to the production of knowledge about race. They serve to both constitute and maintain the idea of what type of social division race is.

Does it make sense to persist with a discourse of race at all? Mac an Ghaill (1999) has criticized conventional sociology for 'over-racializing' particular minorities, while systematically 'under-racializing' whites. This is generally true of the sociology of race, but should it now be an aim to racialize whiteness, as Mac an Ghaill seems to suggest? An alternative perspective would underline the need to destabilize all racial categories. From this viewpoint, stressing whiteness as a 'raced' category could be counter-productive as it re-inscribes the raciology that Gilroy has argued against, in describing it as the 'lore that brings the virtual realities of "race" to dismal and destructive life' (Gilroy, 2000, p.11). In condemning raciology, Gilroy has also been critical of 'anti-racism' because, he argues, it adopts the same 'mythic morphology' of race. For Gilroy a non-racial future can only be reached by doing away with systems of race-thinking in order to transcend race and establish cosmopolitan and transcultural histories freed from raciological bias. His argument has been criticized for adopting a view of race that fixes it with negative meanings and associations. Against that we have seen that race can have shifting meanings. But some degree of changeability and instability co-exists with continuing – though not fixed – patterns of domination and inequality in both ideological and material terms. The key paradox then, as we saw in section 3 in the discussion of the purposes of using racialized census categories, is that it may be necessary to persist with racial categories and discourses because they provide a benchmark against which such patterns can be identified and changed.

References

Abercrombie, N., Hill, S. and Turner, B.S. (2000) *The Penguin Dictionary of Sociology*, London, Penguin Books.

Allen, J. (2000) 'Power: its institutional guises (and disguises)' in Hughes, G. and Fergusson, R. (eds) *Ordering Lives*, London, Routledge.

Banton, M. (1991) 'The race relations problematic', *British Journal of Sociology*, vol.42, pp.115–30.

Blackburn, D. (2000) 'Why race is not a biological concept' in Lang, B. (ed.) *Race and Racism in Theory and Practice*, Lanham, MD, Rowman and Littlefield.

Bonnett, A. (2000) *White Identities: Historical and International Perspectives*, Hemel Hempstead, Prentice Hall.

Cohen, P. (1988) 'The perversions of inheritance' in Cohen, P. and Bains, H. (eds) *Multi-Racist Britain*, Basingstoke, Macmillan.

Curtis, L. (1984) *Nothing But the Same Old Story*, London, Information on Ireland.

Curtis, L.P. (1997), *Apes and Angels – the Irishman in Victorian Caricature*, revd edn, Washington DC, Smithsonian Institution (originally published in 1971).

Fanon, F. (1986) *Black Skin, White Masks*, London, Pluto Press.

Foucault, M. (1977) *Discipline and Punish*, Harmondsworth, Penguin Books.

Foucault, M. (1979) *The History of Sexuality*, Harmondsworth, Penguin Books.

Gilroy, P. (2000) *Between Camps*, London, Allen Lane.

Goldberg, D.T. (1997) *Racial Subjects*, New York, Routledge.

Haraway, D. (1992) *Primate Visions*, London, Verso.

Hetherington, K. and Munro, R. (eds) (1997) *Ideas of Difference*, Oxford, Blackwell.

Jenkins, R. (1997) *Rethinking Ethnicity*, London, Sage.

Kalpagam, U. (2000) 'The colonial state and statistical knowledge', *History of the Human Sciences*, vol.13, pp.37–55.

Kohn, M. (1996) *The Race Gallery: The Return of Racial Science*, London, Vintage.

Lee, S.M. (1993) 'Racial classifications in the US census: 1890–1990', *Ethnic and Racial Studies*, vol.16, pp.75–94.

Mac an Ghaill, M. (1999) *Contemporary Racisms and Ethnicities*, Buckingham, Open University Press.

Macpherson, W. (1999) *The Stephen Lawrence Inquiry*, London, The Stationery Office.

Malik, K. (1996) *The Meaning of Race*, Basingstoke, Macmillan.

Miles, R. (1993) *Racism after 'Race Relations'*, London, Routledge.

Nobles, M. (2000) *Shades of Citizenship*, Stanford, CT, Stanford University Press.

Omi, M. and Winant, H. (1994) *Racial Formation in the United States*, 2nd edn, New York, Routledge.

Parekh, B. *et al.* (2000) *The Future of Multi-ethnic Britain*, London, Profile Books.

Phillips, M. (2001) *London Crossings*, London, Continuum.

Rose, N. (1991) 'Governing by numbers: figuring out democracy', *Accounting, Organizations and Society*, vol.16, pp.673–92.

Rose, N. and Miller, P. (1992) 'Political power beyond the state', *British Journal of Sociology*, vol.43, pp.173–205.

Ware, V. (1992) *Beyond the Pale*, London, Verso.

Warren, J.W. and Twine, F.W. (1997) 'White Americans, the new minority?', *Journal of Black Studies*, vol.28, pp.200–18.

Weiss, S.F. (1987) *Race Hygiene and National Efficiency: The Eugenics of Wilhelm Schallmeyer*, Berkeley, CA, University of California Press.

Winant, H. (1994) *Racial Conditions*, Minneapolis, MN, University of Minnesota Press.

Wray, M. and Newitz, A. (1997) *White Trash: Race and Class in America*, New York, Routledge.

Readings

4.1   Richard Jenkins, 'Categorization and power' (1997)

Groups and categories

If ethnicity is transactional, those transactions are of two basic kinds. First, there are processes of *internal definition*: actors signal to in- or out-group members a self-definition of their nature or identity. This can be an ego-centred, individual process or a collective, group process, although it only makes sense to talk of ethnicity in an individual sense when the identity being defined and its expressions refer to a recognizable collective identity and draw upon a repertoire of culturally specified practices. Although conceptualized in the first instance as internal, these processes are necessarily transactional and social (even in the individual case) because they presuppose both an audience, without whom they make no sense, and an externally derived framework of meaning.

On the other hand there are processes of *external definition*. These are other-directed processes, during which one person or set of persons defines the other(s) as 'X', 'Y', or whatever. This may, at its most consensual, be the validation of others' internal definition(s) of themselves. At the conflictual end of the spectrum of possibilities, however, there is the imposition, by one set of actors upon another, of a putative name and characterization which affects in significant ways the social experience(s) of the categorized.

This process of external definition may, in theory, be an individual act, in which person A defines person or persons B as, say 'X' or 'Y'. For two reasons, however, it is difficult to think about external definition as solely an individual process. In the first place, more than an audience is involved: the others here are the object(s) of the process of definition, and implied within the situation is a meaningful intervention in their lives, an acting upon them. Thus external definition can only occur within active social relationships, however distant or at however many removes. Second, the capacity to intervene successfully in other people's lives implies either the power or the authority to do so. The exercise of power implies competitive access to and control over resources, while authority is, by definition, only effective when it is legitimate. Power and authority are necessarily embedded within active social relationships.

This distinction between internal and external definition is, of course, primarily analytical. In the complexity of day-to-day social life, each is chronically implicated in the other in an ongoing dialectic of identification. The categorization of 'them' is too useful a foil in the identification of 'us' for this not to be the case, and the definition of 'us' too much the product of a history of relationships with a range of significant others (Hagendoorn, 1993). ... Ethnicity – the production, reproduction and transformation of the 'group-ness' of culturally differentiated collectivities – is a two-way process that takes place across the boundary between 'us' and 'them'. At the individual level, in the ongoing production of personal identities, much the same can be said. Individual identity is located within a two-way social process, an interaction of 'ego' and 'other', inside and outside. It is in the meeting of internal and external definition that identity, whether collective or individual, is created.

...

The contrasting processes of identity production, internal and external, can be illuminated further by drawing on concepts derived from the methodology of social research. Basic to the sociological and anthropological enterprises is the classification of human collectivities. One of the most enduringly useful distinctions we employ for this purpose is that between *groups* and *categories*. A group is a collectivity which is meaningful to its members, of which they are aware; a category is a collectivity which is defined according to criteria formulated by the sociologist or anthropologist. A group is a self-conscious collectivity, rooted in processes of internal definition, while a category is externally defined. This distinction is, in the first instance, concerned with the procedures which sociologists and anthropologists employ to constitute the social world as a proper object for systematic empirical inquiry and theorization. As such, it is relevant beyond the study of ethnicity and ethnic relations. Debates about social class, for example, are often characterized by disagreement about which principle of definition is most appropriate for the adequate constitution of classes as objects of/for analysis.

However, social groups and social categories can also be understood as different kinds of collectivities *in the actual social world*, and not just in the abstracted social world conjured up by social scientists. A vivid example of this can be found in Marx's famous contrast between 'a class in itself' (a category) and 'a class for itself' (a group). In this understanding of the development of class consciousness, the working class(es) – a social category that was initially defined, with reference to their immiseration and alienation from the means of production, and to their threat to the established order, by others such as capitalists, agencies of the state or socialist activists – becomes a social group, the members of which identify with each other in their collective misfortune, thus creating the possibility of organized collective action on the basis of that identification.

Social categorization – the identification of others as a collectivity – is no less a routine social process than the collective self-identification of the group. Whereas social groups define themselves, their name(s), their nature(s) and their boundary(ies), social categories are identified, defined and delineated by others. All collectivities can be characterized as, to some extent, defined, and thus socially constructed, in both ways. Each side of the dichotomy is implicated in the other and social identity is the outcome of a dialectical process of internal *and* external definition. Whether, in any specific instance, one chooses to talk about a group or a category will depend on the balance struck between internal and external processes in that situation. It is a question of degree.

Categorization and power

Categorization contributes to group identity in various ways. There is, for example, something which might be referred to as 'internalization': the categorized group is exposed to the terms in which another group defines it and assimilates the categorization, in whole or in part, into its own identity. Put this baldly, however, the suggestion seems to beg more questions than it answers: *why* should the external definition be internalized, for example, and *how* does it happen? At least five possible scenarios suggest themselves.

First, the external categorization might be more or less the same as an aspect of existing group identity, in which case they will simply reinforce each other. It seems altogether plausible that some degree of external reinforcement or validation is crucial to the successful maintenance of internal (group) definitions. Similarly, categorization may be less likely to 'stick' where it is markedly at odds with existing boundaries and identifications.

Second, there is the incremental cultural change which is likely to be a product of any long-standing but relatively harmonious inter-ethnic contact. The ethnic boundary is osmotic, and not just in terms of personnel: languages and cultures may also interact, and in the process identities are likely to be affected. We, for example, may gradually and imperceptibly come to define ourselves somewhat differently in the light of how they appear to define us, and how they treat us (and, equally likely, vice versa).

Third, the external category might be produced by people who, in the eyes of the original group, have the legitimate authority to categorize them, by virtue of their superior ritual status, knowledge, or whatever. Such a situation implies greater social than cultural differentiation – if a distinction posed in terms as crude as this is admissible – inasmuch as legitimate authority necessarily requires at least a minimal degree of shared participation in values or cosmology.

Fourth, is a simpler case, or at least a cruder one: external categorization is imposed by the use of physical force or its threat, i.e. the exercise of power. The experience of violation may become integral to group identification. The categorized, without the physical capacity to resist the carrying of identity cards, the wearing of armbands, or whatever more subtle devices of identification and stigmatization might be deployed, may, in time, come to see themselves in the language and categories of the oppressor. They are certainly likely to behave in an appropriate manner.

Finally, there are the oppressed who do resist, who reject imposed boundaries and/or their content(s). However, the very act of defying categorization, of striving for an autonomy of self-identification, is, of course, an effect of being categorized in the first place. The rejected external definition *is* internalized, but paradoxically, as the focus of denial.

In these five possibilities, a distinction between power and legitimate authority is apparent. However, the contribution of categorization to group identity depends upon more than 'internalization'. The capacity of one group of people to effectively define or constitute the conditions of existence experienced by Others is enormously important in the internal-external dialectic of collective identification. …

To revisit an example given earlier, the categorization of the Mapuche by the Spanish and white Chileans, in particular ways, must be expected to have influenced the behaviour of the Chileans towards the Mapuche: 'native policy' as Stuchlik puts it. The Chileans, like the Spanish before them, because of their eventual monopolization of violence within the local context and their consequent control of resources, were – and, indeed, still are – in a position to make their categorization of the Mapuche count disproportionately in the social construction of Mapuche life. And the internal–external dialectic can be seen at work: resistance to the Spanish was, for example, an important factor creating internal group identification in the shape of military alliances, and generating, between the sixteenth and nineteenth centuries, the wider collectivity of the Mapuche out of a network of small, mutually related kin groups (Stuchlik 1976: 15). In many senses, therefore, what it means to be a Mapuche is in part a consequence of what the Spanish or the Chileans have *made* it mean.

The effective categorization of a group of people by a more powerful 'other' is not, therefore, 'just' a matter of classification (if, indeed, there is any such thing). It is necessarily an intervention in that group's social world which will, to an extent and in ways that are a function of the specifics of the situation, alter that world and the experience of living in it. Just as the Chileans have the capacity to constitute, in part, the experience of 'being a Mapuche', so, for example, employment recruiters in Britain – who are typically white – contribute to the social constitution of the collective experience of growing up as a member of a black ethnic minority....

References

Hagendoorn, L. (1993) 'Ethnic categorization and outgroup exclusion: cultural values and social stereotypes in the construction of ethnic hierarchies', *Ethnic and Racial Studies*, vol.16, pp.27–51.

Stuchlik, M. (1976) *Life on a Half Share: Mechanisms of Social Recruitment among the Mapuche of Southern Chile*, London, C. Hurst.

Source: Jenkins, 1997, pp.53–5 and pp.70–2

 4.2 # Sharon M. Lee, 'Racial classifications in the US census: 1890–1990' (1993)

A two-category system based on perceived skin colour: whites and others

The separation of the US population into a dichotomy based on skin colour (white and non-white) is perhaps the most enduring theme reflected in the census classifications of race examined in this article. Throughout the time span covered in this article, there is just one category, White, for counting people who are popularly considered White but who may vary considerably in actual skin colour and physical appearance, while the remaining categories (sometimes as many as thirteen) referred to groups that are considered non-White.[1] These other groups also varied in terms of skin colour, with some who may well be 'whiter' than some classified as Whites.

It is also noteworthy that who were considered White varied over time, reflecting the influence of racial ideology on census classifications. Prior to 1980 Asian Indians were considered White but are now placed in the Asian/Pacific Islander aggregate.

Mexicans were listed as a separate race or colour in 1930 but from 1940 till recently, Mexicans and other people of Spanish descent were routinely placed in the White group. Now, people of Hispanic origin can be of any race – White, Black, or Other. Such freedom of choice for Hispanics is a new development and demonstrates a degree of political influence not possessed by other groups (see below). This is particularly evident when contrasted against the 'one drop of Black blood and you're Black' rule applied to Black Americans, a rule that was not uniformly accepted prior to 1850 but that gradually had taken hold by 1915 because it was 'crucial to maintaining the social system of white domination' (Davis, 1991, p.63). Blacks also accepted this rule to foster group unity and identity in the face of increased White hostility (Williamson, 1980; Davis, 1991).

While the population counted as White is quite diverse and the largest numerically, all who 'qualified' were placed in a single racial category. When counting non-white groups who were numerically much smaller, considerable effort was expended by providing many categories. A concern with the minority populations was thus very clear from the beginning. The 1890 census's attempt to measure the extent of Black-White mixing with absurd instructions to enumerators to count Mulattos, Quadroons, and Octoroons was certainly doomed to failure. At the same time, these heroic attempts can be seen as efforts to prevent racially-mixed individuals from crossing the racial line into the White population. The mixed-racial categories also represented attempts to measure the extent of racial mixing, a process that inspired much worry among those who feared racial and national decline because of miscegenation.

In the same year the numerically insignificant Chinese and Japanese populations were counted separately. These efforts should be interpreted within the context of prevailing anti-Chinese and anti-Japanese sentiments and restrictive immigration and other policies directed at these groups. In response to intense anti-Chinese sentiment on the west coast, the Chinese Exclusion Act was passed in 1882 to prevent further immigration of Chinese workers to the United States. This was the first federal immigration policy that specifically excluded people on the basis of nationality. ...

Chronic concern with populations defined as non-White is also seen from the addition of more categories of Asian 'races' to the recent 1980 and 1990 census schedules. As a result of changes in US immigration policy in 1965, immigrants to the United States are mostly Asian or Hispanic, and these two populations have grown the fastest over the last twenty years. Signs of revived nativism and anti-immigrant sentiment (directed particularly against the more visible immigrants) are common. It is therefore not surprising that the number of racial classifications for counting Asians have grown since 1980, reflecting political and social reactions to the growing Asian presence in US society.

'Pure' races, mixed-race, and 'other' races

A fundamental rule of measurement is that the categories be mutually exclusive. In the past it was assumed that enumerators could assign individuals to one of the named races by observation; today, individuals are asked to self-identify with one of the listed racial options. Beginning with the 1910 census, a residual 'Other' racial category was provided to increase the response rate to the race question. Even so, enumerators were instructed to write down the

person's race based on observation; or to ask the respondent to choose which one of the listed races he or she identified with; or, in the case of recent mail-back census forms, to write in what his or her race was. These write-in responses were then reassigned to one of the listed racial classifications, and census data on race continue to present data as if people were classifiable with a single race. For example, before 1980, a mixed-race person was assigned the father's race but since 1980, this person is now assigned the mother's race. In cases where the written-in response was, for example, 'Italian', the person would be reassigned to the White race.

Between 1980 and 1990, there was a 45 per cent increase in the number of people who marked 'Other' in response to the race question (an increase from 6.8 million in 1980 to 9.8 million in 1990). According to Word and Spencer (1991), over 95 per cent of these 'Other' race respondents also indicated that they were of Hispanic origin. This has brought about greater effort by census Bureau staff to accommodate these non-standard racial responses, although such efforts are constrained by legal requirements to collect information on the four main racial categories (White, Black, Asian, and Native American) and the Hispanic origin population (US Office of Federal Statistical Policy and Standards 1978, Directive Number 15). For the 1990 census, people who wrote that they were 'multi-racial' or 'bi-racial' were left in the 'Other' race classification. Respondents who wrote 'black-white' were counted as Blacks; those who wrote 'white-black' were counted as Whites. Finally, imputation processes ... are used to assign a standard race to more complicated cases. This usually involves checking the racial responses of other people in the same household or similar households in the neighbourhood, or racial assignment would be based on individuals with other similar characteristics. ...

Over time, therefore, the treatment of non-standard responses to the race question on census schedules has shifted to take into account the increasing numbers of Americans who choose not to fit into one of the standard single race classifications. This represents an important change, given the historical and cultural bias towards single race classification, and contains significant implications for the measurement of race in future censuses. In the past, people were forced into one of the standard racial categories, reflecting the belief that there are 'pure' races.[2] By insisting on placing every person into one of the standard races, the impression of minimal racial mixing could be maintained, an ideology that was important given the opposition to racial mixing (an ideology formally represented by many state anti-miscegenation laws). Furthermore, insisting that those with any Black ancestry were Black also buttressed the 'pure' race ideology and served to maintain the boundary between White and Black. It is only within the last decade that a serious effort has emerged to respond to the growing population of mixed-race Americans. The evolution of census racial classifications can thus be seen to represent both the historical insistence on 'pure' races and the more recent official acknowledgement of growing intermarriage, multiracial Americans and people who are outside the traditional White or Black or American Indian or Asian classifications. The fact that this trend is driven by the growing Hispanic population is also significant. The increased presence of Hispanics in the United States may pose the first real challenge to the traditional Black/White biracial classification, a challenge that may lead to a three-tier racial system (Starr, 1992). Recent shifts that acknowledge mixed-race people also reflect the particular difficulty of 'social classification – that is, the classification of people, their activities, and their attributes … because people typically have their own conceptions of membership' (Starr, 1987, pp.43–4).

Transforming diverse ethnic groups into pan-ethnic races

One function of official racial classifications is to create a sense of group membership or even community where there had been none before. Petersen (1987, p. 218) suggests that 'few things facilitate a category's coalescence into a group so readily as its designation by an official body'. Whether such an outcome was intended is debatable but the consequences are clear. When people of European descent were all classed together in the White category and, furthermore, set apart from people who were placed in the numerous non-White categories, the eventual acceptance of many European ethnic groups that had been viewed with hostility and prejudice when they first migrated to the US was greatly facilitated. When Jewish immigrants arrived in large numbers in the late-nineteenth century, attacks and hostility were common and widespread. Hotels put up signs that said 'No Jews Allowed' and job advertisements specified 'Christians Only'. Italians were called 'a race of simple-minded and often grossly ignorant' and often forced to attend Black schools in the south

(Dinnerstein and Reimers, 1988, pp. 48–9). Yet all were counted as White by the census. While the assimilation of immigrant and ethnic groups into the dominant or majority group is a complicated process that is affected by many factors, we should not discount the influence of an inclusive racial label in this process. In short, the social construction of a pan-ethnic racial group called White served to minimize ethnic differences among the numerous European ethnic groups while fostering a common racial identity.[3] It also hardened the division between White and Others.

A more recent example is seen in the grouping of several Asian and Pacific Islander groups into a larger population called the 'Asian and Pacific Islander (API)' population. Asian ethnic groups, for example, Chinese and Japanese, who have a relatively long history of settlement in the US, tended to identify themselves in ethnically specific ways. In other words, a person of Chinese descent would call himself or herself Chinese American and one of Japanese ancestry would be Japanese American. However, as official classifications such as the census categories of 'Asian American' and now 'API' become more prevalent, can we expect a construction of a pan-ethnic racial community called Asian/Pacific Islander similar to that which occurred among Whites? Or will this unwieldy Asian oblique Pacific Islander label be too transparent an artificial construction to eliminate successfully differences of culture, national origin, socio-economic status, and even 'racial stock' (Asian Indians who are considered 'Caucasoids', Chinese and Japanese who are considered 'Mongoloids', and the mixed peoples of the Pacific, Micronesia, Philippines, and so forth) in this population? The answer will come with time but the influence of official labels on social processes can already be detected in the many individuals of Asian backgrounds who have begun to refer to themselves using the pan-ethnic term, 'Asian American'. Political organizations and action that appeal to such a pan-ethnic base is also increasing. In this way, 'official categories may help to constitute or divide groups and to illuminate or obscure their problems and achievements' (Starr, 1987, p.53). Two specific examples of what Starr refers to would be the 'model minority' image of Asian Americans that obscures serious socio-economic problems of many Indo-Chinese refugees (included as Asian Americans) and the high socio-economic status of Japanese Americans that would be missing in aggregate statistics describing Asians and Pacific Islanders.

Confusing race and ethnicity

This article began by noting that race is social differentiation based on physical criteria and ethnicity is social differentiation based on cultural criteria. The data that have been analysed in this research are census classifications of race. However, it is apparent that the racial classifications offered on census schedules are not classifications of race, defined sociologically. Instead, we observe a medley (indeed, we might emphasize that it is a motley medley) of racial and ethnic terms.

In the 1980 census, Chinese and Japanese are listed as separate races; it would be biologically and sociologically difficult to insist that these are distinct races. In 1930 'Hindu' was offered as a choice in the race question. As noted earlier (see note 4), Hinduism refers to a religious, and therefore, cultural identity. The confusion between race and ethnicity continues into the 1990s. Are Eskimos and Aleuts races, or are they more accurately ethnic groups within the Native American population? Do Native Americans constitute a separate race? If so, what race? Why are Hawaiians (another native or indigenous group) placed under the Asian and Pacific Islander 'race' but not American Indians whose ancestors were of Asian origin? Furthermore, the listing of many Asian ethnic groups under the choices for the race question violates all rules of taxonomy by effectively mixing racial and ethnic domains.[4] This would be as if several European groups (for example, French, English, Dutch, and so on) were offered as choices in the question on race or colour....

Notes

1 The vacuity of racial labels, for example, 'Whites', is clearly seen when we compare a 'white' person's skin colour to the colour white, as in a piece of white paper or white paint. Philip Curtin, a historian at The Johns Hopkins University put it well when he said that 'whites' are really 'pinkish-yellowish.' Similarly, the term 'Blacks' to refer to people of African origin is not too meaningful, given the range in skin colour among African Americans. It is estimated that at least 75 per cent of 'Blacks' have some European ancestry. Williamson (1980) calls these 'brown' Americans the 'new people'.

2 With reference to Canadian census questions on ethnic origin, Kralt (1990, p.27) describes a similar attempt 'to paint a picture of Canadian society that consisted of four large, generally mutually exclusive ethnic or cultural groups.' The image of a society divided into four groups, each of homogeneous ethnic origin, was reinforced every ten years with the release of census data, according to Kralt (1990).

3 It would be interesting to see if the label 'Anglo', that is popular in the south-west of the United States to refer to non-Hispanic Whites, will become another pan-ethnic category. The implications of combining groups as diverse as Jews, Italians, English, Poles, and others into an 'Anglo' group are many and intriguing. Imagine how the English in the United Kingdom would react to an 'Anglo-American' who was of Jewish-Italian-Irish ancestry. Individual Americans also experience shock when confronted with such labels – an Italian American and his wife, who is of Czechoslovakian and Slovenian ancestries, were surprised and amused to be suddenly classified as 'Anglos' on moving from New York state to New Mexico.

4 The list of 'races' offered in the 1980 census was criticized by Petersen (1987, p.204) for violating 'elementary rules for constructing a taxonomy – that the classes be mutually exclusive, that all the classes add up to the whole of the population, and that they be roughly the same order of importance and magnitude'. Since the 1990 census classifications were essentially the same, they too suffered from similar defects.

References

Davis, F.J. (1991) *Who is Black? One Nation's Definition*, University Park, PA, Pennsylvania State University Press.

Dinnerstein, L. and Reimers, D.M. (1988) *Ethnic Americans*, 3rd edn, New York, Harper and Row.

Kralt, J. (1990) 'Ethnic origins in the Canadian census, 1871–1986' in Halli, S.S, Trovato, F. and Driedger, L. (eds) *Ethnic Demography: Canadian Immigrant, Racial and Cultural Variations*, Ottawa, Ontario, Carleton University Press, pp.13–29.

Petersen, W. (1987) 'Politics and the measurement of ethnicity' in Alonso, W. and Starr, P. (eds) *The Politics of Numbers*, New York, Russell Sage Foundation, pp.187–233.

Starr, P. (1987) 'The sociology of official statistics' in Alonso, W. and Starr, P. (eds) *Top. cit.*.

Starr, P. (1992) 'Social categories and claims in the liberal state', *Social Research* (forthcoming).

US Department of Commerce, Office of Federal Statistical Policy and Standards 1978, *Statistical Policy Handbook*, Washington, DC, US Government Printing Office.

Williamson, J. (1980) *New People: Miscegenation and Mulattoes in the United State*, New York, The Free Press.

Word, D.L. and Spencer, G. (1991) *Age, Sex, Race, and Hispanic Origin Information from the 1990 Census: A Comparison of Census Results with Results where Age and Race have been Modified CPH–L–74*, Washington, DC, US Bureau of the Census.

Source: Lee, 1993, pp.81–6

4.3 U. Kalpagam, 'The colonial state and statistical knowledge' (2000)

Colonial governmentality, quantification and statistical knowledge

The advent of colonial rule in India also marked the beginning of a vast documentation project on a hitherto unknown scale of activities and the life of the people. Cohn (1998, 1996) has recently provided a classification of the investigative modalities by which knowledge of Indian society was generated by British colonial rule. These he grouped as the historiographic, the observational/travel, the survey modality, the enumerative, the museological, the surveillance and sanitary modalities. Although he refers to the colonial state, and to state-making as a cultural project, drawing his ideas from Corrigan and Sayer (1985), and invokes the name of Foucault, his investigative modalities are insufficiently integrated with the regulatory activities of the state. As noted earlier, Foucault's conception of 'governmentality' provides a useful framework.[1]

The techniques of government instituted by the colonial state differed greatly from pre-colonial states both in the nature of accountability procedures and in the recording of information. These called for the setting up of new institutions, procedures, calculations, reflections, and tactics giving rise to both a modern state form and to a modern regime of power/knowledge.

The institution of a fully developed colonial state was a process long in the making. In the early years when the East India Company carried on its activities of commerce, the role of governance was insignificant. Even then the Company bureaucracy set in place systems of accountability that consolidated knowledge of the commercial activities. Once the Company acquired the administration of police, justice and revenue, first in Bengal and then in most other regions, the techniques of government were progressively instituted. It was from 1818 onwards, after the defeat of the Mahrattas, that regular and centralized forms of administration were to evolve; Stokes aptly remarked: 'The age of chivalry had gone; that of sophisters, economists and calculators was to succeed' (1989, p.13).

It is of course by now common knowledge that British administrative policy in India did not evolve out of a consensus, not at just one point in time. …

Ultimately, whatever … the local variations in administration, the procedures that got instituted called for an immense recording of information (Bayly, 1996). The hierarchical nature of long-distance government under conditions of coloniality progressively installed a new matrix of calculating rationality. From the latter half of the 19th century, after the 1857 rebellion and the passing of governance from the Company to the Crown, administrative procedures in every department and province became far more systematized. This period was also to launch the project of knowing India 'scientifically', thus ushering in the era of censuses and surveys on various aspects of the social and economic life of the people. No doubt scientific surveying of territories had started from the last years of the 18th century, but population was not the explicit focus of concern.

From the latter half of the nineteenth century, population became the chief concern. Once the population was enumerated, classified and territorially delineated, it could become the target of interventions. As the apprehension of social and economic phenomenon became possible through statistical methods, and as scientific understanding of the nature of causality of a number of these social and economic processes was gained, it became possible to devise modalities of interventions by way of laws and regulations.

The colonial state did not have the developmental concerns of the post-colonial state, and its administrative functions were to regulate the economy and society. Revenue administration, law and order, education, infrastructure-building and a few other activities constituted the bulk of administrative work. But in each of these spheres, the statistical information recorded at various levels and on an ongoing basis provided the means to assess performance, and thus enabled modern social scientific discourses to emerge for the first time.

Statistics was not only a new discourse, but the discursive practices of administration regulated certain spatial and temporal categories, constituted new objects of discourse, generated vast quantities of numbers and classifications, and ushered in new kinds of interventions, new conceptions of causality and new modes of reasoning. It is these new categories that rendered it possible to conceive of narratives and counter-narratives of modernity and progress, and in doing so brought 'India' within the discursive fold of universal science and universal history.

...

... The whole period of 19th century colonial rule in India witnessed numerous surveying and mapping operations as more and more territories were brought under British rule (Kalpagam, 1995). The topographical, trigonometrical and revenue surveys provided the colonial state with the much needed information on geographic locations, boundaries, topographical details, resources, rights on land, etc. Demarcating boundaries of fields and villages was necessary to produce maps, as well as for revenue assessment and verifying claims to land. As administrative power developed from its concerns of territoriality to govermentality with population as its object, the mapping of space performed other functions as well. As carto-statistical techniques developed, it was possible to identify and demarcate aggregates of population for specific kinds of description and intervention. Modern maps thus entered the vocabulary of modern Indians and in so doing shaped their national identities even as it enabled them to identify the nation.

The modern discipline of sociology tracing its heritage to Comtean positivism is derived from the idea that 'society', which is the disciplinary object, is an enumerable aggregate. Colonial governmentality with population as its target, needed the population to be enumerated, spatially demarcated and classified according to a whole range of attributes thus transforming what were once fuzzy communities into enumerated communities. The census classification of population into religious groups, castes, tribes and occupational categories provided this conception of society. Although social attributes such as education, sex rations, infirmities, etc., were made to converge around the trope of caste, thus enabling the apprehension of social fault-lines for purposes of administrative interventions, the study of the frequency of social phenomena and the normalizing of individual behaviour needed a less deterministic and a temporally more frequent data series than the decennial census. The collection of social and civic statistics by the different departments of the administration on a regular annual basis afforded that possibility.

The opportunity provided by the census classification in enabling an empirical view of society made obvious the problem of transforming qualitative attributes and subjectively perceived differences into quantifiable numbers and hierarchically ordered facts. Although categories such as caste and tribe remained stubborn in their differences, under the attempts at typification by social criteria, their unruliness was to some extent tamed by the imposition of racial taxonomy onto them, and their subjection to the dubious methods of anthropometric measurements. Even if caste was eventually given up in the census classification, the classificatory discourse of caste found a permanent status in modern polity.[2] Colonial governmentality and its disciplinarity of counting and classification was thus able to delink what were once primordial loyalties based on kinship, lineage and territorial groupings in a pre-modern sovereignty that was linked to territoriality (Fox, 1971), to modern identities based on religion, caste, tribe and occupation, and which increasingly acquired a pan-national status in the emerging space of the modern state.

Notes

1 For an insightful formulation of 'governmentality' in the colonial context, read Scott (1995).

2 There has been a recent revival of the debate on the census classification of caste. As protective discrimination policies are framed on caste considerations, there have been contending positions on reviving the caste classification at the 2001 census. See Omvedt (1998, p.12), 'Castes and the census'.

References

Bayly, C.A. (1996) *Empire and Information: Intelligence Gathering and Social Communication in India, 1780–1870*, Cambridge, Cambridge University Press.

Cohn, B.S. (1988) 'The anthropology of a colonial state and its forms of knowledge', paper presented at the Wenner-Gren conference on Tensions of Empire: Colonial Control and Visions of Rule, Spain.

Cohn, B.S. (1996) *An Anthropologist among the Historians and Other Essays*, Delhi, Oxford University Press.

Corrigan, P. and Sayer, D (1985) *The Great Arch*, Oxford, Blackwell.

Fox, R.G. (1971) *Kin, Clan, Raja and Rule: State-hinterland Relations in Pre-industrial India*, Berkeley, University of California Press.

Kalpagam, U. (1995) 'Cartography in colonial India', *Economic and Political Weekly* (Review of Political Economy), vol.xxx, no.30, pp.87–98.

Omvedt, G. (1998) 'Castes and the census', *The Hindu*, Saturday 18 July, p.12.

Scott, D. (1995) 'Colonial governmentality', *Social Text*, vol.43, pp.191–220.

Stokes. E. (1989 [1959]) *The English Utilitarians in India*, New Delhi, Oxford University Press.

Source: Kalpagam, 2000, pp.47–51

Sheila Faith Weiss, 'Power through population: Schallmayer and population policy' (1987)

...

Anxiety in the certain decline in the level of Germany's biological fitness as a result of the war prompted Schallmayer and other eugenicists to devise a Bevökerungspolitik – a series of reform plans and programs – to help offset the anticipated quantitative and qualitative population loss. In a chapter entitled 'Volksvermehrungspolitik' (Policy for Population Increase) in his thoroughly revised third edition of *Vererbung und Auslese*, Schallmayer brought together many of his own proposals with several recommended by Gruber, Lenz, and others (Schallmayer, 1918). In addition to the numerous suggestions and plans to remedy the population problem articulated by Schallmayer and others prior to 1914, such as early marriages, the fight against venereal disease, and the campaign to lower infant mortality, the chapter included several novel proposals, of which only five of the most important will be discussed here.

Although it would be difficult to try to rank-order the various proposals cataloged in *Vererbung und Auslese* according to their anticipated effectiveness in replenishing the Reich's stock of human resources, Schallmayer was certainly very favorably impressed by a suggestion first initiated by Gruber to reform Germany's inheritance laws. According to Gruber's plan, a family estate could be inherited in full only if the deceased father had left at least four children. In the event that fewer were reared, a portion of the inheritance would be turned over to relatives – presumably those with children (*ibid.*, p.336). Schallmayer, conscious of the sad state of the national treasury, offered a revised plan whereby a portion of the estate not inherited would be turned over to the Reich (*ibid.*, p.339). Either way, Schallmayer maintained, such an inheritance reform would not only boost population growth but would also encourage a higher fertility rate among the propertied classes – those classes that on the whole were eugenically more desirable.

Another population policy measure adopted by Schallmayer was the creation of free or very inexpensive homes or *Heimstätten* (homesteads) for returning soldiers and, if enough resources became available, for other 'suitable' people (*ibid.*, p.351). The idea behind this plan was to make large families financially feasible for returning disabled soldiers who because they were unable to work could not afford

to marry or have children, even though they were physically capable of providing the Reich with progeny. Schallmayer's scheme was undoubtedly influenced by the far more völkisch plans of Gruber and Lenz. Lenz from the outset had made the *bäuerliches Leben* (rural life) the center of his eugenic program for the biological renewal of Germany. He recommended the creation of rural homesteads and colonies to be built on land taken from Russia in the east (Lenz, 1916). These homesteads would be given free to eugenically desirable couples on the condition that they have at least five children. These estates could be inherited only if the parents lived up to their part of the bargain. In cases where the couple were unable or unwilling to have the requisite number of children, a fixed rent would be established (Schallmayer, 1918, p.352). Although Schallmayer did not necessarily share Lenz's nationalist and imperialist war aims (i.e., to use former Russian territory as a site for a homestead policy designed to stem the tide of the 'Slavic flood'), he did believe that the establishment of such colonies would be desirable for national efficiency.[1] Echoing Lenz, he argued that it was only fair that couples with large families be given free housing and land since such parents 'provide a greater service for the race and state than they would paying rent.' Presumably, if they had to pay rent, they could not afford to have as many children (*ibid.*, p.352). Like the proposal to reform the inheritance laws, the creation of such homes or homesteads, Schallmayer maintained, would enhance the quality as well as the quantity of the German population.

In addition to the two measures just discussed, Schallmayer advanced three further proposals designed to remedy the population problem: (1) the development of a state 'progeny insurance' program whereby all individuals earning enough money to pay taxes would be required to give a portion of their income to a state fund that would be used to help couples with large families pay the expenses of rearing their children; (2) a wage reform for civil servants such that the more children an individual had, the higher his salary, and (3) a reform of the voting laws such that all men over twenty-five would receive as many votes as he had dependent family members (i.e., wife, daughters, and sons not yet old enough to vote) (Schallmayer, 1918, pp. 339–44, 344–50, 357–60). These three proposals, like the two measures described earlier, were articulated and discussed by a number of eugenicists and eugenics-minded reformers in addition to Schallmayer. In fact, these and similar measures became the *Leitsätze* (guiding principles) for the German Society for Race Hygiene in its fight against the declining birth rate.[2]

None of the above-mentioned proposals and programs was ever officially adopted by the government or written into law. They are, however, worth mentioning in detail because they demonstrate the degree to which Schallmayer as well as other prominent German eugenicists viewed a large and 'healthy' population as the prerequisite for national efficiency, or indeed national survival. All eugenicists knew that population, especially a hereditarily healthy population, meant power. Of course, not all population policy measures advanced the cause of biological fitness. Some proposals, like the reform of voting rights, did not discriminate between so-called genetically inferior and superior fathers. Yet on the whole the assortment of plans and programs adopted by Schallmayer and discussed at the meetings of the German Society for Race Hygiene followed Lenz's maxim: 'the largest degree of fitness of the greatest

possible number' (Lenz, 1916, pp.1668). Only by simultaneously encouraging population quantity and quality could Germany hope to escape the biological and political damage brought on by the war.

Notes

1 For an example of Lenz's nationalist views and his fear of Russians, see Lenz (1916–18)

2 These ten 'guiding principles' formulated by the Delegate Committee of the German Society for Race Hygiene in June, 1914, are listed in Schallmayer (1918), pp.359–60.

References

Lenz, F. (1916) 'Rassenhygienische Bevölkerungspolitik', *Deutsche Politik*, 1, p.1665.

Lenz, F. (1916–18) 'Vorschläge zur Bevölkerungspolitik mit besonderer Berücksichtigung der Wirtschaftslage nach dem Krieg', *ARGB*, 12, p.445.

Schallmayer, (1918) *Verebung und Auslese*, 3rd edn, p.352.

Source: Weiss, 1987, pp.143–46

Jonathan W. Warren and France W. Twine, 'White Americans, the new minority?' (1997)

The race to whiteness across black terrain[1]

… [How] has the White category come to include previously defined non-Whites? How did the Celts, Slavs, and Mediterraneans come to be included in the White race? Why were these groups allowed to blend, to intermarry, to move up the socio-economic ladder, to become unhyphenated Americans? The answer, we will argue, rests in large part with the way in which Whiteness is constructed in the United States.

Scholars of Whiteness have found that North American Whites often define Whiteness as a void, as cultureless (Duster, 1992; Frankenberg, 1993). As one White woman put it, 'to be a Heinz 57 American, a white, class-confused American, land of the Kleenex type American, is so formless in and of itself. It only takes shape in relation to other people' (Frankenberg, 1993, p.196). Whiteness is, of course, not formless. On the contrary, it is in many cases 'the norm against

which all are measured and all are expected to fit' (Frankenberg, 1988, p.238). Whiteness does, however, take shape in relation to others.

In their separate studies of nineteenth-century minstrelsy, both Alan W.C. Green and David R. Roediger concluded that Blacks were key to the development of an 'ersatz whiteness, 'which came to incorporate both Catholics and Celts. 'As various types – particularly the Irishman and the German – fused with native-born Americans, the Negro moved into a solo spot centerstage, providing a relational model in contrast to which masses of Americans could establish a positive and superior sense of identity' (Green, 1970, p.395). … Hence, Blacks served as the 'other' against which a popular sense of Whiteness, which cut across ethnicity, religion, and skill, could be generated (Roediger, 1991, p.127).

… This would at least partially explain the Irish's often noted rapid transformation upon arriving in America from friends of the Black to ardent racists

(Rubin, 1978). Their inclusion in the White category was at stake. For the 'Blacker' Blacks were made, the 'Whiter' the Irish became in the eyes of White Americans. In other words, the more vulgar, grotesque, and the obscene simulations of Blackness, the Whiter, the more palatable to Whites the Irish became. Thus, by embracing and producing White supremacist images of Blacks and simultaneously conforming to White norms, the Irish were able to reposition themselves as White.

In the only published ethnography of the Mississippi Chinese, James Loewen (1972/1988) described how Chinese Americans in pre-civil-rights Mississippi were able to successfully transform themselves from Blacks into Whites. As with the Irish, 'Key to their success in making this transition was their ability to define themselves as [non-Black] and thus as fully human, as full citizens' (Loewen, 1972/1988, p.99). As Loewen documents in rich detail, the Mississippi Chinese were able to 'prove' their non-Blackness by cutting off all of their social ties with Blacks, invoking racist representations of Blacks, and culturally imitating the White community.

… In addition to severing their social ties with Blacks, Loewen (1972/1988) also found that the Chinese went to great lengths to model themselves after the southern White community.

> Chinese patterns are being pushed to one side, but there is no patterning from [Black] characteristics among the young. The way they dance, sing, the argot they use, their gestures and mannerisms – all are incredibly free of black influence, when it is remembered that most Chinese children live in [Black] neighborhoods, wait on blacks in the stores, and have more contacts with [Blacks] than with Caucasians of their age groups. (pp.81–2)

…

… In the end, this strategy paid off for the Mississippi Chinese. By the late 1960s, they had almost fully repositioned themselves from a Black to a White status (p.96). Their children could attend White high schools and universities, they could live in White neighborhoods, join the infamous White citizens' councils, become members of White churches, be defined as White on driver's licenses, and the Chinese women could marry White men – all 'privileges' that were denied Blacks.

Implications for the new immigrants

Given that Whiteness expanded and was transformed so that Slavs, Celts, and Mediterraneans could fit snugly into the White box, why would one assume that this process will come to a halt on the European borders? Is it not possible that 'some non-white and Hispanic groups may be beginning to undergo processes similar to those that have undercut ethnic difference among European whites – one thinks in this connection of Cubans, most Asian American groups, and the many Americans of American Indian ancestry who are integrated in the white population' (Alba, 1990, p.9)? In other words, are Whites becoming a minority or will the White category simply continue to expand so that some of today's non-Whites will be tomorrow's Whites? What are the indicators, if any, that the boundaries of Whiteness are continuing to expand?

While in Chicago during the summer of 1993, we visited a White couple who live in Bridgeport. Bridgeport is located on the South Side and has historically been a racist 'White' community of Italian, Irish, and Polish Americans. When we asked how the neighborhood had been changing, we were told that the old, strictly ethnic blocks had been breaking up and that a lot of Mexican and Chinese families had moved into the area. We then asked if that had not created a lot of animosity – knowing the potential of White flight and violence toward any perceived non-White invaders. Our friend responded that there had not been any. She added that 'Blacks are not allowed to move into this area, but Mexicans and Asians are different – they can blend.'

…

A significant segment of the Latino population has been reclassified from a separate race to essentially a White ethnic group. In the 1930s, Hispanics were classified as a separate race by the federal census (Bean and Tienda, 1987, p.18). However, one now sees the emergence of such terms as *non-Hispanic Whites* and *Hispanic Whites*. And this is not a classification that is simply being imposed by the federal government but is also being embraced by a large proportion of the Latino community. In the 1990 census, more than half of the Hispanic population racially self-identified as White (US Bureau of the Census, 1992b, pp.B–1).

Note

1 This subheading is a play on the title of Brackette F. Williams's (1989) article, 'A Class Act: Anthropology and the Race to Nation Across Ethnic Terrain'.

References

Alba, R.D. (1990) *Ethnic Identity: The Transformation of White America*, New Haven, CT, Yale University Press.

Bean, F. and Tienda, M. (1987) *The Hispanic Population of the United States*, New York, Russell Sage.

Duster, T. (1992) *The Diversity Project: Final Report*, Berkeley, University of California Press.

Frankenberg, R. (1993) *White Women, Race Matters: The Social Construction of Whiteness*, unpublished doctoral dissertation, University of California, Santa Cruz.

Frankenberg, R. (1998) *White Women, Race Matters: The Social Construction of Whiteness*, Minneapolis, University of Minnesota Press.

Green, A.W.C. (1970) '"Jim Crow", Zip Coon": The northern origins of Negro minstrelsy', *Massachusetts Review*, vol.11, pp.385–97.

Loewen, J. (1988) *The Mississippi Chinese: Between Black and White*, Prospect Heights, IL, Waveland (Original work published 1972).

Roediger, D.R. (1991) *The Wages of Whiteness: Race and the Making of the American Working Class*, London, Verso.

Rubin, J. (1978) 'Black nativism: The European immigrant in Negro thought, 1830–1860', *Phylon*, Spring, pp.1–17.

US Bureau of the Census (1992b) *The Hispanic Population of the United States: March 1992* (Current Population Reports, p.20–465), Washington, DC, US Government Printing Office.

Source: Warren and Twine, 1997, pp.206–14

Citizenship

Bryan S. Turner

Contents

1	**Introduction: social citizenship and sociology**	**206**
	Aims	
2	**Marshall and the theory of citizenship**	**209**
3	**Three routes of effective entitlement: work, war and reproduction**	**212**
	3.1 Work and citizenship	214
	3.2 War and citizenship	217
	3.3 Reproductive citizenship	2218
4	**Voluntary associations: a fourth way to entitlement?**	**221**
5	**Conclusion: new patterns of citizenship**	**226**
	References	**230**
	Readings	
	5.1: T.H. Marshall, 'Welfare and citizenship' (1950)	**234**
	5.2: Bhikhu Parekh, 'Equality in a multicultural society' (2000)	**239**
	5.3: Diane Richardson, 'Citizenship and sexuality' (2000)	**244**
	5.4: Engin F. Isin and Patricia K. Wood, 'Citizenship and identity' (1999)	**247**

1 Introduction: social citizenship and sociology

Citizenship rights are fundamental because in the last analysis they determine who is included and who is excluded. Citizenship in political and legal terms draws the borders of the national society. How precisely we conceptualize and how violently we defend those borders defines the nature of our society in moral and political terms. No matter how humane and liberal a society may be, it will have to establish a border, and borders produce disputes. The real question is how narrowly and tightly those citizenship criteria are drawn. The claims of asylum-seekers, for example, can reveal society's attitudes – how openly we define our society, and whether we feel any moral obligation to strangers.

citizenship   The aim of this chapter is to explore the changing nature of **citizenship** in modern societies. Citizenship is often examined in a narrow political framework, but in this chapter we shall explore the social foundations of modern citizenship. Social citizenship is defined as the rights and obligations that determine the identity of members of a social and political community, and which as a result regulates access to the benefits and privileges of membership. Social citizenship involves membership of this community, the allocation of resources, the creation of identities and a set of virtues relating to civil obligation and responsibility (Turner, 1997). Social theories of citizenship may be distinguished from the political analysis of citizenship by the fact that sociology is less concerned with formal rights (for example to elect a government) and more concerned with the social and economic conditions that support participation and inclusion in society. In its most elementary form, citizenship refers to the conditions by which people participate in society.

ACTIVITY 1

Do you hold a passport? If so, to what does it entitle you? What protection does it give you? Take a look at your passport, if you have one, and make a list of your entitlements. Are they important?

A United Kingdom passport actually says that 'Her Britannic Majesty's Secretary of State in the Name of her Majesty' requests that the bearer of the passport be permitted 'to pass freely without let or hindrance'. A passport allows people to travel across borders and, at the same time, the absence of a passport (or in some cases, an identity card) prohibits other groups of people from entering 'our' space. A UK passport, in somewhat old-fashioned language, also reminds us of the importance of the Queen in the constitution, and the fact that we belong to a place called the United Kingdom of Great Britain and Northern Ireland. A passport spells out some of the obligations of the state towards its citizens, and implies a set of corresponding responsibilities. Because of migration and inter-marriage, more and more people have conflicting or multiple claims on citizenship. In modern Britain, dual citizenship (for example, having British and Australian passports) is not uncommon. Do such people have divided loyalties?

The contemporary interest in citizenship theory is the product of a variety of social changes: the problems of European integration, the pressure of asylum-seekers on welfare and security systems, the transformation of the welfare state, sexual politics, social movements to protect the environment, the global commercial attempt to patent the genetic information about the human body, the conflict between aboriginal rights, land conservation and the social rights of nation-states, and finally the challenge of new medical technologies to familial relationships. We can summarize the issue behind these diverse social forces in terms of the politics of identity and difference. We can argue that early forms of citizenship made an assumption about the social 'sameness' of individuals within a nation-state. As societies become more complex, this assumption about sameness is challenged. Can citizenship provide a political framework within which social differences are accepted? Conventional forms of citizenship were associated with the modernization of society and with the development of the administrative framework of modern states, and the national structure of citizenship was assumed to have universal relevance. Early forms of citizenship were connected with the evolution of the administrative structure of the state and its need to regulate populations. Ethnic diversity, multiculturalism and the globalization of cultures have challenged the assumptions of administrative modernization and the geo-

Figure 5.1 *An immigrant is detained after being discovered in the back of a lorry at Dover: refugee, asylum-seeker or economic migrant?*

politics of state boundaries (Sassen, 1999). Contemporary societies are diverse, and hence differences between people become critical to modern citizenship. We might say that modern politics involves a politics of recognition.

ACTIVITY 2

The Statue of Liberty in New York harbour, which welcomed thousands of European migrants to the United States, is a symbol of the openness of US society to immigrants. Stop and consider how open modern societies are to mass immigration. What criteria do western countries use to decide whom to allow in? Do these vary in other parts of the world (think of refugees from war and famine in Africa)?

US democracy has been driven by very overt and inspiring ideals. For example, the Statue of Liberty is the 'new Colossus', the Goddess of Liberty that says to the Old World:

Give me your tired, your poor,
Your huddled masses yearning to breathe free,
The wretched refuse of your teeming shore.
Send these, the homeless, the tempest-toss'd to me
I lift my lamp beside the golden door.

This appeal to a principle of universalism and openness is, of course, difficult to convert into a reality. For example, there are important and valid restrictions on the migration of people with criminal records, and the majority of democracies will not be as porous as the Statue of Liberty proclaims. In practice, the United States, like other liberal democracies, places severe limitations on the entrance of foreigners. The US government is currently attempting to regulate its border with Mexico in order to control the flow of Mexican workers into southern California and Texas. In the UK attitudes recently displayed towards asylum-seekers are an indication of the boundaries of British citizenship:

> Since the ferry company P&O started a crackdown on illegal immigrants on 6 December its security guards have discovered 485 people crammed into cars, vans and lorries making the Calais and Dover crossing. P&O Stena believes it may have saved up to £1 million in fines it would have paid if the asylum seekers had been discovered on the British side of the Channel. Anne Widdecombe (Shadow Home Secretary) waded into choppy waters saying on Wednesday that if the Tories win the next election they would lock up all asylum seekers in detention centres.
>
> (*The Observer*, 31 December 2000)

**rights,
welfare state**

In this chapter we will explore the foundations of social citizenship in the UK, looking back to the period after the Second World War. Following the work of the English sociologist T.H. Marshall, we shall examine the historical development of legal, political and social **rights** in the UK, where the institutional core of social citizenship was the **welfare state**: in this welfare system, work, war and parenthood provided the foundation of social entitlements. However, these require re-evaluation in the light of economic, political and technological changes, that have brought about an erosion of citizenship. In contemporary society, social citizenship needs to be more responsive to gender, ethnic diversity and environmental concerns and these issues are explored through the role of voluntary associations, examining the emergence of new forms of citizenship in relation to cultural and environmental rights.

AIMS

The aims of this chapter are:

1   To explore the changing nature of citizenship in modern societies.

2   To examine the historical development of legal, political and social rights, looking at the welfare state as the institutional core of social citizenship and the original basis of entitlement via work, war and parenthood.

3   To explore how economic, technological and political changes have brought about an erosion of citizenship.

4   To show how, in contemporary society, social citizenship needs to be more responsive to gender, sexual orientation, ethnic diversity and environmental concerns.

5   To examine the emergence of new forms of citizenship in relation to cultural and environmental rights.

2 Marshall and the theory of citizenship

While acknowledging that the contemporary study of citizenship owes a great deal to the legacy of the English sociologist **T.H. Marshall**, in this section I shall outline a number of criticisms of his theory in order to grasp the importance of citizenship in modern Britain (Turner, 1990).

Marshall,
Thomas H.

Marshall divided citizenship into three aspects – civil, political and social. The civil component was necessary for the achievement of individual freedoms and included such elements as freedom of speech, the right to own property and the right to **justice**. The political element was constituted by the right to participate in the public exercise of power, in particular the rights to free elections and a secret ballot. Finally, Marshall defined the social component as the right to 'a modicum of economic welfare and security to the right to share to the full in the social heritage and to live the life of a civilized being' (Marshall, 1950, p.69). Alongside these three components, there exists a set of institutions that give these rights social expression, namely the courts of justice, parliament and councils of local government, and the educational system and the social services.

justice

Marshall argues that citizenship modifies the negative impact of the capitalist market by a redistribution of resources on the basis of rights and, as a result, there is a permanent tension between the principles of **equality** that underpin **democracy** and the de facto inequalities of wealth and income that characterize the capitalist market. In post-war Britain, citizenship came to institutionalize the ideals and aspirations of social reconstruction. The rebuilding of British society after the Second World War was influenced by the social and economic ideas of John Maynard Keynes who argued that the government had to play an active role in periods of economic depression through investment in public works (such as building roads). These principles of government involvement, that came to be defined as 'social Keynesianism', are important for citizenship, because they assume that citizenship is enhanced by social policies of full employment. In this sense, citizenship is a status position that mitigates the negative effects of economic class and social inequality within a capitalist society.

equality,
democracy

Citizenship is concerned with one of the fundamental questions of any society: who shall belong? Citizenship is normally acquired through one of three means:

(a) by birth on the soil of the territory of the sovereign, that is by the principle of *jus soli*;

(b) by descent according to blood relationships:the principle of *jus sanguinis*; or

(c) by naturalization through a formal legal process in which some combination of *jus soli* or *jus sanguinis* is embraced.

Societies such as Canada and Australia that have been constituted by **migration** tend to regard citizenship as a means of generating a national community. Societies vary considerably in terms of their criteria for citizenship, and hence differ significantly in terms of their rates of naturalization. While Germany has historically defined citizenship exclusively on a principle of descent, France has had a more inclusive definition on a principle of territoriality and allegiance

migration

to the state (Brubaker, 1992). Citizenship rules thus reflect different conceptions of the nation as either an ethnic community or a political territory.

In terms of traditions of membership, there have been important differences between US and UK citizenship. Whereas in the UK, the main factor behind the growth of social rights has been class inequality in relation to basic resources such as housing, education and social security, the US citizenship debate has been largely inspired by the issues of migration and social mobility (Shklar, 1991). The US experience of citizenship has been about the success and failure to implement civic ideals in a context of racial division and conflict (Smith, 1997). The other major causal feature in the development of citizenship in both the United States and the UK has been the unintended consequence of modern warfare. The idea of a comprehensive health system gained widespread acceptance during the First World War, and after the Second World War the Labour government brought in a national health service that offered treatment free at the point of use for all citizens. The welfare state and social Keynesianism in Britain after the Second World War and the civil rights movement in the US were both responses to the mobilization of society and to its self-critical reflection.

We might call this development of citizenship through the crisis of war the 'Titmuss effect'. In his *Income Distribution and Social Change*, Richard Titmuss observed that:

> The major stimulus to social inquest in Britain during the present century has come from the experience of war. On each occasion this experience was sufficiently mortifying to weaken temporarily the forces of inertia and resistance to change. In the absence of such stimuli in the future, we may have quite consciously to invent and nourish new ways and means of national self-examination. This task may be harder to discharge in the face of rising standards of living and the growing influence of the mass media of complacency.
>
> (Titmuss, 1962, p.188)

Revolutionary struggles, civil war, the destructive consequences of warfare and mass migration have often created the conditions for active involvement, but, as Titmuss recognized, we need to devise new means for national self-examination and public debate in a period when the possibility of nuclear and biological warfare have created the technical means to destroy civilized existence.

In retrospect, the principal weakness of Marshall's theory of citizenship in Britain was that it assumed a somewhat homogeneous society in which regional, cultural and ethnic divisions were not important when compared to social class divisions (Crowley, 1998). Marshall worked in a political context where the unity of the United Kingdom was not a major issue, and where migration had yet to turn it into a multicultural society. The cultural and constitutional problem of 'Englishness' within the devolution of government in modern Britain was hardly imaginable in Marshall's time. In contemporary Britain, by contrast, one person in fifteen is from a minority ethnic group. Multicultural and racial issues have come to dominate domestic policy debate about the rights of citizens.

Finally, for Marshall, citizenship was primarily a matter of entitlement, but he had little to say about duties and obligations. As such, the theory envisaged a passive citizenry in which the state protected the individual from the uncertainty of the market through a system of universal rights. Political economists have criticized Marshallian citizenship as liberal reformism that offered formal rights rather than substantive benefits. Citizenship has often been dismissed as merely

Figure 5.2 *In a democratic society is there a duty on citizens to protest at government decisions perceived as unjust?*

a 'ruling-class strategy' to pacify the working class through the promise rather than the enactment of citizenship (Mann, 1987). How do citizenship rights become effective forms of entitlement? My argument is that citizenship as a status position is not in itself sufficient to guarantee effective entitlement and that effective claims to citizenship have traditionally depended on three crucial foundations: work, war and reproduction.

READING 5.1

Now read an extract from T.H. Marshall's *Class, Citizenship and Social Development*, which you will find reproduced as Reading 5.1.

■ When you have done so, write down what you would see as the major criticisms of Marshall's theory of citizenship.

■ What additions are necessary to make Marshall's theory more relevant to the circumstances of modern-day Britain?

Critics of Marshall would argue that in Britain the liberal beliefs and institutions that underpinned post-war welfare assumed the social and political dominance of a white middle class. As a result, Marshall's model of social citizenship has not been responsive to the social aspirations of minority ethnic groups, especially those communities that we recruited in the 1950s and 1960s from the Caribbean and the Indian subcontinent to service Britain's economy. The question of ethnicity and citizenship is addressed at the end of this chapter, and in Reading 5.4.

SUMMARY OF SECTION 2

1   The importance of T.H. Marshall's contribution to the debate about
     citizenship is that citizenship is seen to modify the negative aspect of the
     capitalist market by redistributing resources on the basis of assumed rights.

2   In retrospect, Marshall's analysis can be criticized on several grounds, notably
     because it treats society as more homogeneous than it is and so, for example,
     overlooks the implications that ethnic diversity might have for notions of
     citizenship.

3 Three routes of effective entitlement: work, war and reproduction

Rather than define citizenship within a static framework of rights and obligations, it is important to understand citizenship as process. Citizenship is both an inclusionary process involving some re-allocation of resources and an exclusionary mechanism involving the creation of identities on the basis of a common or imagined solidarity. Citizenship entitlement provides criteria for the allocation of scarce resources and at the same time forms powerful identities that are not only juridical, but typically involve assumptions about ethnicity, religion and sexuality (Isin and Wood, 1999). National citizenship has been frequently and implicitly constituted around racial divisions, because it excluded outsiders from access to resources on the basis of an (ascribed) ethnic or national identity. A strong sense of national identity is sustained by what sociologists call
social closure   '**social closure**', that is by institutions that specifically exclude 'outsiders'.

Because citizenship is a set of processes for the allocation of entitlements, obligations and immunities within a political community, these entitlements are themselves based on a number of assumptions that describe and evaluate the specific contributions that individuals have made to society, for example through war service, or reproduction, or work.

From a historical perspective, social citizenship has been closely associated with the involvement of individuals (typically men) in the formal labour market. Work was fundamental to the conception of citizenship for the foundation of the welfare state. Individuals could achieve effective entitlements through the production of goods and services, namely through gainful employment which was essential for the provision of adequate pensions and superannuation. These entitlements also typically included work care, insurance cover, retirement benefits and health care. Citizenship for (male) workers characteristically evolved out of class conflicts over conditions of employment, remuneration and retirement. In Britain, class conflict was institutionalized through reformist trade unionism and through various compromises (typically referred to as a 'social contract') between government, employers and workers.

Secondly, service to the state through warfare generates a range of entitlements for the soldier-citizen. Wartime service typically leads to special pension rights, health provisions, housing and education for returning servicemen and their families. War service has been important, as we have seen, in the development of social security entitlements (Titmuss, 1963).

Thirdly, people achieve entitlements through the formation of households and families that become the mechanisms for the reproduction of society through the birth, maintenance and socialization of children. These services increasingly include care for the ageing and elderly as obligations between generations continue to be satisfied through the private sphere. These services to the state through the family provide entitlements to both men and women as parents, that is as reproducers of the nation. These familial entitlements become the basis of family security systems, various forms of support for mothers, and health and educational provision for dependants.

Although the sexual activity of adults in marriage is regarded in law as a private activity, the state and church have clearly taken a profound interest in the conditions for sexual activity. Heterosexual reproduction has been a principal feature of the regulatory activity of the modern state. The values and norms of a household constituted by a married heterosexual couple have provided the dominant ideal of British social life, despite the fact that four in ten live births in 1998 occurred outside marriage (ONS, 2000). In fact, the moral force of the idea of marriage is so compulsive in contemporary

Figure 5.3 William Beveridge, architect of the welfare state after the Second World War

society that in some states of the United States legislation is being enacted that would enable gay couples to form 'civil unions'.

These conditions of effective entitlement also established a pattern of active participation in society, that in turn contributed to civil society through the creation of 'social capital' (Putnam, 1993, 1995). We may define social capital as the investments which people make in society through their involvement in associations such as churches, clubs, professional bodies and sports organizations. Active citizenship supported work-related associations, such as working-men's clubs, trade union organizations and guilds, and political organizations such as the traditional Labour Party. These groups, clubs and societies are 'intermediary associations' (Durkheim, 1992/1890–1900), that is forms of association that mediate between the state and the individual, and provide moral regulation of society and the economy. These associations – chapels, gardening clubs, women's meetings and sports organizations – have been recognized as an essential aspect of social cohesion. While mass warfare in the twentieth century has been profoundly destructive of traditional society, one unintended consequence of these military conflicts was to produce a multitude of (male) associations that provided support and services to ex-soldiers. Ceremonials of male solidarity (Cenotaph parades and other rituals of remembrance) kept alive the comradeship of war, and the 'Dunkirk spirit' continued to be a norm of civilian service and sacrifice. Finally, parenthood has traditionally provided solidaristic linkages to the wider community through women's groups, child-care associations, school-related groups, neighbourhood groups, and church-based groups such as the Mothers' Union. The growth of post-war active citizenship was also associated with activities that contributed to social solidarity. These patterns of citizenship have been attenuated because the three foundations of effective entitlement have been transformed by economic, military and social changes.

The remainder of this section will explore in turn the role of these three entitlements in the growth of social citizenship rights.

3.1 Work and citizenship

It may sound perverse to suggest that in contemporary Britain the decline of economic participation has brought about an erosion of citizenship, when participation in the labour force has been rising continuously since the early 1990s. Increasing economic activity has been especially important for women. Between 1971 and 1999, the percentage of women who are economically active increased from 56 to 72 per cent. However, high levels of economic participation mask a real change in the nature of the economy and obscure a transition from old to new welfare regimes. The new economic regime is based on monetary stability, fiscal control and a reduction in government regulation of the economy.

third way politics

These new policies have often been described, especially in Britain, as **'the third way'**. This phrase attempts to describe a government strategy that provides an alternative to unregulated or liberal capitalism, on the one hand, and regulated socialism, on the other. The third way seeks strategies that will achieve some control over the economy without the dangers of bureaucratic management under socialism. In this new economic environment, one version of the third way strategy involves, not protecting individuals from the uncertainties of the market that had dominated welfare strategies between 1930 and 1970, but helping people to participate successfully in the market through education (life-long learning schemes), flexible employment (family-friendly employment strategies) and tax incentives (Myles and Quadagno, 2000). However, while increasing rates of economic activity have been a positive aspect of economic liberalization, much of this increase in economic participation has required the casualization of the labour force. The number of men in part-time employment doubled between 1984 and 1999, and radical changes in the labour market (job-sharing, casualization, flexibility, down-sizing, and new management strategies) have disrupted work as a career. For employers, functional and numerical flexibility have broken down rigidities in the workplace, but these strategies have also compromised job security (Abercrombie and Warde, 2000, p.81). These changes in work and career structures constitute a significant 'corrosion of character' (Sennett, 1998). Traditional patterns of work permitted workers to establish safe routines and predictable lifestyles: they could organize their domestic activities with some degree of security; their sense of identity ('character') was supported by their work routines. With the obsolescence of the social relevance of the concept of career (even among the professional classes), there is also an erosion of commitment to the company. Workers can no longer depend on a stable life-course or life-cycle. In addition, there has been a major decline in trade-union membership, and work in a life-long career no longer so clearly defines personal identity. Union density (or the proportion

Figure 5.4 *A dole queue – a once-familiar sight*

of people eligible for membership who actually join) has declined steadily since 1979, and by 1996 union membership was lower than at any time since the end of the Second World War. Class-based identities are disappearing along with class-based communities. In Britain, the miners' strike of 1984–5 represented the collapse of working-class communalism that had been the back-bone of British social solidarity as celebrated in texts such as *Coal is Our Life* (Dennis *et al.*, 1962).

Sociological studies of social class suggest that, while levels of unemployment have been falling as a consequence of the economic boom of the 1990s, the contemporary class structure has new components – an 'underclass' of the permanently unemployable (typically, lone-parent welfare claimants), a declining middle class associated with the decline of middle management, and the 'working poor' whose skill levels do not permit upward mobility. These new features of the class structure do not encourage active citizenship through economic entitlement. However, these changes in the nature of employment are perhaps insignificant when compared to the ageing of the population and the social problems of (early) retirement. In 1901, one person in twenty was aged 65; by 1998, it was one in six. Between 1961 and 1996 the number of people aged 85 and over trebled, reaching 1.1 million people, whilst the number of centenarians increased from 300 in 1951 to 5,500 by 1996. The stereotype of the elderly as a dependent and passive population is false, but the greying of the population does have important implications for the shape of the working population and for employment as a basis for entitlement. It has been predicted that by 2030 the dependency ratio of employed to non-working pensioners in Germany and Italy will reach 1:1, and the European economy will continue to be heavily dependent on young migrant labour from outside the European Union. The demand for labour that arises from European economic growth, an ageing population and compulsory retirement is changing the ethnic composition of Europe. There are now, for example, around 13 million Muslims in Europe. These social changes are producing demands for changes in naturalization policies, for dual citizenship and for more porous political boundaries (Aleinikoff and Klusmeyer, 2000).

READING 5.2

Now read 'Equality in a multicultural society' by Bhikhu Parekh, in Reading 5.2. When you have done so, answer the following questions:

1   What are the implications of multiculturalism for citizenship rights?

2   Do we all have to be the same? Should we all be treated the same?

We can argue, following Bhikhu Parekh, that the social rights of citizenship do not always or necessarily imply that all citizens should be treated the same. Justice may require different treatment of people whose circumstances are very different. In this sense, justice is 'fairness' (Rawls, 1971).

Post-war migration to Britain forced various British governments to re-think the nature of British citizenship. The United Kingdom was historically a society in which citizenship was based on residence (the *jus soli* system). All people born in any British territory anywhere in the world could in principle claim British citizenship. However, in the 1960s and 1970s immigration controls were introduced. These controls undermined the broad, liberal view of British citizenship and restricted entry into Britain. The British Nationality Act 1981 recognized this transformation of citizenship. Naturalization of migrants in Britain can occur after three to five years of residence, but naturalization is at the discretion of the Home Secretary and no reason for refusal is required to be given.

One might argue that Britain is a reluctant multicultural society and in cultural terms remains closed to outsiders. It is often said that, while the United Kingdom, recognizes the presence of 'Black British', it does not recognize 'Black English': that is, the host society finds it difficult to imagine that Black citizens could ever acquire the habits and attitudes over time of a 'true' Englishman. However, while Britain as a society may be conservative culturally, it has become de facto a multicultural society, especially in the large urban centres of industrial production.

A further factor in the slow transformation of British identity has been the gradual devolution of power to Scotland and Wales, and the emergence of a peace settlement in Northern Ireland. Entry into the European Economic Community (now the European Union) has also brought about political changes that indicate an erosion of the sovereignty of the state. It is possible to argue

multiculturalism that **multiculturalism** is one factor among many that is changing British identity. One possible consequence of this transformation of national identity might be, not an acceptance of social change, but an effort to restore a narrow or reactionary defence of Englishness.

As we have seen, early theories of citizenship in Europe assumed that class divisions in capitalism were the main source of social conflict and that citizenship could modify these class relationships and produce a new foundation for social solidarity and common identity. An unintended consequence of British economic expansion, labour migration and a greying population has been the growth of a multicultural society, but British social institutions (churches, universities, police force, the military and the professions) have yet to come to terms with ethnic diversity and difference. The fact of multiculturalism – or more specifically the presence of black communities in Britain – has yet to be reflected in national institutions: as Paul Gilroy expressed this absence – 'there ain't no black in the Union Jack' (Gilroy, 1987). It can be claimed that the continuity of institutional racism in the police force was an element in the tragic case of Stephen Lawrence, a black 'A' Level student who was brutally murdered by several white youths at a bus stop in south-east London. The report by Sir William Macpherson of Cluny (1999) not only concluded that the police investigation had been inadequate, but also gave support to the criticism that institutional racism was a feature of government agencies, including the police. Racial violence is a measure of the failure of citizenship to act as a process of social inclusion in British society. The issue of racial violence in Britain is a useful illustration of the interaction between the state and the community over the nature of citizenship as an institution of both social closure and social inclusion. The Lawrence episode can be depicted as indicating exclusion (the murder itself, the flawed police investigation) and inclusion (the setting up of the Inquiry, the official response to the findings of the Inquiry). The social and political boundaries of a society are the effects of social struggles over citizenship entitlements that take place at many levels.

3.2 War and citizenship

In attempting to develop a better understanding of citizenship entitlement, we have briefly considered how changes in the economy have eroded a basic principle of social citizenship, namely the right to work. In addition to changes in the economic foundations of citizenship entitlement, the Titmuss-mechanism of war-related claims to social rights has largely disappeared with the end of mass warfare. The end of the Cold War and nuclear disarmament have meant that the traditional role of the citizen-soldier has given way to a new pattern of warfare involving both professional soldiers and mercenaries as the personnel of modern wars. Unlike France, Britain's military defence of its shrinking empire was modest and Prime Minister Macmillan's vision of peaceful social change in Africa set the scene for gradual disengagement. Aggressive racial views and policies to rebuild imperial Britain, contain Commonwealth immigration and repatriate migrants that were advocated by British politicians like Enoch Powell in the 1960s did not eventually triumph in an emerging affluent society. Modern colonial wars were becoming increasingly expensive in the face of nationalist opposition and 'the British, more by luck than good management, had perceived this truth in time and retired from the business of empire with comparative ease and dignity' (Brogan, 1985, p.672).

The end of conscription and progressive decolonization changed the role of militarism in British society and the brief involvement of British forces in the Falklands/Malvinas War of 1982 was the exception not the rule. Of course, this argument is largely about British society, but, given the technological character of modern warfare, the experience of western states in Korea, Vietnam, Afghanistan, the Gulf and Kosovo suggests that modern wars corrupt and corrode democracies rather than cementing them together. In addition, the modern media have made it more rather than less difficult for any democracy to conduct large-scale military interventions in which there is a significant risk of casualties. The disruptive effect of the Vietnam War on US civil society is the classic example. US media coverage of that war and especially the image of hundreds of 'body bags' returning home dead, young, US soldiers did more to undermine the government's ability to pursue the war effort than actual Vietcong military successes in the countryside. We might argue that we are now into a period of post-heroic wars, when local conflicts tend not to have a larger moral or historical purpose. Ironically, the social result of peace is the erosion of the citizen-soldier as a social role, the decline of servicemen's clubs as part of civil society and the diminution of military ceremonials as part of the secular rituals of civil society and the state. In the age of smart bombs and stealth aircraft, mass involvement in heroic militarism is no longer (fortunately) a significant feature of citizenship formation.

3.3 Reproductive citizenship

Recent writing in the field of citizenship studies (Lister, 1997; Yuval-Davis, 1997; Voet, 1998; Richardson, 2000) has underlined the neglect of gender in the analysis of the national development of citizen entitlements and obligations in the nation-state. We need to extend the discussion of citizenship, nationalism and gender by examining the relationship between parenthood and entitlement.

Reproducing the next generation of citizens through marriage, household formation and socialization is a central means of acquiring comprehensive entitlements of citizenship and fulfilling its corresponding obligations. Contemporary government policies on new reproductive technologies demonstrate implicitly the general importance of eugenics for the modern state. Because the majority of western societies in demographic terms enjoy only modest rates of successful reproduction, the state promotes the desirability of fertility as a foundation of social participation. With an ageing population and a declining birth rate, the UK faces similar problems. Population growth in the United Kingdom since the 1980s has been increasingly dependent on net immigration. The privileged position that is given to heterosexuality is a function of the manner in which public policies seek to normalize reproduction as the desired outcome of marriage. The alternative for a society like Britain is to recruit its working class externally through immigration.

The liberal regime of modern citizenship regards parenthood in nuclear families, rather than heterosexuality as such, as the defining characteristic of the 'average' citizen and as the basis of social entitlement. Reproduction through heterosexual sexual intercourse has simply been, until recently, the only means to achieve the social, cultural and biological goals of parenthood. The technologies of artificial human reproduction introduced from the late 1970s served to underline the manner in which reproduction plays a foundational role in citizenship, because they provide the potential for reproduction without heterosexual sexual intercourse. Despite their widespread acceptance as a treatment for infertility, new reproductive technologies remain controversial medical procedures that continue to receive sensational attention from the popular press. Human artificial reproduction continues to prompt considerable public debate, because these developing technologies promise new means of human fertilization and provide unanticipated options for family formation. The more significant issues which these technologies raise explicitly concern mothering, parenthood and conception. The manner in which governments respond to these technical and social challenges reveals the moral assumptions of the state towards parents and families, namely the system of reproductive values prevalent in society. The concept of 'sexual citizenship' which has been promoted by some sociologists does not adequately describe the relationship between sexuality, reproduction and citizenship. In fact, the state's interest in sexual identity is secondary and subordinate to its demographic objective of securing and sustaining the connection between reproduction and citizenship. The notion that state-building, nationalism and reproductive citizenship describe a set of necessary connections is supported by traditional theories of patriarchy and by the history of the modern state. In the traditional terminology of sociology, citizenship-building is also and necessarily nation-building. The creation of a national community as the basis of national citizenship typically involved the conjunction of the dominance of both ethnic and national identities (Nelson, 1998).

The nation-state presupposed a continuing pattern of patriarchy and patriotism as the dual legacy of monarchy and state-building. The modern matrix of nation, citizenship and masculinity has been changed by the global challenge to national sovereignty, by the transformations of work and warfare in modern societies, and by the transformation of sexuality and parenthood associated with the development of reproductive technology. Despite these fundamental social and political transformations, the foundations of national citizenship and the basis of individual entitlement remain legally and socially connected with reproduction and hence with the family and heterosexuality. A familial ideology of procreation has been a major legitimating support of the contemporary ensemble of entitlements that constitute the social rights of citizenship.

READING 5.3

Now study Reading 5.3, 'Citizenship and sexuality' by Dorothy Richardson. When you have done so, consider the following questions:

1   What do you make of the idea of being only a partial citizen?

2   What do you understand by the notion of 'sexual citizenship'?

3   Richardson makes the distinction between public and private citizen rights. Do you think this is a significant distinction?

Sexual citizenship appears to have two dimensions. The first concerns the rights of women and men to reproduce under conditions that they can choose and control: for example, the right to abortion could be regarded as a 'sexual right'. The second concerns the right to experience intimacy and sexual pleasure under conditions of one's own choosing, and with partners that one can select as legitimate sexual partners: for example, sex between men might be an example of 'intimate' citizenship.

In general these sexual rights have been very closely associated with the women's movement that has fought for female equality. The question of the role of women in the military is problematic. Since the women's movement has generally been against violence, the issue of women's participation in the military is somewhat contradictory. The historical trend has been for women to play an increasingly active role in the military (for example, in Israel, the US and Scandinavia). Is this trend a measure of female equality?

Throughout the twentieth century, women struggled to achieve equal pay, access to education, welfare benefits for children and working women, and equality in retirement benefits and superannuation. They also wanted access to political institutions. These rights were an important aspect of sexual citizenship. Recent comparative research suggests that these aspirations for the equality of women have not been fully satisfied, even where women, as in Denmark, have entered politics in significant numbers (Siim, 2000). Sexual citizenship is ultimately about the right of women to reproduce and to have equal access to the public sphere in terms of political representation and economic participation. In capitalism, there appears to be a permanent tension between the private sphere (such as the home) and the public sphere (such as the workplace).

SUMMARY OF SECTION 3

1   Historically, effective entitlement to social citizenship has been associated with involvement in the labour market, wartime service and the formation of households and families.

2   The prevailing conditions of effective entitlement to social citizenship also established a pattern of active participation in society via associations connected to work, politics, war and family, and these associations served to increase social cohesion. However, the role of these associations has been attenuated by economic, political and technological changes.

3   In the contemporary UK, mass involvement in military activity is no longer a significant element in citizenship formation.

4   The structural changes in economic participation have produced changes in work and career structures that have eroded citizenship. The greying of the population has important implications for employment as a basis for entitlement to citizenship.

5   An unintended consequence of economic expansion, a greying population and inward labour migration has been the growth in the UK of a multicultural society and this development has significant implications for British identity and conceptions of UK citizenship.

6   Despite fundamental social and political transformations the foundations of citizenship and entitlement are connected to reproduction and to the family.

7   The state's interest in sexual identity is less significant than its demographic objective in promoting the connection between reproduction and citizenship.

8   Sexual citizenship concerns the right of women to reproduce *and* to have equal access to the public sphere.

4 Voluntary associations: a fourth way to entitlement?

As section 3 has shown, work and war no longer provide certain or confident cultural identities: the worker-citizen and the soldier-citizen are images of the past. In modern society, especially for poorly educated, culturally deprived, young men and women, reproduction is one of the few remaining opportunities for social recognition – hence the prevalence of teenage pregnancy. Young men without military opportunities to establish an identity as an effective citizen, and without jobs or careers to earn sufficiently to finance the creation of a household, to enjoy conspicuous consumption, or to fund romantic love (Illouz, 1997), are structurally marginalized. These tensions between tenuous membership, casualized employment, consumer affluence and aggressive individualism are what we might call the new 'cultural contradictions of capitalism' (Bell, 1976). The result of these changes has been to reduce the 'social standing' of young people, the unemployed, single people who cannot afford to maintain their own households, the elderly on limited pensions and racially marginalized communities, and thus to reduce their chances of social inclusion (Sennett, 2000).

The erosion of citizenship through the transformations of work, war and parenthood also corrodes the possibilities of participatory or associative democracy. **Alexis de Tocqueville**, a student of American democracy, argued in 1835–40 that **voluntary associations** were crucial to the success of a modern democracy, because they protected the individual from mass opinion (de Tocqueville, 1968). Modern society is no longer constituted by a dense network of associations, clubs, fraternities, chapels, working-men's societies, choirs and communal associations. The decline of social capital is a major index of the erosion of citizenship and trust. The late twentieth century was marked by a major decline in all forms of social participation, at least partly as a consequence of the impact of television on leisure activities. Religious membership, confirmations, baptism and marriages in the mainstream Christian churches have declined considerably since 1970, although there has been an increase in evangelical sects and in non-Christian religions. Membership of political parties and newspaper readership have also declined. Whereas 76 per cent of men and 68 per cent of women claimed to read a newspaper in 1981, newspaper readership had fallen to 60 and 51 per cent respectively by 1998/99. These changes raise questions about the possibilities of participation in contemporary society, and specifically about the level of third-sector institutions such as voluntary associations in providing opportunities for social service and participation. It is generally recognized that individual giving to charities and voluntary associations has steadily declined in the post-war period.

The conventional assumption is that participation in the voluntary sector has, like other forms of social involvement, declined through the twentieth century, but this pessimistic interpretation may underestimate the importance of charities, voluntary associations and philanthropy. For example, *Social Trends* reports that about one-quarter of the British population claim to have participated in a voluntary association in the previous year, and of these about half had spent twenty days or more in voluntary activities. While the membership of

Tocqueville, Alexis de

voluntary associations

some associations has fallen, other associations have grown rapidly. For example, although the membership of the Mothers' Union fell from 308,000 to 177,000 between 1971 and 1990, membership of the National Trust increased from 278,000 to just over two million in the same period (Abercrombie and Warde, 2000, p.330). Membership of voluntary associations increased from 0.73 memberships per capita in 1959 to 1.12 memberships in 1990. Individual involvement in voluntary associations, clubs and leisure groups is probably more robust than the Putnam thesis (1995) about the decline of social capital would suggest. If, however, we simply count the number of voluntary associations and chart their growth, it is evident that voluntary associations, especially in the welfare sector, have expanded significantly in the last twenty years, and in part this growth can be attributed to the decline of state activity in welfare. The Johns Hopkins Comparative Non-profit Sector Project discovered that in the USA, France, Italy, Hungary, Sweden and parts of the Third World, one in every twenty jobs and one in every eight service jobs are accounted for by the voluntary sector.

These changes to society that are illustrated by the decline of social memberships and voluntarism imply that there has been a decline in active citizenship. Various authors, but notably Robert Putnam, have suggested that passivity has been the consequence of consumerism, and especially the dominance of television. Citizens are increasingly passive observers of society rather than active members. The growth of TV ownership has been a major cultural indicator of social change. In the United States in 1946 there were 7,000 TV sets and by 1960 there were 50 million. In Britain by 1960, 75 per cent of British families had television. By bringing the world into our front room, television has transformed society into a spectacle.

In Britain in 1998 people over four years of age watched on average twenty-five hours of television per week. Less than four per cent of the population had, in the previous twelve months, engaged in any political activities such as election campaigns or helping political parties or movements. Because television-watching has often been blamed for a decline in social participation, membership of and participation in voluntary associations are often seen to be important for the vitality of society. In addition, many governments have supported the voluntary sector because it makes an important contribution to welfare services. Voluntary associations are regarded as a training ground for active, altruistic citizens. Voluntarism is therefore seen to represent important moral values of service, philanthropy and altruism.

For many critics of market-driven social policies (variously described as Thatcherism, Reagonomics and Managerialism), the reduction of state support for welfare was automatically taken to be a measure of the decline of social citizenship, but this argument ignores the criticism that many features of the post-war welfare state were bureaucratic, paternalistic and exclusionary. While we should not exaggerate the degree of post-war political consensus as to the role of the state in welfare provision in the immediate aftermath of the Second World War (Sullivan, 1992; Targetti, 1992), criticism of the legacy of social Keynesianism and 'bureaucratic collectivism' became increasingly strident in the 1970s. The state welfare bureaucracy was an obvious target of right-wing criticism in the Thatcher years, but left-wing and liberal critics of bureaucratic welfare were equally antagonistic towards invasive welfare processes, especially means-tested support. In the period leading up to the election of Mrs Thatcher's

Conservative government in 1979, there was a paradoxical agreement between the left and right wings of British politics that the welfare state was in crisis. The solution adopted by the Thatcher and Major governments (1979–1997) was to reduce public expenditure on welfare, to privatize national industries and to cut personal taxation.

The new consensus of the Labour government of Mr Blair places greater emphasis on third-way strategies, part of which involves a quest either for partnerships between government and voluntary organizations or direct encouragement of the voluntary sector to provide local and community-based services. Given dissatisfaction with the negative consequences of the market as a solution to social and political questions, reliance on the voluntary sector is compatible with the search for active citizenship, associative democracy and subsidiarity in service provision. The underlying assumption is that a vibrant democracy is unlikely to flourish without authentic community, but whether or not voluntary associations can provide an effective welfare service is possibly less important than whether they can provide an experience of community involvement that in turn can be a schooling in democracy.

Voluntary associations can provide opportunities for social participation, for democratic involvement at the local level, and thus for active citizenship. They are essential to the survival of the public sphere, and in terms of service delivery, they can provide welfare programmes that are sensitive to local client needs. This positive view of the voluntary sector and active citizenship is often shared by both politicians and academics. Tony Blair has claimed:

> We seek a diverse but inclusive society, promoting tolerance within agreed norms, promoting civic activism as a complement to (but not a replacement for) modern government. An inclusive society imposes duties on individuals and parents as well as on society as a whole.
>
> (Blair, 1993, p.12)

Voluntary associations have the potential to be the principal organizing force in society providing public welfare and the primary means of democratic governance (Hirst, 1994). Indeed, if 'big government' really is part of the problem, then a partnership between voluntary associations and government should prove attractive, since voluntarism can reduce the scale and scope of the affairs administered by the state. Subsidiarity would be achieved through a process of devolution of state functions, authority and funding to a network of voluntary associations. Such a system would support a process where citizen choice is combined with public welfare and, because voluntary associations have the capacity for a high level of communicative democracy, this devolved political structure would allow for widespread consultation, co-operation and collaboration. Voluntary associations are characterized by organizational autonomy from the state and where their internal organizational structures support client involvement, they are better suited to promoting welfare that is targeted to local communities than are state bureaucracies.

These broad claims for the democratic functions of the voluntary sector (Cohen and Rogers, 1995) have to be modified to take into account the extreme variation within the sector. We must in any case start with a definition of voluntary associations. The point of this definition is to suggest that large voluntary associations working closely with government may share characteristics with large profit-making corporations. There is considerable criticism of the notion that voluntary associations can be entrepreneurial, democratic and responsive to client interests. Research suggests that the interests of associative democracy and social inclusion are probably better served by small community groups on the margins of the social order than by large associations that are like corporations apart from the fact that a share of the profits are not distributed to the board of managers (Brown *et al.*, 2000). Despite the extent of the debate about voluntary associations, there has in fact been little agreement about how they might be precisely defined (Sills, 1957).

One definition claims that voluntary associations have five characteristics: they are organized, private, non-profit-distributing, self-governing and voluntary (Salamon and Anheier, 1999, p.69). However, there are some difficulties with this definition of the voluntary sector, because in practice their connections with government are very strong. There are, for example, a variety of funding arrangements in the UK as a result of the close relationships between government and voluntary organizations, and these include direct financial support and tax concessions (Kendall and Knapp, 1996). The national lottery also channels funding into the voluntary sector under the regulation of the government.

There is also considerable ambiguity in the relationship of voluntary associations to the economy. Traditionally, voluntary associations were not expected to function like business organizations and their funding came from philanthropy, bequests and other gifts. Although voluntary associations are still either non-profit and not-for-profit organizations, they are increasingly under economic pressure to marketize and to commodify their services. The growth of 'McWelfare' and 'welfare.com' are likely outcomes of the growth of global welfare websites and commercialized service delivery (Brown *et al.*, 2000, p.212). In order to increase funding, they have to compete for government grants and so there is pressure for these associations to become more professional. They need to hire staff who are not only highly qualified, able to cost and manage projects, and to run large and complex organizations, but who are also knowledgeable about government strategy. These developments tend to create a gap between the board of managers and the rank and file. There appears to be an inherent tension in how voluntary associations are organized, because the growth of professional values may conflict with traditional notions of philanthropy and with the ethos of those attracted to working in this sector.

We can summarize these issues by saying that, especially for large voluntary associations, the voluntary sector is now under the same financial and management pressures that shape capitalist corporations. In particular, voluntary associations are driven by a logic of resource maximization and enhancement (Galaskiewicz and Bielefeld, 1998, p.35); they are forced to employ and promote managerial rationality (and thus to recruit from a pool of generic management); they are also compelled to professionalize their processes of recruitment and training; and they are dependent on rational and professional systems of fund-raising. In the UK and Australia, they are very dependent on their ability to tender successfully for government grants. There is therefore some force to the conventional criticisms of the voluntary sector: it cannot provide a universalistic service; it does not have clear performance criteria; it is not rigorously accountable; and it may not be cost-effective. Worse still, voluntary associations may often function more like social clubs than service agencies, and they may form a social hierarchy of agencies that is a mirror-image of the status hierarchy of society as a whole. Some charities and voluntary associations simply serve the 'expressive needs' of the middle classes and provide social outlets for unpaid work by them (Pearce, 1993).

In both the United States and the UK, there developed a critical research literature in the 1970s that suggested that voluntary associations functioned to restrain wage increases in social services as a result of competition between paid and unpaid workers. My argument from comparative data collected across a number of different societies is that the economic and legal framework within which the voluntary sector operates in the United Kingdom is not conducive to sustaining its more idealistic or Tocquevillian objectives of democratization. For example, voluntary associations that are run by and for local aboriginal communities (in Canada and Australia), or more generally associations that exist to provide a specific service to marginalized social groups (such as HIV-positive gay men), are able to avoid bureaucratization and co-option. Perhaps for rather obvious reasons, voluntary associations that provide a social conduit for activist groups and rights advocacy are less dependent on government funding, more closely associated with community needs, less driven by the norms of generic management, and closer to the model of a participatory democracy recommended by de Tocqueville.

ACTIVITY 3

How much do you think that participation in such voluntary associations contributes to nurturing active citizenship in modern society? Reflect on your own experience (or those of relatives or colleagues) of voluntary associations – the school PTA, running a football team, charity fund-raising and so on.

The theory of social capital suggests that community and voluntary associations are important for building up trust and civic participation. It is assumed that volunteering makes people into better and more active citizens. For example, it has been said that participation in the Methodist chapels made working people more educated and literate, thereby training them for leadership. The early stages of the British Labour Party apparently depended considerably on local Methodist preachers who often had radical social values and provided local leadership of the Labour movement (Thompson, 1963). Critics of the contemporary emphasis on volunteering argue that voluntarism is dependent on the unpaid labour of women.

SUMMARY OF SECTION 4

1   The conventional assumption is that participation in the voluntary sector – which is held to be an important means of promoting active citizenship – declined throughout the twentieth century.

2   A proper assessment of the potential contribution of the voluntary sector to democratic functioning of society should take account of the great variation within the voluntary sector, which ranges from organizations with strong links to government that may be managed in a way which conflicts with conventional notions of philanthropy, to groups less dependent on government funding that are more closely identified with community needs.

5 Conclusion: new patterns of citizenship

The traditional framework through which citizenship rights have been granted has been eroded, because economic changes, technological innovation and globalization have transformed the nature of work, war and the social relations of reproduction. The three routes to effective citizenship no longer provide a firm socio-economic framework within which social rights can be enjoyed. Although the voluntary sector provides partial means for restoring and sustaining civil society, this idealism has to be tempered by a recognition that the sector is also shaped by economic conditions of competition and commercialism that may prove to be incompatible with the objectives of associational democracy. Citizenship in modern societies is 'thin' rather than 'thick' (Tilly, 1995, p.8), partly because the social capital that underpinned the communal basis of social involvement has been diluted by the passive world of television.

There is therefore considerable evidence to support a pessimistic analysis of the prospects of active citizenship in modern society. An alternative view is that a new regime of rights has emerged that reflects these changed social conditions. The social rights of nation-states are being slowly replaced or, better still, augmented by human rights. First, these new forms of citizenship are not specifically located within the nation-state, and are typically connected with human rights legislation rather than with civic rights. The communities that support these rights are often global, virtual and thin, rather than local and thick. Secondly, they arise because of social issues related to global changes and pressures, and in this sense are post-national, and finally they are conceptually interconnected, because they are driven by a common problem of modern society, namely the relationship between the human body and the environment (Turner, 1993). The quest for social security that lay behind the British welfare state has been overtaken by the human need for ontological security (that is, the survival of the human species).

This set of human rights has evolved for two basic reasons. The problems of the global order, such as the spread of AIDS or the pollution of the environment, cannot be solved by the unilateral action of individual governments, and secondly because the social risks of modern society that are created by new technologies (such as cloning or genetically modified food) do not fit easily into the existing politico-legal framework. Although Marshall's paradigm is now sociologically obsolete, I shall conclude by identifying three types of post-national citizenship that parallel the three components of citizenship in his original argument.

Global concern for the negative consequences of industrial capitalism on the natural environment has become a dominant issue of contemporary politics. Individual governments have, at various levels of intervention, attempted to protect their national populations from the effects of the industrialization of agricultural production, carbon dioxide emissions from motor vehicles, contamination from civil nuclear power or oil spillage from shipping disasters. Writing about the development of environmentalism in Britain, Howard Newby (1996) identified four stages in the emergence of 'environmental citizenship'. First, from the 1880s to the start of the twentieth century, there was a concern for preservation as epitomized by the National Trust. Secondly, in the inter-war years there was growing criticism of laissez-faire economics among the middle class and an emphasis on regulation and the provision of amenities. Between the early 1960s and 1970s, environmental concerns were expressed in a third stage through the debate over post-materialism through organizations such as Friends of the Earth and the Ecology Party. While membership of the Mothers' Union slumped between 1971 and 1990, membership of the Royal Society for the Protection of Birds increased from 98,000 to 890,000 and for the WWF, an international nature conservation charity, membership expanded from 12,000 to 219,000. Finally, in the late 1990s the British debate was challenged by the universal dimensions of global warming and, with a new emphasis on sustainability, the traditional language of amenity was replaced by a discourse of global catastrophe. A similar pattern also appeared in the 1960s in the growth of the US environmental lobby where a legal framework was created to regulate industry and protect the environment. This has been the background to the recognition of the importance of *ecological rights*.

ACTIVITY 4

Now take a moment to consider the following question: should we prevent or regulate fox-hunting primarily in the interests of foxes or of citizens?

Figure 5.5 *An anti-hunt demonstration: feelings run high on both pro and anti sides*

This may seem an odd question to ask, but let me suggest how confronting it helps to illuminate modern conceptions of citizenship. In contemporary societies, citizenship is implicitly associated with civilization. The word 'citizen' refers to the idea of a person who lives in a city, that is somebody who is civilized – unlike peasants who live in the countryside. To become a citizen implies an education that transforms somebody into a human being with certain virtues, for example respect for the lives of other citizens. Thus the argument against sports that involve cruelty to animals (fox-hunting, bull-fighting and bear-baiting) is that they corrupt the character of the citizen.

Some writers believe that we should extend rights to animals, especially animals that appear to have consciousness, awareness and even an elementary language, such as dolphins. Peter Singer (1995) argues that animals can suffer and therefore we have a moral obligation to prevent cruelty to animals. Hunting foxes is not only cruel, it reveals a lack of moral concern. More seriously, it points to our own lack of humanity. Michel de Montaigne (the famous sixteenth-century humanist) complained that fox-hunting trained the European aristocracy to be violent and aggressive (Quint, 1998).

The concept of 'risk society' (Beck, 1992) captures the critical dimension of the ecological consciousness as a lack of confidence in expert opinion and lack of trust in government policy. The debate in the UK in 2000–01 about genetically modified food is a perfect example of green politics in which ecological citizenship is expressed as a right to a safe, 'natural' environment. Whereas social rights were often the consequence of class-based activity, contemporary human rights are frequently the result of social or environmental movements and consumer lobbies that have diverse social memberships. Global and national social movements, rather than social class conflicts, appear to be relatively successful in bringing about an expansion of rights. Whereas Marshallian citizenship rights attempted to protect individuals from the vagaries of the market-place, the new regime of global rights attempts to protect humans from the negative consequences of economic growth and technology on their health and safety. It would be more precise to say that the human rights legislative framework is to protect future generations from the contemporary consequences of environmental degradation.

While the environmental lobby and the emergence of environmental or ecological citizenship were shaped by a sociological concern over the impact of industrial capitalism on the environment, the second dimension of this debate involved an anthropological concern with the impact of capitalism and colonial powers, not only on the environment, but on human communities as such. The notion that unrestrained industrial capitalism has had a negative impact on the natural environment was followed by the obvious conclusion that the spread of capitalist agriculture has had devastating consequences for pre-modern tribal society. The destruction of 'primitive society' was not simply a consequence of military encounters or the ravages of European disease; it also involved the removal of aboriginal society from the land in order to create a global market in beef, sheep and cereals. In the nineteenth century, the spread of capitalist agriculture, the destruction of aboriginal cultures and white migration created the characteristics of 'white-settler society' from North America to New Zealand. In the twentieth century, these societies have experienced a common pattern of policy-making designed to acculturate, to assimilate or to accommodate aboriginal peoples.

READING 5.4

Study Reading 5.4, 'Citizenship and identity', and then consider what lessons for citizenship in modern industrial societies can be learnt from the history of white settler societies, the destruction of aboriginal cultures and the disregard of their rights.

Figure 5.6 *An aboriginal group set up an illegal squatter camp in Victoria Park, Sydney, in August 2000 (during the Olympic Games), to draw attention to their situation in Australian society*

Aboriginal societies were typically tribal in their social organization and they did not form nation-states. They also characteristically regarded the land as a collective, not individual, resource. The occupation and control of aboriginal land by colonial states was achieved relatively quickly. In contemporary society, however, aboriginal communities have increasingly resisted incorporation into multicultural societies and have questioned social citizenship, appealing instead to human rights legislation to uphold *aboriginal rights*.

It could be assumed that the tensions between aboriginal human rights and general social rights have little or no relevance to the British Isles. This assumption is mistaken, because understanding the relationship between the exploitation of the land and the destruction of aboriginal cultures has given rise to a wider, and possibly more important, debate about cultural rights. Whereas the Marshallian framework had little analytical light to throw on the problem of ethnic identity, the global aboriginal issue has been a spur to more fundamental discussion of questions relating to identity and difference. The third type of citizenship rights is thus concerned with culture. *Cultural rights* (to language, to a share in the cultural heritage of a community, to freedom of religion and belief, and ultimately to identity) have become central to contemporary politics, but these cultural rights have neither precise nor necessary connections with membership of the nation-state. They depend crucially on international covenants (Boyle and Sheen, 1997).

These emerging rights (to a safe environment, to aboriginal culture and land, and to ethnic identity) point to and are underpinned by a generic right, namely a right to ontological security as a parallel to Marshallian social security. From this perspective, human beings are characterized by their frailty and their vulnerability, and by the precarious character of their social and political arrangements (Turner, 2000; Turner and Rojek, 2001). Where life is nasty, brutish and short, citizenship functions to make the world more secure and civilized, but the irony of globalization is that in many respects our world is becoming more risky and precarious, because the dangers of modern technology often outweigh, or at least question, its advantages. Ontological security is closely connected to questions of human embodiment, but it goes beyond reproductive citizenship and involves entitlement to respect. The right to ontological security underpins the other environmental, cultural and identity claims that have been characteristic of modern social movements. Our ontological security can only be safeguarded by a new set of values that embrace stewardship of the environment, concern for the precariousness of human communities, respect for cultural differences and a regard for human dignity. In short, we need a set of obligations that correspond to the demand for human rights.

These three post-national citizenship rights – ecological, aboriginal and cultural – are identified here as analogous to Marshall's three stages of national citizenship. They form a hierarchy: environment, community and individuals. These new rights are thus conceptually and historically connected by the risks to human embodiment in a global system. Post-national rights of the environment are connected by human frailty and by the fact that the nation-state cannot adequately respond to the vulnerability of human beings within an ecological system that is globally disrupted by modern technology. What is less clear – if we are to continue the parallel with Marshall – is the presence of an institutional structure to which they correspond. Marshallian citizenship rights were matched by the rise of specific institutional structures – the courts of justice, parliamentary institutions, and the welfare state. Environmental rights, aboriginal rights and cultural rights are all enshrined in some components of the Declaration of Human Rights and more recently in the legal recommendations arising from UN conferences on the environment (Rio de Janeiro), population (Cairo) and human settlements (Istanbul), but as yet there is no decisive set of governmental arrangements at the global level that enforce or match these rights. The notion that there should be global governance has been canvassed by numerous social scientists, but for global governance to make sense, we would need to spell out how a global political community could exist. The prospects of such a system are not too promising and thus the question that lies beyond the scope of this chapter is the conditions under which global governance would be both feasible and effective.

References

Abercrombie, N. and Warde, A. (eds) (2000) *Contemporary British Society,* Cambridge, Polity Press.

Aleinikoff, T.A. and Klusmeyer, D. (eds) (2000) *From Migrants to Citizens: Membership in a Changing World,* Washington, DC, Carnegie Endowment for International Peace.

Beck, U. (ed.) (1992) *Risk Society: Towards a New Modernity,* London, Sage.

Bell, D. (1976) *The Cultural Contradictions of Capitalism,* London, Heinemann.

Blair, T. (1993) *The Third Way: A New Politics for the New Century,* London, Fabian Society.

Boyle, K. and Sheen, J. (eds) (1997) *Freedom of Religion and Belief*, London, Routledge.

Brogan, H. (1985) *Longman History of the United States of America*, London, Longman.

Brown, K., Kenny, S. and Turner, B.S. (2000) *Rhetorics of Welfare: Uncertainty, Choice and Voluntary Associations*, Basingstoke, Macmillan.

Brubaker, R. (1992) *Citizenship and Nation in France and Germany*, Cambridge, MA, Harvard University Press.

Cohen, J. and Rogers, J. (eds) (1995) *Associations and Democracy*, London, Verso.

Crowley, J. (1998) 'The national dimension of citizenship in T.H. Marshall', *Citizenship Studies*, vol.2, no.2, pp.165–79.

Dennis, N., Henriques, F.M. and Slaughter, C. (1962) *Coal is Our Life*, London, Eyre & Spottiswoode.

Durkheim, E. (1992) *Professional Ethics and Civic Morals*, London, Routledge. A series of lectures first given by Durkheim in 1890–1900. (English translation, Routledge, 1957.)

Galaskiewicz, J. and Bielefeld, W. (1998) *Nonprofit Organizations in an Age of Uncertainty: A Study of Organizational Change*, New York, Aldine de Gruyter.

Gilroy, P. (1987) *There Ain't No Black in the Union Jack: The Cultural Politics of Race and Nation*, London, Hutchinson.

Hirst, P.Q. (1994) *Associative Democracy*, Cambridge, Polity Press.

Illouz, E. (1997) *Consuming the Romantic Utopia: Love and the Cultural Contradictions of Capitalism*, Berkeley, CA, University of California Press.

Isin, E.F. and Wood, P.K. (1999) *Citizenship and Identity*, London, Sage.

Kendall, J. and Knapp, M. (1996) *The Voluntary Sector in the United Kingdom*, Manchester, Manchester University Press.

Lister, R. (1997) *Citizenship: Feminist Perspectives,* Basingstoke, Macmillan.

Mann, M. (1987) 'Ruling class strategies and citizenship', *Sociology*, vol.21, no.3, pp.339–54.

Macpherson, W. (1999) *A Report into the Death of Stephen Lawrence*, London, Her Majesty's Stationery Office.

Marshall, T.H. (1950) *Citizenship and Social Class and Other Essays*, Cambridge, University of Cambridge Press. (Republished as Marshall, T.H. and Bottomore, T. (1987) *Citizenship and Social Class*, London, Pluto Press.)

Marshall, T.H. (1964) 'Citizenship and social class' in Turner, B.S. and Hamilton, P. (eds) (1994) *Citizenship: Critical Concepts*, Vol.II, London, Routledge, vol.2, Ch.29, pp.5–44. (Originally published in Marshall, T.H. (1964) *Class, Citizenship and Social Development*, Cambridge, Cambridge University Press.)

Myles, J. and Quadagno, J. (2000) 'Envisioning a *Third Way*: the welfare state in the twenty-first century', *Contemporary Sociology*, vol.29, no.1, pp.156–67.

Nelson, D.D. (1998) *National Manhood: Capitalist Citizenship and the Imagined Fraternity of White Men*, Durham, NC, and London, Duke University Press.

Newby, H. (1996) 'Citizenship in a green world: global commons and human stewardship' in Bulmer, M. and Rees, A.M. (eds) *Citizenship Today: The Contemporary Relevance of T.H. Marshall*, London, UCL Press.

ONS (2000) *Social Trends 30*, London, Office for National Statistics.

Parekh, B. (2000) *Rethinking Multiculturalism: Cultural Diversity and Political Theory*, Basingstoke, Macmillan.

Pearce, J.L. (1993) *Volunteers: The Organizational Behavior of Unpaid Workers*, London and New York, Routledge.

Putnam, D. (1993) *Making Democracy Work: Civic Traditions in Modern Italy*, Princeton, NJ, Princeton University Press.

Putnam, D. (1995) 'Bowling alone: America's declining social capital', *Journal of Democracy*, no.6, pp.65–78.

Quint, D. (1998) *Montaigne and the Quality of Mercy: Ethical and Political Themes in the* Essais, Princeton, NJ, Princeton University Press.

Rawls, J. (1971) *A Theory of Justice*, Oxford, Oxford University Press.

Richardson, D. (2000) *Re-Thinking Sexuality*, London, Sage.

Salamon, L.M and Anheier, H.K. (1996) *The Emerging Nonprofit Sector: A Cross-national Analysis*, Manchester, Manchester University Press.

Sassen, S. (1999) *Guests and Aliens*, New York, The New York Press.

Sennett, R. (1998) *The Corrosion of Character*, New York, W.W. Norton.

Sennett, R. (2000) 'Work and social inclusion' in Askonas, P. and Stewart, A. (eds) *Social Inclusion: Possibilities and Tensions*, Basingstoke, Macmillan, pp.278–90.

Shklar, J. (1991) *American Citizenship: The Quest for Inclusion*, Cambridge, MA, Harvard University Press.

Siim, B. (2000) *Gender and Citizenship: Politics and Agency in France, Britain and Denmark*, Cambridge, Cambridge University Press.

Sills, D. (1957) *The Volunteers: Means and Ends in a National Organization*, Glencoe, IL, The Free Press.

Singer, P. (1995) *Animal Liberation*, London, Pimlico.

Smith, R.M. (1997) *Civic Ideals: Conflicting Visions of Citizenship in US History*, New Haven, CT, and London, Yale University Press.

Sullivan, M. (1992) *The Politics of Social Policy*, London, Harvester Wheatsheaf.

Targetti, F. (ed.) (1992) *Privatization in Europe: West and East Experiences*, Aldershot, Dartmouth.

Thompson, E.P. (1963) *The Making of the English Working Class*, London, Gollancz.

Tilly, C. (1995) 'Citizenship, identity and social history', *International Review of Social History*, vol.40, no.3, pp.1–17.

Titmuss, R. (1962) *Income Distribution and Social Change: A Study in Criticism*, London, George Allen & Unwin.

Titmuss, R. (1963) *Essays on the 'Welfare State'*, London, Unwin University Books.

Tocqueville, A. de (1968) *Democracy in America*, Glasgow, Collins. Originally published in two volumes in 1835 and 1840.

Turner, B.S. (1986) *Citizenship and Capitalism: The Debate over Reformism*, London, Allen & Unwin.

Turner, B.S. (1990) 'Outline of a theory of citizenship', *Sociology*, vol.24, no.2, pp.189–214.

Turner, B.S. (1993) 'Outline of a theory of human rights', *Sociology*, vol.27, no.3, pp.489–512.

Turner, B.S. (1997) 'Citizenship studies: a general theory', *Citizenship Studies*, vol.1, no.1, pp.5–18.

Turner, B.S. (2000) 'An outline of a general sociology of the body' in Turner, B.S. (ed.) *The Blackwell Companion to Social Theory*, Oxford, Blackwell, pp.481–502.

Turner, B.S. and Rojek, C. (2001) *Society and Culture: Principles of Scarcity and Solidarity*, London, Sage.

Voet, R. (1998) *Feminism and Citizenship*, London, Sage.

Yuval-Davis, N. (1997) *Gender and Nation*, London, Sage.

Readings

5.1 T.H. Marshall, 'Welfare and citizenship' (1964)

The early impact of citizenship on social class

So far my aim has been to trace in outline the development of citizenship in England to the end of the nineteenth century. For this purpose I have divided citizenship into three elements, civil, political and social. I have tried to show that civil rights came first, and were established in something like their modern form before the first Reform Act was passed in 1832. Political rights came next, and their extension was one of the main features of the nineteenth century, although the principle of universal political citizenship was not recognized until 1918. Social rights, on the other hand, sank to vanishing point in the eighteenth and early nineteenth centuries. Their revival began with the development of public elementary education, but it was not until the twentieth century that they attained to equal partnership with the other two elements in citizenship.

...

Citizenship is a status bestowed on those who are full members of a community. All who possess the status are equal with respect to the rights and duties with which the status is endowed. There is no universal principle that determines what those rights and duties shall be, but societies in which citizenship is a developing institution create an image of an ideal citizenship against which achievement can be measured and towards which aspiration can be directed. The urge forward along the path thus plotted is an urge towards a fuller measure of equality, an enrichment of the stuff of which the status is made and an increase in the number of those on whom the status is bestowed. Social class, on the other hand, is a system of inequality. And it too, like citizenship, can be based on a set of ideals, beliefs and values. It is therefore reasonable to expect that the impact of citizenship on social class should take the form of a conflict between opposing principles. If I am right in my contention that citizenship has been a developing institution in England at least since the latter part of

the seventeenth century, then it is clear that its growth coincides with the rise of capitalism, which is a system, not of equality, but of inequality. Here is something that needs explaining. How is it that these two opposing principles could grow and flourish side by side in the same soil? What made it possible for them to be reconciled with one another and to become, for a time at least, allies instead of antagonists? The question is a pertinent one, for it is clear that, in the twentieth century, citizenship and the capitalist class system have been at war.

It is at this point that a closer scrutiny of social class becomes necessary. I cannot attempt to examine all its many and varied forms, but there is one broad distinction between two different types of class which is particularly relevant to my argument. In the first of these class in based on a hierarchy of status, and the difference between one class and another is expressed in terms of legal rights and of established customs which have the essential binding character of law. In its extreme form such a system divides a society into a number of distinct, hereditary human species – patricians, plebeians, serfs, slaves and so forth. Class is, as it were, an institution in its own right, and the whole structure has the quality of a plan, in the sense that it is endowed with meaning and purpose and accepted as a natural order. The civilization at each level is an expression of this meaning and of this natural order, and differences between social levels are not differences in standards of living, because there is no common standard by which they can be measured. Nor are there any rights – at least none of any significance – which all share in common.[1] The impact of citizenship on such a system was bound to be profoundly disturbing, and even destructive. The rights with which the general status of citizenship was invested were extracted from the hierarchical status system of social class, robbing it of its essential substance. The equality implicit in the concept of citizenship, even though limited in content, undermined the inequality of the class system, which was in principle a total inequality. National justice and a law common to all must inevitably weaken and eventually destroy class justice, and personal freedom, as a universal birthright, must drive out serfdom. No subtle argument is needed to show that citizenship is incompatible with medieval feudalism.

Social class of the second type is not so much an institution in its own right as a by-product of other institutions. Although we may still refer to 'social status', we are stretching the term beyond its strict technical meaning when we do so. Class differences are not established and defined by the laws and customs of the society (in the medieval sense of that phrase), but emerge from the interplay of a variety of factors related to the institutions of property and education and the structure of the national economy. Class cultures dwindle to a minimum, so that it becomes possible, though admittedly not wholly satisfactory, to measure the different levels of economic welfare by reference to a common standard of living. The working classes, instead of inheriting a distinctive though simple culture, are provided with a cheap and shoddy imitation of a civilization that has become national.

It is true that class still functions. Social inequality is regarded as necessary and purposeful. It provides the incentive to effort and designs the distribution of power. But there is no over-all pattern of inequality, in which an appropriate value is attached, *a priori*, to each social level. Inequality therefore, though necessary, may become excessive. As Patrick Colquhoun said, in a much quoted passage:

> Without a large proportion of poverty there could be no riches, since riches are the offspring of labour, while labour can result only from a state of poverty … Poverty therefore is a most necessary and indispensable ingredient in society, without which nations and communities could not exist in a state of civilisation.
>
> (Colquhoun, 1806, pp.7–8)

But Colquhoun, while accepting poverty, deplored 'indigence', or, as we should say, destitution. By 'poverty' he meant the situation of a man who, owing to lack of any economic reserves, is obliged to work, and to work hard, in order to live. By 'indigence' he meant the situation of a family which lacks the minimum necessary for decent living. The system of inequality which allowed the former to exist as a driving force inevitably produced a certain amount of the latter as well. Colquhoun, and other humanitarians, regretted this and sought means to alleviate the suffering it caused. But they did not question the justice of the system of inequality as a

whole. It could be argued, in defence of its justice, that, although poverty might be necessary, it was not necessary that any particular family should remain poor, or quite as poor as it was. The more you look on wealth as conclusive proof of merit, the more you incline to regard poverty as evidence of failure – but the penalty for failure may seem to be greater than the offence warrants. In such circumstances it is natural that the more unpleasant features of inequality should be treated, rather irresponsibly, as a nuisance, like the black smoke that used to pour from our factory chimneys. And so in time, as the social conscience stirs to life, class-abatement, like smoke-abatement, becomes a desirable aim to be pursued as far as is compatible with the continued efficiency of the social machine.

But class-abatement in this form was not an attack on the class system. On the contrary it aimed, often quite consciously, at making the class system less vulnerable to attack by alleviating its less defensible consequences. It raised the floor-level in the basement of the social edifice, and perhaps made it more hygienic than it was before. But it remained a basement, and the upper stories of the building were unaffected. And the benefits received by the unfortunate did not flow from an enrichment of the status of citizenship. Where they were given officially by the State, this was done by measures which, as I have said, offered alternatives to the rights of citizenship, rather than additions to them. But the major part of the task was left to private charity, and it was the general, though not universal, view of charitable bodies that those who received their help had no personal right to claim it.

Nevertheless it is true that citizenship, even in its early forms, was a principle of equality, and that during this period it was a developing institution. Starting at the point where all men were free and, in theory, capable of enjoying rights; it grew by enriching the body of rights which they were capable of enjoying. But these rights did not conflict with the inequalities of capitalist society; they were, on the contrary, necessary to the maintenance of that particular form of inequality. The explanation lies in the fact that the core of citizenship at this stage was composed of civil rights. And civil rights were indispensable to a competitive market economy. They gave to each man, as part of his individual status, the power to engage as an independent unit in the economic struggle and made it possible to deny to him social protection on the ground that he was equipped with the means to protect himself. Maine's famous dictum that 'the movement of the progressive societies has hitherto been a movement from Status to Contract' (1878, p.170) expresses a profound truth which has been elaborated, with varying terminology, by many sociologists, but it requires qualification. For both status and contract are present in all but the most primitive societies. Maine himself admitted this when, later in the same book, he wrote that the earliest feudal communities, as contrasted with their archaic predecessors, 'were neither bound together by mere sentiment nor recruited by a fiction. The tie which united them was Contract' (*ibid.*, p.365). But the contractual element in feudalism co-existed with a class system based on status, and, as contract hardened into custom, it helped to perpetuate class status. Custom retained the form of mutual undertakings, but not the reality of a free agreement. Modern contract did not grow out of feudal contract; it marks a new development to whose progress feudalism was an obstacle that had to be swept aside.

For modern contract is essentially an agreement between men who are free and equal in status, though not necessarily in power. Status was not eliminated from the social system. Differential status, associated with class, function and family, was replaced by the single uniform status of citizenship, which provided the foundation of equality on which the structure of inequality could be built.

When Maine wrote, this status was clearly an aid, and not a menace, to capitalism and the free-market economy, because it was dominated by civil rights, which confer the legal capacity to strive for the things one would like to possess but do not guarantee the possession of any of them. A property right is a not a right to possess property, but a right to acquire it, if you can, and to protect, if you can get it. But, if you used these arguments to explain to a pauper that his property rights are the same as those of a millionaire, he will probably accuse you of quibbling … But these blatant inequalities are not due to defects in civil rights, but to lack of social rights, and social rights in the mid-nineteenth century were in the doldrums. The Poor Law was an aid, not a menace, to capitalism, because it relieved industry of all social responsibility outside the contract of employment, while sharpening the edge of competition in the labour market. Elementary schooling was also an aid, because it increased the value of the worker without educating him above his station.

But it would be absurd to contend that the civil rights enjoyed in the eighteenth and nineteenth centuries were free from defects, or that they were as egalitarian in practice as they professed to be in principle. Equality before the law did not exist. The right was there, but the remedy might frequently prove to be out of reach. The barriers between rights and remedies were of two kinds: the first arose from class prejudice and partiality, the second from the automatic effects of the unequal distribution of wealth, working through the price system. Class prejudice, which undoubtedly coloured the whole administration of justice in the eighteenth century, cannot be eliminated by law, but only by social education and the building of a tradition of impartiality. This is a slow and difficult process, which presupposes a change in the climate of thought throughout the upper ranks of society. But it is a process which I think it is fair to say has been successfully accomplished, in the sense that the tradition of impartiality as between social classes is firmly established in our civil justice. And it is interesting that this should have happened without any fundamental change in the class structure of the legal profession. We have no exact knowledge on this point, but I doubt whether the picture has radically altered since Professor Ginsberg (n.d.) found that the proportion of those admitted to Lincoln's Inn whose fathers were wage-earners had risen from 0.4 per cent in 1904–8 to 1.8 per cent in 1923–7, and that at this latter date nearly 72 per cent were sons of professional men, high-ranking business men and gentlemen. The decline of class prejudice as a barrier to the full enjoyment of rights is, therefore, due less to the dilution of class monopoly in the legal profession than to the spread in all classes of a more humane and realistic sense of social equality.

It is interesting to compare with this the corresponding development in the field of political rights. Here too class prejudice, expressed through the intimidation of the lower classes by the upper, prevented the free exercise of the right to vote by the newly enfranchised. In this case a practical remedy was available, in the secret ballot. But that was not enough. Social education, and a change of mental climate, were needed as well. And, even when voters felt free from undue influence, it still took some time to break down the idea, prevalent in the working as well as other classes, that the representatives of the people, and still more the members of the government, should be drawn from among the *élites* who were born, bred and educated for leadership. Class monopoly in politics, unlike class monopoly in law, has definitely been overthrown. Thus, in these two fields, the same goal has been reached by rather different paths.

The removal of the second obstacle, the effects of the unequal distribution of wealth, was technically a simple matter in the case of political rights, because it costs little or nothing to register a vote. Nevertheless, wealth can be used to influence an election, and a series of measures was adopted to reduce this influence. The earlier ones, which go back to the seventeenth century, were directed against bribery and corruption, but the later ones, especially from 1883 onwards, had the wider aim of limiting election expenses in general, in order that candidates of unequal wealth might fight on more or less equal terms. The need for such equalizing measures has now greatly diminished, since working-class candidates can get financial support from party and other funds. Restrictions which prevent competitive extravagance are, therefore, probably welcomed by all. It remained to open the House of Commons to men of all classes, regardless of wealth, first by abolishing the property qualification for members, and then by introducing payment of members in 1911.

It has proved far more difficult to achieve similar results in the field of civil rights, because litigation, unlike voting, is very expensive. Court fees are not high, but counsel's fees and solicitor's charges may mount up to very large sums indeed. Since a legal action takes the form of a contest, each party feels that his chances of winning will be improved if he secures the services of better champions than those employed on the other side. ...

What, then, has been done to remove the barriers to the full and equal exercise of civil rights? Only one thing of real substance, the establishment in 1846 of the County Courts to provide cheap justice for the common people. This important innovation has had a profound and beneficial effect on our legal system, and done much to develop a proper sense of the importance of the case brought by the small man – which is often a very big case by his standards. But County Court costs are not negligible, and the jurisdiction of the County Courts is limited. The second major step taken was the development of a poor person's procedure, under which a small fraction of the poorer members of the community could sue *in forma pauperis*, practically free of all cost, being assisted by the gratuitous and voluntary services of the legal profession. But, as the income limit was extremely low (£2 a week since 1919), and the procedure did not apply in the County Courts, it has had little effect except in matrimonial cases. The supplementary service of free legal advice was, until recently, provided by the unaided efforts of voluntary bodies. But the problem has not been overlooked, nor the reality of the defects in our system denied. It has attracted increasing attention during the last hundred years. The machinery of the Royal Commission and the Committee has been used repeatedly, and some reforms of procedure have resulted. Two such Committees are at work now, but

it would be most improper for me to make any reference to their deliberations.[2] A third, which started earlier, issued a report on which is based the Legal Aid and Advice Bill laid before parliament just three months ago.[3] This is a bold measure, going far beyond anything previously attempted for the assistance of the poorer litigants, and I shall have more to say about it later on.

It is apparent ... that there developed, in the latter part of the nineteenth century, a growing interest in equality as a principle of social justice and an appreciation of the fact that the formal recognition of an equal capacity for rights was not enough. In theory even the complete removal of all the barriers that separated civil rights from their remedies would not have interfered with the principles or the class structure of the capitalist system. It would, in fact, have created a situation which many supporters of the competitive market economy falsely assumed to be already in existence. But in practice the attitude of mind which inspired the efforts to remove these barriers grew out of a conception of equality which overstepped these narrow limits, the conception of equal social worth, not merely of equal natural rights. Thus although citizenship, even by the end of the nineteenth century, had done little to reduce social inequality, it had helped to guide progress into the path which led directly to the egalitarian policies of the twentieth century.

... Citizenship requires ... a direct sense of community membership based on loyalty to a civilization which is a common possession. It is a loyalty of free men endowed with rights and protected by a common law. Its growth is stimulated both by the struggle to win those rights and by their enjoyment when won. We see this clearly in the eighteenth century, which saw the birth, not only of modern civil rights, but also of modern national consciousness. ...

This growing national consciousness, this awakening public opinion, and these first stirrings of a sense of community membership and common heritage did not have any material effect on class structure and social inequality for the simple and obvious reason that, even at the end of the nineteenth century, the mass of the working people did not wield effective political power. By that time the franchise was fairly wide, but those who had recently received the vote had not yet learned how to use it. The political rights of citizenship, unlike civil rights, were full of potential danger to the capitalist system, although those who were cautiously extending them down the social scale probably did not realize quite how great the danger was. They could hardly be expected to foresee what vast changes could be brought about by the peaceful use of political power, without a violent and bloody revolution. The Planned Society and the Welfare State had not yet risen over the horizon or come within the view of the practical politician. The foundations of the market economy and the contractual system seemed strong enough to stand against any probable assault. In fact, there were some grounds for expecting that the working classes, as they became educated, would accept the basic principles of the system and be content to rely for their protection and progress on the civil rights of citizenship, which contained no obvious menace to competitive capitalism. Such a view was encouraged by the fact that one of the main achievements of political power in the later nineteenth century was the recognition of the right of collective bargaining. This meant that social progress was being sought by strengthening civil rights, not by creating social rights; through the use of contract in the open market, not through a minimum wage and social security.

But this interpretation underrates the significance of this extension of civil rights in the economic sphere. For civil rights were in origin intensely individual, and that is why they harmonized with the individualistic phase of capitalism. By the device of incorporation groups were enabled to act legally as individuals. This important development did not go unchallenged, and limited liability was widely denounced as an infringement of individual responsibility. But the position of trade unions was even more anomalous, because they did not seek or obtain incorporation. They can, therefore, exercise vital civil rights collectively on behalf of their members without formal collective responsibility, while the individual responsibility of the workers in relation to contract is largely unenforceable. These civil rights became, for the workers, an instrument for raising their social and economic status, that is to say, for establishing the claim that they, as citizens, were entitled to certain social rights. But the normal method of establishing social rights is by the exercise of political power, for social rights imply an absolute right to a certain standard of civilization.which is conditional only on the discharge of the general duties of citizenship. Their content does not depend on the economic value of the individual claimant. There is therefore a significant difference between a genuine collective bargain through which economic forces in a free market seek to achieve equilibrium and the use of collective civil rights to assert basic claims to the elements of social justice. Thus the acceptance of collective bargaining was not simply a natural extension of civil rights; it represented the transfer of an important process from the political to the civil sphere of citizenship. But

'transfer' is, perhaps, a misleading term, for at the time when this happened the workers either did not possess, or had not yet learned to use, the political right of the franchise. Since then they have obtained and made full use of that right. Trade unionism has, therefore, created a secondary system of industrial citizenship parallel with and supplementary to the system of political citizenship.

...

Social rights in the twentieth century

...

A new period opened at the end of the nineteenth century, conveniently marked by Booth's survey of Life and Labour of the People in London and the Royal Commission on the Aged Poor. It saw the first big advance in social rights, and this involved significant changes in the egalitarian principle as expressed in citizenship. But there were other forces at work as well. A rise of money incomes unevenly distributed over the social classes altered the economic distance which separated these classes from one another, diminishing the gap between skilled and unskilled labour and between skilled labour and non-manual workers, while the steady increase in small savings blurred the class distinction between the capitalist and the propertyless proletarian. Secondly, a system of direct taxation, ever more steeply graduated, compressed the whole scale of disposable incomes. Thirdly, mass production for the home market and a growing interest on the part of industry in the needs and tastes of the common people enabled the less well-to-do to enjoy a material civilization which differed less markedly in quality from that of the rich than it had ever done before. All this profoundly altered the setting in which the progress of citizenship took place. Social integration spread from the sphere of sentiment and patriotism into that of material enjoyment. The components of a civilized and cultured life, formerly the monopoly of the few, were brought progressively within reach of the many, who were encouraged thereby to stretch out their hands towards those that still eluded their grasp. The diminution of inequality strengthened the demand for its abolition, at least with regard to the essentials of social welfare.

These aspirations have in part been met by incorporating social rights in the status of citizenship and thus creating a universal right to real income which is not proportionate to the market value of the claimant. Class-abatement is still the aim of social rights, but it has acquired a new meaning. It is no longer merely an attempt to abate the obvious nuisance of destitution in the lowest ranks of society. It has assumed the guise of action modifying the whole pattern of social inequality. It is no longer content to raise the floor-level in the basement of the social edifice, leaving the superstructure as it was. ...

...

I said earlier that in the twentieth century citizenship and the capitalist class system have been at war. Perhaps the phrase is rather too strong, but it is quite clear that the former has imposed modifications on the latter. But we should not be justified in assuming that, although status is a principle that conflicts with contract, the stratified status system which is creeping into citizenship is an alien element in the economic world outside. Social rights in their modern form imply an invasion of contract by status, the subordination of market price to social justice, the replacement of the free bargain by the declaration of rights. But are these principles quite foreign to the practice of the market today, or are they there already, entrenched within the contract system itself? I think it is clear that they are.

Notes

1   See the admirable characterization given by R.H. Tawney in *Equality*, pp.121–2.

2   The Austin Jones Committee on County Court Procedure and the Evershed Committee on Supreme Court Practice and Procedure. The report of the former and an interim report of the latter have since been published.

3   The Rushcliffe Committee on Legal Aid and Legal Advice in England and Wales.

References

Colquhoun, P. (1806) *A Treatise on Indigence,* London, Hatchard.

Ginsburg, N. (n.d.) *Studies in Sociology.*

Maine, H.S. (1878) *Ancient Law.*

Tawney, R.H. (1964) *Equality*, London, Allen & Unwin.

Source: Marshall, 1964 in Turner and Hamilton, 1994, pp.17–24,25–6,35

5.2 Bhikhu Parekh, 'Equality in a multicultural society' (2000)

Much of the traditional discussion of equality suffers from a weakness derived from the mistaken theory of human nature in which it is grounded. As we saw earlier, many philosophers understand human beings in terms of a substantive theory of human nature and treat culture as of no or only marginal importance. Broadly speaking they maintain that human beings are characterized by two sets of features, some common to them all such as that they are made in the image of God, have souls, are noumenal beings, have common capacities and needs or a similar natural constitution; and others varying from culture to culture and individual to individual. The former are taken to constitute their humanity and are ontologically privileged. Human beings are deemed to be equal because of their shared features or similarity, and equality is taken to consist in treating them more or less the same way and giving them more of less the same body of rights.

I have argued that this view of human beings is deeply mistaken. Human beings are at once both natural and cultural beings, sharing a common human identity but in a culturally mediated manner. They are similar and different, their similarities and differences do not passively coexist but interpenetrate, and neither is ontologically prior or morally more important. We cannot ground equality in human uniformity because the latter is inseparable from and ontologically no more important than human differences. Grounding equality in uniformity also has unfortunate consequences. It requires us to treat human beings equally in those respects in which they are similar and not those in which they are different. ...

Human beings do share several capacities and needs in common, but different cultures define and structure these differently and develop new ones of their own. Since human beings are at once both similar and different, they should be treated equally because of both. Such a view, which grounds equality not in human uniformity but in the interplay of uniformity and difference, builds difference into the very concept of equality, breaks the traditional equation of equality with similarity, and is immune to monist distortion. Once the basis of equality changes so does its content. Equality involves equal freedom or opportunity to be different, and treating human beings equally requires us to take into account both their similarities and differences. When the latter are not relevant, equality entails uniform or identical treatment; when they are, it requires differential treatment. Equal rights do not mean identical rights, for individuals with different cultural backgrounds and needs might require different rights to enjoy equality in respect of whatever happens to be the content of their rights. Equality involves not just rejection of irrelevant differences as is commonly argued, but also full recognition of legitimate and relevant ones.

Equality is articulated at several interrelated levels. At the most basic level it involves equality of respect and rights, at a slightly higher level that of opportunity, self-esteem, self-worth and so on, and at a yet higher level, equality of power, well-being and the basic capacities required for human flourishing. Sensitivity to differences is relevant at each of these levels. We can hardly be said to respect a person if we treat with contempt or abstract away all that gives meaning to his life and makes him the kind of person he is. Respect for a person therefore involves locating him against his cultural background, sympathetically entering into his world of thought, and interpreting his conduct in terms of its system of meaning. A simple example illustrates the point. It was recently discovered that Asian candidates for jobs in Britain were systematically underscored because their habit of showing respect for their interviewers by not looking them in the eye led the latter to conclude that they were shifty and devious and likely to prove unreliable. By failing to appreciate the candidates' system of meaning and cultural practices, interviewers ended up treating them unequally with their white counterparts. Understandably but wrongly, they assumed that all human beings shared and even perhaps ought to share an identical system of meaning which predictably turned out to be their own. This relatively trivial example illustrates the havoc we can easily cause when we uncritically universalize the categories and norms of our culture.

Like the concept of equal respect, that of equal opportunity, too, needs to be interpreted in a culturally sensitive manner. Opportunity is a subject-dependent concept in the sense that a facility, a resource, or a course of action is only a mute and passive possibility and not an opportunity for an individual if she lacks the capacity, the cultural disposition or the necessary cultural knowledge to take advantage of it. A Sikh is in principle free to send his son to a school that bans turbans, but for all practical purposes it is closed to him. The same is true when an orthodox Jew is required to give up his yarmulke, or the Muslim woman to wear a skirt, or a vegetarian Hindu to eat beef as a precondition for certain kinds of jobs. Although the inability involved is cultural not physical in nature and hence subject to human control, the degree of control varies greatly. In some cases a cultural inability can be overcome with relative ease by suitably reinterpreting the relevant cultural norm or practice; in others it is constitutive of the individual's sense of identity and even self-respect and cannot be overcome without a deep sense of moral loss. Other things being equal, when a culturally derived incapacity is of the former kind, the individuals involved may rightly be asked to overcome it or at least bear the financial cost of accommodating it. When it is the latter kind and comes closer to a natural inability, society should bear at least most of the cost of accommodating it. When it is of the the latter kind and comes closer to a natural inability, society should bear at least most of the cost of accommodating it. Which cultural incapacity falls within which category is often a matter of dispute and can only be resolved by a dialogue between the parties involved.

Equality before the law and equal protection of the law, too, need to be defined in a culturally sensitive manner. Formally a law banning the use of drugs treats all equally, but in fact it discriminates against those for whom some drugs are religious or cultural requirements as is the case with Peyote and Marijuana respectively for the American Indians and Rastafarians. This does not mean that we might not ban their use, but rather that we need to appreciate the unequal impact of the ban and should have strong additional reasons for denying exemption to these two groups. The United States government showed the requisite cultural sensitivity when it exempted the ceremonial use of wine by Jews and Catholics during Prohibition.

Equal protection of the law, too, may require different treatment. Given the horrible reality of the Holocaust and the persistent streak of anti-semitism in German cultural life, it makes good sense for that country to single out physical attacks on Jews for harsher punishment or ban utterances denying the Holocaust. In other societies, other groups such as blacks, Muslims and gypsies might have long been demonized and subjected to hostility and hatred, and then they too might need to be treated differently. Although the differential treatment of these groups might seem to violate the principle of equality, in fact it only equalizes them with the rest of their fellow-citizens.

In a culturally homogenous society, individuals share broadly similar needs, norms, motivations, social customs and patterns of behaviour. Equal rights here mean more or less the same rights, and equal treatment involves more or less identical treatment. The principle of equality is therefore relatively easy to define and apply, and discriminatory deviation from it can be identified without much disagreement. This is not the case in a culturally diverse society. Broadly speaking equality consists in equal treatment of those judged to be equal in relevant respects. In a culturally diverse society citizens are likely to disagree on what respects are relevant in a given context, what response is appropriate to them, and what counts as their equal treatment. Furthermore, once we take cultural differences into account, equal treatment would mean not identical but differential treatment, raising the question as to how we can ensure that it is really equal across cultures and does not serve as a cloak for discrimination or privilege.

...

Equality of difference

In multicultural societies dress often becomes a site of the most heated and intransigent struggles. As a condensed and visible symbol of cultural identity it matters much to the individuals involved, but also for that very reason it arouses all manner of conscious and unconscious fears and resentments within wider society. It would not be too rash to suggest that acceptance of the diversity of dress in a multicultural society is a good indicator of whether or not the latter is at ease with itself.

In 1972, British Parliament passed a law empowering the Minister of Transport to require motor-cyclists to wear crash-helmets. When the Minister did so, Sikhs campaigned against it. One of them kept breaking the law and was fined twenty times between 1973 and 1976 for refusing to wear a crash-helmet. Sikh spokesmen argued that the turban was just as safe, and that if they could fight for the British in two world wars without anyone considering their turbans unsafe, they could surely ride motor-cycles. The law was amended in 1976 and exempted them from wearing crash-helmets. Although this was not universally welcomed, Parliament was right to amend the law. Its primary concern was to ensure that people did not die or suffer serious injuries riding dangerous vehicles, and it hit upon the helmet meeting certain standards as the best safety measure. Since the Sikh turban met these standards, it was accepted as an adequate substitute for the helmet.[1]

This became evident in the subsequent development of the law as it related to Sikhs. Although the Construction (Head Protection) Regulation 1989 requires all those working on construction sites to wear safety helmets, the Employment Act 1989 exempts turban-wearing Sikhs. The latter does so because it is persuaded by its own scientific test that the turban offers adequate though not exactly the same protection as the helmet, and is thus an acceptable substitute for it. One important implication of this argument is that if a turbaned Sikh were to be injured on a construction site as a result of another person's negligence, he would be entitled to claim damages for only such injuries as he would have suffered if he had been wearing a safety helmet. ...

...

The controversy concerning uniforms occurs in civilian areas of life as well, where it raises issues that are once both similar and different. Since no question of national unity or symbolism is involved, the controversy has no political significance. However, it involves far more people, usually women, and has a great economic significance.

Many Asian women's refusal to wear uniforms in hospitals, stores and schools has led to much litigation and contradictory judgements in Britain. A Sikh woman who, on qualifying as a nurse, intended to wear her traditional dress of a long shirt (*quemiz*) over baggy trousers (*shalwar*) rather than the required uniform, was refused admission on a nursing course by her Health Authority. The Industrial Tribunal upheld her complaint on the ground that since her traditional dress was a cultural requirement and did not impede the discharge of her duties, asking her to replace it with a uniform was unjustified. The Tribunal was overruled by the Employment Appeal Tribunal, which took the opposite and much criticized view. Since rules about nurses' uniforms are laid down by the General Nursing Council, the latter promptly intervened under government pressure and made more flexible rules. This enabled the Health Authority to offer the Sikh woman a place on the course on the understanding that as a qualified nurse her trousers should be grey and the shirt white.

This is one of many cases in which lower courts took one view and the higher courts another, or the same court took different views in similar cases. The discrepancy arose because courts used two different criteria in deciding such cases. Sometimes they asked if the job requirements were *plausible* or understandable; that is, if 'good reasons' could be given for them. On other occasions they thought such a criterion justified almost every demand, and insisted that job requirements should be *objectively necessary*; that is, indispensable for discharging the duties of the jobs concerned. ...

Although the test of objective necessity is reasonable, it runs the risk of taking a purely instrumental view of job requirements and stripping the organizations concerned of their cultural identity. Take the case of nurses' uniforms. One could argue that since these are not objectively necessary for carrying out the required medical tasks, anyone may wear anything. This is to miss the crucial point that they symbolize and reinforce the collective spirit of the nursing profession and structure the expectations and behaviour of their patients. The instrumental view of rationality implicit in the test of objective necessity is also likely to provoke resentment against minorities whose cultural demands might be seen to undermine a much-cherished tradition. It is also unjust because, while it respects the cultural identity of the minority, it ignores that of the wider society. The concept of objective necessity should therefore be defined in a culturally sensitive manner and do justice to both the minority and majority ways of life. This means that uniforms should be kept in hospitals, schools and wherever else they are part of the tradition and perform valuable symbolic, inspirational, aesthetic and other functions, but be open to appropriate modifications when necessary. Such an arrangement neither deculturalizes the organizations concerned and renders them bland, nor eclectically multiculturalizes them and renders them comical, but preserves and adapts the tradition to changing circumstances and facilitates minority integration into the suitably opened-up mainstream society.

...

Contextualizing equality

Sometimes we know what is relevant in a given context, but find it difficult to decide if two individuals are equal in relation to it. Take *l'affaire du foulard* which first surfaced in France in September 1989 and has haunted it ever since.[2] Three Muslim girls from North Africa, two of them sisters, wore *hijab* (head scarf) to their ethnically mixed school in Creil, some 60 kms north of Paris. In the previous year 20 Jewish students had refused to attend classes on Saturday mornings and autumn Friday afternoons when the Sabbath arrived before the close of the school, and the headmaster, a black Frenchman from the Caribbean, had to give in after initially resisting them. Worried about the trend of events, he objected to the Muslim girls wearing the *hijab* in the classroom on the grounds that it went against the *laicitée* of French state schools. Since the girls refused to comply, he

barred them from attending the school. As a gesture of solidarity many Muslim girls throughout France began to wear *hijabs* to school and the matter acquired national importance. To calm the situation the Education Minister, Lionel Jospin, sought an opinion (*avis*) from the *Conseil d'Etat*. The *Conseil* ruled in November 1989 that pupils had a right to express and manifest their religious beliefs within state schools and that the *hijab* did not violate the principle of *laicitée*, provided that such religious insignia did not 'by their character, by their circumstances in which they were worn ... or by their ostentatious or campaigning nature constitute an act of pressure, provocation, proselytism or propaganda', the decision on which was to be made by the local education authority on a case-by-case basis.

...

The national debate on the *hijab* went to the heart of the French conceptions of citizenship and national identity and divided the country. Some advocated *laicitée ouverte*, which largely amounted to a search for a negotiated solution with the Muslims. Some others ... saw no reason for banning the *hijab* and advocated the right to difference and the concomitant celebration of plurality. Yet others questioned the rigid application of the principle of *laicitée* and argued for the teaching of religion in schools, both because of its cultural importance and because pupils would not be able to make sense of contemporary global conflicts without some knowledge of it.

These views, however, were confined to a minority. The dominant view was firmly committed to the practice of *laicitée* and hostile to any kind of compromise with the Muslim girls. It was eloquently stated in a letter to *Le Nouvel Observateur* of 2 November 1989, signed by several eminent intellectuals and urging the government not to perpetrate the 'Munich of Republican Education'. As the 'only institution consecrated to the universal', the school must be a 'place of emancipation' and resist 'communal, religious and economic pressures' with 'discipline' and 'courage'. For the signatories to the letter, as for a large body of Frenchmen, France was a single and indivisible nation based on single culture. The school was the central tool of assimilation into French culture and could not tolerate ethnic self-expression. The *hijab* was particularly objectionable because it symbolized both a wholly alien culture and the subordinate status of women. Wearing it implied a refusal to become French, to integrate, to be like the rest. Since *laicitée* was a hard-won principle of long historical standing, the French state could not compromise it without damaging its identity. As Serge

July, the editor of *Liberation*, put it, '... behind the scarf is the question of immigration, behind immigration is the debate over integration, and behind integration the question of *laicitée*.'

The principal argument against allowing Muslim girls to wear the *hijab*, then, was that it violated the principle of *laicitée* and went against the secular and assimilationist function of state schools. If Muslim spokesmen were to argue their case persuasively, they needed to counter this view. While some tried to do so, most realized that it raised many large and complex questions that did not admit of easy and conclusive answers, and that such a debate would take years to settle and did not help them in the short run. As it happened, French state schools did not strictly adhere to the principle of *laicitée*, and allowed Catholic girls to wear the cross and other insignia of religious identity and the Jews to wear the *kipa*. Muslims decided to articulate their demand in the language of equality and argued that, since they were denied the right enjoyed by other religious groups, they were being treated unequally.

Defenders of the ban, including the Minister of Education, rejected the Muslim charge of discrimination on the ground that the *hijab* was not equivalent to the cross, and that the two groups of girls were *not* equal in relevant respects. First, unlike the 'discreetly' worn cross, the 'ostentatious' *hijab* was intended to put pressure on other Muslim girls and entailed 'proselytization'. Second, unlike the freely-worn cross, the *hijab* symbolized and reinforced women's oppression. Third, unlike the unself-consciously worn cross, the *hijab* was an ideologically motivated assertion of religious identity inspired by a wider fundamentalist movement which the schools had a duty to combat.[3]

... The question is not whether the *hijab* is the Islamic equivalent of the Christian cross, but whether in contemporary France wearing the *hijab* has broadly the same religious significance for Muslims as wearing the cross has for Christians. Since we cannot therefore dismiss the ban in the name of an abstract right to equal religious freedom, we need to take seriously the three arguments made in support of it and assess their validity.

As for the first argument, the *hijab* is certainly visible but there is no obvious reason why religious symbols should be invisible or be of the same type. Besides, there is no evidence to support the view that the *hijab* was intended to proselytize among non-Muslims or to put religious pressure on other Muslim girls beyond the minimum inherent in the wearing of religious symbols. Conversely, the cross is not

necessarily discreet for Catholic girls do sometimes display, flaunt and talk about it, it is clearly visible when they engage in sports, swimming and such other activities, and it is visible even otherwise except that we do not see it because of its familiarity. Once the *hijab* is allowed, it too would become invisible.

The second argument which contrast the freely worn cross with the coerced *hijab* is no more persuasive. It assumes that parental pressure is necessarily wrong, a strange and untenable view, and that choices by adolescent girls are always to be preferred over parental preferences, which is no more tenable. ...

...

The third argument for the ban is equally unconvincing, for wearing the *hijab* need not be a form of ideological self-assertion any more than wearing the cross is. As for the fears about the rise of fundamentalism, a term that was never clearly defined, they were speculative and irrelevant to the argument. ...

...

The widely shared belief that the *hijab* symbolizes and reinforces female subordination ignores its complex cultural dialectic. Muslim immigrants in France, Britain and elsewhere are deeply fearful of their girls entering the public world including the school. By wearing the *hijab* their daughters seek to reassure them that they can be culturally trusted and will not be 'corrupted' by the norms and values of the school. At the same time they also reshape the semi-public world of the school and protect themselves against its pressures and temptations by subtly getting white and Muslim boys to see them differently to the way they eye white girls. The *hijab* puts the girls 'out of bounds' and enables them to dictate how they wish to be treated. Traditional at one level, the *hijab* is transgressive at another, and enables Muslim girls to transform both their parental and public cultures. To see it merely as a sign of subjection, as most secular Frenchmen and feminists did, was to be trapped into crude cultural stereotypes and fail to appreciate the complex processes of social change and intercultural negotiation it symbolized and triggered. This is not at all to say that all Muslim girls saw the *hijab* in this way, but rather that at least some did. Since the school and local authorities had no reliable means of ascertaining who wore it for what reasons, and since female subordination is too large an issue to be tackled by banning the *hijab*, they should have restrained their republican zeal and left the girls alone subject to the requirement of non-proselytization.

Notes

1 For a most thorough discussion of some of these cases, see Poulter (1998).

2 For a good discussion of the headscarf controversy, see Galeotti (1993) and Moruzzi (1994). For a similar controversy in Germany, see Mandel (1989).

3 The *Conseil d'Etat*'s decision on 14 April 1995 permits Jewish students to miss Saturday classes to observe the Sabbath. Since this does not violate the principle of *laicité*, the Conseil's attitude to Muslims is puzzling. See *Le Monde*, 16-17 April 1995, pp.1 and 9. The French government heavily subsidizes the 'private' Roman Catholic school system, but refuses public funds to Jewish, Muslim and even other Christian schools.

References

Galeotti, A. (1993) 'Citizenship and equality: the place for toleration', *Political Theory*, vol.21, no.4.

Mandel, R. (1989) 'Turkish headscarves and the "foreigners problem": constructing difference through emblems of identity', *New German Critique*, vol.46.

Moruzzi, N.C. (1994) 'A problem with headscarves', *Political Theory*, vol.22, no.2.

Poulter, S. (1998) *Ethnicity, Law and Human Rights: The English Experience*, Oxford, Clarendon Press.

Source: Parekh, 2000, pp.239–44,246–54

 # Diane Richardson, 'Citizenship and sexuality' (2000)

What do we mean by 'citizenship'?

… The question of the relationship of citizenship to gender, until recently, has been largely absent from much of the debate within the social sciences, and in the case of sexuality almost non-existent. For example, in *Citizenship and Social Theory*, although passing reference is made to the fact that many of the new issues of citizenship 'appear to centre around gender politics' and that 'interesting and radical developments appear to be centred around … the struggle for homosexual rights' (Turner, 1993, p.13), none of the contributors elucidates how the study of such social movements might change notions of citizenship and, more significantly, its presumed relation to social theory. Ken Plummer (1995) makes a similar point in discussing the way in which social theorists have ignored and/or marginalised sociological work on lesbian and gay lives, highlighting the study of social movements and the study of identities as classic examples.

What has been termed a 'gender-blind' understanding of citizenship has been challenged by, in particular, feminist analyses (Lister, 1990, 1996, 1997; Ellis 1991; Phillips, 1991; Walby, 1994, 1997; Voet, 1998). … Underlying this body of work is the assumption that access to citizenship is a highly gendered process and that, despite claims to universality, a particular version of the normal citizen/subject is encoded in dominant discourses of citizenship. Historically, citizenship has been constructed in the 'male image'. Indeed, in ancient Greece, where concepts of civil and political citizenship have their origins, women, along with children and slaves, were excluded from the status of citizenship and, it is argued, have continued to be marginalised in contemporary accounts where the paradigmatic citizen is male (Wilton, 1995). …

In part reflecting these critiques, the Marshallian notion of citizenship as a set of civil, political and social rights has been more broadly criticised in recent years as much too simplistic. Other definitions have emerged in response to social changes in the family and the economy, in particular the idea of citizenship as social membership, as common membership of a shared community. Bryan Turner (1993, p.2), for example, suggests that citizenship may be defined as 'that set of practices (juridical, political, economic and cultural) which define a person as a competent member of society, and which as consequence shape the flow of resources to persons and social groups'. Within this framework citizenship has been traditionally defined in terms of national identity: citizenship as a set of practices which define social membership in a particular society or nation-state. A citizen is someone who belongs, who is a member of a given nation or a member of a given city or particular region within a nation-state. By implication those who are perceived as not belonging to the city-state or the nation-state can be excluded from the rights of citizenship. They are non-citizens, denied the right of membership of, or belonging to, a particular community with a shared identity.

Such an analysis of citizenship raises the question of how 'nationhood' is defined. Rather than understanding 'nation' as an unproblematic, timeless, given, it is argued that most modern nations are of recent invention. For example, Benedict Anderson (1991) has argued that nations are 'imagined communities', systems of cultural representation whereby we come to imagine a shared experience of belonging to a particular community. Although the idea of nation as an invention has received wide theoretical attention, there has been relatively little discussion about how assumptions about gender or sexuality are implicated in the representation and creation of such 'imagined communities'. Joanne Sharp (1996, p.99), for example, argues that gender difference is in-built into Anderson's notion of nations as imagined communities: 'Anderson's thesis of imagined communities assumes an imagined citizen, and this imagined citizen is gendered … Women are scripted into the national imaginary in a different manner. Women are not equal to the nation but symbolic of it.'

…

This idea that nations are (gendered) 'fictions', reproduced across space and time through shared representations and practices, is therefore important to understanding how citizenship status is dependent on practices through which social difference is invented/produced.

…

Sexuality and citizenship

… [C]laims to citizenship status, at least in the west, are closely associated with the institutionalisation of heterosexual as well as male privilege … [W]ithin discourses of citizen's rights and the principle of universal citizenship the normal citizen has largely been constructed as male and, albeit much less discussed or acknowledged in the literature, as heterosexual (Warner, 1993; Phelan, 1995). This latter point is evidenced when the association of heterosexuality with citizenship status, as national identity say, is challenged or threatened. …

Within the traditional and dominant model of *citizenship as a set of civil, political and social rights* it can be argued that lesbians and gay men are only partial citizens, in so far as they are excluded from certain of these rights. This is evidenced by attempts by lesbian and gay movements and campaigning groups to get equal rights – such as, for example, formal marriages and similar legal status within the armed forces – with heterosexuals. A further aspect of civil citizenship, which relates to Marshall's conception of the right to justice, is the lack of protection in law from discrimination or harassment on the grounds of sexual difference/orientation.

…

Social citizenship tends to be interpreted in terms of the social rights of welfare, and once again lesbians and gay men have highlighted their disadvantaged position. For example, in Britain, as in many other parts of the world, same-sex relationships are not officially recognised or sanctioned; this affects pension rights and inheritance rights, and denies lesbian and gay couples the tax perks to which married couples are often entitled. Other areas where access to full social citizenship is (hetero)sexualised include education, parenting, employment, and housing (Rosenbloom, 1996).

In most countries, the law and social policy deny lesbians and gay men full citizenship, what Anya Palmer refers to as the 'sexual equivalent of apartheid' (Palmer, 1995, p.33). Nevertheless, it is important to recognise that the dominant ideology of liberal citizenship in the west has been receptive to certain lesbian and gay rights claims. This has been primarily through the construction of lesbians and gay men as a minority group, different and less than the norm, but who can't help 'being that way' and therefore should not be discriminated against on that basis. …

Legitimate claims to citizenship are here grounded in essentialist understandings of sexuality and a liberal framework for understanding 'rights'. Indeed, the term commonly used in anti-discrimination laws and equal opportunity policies is 'sexual orientation', itself an essentialist concept. It is also a concept that erases the gendered nature of citizenship in collapsing lesbians and gay men's claim to equal rights under one category.

Lesbians and gay men are, then, seen as deserving of certain rights and protections in many western countries; however, the terms on which these 'rights and protections' are 'granted' are the terms of partial citizenship. Lesbians and gay men are entitled to certain rights of existence, but these are extremely circumscribed, being constructed largely on the condition that they remain in the private sphere and do not seek public recognition or membership in the political community. In this sense lesbians and gay men, though granted certain rights of citizenship, are not a legitimate social constituency.

…

This construction of lesbian and gay relations as belonging to the private sphere does suggest a difficulty in addressing citizenship using conventional frameworks that focus almost exclusively on participation in the public. The role of the public/private structuring of social relations in the exclusion of women from full access to the rights of citizenship has been highlighted by feminist theory (Lister, 1996, 1997; Walby, 1997). Such analyses have critiqued traditional conceptions of citizenship which use the private/public divide to draw a boundary around what can usefully be discussed in relation to claims to citizenship. For most social and political theorists, as Sylvia Walby remarks: 'The concept of citizenship depends upon the public sphere; the term has no significant meaning in the private' (Walby, 1997, p.176). Taken to its logical conclusion, this would mean that social relations in the private sphere are considered to be of little or no relevance to understanding citizenship.

There is an interesting tension in the use of the term 'private' to demarcate the boundaries of (homo)sexual citizenship. Whilst lesbians and gay men are banished from the public to the private realm, they are, in many senses, simultaneously excluded from the private where this is conflated with 'the family'. As Alan Sinfield argues (1995), the state withholds various rights of citizenship, 'especially in familial and quasi-familial contexts (partnerships, childbearing, entertainment in the home)', which are facets of the private sphere where lesbians and gay men are supposedly 'licensed'. Thus, notions of privacy, as well as of public space, are exclusionary, the right to privacy being primarily a right of legally married heterosexuals. In this sense, both the public and the private need to be understood as sexualised concepts.

    ....

In so far as the nation-state is constructed as heterosexual, this does not mean that all forms of heterosexuality are necessarily regarded equally. It is heterosexuality as marriage and the traditional, middle-class nuclear family that is commonly held up as a model of good citizenship, necessary for ensuring national security and a stable social order. By implication, other forms of heterosexuality, for instance young women who are single mothers, imperil the nation.

References

Anderson, B. (1991) *Imagined Communities*, London, Verso.

Andrews, G. (ed.) (1991) *Citizenship*, London, Lawrence and Wishart.

Ellis, C. (1991) 'Sisters and citizens' in Andrews, G. (ed.) *op. cit.*.

Lister, R. (1990) 'Women, economic dependency and citizenship', *Journal of Social Policy*, vol.19, no.4, pp.445–68.

Lister, R. (1996) 'Citizenship engendered' in Taylor, D. (ed.) *Critical Social Policy: A Reader*, London, Sage.

Lister, R. (1997) *Citizenship: Feminist Perspectives*, Basingstoke, Macmillan.

Palmer, A. (1995) 'Lesbian and gay rights campaigning: a report from the coal-face' in Wilson. A.R. (ed.) *op. cit.*.

Phelan, S. (1995) 'The space of justice: lesbians and democratic politics' in Wilson, A.R. (ed.) *op. cit.*.

Phillips, A. (1991) 'Citizenship and feminist theory' in Andrews, G. (ed.) *op. cit.*.

Plummer, K. (1995) *Telling Sexual Stories: Power, Change and Social Worlds*, London, Routledge.

Rosenbloom, R. (ed.) (1996) *Unspoken Rules: Sexual Orientation and Women's Human Rights*, London, Cassell.

Sharp, J.P. (1996) 'Gendering nationhood: a feminist engagement with national identity' in Duncan, N. (ed.) *Bodyspace: Destabilizing Geographies of Gender and Sexuality*, London, Routledge.

Sinfield, A. (1995) 'Diaspora and hybridity: queer identities and the ethnicity model', paper presented at the Changing Sexualities Conference, Middlesex University, July.

Turner, B.S. (1993) *Citizenship and Social Theory*, London, Sage.

Voet, R. (1998) *Feminism and Citizenship*, London, Sage.

Walby, S. (1994) 'Is citizenship gendered?', *Sociology*, vol.28, no.2, pp.379–95.

Walby, S. (1997) *Gender Transformations*, London, Routledge.

Warner, M. (1993) 'Introduction' in Warner, M. (ed.) *Fear of a Queer Planet: Queer Politics and Social Theory*, Minneapolis, MN, University of Minnesota Press.

Wilson, A.R. (ed.) (1995) *A Simple Matter of Justice? Theorizing Lesbian and Gay Politics*, London, Cassell.

Wilton, T. (1995) *Lesbian Studies: Setting an Agenda*, London, Routledge.

Source: Richardson, 2000, pp.71–3,75–6,77–8,80

5.4 Engin F. Isin and Patricia K. Wood, 'Citizenship and identity' (1999)

Decentring the nation-state: First Nations and Aboriginal rights

The identities of immigrants are not the only disruption of the nation-state's homogeneous narrative. Unquestionably, there is a real challenge to the authority and sovereignty of the nation-state posed by Aboriginal peoples. Australia, the United States and Canada all became nation-states at the expense of, not with the co-operation of, Native nations already inhabiting those territories. Through wars, land grabs (with and without treaty), disease and starvation, Europeans pushed Native peoples out of the way of their settlement. Actual face-to-face encounters were often unnecessary. In many instances, North American lands changed hands between European powers in situations that had no connection to that land or its inhabitants. This political practice, in its oblivion, was the beginning of a long history of silencing and rendering invisible Native peoples. We now turn to a consideration of the cultural and territorial dislocation of Native peoples under 'aboriginal citizenship' (see also Churchill, 1996).

Kymlicka has noted the central importance of land rights in Aboriginal cultural politics: 'the single largest cause of ethnic conflict in the world today is the struggle by indigenous peoples for the protection of their land rights' (Kymlicka, 1995, p.30). Further, '[t]he survival of indigenous cultures throughout the world is heavily dependent on protection of their land base, and indigenous peoples have fought tenaciously to maintain their land' (*ibid.*, p.43). ...

The Australian state took one of the strongest stances against its Native population through its policy of '*terra nullius*', which denied Aboriginals title to land based on the assumption that they had no connection to their land (because they had not developed a Western property system). *Terra nullius* was implemented even though nothing under British nor international law at the time gave the colonial governments of 1788–1901 the right to alienate Native title. Progress in Aboriginal rights has been slight and very recent. *Terra nullius* was first overturned in 1992 by the Mabo decision, which led, not without controversy, to the creation of the Native Title Act in 1993. This act has yet to grant any land title to any Native community.

A more recent court decision has taken the further step of articulating Native claims. In December 1996, the Australian High Court established in *The Wik Peoples* v. *State of Queensland* that pastoral leases on Crown land did not inherently extinguish Native claims to that territory. The Wik decision does not remove pastoral rights to lease Crown land; indeed, in situations where there is conflict between pastoralists and Natives, pastoral rights supersede Native title. The Australian government, under Prime Minister John Howard, responded with legislation passed in mid-1998 that effectively returns the rights to pastoral land to agriculturalists, the majority of whom are large corporations with large-scale land holdings. Those pastoralists who had previous arrangements with the Crown to lease land for grazing will be granted exclusive rights, regardless of Native claims. More disturbingly, they will also be thus given the ability to rent the land to Aboriginals or evict them entirely. ...

Similarly, a recent Canadian court decision (after thirteen years in the system) regarding Delgamuukw land not covered by treaty asserted that land claims must be negotiated (rather than extinguished) and that oral history may be considered appropriate testimony in the determination of continuous Native residence. This is perhaps the beginning of a small turnaround from the legal and social persecution of Natives in Canada. In addition to issues of land title, the state has a history of misrecognizing Native identity. The creation of 'status Indian' established a model whereby women were stripped of their status as Natives, in the eyes of the law, by marrying non-Natives, while Native men in mixed marriages could maintain their status and even extend it to their wives. This represents a systematic attempt to define for Aboriginals who they are and how they should relate to the nation and to their communities (Richardson, 1993).

Again the question is not how much does this history matter, but how does this history get addressed in terms of political realities and issues of citizenship. As with racial and ethnic minorities, it must be acknowledged that the situation that Natives find themselves in is a product of a particular history, one that cannot be ignored if their situation is to be understood and justly addressed. Moreover, land title disputes are not always a case of 'ancient history' coming back to haunt the present, but are often long-standing claims. In July 1998, the Nisga'a people negotiated a treaty with the Canadian province of British Columbia and thus ended a legal battle that had been ongoing for more than a hundred years. If the treaty, which included financial compensation, land and some self-government rights, is imitated, it may change dramatically the political structure of the nation-state. The immediate response from neoliberals has been telling: in the name of freedom and equality, they have declared the treaty unjust, without a second glance at the history of inequality and systemic injustice Natives have endured.

Historically, Natives in Canada, the United States and Australia have not been given equal civic, social or political rights as citizens, nor have they been invited to participate fully in the polity. Natives demand the right to identification with a group, have this right legally recognized, and have a political capacity to influence the way in which such recognition manifests itself materially. In Canada and the United States, Natives now have the lawyers and politicians to be able to articulate and fight for their goals. Paramount is the demand for some form of self-governance. But this demand is always attached to the actual territory of nationhood. Whether this constitutes the only answer remains to be seen. It is hard to imagine that liberal regimes of government will find a solution, for it entails the undoing of liberalism, whose premise victimized the Natives in the first place.

Kymlicka discusses the efforts of Natives in Canada to be exempt from the Charter of Rights and Freedoms, and places their campaigns in the context of the internal/external group-differentiated rights framework discussed earlier. He suggests that governance from the non-Aboriginals in the application of the Charter is appropriate in the event of, say, internal, tribal councils not defending the rights of women ... It would be interesting if Kymlicka would consider the reverse situation, say where a tribal council affords the political participation or social rights of Native women in a way that non-Aboriginal society does not. Given that Native women were until recently forced under Canadian law to forfeit their citizenship if they married non-Native men, this question merits investigation. Certainly, though, this issue of which level of government has ultimate authority is a fundamental problem: 'What they object to is the claim that their self-governing decisions should be subject to the federal courts of the dominant society – courts which, historically, have accepted and legitimized the colonization and

dispossession of Indian peoples and lands' (p.40). ...

What also deserves further exploration is the lack of opportunities afforded Natives in Canada, the US and Australia to participate in the process of the development or amendment of policies or laws that apply to them. It isn't just that Natives are subject to what may be biased or unsympathetic courts; the legal context of such court decisions is also imposed. Natives have not been invited to participate in the formation of policy and legislation that affects them – which is supposed to be the basis of justice in a democracy, that citizens participate in at least the selection of their legislative representatives. In Canada, Natives have only been voting since 1960. Moreover, a case could reasonably be made for their lack of political voice (such as participation in debates, inclusion in high-level meetings, like the premiers' conferences, media coverage, inclusion in the machinations of party organizations), not because they are not politically organized, but because they are excluded.

If we examine what various groups are actually trying to achieve, we see that it is neither to dismantle the nation nor to be accommodated nor recognized but to reinvent it as a postnational state. This is not the divisiveness and tribalism of which many critics accuse the groups and their identity politics. Neither is it an idle threat. Liberals are right to sense an undermining of their power, for the collective nation [this] previously excluded groups' demand is a fundamental challenge to the nation-state as it is currently manifested. Social justice (both recognition and distribution) calls for the reorganization of the political system, the judicial system – the very social fabric itself. It would undermine basic property rights as the West currently understands them. In other words, group rights cannot really be conceived of without imagining a postnational state.

References

Churchill, W. (1996) 'Like sand in the wind: the making of an American Indian diaspora in the United States' in Crow, D. (ed.) *Geography and Identity: Living and Exploring Geopolitics of Identity*, Washington, DC, Maisonneuve Press.

Kymlicka, W. (1995) *Multicultural Citizenship*, Oxford, Oxford University Press.

Richardson, B. (1993) *People of Terra Nullius: Betrayal and Rebirth in Aboriginal Canada*, Vancouver, BC, Douglas and McIntyre.

Source: Isin and Wood, 1999, pp.64–7

6

Social justice

Peter Braham

Contents

1	**Introduction**	**250**
	Aims	251
2	**The concept of social justice**	**251**
	2.1 The social context of legal justice	254
3	**Social justice in theory**	**257**
4	**Social justice in practice: overcoming inequalities?**	**262**
	4.1 Bussing	265
5	**Perceptions of social justice**	**267**
6	**Immigration, 'race' and social justice**	**269**
	6.1 The rise of the underclass thesis	275
7	**Conclusion**	**278**
	References	**279**

Readings

6.1: Brian Barry, 'Economic motivation in a Rawlsian society' (1989)	**281**
6.2: Stephen Steinberg, 'The underclass: a case of color blindness, right and left' (1999)	**284**

1 Introduction

'Social justice' is often invoked by politicians when they wish to promote their policies as setting out to achieve a more equitable society: the Scottish Parliament, for example, has appointed a Minister and a Committee for Social Justice. The issue of social justice is also a significant source of debate in a number of social sciences – philosophy, political science, psychology and sociology. In other social sciences such as law and social policy, as well as in emerging areas of study such as community mediation, it is a source of both debate and decision-making. What underpins these debates is the general appreciation that comes in any society when its members begin to think about the way in which their lives are arranged and the specific realization that social arrangements are not some natural phenomenon, but are human creations. This produces debate about justice because such a realization inevitably raises the question as to what social arrangements are defensible. With equal inevitability, as Barry argues, this process of thought is connected to the issue of inequality because in every society:

> ... there are those who give orders and those who obey them, those who receive deference and those who give it, those who have more than they can use and those who have less than they need.
>
> (Barry, 1989, p.3)

After a general discussion of issues of justice and social justice, this chapter focuses particularly on social justice associated with 'race', ethnicity and immigration. There are several reasons for this focus. First, inequalities associated with 'race', ethnicity and immigration have been, and often remain, substantial. Second, and in consequence, such inequalities have been widely studied and substantive attempts have been made to counter them through social engineering and legislation. Third, these inequalities are not merely important in themselves, but – to use a medical analogy – they can serve as a 'barium trace' indicating significant patterns of discrimination and disadvantage in the wider society; the attempts to counter these patterns – as, for example, in specific education policies or in the successive Race Relations Acts passed in the UK – can clarify our general understanding of social justice. Fourth, and most importantly, many of these inequities are closely related to matters that are at the heart of debates about social justice, notably: how the position of the least advantaged in society might be ameliorated and on what basis this should be done. In addition to this, such inequities contribute to tension, conflict and lack of social stability and so pose a threat to the inclusionary nature of citizenship (see also Chapters 4 and 5).

To begin with, however, we shall look at the work of the Commission on Social Justice, which was established by the late John Smith, leader of the Labour Party from 1992 until his death in 1994. This examination has the following objectives: it demonstrates the salience of 'social justice' in political and policy debate; it reveals some of the connections between political conceptions of social justice, on the one hand, and various philosophical and sociological conceptions on the other; and it indicates some of the complexities of the issues raised by these debates and conceptions.

The aims of this chapter are:

1   To explore the way in which the distribution of, and access to, differential rewards is regarded.

2   To examine, in particular, views about the condition of the least advantaged in society.

3   To discuss some of the complexities of social justice when proceeding from general conceptions of social justice to the social injustices facing deprived and disadvantaged groups.

4   To focus on questions of social justice in the UK and the USA associated with 'race', ethnicity and immigration.

2 The concept of social justice

The complexity of **justice** in its different dimensions and typologies is indicated by the following list:

justice

- fairness
- propriety or impartiality in procedures
- retributive justice or compensation
- restorative justice
- equity in the way resources are divided between two or more participants in an exchange
- equity in the way resources or access to resources are divided when distributed by some authority, such as a government, and
- justice as equality, especially to treat individuals equally.

This is a long and perhaps daunting list. That this is so reflects the fact that notions of fairness and justice go to the heart of what philosophers have seen as the 'good society' and which they have sought to describe in terms of a universally valid, timeless set of principles. Such an attempt is exemplified by Socrates' statement in Plato's *The Republic*, that justice cannot be a series of empirical practices, but is an ideal concerned with higher aspirations to the good life (Pavlich, 1996, p.17). But it is when we try to turn justice into the empirical practices eschewed by Socrates, when we seek to agree on what is 'just' in a given instance and on the processes by which justice is then to be achieved, that some of the greatest disputes break out.

The contentious nature of what may be considered to be socially just is shown by the range of different concepts that are used to determine whether a decision, procedure or policy should be considered 'just' or 'unjust'. These principles include merit, need, entitlement, **equality**, equality of opportunity and equality of outcome. Not only is it a matter of disagreement as to which of these goals should prevail, but equally contentious is the question of which is the best method of achieving them, even assuming agreement on goals.

equality

citizenship

In 1994 the Commission on Social Justice (henceforth the abbreviation CSJ is used) published its final report, *Social Justice: Strategies for National Renewal.* This report was, of course, a political document, yet it drew extensively on sociology and other social sciences. Though the CSJ's chief focus was on social justice, its treatment of this concept was linked to several other closely related terms, such as need, equality of opportunity and **citizenship** (see Chapter 5) – as is shown by the four principles that it set out in a discussion paper, *The Justice Gap*, published in the previous year, 1993. They were:

1   The foundation of a free society is the equal worth of all its citizens.

2   Everyone is entitled, as a right of citizenship, to be able to meet their basic needs.

3   The right to personal autonomy demands the widest spread of opportunities.

4   Not all inequalities are unjust, but unjust inequalities should be reduced and where possible eliminated.

(CSJ, 1998a/1993, p.48)

These principles may seem to you to be uncontroversial, but even these raise some matters that can be contentious.

First, what is meant by 'basic needs'? Is there an absolute measure of 'need' or is this a relative matter?

Second, what is denoted by the 'widest spread of opportunities' and on what calculation is this based? Is this the same or similar to 'equal opportunities' and, if so, how can equal opportunity be approached or achieved? If it falls short of equal opportunity, what scale of inequality is then countenanced and on what criteria would this inequality be based?

Third, even if we leave aside the probability that there are those in a society who are indifferent to the scale of inequality and need, are there other values that should reasonably take precedence? For example, it can be argued that the equation of justice with equality via the use of redistributive taxation, as manifested in high direct taxes on income, inheritance tax and wealth tax, imposes unwarranted restrictions on individual liberty.

These principles reflected analysis by the CSJ of what UK society had once been, how it had changed and what it should become in the future. According to the CSJ,

> ... [the] welfare capitalist states that developed in Europe after World War II sought to combine social justice and economic prosperity on the basis of a common set of values. However, the ways in which they expressed these values depended on three specific factors: full employment, the nuclear family and the interventionist national state.

(CSJ, 1998b, p.13)

In this context the UK was described by the CSJ as a hybrid: in some respects at the leading edge (as with the national insurance system); in others, lagging behind (in the rights of citizens); part collectivist (council housing); part universal (child benefit); and part means-tested (income support).

The CSJ then considered a number of critical changes that had occurred in the UK since the creation of the welfare state, founded as it was on one form of social justice – the idea of cradle-to-grave protection from need (as was discussed in Chapter 5). These changes, as perceived by the CSJ, comprised (in summary):

an economic revolution that had globalized competition and ended the expectation of a 'job for life'; a social revolution that had transformed women's role in society; and a political revolution that had, *inter alia*, caused people to expect more of a say in the way their lives were ordered. These changes, it was argued, caused an exposure to 'degrees of uncertainty and risk in people's lives that were previously hidden' (Franklin, 1998a, p.3) and which were sufficient to persuade the CSJ that there could be no return to the relative stability and security of the 1950s and 1960s. In these changed circumstances the CSJ sought to use their (revised) conception of social justice to satisfy need and to reconcile rights and responsibilities, though in so doing they referred to other concepts that they saw as relevant, such as equality of opportunity, life-chances and fairness.

The CSJ report raised several key issues that will be explored in this chapter. One issue concerns the extent of change and the nature of that change:

> What we wear, how we vote, what we eat, what job we do, where we live – all these are concerns that, two generations ago, were determined for the population by their birth. This is no longer the case. The UK is more mobile and open, but it is increasingly unequal.
>
> (CSJ, 1998b, p.27)

ACTIVITY 1

Spend a few moments writing down your reactions to this statement and its implications and then compare your reactions with my comments below.

You may have begun by taking another look at what Chapter 1 had to say about the freedom to choose 'where we live' in the UK and about how to measure the various aspects of spatial inequality that Chapter 1 addresses.

You may then have noted – and thought about – the distinction between social mobility and inequality. This is an important distinction because it raises a number of critical questions about social justice. The idea of equal access to unequal positions has been particularly influential in societies like Britain, but is this condition socially just or, alternatively, *generally regarded* as socially just? Later, in section 5, we shall examine these questions with reference to Runciman's seminal work, *Relative Deprivation and Social Justice*.

You would then have considered in what ways might the UK be seen as 'increasingly unequal' and, crucially, how should such inequality be interpreted? Here there has been a growing preoccupation with what has been termed *social* and *economic exclusion*, sometimes referred to as *marginalization*. Indeed, one of the first acts of the 1997 Labour government was to set up the Social Exclusion Unit to explore these problems and how to address them. As the CSJ report put it, in work, transport, education, accommodation and so on, such exclusion '… is an obvious and depressing feature of life in many parts of the UK … [T]he accumulated disadvantages of unemployment, bad housing and poor schooling combine to produce areas where there is simply no economy – no banks, no shops, no work' (CSJ, 1998b, p.28).

Though this may be, in the CSJ's description, 'obvious and depressing', there are several reasons why it nonetheless takes us into fiercely contested territory. As the CSJ acknowledged, it has been argued from the right of the political spectrum that the drive for a fairer society has resulted in 'slow (economic)

Figure 6.1 *A vandalized shop still open in a semi-derelict and all but abandoned row of shops on a council housing estate in Niddrie, East Edinburgh: an example of social exclusion as it is experienced*

growth and slowly increasing equality, and (that) the second caused the first' (*op. cit.*, p.11). If this is so, increasing equality can be regarded as contrary to the interests of the least well-off if it transpires that slow economic growth means that there are fewer resources to redistribute in their direction.

Equally significant is the interpretation in some quarters that the persistence of disadvantage and poverty in conditions of greater social mobility is evidence of a mind-set present in certain sections of the population comprising one or more of the following: recalcitrance, fecklessness, deviance, criminality, idleness and welfare dependency. This view therefore looks at individual and group behaviour and sees responsibility lying with those who exist in such conditions. However, others would argue that this diverts attention from structural causes of homelessness, unemployment, poverty and deprivation that are beyond the control of the disdavantaged. These opposing views of the behaviour of the poor and the deprived are especially evident in debates about the so-called 'underclass' (discussed in section 6).

2.1 The social context of legal justice

justice

In addition to these controversies, the CSJ recognized that there were those – especially on what it called the 'libertarian right' – who do not accept that there is such a thing as 'social justice' at all and who refuse to treat it as a viable concept. From this position it is argued that **'justice'** applies to the law, but that it should not be applied more widely. On this view, what is problematic is the decision to bracket 'justice' with 'social', not the concept of 'justice' *per se.*

One of the foremost exponents of this position is Friedrich Hayek, a prominent economist and political scientist, who came to be particularly associated with anti-Keynesian monetarism. Hayek referred to social justice as a mirage, the pursuit of which, he believed, had done more than anything else to destroy the juridical safeguards of individual freedom. He argued that 'we' (that is, society) had charged legislatures with tasks that enabled them to 'use coercion in the discriminatory manner' which is needed

> ... to assure benefits to particular people or groups. This they are constantly asked to do in the name of what is called social or distributive justice, a conception which has largely taken the place of the justice of individual action. It requires that not the individual but 'society' be just in determining the share of individuals in the social product.
>
> (Hayek, 1986, p.26)

Hayek then went on to say that:

> ... [in a] market economy in which no single person or group determines who gets what, and the shares of individuals always depend on many circumstances which nobody could have foreseen, the whole concept of social justice is empty and meaningless; and there will never exist agreement on what is just in this sense.
>
> (Hayek, 1986, p.26)

However, the question arises: how far can justice be achieved in the legal process in the absence of wider social justice?

ACTIVITY 2

I would like you to spend a few moments writing down what you think each of the following quotations tells us about the impartial application of legal justice and how they help us in distinguishing between 'justice' and 'social justice':

> In England, Justice is open to all, like the Ritz Hotel.
>
> (Lord Justice Sir James Mathew, quoted in Megarry, 1955, p.254)

> [In the USA] those sentenced to death are almost without exception male ... and disproportionately poor and black and their victims are overwhelmingly white. Of the approximately 300 people executed in the United States since 1977, 83% had been convicted of killing a white person, though white people represent only about half of all murder victims. Depending on the state, criminals are anywhere from four to eleven times more likely to be sentenced to death for killing a white person than a black person – hardly a ringing endorsement [of the idea] that justice is blind.
>
> (Bryson, 1998, p.356)

Clearly, both these quotations concern what happens in court. If we apply Lord Justice Mathew's dictum to present-day England, we might say justice is precluded where, for example, an individual does not qualify for legal aid despite having limited resources or where legal aid is unavailable. In the US situation, as recounted by Bryson, injustice might result when judges, lawyers or juries fail for some reason to be 'colour-blind'. If we generalize from each of these scenarios, the main issue might be narrowly legal, such as can a defendant or plaintiff obtain 'justice' irrespective of colour, creed, gender or station in society?

From this standpoint it is sensible to speak of justice or fairness in the decisions of the courts, but justice is restricted to fairness in respect of crime, sentencing, the handling of disputes, and so on. But it makes no sense to speak of fairness or unfairness in the distribution of resources in society. The emphasis of debate is therefore on things like equity in access to the courts and equality before the law. Thus, as Bell argues, with reference to lawyers' concepts: '[I]t is a central theme in much writing that justice involves the impartial application of legal rules without bias and in a way that treats all subjects of law equally and allows them to state their point of view' (Bell, 1994, p.127).

For those who see validity in the concept of 'justice', yet who do not wish to confine it to legal questions, it is conventional to distinguish between questions of 'formal justice' – as in the law – and questions of 'material justice' – as in the processes and politics of deciding the division of or access to resources. There are indeed convincing reasons for treating these areas as overlapping and interconnecting insofar as each is concerned with matters such as due process, impartiality, fairness and distribution on the basis of appropriate and defensible criteria.

However, in each of the cases cited in Activity 2 things become more complicated if we ask how far inequalities and injustices in the surrounding society impinge on what happens in court. The issue is no longer simply why it is that a jury in a specific case should be racially prejudiced, but the more general issue of why black people (especially young black men) are routinely treated more harshly than their white counterparts or why black defendants are unable to afford the best legal expertise. The outcome is that the likelihood of prosecution and the imposition of custodial sentences are both racially disproportionate.

Thus, the unequal imposition of the death penalty, as described by Bryson, might be accounted for not just by prejudice in the courtroom, but by racism within the court system, or on the part of the police which, in turn, may influence whether a case goes to court, and if so, whether it proceeds as a charge which attracts the death penalty. More diffusely, such inequities might reflect a pattern of disadvantage and discrimination that confronts black people in the USA which is so profound that it simply makes their lives more violent than is the norm: after all, according to recent statistics, in the USA the single greatest cause of death for black people in the age range 16–24 is murder. In the UK, in recent years, attention has been devoted to patterned differences between designated 'racial' or ethnic groups not only in connection with 'stop and search', but also in respect of rates of arrest, granting of bail, and type and length of sentence following conviction – differences that have attracted increasing concern in the judiciary and among politicians. We might then ask on what basis a 'patterned difference' – in which there is empirical evidence of, for example, inequality between one group and another – might be connected to 'social justice'?

SUMMARY OF SECTION 2

1   The complexity of 'justice' is indicated by the terms frequently associated with it. These include fairness, equality of opportunity, equality of outcomes, equality and need.

2   To establish what is 'just' in a given case may involve not merely deciding
     on what is meant by 'need' and what degree of inequality is acceptable, but
     on the balance between 'efficiency' and 'equality'.

3   The CSJ sought to establish an appropriate framework for social justice for
     Britain in the 1990s which took account of the substantial changes that had
     occurred since the foundation of the welfare state.

4   In doing this, the CSJ placed particular emphasis on growing inequality and
     social exclusion.

5   Some argue that the concept of social justice is meaningless and that the
     concept of justice should be applied only to the legal system. The problem
     with this view is that it is extremely difficult to prevent societal inequalities
     and injustices from intruding on the legal process and so it may be advisable
     to treat 'formal' and 'material' justice as overlapping.

3 Social justice in theory

We have already outlined the view that redistribution in pursuit of equality, if
taken too far (which may not be very far at all), is self-defeating: this may be
because, by its impact on the better-off, it reduces the total sum of what is
produced in society; and so – in the medium or long term – the worse-off may
actually lose rather than gain. This idea that the worse-off might actually lose
rather than gain by equality might seem to find some support in the general
principle of justice set out by Rawls, known as the 'difference principle'.
This principle provides the most influential modern general treatment of the
concept of social justice. It not only deals with what is meant by this concept,
but deconstructs it and compares the value of social justice with other competing
values, notably liberty.

The essence of Rawls' approach is deceptively simple. First, he calls for an
equal distribution of goods, opportunities and values unless an *unequal*
distribution of any, or all, of these things would be to everybody's advantage.
Second, he examines what constitutes a fair division of 'the cake' (that is of
roles, resources and access to resources in a society). In Rawls' hypothesis, a
fair division would be the division which the members of society would accept
in an imagined 'original position'. What would prompt them to accept such a
division is that they would have no way of knowing what their own share or
position would be in terms of resources and opportunities because they are
precluded from this knowledge by what Rawls visualizes as a 'veil of ignorance'.
It is, then, in their self-interest to adopt a division of resources that produces the
greatest well-being amongst the least-advantaged members of society – precisely
as an insurance policy against discovering that they themselves turn out to occupy
a disadvantaged position. In this case, as the Duc de la Rochefoucauld put it,
'The love of justice in most men is simply the fear of suffering injustice'.

Suppose that we apply the concept of the 'veil of ignorance' to the provision
of health care and education. There seem to be several reasons for saying that it
would be unjust to allow private provision of these resources that is within the

reach of some, but not of others, in the population and which is in some ways superior to state-funded provision. If we follow Rawls' hypothesis, because we would not know in advance which group we were going to be in, we would choose to avoid the risk of being excluded from the benefits of better educational or health provision and therefore support state-funded health care. Also, it could be thought that the existence of private provision might serve to weaken the chances of resources being devoted to the improvement of non-private health care or education. In this event the least well-off would be worse off still and equal opportunity and equal outcomes would be further away than ever.

READING 6.1

You should now read 'Economic motivation in a Rawlsian society' by Brian Barry which is reproduced as Reading 6.1. This reading raises quite complex issues that have to do with whether the justice or injustice of particular economic arrangements can be established and, if they can be established, on what basis?

As you read this extract, think about the following issues:

1   As a matter of principle, how might the pursuit of individual interest in the market be reconciled with the goals of redistribution and the alleviation of poverty?

2   Is the proposition that those with greater capacity produce more, and consequently earn more, compatible with Rawls' idea of a 'just society'?

3   If we assume that a condition of 'ideal justice' – defined as that in which everyone works for equal reward (or without special reward) – cannot be attained, is there, nevertheless, a condition of *relative* justice?

4   What importance does Rawls ascribe to the 'difference principle' and what part does 'fair equality of opportunity' play in it?

Rawls argues that we should take as a benchmark a hypothetical society in which, to begin with, not just rights and duties but, more particularly, income and wealth are evenly shared. If, in this society, certain inequalities, say of wealth, would render everyone better off than in the beginning, then, he argues, it is legitimate to move away from the benchmark position because, 'All social values – liberty and opportunity, income and wealth, and the bases of self-respect – are to be distributed equally unless an unequal distribution of any, or all, of these values is to everybody's advantage' (Rawls, 1971, p.62).

To put this in simple terms, the argument is that everyone stands to gain through some degree of inequality because the incentive to have more or to earn more than one's neighbour will boost production by directing scarce resources to where returns are greatest. If this is so, then 'more' is available to all and the conclusion follows that, if this is true, then (some degree of) inequality must be 'just'. In effect the dispute here is between 'accumulators' and 'redistributors', where accumulators treat the pursuit of equality instead of efficiency and the discouragement of entrepreneurial activity as a cause of slow economic growth – possibly the major cause – and they assert that we all stand to lose as a result.

To say that a degree of inequality is desirable because it is efficient and thus benefits the least well-off sections of society is different from saying that such inequality is desirable because it is right to reward merit. The latter proposition is primarily normative or ideological, even if reward according to merit turns out to be efficient and so ought to be measurable in some way. But the first proposition is largely an empirical matter, which may be supported or contested, for example, by looking at the expansion or contraction of the proportion of a population classed as living in poverty as economic activity fluctuates. This concerns the **distribution of income and wealth** in the population.

distribution of income and wealth

In 1991, according to Donnison, about one in five of the British population was living in **poverty**, where poverty was defined as having to live on less than half the nation's average income; the proportion was even higher if housing costs were taken into account, at about one in four (Donnison, 1998, p.9). Moreover, these figures had been rising for many years, particularly so from the mid-1980s. In 1979 more than four million families in the UK had been living on supplementary benefit (the minimum safety-net income then proposed by the state) and an additional three million families actually fell below that level through low pay or inadequate pension levels and for some reason they did not claim supplementary benefit. The important point, however, is that by 1989 the number living on income support (which by then had replaced supplementary benefit) had risen by two-thirds and the number living in households falling below that level had risen by one-third. In Donnison's opinion,

poverty

> That was not because the country could not afford to be more generous to its poorest people. This increase in poverty, as defined year by year in Parliament (that is to say, by the Department of Social Security) came about at a time when average income for the whole population increased faster than at any time over the previous 18 years. The problem has economic origins ... but it is essentially political in character. It is not a problem arising from lack of resources; it is a problem arising from a lack of shared concern and unity within the nation.
>
> (Donnison, 1998, p.14)

There are two things that Donnison notes that seem especially significant over and above the overall increase in the proportion of the population which was defined as being 'in poverty'. First, between 1979 and 1991/92 there had been an increase from 10 per cent to 33 per cent in the proportion of dependent children living in households in receipt of less than half the average national income. Second, there had been a growing concentration of both poverty and affluence in particular neighbourhoods (see Chapter 1). This concentration was most apparent, not at the level of towns or municipal districts, but at the level of census enumeration districts and it was linked in particular to the growing concentration of poor people in certain large housing estates (Donnison, 1998, pp.17–18; see Chapter 7).

There are several ways to read these statistics. First, we may say that the increase in the numbers of those defined as poor in a time of growing prosperity shows that the proceeds of 'efficiency' do not automatically 'trickle down' to the poor, and that it takes the necessary political will to achieve this effect.

Second, though we may accept that poverty may increase (and thus, by implication inequality increases as well), we might argue that it could or would increase still more if it were not for an increase in general prosperity. Apart from this, it may be that the definition of poverty has changed over time, as it surely will if it is tied to average levels of income.

Figure 6.2 *A council estate in the London Borough of Tower Hamlets: such urban council housing estates tend to have large proportions of their populations living on welfare benefits*

Third, if everyone within a given society was 'in poverty' we might assert that there is no injustice. If, however, we observe that the UK is not a 'poor society' in this sense, yet poverty exists and may be widespread, the question of *distributive justice* (that is, how the cake is fairly divided) arises. This raises the further question of whether analysis of social justice should be confined to what occurs within a specific country, given that measurable inequalities – ranging from access to education and employment to housing provision to expectation of life – are considerably more extreme between nations than they are within nations. As Barry puts it:

> The basic structure of the world – the institutions that … define differential life-chances – is no less open to criticism on the principles of justice than is that of any single country. It is surely obvious that among the most important things that determine people's prospects – including the elementary one of surviving to celebrate their first birthday – is the country in which they were born.
>
> (Barry, 1989, p.237)

sociology of development

Although the **sociology of development** is centred on disparities of economic condition between countries and on the reasons for these disparities, sociological accounts of social justice have been largely intra-national and mainly concerned with distributive justice (see section 4). In this regard, sociological approaches mirror the neglect by philosophers of issues about justice beyond the borders of the individual state, even though international disparities raise significant issues for social justice. For instance, developments in technology and communications have facilitated the relocation of production from more developed countries to countries where labour is relatively cheap, abundant and poorly protected from exploitation, which was described as a 'new international division of labour' (Fröbel *et al.*, 1980). This has had several consequences. Workers in less developed countries obtain employment in manufacturing where previously there was little such work; they, nevertheless, work for very low wages (often below subsistence levels) and in poor conditions and are treated as expendable. Those in the more developed countries who lose their jobs as capital 'migrates' abroad are often among the poorest and least well-paid of the labour force. What would the principle of 'social justice' suggest in these circumstances? Should protectionism be used to retrieve the position of the less advantaged in the developed country or is it preferable to take no action in order to allow less developed countries to accumulate wealth through industrialization in the way in which countries such as the UK once did (CSJ, 1998b, p.20)?

Figure 6.3 *Female workers in a modern, so-called 'world factory' in Taipei, Taiwan: manufacturing jobs have increasingly migrated from the developed world to the industrializing countries of South East Asia*

Another example concerns the aftermath of post-Second World War immigration into Western Europe. This began as a short-term remedy for supposedly temporary labour shortages but, as it turned out, proved a permanent phenomenon. In these circumstances many single immigrant workers wanted their families to join them and this led to 'secondary' immigration on a significant scale. This raises important issues for social justice and human rights – with regard to the right to family life and how the right to family reunification might be reconciled with immigration controls, as well as the difficulty that migrants have in obtaining citizenship. The right to family life has been recognized in a number of international conventions and resolutions, such as the European Convention on Human Rights and Fundamental Freedoms (1950), the

International Covenant on Civil and Political Rights (1966), the Convention on the Rights of the Child (1989), and by a resolution of the UN General Assembly, which stated that:

> ... all Governments, particularly those of receiving countries, must recognise the vital importance of family reunification and ... ensure the protection of the unity of the families of documented migrants... [and which called on] all States to discourage and reverse legislation that adversely affects family reunification ...

> (UN Resolution 49/182, 1994)

By looking at the life-chances of those who emigrated from less developed to more developed countries and the life-chances of their descendants (see section 6), not only can we address some elements of these international inequalities, but we can also encompass the matter of expectations in relation to inequality (see section 5).

SUMMARY OF SECTION 3

1   Rawls' principle of a 'fair division of the cake' posits a 'veil of ignorance' to ensure that the position of the least advantaged in society will be protected.

2   However, Rawls suggests that a degree of inequality is acceptable if this boosts total production and can thus benefit the least well-off in the long term.

3   An empirical analysis of the incidence of poverty in the UK from the late 1970s to the beginning of the 1990s indicates that a growing economy did not lead to an improvement in the situation of the poorest people. In this case 'justice' can be seen as requiring political will rather than a purely economic solution.

4   The sociological treatment of social justice in terms of an unequal distribution of wealth and resources has been largely intra-national; though international inequalities consequent upon movement of labour and capital raise issues of inequality, exploitation and social justice, they have received comparatively little attention.

---

4 Social justice in practice: overcoming inequalities?

Rawls posits a hypothetical society in which there is a principled choice to be made about the optimum distribution of resources. Such a choice is central to the political process. However, as we have seen, the principles of social justice are filtered through the status quo of institutions in a context of a given distribution of resources and a given social structure that together determine the access that individuals and groups within that society have to key resources. Together these create and maintain a whole series of advantages and disadvantages that determine whether individuals acquire or fail to acquire income, wealth, status and other desirables. These institutions include the legal process, which may offer unequal rights and access; the taxation and inheritance system; and the education system, which increases the **life-chances** open to individuals.

life-chances

The essential point is that through the circumstances into which we are born, but also through the working of these institutions, some have excellent prospects and others have poor ones. Thus, if we consider the impact of the educational system in terms of social justice, we would want to know how far **educational attainment** is the key to gaining access to more desirable occupational positions: how far it leaves intact the consequence of being born into more or less privileged surroundings and how far it evens out their impact (this will be discussed further in Chapter 7). The crucial issue from the standpoint of social justice is not the content of education – which we may praise or condemn – but the extent to which education facilitates the acquisition of whatever qualifications may be specified to gain entry to various desirable occupations or professions (Barry, 1989).

educational attainment

To illustrate this point, Barry considers Macaulay's view (expressed in the nineteenth century) that the ability to write with elegance in a foreign language – preferably a dead language – was the ideal way to recruit for the Colonial Civil Service. From the standpoint of social justice, what is critical is not whether Macaulay's criterion was sensible or relevant. What we need to ask is: when Macaulay expressed this opinion, was the teaching of Latin and Greek within the reach of only a minority of children who came from privileged backgrounds (Barry, 1989, p.357)?

If we think about the ramifications of Macaulay's suggestion, we are quickly confronted by a general form of disadvantage or inequality which has been termed 'discrimination *before* the market'. This:

> ... denies those who are discriminated against the same opportunities as others to develop their capability, and to use so much capacity as they do develop in the most advantageous employment for which it qualifies them. ... The differential provision of social services, especially education, and the segregation of residence, prevent the children of a group from developing their potential capacity. They are at a further disadvantage through their parents having been similarly situated, and so having limited ability to develop and to motivate them; this kind of discrimination, once imposed, is thus in a measure self-perpetuating.
>
> (Phelps-Brown, 1977, pp.145–6)

But such inequality is more than simply 'self-perpetuating'. In an advanced industrial or post-industrial economy, when it comes to choosing between job applicants and candidates for promotion, employers tend to apply what Offe has called 'the achievement principle'. This principle assumes that there are qualitative differences between employees and that these can be measured objectively and then used as the basis for recruitment and promotion. The achievement principle is thus integral to the idea and practice of a meritocratic society. However, Offe believes that this principle actually provides a rationalization for procedures that legitimize (irrelevant) inequalities between individuals and groups. This is because its application conceals the frequently subjective interpretations of the requirements of a particular job and of the skills and experience appropriate to performing that job (Offe, 1976, p.90).

This does not apply only to filling the kind of higher-level posts that concerned Macaulay and for which substantial educational accomplishment was judged necessary. On the contrary, 'justice' in selection poses a general problem at all levels and in all sections of the labour market. This point can be illustrated by a study of manual workers in Peterborough which found that:

> ... 95 per cent had no formal educational qualifications. Other indicators of quality are also lacking. ... We have estimated that in Peterborough about 85 per cent of the workers possess the necessary ability to undertake 95 per cent of the jobs ...
>
> (Blackburn and Mann, 1979, p.12)

Indeed, Blackburn and Mann concluded that in the categories of work that they had examined, workers exercised considerably more skill in *driving* to work, than they exercised once *at* work. Given these circumstances, they asked:

> How is this to be reconciled with the fact that employers do search for worker quality? Though employers (that is, in this category of work) do not operate very rigorous selection procedures they do make an attempt to be selective. ... Instead of using direct measures of ability, they use what the economic literature terms 'screening devices', that is they assume that some readily observable characteristics (like race) can serve as an indicator of a certain degree of ability, and select according to that. In the first stage of the selection procedure for the 'good jobs' are weeded out the blacks, the women, those with several jobs over a recent short period, the very young and the very old, the single and the school drop-outs. ...What all these criteria have in common is that they are aimed less at 'ability' than *stability*.
>
> (Blackburn and Mann, 1979, pp.12–13)

In spite of this, universal, compulsory education appears as a watershed in securing social justice. This is because it provides a crucial means of nurturing ability and counteracting inherited advantages and disadvantages unconnected to ability. Yet the pervasive and self-perpetuating nature of discrimination before the market constitutes a formidable obstacle to linking life-chances to ability rather than to circumstances of birth and upbringing. This helps to explain why it is that the goal of 'equal opportunity' – as a measure or constituent part of social justice – is not the weak goal that is sometimes suggested, even though it allows inequality of outcomes. In fact, to achieve equal opportunity would demand extensive and radical change, especially in education, if discrimination before the market is to be neutralized.

Some occupations inevitably offer better pay and conditions than others. But if equality of opportunity is to prevail, then there must be equal means of obtaining these more desirable positions. We can return to Macaulay's view of the appropriate criteria for entry to the Civil Service to explore this further. The first condition would be that there is no arbitrary restriction on who can aspire to occupy these 'unequal' positions. Thus it would be unjust to exclude citizens on grounds of gender, religion, 'racial' or ethnic origin. The second condition would be the introduction of free and universal schooling, without which many will be excluded simply by the inability of their parents to afford the cost of education. Rawls captures the impact that education might have in securing equality of opportunity when he says, 'Chances to acquire cultural knowledge and skills should not depend on one's class position, and so the school system, whether public or private, should be designed to even out class barriers' (Rawls, 1971, p.73).

Much educational reform has been concerned, directly and indirectly, with recognizing and overcoming the various inequalities that lie outside the school gates – between families, communities, localities, groups and classes. Yet there is substantial evidence from the UK and elsewhere to suggest that the effects of these inequalities are extraordinarily difficult to counteract (see Chapter 7).

4.1 Bussing

We can appreciate some of these difficulties by looking in some depth at the reasons that lay behind what was called 'bussing'. This is a policy that has been employed in schools in the UK and the USA. In the US bussing had been introduced after the US Supreme Court declared segregation unconstitutional in 1954. It involved the transportation of black pupils from inner-city areas to schools located in the white suburbs. This device was introduced not simply to comply with the legal decision, but it was designed to deliver a measure of social justice by furthering equality of opportunity in education.

The educational rationale was: first, it assumed that education offered the prospect of social and occupational advancement. Second, schools in black (and Hispanic) neighbourhoods had, as a rule, been run down, poorly funded and understaffed. It therefore seemed reasonable to suppose that bussing would help to equalize educational opportunities by taking students away from inadequate schools to schools with more resources and whose pupils were relatively advantaged. Third, the policy had a symbolic significance. This was not merely because it recognized that inferior education had represented an important element in black subordination in the US, but because the inter-racial contact brought about by bussing promised a more tolerant society with increased contact and better mutual understanding between different groups.

Despite these high expectations, the results of bussing in the USA were disappointing. Not only did bussing meet head-on the embedded practices of racial discrimination and disadvantage in the larger society, but there were several more specific factors. Transporting groups of pupils to schools which were often at a considerable distance from the localities in which they lived was literally 'dislocating' and it took up time better used for studying. Also, many teachers at the schools to which pupils were bussed had low academic expectations of black

Figure 6.4 *Two children look over the sign on a bus sponsored in the name of Pope John XXIII in Boston, Massachusetts, in 1965. In this case parents were themselves organizing and paying for the bussing of their children to schools outside their predominantly black districts*

pupils and saw them as aggressive or threatening. In addition, a major purpose of bussing black pupils to suburban state schools was undermined because their arrival precipitated a movement of white pupils out of these same schools into private schools. This helped to re-create many of the elements of the prior inequality, as the reputation of these formerly all-white schools declined and the withdrawal of white pupils weakened local political support for them in a system where school funding depended on local education taxes being voted for by the (white) population (Kirp, 1982; Coleman, 1990).

Bussing was introduced to mitigate inequalities associated with the areas in which less advantaged groups live. Some of these inequalities reflected differential funding of schools but, if this was the main problem, then such inequalities might have been relatively easy to correct. What has proved a much more difficult problem is the extent to which an advantaged or disadvantaged educational environment consists of the *other children* attending any given school and the inequalities that these children bring with them. It is this dimension of inequality in education that explains why it is that the provision of free education by the state – accessible to all – does not necessarily produce the conditions demanded if equality of opportunity is to exist. As Barry argues:

> Given the tendency of people in a neighbourhood within any city to have similar education and cultural backgrounds, this entails that (at any rate in urban areas) the effects of individual parents on their children's prospects will be multiplied by the likelihood that the other children will have similar parents. *Nothing short of scattering children at random over an entire metropolitan area could avoid this.*
>
> (Barry, 1989, p.221; emphasis added)

Whatever its deficiencies, bussing represented an attempt to counter not just educational disadvantage, but also the more general social and economic exclusion which both contributed to this educational disadvantage and which this disadvantage reinforced. In other words, children were bussed out of areas where work, transport, housing, leisure and commercial facilities were inadequate or crumbling and where they faced a range of disadvantages – unemployment, poor housing conditions, high crime rates, illness related to deprivation and below-average expectation of life – which, as Donnison puts it, at one end of a continuum of inequality are 'heaped on the same kinds of people' (1998, p.7).

The elimination of such locational and environmental inequalities appears, at first sight, to be in keeping with certain key principles of social justice. This is because their eradication would bring us closer to a condition where accident of birth played no part in deciding the qualifications that we are able to achieve and the occupational positions that these qualifications permit us to obtain. However, were they to be eliminated, it would illuminate a key difference about what is 'just' that separates advocates of equality of opportunity from advocates of equality. This difference is explained by Jencks as follows:

> One inevitable result of eliminating environmental inequality would be to increase the correlation between IQ genotype and IQ scores. Indeed, this is often a conscious objective of educational policy. Most schools try to help their students with high 'native ability' realise their 'potential'. In effect, this also means eliminating the unfair advantage of students who have unpromising genes but come from stimulating homes. The idea seems to be that inequality

based on genetic advantage is morally acceptable, but that inequality based on other accidents of birth is not. Most educators and laymen evidently feel that an individual's genes are his [*sic*], and that they entitle him to whatever advantages he can get from them. His parents, in contrast, are not 'his' in the same sense, and ought not to entitle him to special favours. For a thoroughgoing egalitarian, however, inequality that derives from biology ought to be as repulsive as inequality that derives from early socialisation.

(Jencks *et al.*, 1973, p.73)

As this suggests, the closeness of the connection between social justice and social inequality is mediated by *attitudes* towards these institutionalized inequalities – by what is regarded as acceptable or fair. This a central theme of Runciman's book, *Relative Deprivation and Social Justice* (1966) and Runciman's approach, which is discussed in the next section, merits careful consideration.

SUMMARY OF SECTION 4

1   Distributive justice concerns the connections between social justice and social structure.

2   In reviewing a given institution, a critical question is how far it leaves intact the consequence of being born into more or less privileged circumstances and how far and in what ways it modifies what is termed 'discrimination before the market'.

3   The intractability of 'discrimination before the market' can be illustrated by attempts to equalize educational opportunity through what was termed 'bussing'.

4   The elimination of inequalities perceived as unjust may leave untouched other inequalities which are regarded as acceptable.

5   Perceptions of social justice

ACTIVITY 3

Before we look at Runciman, think again about the comment made by the CSJ (quoted earlier on p.253), that 'the UK is more mobile and open, but it is increasingly unequal' (CSJ, 1998b, p.27). Spend a few moments noting down what this suggests to you about the way in which inequalities may be perceived, then compare your notes with Runciman's analysis.

Writing in the mid-1960s, Runciman noted sharply contrasting views about the extent and nature of social inequality in Britain. On one hand, it was said that manual workers had by then caught up with non-manual workers in their level of reward and that careers had 'increasingly opened up to talent'. On the other hand, it was said that educational and social privilege persisted and that 'the distribution of wealth was not as egalitarian as was generally assumed' (Runciman, 1966, pp.4–5).

Clearly, the structure and patterns of inequality in a society have to be examined to establish the truth, but what was of special interest to Runciman was the connection between inequality and 'grievance' – that is, the way in which inequality is regarded. He quotes Durkheim, who had argued that:

> What is needed if social order is to reign is that the mass of men be content with their lot. But what is needed for them to be content, is not that they have more or less, but that they be convinced that they have no more right to more.
> (Durkheim [1959], quoted in Runciman, 1966, p.25)

Runciman therefore began his book by saying that, 'All societies are inegalitarian. But what is the relation between the inequalities in a society and the feelings of acquiescence or resentment to which they give rise? People's attitudes to social inequalities seldom correlate strictly with the facts of their own position' (Runciman, 1966, p.3). In his opinion, the connection between inequality and grievance was much more subtle than the commonly-held view that the under-privileged would be assuaged by rising prosperity. He thought that it was ' … just as difficult for the period after the Second World War as for the 1840s or 1930s to establish what has in fact been the relation between inequality and grievance and how far this relation has been such as would accord with the requirements of social justice' (*ibid.*, p.5).

In fact, Runciman suggested that not only was it apparent that dissatisfaction was *not* felt in direct proportion to the degree of inequality with which rewards and privileges were distributed in a given society, but that many people nearer the top of society were much less content than their position seemed to warrant and many near the bottom were much less resentful than might have been anticipated (*ibid.*, p.3). Why should this be so? Runciman's answer to this paradox was that in most respects one's level of satisfaction depended on *expectations*, and these expectations were obtained – to put it simply – by contrasting one's own position with someone worse-off. This explains why 'steady poverty is the best guarantee of conservatism', whereas, if the poor came to see as obtainable the condition of a more fortunate community, then they will be discontented until they succeed in catching up. To make sense of this concept of 'rising expectations' he used the psychological terms of **relative deprivation** and **reference group** (*ibid.*, p.9).

relative deprivation, reference group

Runciman refers to the most famous study in the literature on reference groups –*The American Soldier*. It found that in the Military Police, where opportunities for promotion were very poor, there was greater satisfaction about this than in the Air Corps, where opportunities for promotion were much greater (Stouffer *et al.*, 1949, pp.250–3; cited in Runciman, 1966, p.18). The reason for this was that those in the Air Corps who had not been promoted would compare themselves with the large number of their fellows who *had* been promoted, while those who had not been promoted in the Military Police would compare themselves with the large number of their fellows who had also *not* been promoted. Runciman makes the point that only in rare instances will the 'frequency' of relative deprivation (that is, the proportion of a group who feel it) be directly related to actual inequality. This raises the question of how a group reacts to being denied access to higher positions in their society: 'If it is true that the sense of inequality depends on the choice of reference groups, then the influences behind reference group choices will be the determinants of the relation between grievance and inequality' (*ibid.*, p.25).

What, then, can disturb reference groups? One way is through the receipt of 'news' – epitomized by the observation that it would be better to close the schools than to create aspirations and then deny them (*ibid.*, pp.24–5). But the most obvious external influence is war – where the underprivileged share in equal measure the experiences and exertions of their 'social superiors' and so they may expect a joint share in a better post-war world (*ibid.*, p.24; and see Chapter 5).

The concept of relative deprivation has particular resonance for immigration and 'race'. In making 'references', the first generation of immigrant workers may focus on conditions in their country of origin rather than look at the opportunities available to indigenous workers, whereas their children may expect to be treated on the same basis as their school-fellows. And a group that faces racial discrimination may adjust their references accordingly: for example, in order to avoid discrimination they may refrain from applying to certain companies of from trying to obtain particular jobs, or they may (reluctantly) accept discrimination as an inevitable part of their daily life. Thus in each case prejudice, discrimination and disadvantage are not just a question of degree, but also a question of perception and expectation. In other words, who these groups see as being 'in the same boat' as themselves is important. We will explore this further in section 6.

SUMMARY OF SECTION 5

1   The structure and patterns of inequality in society are mediated by the way in which inequality is regarded and this, according to Runciman, is at variance with the objective situation.

2   The principal reason for this disjunction can be explained by the fact that people compare their own situation with others whom they see as similar (a reference group) and consider their situation in relation to others (relative deprivation).

6 Immigration, 'race' and social justice

Racial discrimination is a significant element of social and economic injustice not only in the UK, but in other societies as well. In the UK:

> It works in a number of direct and indirect ways, wastes talent and potential, and, by creating bitter feelings of resentment and alienation, undermines respect for and desire to participate in the political system. Discrimination is a brake on the material and social progress of the country as a whole, and while not an absolute bar to the progress of minorities, it prevents success on equal terms or in proportionate numbers to that of the white majority.
>
> (Modood, 1998, p.167)

As far as the UK is concerned, we should ask three questions (McCrudden *et al.*, 1991, p.2):

1   What is the present situation of minority ethnic groups in the UK economy and culture and why do they occupy that situation?

2   What would the 'good' or the 'just' society look like in matters relating to 'race' and ethnicity?

3   By what instruments of policy do we move from position (1) to position (2)?

ACTIVITY 4

My response to the first of these questions focuses on employment. As you read it, start to think how you might answer the second and third questions.

Minority ethnic groups tend to enter the 'host' society at the bottom. A wave of immigration from the New Commonwealth (India, Pakistan and the West Indies) arrived in the UK in the late 1940s, 1950s and early 1960s as a 'replacement' labour force to fill vacancies in those industries and occupations where the indigenous labour force was unwilling or insufficient to meet the demand for labour. The endemic labour shortages that had arisen in the UK in the years after the Second World War had also occurred in other Western European countries, such as Germany who brought in *gastarbeiter* (or guestworkers) from Turkey, for example, to work in their car and manufacturing plants. One result of filling these shortages with imported labour was to rigidify what was termed the *social-job structure*: the recruitment of workers into certain sectors and occupations seemed to confirm and deepen the stigma attached to such jobs, a stigma that had helped cause the initial shortage in the first instance (Böhning, 1981, p.29). This process was most pronounced in Switzerland, where indigenous Swiss workers had abandoned 'arduous, disagreeable, dirty and poorly paid jobs' to foreign workers on such a scale that in terms of the degree of segregation between indigenous and foreign workers, its labour market could be compared to that of a colony (Girod, 1965, p.1).

Figure 6.5 *Jamaican immigrants arriving in the UK on the ex-troopship* Empire Windrush *at Tilbury, 22 June 1948*

In these circumstances, immigrant labour played an important part in creating and perpetuating what is sometimes called a 'dual labour market'. In such a **segmented labour market**, immigrant workers occupy 'secondary jobs' – jobs where wages are lower, where there is little security of employment, training is minimal and prospects for promotion are poor, rather than 'primary jobs' – where pay, conditions and job security are reasonably good (Giddens, 1973, pp.219–20).

labour market segmentation

In addition to the rigidification of the social-job structure, black workers also encountered 'discrimination *within* the market', a process whereby 'workers who are distinguished by some characteristic that does not directly affect their present capability are treated less favourably in a given employment than others who are of no greater capability, but who are not marked off by that characteristic' (Phelps-Brown, 1977, p.145). In other words, racial discrimination, which represents a persistent and sometimes virulent form of discrimination within the market, was superimposed on prior inequality.

One well-tried way to assess the extent of racial discrimination in employment is to use controlled experiments. A frequently used experiment involved 'testers' – identifiable as belonging to different 'racial' or ethnic groups, applying for a range of jobs in writing, by telephone and in person, but doing so in a way that the success rates of each group could be compared. This type of experiment had first been used in Britain in the late 1960s and, with minor variations, much the same methodology was utilized in the following decades. For instance, the testing carried out by Political and Economic Planning (PEP) in the early 1970s covered recruitment of different racial groups for unskilled, semi-skilled and skilled manual jobs and several types of white-collar employment (Smith, 1977, p.105). These tests indicated a pattern of discrimination very much along the lines that might have been predicted given that black immigrant workers had been recruited to fill vacancies unattractive to white workers, and, given the extent to which employers had recruited them with reluctance even then. Later surveys indicated that racial discrimination and inequality in employment remained substantial. For instance, replication in 1984 and 1985 by the Policy Studies Institute of the job application tests carried out in 1973 and 1974 by PEP, demonstrated that at least one-third of private employers discriminated against either African-Caribbean or Asian applicants or against both (Brown, 1984; Brown and Gay, 1985). In the UK the prevailing attitude to the recruitment of (black) immigrant labour can be summed up in the remark of one large manufacturer who said: 'If we could interview queues of English men for our vacancies we would not employ any immigrants at all' (quoted in Allen *et al.*, 1977, p.46).

This discrimination applied at all levels from manual and white-collar jobs (Smith, 1977, p.105) through to the appointment of doctors (Esmail and Everington, 1993, p.691–2). In the latter case a pilot study was carried out using pairs of applications, matched in terms of comparability of CVs, for each post, but one with an English name and one with an Asian: the results showed that English applicants were twice as likely to be shortlisted for interview. Interestingly the researchers were arrested by the fraud squad for making fraudulent applications and were advised not to continue the research. However, other research has shown similar discrimination in the medical profession (McKeigue *et al.*, 1990), as well as more generally in the job market at all levels and continuing today. For example, research commissioned by the University Vice

Figure 6.6 ' *Rooms to let. No coloured men': a common sight in Britain in the 1950s*

Chancellors and academic unions, and carried out by John Carter, Steve Fenton and Tariq Modood (1999) for the Policy Studies Institute, found that ethnic minority staff were concentrated in fixed-term contract posts at the bottom end of the employment scale, with nearly 50 per cent on contracts compared to one-third of their white peers. They found evidence that 'minority ethnic groups experienced discrimination in applications for posts and promotions, harassment and negative stereotyping'. The London Borough of Hackney was actually served with a non-discrimination notice by the Commission for Racial Equality (CRE) after a two-year investigation, and in 2000 Ford Motor Company was faced with a Formal Investigation by the CRE following a tribunal decision about racial discrimination at the Dagenham works, and failure to take effective action in response to complaints about racial harassment.

ACTIVITY 5

In the light of my response to the first question posed by McCrudden *et al.*, now think more carefully about how their second and third questions might be answered. In particular, I would like you to consider the role that education plays in creating a 'socially just society' and where responsibility lies for achieving social justice. As you will see from my comments, I think that these questions raise complex and contentious issues.

Until 1968 racial discrimination in employment was not unlawful, so there was nothing to prevent employers taking on who they wanted, using whatever selection process they wanted to. Explicitly discriminatory advertisements appeared frequently, and it was common for employers to pass instructions to state and private employment agencies specifying 'no coloureds' (Brown, 1992, p.47). However, between the mid-1960s and 1976 three Race Relations Acts were passed in Britain. Although the first Act, in 1965, did not cover racial discrimination in employment, it was covered by the 1968 Act; and, subsequently, the 1976 Act extended the basis of legal intervention somewhat further to include indirect or unintentional discrimination in employment. In addition, the 1976 Act established the CRE, giving it power to mount formal investigations of employers suspected of racial discrimination and to issue non-discrimination notices if it was found that the law had been breached (Brown, 1992, p.55). These interventions were important because: they gave a standard by which public and private behaviour could be measured and judged; they constituted an unequivocal declaration of public policy; and, not least, they assured majority and minority groups that important issues of concern were now being addressed (McCrudden *et al.*, 1991, p.4). All of these aspects of recognizing and contesting racial discrimination and achieving equity can be seen as central to social justice. The Race Relations (Amendment) Act 2000 was aimed at tackling institutional racism, extending the coverage of the 1976 Act to the functions of public authorities that were previously excluded, including law enforcement, the implementation of government policies and services and certain public appointments. In launching the Act, the Home Secretary Jack Straw admitted that ethnic minorities were under-represented in the most senior posts right across the public sector.

The scale and persistence of racial discrimination, in spite of the passing of successive Race Relations Acts, might direct attention to the causes of ethnic and racial disadvantage and the means to remedy these disadvantages, notably via the promotion of educational opportunity. For minorities of relatively recent immigrant origin, education can be said to have had a special significance in that it might fulfil the hopes and expectations of the first generation of minority ethnic groups by allowing their children to progress in a way that they themselves – because of 'newness' and discrimination – could not.

We can see the various strands of this argument if we look at some of the policy statements on equal opportunity issued by the Department for Education and Employment [DfEE]. In the Foreword to the White Paper *Excellence in Schools*, the Secretary of State for Education said that:

> To overcome economic and social disadvantage and to make equal opportunity a reality, we must strive to eliminate, and never excuse, under-achievement in the most deprived parts of our country. Educational attainment encourages aspiration and self-belief in the next generation, and it is through family learning as well as scholarship through formal schooling, that success will come.

> We are talking about investing in human capital in the age of knowledge. To compete in the global economy, to live in a civilised society and to develop the talents of each and every one of us, we will have to unlock the potential of every young person. By doing so, each can flourish, building on their own strengths and developing their own special talents. We must overcome the spiral of disadvantage, in which alienation from, or failure within, the education system is passed from one generation to the next.
>
> (DfEE, 1997, p.3)

Here we have both a clear vision of social justice based on equal opportunity and an indication of some of the obstacles lying in its path. And if the goal of equal opportunity is to be attained, then the tendency for poor educational performance to be passed from one generation to the next in a 'spiral of disadvantage' – along similar lines to those mentioned by Phelps-Brown in his concept of 'discrimination before the market' – must be resisted and transcended.

According to the White Paper one of the most important explanations for poor performance in schools is low expectations of pupils of the kind epitomized by a comment which it quotes: 'you cannot expect high achievement from children in a run-down area like this' (*ibid.*, p.25). Teachers are said to have different expectations of middle-class pupils and working-class pupils. Whereas middle-class teachers were seen to share the same culture as middle-class pupils, 'Working-class culture was thought [by teachers] to be one of cultural deprivation, marked by low aspirations for educational attainment in family and community …' (Abercrombie *et al.*, 2000, p.112).

Apart from class, the DfEE White Paper expressed particular concern about some ethnic minority pupils, who, because of language difficulties, racial harassment, stereotyping, and disproportionate rates of exclusion, were underperforming. It suggested that this underperformance would require targeted action if these groups were to escape 'a cycle of disadvantage'.

It is important, however, to avoid giving the impression that nothing has changed in the period since New Commonwealth immigration to Britain began. As Modood put it, 'Despite the persistence of racial discrimination, the ethnic minorities in Britain are reversing the initial downward mobility produced by migration and racial discrimination' (Modood, 1998, p.168). According to Modood, the experience varies greatly. This is acknowledged in the White Paper:

> There are no national data on achievement by pupils from different minority ethnic groups. But the latest survey of research by OFSTED suggest that there are some common patterns. Indian pupils appear consistently to achieve more highly, on average, than pupils from other South Asian backgrounds and white counterparts in some, but not all, urban areas. Bangladeshi pupils' achievements are often less than other ethnic groups. African-Caribbean pupils have not shared equally in the increasing rate of educational achievement: in many LEAs their average achievements are significantly lower than other groups. The performance of African-Caribbean young men is a particular cause for concern.
>
> (DfEE, 1997, Appendix, para.7)

This is an important matter because how racial disadvantage is best tackled is often influenced by views about the ability or willingness of discriminated against or disadvantaged groups to 'help themselves'. This is evident in the comment:

> Racial discrimination is not necessarily linked to racial disadvantage because some groups migrate with skills and capital, and because some discriminated (against) groups put in extra time and energy, work and study harder, develop self-help and/or other networks to compensate and, therefore, avoid the socio-economic disadvantages that would otherwise result from discrimination.
>
> (Modood, 1998, p.174)

To illustrate his argument, Modood mentions the extent to which some Asian groups in Britain experience discrimination in selection processes. For instance, research carried out in the late 1980s revealed the existence of racial discrimination in recruitment to and progress within a range of professional occupations, accountancy in particular (CRE, 1987a) and graduate professions in general (CRE, 1987b). Yet, the groups in question, though discriminated against to the extent that all minority ethnic groups continue to be employed at levels below those appropriate to their educational qualification, are nonetheless *over-represented* in high-status professions like law and accountancy and in admission to tertiary education. This, Modood asserts, is 'quite a confusing development for race egalitarians' and they 'have in general given it little thought and do not know how to respond to it (except to deny that it exists)' (1998, p.174).

In Modood's view, the problem that arises in the case of an upwardly mobile minority facing discrimination is that attempts to achieve social justice by attacking discrimination directed at (all discriminated against) minorities will *further* increase over-representation in higher education, the professions or management of certain minorities (like the Chinese). This is simply because some of those in the upwardly mobile minority 'presently kept out will get in' (Modood, 1998, p.174).

This raises the question of whether social justice in the form of equal opportunity has to do with processes or with outcomes. This is a real dilemma because most equal opportunity policies (relating to gender as well as to 'race') suggest that the main criterion for judging success is outcome, not process. Thus the yardstick when selecting who is recruited or promoted, or who is admitted to a profession or an institution of higher education, is to 'mirror' the population from which the selection is made. The corollary is that if 'mirroring' or 'proportionality' of a given population is not achieved then the assumption is that discrimination must be taking place. These complexities are well-exemplified by the controversies concerning the numbers and proportions of blacks, whites and certain Asian groups admitted to US universities and the proposed methods of modifying the situation, for example by introducing quotas or specifying lower test scores for under-represented ethnic groups as part of affirmative action programmes.

6.1 The rise of the underclass thesis

It could be said that the UK compares favourably with other labour-importing countries of Western Europe both in terms of assessing and addressing the racial discrimination and disadvantage facing minorities of recent immigrant origin. Yet recognition of the extent of racial discrimination and disadvantage does not signify that these phenomena are separate from other forms of discrimination and disadvantage. In particular, we need to understand how racial inequalities intersect with class inequality, poverty and other forms of social deprivation and exclusion (Modood, 1998, p.180; see also Chapter 2).

I want now to explore some of these intersections. Discussion of poverty raises questions about inequalities, sometimes extreme inequalities, in health, housing and education and other spheres, and the ensuing debate is often contentious. For instance, the Moynihan Report, which enquired into the condition of the 'Negro family' in the USA in the mid-1960s found '… a bleak picture of broken families, of children born out-of-wedlock, of welfare dependency, of school dropouts and delinquency' (Steinberg, 1999, pp.5–6; see also Moynihan, 1967).

If we consider the Moynihan Report's findings, several matters arise. First, since the report was produced, has US society moved towards smaller inequalities in terms of deprivation, opportunities, income and wealth, or have these inequalities increased? As Donnison's (1998) data on UK poverty indicate, increased prosperity at the national level does not necessarily result in reduced poverty.

Second, how should we interpret findings of this sort? Given that poverty is frequently associated with the type of behaviour that contravenes prevailing moral codes, such as criminal activity or truanting from school, the question is how we should view behaviour of this kind in black communities. Do we merely label it 'anti-social' or do we attempt to consider ' … the *linkages* between the behaviour we can observe and the more distant and less visible social forces that are ultimately responsible for the production of the ghetto and its notorious ills' (Steinberg, 1999, p.5; emphasis in original)?

Though it was not widely employed when Moynihan's report was written, a concept that would now often be used to describe the 'bleak picture' that it

underclass

provides of black families and communities in the USA is that of an **underclass**, a concept which focuses on the alleged breakdown of family life and the form that this may take and which has assumed considerable salience in debates about welfare.

READING 6.2

You should now read Reading 6.2, 'The underclass: a case of colour blindness, right and left'. When you have done so, try to answer the following questions:

1   Why is it helpful to distinguish between those who use 'underclass' to refer to structures of poverty and joblessness, and those who use the term to refer to socially dysfunctional behaviour of the poor? What seem to be the policy implications of adopting the first approach rather than the second?

2   Why is it important to distinguish between, on the one hand, saying that socially dysfunctional behaviour explains why a group is in the underclass and, on the other hand, saying that being in the underclass explains socially dysfunctional behaviour? What implications might this difference in emphasis have for formulating effective policies to achieve social justice?

3   How would you summarize the argument that the main problems faced by the black lower classes were essentially 'colour-blind' rather than 'race-specific'? What implications does this 'colour-blind' position have for formulating policies to tackle inequality and promote social justice? And what criticisms may be made of this position?

4   Why, according to Steinberg, were social scientists willing to accept a view of the job crisis afflicting blacks that, in his contention, was so clearly flawed?

5   What remedies are suggested for tackling racial discrimination in the US labour market?

If we apply the questions that McCrudden *et al.* posed about the position of racial and ethnic minorities in Britain – namely: what was their position and why were they in that position? What would the 'good' or the 'just' society look like as far as these minorities were concerned? And, by what policy means could we move from present inequity to future social justice (McCrudden *et al.*, 1991, p.2)? – to the US context discussed by Steinberg, various things become apparent. First, if we look at the extent of black inequality in the modern United States we might begin by referring to the racial inequalities of the past, notably slavery and segregation. On the other hand, if we follow Steinberg's approach, it would be unwise in the extreme to ignore the scale and effect of modern racially-based inequalities and injustices.

The extent of present-day poverty among US blacks might be gauged by referring to the statistic that they account for 12 per cent of the population, but 29 per cent of those defined as living below the poverty line. In fact, the situation is even more acute than this, for at the beginning of 1990s nearly half of all black children under eighteen years of age were being raised in families below the poverty line (as against 16 per cent of white children) (*Statistical Abstracts of the United States*, 1994, p.475; cited in Steinberg, 1999, p.212). Steinberg also mentions a recent study, covering 95 US cities, in which blacks accounted for 58 per cent of those classified as 'severely distressed', a condition defined in terms of low education, single parenthood, poor work history, poverty, and being a recipient of welfare (Kasarda, 1992, pp.49–54; cited in Steinberg, 1999, p.213).

In trying to decide what path to take if inequality on this scale is to be remedied, Steinberg's comment on public discussion of black poverty is highly significant. He argues that this discussion gives the impression that poverty and unemployment among blacks is not merely a black problem in the sense that it impacts disproportionately on blacks, which it manifestly does. In Steinberg's view, public discussion characterizes black poverty as a problem for which black people are *themselves* to blame. In this discussion reference to 'race' or 'racism', though it is not explicit, is conveyed clearly enough in coded language about such contentious issues as the cost to the taxpayer of welfare programmes (Steinberg, 1999, p.212).

In other words, striking as the statistics on black poverty are, they do not speak for themselves. If, therefore, we want to formulate policies to take us from a situation where the incidence of poverty is racially disproportionate, towards a more equal or socially just situation, we need to ask what it is these statistics mean. This raises again the question posed as a matter of principle in respect of Reading 6.1, namely, how might the pursuit of individual interest in the market be reconciled with the goals of redistribution and the alleviation of poverty? In practice, this question is extremely delicate and

Figure 6.7 *A game of dominoes on the sidewalk in New York across from a building that was once the neighbourhood centre for drug trafficking. The Department of Housing Preservation and Development worked with community groups and tenants to drive drug-dealers out of more than 2000 HPD-owned buildings through the 1990s*

we might say that in these circumstances social justice is very much in the eye of the beholder: if black poverty is seen as the consequence of continuing discrimination then the remedy is likely to be to tackle the discrimination. If, on the other hand, black poverty is seen as the consequence of the way an underclass *chooses* to behave – as if it has a tendency to reproduce itself or as if it is a product of the 'black family' rather than of racist structures – then the remedy will be very different.

There are even deeper issues at stake here, however. It has been argued that the inferior position of black people in the United States makes a significant contribution to the perpetuation of prejudice against black communities and the portrait of a black underclass manifesting self-destructive behaviour can be used to illustrate this cycle of cause and effect. Yet if beliefs alone were capable of subjugating a group or people, then the beliefs of a disadvantaged group about an advantaged group would be as effective as those of a privileged group about a disadvantaged group. For this reason, it is insufficient to identify prejudice as a force disembodied from power and social structure; what is also required is to locate the structural basis of prejudice and to understand the ways in which racial beliefs are incorporated in structures of power.

SUMMARY OF SECTION 6

1   The experiences of immigrants and minority ethnic groups illuminated vital aspects of social justice, not least in the way they regarded their own position and in the way they were regarded by others.

2   In their case, what is termed 'discrimination within the market' was superimposed on prior inequalities.

3   The recognition of the inequality faced by minority ethnic groups and attempts to improve their position by direct legislation and through education and other policy initiatives can be seen as central to debates about social justice and what is to be understood by a 'just society'.

4   Initiatives to improve or ameliorate the position of minority ethnic groups or 'racial' minorities can raise controversial issues concerning the differential experience of different groups.

5   There are significant differences in the way the condition of the least-advantaged in society has been interpreted – some approaches stress structures of poverty, while others stress socially dysfunctional behaviour – and these differences suggest different remedies and different views of social justice.

7 Conclusion

This chapter has explored the concept of social justice – and in particular issues of distributive justice – in the context of social divisions, differences and inequalities. This involved considering views about the nature and extent of disadvantage, the situation of different disadvantaged groups and the appropriate means of remedying such disadvantage.

This exploration has encompassed a number of elements. The salience of 'social justice' both in political and policy debate and in sociological and philosophical discussion was established. The complexity of 'social justice' was underlined by citing some of the concepts often associated with it, such as need, merit and equal opportunity – and by citing some of the factors that are held to impede its realization, such as discrimination before the market. This led on to the question of how best to improve the condition of the least well-off in society and was done primarily by considering the present condition and future prospects of minority ethnic groups and those of immigrant origin in the UK and the US in terms of specific policies and general opportunities. Thus, for example, attention was given to bussing groups of pupils from impoverished environments to more affluent locations and to the role that education might play in providing access to more desirable occupations. The final question that was looked at was how society might regard the nature and extent of the discrimination and disadvantage that such groups face and how the position of disadvantaged groups might then be ameliorated. In this context attention was drawn to contrasting views about the willingness or ability of disadvantaged groups – sometimes termed an 'underclass' – to help themselves, and to the implications that these different views might have for overcoming disadvantages that without intervention might be passed from one generation to the next.

References

Abercrombie, N., Hill, S. and Turner, B.S. (2000) *The Penguin Dictionary of Sociology* (4th edn), Harmondsworth, Penguin Books.

Allen, S., Bentley, S. and Bornat, J. (1977) *Work, Race and Immigration*, Bradford, University of Bradford School of Studies in Social Sciences.

Barry, B. (1989) *Theories of Justice*, London, Harvester-Wheatsheaf.Bell, D. (1994) 'Justice and the law' in Scherer, K. (ed.) *Justice: Interdisciplinary Perspectives*, Cambridge, Cambridge University Press.

Blackburn, R. and Mann, N. (1979) *The Working Class and the Labour Market*, Basingstoke, Macmillan.

Böhning, W. (1981) 'The self-feeding process of economic migration from low-wage to post-industrial countries with a liberal-capitalist structure' in Braham, P., Rhodes, E. and Pearn, M. (eds) *Discrimination and Disadvantage in Employment: The Experience of Black Workers*, London, Harper and Row.

Brown, C. (1984) *Black and White Britain: The Third PSI Survey*, London, Heinemann/Gower.

Brown, C. (1992) 'Same difference: the persistence of racial disadvantage in the British labour market' in Braham, P., Rattansi, A. and Skellington, R. (eds) *Racism and Antiracism: Inequalities, Opportunities and Policies*, London, Sage.

Brown, C. and Gay, P. (1985) *Racial Discrimination: 17 Years After the Act*, London, Policy Studies Institute.

Bryson, B. (1998) *Notes From a Big Country*, London, Black Swan.

Carter, J., Fenton, S. and Modood, T. (1999) *Ethnicity and Employment in Higher Education*, PSI Report no.865, London, Policy Studies Institute.

Coleman, J. (1990) *Equality and Achievement in Education*, Boulder, CO, Westview Press.

CRE (1987a) *Formal Investigation: Chartered Accountancy Training Contracts*, London, Commission for Racial Equality.

CRE (1987b) *Employment of Graduates from Ethnic Minorities: A Research Report*, London, Commission for Racial Equality.

CSJ (Commission on Social Justice) (1998a) 'What is social justice?' in Franklin, J. (ed.) (1998b) *op. cit.*.

CSJ (Commission on Social Justice) (1998b) 'The UK in a changing world' in Franklin, J. (ed.) (1998b) *op. cit.*.

Department for Education and Employment (1997) *Excellence in Schools*, Cmnd 3681, London, The Stationery Office.

Donnison, D. (1998) *Policies for a Just Society*, Basingstoke, Macmillan.

Durkheim, E. (1959) *Socialism and Saint-Simon*, quoted in Runciman, W. (1966) *op. cit.*.

Esmail, A. and Everington, S. (1993) 'Racial discrimination against doctors from ethnic minorities', *British Medical Journal*, no.306, pp.691–2.

Franklin, J. (1998a) 'Introduction' in Franklin, J. (ed.) (1998b) *op. cit.*.

Franklin, J. (ed.) (1998b) *Social Policy and Social Justice: The IPPR Reader*, Cambridge, Polity Press.

Fröbel, F., Heinrichs, J. and Kreye, O. (1980) *The New International Division of Labour*, Cambridge, Cambridge University Press.

Giddens, A. (1973) *The Class Structure of the Advanced Societies*, London, Hutchinson.

Girod, R (1965) 'Foreign workers and social mobility in Switzerland', Address to the Symposium on Migration for Employment in Europe, Geneva, 12–15 October (mimeograph).

Hayek, F. (1986) 'Economic freedom and representative government' in Donald, J. and Hall, S. (eds) *Politics and Ideology*, Milton Keynes, The Open University Press.

Jencks, C. *et al.* (1973) *Inequality: A Reassessment of the Effect of Family and Schooling in America*, London, Allen Lane.

Kasarda, J. (1992) 'The severely distressed in economically transforming cities' in Harrell, A. and Petersen, G. (eds) *Drugs, Crime and Social Isolation*, Washington, DC, The Urban Institute press.

Kirp, D. (1982) *Just Schools*, Berkeley, CA, University of California Press.

McCrudden, C., Smith, D., and Brown, C. (1991) *Racial Justice at Work: Enforcement of the 1976 Race Relations Act*, London, Policy Studies Institute.

McKeigue, P.M., Richards, J.D. and Richards, P. (1990) 'Effects of discrimination by sex and race on the early careers of medical graduates during 1981–7', *British Medical Journal*, no.301, pp.961–4.

Megarry, R. (1955) *Miscellany-at-Law*.

Modood, T. (1998) 'Racial equality: colour, culture and justice' in Franklin, J. (ed.) *op. cit.*.

Moynihan, D. (1967) 'The Negro family: the case for national action' in Rainwater, L. and Yancey, W. (eds) *The Moynihan Report and the Politics of Controversy*, Cambridge, MA, MIT Press.

Offe, C. (1976) *Industry and Inequality*, London, Edward Arnold.

Pavlich, G. (1996) *Justice Fragmented: Mediating Community Disputes Under Postmodern Conditions*, London, Routledge.

Phelps-Brown, H. (1977) *The Inequality of Pay*, London, Oxford University Press.

Rawls, J. (1971) *A Theory of Justice*, Cambridge, MA, Harvard University Press.

Runciman, W.G. (1966) *Relative Deprivation and Social Justice*, London, Routledge and Kegan Paul.

Smith, D. (1977) *Racial Disadvantage in Britain (The PEP Report)*, Harmondsworth, Penguin Books.

Statistical Abstracts of the United States (1994) Washington, DC, Government Printing Office.

Steinberg, S. (1999) *Turning Back: The Retreat from Racial Justice in American Thought and Policy*, Boston, MA, Beacon Press.

Stouffer, S. *et al.* (1949) *The American Soldier, I: Adjustment During Army Life*, Princeton, NJ, Princeton University Press.

Readings

 ## Brian Barry, 'Economic motivation in a Rawlsian society' (1989)

In *A Theory of Justice* Rawls himself introduces the topic of economic motivation by asking why the people who are in the original position should be prepared to consider a move from an equal distribution of income to an unequal one. The answer he offers is as follows:

> If there are inequalities in the basic structure that work to make everyone better off in comparison with the benchmark of initial equality, why not permit them? ... If, for example, these inequalities set up various incentives which succeed in eliciting more productive efforts, a person in the original position may look upon them as necessary to cover the costs of training and to encourage effective performance.
>
> (Rawls, 1971, p.151)

Rawls then goes on to address himself to the possible objection that material incentives should not be necessary in a society whose members are committed to justice.

> One might think that ideally individuals should want to serve one another. But since the parties are assumed not to take an interest in one another's interests, their acceptance of these inequalities is only the acceptance of the relations in which men stand in the circumstances of justice. They have no grounds for complaining of one another's motives. A person in the original position would, therefore, concede the justice of these inequalities.
>
> (Rawls, 1971, p.151)

...

... Rawls does not posit a single kind of motivation in a just society. Most institutions require that people internalize norms of justice that require them sometimes to act in a way contrary to their interests. When it comes to economic institutions, however, we get a division of motivation. The institutions themselves (for example, the tax and transfer system) are to be created with the conscious objective of realizing the principles of justice. But the people who are to act within these institutions will, it is assumed, pursue self-interest.

Now, it may be said at once that Rawls is by no means peculiar in this regard. On the contrary, his outlook is quite characteristic of those who support a market system (whether capitalist or socialist or with some mix of public and private ownership) plus a system of taxes and benefits designed to provide a 'safety net' or to increase equality as an end in itself. Thus, James Meade, who clearly functions as something of an economic guru for Rawls in *A Theory of Justice*, wrote the following two years later, in 1973: 'In my view the ideal society would be one in which each citizen developed a real split personality, acting selfishly in the market place and altruistically at the ballot box. [... I]t is, for example, only by such "altruistic" political action that there can be any alleviation of "poverty" in a society in which the poor are in a minority' (Meade, 1973, p.52).

It was suggested by Thomas Grey in a percipient review of Rawls's book that the schizophrenia attributed to people in a Rawlsian society – making whatever money they can get in the market and then voting for a government pledged to instantiate the difference principle – is reflected in the real world by the fact that 'the concept of income redistribution as such has found no strong political favor in any country whose economy is based largely on a market system' (Grey, 1973, p.324). This is, I think, too sweeping a statement, given the degree of support for avowedly egalitarian ends found in market societies such as Norway and Sweden. But even there the strains are apparent and it does seem plausible to suggest that the rise of anti-tax movements in a number of countries in recent years may well have something to do with a conflict between the spirit of individual self-interest fostered by the market and the spirit of collective responsibility for the worst off that is required to maintain support for redistributive programs.

It is important here to distinguish between two claims. One is that there is as a matter of fact a psychological difficulty in switching from self-interested bargaining in the market to the pursuit of equality (or maximizing the minimum) in the voting booth. This seems undeniable. The stronger claim, which Grey also wants to make, is that there is also a moral inconsistency in that the principled rationale for the market determination of incomes is incompatible with the principled rationale for redistribution.

Grey's idea here is that there are two conflicting notions, one of which underwrites equality, the other an entitlement to whatever one makes on the market. On the socialist view, 'bargaining for extra income on the basis of superior productive capacity' is 'a species of extortion.' 'This approach implies a social duty to work, and to work to one's full capacity, without bargaining for extra income in exchange.' The upshot would be 'an equal division of the social product,' which would be compatible with maximum production 'since everyone would work to the limit of his ability without regard to pay' (Grey, 1973, p.323). The second view is 'the free market principle' that 'the person of superior productive capacity is justified in extracting in return for his labors what the market will bear. Under proper market conditions his return will equal his marginal contribution to society' (*ibid.*).

That these two views are inconsistent seems patent. But is it really true that they are the only ones in the field? Grey apparently thinks so, and hence regards Rawls's difference principle as an unconvincing attempt to mediate between them. 'Rawls's attempt to describe the bare bones of an ideal market redistributist state based on moral principles may show the internal inconsistency of the ideal even more clearly than our own frustrating political experience' (*ibid.*, p.325).

Fairly obviously, as a sheer matter of exegesis, one could scarcely attribute either of the alternative positions to Rawls, since he does not put forward the notion of a moral duty to work at maximum capacity without thought of reward and he does not accept any notion of an entitlement to one's market earnings. But what Grey apparently believes is that there is no way of backing differential earnings without the market principle and no way of backing redistribution without the socialist moral outlook.

'How can I justly bargain for more than an equal share by threatening to withhold my scarce talents? It must be because I have some special claim on these talents and their fruits. But if they are considered a social asset – as Rawls apparently regards them – I can have no such special claim. On the other hand, if my talents and the fruits of the use I choose to make of them belong to me, then there can be no justified coercion of me if I do not choose to share them with others' (*ibid.*).

… The claim of inconsistency can be expressed in the following way. On the one hand, when he is seeking to establish equality as the baseline from which departures have to be justified, Rawls relies on the premise that whatever makes people more or less capable of producing is morally arbitrary. On the other hand, in the course of making his move from equality to the difference principle he makes use of the premise that people in a just society will respond to material incentives. But the implication of any system of material incentives is that those who produce more will finish up with more. The charge is that, if it is accepted that productive advantages are unjust, there should be no need for material incentives. For the members of a just society should be motivated by thoughts of the injustice of inequality to work loyally in pursuit of the goal of maximum income equally distributed.

Reasoning along these lines, Jan Narveson (1976, 1978) has devoted a couple of articles to the proposition … that Rawls faces a dilemma. If the first principle, which establishes the basic liberties, includes economic liberty in some full-bodied sense, then there is no room for the difference principle, for in that case people are entitled to what they make in the market. If, alternatively, there is to be a duty to work without reward in order to make the worst off as well off as possible, then again there is no room for the difference principle, for in that case there is no reason for admitting any departure from equal distribution.

So far, Narveson's claim amounts to the same as Grey's: the only internally consistent theories of distribution are the free-market one of entitlement to what one makes and the socialist one of a duty to contribute to social wealth. Narveson goes on to say (surely undeniably) that Rawls plainly does not intend to attribute to everyone a right to the full value of his own product. If he is correct in asserting that there is no middle way between the horns of the dilemma that he seeks to foist on Rawls, Narveson can obviously conclude from this that (in spite of any appearances to the contrary) Rawls must adhere to the second position: that in a truly just society there would be no room for inequality. 'The motives of justice would always direct one to sharing equally with one's fellows' (Narveson, 1978, p.287). So saying that incentives will be needed to get people to produce the optimal amount is simply admitting that they will be actuated not by justice but by greed (*ibid.*, pp.287–9).

This of course means sweeping away Rawls's stipulation that people are not to complain about one another's motives in the economic sphere. The question, Narveson says, is precisely whether or not self-interested motivation should be '"accepted" in the sense that it is allowed as a reason for justifying differentials in social reward' (1976, p.15). It should not be so allowed on Rawls's premises, according to Narveson:

> If it is the case that socially distributable goods ought to be distributed equally unless an unequal distribution is required to improve the prospects of the worst off, and if we all have the option, if we so choose, of sharing equally with others, then does it not follow that if we don't take this option, we are being *unjust*. For in effect, my claim that I 'need' more as an 'incentive' is just a misleading way of saying that I *want* more and that I'm not willing to do as much if I don't get it.
>
> (Narveson, 1976, p.12)

One possible answer that might be given (as Narveson admits) is that, ideally, a just distribution would be an equal one, but that unfortunately we cannot count on people to work at their best without material incentives. …

…

Now, it would of course be quite in accord with this view of incentives as a necessary evil to reintroduce the difference principle as a principle of *relative* justice. We could say: once we abandon ideal justice, we still want to distinguish between more or less just departures from equality. The difference principle can then reasonably be interpreted as the least obnoxious concession to the necessity of incentives. For, although it licenses greed, it at least insists that greed should be harnessed to the improvement of the position of the worst off.

We must be clear that this is not the line Rawls takes. It is true, as I have already noted, that he considers an 'ideal' possibility that people would not require incentives, but the state of affairs he has in mind there is one in which justice would not be necessary because people would work for the common good spontaneously (Mills, 1965, p.210). He does not ever suggest that ideal *justice* would require people to work for the common good.

Again, it is true that Rawls makes use of the notion of the 'strains of commitment' in *A Theory of Justice* (1971, pp.176–8). This is the idea that people who are choosing principles of justice should check to see if some set of principles in other respects attractive is liable to issue in calls on people to make extraordinary sacrifices. Prudence should, Rawls argues, lead to the rejection of principles that may be too hard to live up to. The 'strains of commitment' are deployed as an argument against the principle of maximizing aggregate utility. It is, Rawls says, asking too much of people to expect them to put up with hardship for themselves merely in order to confer somewhat greater benefits on people who are already very well off.

The only alternative to the utilitarian principle considered in this context is the two principles of justice. Rawls argues that these can be lived with by everyone because the worst-off position will be acceptable and 'a fortiori everyone would find the other positions acceptable' (1974, p.653). There is no suggestion here that what is required by strict justice has to be modified to take account of the problems posed by the strains of commitment. Rather, the difference principle, with its attendant inequalities, *is* the principle of ideal justice.

… We would simply say that these inequalities are not ideally just, but that, once we concede the need for incentives, inequalities permitted by the difference principle are the only defensible ones. However, we must be clear that this argument is not Rawls's. Our question now must be whether Rawls can consistently defend the difference principle not as a second best but as what justice really demands.

References

Grey, T.C. (1973) 'The first virtue', *Stanford Law Review*, vol.25, pp.286–327.

Meade, J.E. (1973) *Theory of Economic Externalities: The Control of Environmental Pollution and Similar Social Costs*, Leiden, Sijthoff.

Mills, J.S. (1965) *Collected Works of John Stuart Mill*, vol.2 (ed. J.M. Robson), Toronto, University of Toronto Press.

Narveson, J.F. (1976) 'A puzzle about economic justice in Rawls' theory', *Social Theory and Practice*, vol.4, pp.1–27.

Narveson, J.F. (1978) 'Rawls on equal distribution of wealth', *Philosophia*, vol.7, pp.281–92.

Rawls, J. (1971) *A Theory of Justice*, Cambridge, MA, Harvard University Press.

Rawls, J. (1974) 'Reply to Alexander and Musgrave', *Quarterly Journal of Economics,* vol.88, pp.633–55.

Source: Barry, 1989, pp.393,394–398

6.2   Stephen Steinberg, 'The underclass: a case of color blindness, right and left' (1999)

In the 1980s poverty acquired a new 'voguish stigma' (McGahey, 1982). The term 'underclass' was added to the English language's expanding lexicon of inequality. The term actually originated with Gunnar Myrdal, who borrowed an old Swedish term for the lower class, *underklassen* (Jackson, 1990, p.2). In *Challenge to Affluence*, written in 1962, Myrdal used the term to refer to groups that did not share in the nation's affluence. They were a 'permanent underclass,' which is to say that they languished in poverty even during periods of economic growth and declining unemployment (Myrdal, 1962, p.53). Ken Auletta rescued the term from academic obscurity in 1982 with the publication of *The Underclass*. Suddenly the underclass was a hot topic, the subject of articles in US *News and World Report, The Atlantic, Fortune, Newsweek, Reader's Digest,* and *Time*.[1] By 1988 the term entered the political discourse of the presidential election, as candidates were queried about their policies for dealing with the underclass. ...

Once again, social science lagged behind journalism. In due course, however, the academic wheel was lubricated with foundation grants to measure the size, location, racial makeup, and other germane characteristics of the underclass. Dozens of studies were conducted, and, according to a summary report issued by the Social Science Research Council in 1988, estimates of the size of the underclass ranged from 2 to 8 million people (Gephart and Pearson, 1988, p.4). One widely cited study by Ricketts and Sawhill defined an 'underclass area' as a census tract with a high proportion of high school dropouts; young males outside the labor force; welfare recipients; and female-headed households. On the basis of these criteria, Ricketts and Sawhill estimated that 2.5 million people live in these underclass areas, most of which are in cities. Fifty-nine per cent of their residents are black and 10 per cent are Hispanic (Ricketts and Sawhill, 1988, pp.321–2).

As social researchers scurried about measuring the underclass, the term underwent a conceptual transformation. Myrdal had used 'underclass' to define an objective condition – one that was rooted in the class system and labor market processes, and that manifested itself in the existence of a group so removed from the regular economy that it was unaffected even by surges in the economy, defying the maxim that a rising tide lifts all boats. This idea had a crucially important implication for social policy: it suggested that macroeconomic policies to stimulate

growth and jobs would *not* reach the underclass. In other words, special programs and policies targeted for this castaway population would be necessary.

Once again, however, methodological individualism played havoc with the sociological imagination, reducing a concept that pertained to social structure down to the level of individual behavior. Thus, in the hands of the empiricists the underclass was redefined to refer, not to objective conditions of chronic poverty and joblessness, but to the socially dysfunctional behavior of the poor themselves. In summing up the prevailing view, Ricketts and Sawhill write: 'most observers agree that the underclass is characterized by *behaviors which are at variance with those of mainstream America* (such as joblessness, welfare dependency, unwed parenting, criminal or uncivil behavior, and dropping out of high school)' (1988, p.317; emphasis added).

Although these empirical studies have all the trappings of objective social science, they are riddled with unexamined value assumptions. The class system itself is accepted as a given – an empirical if not normative fact of life. Thus, attention is shifted away from the structures of inequality that produce an underclass, to the attributes of the individuals who inhabit this lowly stratum. Hence, the individual becomes the focal point of change as well. The presumption is that we can eliminate the underclass by rehabilitating its victims.[2]

A still more serious flaw in the concept of the underclass is the conflation of race, class, and culture. The result is a conceptual muddle that obscures the distinctive roles of race, class, and culture in producing the underclass, the explanatory weight that is to be assigned to each, and the dynamic relationships that exist among them. ...

The conflation of race, class, and culture has left the theoretical door open for different theorists to single out whichever factor serves their ideological position. For 'the color-blind right', *culture* is the key factor in explaining the underclass. For 'the color-blind left,' it is *class* – which is to say, the economic factors that keep people trapped in poverty. What these positions have in common is a neglect of *race* – that is, the specifically racist structures that keep racial minorities trapped in poverty.

Like 'underclass,' the term 'race' lumps together groups that are disparate from one another, not only in terms of their historical origins but even in terms of the extent to which they encounter racist barriers to mobility. This sloppy conceptualization has led to specious comparisons between various 'racial' minorities. ... The reification of 'race' has not only blurred these crucial distinctions, but has also had an adverse impact on social policy. Because eligibility for affirmative action generally has been defined in terms of 'historical disadvantage,' rather than in terms of specific injustices visited upon specific minorities, groups with very different historical and moral claims have crowded under the meager umbrella of affirmative action.

In point of fact, there are different underclasses – different in their origins, their social constitution, their circumstances, and their implications for the society at large. To lump these disparate groups together on the basis of common demographic traits is to obscure the historically specific factors that produced these various underclasses, and in particular, the role that racism has played in the production and reproduction of the *black* underclass.

The underclass as culture

... [M]ost studies of the underclass assume aberrant culture and anti-social behavior in the definition of the underclass, thus obscuring cause and effect. The issue here is not whether there is an underclass, or whether its members engage in 'socially dysfunctional behavior.' Rather, the issue is whether their behavior *explains why* they are in the underclass, or, conversely, whether these individuals first find themselves in the underclass (typically as a matter of birth) and only then develop 'socially dysfunctional behavior.' Also at issue is whether this behavior, while clearly dysfunctional for the society at large, is nonetheless functional for the actors themselves, given their restricted life-chances. As Douglas Glasgow wrote in his book *The Black Underclass:*

> Behaviors of younger inner-city Blacks ... are consciously propagated via special socialization rituals that help the young Blacks prepare for inequality at an early age. With maturity, these models of behavior are employed to neutralize the personally destructive effects of institutionalized racism. Thus, they form the basis of a 'survival culture' that is significantly different from the so-called culture of poverty. Notwithstanding its reactive origin, survival culture is not a passive adaptation to encapsulation but a very active – at times devious, innovative, and extremely resistive – response to

> rejection and destruction. It is useful and necessary to young Blacks in their present situation.
>
> (Glasgow, 1981, p.25)

In contrast to Glasgow's careful delineation of the existential sources and functions of cultural patterns associated with the underclass, note how cause and effect are obscured in the following passage from a 1987 article by Myron Magnet in *Fortune* magazine.

> They are poor; but numbering around five million, they are a relatively small minority of the 33 million Americans with incomes below the official poverty line. Disproportionately black and Hispanic, they are still a minority within these minorities. What primarily defines them is not so much their poverty or race as their behavior – their chronic lawlessness, drug use, out-of-wedlock births, non-work, welfare dependency, and school failure. *'Underclass' describes a state of mind and a way of life. It is at least as much cultural as an economic condition.*
>
> (Magnet, 1987, p.130; emphasis added)

In this treatment of the underclass as 'a state of mind and a way of life,' we have a clear retrogression to the culture-of-poverty school of the 1960s, which was itself a retrogression to the cultural deprivation school of the 1950s. The common element is a presumption that the culture of the poor is different from that of middle-class society, and that it is this aberrant culture that keeps the poor trapped in poverty. ...

...

The class interpretation of the underclass

If some observers of the underclass give theoretical primacy to culture, others give theoretical primacy to class. Ever since the publication of *The Declining Significance of Race* in 1978, William Julius Wilson has been in the forefront of those who see the underclass as a by-product of economic dislocations that have transformed the urban economy, wiping out millions of jobs in the industrial sector (Wilson, 1978, 1987). These dislocations, which are themselves the product of larger transformations in the global economy, have had an especially severe effect on blacks since they are concentrated in cities and job sectors most impacted by deindustrialization. According to Wilson, blacks migrating to Northern cities not only encountered a shrinking industrial sector, but they lacked the education and skills to compete for jobs in the expanding service sector. For Wilson, this explains why conditions have deteriorated for the black lower classes during the post-civil rights era, a period of relative tolerance that has witnessed the rise of a large and prosperous black middle class.

Furthermore, Wilson sees this endemic unemployment and underemployment as the root cause of the 'tangle of pathologies' associated with the underclass. Wilson's agenda for change is consistent with his analysis. Because the causes are not race-specific – that is, based on patterns of deliberate racial exclusion – neither can the remedy be race-specific. Thus, in *The Truly Disadvantaged* Wilson proposes 'a universal program of reform' that would attack unemployment and underemployment (Wilson, 1987, Ch.7). Essentially, Wilson's agenda involves a renewal and expansion of the forgotten War on Poverty. Thus, Wilson calls for a macroeconomic policy to promote growth and generate jobs, and improved welfare and social services, including job training, for those who need it.[3]

Over against the culture-of-poverty theorists, Wilson is mindful of the link between culture and social structure. He traces underclass culture primarily to the job crisis that afflicts ghetto workers, particularly males, destroying the basis for stable families and engendering various coping strategies that affront middle-class society. ...

There can be no doubt that deindustrialization has exacerbated the job crisis for working-class blacks. ...

Nevertheless, there is reason to think that Wilson places far too much explanatory weight on deindustrialization as the reason for the job crisis that afflicts black America. As Norman Fainstein has argued in a paper on 'The underclass/mismatch hypothesis as an explanation for black economic deprivation', blacks were never heavily represented in the industrial sector in the first place. ... Fainstein concluded that 'the economic situation of blacks is rooted more in the character of the employment opportunities in growing industries than in the disappearance of "entry-level" jobs in declining industries' (Fainstein, 1986–87, p.439; Waldinger, 1986–87, pp.379–80; see also Stafford, 1985).[4]

...

... [T]he entire thrust of Wilson's analysis is to interpret the growing black underclass as the hapless victims of color-blind economic forces. What role, if any, does racism play? Wilson grants that *past* racism

has left lower-class blacks vulnerable to the economic dislocations of a postindustrial economy, but, consistent with his thesis in *The Declining Significance of Race*, he does not see contemporaneous racism as a major factor in its own right.[5] ... [H]e presents no direct evidence to show that blacks do not encounter racism in job markets. Rather, he *infers* this on the basis of an improved climate of tolerance generally, together with the unprecedented success of the black middle class.

Given the meager empirical foundation on which Wilson's conclusions are based, it is astonishing how widely they have been embraced by social scientists who usually insist upon higher standards of empirical proof. Not only are his major propositions unsubstantiated, but they rest on assumptions that are implausible if not patently false. Specifically:

1   Wilson assumes that if not for the collapse of the manufacturing sector, blacks would have found their way into these jobs. But there is nothing in history to support this assumption since, as we have seen, the entire thrust of Northern racism has been to exclude blacks from blue-collar jobs in core industries. ... The lesson of history is that blacks have gained access to manufacturing only as a last resort – when all other sources of labor have dried up. Now we are asked to believe that blacks would have finally gotten their turn, except that the jobs themselves have disappeared.

2   Wilson assumes that an expansive economy will translate into jobs and opportunities for 'the truly disadvantaged.' Yet his faith in macroeconomic policy has not been sustained by subsequent events. As was noted in a recent story in the *New York Times*, 'even during the robust economic recovery of the late 1980s when the white unemployment rate was – as it is now – under 5 per cent, black unemployment never dipped below 10 per cent, and sometimes topped 12 per cent' (Holmes, 1995, p.A12).[6] ... In point of fact, these economic trends lend credence to Myrdal's concept of the underclass as unaffected by increased prosperity and declining unemployment.

Yet Wilson has not wavered in his faith in universal as opposed to race-specific public policy. At a 1993 symposium at the University of Michigan, he reported the results of recent research in ghetto neighborhoods where the majority of adults are unemployed or have dropped out of the labor force, construing this as evidence of a 'new urban poverty.' Citing the 'resistance to targeted programs for the truly disadvantaged,' he called for policies that 'address concerns beyond those that focus on ... inner-city ghettos' (Wilson, 1994, p.266). Roger Wilkins promptly responded that 'the new American poverty has to be viewed as part of the old American racism,' insisting that 'if we don't face the fact that we have done unique and severe damage to poor blacks, then we will construct broad-based social policy programs where the money will roll away from the poor as it always does. When we had model cities programs for the poor we ended up building golf courses and parks in suburbs. That is the way it works when money is not targeted' (Wilkins, 1994, pp.282,287).[7]

...

3   Wilson assumes that affirmative action has primarily helped the black middle class. As he writes: 'Programs of preferential treatment applied merely according to racial or ethnic group membership tend to benefit the relatively advantaged segments of the designated groups. The truly deprived members may not be helped by such programs' (Wilson, 1994, p.115).[8] Wilson has been widely cited by white liberals to legitimate their own retreat from affirmative action even though he provides no direct evidence to substantiate his claim that affirmative action has primarily been of benefit to the black middle class. Presumably Wilson has in mind affirmative action programs in higher education and the professions that obviously do not reach blacks who are 'truly deprived.' However, as William Taylor has written in the *Yale Law Journal*: 'the focus of much of the effort has been not just on white collar jobs, but also on law enforcement, construction work, and craft and production jobs in large companies – all areas in which the extension of new opportunities has provided upward mobility for less advantaged minority workers' (Taylor, 1986, p.1714).[9] ...

4   Wilson assumes that the principal reason blacks have not been absorbed into the expanding service industries is that they lack the requisite education and skills. As he writes:

> Basic structural changes in our modern industrial economy have compounded the problems of poor blacks because education and training have become more important for entry into the more desirable and higher-paying jobs and because increased reliance on labor-saving devices has contributed to a surplus of untrained black workers.
>
> (Wilson, 1987, p.126)

Here Wilson falls into the familiar trap of assuming that the postindustrial economy is based primarily on an educated and skilled work force. While this holds true for some jobs in a few fast-growing areas of technology, most jobs in the service sector are notable for *not* requiring much education and skills. According to a recent study by the Bureau of Labor Statistics, the following ten occupations account for the largest percentage of projected job growth between 1990 and 2005: retail salespersons, registered nurses, cashiers, office clerks, truck drivers, general managers, janitors and cleaners, nursing aides, food counter workers, and waiters and waitresses (US Department of Labor, 1992). Only two of these – registered nurses and general managers – require a college degree. Other studies show that blacks with a high school degree have a far higher rate of unemployment than whites who have not graduated from high school (for example, Kasarda, 1985, p.57). Given these facts, it makes little sense to blame the scandalously high rate of black unemployment on deficiencies in education and skills.

... Wilson has advanced a class analysis that totally subsumes race to class. The chief problem with this approach is that it obscures the role that racism plays in the production and reproduction of the black underclass.

Racism and the black underclass

...

... Wilson would have us believe that 'if only' blacks had the requisite education and skills, they would encounter few obstacles on the road to success. But this view is predicated on a blanket denial of complex ways that racism prevents blacks from acquiring the requisite education and skills, as well as the persistence of old-fashioned racism that affects even blacks who *have* education and skills. Totally absent from Wilson's analysis of black unemployment is any consideration of racism in occupations and labor markets.

The fault does not lie with Wilson alone. Given the vast literature on racism, one might suppose that there are countless studies on employment discrimination. This is not the case. As the authors of a recent volume assessing the status of blacks in American society observed: 'The extent of discrimination against blacks in the workplace has apparently not been extensively investigated by direct tests similar in design to the audits of residential housing markets' (Jaynes and Williams, 1989, p.146).[10]

...

...

The evidence of widespread employment discrimination against blacks is so overwhelming that even Wilson has recently shifted his position. At least this is what can be garnered from a feature story on

Wilson by Gretchen Reynolds in *Chicago* magazine (Reynolds, 1992, p.81ff). According to Reynolds, Wilson has recently 'rediscovered racism.' With grants lavished on him after the publication of two books that downplayed racism, Wilson and his students have undertaken a series of surveys and ethnographic studies of poor neighborhoods in Chicago. They also interrogated employers about hiring minorities. What they found is that employers do in fact make race central to their hiring decisions, and that, generally speaking, they are predisposed against hiring blacks.[11] Reynolds quotes Wilson as now admitting that 'racism is far more important than I once believed' (Reynolds, 1992, p.128).

This would be a most welcome revision on the part of Wilson, who seems to have convinced the entire Western world (with the exception of the ghetto population whom he had not previously consulted) that racism was 'of declining significance.' However, Wilson adds an ominous caveat to this retraction: 'But cultural factors also play a strong, very strong, role' (*ibid.*). He explains:

> When I say culture is important, I'm not talking about some kind of innate behavior. People are not inherently 'lazy,' or less able to keep a job, as many conservatives would have you believe. Yes, the culture that has developed in many inner-city neighborhoods makes it more difficult for residents there to get and keep jobs. But this culture is not innate. It is a response to bad times. It is not the cause of bad times. It also cannot be ignored. If we are to develop effective antipoverty programs, we must acknowledge the self-destructive behavior so evident in the poorest neighborhoods.

Alas in another reversal of his earlier writing, Wilson seems to have rediscovered not racism but the culture of poverty. Like the culture of poverty theorists of yore, Wilson stipulates that this dysfunctional culture is not innate (even conservatives do not make this claim), but a response to the exigencies of poverty and unemployment. Indeed, Wilson seems to be echoing the view of the employers whom he interviewed, that it is not because of racism that black youth are not hired, but because of their poor work habits.[12]

According to Reynolds, 'some conservatives are greeting this new Wilson with almost smug glee.' Lawrence Mead, for example, is quoted as follows: 'Bill and I used to profoundly disagree about whether economics or culture [was the fundamental cause of poverty]. But look at the results of his own study. Mexicans, with their work ethic, were less likely to remain in poverty. That's strong evidence. Let's face it. I won' (Reynolds, 1992, p.128). Wilson's apparent flip-flop is less surprising in light of the fact that he has consistently had a blind spot to racism. Now that he is confronted with incontrovertible evidence … that employers in fact are averse to hiring blacks, he has accepted the employers' rationalizations at face value. Therefore, Wilson's 'rediscovery' of racism does not lead him to reassess his erstwhile rejection of race-specific public policy and affirmative action in particular. Rather, according to Reynolds, Wilson's new agenda consists of car pools, job-referral services, and scattered-site housing, all designed to integrate blacks into hiring networks. Conspicuously absent from his agenda is any mention of vigorous enforcement of anti-discrimination statutes, much less affirmative action, as a lever for prying open doors that will otherwise be closed to black youth.

By focusing narrowly on the work habits and attitudes of unemployed ghetto youth, Wilson loses sight of the larger picture. Even if one grants his point that the employment prospects of blacks are diminished because of a lack of education and skills, even if one grants that these youth often lack the qualities that employers look for when they make hiring decisions, these 'facts' must be placed in larger historical and social context. How else are we to explain the paucity of skills and other job prerequisites among yet another generation of ghetto youth? These personal deficits are not random or individual events, but are part of a larger pattern of institutionalized racism, reflected in the very existence of racial ghettos and maintained through the complicity of such institutions as the schools, the banks, the housing market, the job market, the welfare system, and the criminal justice system. It is thus a denial of both history and present-day social reality to lump these racial pariahs together with other marginal workers, and on this basis to seek 'universal remedies.' For the black underclass is not merely the accidental by-product of color-blind economic forces, but the end product of a system of occupational apartheid that continues down to the present.

In the final analysis, this is what is most disturbing about Wilson's thesis regarding 'the declining significance of race' and his advocacy of universal, as opposed to race-specific, public policy: it absolves the nation of responsibility for coming to terms with its racist legacy, and takes race off the national agenda.[13]

Notes

1 See Anonymous, 1986; Zuckerman, 1986; Lemann, 1986; Magnet, 1987; Alter, 1988; Hammil, 1988; Stengel, 1988.

2 For a penetrating critique of the underclass discourse and the value assumptions that undergird it, see Reed (1992).

3 Wilson's advocacy of universal policies is forcefully defended by Theda Skocpol (1991); for an opposing argument, see Robert Greenstein (1991). Both articles are in Jencks and Peterson (eds) (1991).

4 According to data on New York City compiled by Roger Waldinger (1986–87), in 1970 17 per cent of whites were employed in manufacturing, as compared to 13 per cent of blacks. By 1980 there were 38 per cent fewer whites employed in manufacturing, whereas the decline for blacks was only 13 per cent. In absolute numbers, 115, 180 whites lost their jobs, as compared to 7,980 blacks.

5 To quote Wilson: 'One does not have to "trot out" the concept of racism to demonstrate, for example, that blacks have been severely hurt by deindustrialization.' Later he writes: 'The problem, as I see it, is unravelling the effects of present-day discrimination, on the one hand, and of historic discrimination on the other. My own view is that historic discrimination is far more important than contemporary discrimination in explaining the plight of the ghetto underclass, but that a full appreciation of the effects of historic discrimination is impossible without taking into account other historical and contemporary forces that have also shaped the experiences and behavior of impoverished urban minorities' (Wilson, 1987, pp.12,32–33).

6 The same article reported that the December unemployment rate for blacks dipped below 10 per cent for the first time in more than two decades (9.8 per cent as compared to 4.8 per cent for whites). As Andrew Brimmer cautioned, however, this could be a temporary aberration, easily reversed with a slowdown in the economy. A spokesman from the NAACP also noted that the government figures leave out the large numbers of blacks who have given up looking for a job.

7 Nor can this be dismissed as political hyperbole. As Hugh Heclo writes: 'the Model Cities proposal, the Great Society's *only* concentrated attack on ghetto poverty, was administratively fragmented and quickly broadened by Congress to include most congressional districts' (1994, p.408). Heclo's assertion is based on a study by Charles Haar (1975).

8 William Julius Wilson amplified his reservations about affirmative action in a subsequent article (Wilson, 1990).

9 Wilson, in fact, quotes this very passage, but still goes on to portray affirmative action as a 'creaming' process that primarily helps 'those with the greatest economic, educational, and social resources' (1987, p.115). Clearly, affirmative action does not reach those worst off, but those who are reached can hardly be characterized as the 'cream' of black society: they are socially and economically marginal, and have few alternative channels of mobility. Besides, given the caste system in occupations, it is imperative that racist barriers be eliminated at *all* occupational strata.

10 'Consequently,' they add, 'the extent of employment discrimination must be inferred from less direct evidence.'

11 These findings are reported in Kirschenman and Neckerman, '"We'd love to hire them, but. ...": the meaning of race for employers' [no details].

12 Wilson's position is also spelled out in a 1992 paper, 'The plight of the inner-city black male'. He begins with the observation that employers in Chicago's neighborhoods regard black men as poor and unreliable workers. Wilson then asserts that 'the deterioration of the socioeconomic status of black men may be associated with increases in these negative perceptions' (p.322). He then asks: 'Are these perceptions merely stereotypical or do they have any basis in fact?' Even though his survey data showed that black men were willing to work for even less than Mexican jobless fathers, he insists, on the basis of his ethnographic studies, that their 'underlying attitudes and values' were different, and that black men exhibited greater hostility and resistance than their Mexican counterparts. On this basis he concludes that 'the issue of race cannot simply be reduced to discrimination' (p.324).

A similar line of reasoning is found in the work of Christopher Jencks, who was one of the early critics of the Moynihan Report and the culture-of-poverty school. However, in Jencks (1993), Jencks states that 'our inability to maintain a tight labor market deserves most of the blame for increased idleness among young blacks.' He adds, however: 'It is not the only culprit' (p.125). Jencks goes on to argue that black youth are not willing to work at low-wage jobs, and that aspects of their culture are off-putting to prospective employers. Because 'moral ideas and norms of behavior have a life of their own,' Jencks reasons, 'institutional reforms must be complemented by a self-conscious effort at cultural change' (p.142). 'Wilson's greatest contribution,' he writes in conclusion, 'may be his discussion of how liberals' reluctance to blame blacks for anything happening in their communities has clouded both black and white thinking about how we can improve those communities' (p.142). For a critique of Jencks's essays in the *New York Review of Books*, see David Wellman (1986).

13 In her profile of Wilson in *Chicago* magazine, Gretchen Reynolds observed: 'In the five years since the publication of his most famous book, *The Truly Disadvantaged*, Wilson has become the darling of centrist politicians for one reason: because he declared, in effect, that the best way to deal with racial issues was not to' (p.82). Later she adds: 'Wilson's prescriptions were of

the grand-scale, society-wide variety. They began with a call for full employment. But what endeared Wilson to many national politicians – what turned Bill Clinton into an acolyte – was his de-emphasis of affirmative action' (p.127).

References

Alter, J. (1988) 'Why we can't wait any longer', *Newsweek*, no.111, 7 March, pp.42–43.

Anonymous (1986) 'A permanent black underclass?', *US News and World Report*, no.100, 3 March, pp.21–2.

Auletta, K. (1982) *The Underclass*, New York, Random House.

Fainstein, N. (1986–87) 'The underclass/mismatch hypothesis as an explanation for black economic deprivation', *Politics and Society*, vol.15, no.4.

Gephart, M.A. and Pearson, R.W. (1988) 'Contemporary research on the urban underclass', *Social Science Research Council Items*, June.

Glasgow, D.G. (1981) *The Black Underclass*, New York, Vintage Books.

Greenstein, R. (1991) 'Universal and targeted approaches to relieving poverty: an alternative view' in Jencks, C. and Peterson, P.E. (eds) *op. cit.*.

Haar, C. (1975) *Between the Idea and the Reality: A Study in the Origin, Fate, and Legacy of the Model Cities Program*, Boston, MA, Little, Brown.

Hammil, P. (1988) 'America's black underclass: can it be saved?', *Readers Digest*, no.132, June, pp.105–10.

Heclo, H. (1994) 'Poverty politics' in Danziger, S.H., Sabdefur, G.D. and Weinberg, D.H. (eds) *Confronting Poverty: Prescriptions for Change*, Cambridge, MA, Harvard University Press.

Holmes, S. (1995) 'Jobless data show blacks joining recovery', *New York Times*, 12 January.

Jackson, W. (1990) *Gunnar Myrdal and America's Conscience*, Chapel Hill, NC, University of North Carolina Press.

Jaynes, G.D. and Williams, R.M. Jr (1989) *A Common Destiny*, Washington, DC, National Academy Press.

Jencks, C. (1993) *Rethinking Social Policy*, New York, HarperCollins.

Jencks, C. and Peterson, P.E. (eds) (1991) *The Urban Underclass*, Washington, DC, Brookings Institution.

Kasarda, J. (1985) 'Urban change and minority opportunities' in Peterson, P. (ed.) *The New Urban Reality*, Washington, DC, Brookings Institution.

Lemann, N. (1986) 'The origins of the underclass', *The Atlantic*, no.257, June, pp.31–55.

Magnet, M. (1987) 'America's underclass: what to do?', *Fortune*, no.115, 11 May, pp.130–50.

McGahey, R. (1982) 'Poverty's voguish stigma', Op-ed page, *New York Times*, 12 March.

Myrdal, G. (1962) *Challenge to Affluence*, New York, Pantheon.

Reed, A. Jr (1992) 'The underclass as myth and symbol', *Radical America*, no.24, January, pp.21–40.

Reynolds, G. (1992) 'The rising significance of race', *Chicago*, no.41, December.

Ricketts, E.R. and Sawhill, I.V. (1988) 'Defining and measuring the underclass', *Journal of Polity Analysis and Management*, vol.7, pp.321–2.

Skocpol, T. (1991) 'Targeting within universalism: politically viable policies to combat poverty in the United States' in Jencks, C. and Peterson, P.E. (eds) *op. cit.*.

Stafford, W.W. (1985) *Closed Labor Markets: Underrepresentation of Blacks, Hispanics and Women in New York City's Core Industries*, New York, Community Service Society of New York.

Stengel, R. (1988) 'The underclass: breaking the cycle', *Time*, no.132, 10 October, pp.41–42.

Taylor, W.L. (1986) '*Brown*, equal protection, and the isolation of the poor', *Yale Law Journal*, no.95.

US Department of Labor (1992) *Bureau of Labor Statistics Bulletin*, no.2402, May.

Waldinger, R. (1986–87) 'Ladders and musical chairs: ethnicity and opportunity in post-industrial New York', *Politics and Society*, no.15.

Wellman, D. (1986) 'The new political linguistics of race,' *Socialist Review*, no.16, May–August, pp.43–79.

Wilkins, R. (1994) 'Progress and policy: a response to William Julius Wilson', *Michigan Quarterly Review*, no.33, Spring.

Wilson, W.J. (1978) *The Declining Significance of Race*, Chicago, IL, University of Chicago Press.

Wilson, W.J. (1987) *The Truly Disadvantaged*, Chicago, IL, University of Chicago Press.

Wilson, W.J. (1990) 'Race-neutral policies and the democratic coalition,' *The American Prospect*, no.1, Spring.

Wilson, W.J. (1992) 'The plight of the inner-city black male', *Proceedings of the American Philosophical Society*, no.136, September, pp.320–25.

Wilson, W.J. (1994) 'The new urban poverty and the problem of race', *Michigan Quarterly Review*, no.33, Spring.

Zuckerman, M.B. (1986) 'The black underclass', *US News and World Report*, no.100, 19 April, p.78.

Source: Steinberg, 1999, pp.137–9,140–44,146–9,151,153–5

Education, housing and social justice

Peter Braham and Norma Sherratt

Contents

1	**Introduction**	**293**
	1.1 Education	294
	Aims	294
	1.2 Housing	295
	Aims	295
2	**Social justice in education**	**295**
3	**The rise and fall of equal opportunities**	**296**
	3.1 Equal opportunities for girls?	298
	3.2 Beyond the 11+	299
	3.3 The breakdown of the consensus in education	301
4	**Patterns of inequality: class, gender and ethnicity**	**302**
5	**Promoting social justice through the education market: a case study**	**307**
	5.1 Material and cultural capital: middle-class advantages	308
	5.2 The reproduction of the middle classes: competition for academic credentials	308
	5.3 Responses by schools to the market	310
6	**Housing and social justice**	**312**
7	**Trends in housing tenure**	**314**
	7.1 The move to state provision of housing	314
	7.2 The move to owner-occupation	317

8   **Housing: a social divider?**   **319**

    8.1 Residualization   319

    8.2 Housing as wealth-creation   321

9   **Conceptualizing the divide**   **325**

    9.1 The concept of the housing class   325

    9.2 Consumption theory   328

10 **Conclusion**   **329**

References   **330**

Readings

7.1: **Sharon Gewirtz, Stephen J. Ball, and Richard Bowe,
     'Choice, equity and control' (1995)**   **333**

7.2: **Stephen J. Ball, Richard Bowe and Sharon Gerwitz:
     'Circuits of schooling: a sociological exploration of
     parental choice of school in social-class contexts' (1997)**   **338**

7.3: **Anne Power, 'Portrait of Broadwater Farm Estate, Britain,
     1966–95' (1999)**   **339**

1 Introduction

In this final chapter we explore education and housing in the light of some of the issues of difference and division with which we started the volume. Earlier chapters dealt with how far place – where we live – may affect opportunities and also explored the significance of and interconnections between divisions of social class, gender and ethnicity on life-chances in contemporary society. A number of concepts such as inequality, exclusion, polarization and deprivation have been used throughout to explain these differences and divisions. Such concepts serve to remind us that assessing social differences and divisions involves more than quantification and measurement, vital as these tasks are. We also need to possess a hypothesis, theory, interpretation or question in order to decide what to connect, quantify or measure. In addition, we need to fix a suitable time-frame within which to take our measurements and apply our hypotheses. Though whatever starting-point we take can seem arbitrary, there are good reasons for beginning our exploration of education and housing with the Beveridge Report of 1942. This set down the key principles of the **welfare** **state**, and its aim of abolishing the 'five giants' of want, ignorance, disease, squalor and idleness (Franklin, 1998, p.3). With this remit in mind, education and housing were to play a central role. Free education provided by the state would banish ignorance and also deliver equal opportunity. It was hoped that providing adequate and affordable housing would eliminate squalor and want, and also reduce diseases associated with overcrowding and lack of facilities.

welfare state

The promise of the welfare state incorporated a particular approach to questions of 'justice', 'fairness' and 'citizenship'. Though the concept of social justice is multi-faceted, as you saw in Chapter 6, in the welfare state it was closely linked to the notion of 'distributive justice' – the way a social structure is organized in terms of the division of and access to resources. Central to this concept of distributive justice is the question of how the position of the less and least advantaged in society can be ameliorated – and on what basis the requisite ameliorative measures can be justified. A distributive-justice perspective characterizes a social structure and its constituent institutions as fair if they promote equality, or equality of opportunity, and facilitate social mobility. They are considered unfair if they fail to achieve these goals, perhaps because of a disjunction between policy and practice. Despite the promise of the welfare state, and the policies that were introduced in pursuit of its aims and objectives, it is noteworthy the extent to which the life-chances of those belonging to different social classes in the UK remain unequal. One reason we could point to is the change in the political climate. This has signalled a move away from the social democratic consensus of the post-war decades towards neo-liberal agendas which has meant that welfare state ideals of universal provision from 'cradle to grave' have given way to an emphasis on greater individual responsibility. This, it can be argued, has applied particularly to health and housing. Welfare is seen increasingly as a 'safety-net' for a minority. A second reason that we find equality persisting between different social classes is that middle-class groups have traditionally been more adept than members of the working class at obtaining advantage from a better provision of resources – especially in health and education. A third reason is that there may be a difference between achieving economic prosperity (and so moving from, say, austerity to affluence) and achieving social justice. There is thus, for example, a distinction to be made between educational expansion which might benefit *all* social classes and the persistence of disparities of educational attainment between different social classes.

In this chapter you will have the opportunity to explore the distribution of opportunities and resources by looking at education and housing. Though the specific issues are different in each of these sectors, there are two basic questions that apply equally to both education and housing sectors:

1   How far have considerations of social justice shaped the way in which educational and housing resources are constructed and delivered?

2   How can we explain the persistence of social differences and divisions in education and housing?

1.1 Education

In 1997 the incoming Labour government declared that its policy for education was 'high quality for the many rather than excellence for the few'. Yet three years later an *Observer* editorial commenting on participation in higher education would note that:

> ... success is still almost entirely determined by class in the British education system ... Despite the government's efforts we are no nearer to establishing a meritocracy than when the comprehensive system was first introduced more than 30 years ago.
>
> (*The Observer*, 8 October 2000)

Is this the case? For over 50 years, there have been attempts to promote social justice in and through education and to promote equality of opportunity for all children. But what do these terms social justice and equal opportunities actually mean in relation to education? In the first part of Chapter 7, our intention is to clarify these questions as we consider key policies and debates of the past and present. Even within the UK there can be significant differences in educational policies, but, as we do not have the space in this chapter to consider these, we have limited our analysis to England and Wales.

AIMS

More specifically, the aims of the first part of this chapter are to:

1   Explore some of the meanings attached to social justice and equal opportunities in relation to education, and show how they can be subject to debate and disagreement.

2   Outline some of the broad trends in educational policy in England and Wales over the past 50 years insofar as they relate to attempts to promote equal opportunities.

3   Delineate the main patterns of differences in educational achievement in terms of pupils' class, gender and ethnic backgrounds.

4   Analyse the extent to which these may be reduced or increased by educational policies which place significant emphasis on market processes.

5   Note the implications of this kind of analysis for wider discussions of social justice.

1.2 Housing

You might think that providing adequate and affordable housing is a basic need, but housing has not enjoyed the same status within the welfare state as have education and health. The second part of Chapter 7 will show that whereas free education was to be made available to all, and health was to be free at the point of need (even if private provision of education and health continued in parallel), direct provision of housing by the state would come to be aimed increasingly towards a narrowing population. And although housing was one of the 'seven pillars of a decent society' identified by the incoming Labour prime minister in 1997 (NHF, 1997), more often housing seems to have been regarded as a 'wobbly pillar of the welfare state' (Torgerson, 1987, cited in Mullins, 1998, p.249). While 'poor' housing may be perceived as a source of social exclusion, housing provision has not been seen as a core responsibility of the state.

AIMS

Our discussion of housing has the following aims:

1   To explore the nature of housing inequality in the UK and the changing balance between public and private-sector housing.

2   To investigate housing as a source of wealth.

3   To address the concept of the 'housing class'.

4   To consider the importance ascribed to owner-occupation and to ask whether the division between owner-occupiers and non-owners represents a significant gulf in society.

---

2 Social justice in education

ACTIVITY 1

As a first step in unpacking some of the key ideas and concepts we will be working with in the first part of this chapter, make some notes about any educational 'injustices' you can think of either in respect of your own educational experiences (or those of your family and friends) or from accounts you may have read about. You may want to think about this Activity in relation to earlier chapters in this volume which alerted you to some of the continuing inequalities in our society, and which introduced concepts of justice (as Chapter 6 did, for instance). But your main aim at this point should be to use your own ideas and experiences.

Our list in response to this Activity would be wide-ranging – encompassing past injustices like the experiences of older family members who had to leave school at the age of 14 because their wages were needed to help support the family? Or women who had wanted to study 'male' subjects but were not allowed to at the time? You may also have listed present-day injustices: one example could be the way in which many inner-city schools seem to offer fewer opportunities to their pupils; another might be research that shows that children excluded from school most often come from particular groups in society. Or you may have noted the small proportion of children from lower-income groups who achieve higher education qualifications.

This is only a start and your list may well be very different from ours. But this kind of Activity can help us to think through the issues involved in any discussion of education and social justice. In particular, it can start us thinking about *definitions* of social justice in relation to education. You will have learnt in Chapter 6 that while there are a variety of ways to understand social justice, perhaps the most common conceptualization is that of distributive justice: its focus is on the question of 'fair' distribution of resources. And as you will see, our list reflects this approach. With regards to education, its concern is with the way in which *access* to different educational experiences or resources is patterned. This is not the only way of thinking about social justice in relation to education – recent debates have also focused on the need to extend the idea of social justice in education to encompass freedom from oppression, marginalization or violence during education. Indeed, your own list may also have recognized that social justice involves 'social structures and relations beyond distribution' (Young, 1990, p.9). Nonetheless, it is this 'distributional' definition that we shall concentrate on in this part of the chapter when we look at different patterns of access to education.

'Fair distribution of resources' would seem to suggest that all children should have access to the same kinds of education. Is it enough, however, to give all children the same opportunities? Is a fair distribution of educational resources 'fair' if it fails to compensate in some way for children's unequal starting-points? What might be a better indicator of social justice is the extent to which there is equality of educational *outcomes*. If we are to examine social justice in education in this light, we must ask what present inequalities in patterns of achievement suggest about the way resources are distributed.

In section 3 we will examine some of the key changes in the English and Welsh education systems over the past 50 years, and focus on attempts to achieve social justice through equality of educational opportunity. In section 4 you will have the opportunity to explore a range of data showing the existence of continuing differences in educational outcomes in terms of class, gender and ethnicity. And in section 5 we will focus on just one aspect of current educational policy – the central role of the market – in order to illuminate the complexities and dilemmas facing attempts to promote social justice in education.

3 The rise and fall of equal opportunities

Ideas of fair distribution of educational resources are comparatively recent. By the end of the nineteenth century the state had already intervened to provide free elementary education, which was compulsory up to the age of 13, for all boys and girls. But this was for children of the working classes. Children of the middle classes and upper classes tended to be educated privately at grammar schools or public schools. And within each class boys and girls received different kinds of education: boys' education focused on their future roles in the work force whilst that of girls was directed by a 'domestic **ideology**', preparing them for their future roles as wives and mothers or as servants or 'mistresses of servants'

ideology

(Paechter, 1998, p.12). According to some commentators, education was therefore 'sharply differentiated to represent and sustain existing social divisions' (Arnot *et al.*, 1999, p.35), with differences of access and resources supported by ideologies of class and gender.

The first half of the twentieth century did see a slow weakening of class ideologies in relation to education, with an 'educational ladder', in the form of scholarships, by which means the very brightest of working-class children might be able to gain access to secondary education. But it was not until the Education Act of 1944 that equality of educational opportunity for all children became an explicit aim. For the first time, free secondary education was now available for all children, as well as allocation to different types of secondary school (grammar, technical or secondary modern) to be decided on results of performance in tests (the 11+) designed to measure aptitude and intelligence. It was the intention of the Act that every individual would have the opportunity to reach their

Figure 7.1 *Preparing to start the 11+ examination*

potential, unconstrained by class background or gender and that individual merit, frequently characterized as the sum of intelligence plus effort, would henceforth be the determinant of a child's access to education and their subsequent position in society.

The primary aim of the 1944 Act was to create a fairer education system by giving working-class children the chance to gain educational qualifications, which, insofar as this improved their occupational opportunities, would create a fairer society. But these reforms were directed not only by a concern for social justice. There was a second aim, which was to use education more effectively to develop the skills of the workforce, to open up a pool of untapped ability needed for economic growth: 'For the first time in the post war period education took a central position in the functioning of advanced industrial societies because it was seen as a key investment in the promotion of economic growth as well as a means of promoting social justice' (Halsey *et al.*, 1980, p.4). And it was this dual aim which was the impetus for two decades of tremendous expansion of education and optimism about its possibilities, not just in the UK, but also throughout Europe.

ACTIVITY 2

meritocracy

As you read the above account of the '**meritocratic**' ideologies that drove education in the early post-war years, a number of questions and doubts may have occurred to you, perhaps based on your work on earlier chapters in this volume as well as on the definitions of equal opportunities that we have been working with so far. (And perhaps based as well on what you yourself know of factors affecting access to education.) Is there anything missing? Any statements which might seem to you unduly optimistic? Make a note of any such doubts and omissions before you continue reading.

3.1 Equal opportunities for girls?

You may have wondered about the lack of explicit references to equal opportunities for girls in the account above. Where do they come into the picture? The short answer is that they do not. Equal opportunities at the time of the Education Act 1944 were couched primarily in terms of class. Thus, 'for a large part of this period, whilst working-class failure was high on the agenda, preoccupation with equal opportunities did not extend to girls and women' (Arnot *et al.*, 1999). Indeed, analysis of the official ideology of educational reports indicates that it was taken for granted through the 1950s and 1960s that the education of boys and girls should differ as they had different interests, aptitudes and futures (Wolpe, 1976).

This was borne out by the Crowther report of 1959. This stated that 'girls needed to be prepared for their likely futures' and that 'the prospect of courtship and marriage should rightly influence the education of adolescent girls' (Crowther, 1959), and reflected the continuation of an ideology of domesticity in relation to girls' education. One way this was highlighted was in the different subject choices offered to girls and boys, for example the assumption that only girls should study domestic science.

Admittedly, there were differences in the educational opportunities offered to middle-class girls compared with those offered to working-class girls.

Figure 7.2 *Girls' domestic science lesson in the 1950s*

Furthermore, explanations of the different curricular routes and choices of girls through schooling involve more than a consideration of educational policy. However, it is clear that:

> ... from the radical Labour government of 1944–51 which was surprisingly resistant to extending such basic rights as equal pay to women . . ., through the high point of social democracy and the extension of the welfare state in the late 1960s to the breakdown of consensus about education and the decline of social democracy towards the end of the 1970s, there was little support for feminist goals or for any other than the broadest notions of sexual equality.
>
> (Weiner, 1994, p.93)

3.2 Beyond the 11+

In responding to Activity 2, you may also have expressed doubts about the effectiveness of the 11+ test as a way of promoting equal opportunity, particularly as debates surrounding its effectiveness have rarely left the public domain during the past 50 years. The use of the 11+ test to allocate children to different types of school came to be increasingly questioned during the 1950s and early 1960s as it became clear it had done little to promote more equal opportunities for working-class children. It is fair to say that some working-class children who might not otherwise have done so gained access to grammar schools.

Nonetheless, middle-class children were significantly over-represented in all selective schools, and a series of sociological studies over this period identified the social factors which resulted in their better performance in so-called objective intelligence tests (Floud *et al.*, 1956; Douglas, 1967). In addition, further sociological research identified, first, the complexities of the relationship between school culture and home culture, which meant that those working-class children who did gain access to a grammar school were less likely to stay on past the school-leaving age; second, the negative effects of selection on those who were allocated to secondary modern schools, in terms of resource allocations and aspiration. With increasing awareness that intelligence was malleable and not fixed – that it would respond to social and environmental factors and that separate differentiated schools were unable to provide equality of opportunity – there was growing acceptance of the argument that only a common educational experience for all would do this. As a result, in 1965 all Local Education Authorities (LEAs) were asked to submit plans for reorganizing secondary schools on comprehensive lines, and this resulted in the gradual replacement of selection by comprehensive schools with similar resources and curricula.

In responding to Activity 2, you may also have felt that you wanted to do more to unpack the notion of equal opportunities. We have noted that in the immediate post-war years it was the promotion of equal opportunities that drove educational reforms, in that the aim was to give every child the opportunity to succeed in and through education. However, as the selective system was replaced by a comprehensive system, and as it started to become clear that this was still not bringing any significant improvement in the educational achievements of working-class children, policies started to be re-thought. It was becoming clear that the provision of equal access would still result in significant *groups* of children being disadvantaged because they had very different starting-points from others and that these were the result of structural inequalities in society. There was, nevertheless, still a consensus between the two major parties during the 1960s, and even into the 1970s, that the aim of education was to achieve 'equality of opportunity'. But during this period there was a shift of emphasis from 'weaker' to 'stronger' versions of equality – from an emphasis on equality of *access* to an emphasis on equality of *outcomes*. In other words, equality of opportunity is a rather 'slippery' concept insofar as it was sometimes defined narrowly, sometimes broadly. As attention came to be given in the 1960s and 1970s, not just to educational prospects of working-class children, but also to the prospects of girls and children from minority ethnic groups, a range of initiatives was introduced that was designed to improve the initial chances of children from a variety of disadvantaged groups. These compensatory education programmes (of which the Educational Priority Area (EPA) programmes were the best known) later came to be criticized for promoting a 'deficit' view of black or working-class culture and family life and for aiming to 'compensate' for a deprivation that did not exist. Chapter 6 has already raised some of the complexity of policy-making in relation to the education of children from minority ethnic groups: the key point we want to emphasize here is how the agenda began to change. As there was a growing recognition that structural and cultural inequalities in society resulted in different starting-points for different groups of children, so equality of opportunity came to be seen as a more complex goal than it had once seemed.

3.3 The breakdown of the consensus in education

Despite the educational expansion of the post-war years, with increasing numbers of children staying on at school and even entering higher education, comparatively little change had been achieved in the patterns of educational achievement. Even in relation to class differences, where the commitment to promoting equal opportunities had been clear and unquestioned, little gain had been made in moving towards a fairer distribution of resources. Certainly, the decades since the war *had been* marked by increasing **social mobility** – whereby some children from working-class backgrounds had achieved higher occupational levels than their parents. However, Goldthorpe (1980) has suggested that this had been due to changes in the occupational structure, most notably the expansion of white-collar jobs, rather than to any marked change in patterns of educational achievement. As a range of research reports and public documents indicated, there had been no radical change in the percentage of working-class children staying on at school to 18 or entering higher education (Halsey *et al.*, 1980). In this vein, Halsey has written:

social mobility

> … despite the expansion in middle-class jobs and an increasingly educated workforce, the guiding idea that everyone would eventually get a middle-class job and that occupation and status would be determined according to merit were myths. The myths were understandable, given the accelerated expansion in middle-class jobs and educational opportunities; but working-class jobs did not disappear, and the privilege of the already-privileged remained. Universities were still dominated by those from professional and managerial backgrounds; and even when intelligence was taken into account, social background remained a significant factor in individuals' life chances.
>
> (*Halsey et al.*, 1997, p.5)

In short, it was middle-class children who were benefiting from the educational policies of the post-war years.

The eventual breakdown of political consensus about the purpose of education was also triggered by factors outside education: in particular by a marked change in the political climate. The voice of the New Right became increasingly powerful in all spheres and in relation to education it took the form of an attack on those policies of the previous decades, which, it was asserted, had been responsible for a decline in national standards. For example, according to the authors of the 'Black Papers', a particularly articulate and powerful voice of the New Right in education, 'the spirit of competition and excellence had been sacrificed in order to make the education system conform to socialist notions of social justice' (Brown, 1997, p.398). What was needed, so these commentators argued, was the defence of 'merit and standards of excellence' against those who had treated schools as 'instruments for equalizing, rather than instructing, children' (Hillgate Group, 1987, p.2).

So with the breakdown of the social democratic consensus in the 1970s, and the emergence of the New Right, the notions of equal opportunity, which had so dominated educational thinking in the decades since the war, took a back seat. The policies and values of the New Right, enshrined eventually in the Education Reform Act of 1988 under a Conservative administration, were centred not on equal opportunity, but on freedom, competition, the individualizing of opportunity, consumerism and parental choice: 'Notions of equality of opportunity whether on grounds of social class, gender or race began to give way to notions of individualism, the ideals of competition, and the reward for performance …' (Arnot *et al.*, 1999, p.95).

It was not until the arrival of the 1997 Labour government that we see, albeit in different shape and form, the re-emergence of some of the terms that had been central to the educational reforms of the post-war years. Yet it was precisely because significant inequalities in educational achievement still existed in terms of social class, gender and ethnic origin that the incoming Labour government faced such a difficult challenge in creating social justice in education. In section 4, you will have the opportunity to look at these inequalities more closely.

SUMMARY OF SECTION 3

The second half of the twentieth century can be described in terms of different approaches to achieving equality of educational opportunity. The focus in this section has been on:

1   The significance of the Education Act 1944 in terms of its emphasis on social justice and a break with previous educational ideologies.

2   The way in which issues of social justice and equality of educational opportunity came to be seen as more complex and problematic during the 1950s, 1960s and 1970s.

3   The breakdown of the social democratic consensus, the emergence of the New Right and the development of a different set of educational aims to those centred on equal opportunity.

---

4 Patterns of inequality: class, gender and ethnicity

One way of measuring achievement is to look at entry into higher education for under 21-year-olds. This is because it reflects continuation beyond the minimum school-leaving age and performance at A level or equivalent. And, as we can see from Table 7.1, children from unskilled and semi-skilled socio-economic groups are still significantly under-represented in higher education. You will see from the table that while the participation rates for the unskilled group more than doubled between 1991/2 and 1998/9, at only 13 per cent it was at a much lower level than that for professional groups, which stood at 72 per cent. It seems therefore that inequalities of *class* remain.

The situation in relation to *gender* is different, however. As you see from Table 7.2, by 1998 girls were outperforming boys at age 16 across all ethnic groups in terms of the crucial marker for continuing on to A levels, namely five or more GSCE grades A to C. And, as Table 7.3 indicates, this gender gap now continues into A level with a higher proportion of girls than boys now achieving two A levels. These are the figures which have been used as evidence for the much publicized closing, and indeed reversal, of the gender gap and the growing concern about boys' under-achievement that has ensued.

Table 7.1 Participation rates[1] in higher education: by social class, Great Britain (%)

	1991/92	1992/93	1993/94	1994/95	1995/96	1996/97	1997/98	1999/99
Professional	55	71	73	78	79	82	79	72
Intermediate	36	39	42	45	45	47	48	45
Skilled non-manual	22	27	29	31	31	32	31	29
Skilled manual	11	15	17	18	18	18	19	18
Partly skilled	12	14	16	17	17	17	18	17
Unskilled	6	9	11	11	12	13	14	13
All social classes	23	28	30	32	32	33	33	31

Note: 1 The number of home domiciled initial entrants aged under 21 to full-time and sandwich undergraduate courses of higher education in further education and higher education institutions expressed as a proportion of the average 18–19-year-old population. The 1991 Census provided the population distribution by social class for all years.

Source of data: Department for Education and Employment; Office for National Statistics; Universities and Colleges Admission Service

Source: *Social Trends 30*, 2000, Chart 3.13, p.56

Table 7.2 Examination achievements of pupils[1] in schools by gender and ethnic origin 1998, England and Wales (%)

	5 or more GCSEs grades A* to C	1–4 GCSEs grades A* to C	No graded GCSEs
Males			
White	43	25	7
Black	23	24	7
Indian	52	23	2
Pakistani/Bangladeshi	29	29	6
Other groups[2]	37	28	11
All males	42	25	7
Females			
White	51	25	6
Black	35	42	7
Indian	55	28	3
Pakistani/Bangladeshi	32	45	6
Other groups[3]	52	31	3
All females	51	26	6

Notes: 1 Pupils aged 16. 2 Includes those who did not state their ethnic group.

Source of data: Youth Cohort Study, Department for Education and Employment

Source: *Social Trends 30*, 2000, Chart 3.16, p.58

Table 7.3 Highest qualification[1] held by gender and ethnic group, 1997–8,[2] Great Britain (%)

	Degree or equivalent	Higher education qualification[3]	GCE A-level or equivalent	GCSE grades A* to C or equivalent	Other qualification	No qualification	All
Males							
Indian/ Pakistani/ Bangladeshi	18	5	16	14	25	22	100
Black	14	6	22	18	24	16	100
White	14	8	32	18	14	15	100
Other groups[4]	20	5	17	15	27	15	100
Females							
Indian/ Pakistani/ Bangladeshi	9	5	11	18	25	33	100
Black	9	12	14	27	22	16	100
White	11	9	16	29	15	20	100
Other groups[4]	12	8	15	17	33	15	100

Notes: 1 Men aged 16 to 64, women aged 16 to 59. 2 Combined quarters: spring 1997 to winter 1997–98. 3 Below degree level. 4 Includes those who did not state their ethnic group.

Source of data: Department for Education and Employment from the Labour Force Survey

Source: *Social Trends 29*, 1999, Chart 3.20, p.65

Table 7.4 Permanent exclusion rates[1] by ethnic group, January 1998, England (%)

White	0.17
Black Caribbean	0.76
Black African	0.29
Black Other	0.57
Indian	0.06
Pakistani	0.13
Bangladeshi	0.09
Chinese	0.05
All	0.18

Note: 1 Number of permanent exclusions as a percentage of the number of full and part-time pupils of all ages.

Source of data: Department for Education and Employment

Source: *Social Trends 30*, 2000, Chart 3.5, p.52

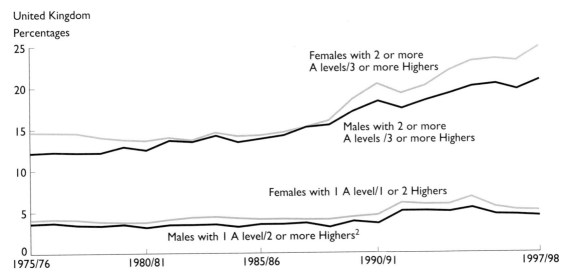

United Kingdom

Percentages

1 Based on population aged 17 at the start of the academic year. Data to 1990/91 (1991/92 in Northern Ireland) relate to school leavers. From 1991/92 data relate to pupils of any age for Great Britain while school performance data are used for Northern Ireland from 1992/93. Figures exclude sixth-form colleges in England and Wales which were reclassified as FE colleges from 1 April 1993. Excludes GNVQ Advanced Qualifications throughout.
2 From 1996/97, figures only include SCE Highers.

Figure 7.3 *Achievement at GCE A-level or equivalent* [1]*: by gender*

Source: *Social Trends 30*, 2000, Chart 3.17, p.58

Finally, underlying the continuation of class differences, and the reversal of gender differences, is the complexity and diversity of achievement by different *ethnic* groups.

ACTIVITY 3

Look again at Table 7.2 and look also at Tables 7.3 and 7.4. Which ethnic group – according to the most commonly used indicators of academic success – seems, on average, to perform least well? As you work through the tables, make a note of any difficulties the data present as far as interpreting them is concerned.

The information we have here is detailed, complex and rich. You will probably have identified a number of low-achieving groups: data from Table 7.3 suggest that it is Indian/Pakistani/Bangladeshi females who present the highest percentage leaving school without qualifications; the information in Table 7.2 indicates that it is 'black' males who make up the lowest percentage with five or more GCSEs; Table 7.4 implies that it is the 'Black Caribbean' group that has the highest rate of exclusion from school. These data are broadly in keeping with the findings of a recent Ofsted Report which, in addition, identified Pakistani/ Bangladeshi and (in some areas) white working-class boys as low achievers. It is important too to note the report's main concern that 'African Caribbean young people – especially boys – have not shared equally in the increasing rates of achievement; [and] in some areas their performance has actually worsened' and that the 'sharp rise in the number of exclusions from school affects a disproportionately large number of black pupils' (Gillborn and Gipps, 1996, p.78).

However, this exercise demonstrates many of the difficulties attached to gathering information of this kind: one such problem is the way in which the use of categories can mask important differences. The linking together of Indian/Pakistani/Bangladeshi (under the umbrella category of Asian) in Table 7.2, for instance, hides significant differences that may be associated with different class/socio-economic positions between, for instance, Indian children and Bangladeshi children. And while the term 'black' is now rarely used to refer to children of all minority ethnic groups, it may still be used in a way which 'fails to distinguish between the pupils with family origins in the Caribbean and those of African ethnic background' (Gillborn and Gipps, 1996). In the same way, the category 'white' hides the immense class differences in terms of achievement that exist within this group – differences that may be of particular relevance when comparisons are made between white and other ethnic groups in particular localities.

In addition, the Ofsted Report draws particular attention to the ways in which class, gender and ethnicity interact to produce specific educational outcomes in different local contexts. Although the great complexity of the patterns revealed here alerts us to the need to be cautious about any broad generalizations, it is worth noting the high levels of achievement of some ethnic groups and the growing gap between those categorized as the highest and lowest achieving groups.

So, how can we explain why it is that the middle classes have been able to hold on to their privileges? And why is it that social class inequalities seem to be so much more intransigent than gender inequalities? And how do we account for the contrasting achievement levels of different ethnic groups? These questions are complex and it is beyond our scope here to attempt to offer complete answers. What we shall do in the next section, however, is to begin to explore them in the context of our discussion of social justice. One significant aspect of government policy has been – and still is – to depend on the market to determine access to schooling within the state education system. In section 5 we will consider the extent to which an analysis of the workings of the market can provide some explanations for the patterns we have been looking at here.

SUMMARY OF SECTION 4

1 Although the data we have here alerts us first and foremost to the complexity of the interactions between class, gender and ethnicity in accounting for patterns of educational achievement, it is still possible to identify a number of key broad trends.

2 Most significantly, whilst education is still acting to express and reaffirm existing class inequalities, there have been important changes in relation to gender, with levels of achievement for girls surpassing that for boys – at least for some groups.

3 Whilst levels of achievement across ethnic groups are wide-ranging, and furthermore cross-cut by divisions of class and gender, there does seem to be at least one clearly identifiable group whose low levels of achievement and relativity high level of exclusions and suspensions is causing concern nationally.

5 Promoting social justice through the education market: a case study

We have already noted the commitment of the Labour government of 1997–2001 to education as a means of promoting social justice, achieving equality of opportunity and combating social exclusion. Some commentators, nevertheless, have raised doubts about whether government policies do bring about real opportunities for all or whether they work to maintain privilege and inequality. Gewirtz, for instance, argues that there are obvious tensions in government policy:

> On the one hand the government is committed to a model of reform which emphasizes markets, compliance, standardization, responsibilization and pedagogic traditionalism and which is based on a belief in the superiority of private sector management practices. On the other hand it allies itself with the need to combat social exclusion, widen participation in the running of schools and to promote through its proposals for citizenship education the values of democracy social justice and respect for cultural diversity.
>
> (Gewirtz, 2001, p.185)

Using notions of the **market** and 'parental choice' as a way of distributing   **market** educational resources has been a central feature of the policies of both the Labour government of 1997–2001 and of previous Conservative governments and this has been justified on the grounds of widening educational opportunities. In this section we will explore the consequences of market-based policies for the patterns of inequality that we identified in section 3. We shall consider how policies which place the concepts of the market and parental choice at the centre of the educational system might work mainly to the advantage of middle-class students and examine to what degree an analysis of market processes can contribute to explanations of other patterns of inequality, including those based on gender and ethnicity.

READING 7.1

Turn now to Readings 7.1 and 7.2. These consist of two extracts, both from work by Gewirtz, Ball and Bowe. The argument in both pieces is that choice, competition and markets will result in further polarization of educational provision and further disadvantage those least able to compete in the market, increasing inequalities even more.

To help clarify the processes involved in the polarization posited by Gerwitz and her colleagues, make notes now in response to the following questions:

1   In what respects are middle-class families advantaged in a market system?

2   What do you understand by the term *reproduction* in this kind of analysis?

3   How do schools themselves respond to the market?

(Note: although Gewirtz *et al.*'s findings are based on a study of London schools within a specific area, these findings have been replicated by other researchers not only in the UK more generally (for example, Noden, 2000), but also in other national contexts (for example, Whitty *et al.*, 1998; Hughes and Lauder, 1999).)

5.1 Material and cultural capital: middle-class advantages

Central to the argument presented here is that middle-class parents are better able to take advantage of the market because they have the resources to enable them to make choices which will give their children access to better schools. These resources are partly material – such as the ability to pay for transport to a more distant school if it has a better reputation – but they are also social and cultural.

cultural capital   As you will have noted as you work through this volume, the idea of **cultural capital**, as developed originally by Bourdieu, has been central to many sociological explanations of inequalities and differences. In Chapter 2, the possession of cultural capital was defined in terms of what gives the middle classes: '[The] skills and attributes to perform well in the educational process and hence convert their dispositions into educational credentials that will allow them to move into privileged jobs' which was seen as involving '[the] inculcation of particular skills and abilities that may bring with them potential rewards, *even though people may be unaware of this, or may misrecognize their cultural capital …*' (Savage in this volume, pp.77,79).

In relation to our concerns here, this means that those defined in this research as the 'privileged/skilled choosers' had the confidence in and knowledge of the educational system to be able to 'play the market' and to decipher the real criteria for admission to schools. They also understand which strategies to use to ensure access for their children to schools of their choice. And most significantly, the model of choice-making advocated by the government was one which corresponded closely to their own construction of choice. As Gewirtz and her colleagues comment, ' … in Bourdieuian terms, the dominant class possesses the necessary cultural code for decoding the cultural [arbitrariness] of the market' (1995, p.183).

The reality of 'school choice', then, is that those with the appropriate economic, social and cultural capital are able to make choices denied to others. In many cases there may not be explicit selection, but it exists in a covert form – in a way which may prove to be more subtle and resilient than explicit selection.

5.2 The reproduction of the middle classes: competition for academic credentials

It is also suggested in these two extracts that the use of the market by middle-class families is a particular 'strategy of reproduction'. The contention here is that few middle-class families today are able to reproduce their privileges by passing on their wealth to their children. The middle classes indeed may be defined not by their ownership of property or wealth but by their occupational success, and the key to occupational success is the possession of the skills, qualifications and experience which command a high price on the market. For large portions of this group, as Giddens (1973) has noted, market power is based on educational qualifications. As a result, the way they ensure that their position and privileges are passed on to the next generation is through giving them the best chance possible of achieving the most valued educational qualifications. Consequently, following Bourdieu, it is more than possible to argue that 'cultural capital in the form of academic credentials is essential to reproduction of middle class privilege'.

A useful extension of this analysis is provided by Brown (1996) who argues that the marketization of education reflects a 'third wave' in principles of provision and selection in British education. Whilst the first wave involved the schooling of working-class children for their predetermined place in society and the second wave can be characterized as involving a shift from social ascription to 'individual merit and achievement' as the basis for provision, the third wave can be characterized in terms of the rise of the 'ideology of parentocracy'. According to Brown, slogans such as 'parental choice', educational standards' and 'the free market' reflect and support the increasing power of parents in determining educational outcomes.

> ... a growing section of the old and new middle classes are undermining the principle of equality of opportunity in the sense that educational outcomes should be determined by the abilities and efforts of pupils not the wealth and preferences of parents. This form of 'social closure' is the outcome of an evaluation by the middle classes that educational success has become too important to be left to the chance outcome of a formally open competition (despite what the research evidence has taught us about social class and patterns of achievement). ...
>
> (Brown, 1997, p.402)

Therefore, this class conflict revolves around educational selection and the achievement of academic credentials. Following this analysis, however, the conflict is hidden because of the way the New Right have claimed moral legitimacy for choice/standards/freedom. These ideas are presented as benefiting all children in a system of open access, what occurs in reality is that the already privileged use their power to exclude others from the opportunity to gain the highest credentials. As a result, prioritizing greater choice, rather than equal opportunities, benefits the middle classes.

Figure 7.4 *School choice?*

5.3 Responses by schools to the market

If, in a market situation, middle-class parents are anxious to use the educational system in order to ensure the success of their children, schools are similarly anxious to use 'able' and 'motivated' children to enhance their own performance and reputation in the local market. The point is that as long as a market system of resource-allocation is in place, students will be valued and selected according to how much they contribute to a school's image and performance, because this has a direct effect on the school's funding. The publication of exam league tables and other performance indicators mean that schools are increasingly anxious to attract enrolments from motivated parents and 'able' pupils, with the consequence that certain groups of children are not being selected for, or are being excluded from, the most highly resourced schools. In addition, within schools, students are increasingly valued according to the contribution teachers judge them capable of making to the school's league-table position. Consequently the adoption of setting and selection practices may mean that those children least likely to contribute to a school's exam performance will be allocated fewer resources.

In effect, as noted by Gerwirtz *et al.*, 'the emphasis seems increasingly to be not what the school can do for the child but what the child can do for the school' (1995, p.176). And this may well be part of the explanation for the underachievement of a number of groups of students. Research in this area is as yet inconclusive, but there are suggestions that the ethos of the educational marketplace and increased competition does have a negative impact on the motivational patterns of some groups of students (see, for example, Gillborn and Gipps, 1996). Before we conclude this section, however, let us look specifically at these ideas in relation to the differences in achievement levels between boys and girls.

ACTIVITY 4

Consider the following two extracts. What is the explanation offered in these for the relative decline in the achievement levels of boys in recent years?

> The emphasis on competition and performance and the heightened visibility of schools has called into play a new concept of the 'good pupil'. Pupils have been required to engage in the improvement of their academic performance for the sake of the school if not themselves. Educational success has been judged predominantly by the number of qualifications achieved at the age of 16, a yardstick which historically many boys have not met or have chosen not to get involved with. This shift in educational values has been successfully exploited by girls, resulting in raised educational performance. It has thus contributed to a decline of the relative advantage of boys over girls.
>
> (Arnot *et al.*, 1999, p.155)

> Evidence from more recent studies suggests that the reform of schooling from the late 1980s to the mid-'90s, at a time when traditional male working-class jobs in the heavy manufacturing industries were in decline, exacerbated rather than reduced school resistance. By increasing emphasis on performance and on competition both within and between schools and by raising the stakes in terms of compliance to a school culture that was class orientated, schools were more rather than less likely to be viewed as hostile institutions. The sorting and selecting functions of schools were made more visible with only weak support

from any legitimating ideology. The reintroduction of streaming and the promotion of setting by school subject for many such boys would confirm their failure to succeed in what were perceived as other people's educational designs. The rising rate of pupils excluded from schools during the 1980s and '90s was closely associated with such a competitive ethos.

(Arnot *et al.*, 1999, p.43)

Of course, any explanation of the decline in achievements of boys relative to girls ought to be multifaceted. There must be recognition, too, of the complexity of these comparisons, not least because the relative gains of girls over boys does not apply to every social grouping.

However, Arnot *et al.*'s account does usefully link the nature of traditional working-class male employment patterns and corresponding lack of interest by some boys in educational qualifications in ways similar to those noted by earlier

Figure 7.5 *Receiving the A level results*

commentators (see, for example, Willis, 1977). She then goes on to suggest how a combination of changes in the employment opportunities open to boys, together with the increased emphasis within schools on qualifications and achievement, may account for the increased hostility and resistance to schooling by boys which, in its turn, results in lower levels of achievement.

SUMMARY OF SECTION 5

The aim of this section has been to demonstrate how an emphasis on choice and markets may work to the advantage of some groups of students and the disadvantage of others and, in particular, how this emphasis may involve the redistribution of educational resources from the least to the most advantaged. It has been shown that this can happen in several ways:

1   As market forces operate, schools become increasingly polarized in terms of resources, reputation and intake. All children do not have equal access to the better resourced and more effective schools

2   Similarly, not all children have equal access to resources within individual schools. Not only is it the case that some groups of white working-class boys may well be less valued by a school in terms of their contribution to examination results and consequently allocated fewer resources, but the same process may also apply to children from some minority ethnic groups, notably African Caribbean boys.

3   Market processes may well also have effects in terms of increased hostility and resistance to school. The ethos of the market may well influence the motivational patterns of some groups of students, with yet further consequences for their valuation by the school and for their own levels of achievement.

6 Housing and social justice

ACTIVITY 5

Spend a few moments writing down what you think the quotations below tell us about housing in Britain of the past:

> At an inquest held by Dr Macdonald, in Spitalfields, upon the death of a baby four months old, evidence was given that the parents and their seven children lived all together in one room about 12 feet square, for which they paid 4s 6d a week. The jury returned a verdict of accidental death, but added a rider to the effect that the sanitary authorities were most lax in their duties to allow a family of nine to live and sleep in so small a room, and that the overcrowding that prevails in the East End ought to be inquired into and something done to alleviate it.
>
> (*East London Advertiser*, 'Overcrowding in Spitalfields', 15 September 1888, quoted in Fishman, 1988, pp.20–1)

> ... fearful conditions of overcrowding were still common. The worst area for them was the north-east coast; in 1899 the counties of Durham and Northumberland had respectively 34 and 38 per cent of their populations overcrowded, while Gateshead, Newcastle and Sunderland were the three most overcrowded towns. The other areas suffering most in this respect were to be found in certain parts of London, in Liverpool near the docks, and on the South Wales coal-field ...
>
> (Ensor, 1960, pp.301–2)

There are four conventional measures of adverse housing conditions in Britain: housing unfit for human habitation or below tolerable standards; housing in disrepair; housing lacking basic amenities; and overcrowded housing. Housing deprivation in the UK has decreased sharply over the last century and access to basic facilities has improved dramatically. For instance, the sole question about housing deprivation in the 1951 Census asked whether a home had an internal hot or cold running-water tap. In contrast, the 1991 Census didn't ask this question – by then, virtually all dwellings had this facility; instead, respondents were asked if their home had central heating (Lee, 1998, p.59). In absolute terms, the most blatant aspects of housing deprivation – households lacking a bath or shower, toilet or central heating, or those where people lived in overcrowded conditions – had been eradicated by the mid-1970s: censuses from 1971 to 1991 reveal a consistent decline in the percentage of households enduring each of the main recorded housing deprivations: households lacking a bath or shower, toilet or central heating, or those living in overcrowded conditions.

This is not to say that deprivation has been eradicated completely, however. By 1991, overcrowding was low by historical standards, yet half a million people (about 2 per cent of the population) lived at a density of more than 1.5 persons per room. Overcrowding was even more common in inner cities (in the larger Scottish cities in particular) and in certain regions. Nine out of the ten local authorities with the most severe overcrowding, for example, were London boroughs. In addition, certain wards in Glasgow, Manchester and Blackburn had rates of overcrowding of between eight and fourteen times the average for the whole of Great Britain (Lee, 1998, p.60). As the Commission on Social Justice remarked: 'In the most disadvantaged parts of the United Kingdom, poverty, unemployment, ill-health and squalor combine to wreck people's chances' (1994, p.50).

Inequality in housing therefore remains, but its character and definition are different. While the association between poor housing conditions and community health has altered, it has not disappeared entirely. In part, this reflects modifications in the definition of housing **deprivation** and also in the way the impact of housing on health is conceived (an example is the inclusion of mental-health consequences of poorly designed housing). In policy debates, however, relatively little attention has been accorded to the impact of housing on other forms of inequality – whether specific, like inequalities in educational outcomes, or more general, such as inequalities in life-chances.

deprivation

In this half of Chapter 7, we explore the role of housing in reflecting, modifying and creating social differences and division. We will start by looking at the trends in housing tenure in the UK, with the shift from private rented to council supply and the ultimate triumph of the market as the supplier of housing on a mass scale. We then go on to consider the reasons for owner-occupation becoming the dominant form of housing in the UK, both in its symbolic importance and in its investment and wealth-creating potential. We then move on to consider the notion of a 'housing class', and conclude by asking whether housing has become a fundamental form of social division within the UK.

SUMMARY OF SECTION 6

1   In the twentieth century there was a marked improvement in housing conditions in the UK.

2   The definition and character of housing deprivation has also changed over this period.

3   This improvement, however, has not ended inequality in housing.

7 Trends in housing tenure

7.1 The move to state provision of housing

citizenship

In 1947 privately rented accommodation still accounted for 61 per cent of housing in England and Wales. Following on from the establishment of the welfare state, the provision of mass housing constituted an especially important component of the 'promotion of the ideal of universal **citizenship**' (Kennett, 1998, p.33). More specifically, as Smith has argued, housing to cater for need – rather than housing to provide profit – 'was regarded by successive governments as one of the more prominent benefits of British citizenship' (Smith, 1989, p.145). The housing situation after 1945 was one of shortage. National resources were, however, limited and the state sector was seen to be the most effective way of increasing the housing stock. The government limited speculative (private) building and new private dwellings had to be licensed. Between 1945 and 1952 over 80 per cent of new homes were built by local authorities. When the Conservatives took office in 1951, this continued, and there were more council houses built in the mid-1950s (180,000 a year between 1951 and 1957) than at any time before or since (Hamnett, 1993, p.151). From 1945 to 1956 the public-sector housing stock (expressed as a proportion of total stock) almost doubled.

Once the situation appeared alleviated, policy was switched to encouraging the private sector and this has increasingly become the basis of government housing policy:

> ... since the last half of the nineteenth century a fundamental change has occurred in the way in which housing has been consumed. In the nineteenth century the most appropriate mechanism for financing housing production and consumption was private landlordism, but for various reasons this situation

Figure 7.6 *Post-war council housing*

has changed. Individual private ownership (owner occupation) has emerged as the most appropriate mechanism in the twentieth century. But the period of transition … involved particular strains and shortages which (through political action) have been offset by state intervention. The development of council housing redistributed housing resources in the interests of the working class and has served the interests of capital and 'social order' by minimising the effects of the restructuring of the private market. By the 1980s it is arguable that the period of transition is over. The transitional role of council housing is therefore being abandoned and its permanent role is a more limited one.

(Murie, 1982, p.35)

Although the public (council) housing sector expanded from 1.5 million households (12 per cent of the total) in 1945 to 6.5 million (31 per cent of the total) in 1979, private owner-occupation (where households are headed by people who own or have mortgages on their homes) grew still faster from 25 per cent in 1945 to 56 per cent in 1979.

The changes in tenure structure in Great Britain between 1914 and 1991 are shown in Figures 7.7 and 7.8 below. Figure 7.7 provides data expressed as a percentage, while Figure 7.8's data are expressed in millions of dwellings. If we look carefully at these figures, we can see that there have been significant changes in tenure structure. For example, in 1914 the private rented sector accounted for approximately 90 per cent of total housing stock, whereas by 1991 it accounted for less than 10 per cent. By contrast, owner-occupation accounted for approximately 10 per cent of the total housing stock in 1914, but by 1991 it made up almost 70 per cent. Meanwhile, the data from Figures 7.7 and 7.8 show that council housing only became a prominent feature of the housing stock after 1945, but its relative importance has recently declined.

The reduction of state provision of housing was boosted further by the introduction by the Conservative administration under Margaret Thatcher of policies that were a radical break with the past. The 'right to buy' scheme allowed existing council tenants to buy their homes from the council with a price discount,

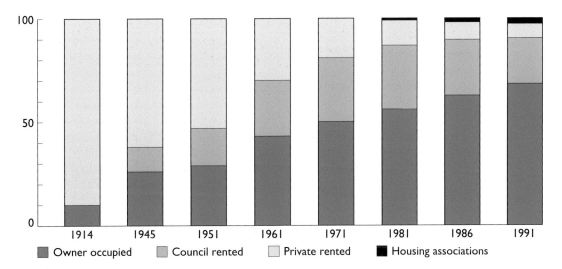

Figure 7.7 *The changing tenure structure of Great Britain, 1914–91 (percentages)*

Source: Drawn from data in Hamnett, 1993, Table 7.1, p.141

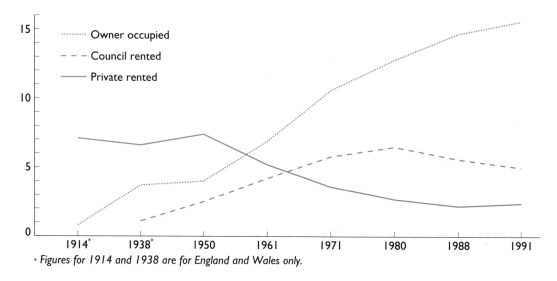

* Figures for 1914 and 1938 are for England and Wales only.

Figure 7.8 The changing tenure structure of dwellings in Great Britain, 1914–91 (millions)

Source: Drawn from data in Hamnett, 1993, Table 7.2, p.141

leading to the transfer between 1979 and 1987 – when the policy was at its zenith – of 1 million homes from the public sector to owner-occupation. Between 1981 and 1991, the sale of council houses to their occupants accounted for 46 per cent of the total growth in home-ownership. In parallel, between 1976 and 1989 housing completions by local authorities fell from 124,512 to 13,555 a year. By 1991 owner-occupation (which we shall examine in more detail in section 7.2) had reached just under 68 per cent of the total housing stock (Kennett, 1998, p.50).

The supply of housing – both quantity and type – is very much a matter of government policy, through its control of housing finance. Between 1979 and 1991, government spending on housing fell by more than half in real terms (Skellington, 1992, p.95). This was part of the Conservative government's attempts to 'roll back the state' and to encourage both the market to step in to supply public goods and individuals to become less dependent on the 'nanny' state.

Private markets now have the key role in the provision of housing in Britain. There is, nonetheless, a significant minority of people who depend on what is termed 'non-market housing', housing that is provided by various organizations operating outside the private sector – by local authorities or, increasingly for new stock, housing associations. Such housing frequently acts as a 'safety-net' for those unable to obtain accommodation privately. The direct provision of housing by the state, by being focused on the most vulnerable people in society, thus could be said to differ from the provision of education and health, each of which purports to cater for everyone (Marsh, 1998, p.7), although, of course, private provision for both education and health are available for those who desire it and can afford to pay.

7.2 The move to owner-occupation

Figure 7.9 *Modern suburban, owner-occupied housing*

As you have seen, at the start of the twentieth century, less than one in ten households in the UK were headed by owner-occupiers. Until the end of the First World War the great majority of the population rented their homes on the private market. Private renting was socially heterogeneous although housing conditions varied widely by class, income and occupation; home-ownership itself was not class-related. By 1945, however, there were 3 million owner-occupiers heading households (making up about a quarter of households) and thereafter the proportion of home-owners grew rapidly, reaching 50 per cent by 1970 and 66 per cent by 1990. Today, we find that almost three-quarters of households are headed by owner-occupiers.

The predominance of owner-occupation can be explained by a number of factors. The decline in rentier landlordism after the First World War had prompted speculative builders to cater for individual home-owners. Rising incomes and the growing infrastructure of mortgage finance enabled people to contemplate buying a house when they might previously not have had the means to do so. Tax relief on mortgage payments and the absence of capital gains tax on the sale of a main residence also worked to make home-ownership attractive. Furthermore, as you have seen in section 7.1, by the 1970s the Conservative government's 'right-to-buy' scheme allowed people who had previously rented from the state to buy their own homes. Compare these figures: in 1945, 25 per cent of homes in the UK were 'owner-occupied'; by 1990, this figure was 66 per cent. As Ball has argued, the state had moved from subsidizing housing provision (in the form of council housing) to subsidizing housing consumption (in the form of owner-occupiers):

> In terms of the social groups receiving state housing subsidies the shift of housing subsidies away from council housing towards owner-occupation consequently has been a shift away from a housing tenure where households increasingly are economically marginalised …
>
> (Ball, 1982, p.63)

ACTIVITY 6

Spend some time thinking about the different kinds of value that a home represents. What is the value of your home to you?

The growth of owner-occupation in Britain has been associated with the term 'property-owning democracy' and the concepts of 'privatism and individualism in contemporary society' (Forrest and Murie, 1995, p.1). The presumption that the wish to own one's home is 'natural' and desirable is evident in a White Paper issued by the Conservative government in the early 1970s: *Fair Deal for Housing* in 1971 (cited in Hamnett, 1989, p.241), which referred to home-ownership as the 'most rewarding form of housing tenure' because it satisfies 'a deep and natural desire' to have 'independent control' and because it builds up 'a capital asset for (the home-owner) himself and his dependants'. Thus, when, after her victory in the 1979 general election, Margaret Thatcher announced the intention to give all council tenants the right to buy, this was the development of already established principles. Nor did the Labour party's attachment to collective provision of housing prevent it proclaiming similar sentiments. The Labour government's *Housing Policy Review* (Department of the Environment, 1977) stated that, given that for most people 'owning one's home is a basic and natural desire', the trend towards home-ownership was better explained in terms of 'the sense of greater personal independence that it brings' than in terms of any anticipated financial advantage (Hamnett, 1989, p.241).

The general subscription to the idea that home-ownership is beneficial, however, overlooks the extent to which the experiences of home-owners are very different 'in different income groups, household types, geographical locations and property types' (Mullins, 1998, p.248).

SUMMARY OF SECTION 7

1   There were dramatic changes in patterns of housing tenure in the UK during the twentieth century, above all the rise in owner-occupation.

2   There was, however, a period after the Second World War when non-market housing was given primacy. Though this was depicted as a benefit of citizenship, others see this period as marking a transition from private landlordism to owner-occupation and from this perspective the large-scale sale of council houses of the 1980s assumes particular significance.

3   Though most housing in the UK is now provided by the private sector, a substantial minority is provided by council housing and other non-market sources.

8 Housing: a social divider?

8.1 Residualization

Does the division between those who own homes and those who do not signify that there is a developing gulf in society between 'haves' and 'have-nots'? The 'residualization' of council housing (that is, its *shrinkage* to a form of housing for those who cannot buy) has focused attention once more on the relationship between housing tenure and deprivation, low income and poverty. In 1967, 45 per cent of households in receipt of means-tested supplementary benefits were council tenants; by 1971 this had risen to 52 per cent, and by 1979 (when council housing accounted for 32 per cent of total housing stock) it stood at more than 60 per cent (Lee, 1998, p.62).

We therefore seem to have two contrasting positions. The first is that most people in the UK today can afford to be owner-occupiers. The second is that there are strong links between housing tenure and social class if measured by income and occupation. We can find evidence to support both positions. On the one hand – since the 1960s especially – owner-occupation has increased significantly among unskilled and semi-skilled categories of workers and also among skilled, managerial and professional categories. On the other, there are now fewer council tenants from professional, managerial and skilled manual categories, while the proportion belonging to semi-skilled and unskilled manual categories has increased markedly.

Figure 7.10 *Broadwater Farm Estate, London*

READING 7.3

You should now turn to Reading 7.3, 'Portrait of Broadwater Farm Estate, Britain, 1966–1995' by Anne Power.

As you read, consider the following questions:

1   What does Power suggest about the types of groups that were housed in Broadwater Farm?

2   Do the experiences in Broadwater Farm corroborate the idea that publicly provided housing is a residualized form of tenure?

3   How do you react personally to the story of Broadwater Farm? Is it reminiscent of your own experience? If it represents an unfamiliar world to you, what is different?

4   What is the story of Broadwater Farm about? Housing? Community relations? Policing? Race relations? 'Have-nots'? Or the effects of concentrated unemployment and social dislocation? Society in general?

5   Consider what you would do to solve the apparent crisis represented by mass housing estates like Broadwater Farm.

In contrast to a time when council housing was seen as a desirable form of housing for working-class people who wanted to escape the privations of the private-rented sector, the contraction of council-house provision today has led to a socially excluded people being concentrated in and residualized by this type of tenure. The proportion of households living in non-market housing has fallen from just over 30 per cent in 1981 to about 22 per cent in 1995 (Burrows, 1999, p.27). Many of those in employment can leave the sector for owner-occupation, but there is also a movement the other way for those who, finding owner-occupation unsustainable, have re-entered the sector. Council houses are now much more likely to be occupied by the less-skilled, unemployed people, or those on welfare benefits – single-parent families, for instance, and some minority ethnic groups (Skellington, 1992). This has brought a change in the characteristics of these households and, significantly, in income: about one half of tenants in this sector are now in the poorest one-fifth of the population.

This trend, it could be argued, was reinforced by the Housing (Homeless) Persons Act 1977, which placed an obligation on councils and local authorities to provide accommodation for those defined as homeless and in priority need. As a result, it prioritized women with children and other groups who were perceived to have difficulty affording housing – such as elderly people and those who had mental or physical disabilities. While this may suggest an *extension* of citizenship rights, Kennett argues that:

> ... the commitment to provide permanent accommodation to those considered eligible within the parameters of the (1977) legislation (a commitment which has since been eroded) also signalled the changing character of council housing which was to evolve from a tenure for middle-income groups to a residualized tenure of last resort.
>
> (Kennett, 1998, p.40)

8.2 Housing as wealth-creation

The other side of the equation of the concentration of poorer people in social housing is the potential of capital accumulation that comes with owner-occupation:

> I believe that, in a way and on a scale that was quite unpredictable, ownership of property has brought financial gain of immense value to millions of our citizens. As house prices rose, the longer one had owned, the larger the gain became ... this dramatic change in property values has opened up a division in the nation between those who own homes and those who do not.
>
> (Michael Heseltine, Secretary of State for the Environment, Debate on the Queen's Speech, 15 May 1979, quoted in Forrest and Murie, 1995, p.60)

As you have seen, the emergence of owner-occupation as the dominant form of tenure in the UK is the outcome of several factors. Nevertheless, these vary demographically. For instance, in 1977, just prior to the sale of council houses under the right-to-buy legislation, 61 per cent of households in South East England owned their own homes while 25 per cent rented publicly, whereas in Scotland only 34 per cent of households owned their own homes while 55 per cent rented publicly – thus Scotland was close to being the inverse of England and Wales (Hamnett, 1989, p.206).

The sale of council homes to tenants was itself quite uneven and mirrored existing variations in owner-occupation – for instance, between social classes and regions. As a result, there were relatively few sales in inner-city areas where a significant proportion of housing consisted of flats, unprepossessing estates and high-rise blocks and where tenants were more likely to have lower incomes. Conversely, sales were heavily concentrated in areas where owner-occupation was already high, especially in suburbs and rural areas that contained relatively desirable housing (Kleinmann and Whitehead, 1987).

While owning a home seems to offer the prospect of accumulation denied to those who rent their homes, the outcome can vary greatly from one period to another, not least because at times there are falling prices, negative equity and repossessions by mortgage lenders. Nevertheless, over the long term, it is assumed that buying a house is a prudent investment. The scale of accumulation of wealth, however, depends on a number of interconnected variables: the wealth, income and occupation of the potential buyer, the initial value of the property, and its locality. It seems safe to say that a wealthy buyer of a costly property should anticipate greater gains from ownership than a low-income buyer of a run-down house in a relatively deprived area. In general this is true, but the disparities in house-price inflation between different parts of the country sometimes confound these expectations. As Hamnett explains, even though prices of expensive houses in favoured areas, such as London and the South East, may well appreciate more quickly than less expensive houses in these areas:

> Both the relative and absolute rate of accumulation has been much greater in the South East and this locational effect has arguably overshadowed price and class related effects *within* regions. To this extent, the impact of house price inflation has been independent of social class, and it has created new inequalities which are not directly class related.
>
> (Hamnett, 1989, p.233; original emphasis)

In other words, given the impact of house-price inflation, it is feasible that a manual worker or lower-middle-class, white-collar worker in London or the South East may own a house that is worth considerably more than the sort of house owned by a well-paid professional or managerial-level worker living in, say, the North of England. This discrepancy points to an important difference between the concepts of 'housing as use' and 'housing as value'. In regions like the South East, where the value of houses has appreciated faster than houses in other regions, this benefits existing owners, but handicaps first-time buyers, because while large profits can be made by selling an existing home, getting on the 'property ladder' is clearly more difficult. Conversely, where prices have appreciated much more slowly, the ratio of average income to average price of property is much more favourable. Thus, in the first case, the degree of accumulation is higher, but in the second the 'use-value' – that is, the 'quantity' and quality of housing that one gets for one's money – is better.

This role of housing as a source and store of wealth can be viewed as perhaps the most significant outcome of the increase in owner-occupation. In the UK the value of dwellings net of mortgage debt grew from 23 per cent of total net personal sector wealth in 1971 to 36 per cent by the early 1990s (Forrest and Murie, 1995, p.2). We should note two key developments here: firstly, as the first generation of home-owners aged, a large number of outright owners emerged; secondly, the value of houses increased at a faster rate than the value of other assets. A strong association consequently emerged between the **distribution of wealth** and the growth of owner-occupation, an association noted by the Royal Commission on the Distribution of Income and Wealth (1977, p.142), which referred to the 'considerable and growing importance of housing in the statistics of wealth'.

distribution of income and wealth

Clearly, a lifetime's existence as an owner-occupier may produce a very valuable asset, but 'the differential accumulation of this form of wealth has implications for social stratification for (a given) generation and for the next generation through intergenerational transfers' (Forrest and Murie, 1995, p.2). According to the Royal Commission, people in the bottom range of wealth-owners (less than £5,000) possessed below-average holdings of dwellings and land, but for those designated in the middle range (£5,000–£20,000) dwellings accounted for 50 per cent of their assets. The significance of these figures is that they underline that 'policies which had principally been expressed as housing policies designed to solve housing problems and provide housing choice, had facilitated a considerable growth of individual wealth' (Forrest and Murie, 1995, p.64).

In this context, sociological attention has concentrated on the role of housing tenure in widening other inequalities and particularly on the social polarization that flows from the residualization of council housing on the one hand and accumulation through ownership – and especially accumulation through inheritance connected to ownership – on the other. For example, Froszteg and Holmans (1993), using Inland Revenue data and data from the General Household Survey, estimated that in 1989–90 about half of the £11.3 billion bequeathed was attributable to the value of dwellings and for those whose inheritance primarily consisted of a dwelling, the mean value was just under £69,000.

The characteristics of beneficiaries indicate the way that existing divisions and differences, both in terms of social class and by region, are likely to be

Figure 7.11 *Desirable properties on display in an estate agent's window*

replicated from one generation to the next:

> A quarter of professional- and managerial-headed households had inherited property at some stage in their lives compared with 15 per cent of junior non manual-headed households, 10 per cent of skilled manual households, 7 per cent of semi and unskilled workers and 5 per cent of economically inactive. Some 17 per cent of home owners had inherited compared with 3 per cent of council tenants. The proportion of households inheriting property was 12 per cent in Great Britain but figures ranged from 19 per cent in the South West and 17 per cent in the South East and Wales, to 9 per cent in the north west and in Greater London and 7 per cent in Scotland ... The sum inherited nationally averaged £22,000 but ranged from £48,000 in London to £13,400 in Yorkshire and Humberside.
>
> (Forrest and Murie, 1998, p.73)

The division is not just between those who inherit property and those who do not. Owner-occupiers can use their property to generate equity within their lifetime to produce loans or gifts to family members, and these can be used to gain a foothold to improve position in the housing market. In either case, however, there is a division between those who have access to funds based on owner-occupation and those who do not and who may become trapped in the rental sector or in low-value owner-occupation.

All this suggests that owner-occupation delivers financial independence and security for owners and their children by creating equity. The level of repossessions and the appearance of negative equity in the late 1980s and 1990s, nonetheless, give reason for some hesitation. In addition, there is a confusion between the benefits of home-ownership *per se*, and the position of different types of home-owners. Owner-occupiers who have entered home-ownership more recently are different from earlier buyers in several key respects. First, they comprise a wider range of occupational groups – there are more low-income workers among their number. Second, given economic restructuring and higher unemployment, they are more vulnerable to interrupted earnings and this is magnified by the erosion of welfare benefits and help with mortgage payments. Third, rising levels of divorce entail division of assets. Fourth, the sale of council housing and the building of low-standard housing has resulted in an increase in the number of lower-value properties (Forrest and Murie, 1998, p.82).

SUMMARY OF SECTION 8

1   Sociological studies of housing have been concerned with the effect of housing tenure in creating social divisions.

2   The nature of the housing market has changed in important respects – on the one hand, need has been substantially alleviated by direct provision; on the other hand, significant amounts of wealth have been created through owner-occupation.

3   Various trends have resulted in council housing becoming a residual tenure of last resort.

4   A by-product of owner-occupation has been its wealth-creation potential which has increased the divide between property-owners and those in rented housing.

9 Conceptualizing the divide

We have seen how the provision of social housing was legitimated in terms of the values of the welfare state – as a fundamental right of citizens to a dwelling and one of a habitable standard. This gradually gave way to a situation where owner-occupation is now the dominant form of tenure and council housing has become a residualized form of tenure. But does the provision of housing by the state or by the market have far-reaching implications for social stratification? Does a person's housing tenure have a material influence on their position in the social structure and on their life-chances? In this section we shall explore two approaches to analysing this by looking at the notion of the 'housing class' and examining what light consumption theory can throw on housing as a social divider.

9.1 The concept of the housing class

Based on their research in inner-city Birmingham in the 1960s, Rex and Moore (1967) posited the notion of 'housing classes', that is, that tenure divisions were the most significant basis of social stratification in urban areas. Their argument was that, though these housing classes were unequal, for example in terms of their market power and the regulation of access to more desirable forms of accommodation, not only were housing classes different from social classes, it was the struggle between housing classes that explained much racial conflict. While Rex and Moore accepted that position in the housing market was to a large degree a reflection of position on the labour market, they argued that, first, it was possible to be in one class position in terms of production and occupation and another in terms of domestic property, and, second, that there were several discernible 'housing classes'. These ranged from the most to the least advantaged: from outright owners of property, then mortgaged owners, then council tenants, and finally those living in single rooms in privately rented accommodation in lodging houses. In their view this was not related solely to occupational class (and most importantly, income) as there were other aspects of access to housing that intervened, creating competition in access to the scarce resource of housing. Membership of a housing class, according to Rex and Moore, determined lifestyle, interests and position in the urban social structure.

The strength of this analysis was that it illuminated specific and general aspects of the housing market, especially as they applied to minority ethnic groups. Its weaknesses were that it seems to have underestimated, first, the extent to which position in the housing market was determined by position on the labour market, and thus by social class and, second, the extent to which those occupying the same housing tenure had different chances of gaining access to more desirable types of tenure or more desirable types of housing within the same tenure. Thus, in the 1960s, black immigrants were constrained by the discriminatory effect of the eligibility criteria used by public housing authorities, which specified a period of local residence that few of them could meet. In consequence, by the mid-1960s only 6 per cent of the overseas-born black population were accommodated in the local authority sector, in contrast to 20 per cent of immigrants born in Ireland and about one-third of the English-born population (Smith, 1989, p.52).

The dramatic increase in the proportion of African-Caribbean households renting from local authorities (from 2 per cent at the beginning of the 1960s to more than 40 per cent by the 1970s) is usually explained in terms of the diminishing impact of residence qualifications and their wish to escape from bad housing conditions in the private-rented sector. However, local authority housing departments have been criticized for continuing to follow policies and practices that result in black people being disproportionately concentrated in the worst council housing on the least desirable estates (CRE, 1984; Ginsberg, 1992). The situation of female-headed African-Caribbean households is different, however. Their disadvantaged position reflects a complex chain of circumstances. They are much more likely than non-African-Caribbean women to experience homelessness, and when classed as homeless they are more likely to be offered temporary bed-and-breakfast accommodation, and usually wait longer to be rehoused. As a rule, they are given no opportunity to refuse the first offer made to them of permanent local authority accommodation, a consequence of which is that they are more likely to live in the least desirable accommodation on the worst estates. All these factors combined to reduce the quality of the accommodation occupied by female-headed African-Caribbean households and thus to diminish the opportunity to purchase their property under right-to-buy legislation (Kennett, 1998, p.46).

Also significant in this context, is Lee's criticism of recent government initiatives to combat the most severe kinds of social exclusion and, in particular, the specific focus on council house estates. These initiatives, he suggests, indicate a belief that housing tenure *per se* does much to explain poverty and exclusion. Lee argues that his findings on the incidence and location of measures of deprivation cast doubt on this

> ... because policies designed around limited perspectives on housing tenure and its interaction with life-cycle, deprivation and incomes can exclude parts of the housing sector where particular social groups face problems which are equally severe ... (and) ... Such policies are not sufficiently attuned to the different housing market experiences of the non-white population in different cities or neighbourhoods.
>
> (Lee, 1998, p.65)

To support his argument, Lee presents data from four major urban areas. This indicates important regional variations of deprivation by tenure and demonstrates that in Birmingham, Bradford and Liverpool the great majority of the non-white population suffering each of several specified types of deprivation were *not* living in council housing (see Tables 7.5 and 7.6). You will notice that Lee uses the categories 'white' and 'non-white'. If you refer back to Chapter 4, you will recall how Karim Murji outlines the way in which the label 'black' has been subjected to frequent redefinition (for example in census data) whereas the label 'white' tends to be treated as unchanging and unproblematic. In the UK, at one time, attempts to measure racial and ethnic discrimination and disadvantage tended to distinguish mainly between 'white' and 'non-white' (or 'black'). Later research regarded this distinction as much too crude and thus broke down the category 'non-white' into 'Asian' and 'Caribbean'. Subsequently, this demarcation itself has become regarded as insufficiently precise, and so 'Asian' was divided into 'Bangladeshi', 'Indian' and 'Pakistani'. The justification for these modifications is that disadvantage, discrimination (and for that matter opportunity

Table 7.5 Percentage of all non-white households (by measure of deprivation) living in council housing

| Non-white headed households with | % of each category living in council housing | | | |
	Tower Hamlets	Birmingham	Liverpool	Bradford
No earner in household	83.9	35.8	23.0	7.8
No car	79.8	33.7	30.3	9.5
Long-term illness in household	84.7	22.0	18.2	8.7
Head of household unemployed	82.1	29.9	27.8	9.6

Source: Lee and Murie, 1997

Table 7.6 Percentage of all white households (by measure of deprivation) living in council housing

| White headed households with | % of each category living in council housing | | | |
	Tower Hamlets	Birmingham	Liverpool	Bradford
No earner in household	70.0	41.4	41.2	30.6
No car	66.4	45.7	42.3	35.2
Long-term illness in household	71.0	39.3	36.8	28.1
Head of household unemployed	67.1	47.4	43.1	38.4

Source: Lee and Murie, 1997

and advancement) do not apply equally to these different groups – for instance, to those of Bangladeshi origin and those of Indian origin. However, even if we need to exercise caution about the categories that we use in dividing the population along 'ethnic' or 'racial' lines, this does not detract from the central point that Lee wishes to make.

These tables show, to take one example, that in Bradford less than 10 per cent of the non-white population without a car lived in council accommodation, whereas the equivalent figure for the white population in Bradford was 35.2 per cent. On the basis of this and other differences, Lee concludes that the polarization between tenures for different income groups is considerably greater in the white population than it is in the non-white population and that it may therefore be misleading to view the relationship between housing and deprivation and poverty solely in tenurial terms (Lee, 1998, p.65). Though owner-occupation is thought to be a privileged form of tenure, for some groups of people this may not be so. Thus Bangladeshi home-owners were found to be disproportionately concentrated in older, low-value, poor-quality dwellings and they also were over-represented among those in mortgage arrears and among those having difficulty meeting housing costs (ONS, 1997).

9.2 Consumption theory

Another way to conceive of the division brought about by housing is by stressing *inequality* rather than class. A consumption perspective would stress that though directly subsidized council housing has alleviated housing shortages, given access to reasonable standards of accommodation, and reduced or eliminated overcrowding for large swathes of the population, the advance of owner-occupation has increased social divisions by producing significant amounts of wealth for privileged households that have been subsidized by tax relief on mortgage payments. In other words, a widespread improvement in housing conditions has been accompanied by a growing division between those who are able and those who are unable to buy private homes. In this way, it could be suggested that the resolution of one inequality – housing as need – has led to another inequality – housing as gain.

What consumption theorists like Saunders would argue is that while housing has something in common with health and education in that they all shape life-chances, housing is the most important factor in determining position in the consumption divide because of the potential that owner-occupation has to realize wealth. Therefore being in the same position in terms of occupation but different positions in terms of consumption may mean occupying different class positions. The argument proposed by consumption theorists is not merely that the present consumption divide emerged as the transitional era of reliance on council house ended, but that it was no longer necessary for the state to provide public housing on a significant scale. Saunders remarks:

> As Rose observes: 'Collective consumption is proving to be not a permanent feature of advanced capitalism but an historically specific phenomenon' (1979, p.23), and the period of collective provision ... may come to be seen in retrospect as a temporary 'holding operation' or period of transition between the decline of the old market mode and the emergence of the new mode of private sector provision which has ... become both possible and attractive for an increasingly large proportion of the population.
>
> (Saunders, 1989, p.210)

For Saunders, the key explanatory factors in this change were the rise in incomes of many middle-class and working-class families and their desire to exercise control over consumption instead of having it directly provided by the state. In his view, the crucial point was that the purchase of housing was not confined to a small minority, but was within the reach of many working-class families. From this, it followed that consumption location, notably the accumulation of wealth associated with owner-occupation and its transfer through inheritance, would rival and even supplant class location as conventionally defined.

However, differences in housing tenure, though they may be influenced by consumption and cultural preferences, nevertheless, remain dependent on the ability to pay and this, in turn, is largely dependent on occupational position, income and terms of employment. The difference between owner-occupation and council housing is in the mode of allocation: the former is allocated primarily by price, but also by occupation and security of employment, whereas the latter is allocated on the basis of need. Thus the comparatively well off move in the direction of one tenure; the comparatively less well off move to the other.

The residualization of council housing therefore deepens – but does not create – this essential difference. It is important nonetheless. Thus, with the selling-off of much of the better stock of council houses, it came about that in many cases those who then *became* council tenants were predominantly those from outside the labour market (and many of these were homeless). For these groups, housing market position often became increasingly intertwined with residential disadvantages. As a result, the debate is no longer just about housing deprivation, but also about the lack of shops, health services and other facilities in certain localities (see Chapter 1 of this volume and Reading 7.3). Saunders (1982) suggests that we need to distinguish between

> … class relations, arising out of the organisation of production, and sector relations, arising out of the social organisation of consumption. The division between owners and non-owners of housing is, in terms of this distinction, one basis of sectoral cleavages … [T]he long-term transition from a socialised to a privatised 'mode of consumption' in Britain is today resulting in a major sectoral cleavage between a privileged majority of households who enjoy access to private provision, and an increasingly marginalised and 'exploited' minority who remain reliant upon the state. This division, it is suggested, not only cross-cuts conventional lines of class cleavage, but in some ways is becoming more significant than class as regards its impact on political alignments and the distribution of life-chances.
>
> (Saunders, 1982, p.i)

SUMMARY OF SECTION 9

1 Housing tenure can be argued to override socio-economic class and may be a better indicator of lifestyle and life-chances, signifying housing classes.

2 It has been argued that inequalities based on consumption – especially divisions between those able and unable to afford owner-occupation – may rival or supersede class divisions.

3 Residential location determines life-chances through access to differential standards of health, educational, leisure and shopping facilities and work opportunities.

10 Conclusion

In this exploration of education and social justice we have traced attempts, since the middle of the last century, to attend to need in UK society and to achieve the 'fair distribution of resources', which we have identified as central to our definition of social justice. We have shown how, despite these attempts, differences still exist along (as well as within) lines of class, gender and ethnicity, in terms of the kinds of education children receive. And we have seen how this is reflected in young people's achievements, at 16+, 18+, or in higher education, with class, gender and ethnic divisions intersecting and cross-cutting each other to produce complex patterns of inequality. We have looked in some detail at market-based policies, as a way of distributing resources, and found these unlikely either to reduce class differentials or to improve the achievements of the lowest performing groups. Returning to our original question of what has been achieved by the welfare state, the answer must be that there is a lack of evidence, in relation to education at least, that life-chances have become more equal. The reasons for this are complex, as you have seen. But *one* of the mechanisms that has enabled the privileged to maintain their position, and which has worked to the disadvantage of some other groups, has undoubtedly been the use of market-based policies within the welfare state.

Of course, the concept of the 'market' is more readily associated with housing than it is with education. In our discussion of housing and social justice we have explored the different ways in which housing has been approached through direct state intervention and private provision. You will have seen that housing raises two different aspects of the state's relationship to social justice: on the one hand, the idea of securing fair and equitable access to a key resource in order to satisfy need and reduce squalor and, on the other, the notion of facilitating individual freedom to allow gain through investment and as a source of independence.

If the question is 'How have developments in housing policy affected the life-chances of different groups?' the answer is that in the twentieth century housing deprivation – though by no means eliminated – has been reduced sharply. Nonetheless, new forms of inequality – particularly inequalities associated with owner-occupation or the lack of it – have emerged, and a gulf has developed between two groups: council-house tenants and owner-occupiers. We have shown that council-house tenants comprise disproportionate numbers of unemployed people and welfare recipients (although we should be cautious before we equate housing tenure with poverty and exclusion). Even so, where once council housing was sought after, it has now been residualized, and this was symbolized by the transformation of council-house tenants into owner-occupiers under 'right to buy' legislation. By contrast, owner-occupiers are able to amass substantial equity and a result of this is the widening of inequalities across generations. What we have shown is that while there has been a reduction of inequality based on deprivation, overcrowding and need in housing in the UK today, a new inequality has emerged – one based on the generation of wealth.

References

Arnot, M., David, M. and Weiner, G. (1999) *Closing the Gender Gap*, Cambridge, Polity Press.

Ball, M. (1982) 'Housing provision and the economic crisis', *Capital and Class*, no.17, pp.60–77.

Ball, S.J., Bowe, R. and Gewirtz, S. (1997) 'Circuits of schooling: a sociological exploration of parental choice of school in social class contexts' in Halsey, A.H. *et al.* (eds) *op. cit.*. First published in *Sociological Review*, vol.43, 1995.

Brown, P. (1997) 'The 'third wave': education and the ideology of parentocracy' in Halsey, A.H. *et al.* (eds) *op. cit.*.

Brown, P., Halsey, A.H., Lauder, H. and Wells, A. (1997) 'The transformation of education and society: an introduction' in Halsey, A.H. *et al.* (eds) *op. cit.*.

Commission on Social Justice (1994) *Social Justice: Strategies for National Renewal*, London, Vintage.

CRE (1984) *Race and Council Housing in Hackney: Report of a Formal Investigation*, London, Commission for Racial Equality.

Crowther Committee (1959) *15 to 18*, London, HMSO for Department of Education and Science.

Douglas, J.W.B. (1967) *The Home and the School*, London, Panther.

Ensor, R. (1960) *England: 1870–1914, Oxford History of England, Vol. XIV*, London, Oxford University Press.

Floud, J.E., Halsey, A.H. and Martin, F.M. (1956) *Social Class and Educational Opportunity*, London, Heinemann.

Fishman, W. (1988) *East End 1888*, London, Duckworth.

Forrest, R. and Murie, A. (1995) 'Accumulating evidence: housing and family wealth' in Forrest, R. and Murie, A. (eds) *Housing and Family Wealth: Comparative International Perspectives*, London, Routledge.

Franklin, J. (1998) 'Introduction: social policy in perspective' in Franklin, J. (ed.) *Social Policy and Social Justice*, Cambridge, Polity Press.

Freeman, A., Holmans, A. and Whitehead, C. (1996) *Is the UK Different? International Comparisons of Tenure Patterns*, London, Council of Mortgage Lenders.

Froszteg, M. and Holmans, A. (1993) 'Inheritance of house property', *Economic Trends*, no.481, London, HMSO.

Gewirtz, S. (2001) *The Managerial School: Post Welfarism and Social Justice in Education*, London, Routledge.

Gewirtz, S., Ball, S. and Bowe, R. (1995) *Markets, Choice and Equity in Education*, Buckingham, Open University Press.

Giddens, A. (1973) *The Class Structure of Advanced Societies*, London, Hutchinson.

Gillborn, D. and Gipps, C. (1996) *Recent Research on the Achievements of Ethnic Minority Pupils*, London, HMSO.

Ginsberg, N. (1992) 'Racism and housing: concepts and reality' in Braham, P., Rattansi, A. and Skellington, R. (eds) *Racism and Antiracism*, London, Sage.

Goldthorpe, J.H. *et al.* (1980) *Social Mobility and the Class Structure in Modern Britain*, Oxford, Clarendon Press.

Halsey, A.H., Heath, A.F. and Ridge, J.M. (1980) *Origins and Destinations*, Oxford, Clarendon Press.

Halsey, A.H., Lauder, H., Brown, P. and Wells, A. Stuart (eds) (1997) *Education: Culture, Economy, Society*, Oxford, Oxford University Press.

Hamnett, C. (1989) 'Consumption and class in contemporary Britain' in Hamnett, C., McDowell, L. and Sarre, P. (eds) *The Changing Social Structure*, London, Sage.

Hamnett, C. (1993) 'Running housing policy and the British housing system' in Maidment, R. and Thompson, G. (eds) *Managing the United Kingdom: An Introduction to its Political Economy and Public Policy*, London, Sage/The Open University.

Hillgate Group (1987) *The Reform of British Education*, London, Claridge.

Hughes, D. and Lauder, H. (1990) *Trading in Futures: Why Markets in Education Don't Work*, Buckingham, Open University Press

Kennett, P. (1998) 'Differentiated citizenship and housing experience' in Marsh, A. and Mullins, D. (eds) *Housing and Public Policy*, Buckingham, Open University Press.

Kleinmann, M. and Whitehead, C. (1987) 'Local variations in the sale of council houses in England', *Regional Studies*, vol.21, no.1, pp.1–12.

Lee, P. (1998) 'Housing policy, citizenship and social exclusion' in Marsh, A. and Mullins, D. (eds) *op. cit.*.

Lee, P. and Murie, A. (1997) *Poverty, Housing Tenure and Social Exclusion*, Bristol, Policy Press.

Marsh, A. (1998) 'Processes of change in housing and public policy' in Marsh, A. and Mullins, D. (eds) *op. cit.*.

Marsh, A. and Mullins, D. (eds) (1998) *Housing and Public Policy*, Buckingham, Open University Press

Mullins, D. (1998) 'Incentives, choice and control in the finance of council housing' in Marsh, A. and Mullins, D. (eds) *op. cit.*.

Murie, A. (1982) 'A new era for council housing' in English, J. (ed.) *The Future of Council Housing*, London, Croom Helm.

NHF (1997) *The Fifth Pillar: Towards New Housing Policies*, London, National Housing Federation.

Noden, P. (2000) 'Rediscovering the impact of marketization: dimensions of social segregation in England's secondary schools, 1994–1999', *British Journal of Sociology of Education*, vol.21, no.3, pp.371–90.

ONS (1997) *Ethnic Minorities*, Office For National Statistics, London, Stationery Office.

OPCS (1991) quoted in Lee, P. (1998) *op. cit.*

Paechter, C.(1998) *Educating the Other*, London, Falmer Press.

Pahl, R. (1975) *Whose City?* (2nd edn), Harmondsworth, Penguin Books.

Power, A. (1999) *Estates on the Edge: The Social Consequences of Mass Housing in Northern Europe*, Basingstoke, Macmillan.

Rex, J. and Moore, R. (1967) *Race, Community and Conflict: A Study of Sparkbrook*, London, Oxford University Press.

Rose, D. (1979) 'Toward a re-evaluation of the political significance of home-ownership in Britain', Paper presented at the Conference of Socialist Economists Political Economy of Housing Workshop, Manchester (February).

Royal Commission on the Distribution of Income and Wealth (1977) Cmnd 6999, London, HMSO.

Saunders, P. (1982) 'Beyond housing classes: the sociological significance of private property rights in means of consumption', Urban and Regional Studies Working Paper 33, Brighton, University of Sussex.

Saunders, P. (1989) 'Beyond housing classes: the sociological significance of private property rights in means of consumption' in MacDowell, L., Sarre, P. and Hamnett, C. (eds) *Divided Nation: Social and Cultural Change in Britain*, London, Sage/The Open University.

Skellington, R. (1992) *'Race' in Britain Today*, London, Sage/The Open University.

Smith, S. (1989) 'Society, space and citizenship: a human geography for the new times?', *Transactions of the Institute of British Geographers*, vol.14, pp.144–56.

Torgerson, U. (1987) 'Housing: the wobbly pillar under the welfare state' in Turner, B., Kemeny, J. and Lundquist, L. (eds) *Between the State and the Market: Housing in the Post-Industrial Era*, Stockholm, Almquist and Wiksell.

Weiner, G. (1994) *Feminisms in Education*, Buckingham, Open University Press.

Whitty, G., Power, S. and Halphin, D.(1998) *Devolution and Choice in Education: The School, The State, and The Market*, Buckingham, Open University Press

Willis, P. (1977) *Learning to Labour: How Working Class Kids get Working Class Jobs*, London, Saxon House.

Wolpe, A.M. (1976) 'The official ideology of education for girls' in Flude, M. and Ahier, J., *Educability, Schools and Ideology*, London, Croom Helm.

Young, I.M. (1990) *Justice and the Politics of Difference*, Princeton, NJ, Princeton University Press.

Readings

7.1   Sharon Gewirtz, Stephen J. Ball, and Richard Bowe, 'Choice, equity and control' (1995)

Introduction

Thorough analysis of public service markets can never be easy or straightforward. Such markets are diverse, complex and unstable. As we have demonstrated, in practice, education markets are also highly localized. They display the effects of both planning and chance, and they have their own histories and idiosyncracies. Nonetheless, the importance of the specifics of local circumstances should not be allowed to obscure general patterns and trends that are evident across settings. In designing the study reported here, we deliberately sought out settings in which the dynamics of the market – choice and competition – would be to the fore. From observation of these settings over three years, we have identified some key, general features and trends at work in the operation and effects of market forces in education. Our analytical focus has been throughout not so much on the schools and parents we have researched as *market players* but on the *policies and the market complex within which they function*. Nevertheless, we see school teachers, managers and parents as bringing different priorities, values and skills into play within the particular structures and disciplines of the market in which they find themselves located.

Two main research concerns underpinned this account of our study. One was to identify, unpack and examine the main features of the workings of local education markets, to begin to make some sense of, to describe and conceptualize, choice and competition in practice. The other was to tease out some of the implications and effects of the operation of local markets for equity and the distribution of access to educational resources. As regards the latter in particular, there is further work needing to be done, but we feel confident that we have captured some of the key aspects of the consequences of the education market in terms of inequalities.

We have identified two competing definitions of equity implicit in the arguments advanced in favour of choice in education. One definition conceptualizes equity in desert-based terms. The contention here is that goods should be distributed according to merit or desert where the 'deserving' are defined as those families motivated to take advantage of the policy of open enrolment. The other definition views equity in needs-based terms – meaning that educational resourcing should favour those with greater educational need and those with fewer private resources in the home and community to be able to meet educational needs (Levin, 1990). In what follows we will tease out and pull together the central threads of our argument to evaluate the market in terms of these two definitions of equity. Our emphasis is primarily upon the needs-based conception.

The main findings of the study can be simply summarized in four general statements.

1. The market is a middle-class mode of social engagement.
2. Parental choice of school is class- and 'race'-informed.
3. Schools are increasingly oriented towards meeting the perceived demands of middle-class parents.
4. The cumulative impact of findings 1–3 is the 'decomprehensivization' of secondary schooling.

The market as a middle-class mode of social engagement

Our interviews with parents indicate very striking class-based differences in family orientations to the market both in terms of parental *inclination* to engage with it and their *capacity* to exploit the market to their children's advantage. These differences are starkly represented by the three types of parents which emerged from our coding of the data – the privileged/skilled choosers, the semi-skilled choosers and the disconnected.

The *privileged/skilled choosers*, who are almost exclusively professional middle class, have always been advantaged in terms of access to educational resources. They were well-placed to get their children into schools of their choice prior to the Education Reform Act 1988 but we argue they occupy an even more favourable position post-1988. The privileged/skilled choosers are inclined to a consumerist approach to choice of school, that is, the idea and worth of having a choice between schools is valued and there is a concern to examine what is on offer and seek out 'the best'. These choosers demonstrate a marked capacity to engage with and utilize the possibilities of choice. Their economic, social and cultural capital enable them to 'decode' and operate to their children's advantage school systems and organizations. In making their choice of school, they are engaged in a process of child-matching. The privileged/skilled choosers are oriented to high profile, élite, often selective, cosmopolitan maintained schools which recruit some or often many of their students from outside of their immediate locale. These schools are usually oversubscribed and are often considered by privileged/skilled choosers alongside the 'local' system of private day schools. Some are more committed to the state sector, others express serious doubts about state schools and some waver uneasily between the two systems. Despite this, choice of secondary school is typically linked to long-term educational and career planning.

The *semi-skilled choosers* tend to emanate from a variety of class backgrounds, but most importantly for the purposes of the current discussion, this group is likely to include those families which we suggest are targeted by Conservative education policy – working-class families, disadvantaged by the system of 'selection by mortgage', who are strongly motivated to make the most of the 'opportunities' for choice afforded to them by open enrolment. Semi-skilled choosers are strongly inclined to engage with the market, but they do not have the appropriate skills to exploit it to maximize their children's advantage. These families talk about potential school choices as outsiders, often relying, at least in part, on the comments and perceptions of others. Recently immigrant families are among those who fit this profile. Their lack of direct experience and knowledge of the English school system and/or lack of necessary cultural or linguistic resources inhibit them in the fulfilment of their aspirations for their children. Semi-skilled choosers may also be hampered by finance-related considerations including time and transport constraints. The mismatch between inclination and capacity amongst the semi-skilled choosers are oriented to the cosmopolitan maintained schools but may have to 'settle' for the local, community, comprehensive schools.

The disconnected choosers are almost exclusively working class. The market is of limited relevance to this group because they tend not to be inclined to participate. Disconnected choosers are primarily oriented to the local comprehensive schools, partly as a result of a positive attachment to the locality and to going to school with friends and family. In addition, school has to be 'fitted into' a set of constraints and expectations related to the demands of work and household organization. For low-income families on time-constrained budgets, the limitations of private and public transport play a key role in decision-making. Such choosers have limited capacity for participation in the education market but they are making active and positive choices. However, these are not made in ways that reflect the primary values of competitive consumerism which are embedded in the English market complex.

The three 'types' of chooser illustrate two ways in which families may be privileged or disadvantaged in the market. First, competition between parents for schools disadvantages those families who are inclined to enter the competition but who are not well placed to exploit the market to their advantage, either because of insufficient finances or inappropriate cultural and social capital. Second, choice has different meanings in different class and cultural contexts; it is a socially and culturally constructed phenomenon; and families are disadvantaged or privileged as a consequence of the values which inform their conceptions of choice-making. The model of choice-making advocated by the government and encapsulated in the *Parent's Charter* (DES, 1991; DFE, 1994) represents only one model, i.e. the consumerist version so comfortably embraced by the privileged/skilled choosers and perhaps less comfortably – if equally enthusiastically – by semi-skilled choosers. However, this particular construction of choice-making is much less relevant to the disconnected or local choosers. Because they value locality over and above other considerations when it comes to choosing a school, they are not inclined to spend time immersing themselves in consumerist activity and agonizing over a range of possible options. There is, therefore, a mismatch between the culture of consumption of the local school choosers and the culture of provision. The culture of provision is much more closely matched to the culture of consumption of the privileged chooser. To use Williamson's (1981) terminology, the market form of school provision reflects the 'ideal of cultivation' of the dominant group. Or in Bourdieuian terms, the dominant class possesses the necessary cultural code for decoding the cultural arbitrariness of the market.

Here we can see the actual realization of social advantage through effective activation of cultural resources (Lareau, 1989, p.178). Because schools are funded on the basis of how many students they have, 'locality' is not a value which the market system rewards. The high-profile, élite, cosmopolitan, maintained schools to which the skilled and some semi-skilled choosers orient themselves, are likely to be oversubscribed and therefore favourably staffed and resourced. Such schools can benefit from the economies of scale that being full offers them. The local, community, comprehensive schools, on the other hand, may be – although will not necessarily be – undersubscribed. They will have similar overheads in terms of building maintenance, fuel bills, etc. as the oversubscribed schools and have to offer the same range of courses but to student bodies which may have higher levels of need (because of their socio-economic profiles, families histories, linguistic backgrounds). However, undersubscribed schools will have less money to work with and are therefore likely to be underresourced and understaffed. This will make it extremely difficult for local schools to match the perceived quality of service of the cosmopolitan schools. By the linking of biography to social structure, our analysis of school choice in relation to class and capital illuminates the reproduction of class position and class divisions and points up the changing form and processes of class struggle in and over the social field of school choice. As we argue, viewed in these terms, the market and parental choice is a class strategy.

> The definition of the legitimate means and stakes of struggle is in fact one of the stakes of the struggle, and the relative efficacy of the means of controlling the game (the different sorts of capital) is itself at stake, and therefore subject to variations in the course of the game.
>
> (Bourdieu, 1986, p.246)

The political and social construction and maintenance of the educational field (of parental choice and diversity of schools in this instance) is the outcome of political and class struggles. Its operation, via processes of individualization (choice) and the characteristics of the requisite cultural and social capital (how and what to choose and who and what you know), are classic examples of Bourdieu's notion of symbolic violence: 'the violence which is exercised upon a social agent with his or her complicity' (Bourdieu and Wacquant, 1992, p.167).

...

Schools and the perceived demands of middle-class parents

In the English education marketplace, schools have a primary incentive to maximize their examination league table performance at minimum cost. Because the bulk of school funding is allocated by formula on the basis of pupil numbers and not need, those children designated as more 'able' are worth more to schools than those with learning difficulties. Filling up a school with 'able' children and keeping children with SEN to a minimum is the cheapest and most labour-efficient way of enhancing league-table performance. Critical commentators have suggested that the logic of the market implies that children with SEN will increasingly be viewed as a liability in the marketplace and that resources will flow to the most 'able' (Willey, 1989; Lee, 1992; Housden, 1993). That is the 'logic' of the market, but what is the practice?

As we have indicated, within our case-study schools, particularly undersubscribed ones, it was firmly believed that survival in the marketplace makes it necessary not only to fill the school to capacity but also to retain or create 'balanced' intakes and to raise the raw-score performance potential of student bodies. School managers and staff typically speak about the need to target those sections of the population likely to enhance their league-table performance in various ways. Some refer to the need to attract more 'able' pupils and others, because of the association between measured ability and social class, talk about a desire to appeal to more middle-class families. Others, more reticent about using the language of class, speak euphemistically about targeting more 'motivated' parents. However, whatever the language employed, schools are adopting a number of strategies in order to raise the raw-score performance potential of their intakes, and, because of the correlation between measured ability and social class, school policies on a variety of issues are being increasingly influenced by a desire to attract more middle-class and, in some cases, aspiring working-class parents. Although the desire to appeal to the middle-class parent is usually only one amongst several rationales for the development of such policies. Some examples of policies designed, at least in part, to make school more attractive to middle-class parents include the re-introduction of setting, the devalorization of SEN and the increasing use of selection and exclusions. Developments in Northwark are of particular interest because the authority is attempting to put into practice the policies of selection and specialization which the Education Act 1993 appears designed to promote. The selective and exclusionary practices of schools, working in association with the class-biased nature of the market as a form of social engagement and the selection of schools by parents according to class- and 'racially'-based criteria, appear likely to intensify the social segregation of schooling.

…

The 'decomprehensivization' of secondary schooling

In the two decades preceding the Education Reform Act 1988, it has been possible to speak of a process of comprehensivization within school education in England. A comprehensive system of educational provision is based on the principles that it is socially and educationally advantageous for all children, whatever their ability, class or ethnic background, to be educated together in a 'common school' and in mixed-ability groups, and that all children should have access to a learning environment which enables them to realize their potential. Since the Warnock Report (1978), a central tenet of English comprehensivism has been that the majority of children with SEN are better achievers when integrated in mainstream schools and in mainstream classes. This is predicated on the argument that 'the higher the range of achievement and expectation within an educational community, the higher standards all children will reach' (Housden, 1993, p.8). The available evidence suggests that comprehensivization is of particular benefit to working-class children. The school 'context' (or social class nature of the pupil composition) has been shown to be an important factor in affecting achievement (Coleman, et al., 1966; Bridge, et al., 1979). Data from Scotland suggest that

> comprehensive reorganisation sub-
> stantially reduced between-school SES
> [socio-economic status] segregation …
> This gave manual pupils access to more
> 'favourable' school contexts, and is
> probably one reason why levels of
> attainment rose faster for manual pupils
> up to the mid-1980s that for non-manual
> pupils.
>
> (Echols et al., 1990, p.217)

However, England has never had a completely comprehensive system (comprehensivization was more thorough in Scotland): status hierarchies persisted throughout the so-called comprehensive era; only a minority of schools had fully comprehensive intakes; a few LEAs never undertook comprehensive re-organization; and middle-class families have always benefited disproportionately within this continuingly diverse educational provision (Mortimore and Blackstone, 1982). This situation, which is replicated in other areas of welfare, is used by supporters of public sector markets to bolster their arguments. Gray (1993, p.104), for instance, claims: 'There is no persuasive ethical justification for the massive, over-extended welfare states of most modern societies, which often involve perverse redistributions to the middle classes. Such 'perverse distributions' have led a number of observers to question why those on the left are so opposed to the recent welfare reforms. We would argue, however, with respect to education, that although the pre-1988 English education system was far from perfectly comprehensive, many schools were able to maintain relatively mixed intakes and to develop, often in conjunction with LEAs, policies and strategies designed to promote equal opportunity for students on the basis of class, 'race', gender and ability. We share the view of Housden (1993, p.13): 'However flawed the concept may originally have been, the comprehensive structure has created the conditions for the further development of inclusive strategies.'

Our evidence suggests that the processes of the English market seem to be halting and reversing such developments and contributing to a process of 'decomprehensivization'. As we have indicated, parents participate differently in the education market and for some children the costs of these differencies are considerable. Across schools, we appear to be seeing an intensification of status hierarchies, provisional differentiation and segregation within the state system. Working-class children, and particularly children with SEN, are likely to be increasingly 'ghetto-ized' in underresourced and understaffed low-status schools. The effects of school 'context' on pupil achievement, together with the under-resourcing and understaffing of such schools, are likely to significantly impair the learning achievements of the children attending them. Because ethic-minority children are disproportionately represented amongst the economically disadvantaged sections of the population, they are likely also to be disproportionately represented in the underresourced and understaffed schools. The re-introduction of setting and the devalorization of SEN means that within schools, segregation and provisional differentiation also seem to be occurring.

Conclusion

Effectively, the market system of education and the concomitant processes of decomprehensivization mean that resources are flowing from those children with greatest need to those with least need. Thus we are seeing a growing inequality of access to the quality of provision necessary for children to succeed educationally. This is perhaps not surprising given that the architects of the English market were not primarily committed to needs-based equity. However, our research also indicates that the English market fails the desert-based equity test ... because success in the marketplace is not primarily a function of family motivation but rather of parental skill, social and material advantages, the perceived raw-score potential of the child, and, to some extent, pure chance.

In many ways, the education markets we have been researching are peculiar and specific to metropolitan areas within England where parents have access, geographically, to a range of schools and where there is genuine competition between schools for children. However, we believe that there are lessons to be learned from our research, lessons which are of relevance across and beyond England. The class nature of the market as a mode of social engagement, and the advantages it thereby offers to the middle classes, are likely to be replicated whatever the particular market form adopted. Middle-class parents, we suggest, will always be most inclined to engage with the market and best skilled to exploit it to their children's advantage. The market is a perverse system of education income allocation in this respect, in that children are rewarded largely in proportion to the skill and interest of their parents. That some parents make choices on the basis of the class and 'racial' composition of schools is also likely to be a general characteristic of markets in socially and culturally diverse societies. That schools are increasingly oriented towards meeting the perceived demands of middle-class parents, however, may well be a more specific product of the English market. It is the outcome of a market where funding takes minimal account of pupils' needs, where there is a highly regulated curriculum and regime of testing which encourages segregation and provisional differentiation, where schools are made to feel they are going to be primarily judged on their raw examination scores, and where the devices of selection and exclusion are permitted as means of controlling pupil compositions.

Typically, advocates of choice in education respond to the English 'market-in-practice' as being a deformed version of their 'market-in-theory'. However, the market-in-theory is a utopian vision which is constructed outside of the political and financial realities of modern education systems. ...

Given the above, it still might be possible, with some imagination, to regulate an education market in ways which encourage a more equitable outcome on a needs-based definition of equity. By adopting needs-led funding, more educationally useful performance indicators and assessment procedures, and by completely removing from schools the right to control their own pupil compositions, it may well be possible to curb the iniquities associated with relatively uncontrolled choice and competition, for example by the recommendations made by Adler (1993) and Walford (1993). In a market system divested of provisional and intake differentials, however, it is highly questionable whether any demand for choice in education would be sustained. This is because, on the whole, parental desire for choice is a response to inequitable provision. But choice, however regulated, is not the *solution* to inequity. From a needs-based perspective, primacy needs to be given to establishing comprehensive pupil intakes, to allocating resources in ways which will facilitate the realization of children's learning potentials, and to making schools responsive to the values and cultures of the children that go to them. It is regulation, commitment and flair, not choice, that is necessary for the realization of these goals. As far as equity is concerned, choice is a dangerous irrelevance.

References

Adler, M. (1993) 'An alternative approach to parental choice' in *Briefings for the Paul Hamlyn Foundation National Commission on Education*, London, Heinemann.

Bourdieu, P. (1986) *Distinction: A Social Critique of the Judgement of Taste*, London, Routledge.

Bourdieu, P and Wacquant, L. (1992) *An Invitation to Reflexive Sociology*, Oxford, Polity Press.

Bridge, R.G., Judd, C.M. and Moock, P.R. (1979) *The Determinants of Educational Outcomes: The Impact of Families, Peers, Teachers and Schools*, Cambridge, MA, Ballinger.

Coleman, J.S., Campbell, E.Q., Hobson, C.J., McPartland, J., Mood, A.M., Weinfeld, F.D. and York, R.I. (1966) *Equality of Educational Opportunity*, Washington, DC, US Government Printing Office.

DES (1991) *The Parent's Charter*, London, Department of Education and Science.

DfE (1994) *Our Children's Education: The Updated Parent's Charter*, London, Department for Education.

Echols, F., McPherson, A. and Willms, J.D. (1990) 'Parental choice in Scotland', *Journal of Educational Policy*, vol.5, no.3, pp.207–22.

Gray, J. (1993) *Beyond the New Right: Markets, Government and the Common Environment*, London, Routledge.

Housden, P. (1993) *Bucking the Market: LEAs and Special Needs*, Stafford, Nasen.

Lareau, A. (1989) *Home Advantage: Social Class and Parental Intervention in Elementary Education*, Lewes, Falmer Press.

Lee, T. (1992) 'Local management of schools and special education' in Booth, T., Swann, W., Masterson, M. and Potts, P. (eds) *Policies for Diversity in Education*, London, Routledge.

Levin, H.M. (1990) 'The theory of choice applied to education' in Witte, J. and Clune, J. (eds) *Choice and Control in American Education*, vol.1, *The Theory of Choice,*

Decentralization and School Restructuring, Basingstoke, Falmer Press.

Mortimore, J. and Blackstone, T. (1982) *Disadvantage and Education*, London, Heinemann.

Walford, G. (1993) 'Selection for secondary schooling' in *Briefings for the Paul Hamlyn Foundation National Commission on Education*, London, Heinemann.

Willey, M. (1989) 'LMS: a rising sense of alarm', *British Journal of Special Education*, vol.16, no.4.

Williamson, B. (1981) 'Class bias' in Warren-Piper, D. (ed.) *Is Higher Education Fair?*, Guildford, Society into Research into Higher Education.

Source: Gewirtz, Ball and Bowe, 1995, pp.180–84,185–6, 187–90

Stephen J. Ball, Richard Bowe and Sharon Gewirtz: 'Circuits of schooling: a sociological exploration of parental choice of school in social-class contexts' (1997)

7.2

We want to attempt to 'place' the education market sociologically in more general terms by applying to it an analysis developed in relation to a somewhat different but related set of changes by Bourdieu and Boltanski. In Bourdieu and Boltanski's (1979, p.197) language the use of the market by 'cosmopolitan', middle-class families, as outlined above, is a particular strategy of reproduction. That is, a strategy by which members of classes or class fractions 'tend, consciously or unconsciously, to maintain or improve their position in the structure of class relations' (p.198). In our case, three factors 'trigger' or provide for the increased emphasis on strategic choice within the middle class families reported here. First, there is the steady inflation of academic qualifications and their correlative devaluation. Second, and related, is the increased democratisation of schooling, by comprehensivisation. Both of these pose threats to the maintenance of class advantage by reducing educational differentiation and by changing patterns of access to higher education and the labour market. Third, is the new possibilities offered in and by the policies of school specialisation and increasing selection and choice within a market framework, being pursued by the Conservative government. That is to say, the middle classes here are making the most of the new opportunities which these policies offer to re-establish their historic economic advantages or newly achieved status position. Or, in other words, changes in educational opportunity have 'compelled

the classes and class fractions whose reproduction was chiefly or exclusively assured by the school to increase their investments in order to maintain the relative scarcity of their qualifications and, in consequence, their position in the class structure' (Bourdieu and Boltanski, 1979, p.220). All of this might be taken as a perverse example of the arguments made by Halsey *et al.* (1980). They suggest that educational growth, at least initially, tended to increase inequality because new opportunities are taken up first and disproportionately by the middle classes. Further, they argued that in relation to inequality, 'scarcity of places was the crucial factor' (p.217). The market is a new 'opportunity' for the middle classes, particularly related in its operation to the conversion of their habitus; and its infrastructure of 'desire' is driven by patterns of scarcity. It must also be noted that all of these factors are set within a context of financial retrenchment in education and general economic depression and unemployment. In relation to both relative educational advantage takes on added significance. What is important here then is the 'utilisation of the specific powers of the educational system as an instrument of reproduction' (Bourdieu and Boltanski, 1979, p.205). Furthermore, within the education market-place this 'mechanism of class transmission' is 'doubly hidden'; it is obscured first of all by the continuing assumptions about the neutrality of patterns of achievement in education and second, by assumptions about the neutrality of the market itself and by the model and distribution of the 'good parent' upon which it trades. The working-class families are also engaged in a process of social reproduction; but their 'use' of the school system is driven by a different set of purposes, values and objectives. Their utilisation of the specific powers of the education system is accommodative rather than strategic.

The market orientations of the cosmopolitan, middle-class families quoted above involve the reinvestment of cultural capital for a return of educational capital.

> The educational market thus becomes one of the most important loci of the class struggle … Strategies of reconversion are nothing but the sum of the actions and reactions by which each group tries to maintain or change its position in the social structure or, more precisely, to maintain its position by changing … the reproduction of the class structure operates through a *translation* of the distribution of academic qualifications held by each class or section of a class …

which can conserve the *ordinal ranking* of the different classes.
> (Bourdieu and Boltanski, 1979, pp.220–1)

While the analysis of the role and functioning of the market in education undoubtedly needs further test and development it begins to bring policy, agency, class relations and social structure together in a powerful way. It allows us to see the link between the ideological and structural aspects of a public service market and the reproduction of class relations and relative economic change. These are the beginnings of a sociological analysis of parental choice.

References

Bourdieu, P. and Boltanski, L. (1979) 'Changes in social structure and changes in the demand for education', *Information sur les Sciences Sociales*, vol.12 (5 October), pp.61–113.

Halsey, A.H., Heath, A. and Ridge, J. (1980) *Origins and Destinations*, Oxford, Clarendon Press.

Source: Ball, Bowe and Gewirtz, 1997, pp.419–21

 # 7.3 Anne Power, 'Portrait of Broadwater Farm Estate, Britain, 1966–95' (1999)

…

An inauspicious beginning

The decision to build Broadwater Farm in 1966 was taken by Haringey Council under strong political pressure from central government to develop large-scale housing estates to help the inner-city clearance programme.

Within the borough of Haringey where the estate is located, there was a high proportion of poor quality, private rented accommodation – estimated at over 50 per cent of the housing stock in 1965 – and a large ethnic minority population. Housing need was severe.

…

Lettings were difficult from the outset. The flats were designated for Haringey's clearance families, but only half the units could be filled this way as the slum clearance programme itself was running out of steam. The rest went to low priority cases, lone mothers, and young single people. A mixture of young and old in

one of the two 18-storey tower blocks proved a disastrous mistake. By 1973, the estate had a reputation for crime, insecurity and poor services.

The estate was 20 minutes from a station and not well linked to centres of employment. Many of its residents were poor, often with a background of homelessness; increasingly they were black. Lettings problems increased its stigma and isolation. By 1976, the refusal rate was 55 per cent and the estate had twice the turnover of the borough as a whole. There were six times the level of referrals to social services (Power, 1987). As conditions on the estate plummeted, the Housing Committee took strong remedial action, blocking all lettings to homeless families and single parents, unless they specifically asked for Broadwater Farm. The idea was to create positive identification with the estate and a sense of belonging. The new lettings policy produced an almost immediate turnaround and, within two years, the estate had improved to such an extent that the access policies were relaxed again.

Investigation of difficult-to-let estates

It was in the middle of this period that the Department of the Environment visited Broadwater Farm, as one of its case studies in the nationwide investigation of difficult-to-let housing estates. There was a mixture of positive and negative findings, the most salient of which were that caretaking and cleaning services were to a high standard and the interracial community contact appeared relaxed and friendly. But roofs and decks leaked, crime and insecurity were big issues, lettings policies seriously stigmatised the estate, the design and layout of the estate were 'monotonous' and overwhelming in scale. The investigation concluded that demolition within a few years must be a serious possibility because of the generally harsh conditions and inhuman proportions.

In 1979, when the Priority Estates Project was set up, Haringey Council applied to join the experiment, proposing Broadwater Farm as the participant estate. This was rejected mainly on the grounds of the extreme severity of the social-management and security problems. Both staff and residents appeared swamped. The estate was not regularly policed. Most of the 12 shops were empty. The doctor had left the estate. The Tenants' Association was all-white in spite of nearly half the population being of minority origin. The small community hall was bleak and decayed in the extreme. Security doors on the tower blocks were broken. Decks were flooded. The walk-ways appeared desolate and abandoned:

> There is no feeling of movement about the estate in spite of the number of people.
>
> (Power, 1979)

There was little ground for believing that the estate could be made to work as a demonstration project for the national rescue of unpopular estates. Conditions appeared unsalvageable.

Between 1979 and 1982, the estate took a nose-dive into deeper troubles. The police were frequently called in to emergencies on the estate. They used the now disbanded and ill-reputed Special Patrol Group as reinforcement, creating deep resentment among young people, particularly black youth. In 1981 and 1982, there were clashes and disorders on several occasions and relations between the police and the black community became tense and often hostile. This division came to include many other older, more established residents, particularly mothers. By 1982, the shopping precinct around the base of the Ziggurat or scissor block, Tangmere, was virtually derelict and the large podium which housed the shops was a windswept, bleak no-man's-land on stilts. There were 75 empty flats on the estate. ...

New initiatives instigated by residents

In 1982, the Labour council lost control of Broadwater Farm ward. It had been considered a safe Labour area and electoral defeat shook the council. The council suddenly started to listen and react. In 1983, in response to pressure from the all-white Tenants' Association, the council agreed to the police setting up a base in one of the abandoned shops in the precinct. This provoked a major outcry from the suspicious and now alienated black community. The police move was stopped in its tracks. Instead, a shop front was given over to the newly formed and predominantly black Youth Association, set up by a long-time resident of Jamaican origin and mother of six.

...

The council then began to decentralise its housing service, placing more staff in the mid-Tottenham area. It found funding for improvements, particularly security; it agreed to open an office on the estate; and it introduced a special lettings' system for Broadwater Farm with local accompanied viewings and more choice for homeless applicants, so that people were no longer forced to move there. It abandoned its block on internal estate transfers to relieve tenant dissatisfaction.

By 1983, the council had set up a full-time neighbourhood office on the estate; had upgraded the caretaking service by appointing a resident estate superintendent, after sending him on a year's training course; allocated twice the ratio of management and administrative staff to the estate, compared with other areas; based a full-time repairs team on the estate; and set up a special panel, with councillors, neighbourhood staff and residents to take control of conditions, directly answerable to the Chief Executive of the council. The Broadwater Farm Panel effectively cut out layers of bureaucracy and left the local staff clearly in control.

At the same time, the council approached the Department of the Environment with the renewed aim of collaborating with the Priority Estates Project (PEP). This time, PEP agreed to help with tenant consultations on capital improvements. Over time PEP became deeply enmeshed in the fortunes of the estate. PEP played the role of honest broker, running block consultations over improvements, supporting key tenants' leaders and the local office, working with the Broadwater Farm Panel, the energetic and go-ahead Director of Housing and other services.

Residents' representatives were given a unique say in staff appointments to the estate under the new local management system. They were represented on all interview panels as a way of ensuring the selection of sympathetic and committed staff. There was a Council decision to offer the maximum number of estate-based jobs to residents and to recruit black staff. Half the new locally based team were residents and half were black. By 1985, there were 40 local staff, including repairs workers and caretakers.

All these changes were little short of revolutionary in council terms. They had a dramatic impact on conditions. The number of empty units dropped from 75 down to 15. …

The positive changes were underpinned by two other important factors. Firstly, the caretaking and cleaning service was intensified and upgraded. The goals were clear – lift cleaning and checking daily; deck and walkway cleaning and patrolling all day; graffiti removal daily; and staircase cleaning three times a week. These targets were strictly enforced by the outstanding resident estate superintendent, using some of the most advanced and efficient equipment. His one-year training course in cleaning and caretaking supervision had a remarkable effect on confidence and performance. All staff had walkie-talkie radios and kept in constant contact. They could be called on to help with any emergencies and were expected to back each other up. This caretaking system, with nine staff, made Broadwater Farm one of the cleanest and best maintained estates of its kind in the country. Visitors from all over the world came to study its style of service, of community involvement, of youth action and of local control.

The physical upgrading began as soon as the local office was set up. Over two years, more than £1,000,000 was spent on replacing all glass in common areas (mostly broken) with diamond glaze, unbreakable glass – causing a revolution in appearance and condition. Floor surfaces were covered with rubberised material to dull sound and to facilitate cleaning. Corridor walls were brightly painted. Most importantly, flimsy and insecure individual front doors, often on internal corridors where intruders could operate unseen, were replaced with strong steel framed doors and extra security locks.

The crime rate on the estate came tumbling down and, by 1984, Broadwater Farm was no longer hard to let. …

There were, however, several missing ingredients.

Rent arrears for the estate remained absurdly high. The debt was on average £350. Local staff explained this partly by the fact that over 80 per cent of the population was in receipt of benefits. But this did not satisfactorily account for the high debts, given the 100 per cent housing benefit rules at that time. …

Police problems

The most serious, missing ingredient was the failure to establish constructive police relations. All local services attended and reported to the Broadwater Farm Panel, except the police. The police did not share the general enthusiasm for some of the Youth Association activities, and they had only poor and infrequent liaison with the young leaders. Staff on the estate were wary of close links with the police for fear of losing the confidence of young black residents. One of the Youth Association's stated goals was to win young people away from crime to more constructive community activities. But this inevitably meant that they communicated with actual or potential 'bad guys'. The police interpreted this as 'harbouring criminals' and 'shielding crime'. It was shown in a survey in 1986 that young black men on the estate were nearly five times as likely as their white counterparts to be stopped and searched by the police on the estate (Gifford, 1986). This was the police response to what they saw as high black crime. The police seemed to see the Youth Association as a potential threat to their control over criminal activity; whereas the Youth Association often saw the police as hostile invaders of their hard-won centre and workshops. Relations were tense.

By 1985, conditions on the estate had improved remarkably. Crime had plummeted, according to police records (Mid-Tottenham Police, 1985). In the summer of 1985, the Youth Association and most of the active leaders went on a Jamaican Youth exchange. It seems that a vacuum arose. Drug dealing appeared openly in the unsupervised and unused underground garages on the estate, mainly carried on from cars driven onto the estate, then off again. …

Tensions mounted as community leaders tried to get the police to act against the drug pushers. …

Meanwhile, riots took place in September 1985 in Handsworth, Birmingham, and in Brixton for a second time within five years, after a black woman was shot in her home by a police officer. Tensions on the estate rose even further and rumours abounded that Tottenham would be the next area to riot.

On 1 October, the local police began a stop and search action on all cars entering and leaving the estate. It was a sudden, blanket action that residents and staff interpreted as provocation and over-zealous. They knew which cars needed stopping and searching. The action was called off under pressure, as young black residents showed mounting resentment of the police. Community leaders on the estate were still reporting to the police and were greatly alarmed by the sudden appearance on the estate of well-known troublemakers with serious criminal records (Zipfel, 1985).

The riot

On the weekend of 5 October 1985 the police raided a house near the estate, looking for a young man, active in the Youth Association, for a minor traffic offence. In the course of the raid, his mother, the occupier, died of a heart attack. News spread like wildfire that the police raid had led to the death of Cynthia Jarrett and, by Sunday afternoon, residents were demonstrating at Tottenham police station. After an angry meeting on the estate, a crowd of young people, mainly male and mainly black, tried to set off again for the local police station to demand a proper explanation for the death. They found exits to the estate blocked by police vans bringing in police reinforcements in riot gear. By then it was dusk.

There erupted an almighty confrontation, with burning cars, petrol bombs, police occupying defensive positions, enclosing the estate and youth moving around the decks and walk-ways, either attacking the police or trying to escape. Much of the clash was televised and the nation was appalled by the spectacle of sheets of flames leaping up past the concrete blocks and seemingly within inches of an unarmed police force crouching behind protective plastic shields, helmets and visors. Shops were set on fire, a totally chaotic and violent situation raged for seven hours and in the course of it a community policeman, PC Blakelock, was knifed to death with many stab wounds while trying to protect firemen who went into Tangmere precinct, where an Asian shop had been fire-bombed.

The anger of the police and the nation at the killing of a young policeman who had been well-respected and who left behind a family, was overpowering. The young black men who had been so angered by the death of their friend's mother were sobered by the enormity of the violence and disorder. They were deeply upset by the loss of so much that they had fought for and gained, particularly respect and support from the wider community. Their violent protest was short-lived and within hours of the

disorder subsiding, local leaders were laying even more ambitious plans for the rebuilding of their estate's reputation as a successful multiracial model. Many, including Margaret Thatcher, called for its demolition. Its name became a byword in bad design, yet in many ways, the people 'bounced back'.

...

Struggle to rebuild

...

Government officials showed their continuing support for the estate by providing a further £3,000,000 in Estate Action money between 1986 and 90 for environmental and landscaping work, for painting the walkways, for vast murals and a mosaic. Much of this work was carried out by the community co-operative set up to help young people from the estate. In all, 60 new jobs were created for residents in 1986. Contractors working on the estate were pressed into hiring local labour.

Money seemed to be gravitating to the estate in support of community initiatives. Slowly, relations were rebuilt with the police, who in 1986 agreed, for the first time, to come and report to the Broadwater Farm Panel. In spite of the bitterness among many police and many young black people, enlightened leaders on both sides worked towards calm and improved communication.

In a symbolic gesture of large proportions, the Residents and Youth Association dedicated a carefully created garden, built on the edge of the estate by the youth co-operative, to the mother and the policeman who both died in that tragic weekend of 5/6 October 1985. ...

New money from government

...

Footpaths would develop at ground level. The Department of the Environment and Haringey Council allocated £33,000,000, to be spent over eight years on the walk-way removal and ground-level reinstatement plan.

By the time these works beautifying the estate began to show, much had changed of Haringey Council. ... Both the Chief Executive and the Director of Housing had left and were replaced by people whose brief was to prioritize other areas. Cuts were in the air, as Haringey Council was forced to set the highest poll tax in the country to try and balance its budget. There was a feeling among the new leaders in Haringey Council that Broadwater Farm had received too many privileges, and was an 'unaffordable extravagance'.

Not only were deep government cuts to London local authorities taking their toll, but Haringey in particular was showing signs of a critical management and financial crisis. Arrears on Broadwater Farm had moved towards £1000 per tenant. Much of this could be traced directly to the breakdown of financial and staff management within parts of the Council. Frozen posts, cuts in repairs, withdrawal of community services, loss of grants to community groups, all meant that tenants and staff became increasingly demoralised and cynical about the Council.

...

In 1989, the Council reverted, after years of successful local lettings, to its 'homeless only, one offer only policy'. It immediately set in train again the previous scenario of refusals, polarisation and rising voids. By 1991, there were 60 empty flats on the estate, yet the restrictive policy was ostensibly to help house homeless people! This was the third time in its brief history that Broadwater had been pushed into a cycle of polarised and insensitive lettings.

References

Gifford, Lord (Chairman) (1986) *The Broadwater Farm Inquiry Report: Report of the Independent Inquiry into disturbances of October 1985 at the Broadwater Farm Estate, Tottenham*, chaired by Lord Gifford QC, London Borough of Haringey.

Mid-Tottenham Police (1985) *Information given by Chief Superintendent Stainsby to the Broadwater Farm Panel*, 24 March.

Power, A. (1979) Notes on Visit to Broadwater Farm, Haringey.

Power, A. (1987) *Property before People: The Management of Twentieth Century Council Housing*, London, Allen & Unwin.

Zipfel, T. (1985) *Broadwater Farm Estate, Haringey: Background and Information Relating to the Riot on Sunday 6th October 1985*, London, PEP.

Source: Power, 1999, pp.195–218

Readings in social differences and divisions

Contents

Reading A
Karl Marx and Friedrich Engels: 'The Manifesto of the Communist Party' (1848)   346

Reading B
Max Weber: 'Class, status, party' (1922)   349

Reading C
Gunnar Myrdal: 'Caste and class' (1964)   355

Reading D
Lynne Segal: ' Only contradictions on offer: feminism at the millennium' (1999)   359

Reading E
Gordon Marshall: 'Social class and underclass in Britain and the USA' (1997)   367

Reading F
Stephen Castles and Godula Kosack: 'Immigrant workers and class structure in western Europe' (1973)   374

Reading G: T.H. Marshall: 'Value problems of welfare-capitalism' (1972)   378

Karl Marx and Friedrich Engels: 'The Manifesto of the Communist Party' (1848)

Bourgeois and proletarians[1]

The history of all hitherto existing society[2] is the history of class struggles. Freeman and slave, patrician and plebeian, lord and serf, guild-master[3] and journeyman, in a word, oppressor and oppressed, stood in constant opposition to one another, carried on an uninterrupted, now hidden, now open fight, a fight that each time ended, either in a revolutionary reconstitution of society at large, or in the common ruin of the contending classes.

In the earlier epochs of history, we find almost everywhere a complicated arrangement of society into various orders, a manifold gradation of social rank. In ancient Rome we have patricians, knights, plebeians, slaves; in the Middle Ages, feudal lords, vassals, guild-masters, journeymen, apprentices, serfs; in almost all of these classes, again, subordinate gradations.

The modern bourgeois society that has sprouted from the ruins of feudal society has not done away with class antagonisms. It has but established new classes, new conditions of oppression, new forms of struggle in place of the old ones.

Our epoch, the epoch of the bourgeoisie, possesses, however, this distinctive feature: it has simplified the class antagonisms. Society as a whole is more and more splitting up into two great hostile camps, into two great classes directly facing each other – bourgeoisie and proletariat.

…

In proportion as the bourgeoisie, i.e. capital, is developed, in the same proportion is the proletariat, the modern working class, developed – a class of labourers, who live only so long as they find work, and who find work only so long as their labour increases capital. These labourers, who must sell themselves piecemeal, are a commodity, like every other article of commerce, and are consequently exposed to all the vicissitudes of competition, to all the fluctuations of the market.

Owing to the extensive use of machinery and to division of labour, the work of the proletarians has lost all individual character, and, consequently, all charm for the workman. He becomes an appendage of the machine, and it is only the most simple, most monotonous, and most easily acquired knack, that is required of him. Hence, the cost of production of a workman is restricted, almost entirely, to the means of subsistence that he requires for his maintenance, and for the propagation of his race. But the price of a commodity, and therefore also of labour, is equal to its cost of production. In proportion, therefore, as the repulsiveness of the work increases, the wage decreases. …

Modern industry has converted the little workshop of the patriarchal master into the great factory of the industrial capitalist. Masses of labourers, crowded into the factory, are organized like soldiers. As privates of the industrial army they are placed under the command of a perfect hierarchy of officers and sergeants. Not only are they slaves of the bourgeois class, and of the bourgeois state, they are daily and hourly enslaved by the machine, by the overlooker and, above all, by the individual bourgeois manufacturer himself. The more openly this despotism proclaims gain to be its end and aim, the more petty, the more hateful and the more embittering it is.

…

The lower strata of the middle class – the small tradespeople, shopkeepers, and retired tradesmen generally, the handicraftsmen and peasants – all these sink gradually into the proletariat, partly because their diminutive capital does not suffice for the scale on which modern industry is carried on, and is swamped in the competition with the large capitalists, partly because their specialized skill is rendered worthless by new methods of production. Thus the proletariat is recruited from all classes of the population.

The proletariat goes through various stages of development. With its birth begins its struggle with the bourgeoisie. At first the contest is carried on by individual labourers, then by the work people of a factory, then by the operatives of one trade, in one locality, against the individual bourgeois who directly exploits them. They direct their attacks not against the bourgeois conditions of production, but against the instruments of production themselves; they destroy imported wares that compete with their labour, they smash to pieces machinery, they set factories ablaze, they seek to restore by force the vanished status of the workman of the Middle Ages.

At this stage the labourers still form an incoherent mass scattered over the whole country, and broken up by their mutual competition. …

But with the development of industry the proletariat not only increases in number; it becomes concentrated in greater masses, its strength grows, and it feels that strength more. The various interests and conditions of life within the ranks of the proletariat are more and more equalized, in proportion as machinery obliterates all distinctions of labour, and nearly everywhere reduces wages to the same low level. The growing competition among the bourgeois, and the resulting commercial crises, make the wages of the workers ever more fluctuating. The unceasing improvement of machinery, ever more rapidly developing, makes their livelihood more and more precarious; the collisions between individual workmen and individual bourgeois take more and more the character of collisions between two classes. Thereupon the workers begin to form combinations (trade unions) against the bourgeois; they club together in order to keep up the rate of wages; they found permanent associations in order to make provision beforehand for these occasional revolts. Here and there the contest breaks out into riots.

Now and then the workers are victorious, but only for a time. The real fruit of their battles lies, not in the immediate result, but in the ever expanding union of the workers. This union is helped on by the improved means of communication that created by modern industry, and that place the workers of different localities in contact with another. It was just this contact that was needed to centralize the numerous local struggles, all of the same character, into one national struggle between classes. …

Notes

1   By bourgeoisie is meant the class of modern capitalists, owners of the means of social production and employers of wage labour. By proletariat, the class of modern wage labourers who, having no means of production of their own, are reduced to selling their labour power in order to live.

2   That is, all *written* history. In 1847 the pre-history of society, the social organization existing previous to recorded history, was all but unknown. Since then Haxthausen (August von, 1792–1866) discovered common ownership of land in Russia, Maurer (Georg Ludwig von) proved it to be the social foundation from which all Teutonic races started in history, and, by and by, village communities were found to be, or to have been, the primitive form of society everywhere from India to Ireland. The inner organization of this primitive communistic society was laid bare, in its typical form, by Morgan's (Lewis Henry, 1818–81) crowning discovery of the true nature of the *gens* and its relation to the *tribe*. With the dissolution of these primaeval communities, society begins to be differentiated into separate and finally antagonistic classes. I have attempted to retrace this process of dissolution in *Der Ursprung der Familie, des Privateigenthums und des Staats* (*The Origin of the Family, Private Property and the State*), second edition, Stuttgart, 1886.

3   Guild-master, that is a full member of a guild, a master within, not a head of a guild.

Source: Karl Marx and Friedrich Engels, 'The Manifesto of the Communist Party' in *The Essential Left: Four Classic Texts on the Principles of Socialism – Marx, Engels, Lenin*, London, Unwin Books, pp.14–15, 21–23. First published in 1848.

Max Weber:
'Class, status, party' (1922)

Determination of class-situation by market-situation

In our terminology, 'classes' are not communities; they merely represent possible, and frequent, bases for communal action. We may speak of a 'class' when (a) a number of people have in common a specific causal component of their life chances, in so far as (b) this component is represented exclusively by economic interests in the possession of goods and opportunities for income, and (c) is represented under the conditions of the commodity or labor markets. (These points refer to 'class situation', which we may express more briefly as the typical chance for a supply of goods, external living conditions and personal life experiences, in so far as this chance is determined by the amount and kind of power, or lack of such, to dispose of goods or skills for the sake of income in a given economic order. The term 'class' refers to any group of people that is found in the same class situation.)

It is the most elemental economic fact that the way in which the disposition over material property is distributed among a plurality of people, meeting competitively in the market for the purpose of exchange, in itself creates specific life chances. According to the law of marginal utility this mode of distribution excludes the non-owners from competing for highly valued goods; it favors the owners and, in fact, gives to them a monopoly to acquire such goods. Other things being equal, this mode of distribution monopolizes the opportunities for profitable deals for all those who, provided with goods, do not necessarily have to exchange them. It increases, at least generally, their power in price wars with those who, being propertyless, have nothing to offer but their services in native form or goods in a form constituted through their own labor, and who above all are compelled to get rid of these products in order barely to subsist. This mode of distribution gives to the propertied a monopoly on the possibility of transferring property from the sphere of use as a 'fortune', to the sphere of 'capital goods'; that is, it gives them the entrepreneurial function and all chances to share directly or indirectly in returns on capital. All this holds true within the area in which pure market conditions prevail. 'Property' and 'lack of property' are, therefore, the basic categories of all class situations. It does not matter whether these two categories become effective in price wars or in competitive struggles.

Within these categories, however, class situations are further differentiated: on the one hand, according to the kind of property that is usable for returns; and, on the other hand, according to the kind of services that can be offered in the market. Ownership of domestic buildings; productive establishments; …

disposition over products of one's own labor or of others' labor differing according to their various distances from consumability; disposition over transferable monopolies of any kind – all these distinctions differentiate the class situations of the propertied just as does the 'meaning' which they can and do give to the utilization of property, especially to property which has money equivalence. Accordingly, the propertied, for instance, may belong to the class of rentiers or to the class of entrepreneurs.

Those who have no property but who offer services are differentiated just as much according to their kinds of services as according to the way in which they make use of these services, in a continuous or discontinuous relation to a recipient. But always this is the generic connotation of the concept of class: that the kind of chance in the *market* is the decisive moment which presents a common condition for the individual's fate. 'Class situation' is, in this sense, ultimately 'market situation'. ...

Those men whose fate is not determined by the chance of using goods or services for themselves on the market, e.g. slaves, are not, however, a 'class' in the technical sense of the term. They are, rather, a 'status group'.

Communal action flowing from class interest

According to our terminology, the factor that creates 'class' is unambiguously economic interest, and indeed, only those interests involved in the existence of the 'market'. Nevertheless, the concept of 'class-interest' is an ambiguous one: even as an empirical concept it is ambiguous as soon as one understands by it something other than the factual direction of interests following with a certain probability from the class situation for a certain 'average' of those people subjected to the class situation. The class situation and other circumstances remaining the same, the direction in which the individual worker, for instance, is likely to pursue his interests may vary widely, according to whether he is constitutionally qualified for the task at hand to a high, to an average, or to a low degree. In the same way, the direction of interests may vary according to whether or not a *communal* action of a larger or smaller portion of those commonly affected by the 'class situation', or even an association among them, e.g. a 'trade union', has grown out of the class situation from which the individual may or may not expect promising results. (Communal action refers to that action which is oriented to the feeling of the actors that they belong together. Societal action, on the other hand, is oriented to a rationally motivated adjustment of interest.) The rise of societal or even of communal action from a common class situation is by no means a universal phenomenon.

... The degree in which 'communal action' and possibly 'societal action', emerges from the 'mass actions' of the members of a class is linked to general cultural conditions, especially to those of an intellectual sort. It is also linked to the extent of the contrasts that have already evolved, and is especially linked to the *transparency* of the connections between the causes and the consequences of the 'class situation'. For however different life chances may be, this fact in itself, according to all experience, by no means gives birth to 'class action' (communal action by the members of a class). The fact of being conditioned and the results of the class situation must be distinctly recognizable. For only then the contrast of life chances can be felt not as an absolutely given fact to be accepted, but as a resultant from either (a) the given distribution of property, or (b) the structure of the concrete economic order. It is only then that people may react against the class structure not only through acts of an intermittent and irrational protest, but in the form of rational association. …

Types of 'class struggle'

Thus every class may be the carrier of any one of the possibly innumerable forms of 'class action', but this is not necessarily so. In any case, a class does not in itself constitute a community. To treat 'class' conceptually as having the same value as 'community' leads to distortion. That men in the same class situation regularly react in mass actions to such tangible situations as economic ones in the direction of those interests that are most adequate to their average number is an important and after all simple fact for the understanding of historical events. Above all, this fact must not lead to that kind of pseudo-scientific operation with the concepts of 'class' and 'class interests' so frequently found these days, and which has found its most classic expression in the statement of a talented author, that the individual may be in error concerning his interests but that the 'class' is 'infallible' about its interests. Yet, if classes as such are not communities, nevertheless class situations emerge only on the basis of communalization. The communal action that brings forth class situations, however, is not basically action between members of the identical class; it is an action between members of different classes. …

…

Status honor

In contrast to classes, *status groups* are normally communities. They are, however, often of an amorphous kind. In contrast to the purely economically determined 'class situation' we wish to designate as 'status situation' every typical component of the life fate of men that is determined by a specific, positive or negative, social estimation of *honor*. This honor may be connected with any quality shared by a plurality, and, of course, it can be knit to a class situation: class distinctions are linked in the most varied ways with status distinctions. Property as such is not always recognized as a status qualification, but in the long run it is, and with extraordinary regularity. …

Both propertied and propertyless people can belong to the same status group, and frequently they do with very tangible consequences. This 'equality' of social esteem may, however, in the long run become quite precarious… .

Guarantees of status stratification

In content, status honor is normally expressed by the fact that above all else a specific *style of life* can be expected from all those who wish to belong to the circle. Linked with this expectation are restrictions on 'social' intercourse (that is, intercourse which is not subservient to economic or any other of business's 'functional' purposes). These restrictions may confine normal marriages to within the status circle and may lead to complete endogamous closure. As soon as there is not a mere individual and socially irrelevant imitation of another style of life, but an agreed-upon communal action of this closing character, the 'status' development is under way.

...

'Ethnic' segregation and 'caste'

Where the consequences have been realized to their full extent, the status group evolves into a closed 'caste'. Status distinctions are then guaranteed not merely by conventions and laws, but also by *rituals*. This occurs in such a way that every physical contact with a member of any caste that is considered to be 'lower' by the members of a 'higher' caste is considered as making for a ritualistic impurity and to be a stigma which must be expiated by a religious act. Individual castes develop quite distinct cults and gods.

In general, however, the status structure reaches such extreme consequences only where there are underlying differences which are held to be 'ethnic'. ...

A 'status' segregation grown into a 'caste' differs in its structure from a mere 'ethnic' segregation: the caste structure transforms the horizontal and unconnected coexistences of ethnically segregated groups into a vertical social system of super- and subordination. Correctly formulated: a comprehensive societalization integrates the ethnically divided communities into specific political and communal action. In their consequences they differ precisely in this way: ethnic coexistences condition a mutual repulsion and disdain but allow each ethnic community to consider its own honor as the highest one; the caste structure brings about a social subordination and an acknowledgement of 'more honor' in favour of the privileged caste and status groups. This is due to the fact that in the caste structure ethnic distinctions as such have become 'functional' distinctions within the political societalization. ...

...

Status privileges

...

The decisive role of a 'style of life' in status 'honor' means that status groups are the specific bearers of all 'conventions'. In whatever way it may be manifest, all 'stylization' of life either originates in status groups or is at lest conserved by them. Even if the principles of status conventions differ greatly, they reveal certain typical traits, especially among those strata which are most privileged. Quite generally, among privileged status groups there is a status disqualification that operates against the performance of common physical labor. This disqualification is now 'setting in' in America against the old tradition of esteem for labor. Very frequently every rational economic pursuit, and especially 'entrepreneurial activity', is looked upon as a disqualification of status. Artistic and literary activity is also considered as degrading work as soon as it is exploited for income, or at least when it is connected with hard physical exertion. An example is the sculptor working like a mason in his dusty smock as over against the painter in his salon-like 'studio' and those forms of musical practice that are acceptable to the status group.

...

Parties

Whereas the genuine place of 'classes' is within the economic order, the place of 'status groups' is within the social order, that is, within the sphere of the distribution of 'honor'. From within these spheres, classes and status groups influence one another and they influence the legal order and are in turn influenced by it. But 'parties' live in a house of 'power'.

Their action is oriented toward the acquisition of social 'power', that is to say, toward influencing a communal action no matter what its content may be. In principle, parties may exist in a social 'club' as well as in a 'state'. As over against the actions of classes and status groups, for which this is not necessarily the case, the communal actions of 'parties' always mean a societalization. For party actions are always directed toward a goal which is striven for in planned manner. This goal may be a 'cause' (the party may aim at realizing a program for ideal or material purposes), or the goal may be 'personal' (sinecures, power, and from these, honor for the leader and the followers of the party). Usually the party action aims at all these simultaneously. Parties are, therefore, only possible within communities that are societalized, that is, which have some rational order and a staff of persons available who are ready to enforce it. For parties aim precisely at influencing this staff, and if possible, to recruit it from party followers.

In any individual case, parties may represent interests determined through 'class situation' or 'status situation', and they may recruit their following respectively from one or the other. But they need be neither purely 'class' nor purely 'status' parties. In most cases they are partly class parties and partly status parties, but sometimes they are neither. They may represent ephemeral or enduring structures. Their means of attaining power may be quite varied, ranging from naked violence of any sort to canvassing for votes with coarse or subtle means: money, social influence, the force of speech, suggestion, clumsy hoax and so on to the rougher or more artful tactics of obstruction in parliamentary bodies.

The sociological structure of parties differs in a basic way according to the kind of communal action which they struggle to influence. Parties also differ according to whether or not the community is stratified by status or by classes. Above all else, they vary according to the structure of domination within the community. For their leaders normally deal with the conquest of a community. They are, in the general concept which is maintained here, not only products of specially modern forms of domination. We shall also designate as parties the ancient and medieval 'parties', despite the fact that their structure differs basically from the structure of modern parties. By virtue of these structural differences of domination it is impossible to say anything about the structure of parties without discussing structural forms of social domination per se. Parties, which are always structures struggling for domination, are very frequently organized in a very strict 'authoritarian' fashion…

Concerning 'classes', 'status groups' and 'parties', it must be said in general that they necessarily presuppose a comprehensive societalization, and especially a political framework of communal action, within which they operate. This does not mean that parties would be confined by the frontiers of any individual political community. On the contrary, at all times it has been the order of the day that the societalization (even when it aims at the use of military force in common) reaches beyond the frontiers of politics. This has been the case in the solidarity of interests among the Oligarchs and among the democrats in Hellas, among the Guelfs and among Ghibellines in the Middle Ages, and within the Calvinist party during the period of religious struggles. It has been the case up to the solidarity of the landlords (international congress of agrarian landlords), and has continued among princes (holy alliance, Karlsbad decrees), socialist workers, conservatives (the longing of Prussian conservatives for Russian intervention in 1850). But their aim is not necessarily the establishment of new international political, i.e. *territorial*, dominion. In the main they aim to influence the existing dominion.[1]

Note

1   The posthumously published text breaks off here. We omit an incomplete sketch of types of 'warrior estates'.

Source: Excerpts from Max Weber, *Wirtschaft und Gesellschaft*, 1922, reprinted in Hans Gerth and C. Wright Mills (eds and trans.), *From Max Weber: Essays in Sociology*, Oxford University Press, 1946, pp.180–95; taken from Kenneth Thompson and Jeremy Tunstall (eds) *Sociological Perspectives: Selected Readings*, Harmondsworth, Penguin Books, 1971, pp.250–4, 256–60, 262–4.

Gunnar Myrdal:
'Caste and class' (1964)

The concepts 'caste' and 'class'

...

It should, however, be clear that the actual content of the Negro's lower caste status in America, that is, *the social relations across the caste line, vary considerably from region to region within the country and from class to class within the Negro group. It also shows considerable change in time.* But variation and change are universal characteristics of social phenomena and cannot be allowed to hinder us from searching for valid generalizations. It will only have to be remembered constantly that when the term 'caste relations' is used in this inquiry to denote a social phenomenon in present-day America, this term must be understood in a *relative* and *quantitative sense.* It does not assume an invariability in space and time in the culture, nor absolute identity with similar phenomena in other cultures. It should be pointed out, incidentally, that those societies to which the term 'caste' is applied without controversy – notably the *ante-bellum* slavery society of the south and the Hindu society of India – do not have the 'stable equilibrium' which American sociologists from their distance are often inclined to attribute to them.[1]

Much of the controversy around the concept caste seems, indeed, to be the unfortunate result of not distinguishing clearly between the caste *relation* and the caste *line.* The changes and variations which occur in the American caste system relate only to caste relations, not to the dividing line between the castes. The latter stays rigid and unblurred. It will remain fixed until it becomes possible for a person to pass legitimately from the lower caste to the higher without misrepresentation of his origin. The American definition of 'Negro' as any person who has the slightest amount of Negro ancestry has its significance in making the caste line absolutely rigid. Had the caste line been drawn differently – for example, on the criterion of predominance of white or Negro ancestry or of cultural assimilation – it would not have been possible to hold the caste line so rigid.

The general definition of caste which we have adopted permits us to infer a concrete definition for our particular problem. When we say that Negroes form a lower caste in America, we mean that they are subject to certain disabilities solely because they are 'Negroes' in the rigid American definition and not because they are poor and ill-educated. It is true, of course, that their caste position keeps them poor and ill-educated on the average, and that there is a complex circle of causation, but in any concrete instance at any given time there is little difficulty in deciding whether a certain disability or discrimination is due to a

Negro's poverty or lack of education, on the one hand, or his caste position, on the other hand. In this concrete sense, practically the entire factual content of the preceding parts of this book may be considered to define caste in the case of the American Negro.

We conceive of the social differentiation between Negroes and whites as based on tradition and, more specifically, on the traditions of slavery society. We have attempted to trace this cultural heritage in various spheres of life. The caste system is upheld by its own inertia and by the superior caste's interests in upholding it. The beliefs and sentiments among the whites centering around the idea of the Negroes' inferiority have been analyzed and their 'functional' role as rationalizations of the superior caste's interests has been stressed. The racial beliefs and the popular theory of 'no social equality' were found to have a kernel of magical logic, signified by the notion of 'blood'. We have been brought to view the caste order as fundamentally a system of disabilities forced by the whites upon the Negroes[2], and our discussion of the Negro problem up to this point has, therefore, been mainly a study of the whites' attitudes and behavior. And even when we proceed to inquire about the internal social structure of the Negro caste, about Negro ideologies, Negro leadership and defense organizations, the Negro community and its institutions, Negro culture and accomplishments, and Negro social pathology, we shall continue to meet the same determinants. Little of this can be explained in terms of Negro characteristics. The Negro problem is primarily a white man's problem. In this part we shall find that *the class order within the Negro caste is chiefly a function of the historical caste order of America*.

    ...

Caste, as distinguished from class, consists of such drastic restrictions of free competition in the various spheres of life that the individual in a lower caste cannot, by any means, change his status, except by a secret and illegitimate 'passing', which is possible only to the few who have the physical appearance of members of the upper caste. Caste may thus in a sense be viewed as the extreme case of absolutely rigid class. Such a harsh deviation from the ordinary American social structure and the American Creed could not occur without a certain internal conflict and without a system of false beliefs and blindnesses aided by certain mechanical controls in law and social structure. To the extent, however, that false beliefs in Negro inferiority are removed by education and to the extent that white people are made to see the degradations they heap on Negroes, to that extent will the American Creed be able to make its assault on caste.

Within each caste, people also feel social distance and restrict free competition, so that each caste has its own class system. The dividing line between two castes is by definition clear-cut, consciously felt by every member of each caste, and easily observable. No arbitrariness is involved in drawing it. The class lines, on the other hand, are blurred and flexible. The very fact that individuals move and marry between the classes, that they have legitimate relatives in other classes and that competition is not nearly so restricted in any sphere, blurs any division lines that are set. Lines dividing the classes are not defined in law or even in custom, as caste lines are. Therefore, it is probably most correct to conceive of the class order as *social continuum*. ...

    ...

The caste struggle

The Marxian concept of 'class struggle' – with its basic idea of a class of proletarian workers who are kept together in a close bond of solidarity of interests against a superior class of capitalist employers owning and controlling the means of production, between which there is a middle class bound to disappear as the grain is ground between two millstones – is in all Western countries a superficial and erroneous notion. It minimizes the distinctions that exist within each of the two main groups; it exaggerates the cleft between them, and, especially, the consciousness of it; and it misrepresents the role and the development of the middle classes. It is 'too simple and sweeping to fit the facts of the class-system' (MacIver, 1931, p.89). In America it is made still more inapplicable by the traversing systems of color caste. The concept of 'caste struggle', on the other hand, is much more realistic. Archer talked of a 'state of war' between Negroes and whites in the United States (Archer, 1910, pp.234 ff); James Weldon Johnson spoke about 'the tremendous struggle which is going on between the races in the South' (Johnson, 1927, pp.75–6).[3] The caste distinctions are actually gulfs which divide the population into antagonistic camps. And this is a conscious fact to practically every individual in the system.

The caste line – or, as it is more popularly known, the color line – is not only an expression of caste differences and caste conflicts, but it has come itself to be a catalyst to widen differences and engender conflicts. To maintain the color line has, to the ordinary white man, the 'function' of upholding the caste system itself, or keeping the 'Negro in his place'. The color line has become the bulwark against the whites' own adherence to the American Creed, against trends of improvement in Negroes' education, against other social trends which stress the irrationality of the caste system, and against the demands of the Negroes. The color line has taken on a mystical significance: sophisticated Southern whites, for example, will often speak with compassionate regret of the sacrifices the Negroes 'have to' make and the discriminations to which they 'have to' submit – 'have to' in order to preserve the color line as an end in itself. This necessitates a constant vigilance. Southern whites feel a caste solidarity that permits no exception: some of them may not enforce the etiquette against all Negroes in all its rigor, but none will interfere with another white man when he is enforcing his superiority against a Negro. A white man who becomes known as a 'nigger lover' loses caste and is generally ostracized if not made the object of violence. Even a Southern white child feels the caste solidarity and learns that he can insult an adult Negro with impunity (Moton, 1929, p.8).

An extreme illustration of white solidarity in the South is given every time the whites, in a community where a lynching has occurred, conspire not to let the lynchers be indicted and sentenced.[4] In less spectacular cases it operates everywhere.

Notes

1   A Hindu acquaintance once told me that the situation in the United States is as much, or more, describable by the term 'caste' as is the situation in India.

2   The voluntary withdrawal and the self-imposed segregation were shown to be a secondary reaction to a primary white pressure.

3   Johnson continues:

It is a struggle; for though the black man fights passively, he nevertheless fights; and his passive resistance is more effective at present than active resistance could possibly be. He bears the fury of the storm as does the willow-tree. It is a struggle; for though the white man of the South may be too proud to admit it, he is, nevertheless, using in the contest his best energies; he is devoting to it the greater part of his thought and much of his endeavour. The South today stands panting and almost breathless from its exertions.

4   As this is being written the Negro press is still vibrating over the first lynching for the year 1942, which occurred in Sikeston, Missouri, January 25. The National Association for the Advancement of Colored Peoples reports that:

White citizens in Sikeston will not testify against each other in any prosecution for guilt in the lynching … and they use the threat of a race riot to prevent further investigation and publicity …

The make-up of the mob was described as being 'just folks' … The investigators said: 'We were given the definite impression that the lynchers would not be ostracized by the community; on the other hand those who might *testify against* the lynchers would be ostracized,' …

Young Prosecuting Attorney Blanton will hardly sacrifice both his career and personal friends, by prosecuting those friends who elected him to office. Even the most liberal of planters said he would 'not be inclined to testify.'

(NAACP Press Release [February 13, 1942], pp.1–2)

Although Governor Forrest C. Donnell of Missouri ordered an immediate investigation, and the Federal Bureau of Investigation sent their investigators into Sikeston, no indictments were ever brought. The way in which this solidarity on the white side elicits a corresponding solidarity on the Negro side is beautifully illustrated in this case. Negro columnists are complementing the American war slogan: 'Remember Pearl Harbor' with the Negro slogan: 'Remember Sikeston'.

References

Archer, W. (1910) *Through Afro-America.*

Johnson, J.W. (1927, first edition 1912) *Autobiography of an Ex-Coloured Man.*

MacIver, W.M. (1931) *Society: Its Structure and Changes.*

Moton, R.R. (1929) *What the Negro Thinks.*

Source: Gunnar Myrdal (with the assistance of Richard Sterner and Arnold Rose), *An American Dilema*, Vol. 2: *The Negro Social Structure*, New York, McGraw-Hill, 1964, pp.668–9, 674–5, 676–7.

Lynne Segal:
'Only contradictions on offer: feminism at the millennium' (1999)

Snapshots of gender

The differing faces of feminism in the media, the academy and politics reflect competing aspects of women's lives today. Depending on our framing, we find two deeply contrasting images: one is gloomy; the other cheerful. Since the 1980s, at a time of mounting economic instability worldwide, there has been a huge expansion in low-waged, insecure jobs in Britain and the USA – the two countries with which I am most familiar. This has occurred alongside continuing attacks on welfare benefits, including the specific targeting of state assistance for single mothers and the disabled, as part of the spread of the low-tax, free-market tenets of economic neo-liberalism, which has accompanied global economic restructuring. The rolling back of social welfare has in turn incited a renewed emphasis on the importance of traditional family life and, in particular, fathers' rights and responsibilities. Women, overall more engaged in the work of childcare and nurturing, suffer specifically, or disproportionately, from welfare cutbacks and paternalistic rhetorics, and many remain at the harshest end of deepening inequalities worldwide, in low-paid, low-status jobs. Those who have researched the effects of the last two decades of change on women in Britain and North America, for example, report that while many women have made considerable progress since the 1980s, the lives of certain other women, especially single parents and the elderly (with a majority of women in both groups) were getting worse and worse (Bashevkin, 1998; Glendinning and Miller, 1992). Moreover, receding expectations of social provision serve to undermine precisely those goals for which the women's movement in the 1970s fought so vigorously, leading to a turning away from militant protest and the disparaging of collective action. Thus, organized resistance to changes in government spending dramatically decreased over this period. Sylvia Bashevkin writes of the 'triple whammy' effect on many women in Britain, the USA and Canada: 'Work pressures, cuts to government spending, and the advocacy crunch – taken together – meant many women faced low pay, no job security, less of a government safety net on which to rely when they were old, sick or unemployed, and fewer opportunities to protest' (Bashevkin, 1998, p.95). Those facing the harshest extremes of poverty were also less and less likely to be white, as racial disadvantage deepened in times of increasing inequality.

   …

   Back to basics, in the UK, women's pay as a percentage of men's has remained relatively stable, with women's average earnings still at least a third less than men's (women working part-time average only 58 per cent of men's hourly earnings; full-timers' hourly average has risen to 80 per cent of men's, but their weekly wage remains over a third less, due to men's longer hours, overtime and additional benefits).[1] Indeed, women's lower wages relative to men persists throughout the world, and where women's share has risen (from around 62 per cent to 72 per cent in the USA since the 1970s) it is mainly attributable to the decline in men's wages (see Kim, 1993). Meanwhile, housework and childcare are still primarily seen as women's responsibility in the overwhelming majority of households – including dual-income families (Bagilhole, 1994, p.1). A more demanding workplace makes it harder than ever to harmonize jobs and outside commitments, especially for mothers (see Franks, 1999a). Thus, research consistently indicates that women have far less leisure time than men, and many feel guilty about neglecting their children's needs due to the demands of their jobs (Bashevkin, 1998, p.120; Lovendeski, 1996, p.10). Even in the poorest families living on benefit, men still have pocket money for themselves, while women do not, according to a recent report from the Policy Studies Unit in Britain (reported in McIntosh, 1998, p.5). Men's violence against women and sexual abuse remain endemic. Indeed, the reporting of rape, child sexual abuse and serious violence against women has been increasing since the mid-1980s, yet conviction rates have been decreasing; meanwhile, funding for rape-counselling, women's refuges and the rehousing of battered women and their children has shrunk in both Britain and North America (Bashevkin, 1998, pp.60,116; Lees, 1996). Some might well wonder, some *do* wonder, has feminism been on a hiding to nothing?

Yet, tilt the frame just a little, and the picture that comes into focus is much more optimistic. Welfare reform, new policies for single mothers and an emphasis on paternal responsibilities are characteristically couched in the language of autonomy and responsibility which was at the heart of seventies feminist rhetoric. Indeed, as others have noticed – and the mourning for Princess Diana in Britain encapsulated – the espousal of a new type of 'feminized', personalized or therapeutic rhetoric abounds today on radio, television and in a plethora of self-help books, borrowing the feminist consciousness-raising discourses of disclosure and shared pain. Moreover, the choices open to women have increased remarkably in the closing decades of the twentieth century, mostly undermining former patriarchal presumptions: many women now delay motherhood; more cohabit and marry later; more divorce and separate; more remain childless; more raise children on their own.[2] This has been made possible primarily by what has been called the 'feminization' of the economy. Full-time jobs in many manufacturing industries have been disappearing, as jobs in the service sector keep expanding. Clerical jobs still account for the largest group of women workers in developed countries, but women have also made rapid progress within most professional and managerial jobs, especially as doctors, lawyers, accountants and business administrators – even if rarely reaching the top levels (Castells, 1998, pp.165–70). Indeed, rather than flaunting any observable or intrinsic 'difference' from men, childless young professional women are working longer hours, and earning slightly more (104 per cent) of equivalent men's earnings. They are, as Suzanne Franks' (1999b) study reveals, 'the most desirable workers of all'.

Meanwhile, the domain of women's lives, once near-invisible, has moved closer to the forefront of international politics, in dialogue which has become more blind to 'class', and more equivocal about 'race'. 50,000 people (mostly women) attended the United Nations Fourth World Conference on Women in 1995 in Beijing, and the associated Non-Governmental Organization (NGO) Forum held nearby. The consequent Beijing Declaration and Platform for Action, built upon twenty years of planning, debates and action, is an impressive statement urging the promotion of women's interests worldwide.[3] Assessing its impact on government actions internationally a few years later, Charlotte Bunch concluded from her Center for Global Leadership at Rutgers University: 'The energy, the activity of Beijing, has not gone away' (Charlotte Bunch cited in Crossette, 1998). As two other early women's liberation activists from the USA insist, the world really has changed:

> It's hard now to evoke the sea of misogyny in which more than one generation of women struggled before the women's movement. ... One general claim feels solid: gross and unapologetic prejudice against women is no longer an unremarked-upon given of everyday life. In the long years before second-wave feminism, women and girls were unquestionably belittled. ... Humiliation seemed fitting and pride made one faintly ridiculous. The prevailing assumption of the inferiority of women was the starting point from which one planned one's moves and shaped one's life – whether acquiescent or angry. The very difficulty of describing this prefeminist atmosphere today is a measure of how dramatically things have changed.
>
> (Duplessis and Snitow, 1998, p.4)

What are we to make of these radically contrasting configurations? How we respond – whether we see little progress, or believe feminism has got what it wanted and should perhaps retire gracefully – will clearly depend upon the type of feminism we espouse. ...

The subject of dependency

...

The continuing offensive against welfare provides, perhaps, the single most general threat to Western women's interests at present – at least for those many women who are not wealthy, and who still take the major responsibility for caring work in the home. ...

Increasingly in Britain, as in the USA, the new myth of 'dependency culture' is used to condemn those receiving any form of state service, marking them out as vulnerable to 'welfare dependency'. Yet, as Mary McIntosh (1998, p.5) reports, despite the hassles and indignities they now face, surveys of single mothers have shown that a majority would still prefer dependence on the state to their experience of dependence on a man. However, that option is disappearing. In alliance with Reagan and the American Right, there was no doubting Margaret Thatcher's determination to overturn all traces of the post-war Keynesian economic orthodoxy with its support for spending on welfare – while upholding and abetting spending on warfare. What is somewhat less clear is the extent to which the Blair government like Clinton's 'New' Democratic Party, is simply a continuation of the same pro-scarcity neo-liberal policies undermining the public realm, while encouraging market forces into every institutional domain.

...

Family values

In stark contrast with the repeated avowal of the 'pathologies' of 'welfare dependency' is the steadfast disavowal of knowledge of the actual casualties when women and children are most financially dependent on familial male authority. Such denial has been strenuously cultivated by the growing strength of 'family values' campaigners since the 1980s. 'Profamily' movements first arose in the 1970s as part of an explicit New Right backlash against feminism and sexual liberation, soon to be underwritten by Reagan and Thatcher. Two decades later, however, this neo-conservative rhetoric seems ubiquitous across the political spectrum. 'Strengthening the family has to be a number-one social priority', Tony Blair announced at the Labour Party Conference in Britain in 1995, embracing the double-dealing Communitarian Agenda of the American sociologist Amitai Etzioni, and echoing the sentiments of that other fading patriarch, Bill Clinton. ...

Meanwhile, the knowledge that the traditional heterosexual marriage can create a living hell of cruelty, neglect and abuse is beaten back by what the American sociologist Judith Stacey calls the 'virtual social science' of distorted data about the dangers of 'fatherless', 'divorced' or 'lone-parent' families being constantly disseminated by the media (Stacey, 1996, Ch.4; 1998). This encourages the continuing denial of lesbian and gay rights (as in campaigns to restrict custody and adoption rights to married heterosexuals) and obstructs official recognition of same-sex relationships. Furthermore, it dismisses the often invaluable role of friendships, community resources and wider structures of social support, which may be all that many individuals have to rely upon to keep them sane when most dependent on the family, for example those for whom childhood is, at the very best, a time of gritting the teeth and enduring. ...

...

Yet pessimism is not entirely appropriate. It is false to claim that women's situation has stayed much the same, and even more misleading to suppose it has worsened. Women's growing economic independence has continued to undermine all the old structures of male domination, removing privileges which men could once take for granted at home and at work, and enhancing women's expectation – though not, perhaps, the practical choices open to them. Moreover, as Manuel Castells has exhaustively analysed, the displacement of the 'patriarchalism' which had ruled for millennia is increasingly global – notwithstanding its clashing and vicious entrenchment in certain nationalistic struggles.[4] The dilemmas of the cultural transitions in gender practices indicate that new strategies are urgently needed to solve the increasing imbalance between caring commitments, employment practices and the rest of life. Everywhere gender relations still matter, generating conflict and anxiety for both sexes. They matter for women, who are usually the most directly affected by the conflictual demands of home and work. They matter for men: for the minority who attempt to participate in the home on equal terms, often with considerable strain; for the majority who have been slower to change, and face the resentment (and increasing levels of divorce and eviction) if they cannot, or will not, sustain more egalitarian relations. Most of all, gender issues matter for children and other dependent people in the home, who bear the brunt of poverty, overstretched and guilt-ridden carers and inadequate public services. It is clear that feminist concerns cannot be separated from struggles for an alternative vision and politics to those currently in command. ...

Switching to the subject

...

... It is no secret that the theorizing of 'difference' paradigms in feminism, rightly suspicious of the chauvinisms, gaps and silences in old emancipatory rhetorics and practices of class, have tended to overshadow material differences within oppressed subject groups. Inside the Western academy, the intellectual prestige of post-structuralism and deconstruction led prominent feminist theoreticians to emphasize the discursive formations of selfhood via logics of exclusion and repudiation. Primarily concerned with ways of displacing or subverting the negation or subordination of the 'feminine' in language, or the silencing of women's voices in culture, the focus on identities, their affirmations and negations, has directed attention away from questions of redistributive justice and social restructuring, which were once central to socialist feminism – that current which is now so often excised from feminist texts, abridged into the retrospectively constructed 'equality' paradigm.

...

Activist challenges

Do not misunderstand me. I am well aware of the importance of the study of identities and differences: whether to explore how they are constructed and reconstructed, or to draw attention to all those subordinated and excluded by previously uncontested universalisms. Hierarchically gendered, sexualized, racialized or hybridized productions of identity are all *material* in their injurious effects, and usually, though not necessarily, and in differing ways, tied up with the structuring of economic disadvantage and marginalization. Furthermore, it is identity-based politics which have so often inspired the cultures of activism which, in the best of times, form part of, or in other ways service, class-based trade-union and community struggles for better lives (Salzman, n.d.; Johnston and Klandermans, 1995). As most feminists were once well aware, the really difficult challenge remains that of building culture and class coalitions, where sexism, racism and the radical complexities of their forms of exclusion or invalidation can find a place on the agenda. ...

...

Cultural imperatives

...

Economic realities and the shifting fortunes of women worldwide are, everywhere, enmeshed within cultural understandings of sexual difference, which still, on all sides, help to promote male paranoia, misogyny, homophobia and related violence against women, gays and other subordinated or dissident men. ... There is no other way to understand the pervasive sense that women in the West are now the 'winners', and men the 'losers', in an ongoing battle of the sexes (Mount, 1997, p.15). We need to understand that it is this very terminology – the positioning of the sexes as embattled primarily with each other – which is quintessentially cultural, and which defers recognition that men, like women, are disparately affected by wider forces of economic restructuring, downsizing and increased job insecurity. Perceiving men as 'losers' obscures an array of crucial questions: which men are losing out? according to what criteria? (See, for example, Epstein *et al.*, 1998.) We will never understand what is at stake here in generating defensive masculinities by posing men as inferior to the very group over whom their 'manhood' should render them superior, without attention to 'the cultural' and its material embeddedness. The burgeoning literature on men and masculinities can reveal little about the predicament and anxieties of men unless it understands the dynamics of power which have hitherto structured gendered meanings and institutional practices. The one cannot be parted from the other – at least, not until women are everywhere already seen as commensurate to men.

Feminism without politics

In Britain in the late 1990s, widespread publicity accompanied the appearance of a book declaring the dawn of a 'New Feminism': this time as a mainstream, majority movement in which women – from the Spice Girls to Cherie Blair and her husband's hundred new women MPs – can celebrate their own sudden power and achievements (in part thanks to Margaret Thatcher for normalizing female success). Its author, the journalist Natasha Walter, like Naomi Wolf before her, offers a form of power-feminism, applauding women's growing success, identification with their jobs and their ability to help each other. She reports on the penetration of feminist beliefs throughout society, reflected in mainstream culture and evident in the increasing support by men for women at home – if still from only a minority. Her book is useful, not only in outlining the real progress many women have made, but also in highlighting how much is still to be done. It is packed with pertinent statistics and the words of a diversity of women. Listing the multiple problems women still face, from grinding poverty, meagre childcare, dead-end jobs, inadequate public services to absence from power-elites, she wants more change to enable all women to find a place, where she hopes to see them, 'in the corridors of power'. However, her sketch of women's lives is one emptied of political theory or any specific strategies for combating the many obstacles she describes still confronting the majority of women. Instead, she appears to believe that it is feminism itself which has failed to deliver change for women, and this is because it 'gradually became primarily associated with sexual politics and culture (Walter, 1998, p.4).

But quite how 'feminism' will manage to deliver, once it remedies its ways and adopts 'a new, less embattled ideal', remains mysterious. Walter's analysis promotes no particular collective political formations or affiliations. We are simply told: 'We must understand that feminism can give us these things now, if we really want them'. Fingers crossed! Although pleasantly symptomatic of many women's goodwill towards a 'feminism' they feel free to fashion, it lacks the very thing it hopes to promote: political seriousness (Walter, 1998, pp.9,34). Introducing her follow-up collection a year later, again offering us 'feminism for a new generation', Walter is even more confident that feminism is 'on the move', evident in women's strong desire for a more equal society. The fact that our society is actually becoming ever more *unequal*, and her authors often committed to a wholly individualistic ethic (one of them offers an exemplary tale of her heroine, Jade Beaumont, who believes that 'people should deal with their own problems; you shouldn't get yourself into situations you can't handle and then slop all over everybody else') does not give her pause for thought about the significance of the political ravine between personal declarations in favour of a fairer world, and its attainment. It should (Simpson, 1999, p.111).[5]

Political futures

...

Given the diversity of reformist, identitarian, deconstructive, activist, therapeutic and power feminisms, it is true that we can indeed take many different routes as feminists leaving the twentieth century. We need to learn from each other's journeys, and to recognize that what will engage the attention and further the interests of one group of women will not be most relevant to the needs of another. The political never simply reduces to the personal, nor to the unfettered analysis of culture, even though attention to desire, discourse and the promotion of caring and responsible sexual politics remains one of the crucial resources feminism delivers to politics. It is only by finding ways to foster effective vehicles for change that feminists can still hope to open spaces for more women to flaunt the diverse pleasures, entitlements and self-questioning to which recent feminist thinking has encouraged us to aspire (often, disconcertingly, in line with late capitalist consumerism). This means women collectively cherishing the existence of the left: whether in alliance with social democratic forces (fighting to preserve their redistributive egalitarian instincts, which will never be smoothly compatible with commercial entrepreneurialism, while opposing their traditional paternalism); with trade unions (continuing to overturn their erstwhile straight, white, male hegemony); with whatever manifestations of local or international struggles emerge to defend those at the sharpest end of market forces or regressive nationalisms, persisting racisms and xenophobia. Why feminism? Because its most radical goal, both personal and collective, has yet to be realized: a world which is a better place not just for some women, but for all women. In what I still call a socialist feminist vision, that would be a far better world for boys and men, as well.

Notes

1   These figures come from the Incomes Data Service, 77 Bastwick Street, London, EC1V 3TT, February 1999.

2   Information from *Social Focus on Women,* quoted in Oakley and Mitchell (1997).

3   The declaration condemns violence against women, especially systemic rape in warfare, and encourages assistance for female victims of violence; recommends enactment of legislation to guarantee the right of women and men to equal pay for equal work; supports the promotion of businesses run by women and women's media networks; calls for women's equal participation in governments; promotes research on women's health, and so on. See a variety of reports from the Beijing conference in *Signs*, vol.22, no.1, 1996, pp.181–226.

4   For the fullest overview see Castells (1998).

5   In her introduction, Walter (1999, p.3) refers to Jade Beaumont as providing 'a heroine for our time'.

References

Bagilhole, B. (1994) *Women, Work and Equal Opportunity*, Aldershot, Avebury.

Bashevkin, S. (1998) *Women on the Defensive: Living through Conservative Times*, Chicago, IL, University of Chicago Press.

Castells, M. (1998) 'The end of patriarchalism: social movements, family, and sexuality in the information age' in *The Information Age: Economy, Society and Culture*, vol.II: *The Power of Identity*, Oxford, Blackwell, pp.165–70.

Crossette, B. (1998) 'Women see key gains since talks in Beijing', *New York Times*, 8 March.

Duplessis, R. Blau and Snitow, A. (1998) 'A feminist memoir project' in Duplessis, R. Blau and Snitow, A. (eds) *The Feminist Memoir Project: Voices from Women's Liberation*, New York, Three Rivers Press.

Epstein D., Elwood, J. and Hey, V. and Maw, J. (eds) (1998) *Failing Boys: Issues in Gender and Achievement*, Buckingham, Open University Press.

Franks, S. (1999a) 'Vital statistics', *The Guardian*, 11 January, p.7.

Franks, S. (1999b) *Having None of It: Women, Men and the Future of Work*, London, Granta.

Glendinning, C. and Miller, J. (eds) (1992) *Women and Poverty in Britain: the 1990s*, London, Harvester.

Johnston, H. and Klandermans, B. (eds) (1995) *Social Movements, Protest, and Contention*, vol.4: *Social Movements and Culture*, Minneapolis, MN, University of Minnesota Press.

Kim, M. (1993) 'Comments' in Cobble, D. (ed.) *Women and Unions: Forging a Partnership*, New York, International Labour Review Press.

Lees, S. (1996) *Carnal Knowledge: Rape on Trial*, Harmondsworth, Penguin Books.

Lovendeski, J. (1996) 'Sex, gender and British politics', *Parliamentary Affairs*, vol.49, no.1, January.

McIntosh, M. (1998) 'Dependency culture? Welfare, women and work', *Radical Philosophy*, no.91, September–October.

Mount, F. (1997) 'Death and burial of the utopian feminist', *Sunday Times*, 14 December.

Oakley, A. and Mitchell, J. (eds) (1997) *Who's Afraid of Feminism? Seeing Through the Backlash*, Harmondsworth, Penguin Books.

Salzman, C. (n.d.) *In the Shadows of Privilege: Women and Unions at Yale*.

Simpson, H. (1999) 'Lentils and lilies: a story' in Walter, N. (ed.) *op. cit.*.

Stacey, J. (1996) *In the Name of the Family: Rethinking Family Values in the Postmodern Age*, Boston, MA, Beacon Press.

Stacey, J. (1998) 'Families against the family', *Radical Philosophy*, no.89, May–June.

Walter, N. (1998) *What is the New Feminism?*, London, Little, Brown.

Walter, N. (ed.) (1999) *On the Move: Feminism for a New Generation*, London, Virago.

Source: Lynne Segal, *Why Feminism? Gender, Psychology, Politics,* Cambridge, Polity Press, 1999, pp.201–10, 214–18, 224–5, 228–9, 231–2.

Gordon Marshall:
'Social class and underclass in Britain and the USA' (1997)

Class analysis: the missing millions

… Is class analysis seriously undermined by its apparent neglect of large numbers of people who do not form part of the analysis, but are affected by class processes, and surely therefore an important component of the class structure?

There is a sizeable lobby of critics who have argued strongly to this effect. For example, in their critical review of studies of class in British sociology, Vic Duke and Stephen Edgell (1987) complain that almost all operationalizations of the central concept exclude economically inactive adults. This yields a 'restrictive and distorted view of the class structure' since it excludes something like 40 per cent of the adult population of Britain. In the view of these authors, 'generalisations about the class structure and class relationships are likely to be less than "totally" valid when they are based on such a small and unrepresentative section of the adult population', and so 'it should be routine to obtain relevant data for the economically inactive as well as the economically active.'

Duke and Edgell are not alone in voicing such criticisms. Others have insisted that welfare dependants and the retired should be questioned about their previous jobs so that these groups can be incorporated within any class analysis. Many have argued that last job serves equally to classify unwaged domestic labourers, although some maintain that this is a poorer indicator of a woman's class than is occupation held prior to the birth of her first child, while a few are in favour of treating 'housewife' as a class category in its own right. parallel arguments are commonly made about unemployment. A number of critics make a distinction between the short-term and long-term unemployed, treating the former in terms of previously held occupations, and the latter as an underclass having their own distinct class location. Various multiple indicator approaches have also been proposed. These apply additional criteria – such as family consumption patterns, income, educational attainment, and presence of dependent children – in determining the class standing of both households and their constituent members.[1]

It is clear that critics do not agree about a preferred alternative to what they take to be the status quo of class analysis. Some maintain that the various groups hitherto excluded can satisfactorily be incorporated within existing approaches and theories. Others argue that the social classes of men and women should be classified separately. Radicals would abandon the whole enterprise of class analysis altogether. The various proposals are not easily reconciled.[2]

...

... [T]here is widespread agreement among a large number of otherwise diverse commentators that exclusion of non-employed individuals from contemporary class analysis greatly restricts its usefulness, because it is allegedly misleading to generalize about the class characteristics of populations on the basis only of a sample of those in employment. Not everyone has an occupation. Class theories which are rooted in the sphere of employment are likely therefore, according to their critics, to give a partial or distorted picture of the processes of class formation. In this chapter we wish simply to explore whether or not this accusation is well founded.

...

The underclass

... Might it not be the case, as is increasingly suggested, that the really serious problem for social class research is created by the large numbers of impoverished welfare dependants who are not in employment, at least not on a regular basis, and have therefore fallen through or dropped out of the class structure entirely? Are there not growing numbers of people who are so irregularly in work, and therefore so marginal to civil society, that they constitute a discrete group, whose existence is simply overlooked in the conventional class literature, and whose class-related attributes are so distinct that they require separate treatment in a class analysis?

Reasoning along these lines, W.G. Runciman (1990, pp.381, 388) has argued that there are seven classes in British society: an upper class, three middle classes (upper, middle and lower), two working classes (skilled and unskilled) – and an underclass. The latter embraces 'those who are excluded from the labour market entirely, whether through debt, disability or a lack of any minimal skill in consequence of which they are permanently consigned to the category of the long-term unemployed'. Note that this is not a group of workers disadvantaged within the labour market. It is, rather, those members of society 'whose roles place them more or less permanently at the economic level where benefits are paid by the state to those unable to participate in the labour market at all'. Many of these individuals are members of ethnic minorities, and many are women (particularly single mothers), but it is their long-term unemployment and therefore welfare dependency (rather than ethnicity or gender as such) that defines their membership of the underclass. Runciman – like many others (for example, Rex, 1986, pp.75–6) – believes that the class characteristics (including the class identities and voting behaviour) of these people are distinct from those of the working classes. Is this in fact the case? To what extent is the class analysis programme compromised by its failure to deal with the contemporary underclass?

The now extensive debate about the underclass stems from a predominantly American literature which addresses two phenomena that are argued to be related; namely, high levels of youth unemployment, and an increasing proportion of single-parent households. The black population is disproportionately affected by both joblessness and single parenthood. The term 'underclass' itself suggests a group which is in some sense outside the mainstream of society – but there is little or no agreement about the nature and source of the exclusion. One interpretation, advanced by writers such as Charles Murray (1984), is that overly generous welfare provision promotes dependency, the break-up of the nuclear family household, and socialization into a counter-culture which devalues work and encourages criminality. An alternative view, proffered by Douglas Glasgow (1980) and others, emphasizes the failure of the economy to provide equal opportunities for secure employment, and the consequent destabilization of the male-breadwinner role. Murray locates the source of exclusion in the attitudes and behaviour of the underclass itself whereas Glasgow points to the structured inequality that disadvantages particular groups in society.

The precise natures of both the structural disadvantages and the cultural attributes in question are themselves a matter of dispute. One disagreement is about whether the problems of the disadvantaged black population originate in their colour or their class position. Early in his work, William Julius Wilson (1978, p.1) makes reference to 'a vast underclass of black proletarians – that massive population at the very bottom of the social class ladder, plagued by poor education and low-paying, unstable jobs'. This depicts the underclass as a black phenomenon, defined in terms of vulnerability in the labour market, and without reference to behavioural or attitudinal factors. However, in a later study he writes about 'individuals who lack training and skills and either experience long-term unemployment or are not members of the labour force, individuals who are engaged in street crime and other forms of aberrant behaviour, and families that experience long term spells of poverty and/or welfare dependency' (Wilson, 1987, p.8). In other words, unstable unemployment has become absence of employment; there is now no explicit reference to race; and, furthermore, the definition has been expanded to include criminality and welfare dependence – thus acknowledging that the socially undesirable attributes of underclass life that are central causes in Murray's account can in fact follow as consequences in Wilson's essentially structural approach.

Although discussion about the nature and extent of underclass membership has been most fully developed in the United States, the issues have also been debated at length in Britain, and no less acrimoniously. For example, in a more recent work, Murray (1990) has argued that the difference between the USA and Britain is simply that the former 'reached the future first'. Using metaphors of social pathology, he suggests that an underclass defined by illegitimacy, violent crime and dropout from the labour force is growing, and will continue to do so because there is a generation of children being brought up to live in the same way. By contrast, Duncan Gallie (1988) has explored the potential for cultural cohesion and collective self-awareness as defining characteristics of the underclass, and concluded that the non-standard employment patterns and long-term unemployment of the 1980s may have provided a structural basis for a distinctive underclass, but that there is no real evidence for its cultural underpinning.

It is not our purpose here either to review the extensive literature on the underclass or to attempt an authoritative definition of this seemingly elusive sociological subject. However, in order to facilitate our investigation of the socio-political characteristics of those normally included within and conventionally excluded from class analysis, the following observations must perforce be recorded.

First – and leaving aside the (many) studies of the underclass which simply fail to define the term precisely – current research reflects two basic approaches to the phenomenon. Either the underclass is characterized as being excluded from civil society on account of its extreme deprivation (due to poverty or lack of employment); or, alternatively, it is seen as being at variance with mainstream behaviour and attitudes (as testified to by the prevalence of voluntary joblessness, welfare dependency, unwed parenting, juvenile delinquency and crime generally). Possible links to ethnicity and residence in 'extreme poverty areas' are merely variations on this basic theme. Dispute then turns on the causality that is deemed to prevail between social structure, poverty, behaviour and attitudes (see Auletta, 1982, pp.50, 253, 265–8; Gans, 1993).

Second, in practice most commentators associate the underclass with either extreme poverty or long-term unemployment, although there is no consensus about how these circumstances arise. As Robert Aponte (1990, p.132) puts it, 'on the one hand, there are those that see self-defeating attitudes and behaviour – as in the long discredited "culture of poverty" thesis – as the primary cause of poverty. On the other, there are those that argue that we must look to the structure of opportunities for the explanation of poverty and the often accompanying pathologies.'

Finally, these unresolved disputes about causality notwithstanding, it is widely (though not universally) held that the underclass shares in a distinctive subculture of cynicism, resignation and despair. As Aponte suggests, some have drawn parallels between this particular 'culture of fatalism' and earlier apparently similar sociological constructs, such as the 'culture of poverty' (much discussed in the United States during the 1960s) and the 'dependency culture' transmitted by so-called cycles of deprivation (a focus of controversy in Britain in the 1970s). Others argue that the debate about the underclass is distinguished by its explicit concern with the relationship between racism and poverty. In both cases, however, the overwhelming impression conveyed by the literature is of an underclass culture comprising largely negative traits which include apathy, indifference towards authority, and defeatism.[3]

It may well be, as some have suggested, that at this level the debate is as much about the politics of social policy – about the need for privileged classes to justify their place in society by pointing to the individual failings of the poor and unemployed – as it is about reasoned sociological analysis (see, for example, Bagguley and Mann, 1992; Morris, 1993; Westergaard, 1992). Nevertheless … we think it is possible to explore empirically some of the issues surrounding the concept of the underclass – specifically from the point of view of determining whether or not the poorest and most persistently unemployed people in the American and British samples are culturally distinct from the wider population in the terms implied by the thesis of the underclass 'culture of fatalism'. Is there a distinctive underclass subculture or do the processes of socio-political class formation transcend the alleged boundaries imposed by poverty and unemployment?

     …

Contrasting interpretations of fatalism

Our results thus far would tend to support the view of those critics who have denied that the poorest members of society constitute an underclass. But, as Alan Walker (1990, p.55) points out, the essence of the argument about the underclass is that the latter consists not necessarily of the poorest people, but of people who *act* differently, and not just from the middle class but from other poor people as well. The underclass is defined, not only by its poverty, but additionally by it propensity for deviant parental, educational, and labour-market behaviour. To what extent do our data support this version of the underclass thesis? In other words, does belonging to these sorts of allegedly underclass groups significantly influence attitudes towards political and economic processes in society, over and above any effects attributable merely to poverty itself? Ultimately, it is the answer to this question that separates those (such as Murray) who favour a behavioural version of underclass theory, from those (such as Walker) who offer a structural interpretation.

One influential (and entirely typical) behavioural definition of the underclass is advanced by Erol Ricketts and Isabel Sawhill (1988), who argue that 'underclass areas' in the United States are those with relatively high proportions of high school dropouts, prime-aged males not working regularly, households with children headed by females, and those receiving public assistance.[4] We therefore considered, for our American and British data, the attitudinal characteristics of single females with children; individuals in households receiving welfare benefits or social security; respondents in the lowest standard age-group (aged less than 25) with no formal educational qualifications; and those who claimed to have been unemployed in the long term (for more than the previous twelve months) or, separately, out of work for at least two years of the previous ten. Afro-Caribbean and Asian interviewees were also identified in order to address the issue of race. Is it the case that any of these characteristics have a further influence on the attitudes that we take to be indicative of the underclass culture of fatalism, once the limited effects of poverty itself are controlled for, again using weighted household income as a proxy for the latter? If this were in fact true, one might be led to conclude that fatalistic attitudes would then have to be viewed as, to some degree, particular to the various groups said by Ricketts and Sawhill to constitute an underclass.

Notes

1   See, for example, Dale *et al.* (1985), Dex (1985, p.150–1), Hagan and Albonetti (1982), Harris and Morris (1986), Heath and Britten (1984), Murgatroyd (1982), Roberts and Barker (1986) and Walby (1986).

2   Compare, for example, Acker (1973), Garnsey (1978), Haller (1981), Murgatroyd (1984), Pahl (1984) and Wright (1989).

3   See, for example, Saunders (1990, pp.122–4) and Stafford and Ladner (1990, pp.138–40). On the earlier debates about the culture of poverty and transmitted deprivation see, respectively, Valentine (1968) and Rutter and Madge (1976).

4   For methodological criticisms of this work see Aponte (1990, pp.126–30).

References

Acker, J. (1973) 'Women and social stratification: a case of intellectual sexism', *American Journal of Sociology*, vol.78, pp.936–45.

Aponte, R. (1990) 'Definitions of the underclass: a critical analysis' in Gans, H.J. (ed.) *op. cit.*, pp.117–37.

Auletta, K. (1982) *The Underclass*, New York, Random House.

Bagguley, P. and Mann, K. (1992) 'Idle thieving bastards? Scholarly representations of the "underclass"', *Work, Employment and Society*, vol.6, pp.113–26.

Dale, A., Gilbert, G.N. and Arber, S. (1985) 'Integrating women into class theory', *Sociology*, vol.20, pp.384–409.

Dex, S. (1985) *The Sexual Division of Work*, Brighton, Wheatsheaf.

Duke, V. and Edgell, S. (1987) 'The operationalization of class in British sociology: theoretical and empirical considerations', *British Journal of Sociology*, vol.38, pp.445–63.

Gallie, D. (1988) 'Employment, unemployment and social stratification' in Gallie, D. (ed.) *Employment in Britain*, Oxford, Blackwell, pp.465–74.

Gans, H.J. (ed.) (1990) *Sociology in America*, Newbury Park, CA, Sage.

Gans, H.J. (1993) 'From "underclass" to "undercaste": some observations about the future of the postindustrial economy and its major victims', *International Journal of Urban and Regional Research*, vol.17, pp.327–35.

Garnsey, E. (1978) 'Women's work and theories of class stratification', *Sociology*, vol.12, pp.223–43.

Glasgow, D.G. (1980) *The Black Underclass: Poverty, Unemployment, and the Entrapment of Ghetto Youth*, San Francisco, CA, Jossey-Bass.

Hagan, J. and Albonetti, C. (1982) 'Race, class and the perception of criminal injustice in America', *American Journal of Sociology*, vol.88. pp.329–55.

Haller, M. (1981) 'Marriage, women and social stratification: a theoretical critique', *American Journal of Sociology,* vol.86, pp.766–95.

Harris, C.C. and Morris, L.D. (1986) 'Households, labour markets and the position of women' in Crompton, R. and Mann, M. (eds), *Gender and Stratification*, Cambridge, Polity Press, pp.86–96.

Heath, A. and Britten, N. (1984) 'Women's jobs do make a difference', *Sociology*, vol.18, pp.475–90.

Morris, L.D. (1993) 'Is there a British underclass?', *International Journal of Urban and Regional Research*, vol.17, pp.404–12.

Murgatroyd, L. (1982) 'Gender and occupational stratification', *Sociological Review*, vol.30, pp.573–602

Murgatroyd, L. (1984) 'Women, men and the social grading of occupation', *British Journal of Sociology*, vol.35, pp.473–97.

Murray, C. (1984) *Losing Ground: American Social Policy, 1950–1980*, New York, Basic Books.

Murray, C. (1990) *The Emerging British Underclass*, London, Institute of Economic Affairs.

Pahl, R.E. (1984) *Divisions of Labour*, Oxford, Blackwell.

Rex, J. (1986) 'The role of class analysis in the study of race relations – a Weberian perspective' in Rex, J. and Mason, D. (eds), *Theories of Race and Ethnic Relations*, Cambridge, Cambridge University Press, pp.64–83.

Ricketts, E.R. and Sawhill, I. (1988) 'Defining and measuring the underclass', *Journal of Policy Analysis and Management*, vol.7, pp.316–25.

Roberts, H. and Barker, R. (1986). 'The social classification of women', London, City University Social Statistics Research Unit.

Runciman, W.G. (1990) 'How many classes are there in contemporary British society?', *Sociology*, vol.24, pp.377–96.

Rutter, M. and Madge, N. (1976) *Cycles of Disadvantage*, London, Heinemann.

Saunders, P. (1990) *Social Class and Stratification*, London, Routledge.

Stafford, W.W. and Ladner, J. (1990) 'Political dimensions of the underclass concept' in Gans, H.J. (ed.) *op. cit.*, pp.138–55.

Valentine, C.A. (1968) *Culture and Poverty*, Chicago, IL, University of Chicago Press.

Walby, S. (1986) 'Gender, class and stratification' in Crompton, R. and Mann, M. (eds), *Gender and Stratification*, Cambridge, Polity Press, pp.23–39.

Walker, A. (1990) 'Blaming the victims' in Murray, C. H. (ed.), *The Emerging British Underclass*, London, Institute of Economic Affairs, pp.49–58.

Westergaard, J. (1992) 'About and beyond the "underclass", some notes on influences of social climate on British sociology today', *Sociology*, vol.26, pp.575–87.

Wilson, W.J. (1978) *The Declining Significance of Race: Blacks and Changing American Institutions*, Chicago, IL, University of Chicago Press.

Wilson, W.J. (1987) *The Truly Disadvantaged: The Inner City, the Underclass, and Public Policy*, Chicago, IL, University of Chicago Press.

Wright, E.O. (1989) 'Women in the class structure', *Politics and Society*, vol.17, pp.1–34.

Source: Gordon Marshall, *Repositioning Class: Social Inequality in Industrial Societies*, London, Sage, 1997, pp.86–8,93–6,100–1.

Stephen Castles and Godula Kosack: 'Immigrant workers and class structure in western Europe' (1973)

Some observers designate the immigrants as a new proletariat, separate from the indigenous working class. For instance Albert Delpérée, General Secretary of the Belgian Ministry of Social Welfare, has said:

> Of course there is frequent talk of equal rights, human dignity, workers' solidarity. But in practice there remain unavoidable conditions of discrimination, inequality, handicaps. Foreign employees are often the true proletarians of this second half of the twentieth century.
>
> (Delpérée, 1965, p.71)

Similarly an article in the organ of the German Social Democratic Party asserts:

> The foreign workers can be designated as a new proletariat because they live on the margins of our society, increasingly form its 'lowest class' and because they suffer social discrimination through being given mainly the most physically demanding manual jobs. They enjoy neither political nor social equality – this is hindered by the natural obstacle that they are not German citizens. Another special characteristic of the new proletariat is its isolation with regard to both language and housing.
>
> (Bartsch, 1963)

But many social scientists would disagree with such popular views. For instance, Henri Bartoli writes: 'Rather than the birth of a new working class, we are witnessing a restructuring of the working class between a sub-proletariat (external and internal migrants) and a proletariat with a higher standard of living, but with depersonalized living and working conditions' (1965, p.2). The discussion here does not involve any disagreement on the fact that immigrant workers have the lowest social position, but rather on the nature of class structure and on the criteria which should be used to designate and to distinguish social classes. …

…

The impact of immigration

… Our study has shown that immigrant workers in all the countries concerned share the same basic position; they have the poorest conditions and lowest status in every social sphere.

On the labour market, which is the key area for determination of class position, immigrants are highly concentrated in a limited range of occupations and industries: those offering the lowest pay, the works working conditions, and the lowest degree of security. An analysis of socio-economic status showed that immigrant workers are considerably overrepresented in the lowest categories. The overwhelming majority are manual workers – mainly unskilled or semi-skilled – and very few are employed in white-collar occupations. Immigrant workers tend to suffer more severely than their indigenous colleagues from unemployment at times of recession.

Immigrants have a similar disadvantageous position outside work. They experience great difficulty in obtaining housing, and generally have to pay high rents for run-down accommodation seriously lacking in amenities. In some countries, there are special housing schemes for immigrant workers. These are insufficient to meet the demand, and often do not provide satisfactory material conditions, particularly when the housing is provided at the expense of the employer. Moreover, such housing tends to segregate immigrants from the rest of the population, and may expose them to the risk of pressure from the employer during industrial disputes. In France the housing situation is so acute that large shanty-towns have developed. Despite the atrocious conditions prevailing, these form the only refuge for tens of thousands of immigrants. Here there is a clear tendency to ghetto-formation, but elsewhere as well immigrant enclaves are becoming established in the older slum areas of large cities, and in the cellars, attics, and shacks which form typical immigrant habitations.

Such housing conditions are reflected in serious health problems. Tuberculosis, rickets, and other diseases associated with poverty are much more prevalent among immigrants in all four countries than among the rest of the populations. Other difficulties encountered by immigrants, with regard to education, leisure activities, and family life, are also closely related to their economic and social conditions.

Low income, insecurity, bad housing, social problems; these characteristics of immigrants were also regarded as typical of the nineteenth-century European proletariat. Does this justify classifying immigrant workers as a separate class, a new sub-proletariat or *lumpenproletariat*? The answer depends on the concept of class structure which is adopted. In the functionalist model, in which classes are replaced by a profusion of 'status groups'. Immigrant workers would form one such group. Because of their inferior occupational position, the low material standards which characterize their 'life-style', and their lack of prestige, they would be regarded as one of the lowest status groups. In terms of functionalist theory, the presence of an immigrant group occupying such a subordinate position could be regarded as a rational feature of society. Immigrants would fulfil a necessary societal function by providing essential labour for menial tasks. Their remaining in this position could thus be seen as a necessary and more or less permanent feature of social stratification, although upward social mobility might be possible for the most talented individuals.

A representative of the *embourgeoisement* theory might regard immigrant workers as a new proletariat. While the indigenous workers have achieved incomes comparable to those of the middle class, and have accordingly taken on middle-class consumer habits, values and aspirations, the immigrants have characteristics similar to those of the proletarians in the period immediately following industrializaiton. But for the *embourgeoisement* theory, the inferior position of immigrants is only an irregularity in the overall process of the workers' advancement and integration into the middle class. Immigrants fill the gaps left by indigenous workers who have gained promotion out of low-paid and unpleasant jobs. Technological progress may be expected to eliminate such jobs, and the type of labour at present provided by immigrants will cease to be necessary. Large-scale immigration may then be expected to stop, and those immigrants already present who decide to stay will participate in the general upward mobility.

But according to the concept of class structure which we have argued to be the correct one, immigrant workers cannot be regarded as a distinct class. A group which makes up 10, 20, or even 30 per cent of the industrial labour force is neither marginal nor extraneous to society and certainly does not constitute a *lumpenproletariat*. Nor are immigrant workers a 'new proletariat' or a 'sub-proletariat'. The first term implies that the indigenous workers have ceased to be proletarians and have been replaced by the immigrants in this social position. The second postulates that immigrant workers have a different relationship to the means of production from that traditionally characteristic of the proletariat. All workers, whether immigrant or indigenous, manual or non-manual possess the basic characteristics of a proletariat: they do not own or control the means of production, they work under the directions of others and in the interests of others, and they have no control over the product of their work. The basic long-term interests of immigrant and indigenous workers are common ones: the collective improvement of the living and working conditions of all workers, and the abolition of a capitalist system which creates distinctions between different categories of workers which assists in maintaining its own domination.

Immigrant workers and indigenous workers together form the working class in contemporary Western Europe, but it is a divided class. The immigrants have become concentrated in the unskilled occupations and the indigenous workers have tended to leave such jobs. Immigrants have lower incomes and inferior housing and social conditions. The two groups are more or less isolated from each other, through differing positions and short-term interests. This objective split is reproduced in the subjective sphere: a large proportion of indigenous workers have prejudiced and hostile attitudes towards immigrants. They lack solidarity with their immigrant colleagues and favour discriminatory practices. Often immigrants find themselves isolated and unsupported when they take collective action to improve their conditions. We may therefore speak of two strata within the working class: the indigenous workers, with generally better conditions and the feeling of no longer being right at the bottom of society, form the higher stratum. The immigrants, who are the most underprivileged and exploited group of society, form the lower stratum.

It is not to be expected that immigrants will rapidly gain promotion to better occupations and thus cease to form the lowest stratum. The labour market developments of the last two decades show that modern industrial expansion creates demand for both skilled and unskilled workers. Many menial jobs cannot readily be eliminated by mechanization. Even where this possibility exists, it may be more profitable to continue labour-intensive forms of work-organization, particularly where immigration tends to keep down the wages for unskilled labour. …

…

The restructuring of the working class into an indigenous stratum and an immigrant stratum is immigration's most important impact on society. It is through this restructuring that the principal societal effects of immigration are mediated. These effects may be divided into three categories.

Firstly, there are economic effects. … The existence of an industrial reserve army in underdeveloped areas, which can be brought in to take unskilled jobs in Western Europe, tends to hold back increases in the wages for unskilled work. This effect may be great enough to hold down the general wage rate for the whole economy. In this case, immigration brings considerable gains for capitalists: in a situation of expansion, stagnant wage rates are matched by growing profits. In the long run, however, it is possible that indigenous labour may also benefit from the dynamic expansion allowed by immigration.

Secondly, there are social effects. By coming in at the bottom of the labour market, the immigrants have allowed many indigenous workers to move out of unskilled jobs and to achieve real social promotion. The number of white-collar workers has grown, while the number of indigenous manual workers has shrunk. This promotion has had important effects on the consciousness of indigenous workers. Those who have obtained better jobs no longer feel that they belong to the lowest group of society and that improvements can only be achieved collectively. Their advancement is taken as a sign that individual merit can bring gains, while the real causes for the upward movement are not perceived.[1] At the same time, such workers tend to distance themselves from the immigrants, who might in the long run threaten their newly-won privileges if allowed equal opportunities. Moreover, even those indigenous workers who have remained in unskilled occupations do not feel solidarity with immigrant workers. This group fears competition from immigrants and is afraid – not without justification – that they may be used by employers to put pressure on wages and conditions. At the same time the attempt to stigmatize immigrants as intrinsically inferior is an effort by such unskilled workers to maintain a higher social status for themselves, even though no objective basis for this exists. Analogies may be found in the well-known 'poor white' mentality in the Southern states of the USA, and in the attempts of low-level clerks to maintain their higher status position against blue-collar workers who often have higher earnings. The main roots of working-class prejudice towards immigrants are to be found in these relationships of competition. The result is that class consciousness is weakened, and tends to be replaced by a 'sectional consciousness', based on real and apparent conflicts of interest between the two strata within the working class.

Thirdly, immigration has political effects. The change in consciousness among indigenous workers lessens the political unity and strength of the working class. …

Note

1   We do not mean to suggest that immigration has been the only factor causing changes in the conditions and consciousness of the working class. We wish merely to emphasize that it has been one important factor which has been generally neglected.

References

Bartoli, H. (1965) *Liasons Sociales – Documents*, No.119/65, 17 November.

Bartsch, G. (1963) 'Das neue Proletariat', *Vowärts*, 27 November.

Delpérée, A. (1965) 'Die Wanderung von Arbeitnehmern', *Deutsche Versicherungs-zeitschrift,* March.

Source: Stephen Castles and Godula Kosack, *Immigrant Workers and Class Structure in Western Europe*, London, Oxford University Press, 1973, pp.463–4,474–9.

T.H. Marshall:
'Value problems of welfare-capitalism' (1972)

In contrast to the economic process, it is a fundamental principle of the welfare state that the market value of an individual cannot be the measure of his right to welfare. The central function of welfare, in fact, is to supersede the market by taking goods and services out of it, or in some way to control and modify its operations so as to produce a result which it would not have produced of itself. The life-history of a policy decision in welfare, as in any other sphere of democratic government, begins in a general election and is marked at various stages by the use of the political instrument of the majority vote. But this in all cases is only a part of the process by which vital choices are made, and in some cases it is less in tune with the true nature of those choices than in others. Some political decisions, that is to say, could more appropriately be submitted to a plebiscite than others. The relation between majority voting and policy decisions in welfare is very equivocal. Democratic voting is egotistic; most voters voice what they believe to be their own interests. The more comprehensive the franchise, the more legitimate this seems to be, because everybody can speak for himself. Welfare decisions depend on altruism – both concern for others and mutual concern for one another. In Victorian bourgeois democracy this was obvious, because the enfranchised were persons of property and the needy were voteless. Not that the former were conspicuously altruistic, but it was only to their social conscience that reformers could appeal in support of measures which were not vote-catchers. Dicey was convinced that if pensioners were allowed to vote – if, that is, the beneficiaries could put pressure on their benefactors – government would be corrupted and the foundations of democracy undermined.

That idea no longer holds, and the appeals of politicians to the self interests of voters are frank and loud. It is possible that the legitimacy of democratic egotism partly, at least, accounts for the obstinate blindness of total democracy to the urgent needs of minorities which, for various reasons, are not psephologically significant? When everybody is represented, it is easy to assume that everybody has been taken care of. …

But even egotism is often a poor judge of its own interests, because, in the sphere of welfare, provision is being made at the expense of one set of people for the immediate needs of others, and for what may seem remote or hypothetical contingencies, as far as they themselves are concerned, to those who are paying. …

Welfare decisions, then, are essentially altruistic, and they must draw on standards of value embodied in an autonomous ethical system which, though an intrinsic part of the contemporary civilisation, is not the product either of the summation of individual preferences (as in a market) or of a hypothetical majority vote. It is impossible to say exactly how these ethical standards arise in a society or are recognised by its members. Total consensus with regard to them is unthinkable, outside a devout religious community, but without a foundation of near-consensus, no general social welfare policy would be possible. ... It would be dishonest to pretend that there is not about welfare policy decisions something intrinsically authoritarian or, to use a less loaded but rather horrible word, paternalistic. Dahrendorf, for example, writes that 'in a certain sense the authoritarian state is always a welfare state, just as, the other way round, the welfare state always contains authoritarian element' (1964, p.238). For one thing, welfare policy would be of little use if it did not actively help to create standards of value in its field and promote consensus on them. It is by nature educational, not only in schools and colleges, but in its health service and welfare centres, and in everything it does to impress upon the public and the politicians the true significance, in real terms, of the disabilities under which many categories of citizen suffer. In all this it is creating and, quite frankly, inculcating concepts and standards of welfare which are not yet universally accepted. ...

...

... [T]he responsibility of government in the field of welfare is more immediate and compelling than it is, generally speaking, in economic affairs. One of the virtues claimed for capitalist private enterprise is that it can take risks, and it earns a considerable part of its substantial rewards by doing so. But a government cannot allow risk-taking in welfare – or only minimally. It cannot leave any important part of its overall responsibilities in the hands of private agencies unless it takes steps to limit risk by regulation, supervision, inspection or safety-nets, as when a basic state pension underpins private ones. It was, in fact, the disastrous effects of the frequent failure of private savings and pension schemes which forced European governments to intervene in this field in the nineteenth century. Thus the distinction between public and private enterprise in welfare is not as sharp as one might imagine; it is a matter of degree.

My second qualification starts from this and leads on to a new point. Where there is in a major service like health or education a division, or, if you like, a partnership between the public and the private sectors, with the state taking very much the larger share, the public service must be potentially comprehensive. By this I mean that it must make its service accessible to all by spreading it nation-wide, and it must be ready to provide for anybody who comes back to it from the private sector (for financial or other reasons), and also to cater for a possible shift of the balance of demand in its direction in the rising generation. The larger the private sector, the more difficult it is to meet this responsibility, especially in the case of personal service. On this rests one objection to the proposal to allow people to 'opt out' of the national health and education services, taking with them part of their contribution to their cost. In the circumstances I have described 'fair competition' between the public and the private sectors is not possible, since the transfer of clients from the former to the latter would reduce the income of the public service without permitting a corresponding economy of expenditure, and, by splitting resources, would lower the standard of efficiency attainable in it.

But it is not only a question of efficiency. Two major issues of value are involved. First, quantitative change would inevitably lead, very rapidly, to qualitative change. A point would soon be reached at which the whole conception of a community dedicated to providing for the vital needs of its members by systems of mutual aid would be lost, and the balance between the elements constituting the democratic-welfare-capitalist society destroyed. Secondly, it is beyond dispute that medical care and education, which enter into the lives of all citizens, are areas in which differences of opportunity and experience, and particularly an institutionalised dual standard (which would inevitably follow), do more to create and sustain class distinctions than any other. It proved possible to establish a democratic welfare state in this country without abolishing or drastically altering the status of the public schools, but the two cannot coexist indefinitely in their present form. Any deliberate enlargement or extension of this kind of social distinction by a democratic policy decision would signify not so much a conflict between the elements of the hyphenated society as an abandonment by the majority of the very concept itself.

...

I want to turn now to an aspect of welfare at the micro-level of the individual case, and ... I start by quoting [the] economist ... Adam Smith. He began his discussion of value by distinguishing between 'value in use' and 'value in exchange', and then devoted his whole attention to the latter, because it was the only kind with which an economist was concerned. But for welfare, value in use is vital. Smith referred to it also as 'utility', but not in the modern sense (to quote Jacob Viner) of 'an attempt to explain price-determination in psychological terms' (quoted in Page, 1968, p.123). It was not subjective in this individual sense. For, in his famous illustration he said that, in contrast to water, diamonds had 'scarce any value in use'. This must refer, not to their value in the eyes of those who wear them, which is great, but to some common estimation of the capacity to satisfy a human need, which is negligible. Welfare, as I have already said, must base its action on value of this kind, and cannot simply react directly to individual, subjective desires. When the discrepancy between these two kinds of value is insuperable and the consequences intolerable, welfare steps in and takes over from the market. My example is housing. A house is a commodity to the landlord but to the occupant it is a home, and these are two quite different objects. When houses are scarce and incomes low, governments of all countries have stepped in to assert what we might call the welfare value of a home over the market value of a house by controlling or freezing rents and by suspending the normal rights of property and contract so as to guarantee security of tenure. The methods were crude, devoid of any principle of valuation, subjective or objective, and operated unilaterally for tenant against landlord. The result was a mess.

The invention by the Labour government of the 'fair rent' standard of value is extraordinarily interesting. Looking back over the past five years or so *The Times* (leader, 3 March, 1971) remarked that 'considering that the "fair rent" formula in the 1965 Rent Act is theoretically nonsensical ... it has worked remarkably well to bring about a sort of rough justice between landlords and tenants'. Quite apart from the fact that this is much better than the rough injustice which prevailed before, I do not agree that the formula is nonsensical. It provides a means of arriving at a bilaterally conceived evaluation through which the different types of value can be reduced to a common denominator. What it does is to strike an acceptable balance between 'value in use', or welfare value and 'value in exchange', or market value through the intermediary concept of the value of the thing itself seen in terms of its physical properties – size, structure, accommodation, equipment, etc. – estimated, not objectively as a commodity in the market nor subjectively as a home in use, but as a thing *for* use, which can be classified and valued in relation to others of its kind. The formula took account of the interests of both parties, as must be done if the state continues to depend in part on a private housing sector to meet its responsibilities towards its citizens and their families.

For my last illustration I take the subject of poverty and inequality. There has been evident for some time past a reaction against the idea of the 'poverty line' in favour of the view that the concept 'poverty' has no meaning except in a relative sense, whereas the 'poverty line' implies that it can be conceived in absolute terms. This has been accompanied by the contention that the real problem is not poverty, but inequality. If this means that poverty is relative to the standard of civilisation of the country concerned, it is beyond dispute. If it means that I may not say that *A* is poor, but only that he is poorer than *B*, I cannot accept it. If it means that inequality is a major social issue of which poverty is a part, that is beyond dispute. But if it means that the problems of poverty and inequality are identical and inseparable, so that one could not eradicate poverty without solving the problem of inequality, then I cannot accept that either. What I said above about welfare value and welfare standards implies the belief that it is possible and necessary, in the present state of society, to envisage a state of destitution or deprivation which must be condemned as intolerable and, even though no exact measurement or definition of this condition can be given, we may refer to it as 'poverty'. The poor remain a category, and the fact that its boundaries would be different in another place or age does not make it any the less absolute for the country in which it exists. Nor does the recognition of poverty as a problem and the poor as a category imply that all forms of poverty are the same; on the contrary, it emphasises the value of making subtle studies of its distinguishing features. The common factor in the state of the poor is the urgency of their need.

At this point the complexity of the subject obliges me to adopt an 'ideal type' approach and ask what place poverty and inequality would occupy in a democratic-welfare-capitalist society which had, so to speak, fulfilled itself. The simply answer is that in such a society poverty is a disease, but inequality is an essential structural feature. We, who are now enmeshed in this composite social system, have long ago rejected the theory of the necessity of poverty, as expressed by Patrick Colquhoun (1806, pp.7–8) when he described poverty as 'a most necessary and indispensable ingredient in society', because 'it is the source of wealth'. We have abandoned belief in the evolutionary benefits of poverty, as a weeder-out of the unfit. We no longer accept poverty as the inevitable and perpetual deposit of personal failures in the competitive struggle, and we do not even rely greatly on the fear of poverty as an incentive to work, as witness unemployment benefits and redundancy payments. It has no logical place in the system, but it obstinately remains with us, so we relieve it – when we notice it. Not very long ago it became almost invisible, but now it has reappeared. The invisibility of poverty has been a recurrent phenomenon in the western world.

The task of banishing poverty from our 'ideal type' society must be undertaken jointly by welfare and capitalism; there is no other way. Not only is there no evidence in history or in contemporary affairs to suggest that conflict between these two components must frustrate any effort at a joint solution but, on the contrary, it is clear that our particular type of social system has got nearer to achieving this objective than any that has gone before or now exists – unless one takes a totally relative view and asserts that poverty has been abolished in societies in which everybody is poor. Furthermore, the mechanics of the process are understood, the instruments have been forged or are on the drawing-board, and all that is needed is the will to use them and a period of economic calm and stability long enough to allow the complexities of the problem to be mastered and the large variety of exceptional and abnormal cases to be brought within the scope of the operation. It is not necessary for me, nor have I the space, to give an exposition of these mechanics and instruments, the range and potentialities of which are well known in this country, thanks to the writings of Peter Townsend and others. So I will press on to my final problem, that of inequality, an area in which the different principles and pressures of the three components of the hyphenated society are most difficult to reconcile with one another.

Democracy stands for equality of citizenship rights. The aim of welfare services is to give equal care to similar cases. 'Capitalism' – or the market – lives by recognising and rewarding inequalities, and depends on them to provide the motive force that makes it work. When this process was given free rein and welfare picked up the casualties, there was no problem. The shape of inequality was rough-hewn by the market. But two things have happened since then. Democracy took a hand. First, it made collective bargaining possible and this led in turn to the formal recognition of differentials, both within and between units of labour. Then it developed, somewhere in the socio-economic atmosphere, the notion that, by correctly reading the cultural signs, one could tell what a certain sort of man ought to be paid, especially if he was in the civil service or one of the professions. Differentials were given an ethical flavour. Thirdly it made a show of cutting inequalities down to the ethical scale, as far as money incomes were concerned, by heavy progressive taxation. Democracy, one might say, legitimised inequality (since you do not tax stolen goods), with the help of the trade unions.

The second thing that happened was that social security in the typical affluent western countries tied itself to the inequalities of the market by relating its whole system of contributions and benefits to differences in earnings, up to a limiting ceiling. Since social security contains, as I have said, a welfare element and forms the bridge between 'capitalism' and welfare, one may say that welfare, like democracy, legitimised inequality. There was nothing conspiratorial in all this. It represents the convergence without which the composite social system would have had little chance of stabilising itself. And there could have been no 'end of ideology'. It certainly does not imply approval of any particular scale of inequality.

So we have a position where all three components accept inequality, but without agreement as to its pattern in any detail. Obviously there could not be any fixed pattern, or the whole economic system would be ossified. But there is no agreement even about the principle to apply in drawing a pattern or any clear idea where to look for such a principle. A high growth-rate can cover a multitude of sins, but with our low rate, the confusion is patent and the disruption of life serious. Prestige, politics and bargaining-power overlay the simpler facts of relative productivity, creating a state of uncertainty in which jealously and 'relative deprivation' flourish – not only at the bottom, but right up the scale, and probably least of all among the poor. That is why I said that poverty and inequality were different problems, when viewed structurally. Poverty is a tumour which should be cut out, and theoretically could be; inequality is a vital organ which is functioning badly.

…

The failure to solve the problem of economic inequality is evidence of the weakness of contemporary democracy. Since the task of maintaining the balance between the component elements of the system falls on democracy, this weakness is dangerous, but it is not critical nor, one hopes, irremediable. The outstanding needs are for better two-way communication to remedy the lack of contact had understanding between politicians, bureaucrats and the public, and for a reconciliation of the roles of the two competing democracies, the political and the industrial, in the power structure. At the moment it may seem that, in our own country, the spirit of pre-welfare-state capitalism is gaining ascendancy over the democratic component and, through it, threatening the status of welfare in the system. But this, too, has all the appearance of being a transitory aberration, the reaction to which is already showing itself in the deep recesses of the popular conscience. Capitalism is most dangerous when it is weak and frightened, not when it is strong and confident, and recent measures taken to economise on welfare are in large part a hasty response to capitalist alarmism and, as such, unlikely to be built into the system. I firmly believe that the main effect of thinking of school meals only as an expense item will be to initiate a study of the real function of school meals in relation to the health of the children and the social life of the school and the family. One might almost say that this has already begun.

References

Colquhoun, P. (1806) *A Treatise on Indigence*, London, Hatchard.

Dahrendorf, R. (1964) *Gesellschaft und Freiheit*, Munich, Piper.

Page, A.N. (1968) *Utility Theory: A Book of Readings*, New York, Wiley.

Source: T.H. Marshall, *The Right to Welfare and Other Essays*, London, Heinemann Educational Books, 1981, pp.107–12, 115–20. Originally published as 'Value problems of welfare capitalism', *Journal of Social Policy*, January 1972.

Acknowledgements

Grateful acknowledgement is made to the following sources for permission to reproduce material in this book:

Text

pp.5–8: Type 8 Home owning areas, well-off older residents' and 'Type 45 Low rise council housing, less well-off families', *The Acorn User Guide Index*. CACI Limited. Copyright © CACI Limited 2000. All rights reserved. ACORN and CACI are registered trademarks of CACI Limited; *Reading 1.1:* Damer, S. (1989) 'Problem places and problem people', *From Mooorpark to 'Wine Alley'*. Edinburgh University Press; *Reading 1.2:* From *The Celebration Chronicles* by Andrew Ross, PhD. Copyright © 1999 by Andrew Ross, PhD. Used by permission of Ballantine Books, a division of Random House, Inc.; *Reading 1.3:* 'Truman didn't sleep here' from *Celebration, USA* by Douglas Frantz and Catherine Collins. © 1999 by Douglas Frantz and Catherine Collins. Reprinted by permission of Henry Holt and Company, New York; *Reading 1.4:* Taylor, I. *et al.* (1996) 'Out on the town: Manchester's Gay Village', *A Tale of Two Cities*. Routledge/Taylor & Francis Books; *Reading 2.1:* Savage, M. *et al.* (2001) 'Ordinary, ambivalent and defensive: class identities in the North West of England', *Sociology,* November. © BSA Publications Limited, published by Cambridge University Press; *Readings 2.2 and 2.3:* Crompton, R. (1991) 'The classic inheritance and its development ', *Class and Stratification: An Introduction to Current Debates*. 2nd edn. Polity Press. By permission of Blackwell Publishers Ltd; *Reading 2.4:* Bourdieu, P. *et al.* (1999) 'With an employee from the central sorting post office' in *The Weight of the World: Social Suffering in Contemporary Society* (Ferguson, P. Parkhurst, trans.). Polity Press. By permission of Blackwell Publishers Ltd.; *Reading 3.1:* Charles, N. (1990) 'Women and class – a problematic relationship?', *Sociological Review*. Vol.38. Routledge/Blackwell Publishers Ltd. Copyright © The Editorial Board of Sociological Review; *Reading 3.2:* Bradley, H. (1996) 'Gender: rethinking patriarchy', *Fractured Identities: Changing Patterns of Inequality*. Blackwell Publishers Ltd; *Reading 3.3:* Reprinted by permission of Sage Publications Ltd from Beverley Skeggs, '(Dis)Identification of class: on not being working class', *Formations of Class and Gender*. Sage Publications Ltd, 1997; *Reading 4.1:* Reprinted by permission of Sage Publications Ltd from Richard Jenkins, 'Categorization and power', in *Rethinking Ethnicity*, Copyright © 1997 Richard Jenkins; *Reading 4.2:* Lee, S.M. (1993) 'Racial classification in the US census: 1890–1990', *Ethnic and Racial Studies*, vol.16, no.1, January 1993, Taylor & Francis Ltd, PO Box 25, Abingdon, Oxfordshire, OX14 3UE; *Reading 4.3:* Reprinted by permission of Sage Publications Ltd from Kalpagam, U. 'The colonial state and statistical knowledge', in *History of the Human Sciences*, vol.13, no.2,

May 2000, Copyright © 2000 Sage Publications Ltd; *Reading 4.4:* Weiss, S.F. (1987) 'Power through population: Schallmayer and population policy', *Race Hygiene and National Efficiency:, The Eugenics of Wilhelm Schallmayer*, University of California Press. Copyright © 1987 by The Regents of the University of California; *Reading 4.5:* Warren, J. W. and Twine, F. W. (1997) 'White Americans, the new minority?', *Journal of Black Studies*, vol.28, no.2, November 1997, pp.206–14. Copyright © 1997 Sage Publications, Inc. Reprinted by permission of Sage Publications, Inc.; *Reading 5.1:* Marshall, T. H. (1964) 'Citizenship and social class', in Turner, B.S. and Hamilton, P. (eds) *Citizenship: Critical Concepts*, Volume II, Routledge. Reprinted by permission of Routledge, a division of Random House, Inc.; *Reading 5.2:* Reprinted by permission of Palgrave Publishers Ltd and Harvard University Press from *Rethinking Multiculturalism: Culture Diversity and Political Theory* by Bhikhu Parekh, Cambridge, MA: Harvard University Press, Copyright © 2000 by Bhikhu Parekh; *Reading 5.3:* Reprinted by permission of Sage Publications Ltd from Richardson, D., *Rethinking Sexuality*, Copyright © Diane Richardson 2000; *Reading 5.4:* Reprinted by permission of Sage Publications Ltd from Isin, E.F. and Wood, P.K., *Citizenship and Identity*, Copyright © Engin F. Isin and Patricia K. Wood 1999; *Reading 6.1:* Barry, B. (1989) *Theories of Justice*, Harvester-Wheatsheaf, reprinted by permission of Pearson Education Limited; *Reading 6.2:* from *Turning Back* by Stephen Steinberg, Copyright © 1995, 2001 by Stephen Steinberg. Reprinted by permission of Beacon Press, Boston, MA; *Reading 7.1:* Gewirtz, S., Ball, S. J. and Bowe, R. (1995) *Markets, Choice and Equity in Education*, Open University Press; *Reading 7.2:* Ball, S. J., Bowe, R. and Gewirtz, S. (1995) 'Circuits of schooling: a sociological exploration of parental choice of school in social-class contexts', in *The Sociological Review*, 43, pp.52–78, reprinted by permission of Blackwell Publishers. Copyright © the Editorial Board of The Sociological Review, 1995; *Reading 7.3:* Power, A. (1999) *Estates on the Edge: The Social Consequences of Mass Housing in Northern Europe*, reprinted by permission of Macmillan Ltd. Copyright © Anne Power, 1997, 1999; *Reading B:* 'Class, status, party', pp.180–95, from *Max Weber: Essays in Sociology* by Max Weber, edited by H.H. Gerth and C. Wright Mills, translated by H.H. Gerth and C. Wright Mills, copyright 1946, 1958 by H.H. Gerth and C. Wright Mills. Used by permission of Oxford University, Inc.; *Reading C:* Myrdal, G. (1964) *The American Dilemma, Volume 2: The Negro Social Structure*, McGraw-Hill Book Company. Copyright © Gunnar Myrdal; *Reading D:* Segal, L. (1999) *Why Feminism? Gender, Psychology, Politics*, Polity Press. Copyright © Lynne Segal 1999; *Reading E:* Marshall, G. (1997) *Repositioning Class – Social Inequality in Industrial Societies*, Sage Publications Ltd. Copyright © Gordon Marshall 1997; *Reading F:* Castles, S. and Kosack, G. (1973) *Immigrant Workers and Class Structure in Western Europe*, Oxford University Press, reprinted by permission of The Institute of Race Relations; *Reading G:* Marshall, T.H. (1972) 'Value problems of welfare capitalism', *Journal of Social Policy*, I, January 1972, pp.15–32, Cambridge University Press.

Figures

Figure 1.1: Baldwin, P. (1999) 'Postcodes chart growing income divide', *The Guardian,* 25 October, 1999. Guardian Newspapers Limited; *Figure 1.2:* 'Postcode guide to services at grassroots', *The Guardian,* 14 July 2000. Guardian Newspapers Limited; *Figure 1.3:* Shaw *et al.* (1999) 'Premature deaths in the extreme areas of Britain', *The Widening Gap.* The Policy Press; *Figure 1.5:* Macduff Everton/Corbis; *Figure 1.6:* From Collison, P. (1963) *The Cutteslowe Walls: A Study in Social Class,* Faber & Faber. Copyright © 1963 by Peter Collison; *Figures 1.7 and 1.8:* Ross, A. (1999) *The Celebration Chronicles: Life, Liberty and the Pursuit of Property Value in Disney's New Town.* Ballantine Books; *Figure1.9:* Nathan Cox; *Figure 2.1:* BBC Picture Archives; *Figure 2.2 (a),(b),(c),(d):* Nathan Cox; *Figures 2.3,2.4 and 2.5:* AKG London; *Figure 2.6:* College de France website; *Figure 3.1:* Third World Newsreel; *Figures 3.2,3.3,3.4 and 3.5:* Office for National Statistics, *Social Trends 30,* 2000. Crown copyright material is reproduced under Class Licence Number C01W0000065 with the permission of the Controller of HMSO and the Queen's Printer for Scotland; *p.109 cartoon:* © Viv Quillan; *Figures 3.6,3.7 and 3.10:* Office for National Statistics, EOC, 2000. Crown copyright material is reproduced under Class Licence Number C01W0000065 with the permission of the Controller of HMSO and the Queen's Printer for Scotland; *Figure 3.8:* D.C. Thomson & Co. Ltd; *Figure 3.9:* Taken from Holdsworth, A. (1988) *Out of the Doll's House.* BBC Books. Photographer unknown; *Figure 3.11:* © Museum of London; *Figure 3.12:* © Mary Evans Picture Library; *Figure 3.13:* © Sally Fraser; *Figure 3.14:* © Hulton Getty Picture Library; *Figure 3.15:* Jenny Matthews/Format Photographers; *Figure 3.16:* © Hulton Getty Picture Library; *Figure 3.17:* Smith College, Maryland; *Figure 3.18:* Pam Isherwood/Format Photographers; *Figure 3.19:* The Advertising Archives; *Figure 4.1:* Simon Baron-Cohen as 'Ali G' Copyright © Rex Features; *Figure 4.2 (left):* Michael Jackson as part of The Jackson Five group – CBS TV (Courtesy Kobal); *Figure 4.2 (right):* Michael Jackson at Jackson Geller book launch, RIBA, London, 5 March 2001. Photo: William Conran/PA Photos Ltd; *Figure 4.3:* Ethnic Group Question to be asked in England and Wales, *Census 2001,* Office for National Statistics. Crown copyright material is reproduced with the permission of the Controller of Her Majesty's Stationery Office; *Figure 4.4:* Courtesy of Sega Europe Ltd; *Figure 4.5:* from Curtis, L. (1984) *Nothing But The Same Old Story,* Information on Ireland Publications; *Figure 4.6:* Browne, A. (2000) 'UK Whites will be a minority by 2100', *The Observer,* 3 September 2000. Copyright © The Observer; *Figure 5.1:* Sean Dempsey/PA Photos Ltd; *Figure 5.2:* PA Photos Ltd; *Figure 5.3:* Haywood Magee/Hulton Archive; *Figure 5.4:* John Harris; *Figure 5.5:* John Harris/Report Digital; *Figure 5.6:* EPS/PA Photos Ltd; *Figure 6.1:* Jess Hurd/Report Digital; *Figure 6.3:* Tom Hanley; *Figure 6.4:* Associated Press, AP; *Figure 6.5:* Press Association Ltd; *Figure 6.6:* Shelton Taylor and Malcolm Aird/Hulton Archive; *Figure 6.7:* Associated Press; *Figure 7.1:* CPL/Popperfoto; *Figure 7.2:* Hulton Archive; *Figure 7.3:* Office for National Statistics, *Social Trends 30,* 2000. Crown copyright material is reproduced under Class Licence Number C01W0000065 with the permission of the Controller of HMSO and the Queen's Printer for Scotland; *Figure 7.4 (a) and (b):* John Harris/Report Digital; *Figure 7.5:* Howard Walker; *Figure 7.6:* Hulton Archive; *Figure 7.9:* Joy Wilson; *Figure 7.10:* Adam Butler/Press Associated Ltd.

Tables

Table 1.1: 'The *acorn*® targeting classification 2000', The *Acorn User Guide Index*. CACI Limited. Copyright © CACI Limited 2000. All rights reserved. ACORN and CACI are registered trademarks of CACI Limited; *Table 1.2:* Shaw *et al.* (1999) 'Constituencies where people are most and least at risk of premature death (mortality rates under 65) in Britain (1991–95)', *The Widening Gap.* The Policy Press; *Tables 2.1 and 2.2:* Office for National Statistics, New Earnings Survey, 1998. Crown copyright material is reproduced under Class Licence Number C01W0000065 with the permission of the Controller of HMSO and the Queen's Printer for Scotland; *Tables 3.1, 3.2 and 3.3:* Office for National Statistics, *Social Trends 30,* 2000. Crown copyright material is reproduced under Class Licence Number C01W0000065 with the permission of the Controller of HMSO and the Queen's Printer for Scotland; *Tables 3.4, 3.5, 3.6 and 3.7:* Office for National Statistics, EOC 1998. Crown copyright material is reproduced under Class Licence Number C01W0000065 with the permission of the Controller of HMSO and the Queen's Printer for Scotland; *Table 4.1:* Blackburn, D.G. (2000) 'Why race is not a biological concept', Lang, B. (ed.) *Race and Racism in Theory and Practice.* Copyright © 2000 by Rowman & Littlefield Publishers, Inc. This material is used by permission of John Wiley & Sons, Inc.; *Table 4.2:* Copyright © 1997 from *Racial Subjects: Writing on Race in America* by David Theo Goldberg. Reproduced by permission of Routledge, Inc., part of The Taylor & Francis Group; *Tables 7.1, 7.2 and 7.4:* Office for National Statistics, *Social Trends 30,* 2000. Crown copyright material is reproduced under Class Licence Number C01W0000065 with the permission of the Controller of HMSO and the Queen's Printer for Scotland; *Table 7.3:* Office for National Statistics, *Social Trends 29,* 1999. Crown copyright material is reproduced under Class Licence Number C01W0000065 with the permission of the Controller of HMSO and the Queen's Printer for Scotland; *Tables 7.4 and 7.5:* Lee, P. and Murie, A. (1997) *Poverty, Housing Tenure and Social Exclusion,* Policy Press.

Cover photographs

Front cover, middle, right (Chinese guards of gated community): Macduff Everton/Corbis. All other photographs United National Photographers (UNP): Boy on housing estate © Charles Knight/UNP; Tony Blair shaking hands © Kiran Ridley/UNP; Children painting © Nigel Hillier/UNP; Hospital corridor with porters © Nigel Hillier/UNP; Women sewing in prison © Charles Knight/UNP; Muslim group of men © Alex Cave/UNP; Muslim girl in call centre © Alex Cave/UNP.

Every effort has been made to trace all the copyright owners, but if any has been inadvertently overlooked, the publishers will be pleased to make the necessary arrangements at the first opportunity.

Index

Abbott, Pamela, 102–3
aboriginal rights, and citizenship
    xviii, 207, 225, 228–30, 247–8
abortion rights 219
ACORN (A Classification of
    Residential Neighbourhoods)
    11–14
    and patterns of ill health 19
    Type 45 7–9
    Type 8 5–7
activist groups, and participatory
    democracy 225
affluent manual workers, and class
    identities 65, 76
age
    and class identities 60, 75
    and economic activity rates 108
    and gay men in Manchester's
        Gay Village 36
    and gender 103
    population of working age, by
        employment status and gender
        107
    problems of identification 163
ageing population, and citizenship
    215–16, 217, 218
aggregate data, on employment and
    gender inequalities 122–3
Ali G (Sacha Baron Cohen) 168
Althusser, Louis 93
Anderson, Benedict 245
Aponte, Robert 370
Arnot, M. 310–11
Asian children, and educational
    performance 305–6
Asian people
    Asian Americans and Whiteness
        203
    and ethnicity 161
    naming and categorizing 168,
        169
    and housing 326–7
    in the US census 173, 174, 175,
        195, 197, 198
Asian women, and uniforms 241–2
asylum-seekers xvii–xviii, 60
    and citizenship 206–7, 208

attitudes
    changing attitudes towards
        women working 131–2
    to inequality 64
Australia
    citizenship in 209
    and aboriginal rights 247, 248

Bagnall, Gaynor see Savage, Mike,
    Bagnall, Gaynor and Longhurst,
    Brian
Ball, S. 317–18
Ball, Stephen J. see Gerwitz, Sharon,
    Ball, Stephen J. and Bowe,
    Richard
Banton, Michael 164, 165
Barry, Brian, 'Economic motivation
    in a Rawlsian society' 250, 258,
    260, 266, 281–3
Bartsch, G. 374
BBC 'social class' website ix
Beauvoir, Simone de xi
    The Second Sex 118
Beechey, Veronica 147
Bell, D. 256
Bennett, Tony 20, 37, 135
Beveridge Report (1945) xx, 213,
    293
bio-power, and population 188
black children, bussing of 265–7
black feminism xvi, 128–9, 130, 133,
    134, 138
    and racial discrimination in
        employment 270–3
black people
    on Broadwater Farm Estate 340,
        341–2
    and Celebration 36, 46–7, 48
    and Chinese Americans 203
    and the Irish 185, 186, 202–3
    and legal justice 255, 256
    naming and categorization of
        166–6, 168, 169
    in the US census 172–3, 174,
        175, 195, 196, 197
    and racial identity 161
    and the underclass 275–8, 285–8,
        368, 369

Black Report on Health Inequalities
    68
Blackburn, R. 264
Blair, Tony 16, 60, 223
    see also Labour government
        (1997)
Blakely, E.J. and Snyder, M., Fortress
    America 25, 26
bodies
    and race 160, 161, 164–6
    and representations of class 136,
        137, 153–5, 156
Bonnett, A. 182, 183, 187
Booth, Charles 20, 238
    Poverty Map 21
Bourdieu, Pierre xvi, 37, 135, 136,
    308, 309, 335
    on class 61, 76–7, 79, 81, 82, 83,
        88, 153
    Distinction 61
    habitus and fields 61, 80
    The Weight of the World 80, 81,
        97–100
    see also cultural capital
Bowe, Richard see Gerwitz, Sharon,
    Ball, Stephen J. and Bowe,
    Richard
boys, and educational achievement
    302, 303, 304, 305, 310–11
Bradley, Harriet 65, 121, 135
    'Gender: rethinking patriarchy'
        127, 129, 134, 146–9
British Empire, and changing
    patterns of warfare 217
British identity, and citizenship
    216–17
'Britishness', concept of 169
Broadwater Farm Estate 319, 320,
    339–43
    government money for 342–3
    and the police 340, 341–2
    rebuilding 342
    riot (1985) 342
Brown, P. 309
Bryson, Bill 255
Bunch, Charlotte 361
Bush, George W. 139
Byrne, D. 45

Canada
  citizenship in 209
  and aboriginal rights 247, 248
capitalism
  and class 82
    Marxist analysis of 71–3, 91–4
    Weberian analysis 95
  and feminism 128
  Marshall on value problems of
    welfare-capitalism 378–83
  and socialist feminists 121–2
  see also markets
caste
  Myrdal on class and 355–8
  Weber on status segregation and
    352
Castells, M. 54, 55
Castles, Stephen and Kosack,
  Godula, 'Immigrant workers and
  class structure in western Europe'
  374–7
Catholicism
  and British race-thinking 185
  and whiteness in America 189,
    202
Celebration, Florida xv–xvi, 4,
  27–32, 33, 46–52
  architecture 28–9, 31, 50, 51, 52
  community restrictions 50
  downtown area 29, 31
  and ethnic minorities 31, 32,
    35–6, 46–9
  Health Centre 29
  housing density 27
  and lifestyle 37
  lottery 30, 46
  and New Urbanism 28, 32, 36, 37
  School 29, 31, 47, 52
  and social exclusion 31, 50–1
  and social inclusion 32
  and technology 52
Celts, and whiteness in America 189,
  202, 203
censuses
  and occupational classification in
    the UK (2000) ix
  and racial categorization 172–6,
    177, 178, 179, 180, 181, 195–8,
    200
Champley, Henry, *White Women,
  Coloured Men* 186–7
Charles, Nicola, 'Women and class –
  a problematic relationship?'
  123–5, 137, 142–5
Chicago School of sociology 22
childcare
  and the gender division of labour
    114–16, 148
  and women in paid work 109,
    122

Chinese people
  Americans
    categorization in the US census
      174, 175, 196, 197, 198
    and whiteness 189, 203
  and skin colour 182
cities, choosing as a place to live 2
citizenship xvii–xviii, 205–48
  and aboriginal rights xviii, 207,
    225, 228–30, 247–8
  and asylum-seekers 206–7, 208
  in Celebration 50
  and civil rights 234, 235–8
  and class 215, 234–8
  and cultural rights 229, 230
  cultural differences within xviii,
    229
  decline in active 222–3
  dual 206, 216
  early forms of 207
  and ecological rights 227, 230
  environmental xviii, 208, 226–8
  erosion of 208
  and European integration 206
  and gated communities 27
  and housing xxi, 314
  and immigration into the EU
    xvii–xviii
  and liberal feminism 117
  Marshall's theory of xviii, 208,
    209–12, 228, 230, 234–9, 244–5
  means of acquiring 209–10
  and multiculturalism 207, 210,
    216–17, 229, 239–44
  new patterns of 226–30
  political xviii, 209, 234, 236–8
  and racial discrimination xviii
  and reproduction xviii, 213–14,
    218–20
  sexual xviii, 219, 220, 244–6
  social xv, xviii, 68, 209, 210, 217,
    222, 234, 238–9
  and social justice 252
  social theories of 206–8
  in the UK 206, 208, 210
    and British identity 216–17
  in the USA 207–9, 210
  and voluntary associations 208,
    213–14, 221–5, 226
  and war 212, 213, 217–18, 221
  and work 212, 214–17, 221
  see also social citizenship
civil rights, and citizenship 234,
  235–8
class xiii–xiv
  awareness and identities 61–5,
    71, 82–3, 86–91
    and cultural capital 79–80, 89
    defensiveness of 88–9

  habitus and fields 80
  and the individual 87–8
  and reflexivity 89–90
  snobbishness and ordinariness
    90–1
  and Weberian analysis 73, 74–6
  and women 123–5, 135–6, 138,
    142–5, 150–7
BBC 'social class' website ix
Britain as a classless society 61,
  69, 86–7
consciousness 64, 65, 71, 73, 83
conundrum of 60–1, 69, 73, 83
distinctions and cultures xvi,
  76–82
  food consumption 77–9
  high and low culture 77
and education
  and gender 298
  ideologies of 296–8
  inequalities 302, 303, 306
  and the market 306, 307,
    308–10
  and parental choice 333–7,
    338–9
and feminism xvi–xvii
and gated communities 25–6, 27
and gender 103
health and life expectancy 19
and housing xi
  home ownership 332–4
  tenure 319–20
and immigrant workers xix–xx,
  374–7
inequalities 60, 66–9, 82, 83, 86
  attitudes to 64
  and citizenship 215, 234–7,
    238–9
  and educational performance
    302, 303, 306
  and Marxism 71–3
  and social rights 210–11
  Weberian analysis of 73–6
Marxist analysis of xvi, 60–1, 70,
  71–3, 75, 76, 80–1, 91–4, 96
  and caste 357
  in the Communist Manifesto
    x–xi, 91, 346–8
Myrdal on caste and 355–8
and place 2, 4, 14
  Celebration 50–1
and race 60, 75, 160, 163, 186,
  190
and social exclusion xvi, 60
and social justice xix–xx, 293–4
Weberian analysis of xi, xvi,
  60–1, 70, 73, 80–1, 94–6,
  349–54
and women 3, 123–5, 142–5

young working-class women 79–80, 135–6, 138, 150–7
see also middle class; occupational groups; underclass; working classes
Cobb, J. 150
Cockburn, Cynthia 147–8
Cohen, P. 185
Collins, Catherine *see* Frantz, Douglas and Collins, Catherine
colonial states, government of 180, 199–200
colour
and race 164, 170–1, 182
see also black people; whiteness
Colquhoun, Patrick 235, 381
Commission for Racial Equality (CRE) 23, 272
Commission on Social Justice (CSJ) 250, 257, 313
Social Justice: Strategies for National Renewal 252–4
communal action, Weber on class interest and 350–1
communist politics, and Marx 71
community, and place 11
community studies, of working-class identity 74–5
Conservative governments, and class 60, 61
consumer culture, and Manchester's Gay Village 33, 35, 36, 38, 53, 54
consumption
and class ix
place, identity and lifestyle 35–8
consumption theory, and housing 328–9
countryside, choosing as a place to live 2–3
Crompton, Rosemary, 'The classic inheritance and its development' 70, 71, 72, 91–6
CSJ *see* Commission on Social Justice (CSJ)
cultural capital 37–8, 76–82
and class ambivalence 79–80, 89
and the educational market 308, 309, 339
and food consumption 77–9
high and low culture 77
and working-class women 135, 136, 137, 153, 154, 155–6
cultural rights xviii, 208, 229, 230

Dahrendorf, R. 379
Damer, Séan, 'Problem places and problem people' 22, 23, 42–5
Danziger's Britain 20
Davies, Nick, *Dark Heart* 20

death penalty, in the United States 255, 256
death rates
men, and class inequalities 68–9
patterns of in relation to place 15, 17–19
Declaration of Human Rights 230
Delpérée, Albert 374
democracy
and citizenship 209, 226
property-owning 318
and voluntary associations 223–5
and welfare-capitalism 378–9, 382, 383
Department for Education and Employment (DfEE), *Excellence in Schools* 273–4
deprivation, and housing 312–13
development, and social justice 260–1
Devine, F. 65
difference, equality of 241–2
difference principle, and the theory of justice 257–8
discourse
Foucault's concept of and feminism 131–3
and race 177, 190
discrimination
before the market 263
and place 22–3
within the market 271
see also racial discrimination
distribution of income and wealth
inequalities in 66, 259, 267
and owner-occupied housing 322
division of labour *see* sexual division of labour
domestic labour
and the gender division of labour 112–13, 148, 360
and socialist feminists 122
Donnison, D. 259, 266, 275
Doyle, Roddy, *The Commitments* 167
dualistic thinking, and feminism 133
Duke, Vic and Edgell, Stephen 367
Duplessis, R. 361

East India Company 199
Echols, F. 336
economic activity rates
and age 108
and ethnicity 108
and gender 106, 108, 109, 115
women and citizenship 214
economic capital 37, 38, 77, 308
economic growth

and equality 253–4
and post-war education 298
economic motivation, and social justice 257–8, 281–3
Edgell, Stephen *see* Duke, Vic and Edgell, Stephen
education
Celebration School 29, 31, 47, 52
and citizenship rights xviii
class, gender and ethnic inequalities 302–6
compensatory education programmes 300
comprehensive schools 300, 309
and cultural capital 81, 137, 153
'decomprehensivization' of secondary schooling 336
and the educational market 307–12, 333–9
equal opportunities in xix, xx, 264–7, 294, 296–302
grammar schools 296, 297, 299–300, 309
levels of, and women's perception of class 124, 142, 143
local authority budgets 16
post-school, and place classification 14
school exclusion rates 304, 305
and social justice xix, xx, 262–7, 273–4, 293, 294, 295–6, 329–30
affirmative action programmes 275
and the educational market 311–12
and third way politics 214
Education Act (1944) xx, 297–8
Education Reform Act (1988) 301
Eisner, Michael 51
employment
and citizenship
and changing patterns of work 212, 214–17
policies of full employment 209
and discrimination before the market 263
and discrimination within the market 271
gender inequalities in 105–9, 115–16, 122
part-time 107, 109, 111, 122, 214
and place discrimination 23
rates for parents 115
and social justice
new international division of labour 260–1
and racial discrimination 270–3, 274
and the underclass 287–8

in the voluntary sector 222
Engels, Friedrich 68, 92, 185
    see also Marx, Karl and Engels,
        Friedrich
the Enlightenment, and feminism
    102
Ensor, R. 312
environmental citizenship xviii, 208,
    226–8
equal opportunities
    in education xix, xx, 264–7, 294,
        296–302
    legislation 119, 138
    and multiculturalism 240
    and social justice 251, 252, 253,
        258, 293
equality
    and citizenship, in a multicultural
        society 216, 239–44
    equality (liberal) feminism xvi,
        117–20
    and Marshall's theory of
        citizenship 209
    and social justice 251, 293
    see also inequalities
equality of outcome, and social
    justice 251, 275
essentialism, and race 169
ethnic cleansing 162
ethnicity ix, x, xii, xvi
    Asian 161
    and citizenship 207, 210, 211,
        212, 216–17, 239–44
    and class identities 75
    and class inequality 60
    and economic activity rates, and
        gender 108, 109
    and education
        access to resources 312
        ethnic minority pupils in
            schools 274
        performance 303, 304, 305–6
        school exclusion rates 304, 305
    ethnic group question in the UK
        census 179
    and gated communities 27
    and gender 103
    health and life expectancy 19
    and housing 325–7
    and place 2, 4
    and race 161
    and social justice 250
    in the UK 161–2
    Weber on 'ethnic' segregation
        and 'caste' 352
    see also race
eugenics 187–8, 201–2, 218
European Union
    and citizenship 216

and migrant labour 215–16
Evans, Karen *see* Taylor, Ian, Evans,
    Karen and Fraser, Penny

Fainstein, Norman 286
fairness
    and legal justice 255–6
    and social justice 251, 252, 253
family values campaigns, and
    feminism 362
Fanon, Franz, *Black Skin, White
    Masks* 165
Featherstone, Mike 36–7, 38
feminism xvi–xvii, 101–57
    activist challenges 363
    black feminism xvi, 128–9, 130,
        133, 134, 138
    and citizenship 244, 246
    and class xvi–xvii
    diversity and heterogeneity of
        102
    and family values campaigns 362
    'first-wave' 118
    and Freudian analysis 127–8
    future of 104–16, 359–66
    images of 359
    lesbian 128
    liberal (equality) xvi, 117–20, 127
    and men and masculinities 363–4
    modernity and the
        Enlightenment 102
    and 'new genetics' 139
    and politics 365
    and post-feminism xvi, 105, 116,
        138, 139
    and post-modernism xvi, xvii,
        130, 133–4, 146-7, 148
    and post-structuralism xvi, 130–3,
        134
    radical xvi, 125–7, 146
    'second-wave' 120–7
    socialist xvi, 120–5, 128, 146
    and the suffrage campaign 118,
        120
    white feminism 128, 129
    women's empowerment and
        'new feminist' commentators
        xvii
    see also gender; women
filtering-down representation of
    place 42, 45
financial exclusion, and place
    discrimination 23
Fishman, W. 312
food consumption, and class 77–9
Ford Motor Company, and racial
    discrimination 272
Forrest, R. 324
'Fortress Europe' xviii

Foucault, Michel
    and bio-power 188
    and discourse, and feminism
        131–3, 138, 147
    and governmentality 180, 199
    and knowledge/power 161, 171,
        178
fox-hunting, and environmental
    citizenship 227–8
France
    citizenship in 209
    Muslim girls and the headscarf
        242–3
Frantz, Douglas and Collins,
    Catherine
    Celebration, USA 28, 31
    'Truman didn't sleep here' 32,
        49–52
Fraser, Charles 51
Fraser, Penny *see* Taylor, Ian, Evans,
    Karen and Fraser, Penny
Freudian analysis, and feminism
    127–8
Friedan, Betty, *The Feminine
    Mystique* 120

Gallie, Duncan 369
gated communities xv, 4, 24–7, 33,
    35, 39
Gates, Henry Louis 185
gay communities
    in Celebration 31
    Manchester's Gay Village xvi, 4,
        33–5, 53–7
    and sexual citizenship 245–6
    and voluntary associations 225
gender
    and class identities 60, 75
    differences, and sex differences
        103
    feminist perspectives on xvi–xvii,
        101–57
    health and life expectancy 19
    and identity xii
    inequalities 102, 138
        aggregate data on employment
            and 122–3
        and childcare 114–16
        and domestic labour 112–13,
            122, 148
        and education 296, 297, 302,
            303, 304, 305, 306, 310–11
        and employment rates 115
        and feminism 105, 117–20,
            120–5
        and income 110–11, 116
        and paid work 105–9, 116, 122
    and place 2, 4
    and race 103, 160, 163, 190

whiteness 186–7
relations 102–4
relationship between sex and 117–18
and the sexual division of labour 122, 127, 147–8
social construction of xi–xii
sociology of 102
see also feminism; men; women
gentrification 3
German eugenicists 187–8, 201–2
Germany
    ageing population 215
    citizenship in 209
    immigrant workers 270
Gerth, H. and Mills, C. Wright 94, 95
Gerwitz, Sharon, Ball, Stephen J. and Bowe, Richard 308, 310
    'Choice, equity and control' 307, 333–8
    'Circuits of schooling' 307, 338–9
Giddens, Anthony 308
Gilligan, C. see Wilson, R.M.S., Gilligan, C. and Peason, D.
Gilroy, Paul 165, 166, 167, 191, 217
girls
    education of
        educational performance 302, 303, 304, 305, 311
        and equal opportunities 296, 298–9
Glasgow, place stigmatization in 22, 42, 45
Glasgow, Douglas, The Black Underclass 285, 369
globalization of cultures, and citizenship 207
Goldberg, David 171, 176, 177, 178
Goldthorpe, J.H. 71, 75, 76, 122–3, 301
grammar schools 296, 297, 299–300, 309
Greer, Germaine, The Whole Woman 104–5, 116
Grey, Thomas 281–2
grievance, and inequality 268
The Guardian, articles on postcode inequalities 9–10, 16

Hague, William 16
Halsey, A.H. 301
Hamilton, Peter 31
Hamnett, Chris 321
Haraway, Donna 163, 171, 177, 181, 182
Harvey, David 11
Hayek, Friedrich 255
health problems, of immigrant workers 375

health service in Britain
    budgets 16
    and citizenship 210
    inequalities
        and class 68–9
        and the postcode lottery 15, 17–19
        and social justice 295
Hemmings, S., Silva, E.B. and Thompson, K. 112
Henley Centre, on consumer segmentation 14
Heseltine, Michael 321
Higher Education Funding Council for England (HEFCE) 14
Hispanic population, categorization in the US census 173, 195, 197, 203
Hobsbawm, Eric 45
hooks, bell 128
households, and changing forms of sexual citizenship xviii
housewives, class position of 144, 145
housing 312–30
    and class xi, 319–20, 332–4
    and consumption theory 328–9
    deprivation and overcrowding 312–13
    and immigrant workers 375
    inequalities in 313, 319–24, 328–9, 330
    owner-occupation 313, 315, 317–18, 328
        profile of well-off older residents 5–7, 8–9
        as wealth-creation 321–4
    and poverty 3, 324, 326, 330
    private rented sector 314, 315, 317
    and social justice xx–xxi, 259, 260, 293, 295, 312–14
    and the welfare state 295
    social/council xviii, xxi, 314–16
        Broadwater Farm Estate 319, 320, 339–43
        and ethnic minorities 325–7
        profile of less well-off families 7–9
        residualization of 319–20, 322, 329
        'right to buy' scheme 315–16, 317, 318, 321
    and welfare capitalism 380–1
Hughes, Simon 16
human capital, and income inequality 67–8
human rights
    and citizenship 226, 228, 229, 230
    and immigrant workers 261–2

humanist Marxism 92–3
Humphries, J. 147

identity
    British, and citizenship 216–17
    and place of residence 3
    and race xii, 160, 161, 162–72
        naming and categorization 166–72, 193–5
        vision and division 163–6
    and the social divisions perspective xii–xiii
ill-health, patterns of in relation to place 15, 17–19
'imagined communities', nations as 245
immigrant workers
    and class xix–xx, 374–7
    and relative deprivation 269
    and social justice 261–2, 269–73
incomes
    distribution of 259, 322
    inequalities
        and class 66–8
        and gender 110–11, 116, 359–60
        and social justice 259, 267
        and women's perceptions of class 144
India, government of colonial 180, 199–200
inequalities xii, xiii–xiv, xv
    in the distribution of wealth 66
    economic
        and class 73, 80–1
        and the welfare state xx
    health 15, 17–19, 68–9
    housing 313, 319–24, 328–9, 330
    income
        and class 66–8
        and gender 110–11, 359–60
        and social justice 259, 267
    labour market 68, 122–3, 264
    and legal justice 255, 256
    and liberal feminism 117–20
    and place
        gated communities 25
        geographical differentiation 4, 11, 19, 23
    and race 190, 191
        and educational performance 303, 304, 305–6
        and social justice 250, 257–62, 281–3
        and education 263–7, 296–306
        perceptions of 267–8
        and poverty 259–60
        and social mobility 253–4
        and the underclass 275–8

and welfare capitalism 381, 382–3
see also class, inequalities;
gender, inequalities
internet
checking progress on public
services in particular locales 15,
16
communities 3
Irish people
and British race-thinking 185, 186
in Northern Ireland 165
and whiteness in America 189,
202–3
Isin, Engin F. and Wood, Patricia K.,
'Citizenship and identity' 228,
247–8
Italy, ageing population 215

Jackson, Michael 168, 169
Japan, class awareness and
identification 62, 64, 65
Japanese Americans, and census
categorization 174, 175, 196, 197,
198
Jencks, C. 266–7
Jenkins, Richard 161, 164
'Categorization and power' 167,
193–5
Jews, and whiteness 184–5
Jordan, T. 3, 11, 20
journalistic 'travelogues' 20–1
justice
and Marshall's theory of
citizenship 209
social context of legal 254–6
see also social justice

Kalpagam, U., 'The colonial state
and statistical knowledge' 180,
199–200
Keith, Sir Arthur, *Peoples of All
Nations* 182
Kennett, P. 320
Keynes, John Maynard 209
knowledge/power, and race xvii,
161, 177–80, 182
Kosack, Godula *see* Castles, Stephen
and Kosack, Godula
Kuper, L. 44–5

La Rochefoucauld, Duc de 257
labour of division, and race 160
Labour government (1997)
and education 301–2, 307
and family values 362
housing policy 318
and social exclusion 15, 60
and welfare spending 361
labour market
and citizenship xviii, 212, 215–16

and cultural capital 81
inequalities
educational 264
gender 122–3
income 68
new international division of
labour 260–1
segmentation 271
and the sexual division of labour
147–8
see also employment; immigrant
workers; occupational groups
labour theory of value 72–3, 92
Lawless, P. and Smith, Y. 23
Lawrence, Stephen 166, 217
Le Corbusier 51
Lee, P. 326, 327
Lee, Sharon M., 'Racial classifications
in the US census' 172, 173, 195–7
legal justice, social context of 254–6
Lenz, X. 201
lesbian feminism 128, 148
lesbians
and Manchester's Gay Village 35,
36, 55–6
and sexual citizenship 245–6
Leyshon, Andrew and Thrift, Nigel
23
liberal feminism xvi, 117–20, 127
life-chances
and class inequalities 69, 75, 82,
96
differences in, and place 10–11
and social justice 253, 293
in education 263, 330
in housing 330
life-cycle, and place 2
lifestyle
and place 33–8
and consumption 35–8
Lister, Ruth xv
Loewen, James 203
London, City of 23
lone parents
in Celebration 31
employment rates 115
single mothers 3, 31, 115, 361,
368
Longhurst, Brian *see* Savage, Mike,
Bagnall, Gaynor and Longhurst,
Brian
Lorde, Audre 103

Mac an Ghaill, M. 190
Macmillan, Harold 217
Macpherson report (1999) 166, 217
Maine, H.S. 235–6
Major, John 60, 223
Malcolm X 49

Manchester
class awareness and
identification 63
Gay Village xvi, 4, 33–5, 36, 37,
39, 53–7
and consumer culture 33, 35,
36, 38, 53, 54
in the larger Manchester 56–7
and lesbians 35, 36, 55–6
location 53–4
Mann, N. 264
Mapuche, racial categorization of
the 195
markets
in education 307–12, 333–9
Weber on class and 349–50
see also capitalism
marriage
and feminism 148
heterosexual reproduction and
citizenship 213
and working-class women 153
Marshall, Gordon 65, 75, 95
'Social class and underclass in
Britain and the USA' xix,
367–73
Marshall, T.H.
theory of citizenship xviii, 208,
209–12, 228, 230, 244–5
*Class Citizenship and Social
Development* 211, 234–9
'Value problems of welfare-
capitalism' xx, 378–83
Marx, Karl
class analysis x–xi, xvi, 60–1, 70,
71–3, 75, 76, 80–1, 91–4, 96,
346–8
and caste 357
*A Contribution to the Critique of
Political Economy* 92
and Engels, Friedrich, 'The
Manifesto of the Communist
Party' x–xi, 91, 346–8
The Power of Philosophy 92
and social categories 194
Marxist feminists 120–5, 146, 147
masculinity 139, 363–4
materiality and meaning
and feminism 130–6, 363
and women's subjective
experience of class 124
Mathew, Lord Justice 255
Maynard, Mary 134
Meade, James 281
medical profession, discrimination
in the 271
men
and citizenship
and war service 212, 213
and work 212, 214

and feminism 363–4
gay men and Manchester's Gay
    Village 35, 36, 38, 54–6, 57
and the gender division of labour
    112, 114
and gender identity 102–3
and gender roles 105
and health inequalities 68–9
incomes 110, 111
occupational groups 106
    and income inequalities 66, 67
and paid work 105–9, 116
    aggregate data on 122–3
    and parenthood 115–16
unemployment, and the
    domestic division of labour 148
working-class 150
meritocratic ideologies in education
    298
Methodist chapels, and working-
    class voluntarism 225
middle class
    awareness and identities 62, 63,
        64–5, 75–6
    black people in the USA 286, 287
    declining 215
    and education, and the market
        306, 307, 308–10, 333–6, 338–9
    and food consumption 79
    jobs, and human capital 68
    and Marshall's theory of
        citizenship 211
    suffragettes 118
    and voluntary organizations 225
    women
        and feminism 128, 134
        mothers 3
Middle Eastern people, and skin
    colour 182
migration
    and citizenship 209
    migrant labour 215–16, 218
Miles, Robert 165, 167, 183, 184
Mill, John Stuart 118
Mills, C. see Gerth, H. and Mills, C.
mind/body dualism, and whiteness
    182
Mitchell, Juliet 127–8
Mitchell, R. 19
modernity, and feminism 102
Modood, Tariq 269, 272, 274–5
Montaigne, Michel de 228
Morgan, Robin 125
Mothers' Union 214, 222, 227
multiculturalism, and citizenship
    207, 210, 216–17, 229, 239–44
Murie, A. 315, 324
Murji, Karim 326
Murray, Charles 369

Muslims in Europe 216
Myrdal, Gunnar xiv, 284
    'Caste and class' 355–8

Narveson, Jan 282–3
national identity, and citizenship
    244–5
National Institute for Clinical
    Excellence 19
national lottery 224
National Trust membership 222, 226
nationality, and gender 103
Native Americans, categorization in
    the US census 198
new genetics, and feminism 139
New Right politics
    and education 301, 309
    and feminism 362
    and structural Marxism 93
    and the welfare state 222–3
Newby, Howard 226
newspaper readership, decline in 221
Nobles, Melissa 173, 176
north–south divide in Britain 9, 10, 15

Oakley, Ann, Housewife 122, 148
occupational groups
    and food consumption 77–9
    and gender 106, 109, 123
    and housing tenure 319–20, 324
    and income inequalities 66–7, 71
    and projected job growth 287
    and social mobility 301
    and women's perception of class
        124, 142–4
Offe, C. 263
Office of Fair Trading 23
Omi, Michael, and Winant, Howard
    162, 163, 166
ontological security, right to 229–30
Oxford, Cutteslowe Walls,
    Summertown 25–6

Parekh, Bhikhu, 'Equality in a
    multicultural society' 216, 239–44
parental occupations, and women's
    perceptions of class 144
parenthood
    and citizenship 213–14, 218–20
    and gender inequalities 114–16
parents, and the educational market
    333–7, 338–9
Paretsky, S. 24
part-time employment 107, 109, 111,
    122, 214
parties, Weber on classes and 353–4
patriarchy, and feminism 121–2, 127,
    128, 132–3, 146–7
Payne, Geoff x, xiii, 102

Peason, D. see Wilson, R.M.S.,
    Gilligan, C. and Peason, D.
people of colour, and racial
    differences 164–5
Phelps-Brown, H. 263, 273
phenotypical differences, and race
    164–5
Phillips, Mike 161
place xv–xvi, 2–57
    and class inequality 60
    classification 5–9, 11–15
        council housing, less well-off
            families 7–9
        home-owning, well-off older
            people 5-7, 8–9
    differences in life-chances 10–11
    gated communities xv, 4, 24–7,
        33, 35, 39
    and lifestyle 33–8
        and consumption 35–8
        Manchester's Gay Village xvi, 4,
            33–5, 36, 37, 38, 39, 53–7
    north–south divide 9, 10, 15
    and the postcode lottery xv, 5,
        9–10, 39
    patterns of ill health and death
        rates 15, 17–19
    representation of 22–4
        problem places 22, 23, 42–5
    and sociology 20–4
    see also Celebration, Florida
Plato, The Republic 251
police
    and Broadwater Farm Estate 340,
        341–2
    and institutional racism 217
Policy Studies Institute 271, 272
political class formation 74
political parties, membership of 221
polygenesis, and whiteness 182
Poovey, Mary 20
post-feminism xvi, 105, 116, 138, 139
post-modernism
    class and gender 135
    and feminism xvi, xvii, 130,
        133–4, 146–7, 148
    and gated communities 26
    and race 168
    and the social divisions
        perspective x, xii
post-neotraditionalism, and
    Celebration 51
post-structuralism, and feminism xvi,
    130–3, 134
poverty
    and housing 3, 324, 326, 330
    and inequality 235
    and social justice 254, 259–60, 262
    and the underclass 275, 276–7,
        288, 370

and welfare capitalism 381–2
Powell, Enoch 217
power
    and the construction of place 39
    and discourse, and feminism
        132–3
    and patriarchy 146–7
    and race 160–1, 190
        eugenics and population 187–8
        and knowledge 177–80, 182
        naming and categorizing 167,
            193–5
Power, Anne, 'Portrait of Broadwater
    Farm Estate' 320, 339–43
Protestantism, and British race-
    thinking 185
public agencies, and place
    classification 14–15
public/private spheres
    and feminism 119, 127
    and sexual citizenship 246
Putnam, Robert 222

race xiv, xvi, 159–204
    anti-racism 191
    black feminism xvi, 128–9, 130,
        133, 134, 138
    and British identity in the UK 169
    and class 60, 75, 160, 163, 186,
        190
        and the underclass 275–8,
            284–8
    and gender 103, 160, 163, 186–7,
        190
    and governmentality 172–80
        census categories 172–6, 177,
            178, 179, 180, 181, 191, 195–8,
            200
        and the colonial state 180,
            199–200
        power through population 188
    and identity xii, 160, 161, 162–72
        naming and categorization
            166–72, 193–7
        vision and division 163–6
    inequalities 190, 191
    institutional racism and the
        police 217
    and knowledge/power xvii, 161,
        177–80, 182
    and the labour of division 160
    mixed race people 168, 177
    and place, Celebration 31, 32,
        35–6, 46–9
    and power 160–1
    racial naturalism 177
    scientific racism 171
    and social citizenship xviii
    and social justice xix, 160, 250

immigrant workers 261–2
    and the underclass 275–8,
        284–8
    sociology of 160
    and the underclass xix, 275–8,
        284–8, 285–8, 368, 369, 370, 371
    see also Asian people; black
        people; ethnicity; whiteness
Race Relations Acts in Britain 272–3
racial discrimination
    and citizenship xviii
    and social justice xix, 269–75
        bussing 265–7
        in employment 270–3, 274
radical feminism xvi, 125–7, 146
rave communities 3
Rawls, John
    on education and equality of
        opportunity 264
    theory of justice 257–8, 262,
        281–3
reference groups, and social justice
    268–9
reflexivity, and class identities 89–90
relative deprivation, and social
    justice 268–9
religion
    membership of religious
        organizations 221
    and race 177
        and Jews 184–5
        racial categories in the US
            census 173
Rendall, Jane, *The Origins of
    Modern Feminism* 102
reproduction, and citizenship
    213–14
reproductive citizenship xviii,
    213–14, 218–20
respectability, and working-class
    women 135–6, 154–5
Reynolds, Gretchen 288
Rich, Adrienne 148
Richardson, D., 'Citizenship and
    sexuality' 219, 244–6
Ricketts, Erol 371
rights, citizenship 208
risk society, and environmental
    citizenship 228
Rose, N. 178
Ross, Andrew
    The Celebration Chronicles 28,
        30, 31
    'Sure tried' 32, 46–9
Rowntree, Joseph 68
Royal Commission on the
    Distribution of Income and
    Wealth 322
Royal Society for the Protection of

Birds 227
Runciman, W. 368
    *Relative Deprivation and Social
        Justice* 253, 267–9
Rwanda 162, 165

Saunders, P. 64, 328, 329
Savage, Mike 308
    Bagnall, Gaynor and Longhurst,
        Brian, 'Ordinary, ambivalent
        and defensive' 63, 64, 86–91
Sawhill, Isabel 371
Schallmayer, Wilhelm, and
    population policy 187–8, 201–2
scientific Marxism 92, 93
Scottish Parliament 250
Segal, Lynne
    'Only contradictions on offer:
        feminism at the millennium'
        xvii, 359–66
    Why Feminism? 139
segmented labour market 271
Semmel, Bernard 186
Sennett, R. 150
sex differences, and gender
    differences 103
sexual citizenship xviii, 219, 220,
    244–6
sexual division of labour, and
    feminism 122, 127, 147–8
sexuality
    and feminism 125, 126, 127
        compulsory heterosexuality
            127, 146, 148
        lesbians 128, 148
    and gender 103
    heterosexual reproduction and
        citizenship 213
    heterosexuality and equality 246
    and place 2, 4
    and working-class women 135–6,
        153
Sheffield
    gay venues 56
    place discrimination in 23
Sikhs, and crash-helmets 241
Silva, E. *see* Hemmings, S., Silva, E.B.
    and Thompson, K.
Singer, Peter 228
single parents *see* lone parents
Skeggs, Beverley xvi–xvii, 37, 79–80,
    88, 90
    Formations of Class and Gender
        135–7, 138, 150–7
Smith, Adam 380
Smith, John 250
Smith, Y. *see* Lawless, P. and Smith, Y.
Snitow, A. 361
social capital 37

and citizenship 213, 225, 226
and education 308
social change
and class 82
and Marxism 72
and social justice 252–3
social citizenship xv, xviii, 209, 210, 217, 222, 234, 238–9
and the National Health Service 68
social class *see* class
social closure, and citizenship 212
social constructionism xi–xii
and gender 103, 117–18, 126, 139
and place 3
and whiteness 189
social Darwinism 186
social-democratic representation of place 22, 42, 44–5
social exclusion xvi
and citizenship 212, 217
and class 76
and housing 295, 320, 326, 330
language of 60
and place 15, 24, 39
Celebration 31, 50–1
and social justice 253–4, 266
social inclusion
and citizenship 212, 221, 224
and class identities 74
language of 60
and place 24
Celebration 32
social justice xix–xxi, 249–90, 293–5
and class xix–xx, 293–4
concept of 251–7
and distributive justice 293, 296
and education xix, xx, 262–7, 273–4, 293, 294, 295–6, 329–30
affirmative action programmes 275
and the educational market 311–12
and the good society 251
and housing xx–xxi, 259, 260, 293, 295, 312–14
institutions and the distribution of resources 262–3
perceptions of 267–9
and race xix, 160, 250, 269–78
immigrant workers 261–2
and the underclass 275–8, 284–8
in theory 257–62, 281–3
and the underclass 254, 275–8, 279
social Keynesianism 209, 210, 222
social mobility
and education 301

and social justice 253–4, 293
social movements
and citizenship 207
and feminism 117, 120
social sciences, and social justice 250
socialism
and Marxism 71, 93
socialist feminists xvi, 120–5, 128, 146
socio-cultural class formation 74
sociology
and citizenship 206–8
of development 260–1
of race 160, 190–1
Soja, Ed 22
Stacey, Judith 362
state representation of place 42–4
Statue of Liberty, and citizenship 207–8
status
and cultural capital 79
and income inequality 67
and Weberian class analysis 73, 74, 95–6, 351–2
Steinberg, Stephen, 'The underclass: a case of colour blindness, right and left' 276–7, 284–90
stratification x, 76
Weber on status stratification 351–2
see also class
structural Marxism 93
structural-functionalist perspective x
suffragettes 118
Switzerland, immigrant workers in 270
symbolic capital 37

taxes, redistributive 252
Taylor, Harriet 118
Taylor, Ian, Evans, Karen and Fraser, Penny, 'Out on the town' 34, 35, 53–7
Taylor, William 287
Tebbit, Norman 169
technological developments, and social justice 260–1
technology
new reproductive technologies 218–19
and the sexual division of labour 147–8
television viewing, and the decline of voluntarism 222
temporary employment, and gender 107, 109
Thatcher, Margaret 53, 61, 150, 222–3, 315, 318, 342, 361, 364

third way politics, and citizenship 214, 223
Thompson, K. see Hemmings, S., Silva, E.B. and Thompson, K
Thrift, Nigel 23
Titmuss effect, and war-related claims to social rights 210, 217
Tocqueville, Alexis de 221, 225
trade unions, decline in membership 214–15
Truth, Sojourner 128

underclass xix, 76, 151, 215, 254, 275–8, 279, 284–8
and class analysis 285–7, 367–8
as culture 285, 370
and fatalism 370–1
unemployment
and gender 115
and housing 324
and place 16
and the underclass 277, 286, 368, 369, 370
United States
caste and class 355–8
citizenship 207–8, 210
civil rights movement 210
class awareness and identification 62, 64, 65
gated communities 24, 25
gay couples and 'civil unions' 213
Moynihan Report 275, 276
and race
Italian immigrants 183
naming and categorizing 167
racial categories in the census 172–7, 179, 181, 195–7
waves of immigration 181
white people as a minority 188, 202–4
and social justice
bussing of black children 265–8
unequal imposition of the death penalty 255, 256
and the underclass xix, 275–8, 368–71
and the Vietnam War 217, 218
see also Celebration, Florida
urban sociology, and the Chicago School 22
utopian communities, and Celebration 28

Victoria, Queen 117
Vietnam War 217, 218
voluntary associations 208, 213–14, 221–5, 226
defining 223–4

and the economy 224–5
participation in 221–2
and the welfare state 222–3

Walby, Sylvia 146
Walker, Alan 370–1
Walter, Natasha 364–5
war
  and citizenship 212, 213, 217–18, 221
  reference groups and social justice 269
  and women in the military 219–20
Warde, A., study of food consumption and class 77–9
Ware, V. 187
Warren, Jonathan W. and Twine, France W., 'White Americans, the new minority?' 189, 202–4
Watson, Diane 20, 135
Weber, Max 10
  class analysis xi, xvi, 60–1, 70, 73, 80–1, 94–6
  'Class, status, party' x, xi, 249–54
  Economy and Society 95
  The Protestant Ethic and the Spirit of Capitalism 95
Weiner, G. 299
Weiss, S.F., 'Power through population' 187–8, 201–2
welfare state
  and the Beveridge Report xx, 213
  decline of
    and feminism 359
    and jobs in the voluntary sector 222
    and the 'dependency culture' 361, 370
  and education 299, 330
  and housing 314
  and the market xx, 222–3
  and social citizenship rights xv, 207, 208, 210
  and social justice 252, 293
    and housing 295
  and wartime service 212
welfare-capitalism, Marshall on value problems of 378–83
White, Charles 182, 186
whiteness 181–90
  categorization in the US census 173, 174, 175, 195, 203

and eugenics 187–8
fractured nature of 183–7
hegemonic (dominant) status of 160, 181–3, 190
invisibility of 163
and 'othering' 165
racialization of 190–1
white feminism 128, 129
white people as Caucasians 166, 170, 182
white people as a minority 188–90
Wilkins, Roger 286–7
Willis, P., *Learning to Labour* 81
Wilson, R. and Wylie, D., *The Dispossessed* 20–1
Wilson, R.M.S., Gilligan, C. and Peason, D. 11
Wilson, William Julius, *The Declining Significance of Race* 285–6, 287, 288, 369
Winant, Howard
  Racial Conditions 160
  see also Omi, Michael and Winant, Howard
Wollstonecraft, Mary, *Vindication of the Rights of Woman* 117, 118
women xi–xii
  Asian women and uniforms 241–2
  attitudes to
    ACORN Type 8 7, 8–9
    and work 132
  and childcare 114, 115, 122, 148
  choices open to 360
  and citizenship 214, 220, 246, 248
  and class 3, 123–5, 142-5
    young working-class women and class identity 79–80, 135–6, 138, 150–7
  and health inequalities 69
  and housing, female-headed African-Caribbean households 326
  incomes 110, 111, 359–60
  occupational groups and income inequalities 66, 67
  and reproductive rights 139
  role of in the military 219–20
  single mothers 3, 31, 115, 361
    as the underclass 368
  violence against 360
  and welfare benefits xvii, 359

white 186–7
and work
  attitudes to 132
  and citizenship 214
  paid 105–9, 112, 115, 119, 122, 360
  unpaid, domestic 112–13, 122, 148, 360
  see also feminism
Women's Liberation Movement (WLM) 120–1
Wood, E. 93
Wood, Patricia K. *see* Isin, Engin F. and Wood, Patricia K.
Woods, Tiger 168
work
  and citizenship 212, 214–17, 221
  see also employment; women, and work
working classes
  awareness and identities 62, 63, 65, 74–5, 75–6
  and British race-thinking 186
  and citizenship rights 211
  collapse of communalism 215
  and education
    and boys' underachievement 310–11, 312
    and equal opportunities 297–8, 299–300, 309, 336
  and immigrant workers xix–xx, 375–6
  jobs, and human capital 68
  manual workers and educational qualifications 264
  and Marxism 71
  men 150
  and Methodism 225
  and 'problem' families/estates 43–4, 45
  sociological studies 20–1, 74–5
  women, and class identity 79–80, 135–6, 150–7
Wright, Eric 93
Wright, Frank Lloyd 51
WWF 227
Wylie, D. *see* Wilson, R. and Wylie, D.

Young, K. 61–2
young people
  and citizenship 221
  and urban life 2

Social Differences and Divisions

Sociology and Society

This book is part of a series produced in association with The Open University. The complete list of books in the series is as follows:

Understanding Everyday Life, edited by Tony Bennett and Diane Watson

Social Differences and Divisions, edited by Peter Braham and Linda Janes

Social Change, edited by Tim Jordan and Steve Pile

The Uses of Sociology, edited by Peter Hamilton and Kenneth Thompson

The books form part of the Open University course DD201 *Sociology and Society*. Details of this and other Open University courses can be obtained from the Course Information and Advice Centre, PO Box 724, The Open University, Milton Keynes MK7 6ZS, United Kingdom: tel. +44 (0)1908 653231, e-mail ces-gen@open.ac.uk

For availability of other course components, contact Open University Worldwide Ltd, The Open University , Walton Hall, Milton Keynes MK7 6AA, United Kingdom: tel. +44 (0)1908 858785; fax +44 (0)1908 858787; e-mail ouwenq@open.ac.uk; website http://www.ouw.co.uk